More Praise for *Talent Development and Training in Healthcare Handbook*

"Healthcare is a people business, and its sole success is dependent upon a highly engaged and well-trained workforce. This book enlightened me to the necessary elements to ensure that my professional colleagues are prepared to be successful in an ever-changing and challenging healthcare environment."

—Frederick Borrelli, Chief Administrative Officer, Yale Medicine

"This book provides a thorough and wonderful framework for understanding the basics of change management. Reading it will enable those involved in change efforts to better plan, implement and track the results of their change initiatives."

—Jay Morris, Vice President, Education, Yale New Haven Health

"A truly impressive work of breadth and depth. This comprehensive handbook provides the best contemporary thinking and practical ideas from a diverse set of expert voices. What a valuable resource for healthcare talent development and training professionals as well as leaders who want to improve our healthcare delivery system."

—Michael Wukitsch, Chief Human Resources Officer, Lee Health

Talent Development and Training in HEALTHCARE Handbook

Gregory Rider, Jacqueline Burandt, and Niranjani Chidamber Papavaritis, Editors

PRESS
Alexandria, VA

CONTENTS

Part 3. Employee Development

Part 4. Business Acumen for the Health System

Part 5. Digital Transformation and Literacy

PREFACE

We are thrilled to bring you this handbook on talent development and training for healthcare provider spaces. Our goal was to create an evergreen resource for healthcare trainers and practitioners that shared best practices from seasoned professionals. The Association for Talent Development (ATD) has been creating training resources since 1943, and in early 2020, released a new content model to effectively cater material to healthcare audiences. Aligning with TRIAGE (training resources, ideas, and analysis guided by experts), this handbook encompasses key topics in learning and development and homes in on crucial areas specific to the industry. We envision it as a guide that every practitioner can have at their desk or working space to turn to whenever they need tried-and-true advice from subject matter experts (SMEs) and peers in the field.

The demands for talent development in healthcare are ever-increasing, and more healthcare organizations are realizing that their success as a business depends on the success of their talent development professionals, regardless of where they reside within the organizational chart or what their scope of responsibilities encompasses. As the function grows in importance, and continues to touch every nook and cranny of the healthcare organization, it will be asked to do more with the (sometimes limited) resources and support available. Fortunately, there's a burgeoning community of skilled and knowledgeable talent development practitioners who are willing and ready to impart their expertise.

Thus, it was important for us to make this a collective effort—to consult SMEs from key areas to discuss their findings, experiences, observations, and recommendations. We each brought our strengths and backgrounds from the field to bring an idea to life. Jacqueline Burandt, having served as the former executive director of the Center for Learning Excellence at University Health, brought decades' worth of TD experience and leadership. Gregory Rider, currently the director of corporate compliance at EmblemHealth, brought expertise from the various TD roles he's held in the past 20+ years across several segments of the healthcare industry. Niranjani Chidamber Papavaritis, having engaged with healthcare executives through a former role at UnitedHealth Group/Optum and serving as the content manager for healthcare training content at ATD, brought experience creating solutions for improved leadership development and training practices at health systems. Together, we had the perfect blend of past experiences, ongoing advancements, and the bond of a shared passion to contribute to the growth of the field.

We wanted to include a diverse group of contributors from within the industry to bring together the best stakeholders and provide perspective from different angles. We reached out to 25 healthcare professionals—including trainers, clinicians, executives, and consultants—with the goal of creating a book written "by the people, for the people." And we are honored to highlight each SME's wisdom and voice through their respective chapters.

While working with each contributor, we had many exchanges to refine their ideas—from the formation of scope to reviewing drafts and offering feedback and insight—striving to bring out the best of each content area. As worlds came together and collided, our contributors began to bond with one another as well, a harmony of talent development and healthcare, mirroring themes and topics within the book. The incidental overlap with the COVID-19 pandemic allowed for serendipitous closeness, as we shared our ups and downs, changing routines, and the direct impact we felt from the virus. We conversed about the way COVID-19 was shifting trends before our eyes and significantly affecting how we were designing, delivering, and evaluating training. And we exchanged thoughts on how our priorities were changing not just daily, but minute by minute.

We want to give a special note of appreciation to the mastermind behind this entire project—Ryan Changcoco. Serving as senior content manager for industry verticals, including healthcare, Ryan had envisioned this handbook years before its creation. He brought the three of us together on a shared mission, and provided endless support throughout the process as an advisor, colleague, and dear friend. We are extremely grateful to have been given the chance to work on this unique project and to have had Ryan's enthusiasm bring this book to life.

To quote Jane Goodall: "What you do makes a difference, and you have to decide what kind of difference you want to make." We have cherished this experience and hope that we can make a smidge of a difference to the growth of learning and development for healthcare providers. We are grateful, humbled, and inspired, and will continue to cheer on our fellow trainers, talent development professionals, and practitioners in the life-changing work they do.

Greg Rider, Jacque Burandt, and Niranjani Chidamber Papavaritis
November 2021

INTRODUCTION

"State of the Union"

Healthcare is one of the largest growing industries, with constantly evolving job opportunities, technological advancements, medical breakthroughs, and shifting trends. According to the US Bureau of Labor Statistics, employment in healthcare occupations is projected to grow 15 percent from 2019 to 2029; with approximately 2.4 million jobs added that's a rate much faster than other occupations (BLS 2021).

In addition to this rapid growth, the industry tackles constant disruption, providing a textbook case of a VUCA (volatile, uncertain, complex, and ambiguous) environment that must acquire, use, and grow talent to thrive. During this book's development the COVID-19 pandemic caused unprecedented changes and job loss to the workplace, and healthcare facilities in particular. But by the end of 2020 the healthcare industry had already regained two-thirds of the jobs lost that year (Turner 2021). The pandemic also reshaped the role of talent development and HR in healthcare organizations.

The healthcare workforce includes staff from multi-generational backgrounds and a variety of disciplines, both clinical and nonclinical. The area that ties a health system together—the array of employees, departments and specialties, providers, and patients alike—is human resources. The role of talent development and HR requires agility, resilience, and proficiency in integrated reasoning (critical thinking) and high-touch skills (communication, empathy) to manage the organization's mission, departmental goals, employee development, and patient care. The growing demand for healthcare workers results in fierce competition, and talent development professionals are responsible for attracting, retaining, and further cultivating that talent. This brings even more challenges. The healthcare industry balances numerous critical demands 24 hours a day, 7 days a week, 365 days a year, while aiming to provide the highest quality patient care, maintain profitability, and juggle fast-paced procedures and turnarounds. Talent development professionals must ensure employees develop the skills they need to succeed and maintain their mental health, while managing their busy schedules, the demands of shift work, and the need to maintain staffing ratios, among other factors.

The Talent Development and Training in Healthcare Landscape

When ATD transitioned from the American Society of Training & Development to the Association for Talent Development in 2014, the talent development and training industry was beginning to recognize that developing employees was a collective responsibility of the entire organization. Developing talent was, and continues to remain, a key feature of the HR function, which helps organizations run more efficiently, optimally, and compliantly, according to the high standards expected of the healthcare industry. The vast influence talent development has—far beyond foundational onboarding topics and mandatory training programs—is highlighted throughout this book. Effective development of staff is the thread that weaves through the various departments to ensure that a healthcare organization is meeting standards with latest practices in patient care, while providing a safe and engaging environment for their practitioners.

Training, learning, and development are important to the success of any organization. However, they are *crucial* to health systems specifically. Talent development professionals in healthcare have consistently maintained that they are unique—that the demands and requirements of this industry are vastly different from those in other major fields, such as finance, IT, or retail. Here are some of the salient characteristics found in healthcare organizations that can affect talent development.

Employees in healthcare provider spaces are typically siloed within their own territory, as practitioners work with patients, directors lead departments, and executives run the overall business. Talent development professionals and trainers, on the other hand, work with every department, specialty area, and employee in a health system. They handle employee career advancement, while also bringing the business together as a whole. Without training, practitioners may remain stagnant in their roles, and health systems may not thrive and keep up with the ever-evolving industry. In the most extreme cases, improper or nonexistent training can severely affect patient care.

Healthcare is inherently dependent on interprofessional teams. To be successful in providing services, clinical outcomes, or financial sustainability, healthcare workers must collaborate. Front-line staff and highly credentialed physicians and researchers work side by side to deliver the highest quality care and best patient and stakeholder experience. Training and coaching teams on interprofessional communication is a major focus of talent development in healthcare. Models, such as TeamSTEPPS and High Reliability Organizations (HROs), improve communication and teamwork skills among healthcare workers and provide a structure to promote patient safety.

This mix of interprofessional team members also makes credibility a factor in the workplace. For example, nonclinical talent development professionals can achieve credibility by investing time in the clinical area and serving on interdisciplinary teams with clinicians to better understand the issues and situations that occur. Talent development professionals share their expertise through a variety of formal and informal methods, just as clinicians share their expertise with those in talent development. Each group has valuable expertise to bring to the table in finding solutions to business problems.

Healthcare is a highly regulated industry, which dictates extensive training on required topics such as HIPAA, Medicare, and Medicaid best practices; preventing fraud, waste, and abuse; and avoiding conflicts of interest. There are also compliance requirements covering more procedural topics, such as infection control, safety, and emergency preparedness. Some of this training is required for all employees and must be completed successfully upon hire and at regular intervals; other training requirements target specific employee populations and have separate completion deadlines. In addition to designing, implementing, and evaluating compliance training, talent development professionals must maintain accurate documentation for all completed training. This is essential to keep the organization in compliance with various local, state, and federal regulatory agencies and to maintain employee and organizational accreditation. Failure to maintain this documentation can have severe consequences, including financial penalties, sanctions, and even closure.

Intense pressure to get healthcare workers on the job quickly often conflicts with the amount of information new employees need to learn (much of which is required by regulatory agencies). There's a delicate balance between time spent "off the unit" in onboarding (usually categorized as nonproductive time) and time spent ensuring employees are competent to perform their assigned tasks. This speed-to-competence dilemma is further evidenced by the need for more job-specific orientation sessions for unique employee populations, such as nurses. Mentoring, precepting, internships, and fellowships have long been a fundamental part of healthcare. They sometimes involve additional pay or academic credit and can be leveraged by talent development as part of the learning portfolio.

Although they're a critical component of health systems, talent development and training are often underrated and underutilized in hospitals. To accommodate the fast-paced, stressful, hectic, and varying schedules of employees, training is often condensed to meet bare minimums and focus primarily on mandatory areas (such as compliance training). Other, softer topics, such as personal and organization development, are often overlooked. Trainers have limited resources and time, and practitioners don't know how to address areas for growth and development on their own. Instructional design is swept aside—full of potential and innovation that everyone is too busy to tap into.

Fortunately, ATD's *2021 State of Healthcare Training* found that healthcare organizations plan to increase direct training expenditures per employee in comparison to the numbers reported in 2019. Healthcare organizations reported an average direct training expenditure of $651 per employee, and of the 48 organizations surveyed (half representing acute-care hospitals, half representing nonacute facilities), 69 percent expected to maintain or increase the expenditure for the next fiscal year. The average organization used 65 percent of its total direct learning expenditure for internal services—such as talent development staff salaries and administrative costs—while 20 percent went toward learning suppliers and 15 percent went toward tuition reimbursement and continuing education. As direct expenditure increases, the aim is to also increase funds for learning suppliers and continuing education to promote career development and advancement for employees.

Healthcare is a highly technological field, and that factors into talent development and training design and delivery. Electronic medical records (EMR) systems are playing increasingly larger roles in transforming healthcare, and maintaining these systems across organizations is becoming more of a challenge. Healthcare training professionals are often caught between various system "owners"—including clinicians, IT and systems teams, security teams, HR, compliance, and legal—and they must navigate successfully among these shareholders to design, develop, implement, and evaluate effective training.

Digital transformation and mobile technologies have allowed training delivery and impact to be taken to the next level—with e-learning, customized lessons, and synchronous and asynchronous learning. Of the organizations surveyed in the *2021 State of Healthcare Training* report, 38 percent were already using mobile technology in their talent development programs and

39 percent planned to do so in the next year, incorporating various mediums such as virtual reality, augmented reality, and mixed reality.

Most importantly, healthcare organizations face enormous responsibilities to ensure both patient and employee safety. In response to the COVID-19 pandemic, safety measures were reformed and norms have shifted for the long term. Organizations have implemented new infection control measures, and 80 percent of those that responded to the *2021 State of Healthcare Training* report planned to continue employing some, if not all, of these measures as part of their routine training curriculum.

These unique characteristics present opportunities and challenges for healthcare talent development professionals. ATD's *Talent Development and Training in Healthcare Handbook* can serve as a ready resource when these issues occur.

Focus Areas in This Book

Talent development professionals in healthcare go by many titles—preceptor, clinical trainer, clinical nurse specialist, nurse educator, learning or performance consultant, director of training or HR, and IT trainer. Regardless of title, all practitioners have a universal need to find resources quickly. As one of the few resources in this space, this book is designed for all talent development professionals in healthcare, whether they are new to the field or seasoned practitioners.

The increasing job opportunities, direct expenditures, and prioritization of training and talent development in healthcare is driving a need to reexamine this role within the healthcare organization. Talent development initiatives in healthcare, like in many other industries, are often the first to be cut when budgets are tight and the first to be brought back when things are going well, which results in inconsistent employee development. In many cases, talent development is under prioritized, underutilized, and underrated—"throwing training at something" is often used as a band-aid for deeper skills gaps and employee engagement issues. This handbook systematically explores the key areas of training within healthcare to promote organizational and employee success. Rather than presenting training as a short-term fix, it aims to provide guidance on using talent development and training as a long-term strategy for overall organizational success.

In early 2020, ATD launched a new content model for the healthcare community, combining core areas of learning and development with topics unique to the industry. Aptly named the TRIAGE Model (training resources, ideas, and analyses guided by experts), this content model became the foundation for sharing training best practices, insights, and experiences from SMEs within the industry.

Figure I-1. ATD's TRIAGE Model

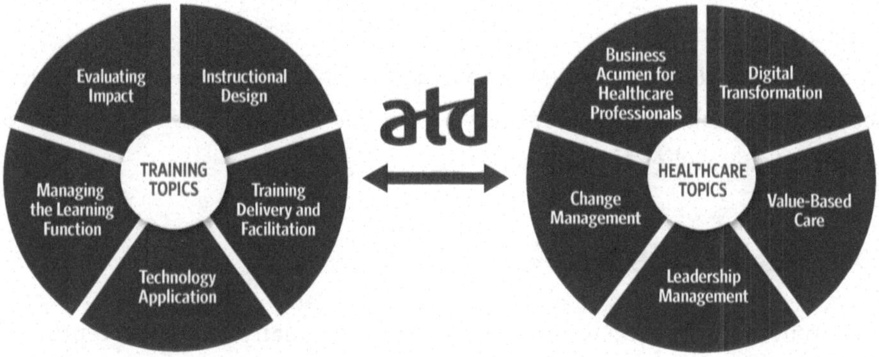

This handbook explores a vast array of resources and assets that align with this model to assist trainers who are working with clinical and nonclinical employees. As mentioned earlier, talent development professionals have the unique role of tying together organizational and employee advancement—this book likewise covers areas for business and professional evolution. The topics included represent the needs expressed by talent development professionals and clinicians from health systems across the nation.

The chapters are divided into six parts:

- Learning and development basics
- Organizational development
- Employee development
- Business acumen for the health system
- Digital transformation
- Patient-centric care

These broad areas each cover a sector of employment and organizational goals that every health system faces, and encompass insights geared toward clinical and nonclinical employees, as well as varying levels of seniority and skill set. Each chapter is written by a subject matter expert, allowing for a thorough exploration and analysis by trial, application, and practicality.

As evidenced by the chapters in this book, talent development is not solely confined to "training." Within the healthcare industry talent development represents an overarching and ongoing initiative to ensure that institutions are functioning at the highest level possible. From doctors to nurses and from registration to staff, effective talent development practices will affect all members of the healthcare organization. Our hope is that you use this tool to not only maximize the impact of your work, but also instill ways to improve your ability to deliver the highest level of care possible to every patient you serve.

PART 1

LEARNING AND DEVELOPMENT BASICS

CHAPTER 1

TRAINING DELIVERY AND FACILITATION

NAOMI J. KINNEY, CPTD

Mary is a facilitator and trainer at a local hospital and is about to deliver the last training session of the year. It is a weekly session that's mandatory for all hospital staff, and is part of an annual cycle all hospitals are required to provide to ensure staff are up to par on the safety and overall best practices. Feeling relieved that this is the final session, Mary still wants to provide the same level of quality she did in her first. In addition to her basic presentation preparations (including a sign-in sheet, ample handouts, and room set-up), Mary wants to study her audience. She knows to never take for granted the individual and common needs of her learners, who are comprised of different staff members from across the facility. However, she does know that they all have one thing in common: They're part of a healthcare team that is critical to the hospital's ability to manage all emergency situations.

Here are just a few things all healthcare workers commonly do on a daily basis:

- Stay on their feet and cover a lot of ground, adding to their physical strain each day.
- Stay alert (a constant state of readiness) so they can manage each emergency within the hospital and within the local community.
- Accurately document a lot throughout the day to maintain hospital compliance.
- Maintain proper infection control and safety practices in each aspect of their work for the safety of everyone within the hospital environment.
- Manage each patient's unique personality and needs (and those of their families).
- Maintain themselves physically and mentally so they're able to be the best care provider they can be.
- Manage the needs of their personal lives to accommodate their family and loved ones.

So, Mary's training not only has to be accurate and follow the latest regulatory guidelines to keep the hospital compliant, but more specifically, her *facilitation and the delivery of the training* requires some finesse with this unique audience and their demands. Mary's audience could include a combination of doctors, nurses, technicians from the hospital's various diagnostic areas; experienced, highly degreed hospital administrators and clinical staff; and the nonclinical, operational staff who run and maintain the facility and the grounds of the hospital, along with administrative, financial staff, and volunteers. Remember: At a hospital or nursing home, the lights never go out! Therefore, training facilitators must deliver training programs for all shifts, and each employee must complete and meet the same mandatory learning objectives required of the institution. They need to follow state and federal regulatory best practices consistently across all facilities that bear the hospital's name.

If Mary delivers the in-person training with finesse, it can go a long way in making important messages stick with this highly technical audience, ensuring that the hospital passes its next impromptu regulatory visit or survey from inspectors of the Joint Commission on Accreditation of Healthcare Organizations (JCAHO). It will also allow her to connect with the learners (who are also her co-workers) in ways that benefit the staff and the organization in the long run.

Being an experienced talent development professional who has designed many training programs and delivered much in-person, instructor-led training in healthcare (and more specifically in hospitals), I've been in Mary's shoes many times. I've had a number of interesting experiences during the delivery and facilitation of the mandatory training (as well as training on professional development subject matter) that were both rewarding and challenging with this particular audience. In this chapter, I'll share some of these experiences (and lessons learned), along with training and facilitation techniques I used in the hospital and healthcare setting while maintaining the hospital's educational requirements.

Knowing Your Audience

A very important aspect of designing learning is knowing who's in the audience. For whom is this training being designed, and what are the objectives? Sometimes you'll have the luxury of knowing who the participants are before they arrive. That allows you to adjust your delivery and facilitation game for each session. Like Mary, I was responsible for the annual mandatory training of all hospital, nursing home, and remote staff. In addition, I also designed and delivered the new employee orientation program. So, I recognized many of the faces I saw in the annual training sessions from orientation.

Trainers should study their rosters before their class to determine which audience members will be assets as they deliver the training message. If you know the participants well (either via previous learning events or from around the hospital), you can use this to your advantage. For example, my hospital's leaders had special mandatory training sessions to attend annually, but they occasionally also attended the regular sessions with their staff to serve as role models and encourage attendance. I enjoyed calling on them to answer questions or lead discussions on a mandatory topic (like patient safety) or share how they apply safety policies in their area of the hospital.

You would ideally adjust your delivery if members of the leadership team are in your audience. Encourage their input so they can demonstrate their support of the policies and procedures throughout the training program. Poll the audience at the beginning of the class to see who knows what about these policies (which are taught annually, but don't often change much from year to year). Most leaders love to speak out when given the opportunity. So, consider setting aside some time to impart their knowledge and experience during the class (assuming they're present and willing) to keep the repetitive subject matter interesting.

When the trainer connects with their audience and customizes the delivery for each session, it creates a more accommodating and engaging experience for the learners. This leads to an ideal learning environment where the audience is open to participating, sharing, and learning with their co-workers.

If the audience remembers a lot of the content from last year, you can ask them to share their experiences on a hot topic (for example, consistently applied infection control best practices) to generate some dialogue. A good group facilitator will ask thought-provoking questions to probe the audience's knowledge and generate discussion.

As an instructional designer, I have designed games like *Safety Jeopardy*, which can turn boring, repetitive facts into a fun competition. People can play *Kahootz* and similar games using their cell phones or other mobile devices. I like to use the participants' names during these to further connect with my audience (and to help me remember their names).

These are all good ways of bringing hospital staff (clinical and nonclinical) together and keeping them talking about the subject matter even after the training ends (whether the subject was mandatory or a professional development class). They get to know one another more, they share their knowledge during training while having fun, and together they learn about the rules they all must consistently follow wherever they work. They can also apply and share best practices on nonmandatory subject matter.

Another way to get to know your audience while determining learning needs is to use a pre-class assessment to gauge knowledge levels and commonalities. Once you know what the audience knows, you can adjust your facilitation techniques to maximize your impact and save time. Many of these assessment tools are found online and are ideally used *before* the training starts so the trainer can use this information to structure the class accordingly. Here are some examples of pre-assessment tools you can use to tailor the training program to meet the learning objectives more effectively:

- **Customized pre-assessment worksheets** for the organization or the course can allow certain employees to test out of parts of the training program. (For example, I once worked at a hospital that allowed new hires to test out of a segment of orientation and annual training based on their previous knowledge of OSHA safety best practices.)
- **Leadership assessments** are often used to prepare for leadership development training. They allow trainers to gauge experience levels, leadership style, and knowledge of leadership principles before they start the program.
- **Strength-finders surveys** assess individual strengths on which to focus, as well as allow members in a group to see how their preferences can be leveraged in combination in the workplace.
- **Individual personality assessment tools** like DiSC and Myers-Briggs Type Indicator (MBTI) are good pre-assessment tools for teambuilding training, to gauge the nuances of team personalities, and to show anticipated interactions among certain team members.

Other pre-assessments are performed at the beginning of the class, either on paper or using electronic audience polling tools or gaming consoles. You can also use them intermittently during the course to quiz the audience on their sentiments or knowledge of a topic. I used them in a sexual harassment training program I gave at a children's hospital I worked at years ago; they were very effective for this sensitive subject matter that many struggle to openly discuss.

Trainers should consider all the tools available to them that allow for a close audience connection, a good exchange and sharing of information among the participants, and an open, honest, relaxed training environment overall.

Key Takeaways

- Study the audience before the training delivery—review the roster, use pre-assessments, or poll the audience. This can be done as pre-work before the session or at the beginning of the session.
- Adjust the facilitation and content delivery as needed, depending on who will be in the audience (but be careful about making any changes to the actual training content).
- Call on familiar participants where possible, but find ways to involve *all* participants (especially leadership and quiet learners), depending upon their background and experience.
- Use fun training tools and activities to consistently convey the same content to all staff while keeping them engaged, participating, and enjoying their learning experience.

Bottom Line Up Front

Time is very precious to all employees, especially healthcare workers caring for patients whose status can change in minutes. Additionally, their jobs have a *lot* of requirements, and training is just *one* of them. I've found it best to be open and honest about what their annual requirements are (before training begins) as well as what I'm going to deliver at the start of the training: Cut to the chase. I like the term *BLUF* (bottom line up front), which is often used in the military.

Since many healthcare workers are used to giving good or bad news to patients and their families, they understand this concept fully: People want you to tell them what's going on right away. So, do the same when you facilitate and deliver training. This can help you connect with the participants and demonstrate humanity from the beginning of the session and throughout. They should immediately hear the objectives of the training, why they're there, and how long it will take. When this information is clearly conveyed (especially the purpose, such as following regulatory guidelines or how to handle themselves when hospital inspectors come around) participants are more likely to focus and listen. Most training programs start with a review of the objectives and some light banter, but when your audience is overly scheduled individuals, it's best to focus on the delivery of those salient points that qualify as "Need to have," rather than "Nice to have." So, acknowledge who's in the audience, get right to the point of why they're there (the BLUF), ask if there are any initial questions, and then proceed with delivering all the content, facilitating with finesse, and keeping the audience engaged as if you're holding a conversation with a valued colleague.

In addition to starting the program with BLUF, you might want to explain the organizational "lingo." Each industry and workplace has its own culture, mission, and language. The use of acronyms in healthcare is rampant, and you should level the playing field (especially for new hire training) by clearly defining and explaining any terms, acronyms, and other jargon that are unique to your organization. Misuse or misunderstanding of key terms in healthcare can even become a safety issue. For some new employees, tackling this long list of new terms and acronyms during onboarding can be a daunting. Provide a glossary of terms within the training materials (for new and current staff) and use or define them often in the content and training delivery (even incorporate them into exercises) to encourage consistent use. Ensuring that the learners are all defining key terms and acronyms in the same way will mean consistency in communications when they hit the floor working with other tenured staff, which will make for better communications, smoother patient hand-offs, and a safer work environment for all.

By using the BLUF concept and defining key terminology or acronyms at the onset of training, you can immediately set the stage for the content and pace of the learning, and it can help you establish a common baseline among the learners. You should strive for all your learners to be on the same page so they're not left wondering, guessing, or filling in the blanks incorrectly about their learning path.

Key Takeaways

- Immediately engage learners with BLUF (Bottom Line Up Front), regardless of the delivery method, by focusing on the subject and not wasting participants' valuable time.
- In addition to clearly stating the course objectives at the beginning of each training delivery, poll the audience to determine their individual objectives.
- Start the session with a trigger video, a thought-provoking question (or two), or an activity that activates the group and proves the message you're trying to convey. (For example, I've kicked off cultural diversity and inclusion classes by asking everyone to share a diversity moment; this validated the objectives and the need for training.)
- Never assume that the audience knows the lingo. Clearly define key terminology and common acronyms to ensure that all employees (particularly new hires) are speaking the same language and can work together smoothly and congruently.

Bringing Training to Them

In a hospital environment, there is an obligation to provide *all* employees with the annual mandatory training, which covers several key subjects, such as patient and employee safety, infection control, fire safety, and emergency preparedness. However, sometimes you must *go to the employees* to provide the training they need within their immediate work area (and keeping in mind infection control best practices). By delivering the training in-person at their site, you're able to reach everyone in that work area, which allows them to ensure continuous staff coverage (that is, no one has to leave, patients and departmental processes are still monitored, and each employee is present and accounted for in the eyes of the department manager). Nurse managers and department directors loved the fact that my staff and I could train their staff at a time and location that was ideal for them. It was more convenient for the leaders because they did not have to coordinate who went to annual mandatory training. We were able to include the training at the end of a typical staff meeting, which meant the leader (who was also present) would simply confirm in person who was present for the session.

As the director of hospital education for a major hospital in Washington, DC, I was responsible for documenting the mandatory requirements and policies for the hospital and Carroll Manor nursing home employees, as well as developing and delivering all training content. I collaborated with other leaders across the organization while having minimal training resources (and only two other trainers to assist me) for a staff of more than 3,000 employees. We worked with leaders and nurse educators in the hospital and nursing home to meet an organization-wide objective of ensuring everyone completed their training before the subsequent regulatory visit.

This was quite a task, but we worked together as a leadership team to coordinate and make sure all employees received the annual mandatory training. However, the training delivery sometimes happened in very unexpected locations around the hospital and nursing home campus and beyond:

- The PACU (post-anesthesia care unit) staff cannot always readily leave their work posts (beside a patient bed) for very long, and a patient's condition can change constantly and in an instant, especially if they're recovering from surgery. So, I went to the work area of these employees. I dressed up in the required personal protective equipment (PPE) to prevent infection control breaches for the patients and delivered the training in an adjacent care area using a flipchart. We not only had to maintain the safe practices of patient care while being so close to the process, but we also had to "quiet" our delivery in those areas. We had to cover the content quickly and thoroughly, keep everyone interested and engaged, and be mindful everyone was also closely monitoring their nearby patients' recovery. This could be quite a balancing act, but everyone was flexible. They expressed how much they appreciated that we met them in their area and worked with us to make sure we had ample safe space, lighting, and, most importantly, that all staff who needed to be there were present.

- Sometimes the training staff had to go to a remote facility off the hospital campus, this included a local elementary school with a medical office, two senior living facilities with senior care centers, and two drug rehabilitation facilities.
- We also delivered mandatory training in the hospital nursing facility's conference and meeting rooms. I gave an annual training session for the speech and rehabilitation department staff right in the rehab area's gym next to the swimming pool. This was one of the most interesting experiences I've had, but it was still safe and met the needs of the staff. The training was delivered between appointments, so no patients or residents were in the pool or in the gym area, which maintained their privacy and kept everyone safe.

Throughout the year we would regularly book hospital auditoriums or meeting halls to gather a group for training on various subjects (both mandatory training and professional development). Some of the subjects included new employee orientation, annual mandatory training (JCAHO preparedness), fire safety, infection control and bloodborne pathogens training, emergency preparedness subjects, OSHA safety training subjects (such as back safety and slips, trips, falls), supervisory training and leadership development, cultural diversity and inclusion, customer service, teambuilding (including conflict resolution and communications), presentation skills, introduction to PowerPoint, and flowcharting and cause-and-effect diagrams (statistical reporting).

However, we would always make an attempt to be very flexible with mandatory training and provide other options to accommodate the date, timing, and location of the training delivery. This was particularly important if the employees worked third shift, worked on-call or part-time, or had other scheduling challenges. For JCAHO preparedness we even put some segments of the training on video and added informational fliers to staff breakroom bulletin boards to raise awareness and educate the staff "on the fly" about key policies or procedures (such as 30-second handwashing). Our main objective was to get as many hospital staff trained as possible each year, and we did that successfully and repeatedly using a combination of creative delivery approaches, cooperation among all hospital leadership, and delivering training in various locations across the hospital campus.

Key Takeaways

- Adjust the training delivery format (but not the content) to accommodate the work area or workspace (for example, you could be near sensitive equipment, an infection-sensitive area, or exposed to personal health information). To limit "travel time" (especially across large hospital campuses) and ensure greater attendance, many department leaders appreciate the convenience of training coming to them.
- Collaborate with healthcare leaders to reach the common goal of regulatory compliance and high attendance numbers in annual mandatory training. The result is a knowledgeable, well-prepared workforce that can provide the best care to their patients and the communities they serve using industry best practices.
- Meeting the employees where they are and delivering the training directly in their work areas not only builds teams across departments, but it also ensures hospital compliance in team fashion, which regulatory authorities find impressive.

Efficient Use of Classroom Tools

All training tools can be challenging if nerves, lack of planning, or plain old clumsiness get in the way. However, they have evolved to the benefit of both the trainer and the learner, making facilitation easier and simpler. *Sometimes!*

When I first started working at the hospital in DC in 1997, they were still using an overhead projector for the new employee orientation program. I knew that had to change, and soon. I was responsible for the orientation program's delivery and facilitation to about 60 to 75 new employees on a monthly basis. Upgrading the training equipment would not only impress new hires, but it would also make the program flow more efficiently for those delivering the training. My past experiences with PowerPoint presentations displayed via an LCD projector had always been positive; so I immediately tossed the overheads in favor of the LCD projectors. Then I met with the guest speakers (leaders from various departments, including the CEO), redesigned their presentations into a smooth-flowing PowerPoint deck, and provided some coaching on the new delivery method. The new employee orientation program improved drastically! It was also much easier for the trainers (myself included) to set up, deliver, and customize or edit each month. The participants enjoyed the smooth flow of information, and each speaker simply had to show up (at their assigned time) and present their information without having to worry about fumbling with media or training tools (the facilitators would advance the slideshow so the speakers didn't have to). We made sure to keep a flipchart handy for impromptu note taking, but no other media or training tools were necessary, which made for a smoother eight-hour training program. From then on, the hospital education department received positive marks about the new delivery method and the progress of the orientation program from hospital employees and the leadership team (especially those who served as speakers and subject matter experts in the program).

Sometimes the very image of training can be changed simply by enhancing the delivery tools used. The quality of training is often gauged by *how* you use those tools most effectively to meet the overall training objective. While mishaps with media and training tools can be both funny and disastrous, the lessons learned are important in the long run for a trainer.

Many trainers use PowerPoint for their online and in-person training delivery methods. If they're also an instructional designer (or work closely with one), they may use other instructional design tools like Articulate 360 to edit and deliver training content and design asynchronous web-based training (which guides the learner through the program). Either tool allows for making quick edits to the training materials when there are changes in organizational policies, processes, and system modifications.

During the delivery of in-person (synchronous) online presentations, which often occur via Zoom, Skype, Webex, and MS Teams, trainers have many options to keep their audiences engaged (although they should be used carefully, efficiently, and in a timely manner):

- **Roll call.** Begin with roll call, which will bring participants to attention when they hear their names called.
- **Navigation instructions.** Tell participants where to find the delivery tools like the hand-raising feature, providing comments or questions, and so on. This allows learners to stay active during the training.
- **Online training delivery tools.** Explain each tool to the learners so they can use them effectively during the session:
    - Share option allows you to share documents you have on file.

  - The polling feature allows the trainer to survey the audience intermittently to help maintain their participation. Audiences love to provide their opinions or to vote on a potentially divisive issue via a poll.
  - Audience annotations are possible in some delivery tools like Zoom, which offer a virtual whiteboard. Participants can use these to write responses and collaborate. You can also use it to show diverse and colorful polling responses.
  - A chat window now is available in most apps and this feature allows participants to send text messages to everyone or to specific individuals within the group. You can also use chat to solicit poll responses or to allow participants to express themselves in the moment throughout the session.
- **Virtual flipchart.** In the past, I have simply "shared" a blank piece of paper with the audience, gathered their input, and summarized everyone's thoughts by typing them out on the virtual flipchart for everyone to see. You can use this technique to document participant responses when you quiz them verbally (by typing their responses in real time).
- **Audience awareness.** Observe participants and what they are doing throughout the training delivery. Are they tapping their pencil, holding their head, wrinkling their brow, or looking elsewhere daydreaming? Stay alert and watch their body language.
- **Audience activation.** If participants seem a bit dazed, you can regain their attention by:
  - Calling on them to answer a question, read something, or complete an exercise.
  - Assign a role like timekeeping or note taking. Call on them at the end of the session to give a recap or summary and thank them.
  - Ask a thought-provoking question or for summary or recap statement that keeps participants thinking about what you just taught them.
  - Ask participants to quiz *you!* If you're the subject matter expert, turn the tables and have them challenge you with questions.
  - Whenever you say "quiz!" people tend to perk up. Give a brief recap quiz at the end of the session to confirm comprehension and get them to focus on the content throughout. They'll also likely pay even more attention if you say, "We'll be verbally reviewing the answers to the quiz afterward, and I'll be calling on each of you!"

The use of technology for training delivery in healthcare is even more important with today's increased focus on safety and infection control management (especially in light of the COVID-19 pandemic). Your facilitation skills need to be even sharper to manage a diverse remote audience of busy healthcare workers who are mentally and physically challenged daily and often exhausted as a result. Using the delivery tool's features can help you keep them engaged. By using these facilitation tips (and many other audience engagement tactics) you'll ensure a good application of the technology, quality content delivery, and that the overall course objectives are met.

Key Takeaways

- Use more current media tools to deliver training. They support your ability to set up quickly and can help facilitate training delivery. These tools also make it easier to edit or change training content so you can facilitate a customized delivery every time.
- Media and delivery tools, when used properly, keep participants engaged, involved, and interested. Some tools are part of the application, while others are things you can do or say to connect directly with each learner.
- If using online communication tools (such as Zoom, WebEx, or Microsoft Teams), make sure to test them before the session for maximum credibility. Show learners how to navigate the tools at the beginning of delivery (or use a poll to see if they already know) and encourage them to use them as appropriate.

Managing the Expectations of All Learners

You are bound to occasionally come across those "interesting" participants who want to question your training materials or challenge the learning solutions. You need to try to recognize this behavior as soon as possible, perhaps through introductions or by polling the audience for what they know. If you work in a hospital or healthcare facility, many of your participants will have advanced degrees, be very experienced at their jobs, be very knowledgeable about the organization, and will not hesitate to speak up if something is incorrect.

You need to make sure you've studied the organization's policies, procedures, and processes so you're able to speak intelligibly in this regard and are ready to answer any questions that arise. Start by developing relationships with the staff to further understand processes and procedures, as well as how departments work together to maintain an environment that is customer friendly, infection free, safe, and well prepared. This is the primary objective of the annual mandatory safety training required of healthcare workers.

If, by chance, you are adversely challenged by an audience member, there are things you can do to manage the classroom positively and avoid any disruption of the learning:

- **Politely bring attention to the behavior (without calling them out).** Every adult learner should come to training ready to learn and be a cooperative participant. If someone is being outwardly rude and says something out of line, you should take control, get everyone's attention, and firmly acknowledge that the behavior was inappropriate by addressing everyone and saying something like, "Now, everyone. Let's please keep our focus; our discussions during this class should be more positive." You can also affirmatively direct the audience toward the kinds of responses you were expecting by saying something like, "What I'd like to hear from you is your feedback on this subject while staying positive and constructive as we do so; let's stay solution-focused. Who else would like to share with the group?" These tactics can keep the group moving toward a more productive conversation instead of having one disruptive person rule the show.
- **Involve this knowledgeable person in the training in some way.** If the "very difficult person" is simply trying to show how much they know, you can call on them to share their take on an organization-wide process or procedure or to answer a question. Then add in whatever they may have left out or clarify a concept they might have overlooked. Use their name in your additional explanation (commenting on their input), and then thank them for the additional input explaining the process or procedure to the (less tenured) audience. You can follow that up with, "Let's hear from some others we have not heard from yet."
- **Talk to this person during the break.** Acknowledge their experience and expertise, but also remind them of more appropriate ways to share what they know, without disrupting the class or being inconsiderate of the trainer and the participants. Ask if they would be willing to help you in future sessions they attend. If the person truly wants to share their knowledge and experience, provide the time and venue to do so during a future training session.
- **Notify their supervisor if behavior continues.** If the person's intent is not positive or constructive, or if the person is insulting, rude, or offensive, it's time to escalate the

situation and report their behavior. Leadership in most organizations want to know how their staff members behave while on the job or at training. If this person is in violation of basic employee conduct policies, you should report their actions to their supervisor immediately, especially if they are a new employee. If this person comes from outside the organization, then follow the proper procedures for reporting it.

However, some healthcare workers are just tired or are dealing with some kind of major challenge and may not be being intentionally difficult. Or perhaps they're a third-shifter who thought they could power through an early morning training session and stay focused after a long overnight shift. Facilitators must maneuver these participants as well, while consistently delivering this critical information to all hospital staff members. Here are some techniques I have used to enliven my delivery and facilitation while keeping the training interesting, engaging, and fun:

- **Empathize with the audience.** When training healthcare workers, you need an extra level of understanding if staff don't show up for training or show up tired. Having never worked in healthcare before, I took this personally until I developed a level of empathy toward the staff and their personal and patient care demands. Remember, they are taking on a lot personally and professionally; try walking the floors of the hospital and observing them in action to better understand their challenges. For example, I worked directly with many patient care providers while performing interpreter services, and I've been between the doctor and patient directly facilitating the care process. This allowed me to see and experience some of the challenges that care-providers have to manage while dealing with patients and family members. And it won't matter when the training is planned or delivered, your audience will likely be strained, exhausted, and distracted—so work with them during the delivery and acknowledge these struggles. In fact, I urge you to say it directly and let them know they are appreciated with, "I know everyone is working hard every day to meet our patients' and families' needs; we thank you for this!"
- **Increase your physical presence.** Work the room by moving around, rather than standing behind the podium while delivering your message. The audience wants a conversation and eye contact; if you do that, the engagement will surely come. Trainers should call on those they know by name (and read the name badges of others) to encourage involvement. If anyone is caught dozing or sleeping, I'll move closer to

them while speaking and continue to project my voice. If I know them personally (and only then!) I might give them a soft double pat on the shoulder as I'm walking by (while speaking) to let them know that I know they're sleepy and tired.

- **Maintain your voice's volume and presence.** In addition to physical presence, you should maintain prominent voice projection, volume, and intonation. Use body language and inflect your tone to emphasize a key point or you could slow down your delivery of the message for greater emphasis (Wash . . . Your . . . Hands!!!). Increasing your voice volume is another option for conveying key points (Wash your hands for at least 30 SECONDS!!). Using your voice to add emphasis can alert the audience to the importance of that piece of information.
- **Finish the trainer's thought.** A lot of OSHA and other regulatory safety practices don't vary much from year to year. As a result, most experienced healthcare audiences already know this stuff. Encourage audience participation in what could feel to them like a dull repeat of last year's program by letting the learners help deliver the content. For example, you could ask the audience, "What do we already know about proper hand washings?" or "Who would like to demonstrate how to properly wash your hands?" Involve the audience when reviewing content they learned during last year's mandatory training (or make it into a game, like Safety Jeopardy). Use questions to prompt a good group discussion about how things are done consistently (or not) across departments or shifts.
- **Offer offline assistance.** If someone is just not getting it or struggling with the content, or if you're concerned they weren't paying attention during the delivery of certain content, you can offer the employee (or group) additional training offline and in another setting. You can make the offer directly to the employee to see if they're responsive and think it's something they need, or you can suggest it directly to their supervisor.

When you involve the audience, you make your job much easier. However, you still have to demonstrate authority over the participants (regardless of their background or title), and you need to maintain a pleasant and productive learning environment. Your true facilitation talents are exposed when you help the audience share knowledge among themselves through great group facilitation. You can also use this as an opportunity to develop good relationships with your co-workers who could serve as subject matter experts (SMEs) in the future.

Key Takeaways

- Know the content well enough to adapt it to a specific learner's level of understanding and expertise. Be ready to answer questions, but also rely on the audience to confirm whether these practices are being performed *consistently* across the organization. Provide feedback to hospital leadership if you're hearing otherwise.
- Use group facilitation techniques to maintain control of the audience and manage any staff who are impolite, distracting, or not supporting the learning environment. There is no excuse for poor employee conduct, so if staff members are disruptive, report their behavior through the proper channels.
- You may encounter difficult and challenging people in the audience, especially if healthcare workers are under strain or exhausted from the day's work (and many are, especially now). Prepare accordingly—empathize with hospital staff but continue to hold them to the same employee behavior expectations. Determine how to communicate the importance of the information they're receiving, why it is important, and how they should apply it. Let compliance and human resources policies be your guide during these tricky situations.
- If your healthcare audience is strained or exhausted, be empathetic and use group facilitation techniques—such as increased instructor presence, heightened voice intonation, and audience engagement with fun activities—to maintain a quality training delivery, especially when dealing with repetitive subject matter.

Collaborative Delivery and Facilitation

The best thing about training facilitation is that you can coalesce a group of professionals and guide them through a quality learning experience. It can be amazing to see them apply what you have taught and do so together as a team, all in the name of patient care, emergency planning, and best practices for all. But I've found it even more rewarding to collaborate with nurse educators to design and deliver annual mandatory training sessions. We created a unity in practice by merging our skills to maintain the program and keep the hospital federally and locally compliant for years.

The collaboration of the clinical and nonclinical staff at the hospital was strong, and everyone understood that much more could be accomplished collectively than individually. We often had to deliver and facilitate the annual mandatory training to all hospital staff (a mixed audience of clinical and nonclinical staff). Everyone understood their interdependence in providing patient care, had great care for one another, and respected the role they played (clinical and nonclinical); we referred to this as "Joy, Care, Respect." We all knew that it took a team of people working together to ensure quality patient care, emergency plans, and employee safety practices.

Another great example of training delivery collaboration came about when I worked at the headquarters of a major grocery chain in HR as an instructional designer and trainer. The company had more than 300,000 employees nationwide at the time. Our team was responsible for developing training content about store processes. So, we created two-by-two-foot table-top flipcharts that showed graphical process flows for various processes (such as the standard store layout, cash management processes, and customer interaction expectations) and produced training videos on safety and food handling. We then delivered a train-the-trainer session to all store managers by region and shared the table-top posters and training videos. The managers used these tools to deliver consistent training content to the store employees. This training often occurred in the store's small breakroom, which was typically cluttered with boxes, products, and store cleaning equipment. These customized tabletop orientation tools helped the company ensure staff used consistent best practices, procedures, and standard processes across all stores.

This idea of tabletop learning originally came from my time working with nurse educators while serving as director of hospital education at a major hospital. Nurse educators are a profession of their own, who strongly support consistent care across all nursing specialty areas (including critical care, ICU, emergency nursing, prenatal and obstetrics nursing, and wound care nursing). Each unit at the hospital is assigned a nurse educator with skills unique to that unit who ensures all clinical staff in that area consistently and compliantly learn and practice the same patient care practices and processes. Three nurse educators were assigned to my team, and we collaborated for many years as a cross-functional team to deliver annual mandatory training to nearly 2,500 hospital and nursing home staff.

It was while working with the nurse educators that I realized training and facilitation doesn't have to occur in a classroom or formal setting. They helped change my perception and influenced my flexibility in where and when I delivered learning content. They also taught me about table-top training—a technique they commonly used to train (especially new) nurses in their tight, limited workspace or in a breakroom (not always a classroom). They used these sessions as pop-up impromptu training to teach critical components of care for their area of the hospital. My team delivered new employee orientation; once that was over, I would hand clinical staff over to the nurse educators who led table-top sessions in their areas. We also developed and delivered 25 three-hour mandatory training sessions annually to all current hospital staff—a process we followed successfully for close to a decade.

One year we decided to take the hospital's annual mandatory training outside the classroom and ramp up the table-top training delivery method using a large poster board presentation. Normally, my staff and the nurse educators would meet for a strategic planning day in January to determine the "hot mandatory topics" for the year and set the 25 training dates and times. We also assigned who would cover each session's delivery, and agreed that we wanted a nurse educator (clinical) and trainer (nonclinical) to co-deliver the large sessions we held for all shifts of the hospital (even the overnight sessions).

This time our delivery method was different. We set up the poster board presentation in a rarely used area of the hospital: the hallway to the loading docks. Despite the location, we still scheduled clinical and nonclinical staff so someone was present all times and ready to facilitate individuals and groups through the learning process. This ensured consistency in practice and allowed us to answer any questions from staff. Our process worked like this:

- Hospital staff would come to the hallway when convenient and grab a test sheet.
- A nurse educator or trainer would explain the new delivery method and get them started with verbal instructions.
- The nurse educator or trainer would maintain a presence by telling learners what to focus on as they reviewed the 10 posters and answered the test questions on each.
- Relevant handouts were stationed under each poster board, so participants could continue learning even after they left the area and returned to their workspace.
- After the employees reviewed the boards and answered the test questions, the trainer would assess their test sheet for completeness before placing it in a lockbox on the wall.
- On a weekly basis, trainers and nurse educators then took turns emptying a secured lockbox, grading exams, and tallying the results. (If an employee failed, the trainer or nurse educator would notify their supervisor, who then had to walk their employee through a second attempt while providing coaching.)

Everyone enjoyed this format:

- Hospital employees could complete the training with a co-worker at a time convenient for them. It was a much shorter learning process than the previous three-hour in-person training sessions.

- Leadership team was happy that the annual mandatory training numbers drastically improved, and employees were making good, productive use of an often misused and abused remote area of the hospital.
- The hospital and nursing education departments were able to complete mandatory training delivery for all staff, and we were all proud of being able to jointly contribute our knowledge to a learning process that benefitted clinical and nonclinical staff.
- Regulators admired the collaboration between the hospital's clinical and nonclinical entities of and appreciated the convenient, safe, and fun method used for training hospital staff on critical topics.

The Joint Commission encourages healthcare leaders to formulate cross-functional teams to make objective house-wide decisions that are high-impact to their patients, customer base, and the local community. These processes require the cooperation and coordination of clinical and nonclinical staff in a healthcare facility, who must learn how to work together and do so smoothly in the name of patient care. The nurse educators and hospital education trainers demonstrated this collaborative spirit by creating this poster board training process and facilitating hundreds of staff members (individually and in groups) through the learning process according to their unique needs in that moment.

Key Takeaways

- In the name of patient care, clinical and nonclinical educators and trainers often share and encourage a unity of practice teambuilding concept. This is admired by leadership and regulators, and hospital staff benefit during the resulting training sessions (regardless of the delivery method).
- Clinical and nonclinical teams work together to jointly and consistently maintain the organization's processes and procedures. When they collaborate to support the organization's compliance efforts, everyone experiences greater productivity, more employee engagement, increased employee knowledge, and a more positive atmosphere across the hospital. The result leads to overall positive patient, customer, and family experiences during their care continuum.
- Talent development professionals should design and deliver quality annual mandatory training in a manner that not only engages the staff, but helps the organization maintain compliance and its customer base. In this role you orchestrate the learning process with staff, and in tandem with leadership, to keep the organization safe, compliant, and in a constant state of readiness.

Conclusion

Yesterday, today, and tomorrow working in healthcare will always be challenging, and regular training will always be necessary. In this, the clinical and nonclinical in-house educators play a critical role in supporting the knowledge, skills, and abilities of healthcare workers who go on to play a critical role in keeping everyone healthy and safe.

Talent development professionals in healthcare can apply a variety of training delivery and facilitation techniques to enhance the quality of the training provided, but the training must be effective for the course's learning objectives. You can:

- **Study the audience and their specific learning needs.** Perform a proper needs assessment and design quality training accordingly. Use this information during delivery to engage and encourage participation across the diverse healthcare audience.
- **Plan for challenging questions and individuals** who might know more than you. Without bringing too much attention to them, use group facilitation techniques to include these individuals into the learning, as well as bring the quiet learners into group discussions.
- **Understand and empathize with the audience**—remember that they are under a lot of personal strain, on the clock, and caring for patients or customers 24/7. Offer to come to them to facilitate training. Maximize your time by immediately stating the objectives and efficiently delivering the training content.
- **Use a variety of training and facilitation techniques**, regardless of the delivery method, to maintain audience control and keep learners engaged and involved.

My extensive history of facilitating and delivering training in the hospital setting has always been a win for me, for my fellow nurse educators and trainers, for the healthcare workers we trained, for hospital leadership, and for the patients and local community. We all benefited from the knowledge exchanged, respectful comradery, and our combined support of the organization's total compliance and educational efforts. Working as a team, applying training industry practices, studying the needs of the organization, collaborating with subject matter experts, and planning and executing quality training has always been the focus. And that has turned out to be a winning recipe in the hospital setting.

CHAPTER 2

ADDITIONAL TECHNIQUES FOR TRAINING DELIVERY AND FACILITATION

DENISE HICKEN

Noncompliance training in a healthcare setting often falls within one of five areas: leadership development, new employee orientation, equipment, procedures, or software training. The last three call for straightforward, to-the-point facilitation. Many of the principles used in these more linear courses align with compliance training. However, classes that fall under soft skills (such as leadership and communication) thrive on open and experiential learning facilitation models, which allow learners to explore the topic within a safe environment and apply the information to their specific situations.

In this chapter, I'll walk through three things facilitators need to ensure learning is successful. Then, I'll highlight two of the roles facilitators can play to make that happen. Finally, I'll wrap up with some facilitation best practices.

Creating a Learning Environment

Let's start with an example. A talent development (TD) professional developed and facilitated a leadership series called Transition to Leadership for a health system's new and emerging leaders. The audience was a mixture of clinical and nonclinical employees with varying leadership and work experiences. As the series progressed and participants discovered they had similar challenges, they developed a synergy where they could share possible solutions for those leadership challenges. This open model allowed the class freedom to learn from each other and provided a haven where they could share, admit struggles, and seek help from others.

In the Transition to Leadership series, the facilitator would conduct roundtable discussions and invite participants to share challenges within their role. The class would then discuss, using the material they'd learned so far in the series and their personal work experiences; those insights would often spark even further discussion. It was a wonderful learning experience for the entire class. Not only did they use what they had learned in the series, they deepened their bonds and continued their friendships and knowledge sharing beyond the series.

A crucial skill for a facilitator, especially in a noncompliance course, is the ability to create a safe, inclusive environment for participants so that bonding can occur. Whether the course is virtual or in person, if participants don't feel safe, they won't allow themselves to fully participate.

Maslow's hierarchy of needs highlights this point (Figure 2-1). The need to feel safe (located near the bottom of the pyramid) must be met before participants develop a feeling of belonging. Closer to the top of the pyramid sits esteem needs; that is to feel good about one's self and abilities. The top of the pyramid is self-actualization, which looks different for each person, depending upon their desire to achieve in a particular area of interest. Noted neuropsychologist Kurt Goldstein stated in his book, *The Organism: A Holistic Approach to Biology Derived from Pathological Data in Man* (1934), that self-actualization involves the tendency to actualize an organism's individual capabilities as well. This aligns with the thought that participants in a leadership course would seek to improve their performance.

Figure 2-1. Maslow's Hierarchy of Needs

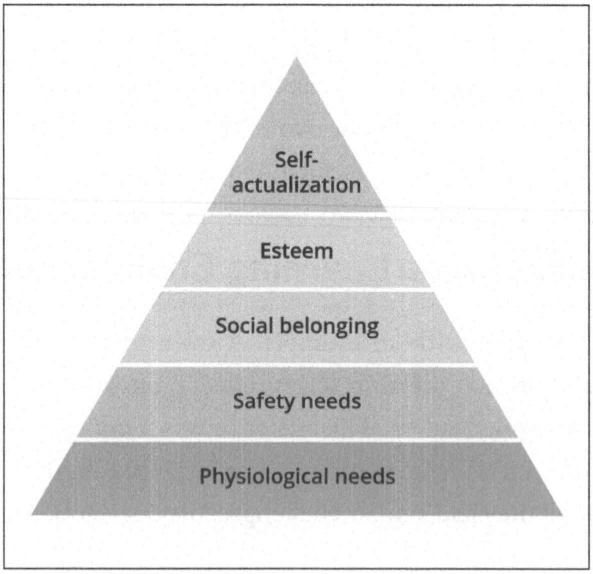

Creating Connection With Participants

Safety supports the creation of connection. Craig Abrahamson's research into the connection between a professor and their class supports this premise: "There must be a relationship between students and the instructor that is founded on mutual sharing of personal experiences, values, beliefs and course content" (2011).

Naturally curious facilitators want to ask questions to understand each participant's needs and desires for the class. The facilitator in the Transition to Leadership series chose to begin building these connections prior to the first session by speaking with the participants' managers and contacting participants directly. Speaking with their managers provided a wealth of information about the participant's role and the manager's reasons for recommending the course; speaking with participants provided more insight into their leadership challenges and what they wanted to take away from the series.

Icebreakers can be more than a simple introductory tool; they are excellent vehicles for creating connection. Run a quick internet search for "training icebreakers" and you'll find a plethora of suggestions. Icebreakers seem to have one thing in common: They encourage participants to share something about themselves. For participants, this provides an initial test of the class environment, so it is imperative for the facilitator to demonstrate, through comments and body language, an interest in the individuals during the exercise and debrief.

Creating a Comfort Zone

To get into a connection frame of mind, participants need to feel comfortable. Frontline healthcare workers and their managers often struggle with physical and mental exhaustion, high stress, and long shifts. Facilitators must transport them to a different mental space to help them focus on the class. In addition, consider that clinical participants are accustomed to evidence-based learning that's scientific and precise—symptoms are present, the illness is diagnosed, and the plan of care dictates specific medicines and procedures. Even a dynamic emergency situation has procedures and protocols. When running a soft skills or noncompliance class, facilitators must consider that, in addition to the stressors already addressed, they may be pulling participants out of their comfort zones and must facilitate accordingly.

Understanding your audience is a given for any facilitation opportunity; however, there is also value in digging deeper into the makeup of your healthcare audience. This is especially true if you are facilitating a smaller class where the participants fall into a wide range of skill levels. Understanding the skill diversity helps you prepare content that's inclusive of all levels.

If there is a concern about participants' prior topic knowledge and skill level, facilitators can send out a pre-class content survey or a knowledge check. They can then use the responses to create a knowledge and skill-level baseline, as well as to learn more about the participants, their job responsibilities, and their expectations for the course. The information allows the TD professionals to tailor their facilitation plans to meet the participants' needs by identifying who may need additional guidance, and who can provide contributions to enhance the course experience.

It's helpful to reach out to participants with a higher level of topic knowledge or experience prior to class for a couple of reasons: The facilitator can ask more specific questions about the participant's expectations for the course, and gauge their comfort in sharing their lessons learned. Usually, participants are more than happy to oblige and are flattered you reached out to them. In addition, knowing their expectations for the class provides an opportunity to make tweaks to ensure the content is meaningful to the entire class.

Facilitating a soft skills class, such as communication, for a group of clinical participants can be especially challenging for a nonclinical facilitator. The facilitator may initially lack credibility because they lack a shared job experience, which can cause participants to doubt the facilitator's ability to relate to their workplace struggles. To combat this, TD professionals should include extra time for building rapport and reaching out to participants on a personal level—ask them to share experiences around the class topic to allow you to better understand their perspective. Share pertinent, meaningful information about yourself to build a human connection, which can increase credibility. It's incumbent on the facilitator to look for similarities and determine how to make the emotional tie with the class.

Creating a learning environment, creating connection with participants, and creating a comfort zone are three essential tasks for successful trainers and facilitators. To that end, we can think of the facilitator as filling two roles: guide and coach. Let's tackle each.

Key Takeaways

- Successful facilitators make sure participants experience a safe, open environment for learning, have opportunities to connect with the facilitator and other participants, and are comfortable with the training content.
- What are some steps you can take to ensure your training delivery and facilitation meets the needs of your participants? Can you invite participants to share challenges within their role? Can you reach out to participants to learn more about them before the session even starts? Then, can you use that knowledge to tailor the facilitation plan to meet their needs?

Facilitator as Guide

To change outcomes, you must change behavior. A change leader, the role the talent development professional plays, guides the class by introducing new ideas and approaches to change behavior through listening, discussing, and encouraging skill practice with thoughtful feedback. This allows participants to begin making the connection between current behavior and the desired behavior. This aligns with John Dewey's constructivist learning theory, which states that participants construct knowledge for themselves, rather than just passively taking in information. The new information builds upon pre-existing knowledge.

One tactic to create discussion and allow participants to consider new ideas is Socratic, or reflective, questioning. Socratic questions are concise, open-ended questions that invite discussion without expecting the learner to have an answer. They are also neutral; they don't suggest a correct or preferred answer. Some Socratic questions around soft skills include:

- How would this affect someone?
- What are the long-term implications?
- What caused you to feel that way?
- Is there any other information needed?

These questions are intended to spark self-reflection and promote interest in a deeper understanding. In a healthcare setting, Socratic questioning is beneficial when asking participants to share a situation where communication with a patient or family member was challenging. Facilitators can use these questions to guide participants through self-discovery of how their actions and words affected the communication and its outcome. This insight may create an understanding and willingness to change behavior.

Guidance played a key role in the Transition to Leadership series. Each participant was tasked to explore their department's contribution to the health system and then develop mission and vision statements for their department. When they met with the facilitator one-on-one to discuss, they were urged to expand their view of the department from day-to-day to a 30,000-foot view. The facilitator began the discussion by asking what role the participant's team played within the organization. Initially, they all gave very day-to-day task-oriented explanations. For example, a blood bank manager responded that her department typed and prepared blood to be used on the units. When the facilitator asked "What would happen if your team didn't do you its job well?" it allowed the manager to see the larger impact of her team. If her staff didn't do their jobs well, patients would be in jeopardy. With additional questioning and discussion, she began to see her department from a different vantage point.

This was a revelation for many in the Transition to Leadership program because they had never viewed their department through this lens. In another example, a housekeeping supervisor's initial mission statement was rudimentary, given to day-to-day tasks. However, when he removed himself from the daily tasks and considered the team's broader impact, he realized that "to create a healing environment" was a better mission statement they could all embrace.

Facilitator as a Coach

At times, a facilitator must transcend being a guide and become a coach. In sports, a coach takes their team and develops strengths while minimizing weaknesses. It's an art as much as a science to harness and develop raw talent. Talent development professionals also use coaching to help participants develop strengths by minimizing weaknesses. In healthcare, one focus for coaching is on improving the patient experience. Research indicates that the patient experience correlates to patient outcomes. It also drives HCAHPS (Hospital Consumer Assessment of Healthcare Providers and Systems) scores, which affect the amount of reimbursement hospitals receive for Medicare and Medicaid. Scores on the communication portion of the HCAHPS survey carry significant weight, especially questions about communication between the patient, the nurse, and the provider. (For more on the importance of the patient experience, see chapter 23.)

Coaching participants to change their communication skills aligns with constructivist theory. SBAR (situation, background, assessment, recommendation) is a tool that helps nurses communicate more efficiently with physicians concerning a patient's status. There may be an initial reluctance to change behavior if the participant doesn't see the benefits; as their coach, it's incumbent to establish the "why." Adults want to understand both the impact of the change and how it affects them. The WIIFM (what's in it for me?) clarifies why the effort to change is worthwhile, so the coach should make sure to discuss the benefits and alleviate voiced concerns.

Establishing a comfort level with behavior change also requires skill practice, such as through role play. When psychological safety is established within the training environment, facilitators may move away from traditional role-play skill development by incorporating the fishbowl technique. In this activity, volunteers complete the exercise or discussion in front of the rest of the class—like they're in a fishbowl. For example, the coach may provide participants with different scenarios and ask them to consider how they will use SBAR in each. The participants then share their SBAR statements while the rest of the class watches and listens. In addition to facilitator coaching, their classmates can also provide supportive feedback.

In the healthcare setting, communication and service behaviors that influence patient experience are often taught during orientation and then reinforced on a continual basis. Thus, poor performance in this area is likely not caused by a knowledge deficit or lack of skill—it may simply be caused by the person's attitude. Perhaps it's not a priority for the employee, or worse, the employee believes they already exhibit the behavior satisfactorily. Define what success looks like in their world. Use case studies and examples to demonstrate how good communication and excellent service lead to better outcomes. Coach them to understand that amazing care includes excellent communication and strong service behaviors. If successful, participants will see how care, communication, and service create a trifecta that improves patient outcomes. That understanding will, hopefully, motivate a change in behavior.

Key Takeaways

- Do you assume the role of guide with your learners? Do you employ reflective questions to invite discussion and allow learners to make their own discoveries?
- Do you coach learners when appropriate? Do you work to establish the "why" so participants understand why they need to learn new skills, change their behavior, and so on?

Noncompliance Facilitation Best Practices

Healthcare is a unique beast. Ever-changing demands, especially with clinical staff, lead to a higher number of participant cancellations and interruptions during class. This is especially true during the winter months, when admission rates rise and clinical staff are caring for sicker patients. As a facilitator, flexibility is essential.

However, some facilitation principles will always be valid. These best practices apply to both in-person and virtual facilitation.

- **Start on time; end on time.** Healthcare leaders are booked with meetings, round on patients, manage units, and coach staff. They're pulled in every way possible, and they depend on the fact class will start and end when expected. That said, leaders often gather for a few minutes after the official end of class to discuss take-aways.
- **Be set up and ready.** Plan to spend a minimum of 30 minutes getting set up prior to the start of a class. As a rule, set up and test the technology, including your presentation and audio, prior to the session if applicable. Check anything that could impede your delivery. In doing so, you give yourself time to take a breath and mentally prepare to facilitate your best class.
- **Warmly greet and engage with the participants.** Pay particular attention to anyone you have not met previously. Your interaction with the class early on sets the tone for the session. This also applies to virtual classes. Participants who feel welcomed and like they're in a safe environment will engage at a deeper level. This can make or break your session! If there's little or no discussion because the class doesn't feel safe to engage, the program will not achieve its objectives. Consider Maslow's hierarchy—the need to feel safe is paramount. To enhance safety, set the expectation that anything said during class, stays in class. If discussing current leadership challenges, do not disclose employee names.
- **Use PowerPoint as an enhancement.** If PowerPoint is the primary source of information, the class will not stay engaged. It's common presentation knowledge that we shouldn't read the screen, but it can be tempting to simply read the bullet points if you're not completely comfortable with the material. This is especially common in when trainers facilitate courses for the first time, especially if it's material they didn't design. Using images, rather than words, is more captivating than bullet points. The images can be photos, clip art (watch copyright), or something created in Adobe Photoshop or PowerPoint.

- **Keep it fresh.** For in-person classes, change the interaction every seven to eight minutes to enhance engagement. The facilitator must continually provide opportunities for class interaction. In an in-person environment, the participants have several visual interests—the facilitator's words and actions, educational elements, and other participants. In the virtual environment, there is just a screen filled with a visual element, such as PowerPoint, and perhaps also head shots of the facilitator and participants. In addition, it's extra tempting for participants to multitask while participating in virtual training, especially when it comes to checking their email.
- **Let the technology help participants focus.** Whiteboards, chat, and polling can promote engagement. Some virtual applications allow for participants to gather in breakout rooms for small group interaction, collaboration, and discussion. These also provide a perfect opportunity for to groups to review scenarios for problem solving. Once the activity is over, participants can come back into the main session and each group can share what they developed or learned.
- **Pump up your energy.** Virtual facilitation presents its own energy challenges. When you're training an in-person session, you can work the room and walk around to feed off participants' energy. When training is virtual, you're sitting at a laptop in a room by yourself. It's difficult to maintain a classroom level of energy when you're sitting, so it's important to push an extra level of energy and not allow yourself or your vocal tone to lag. Record yourself as you practice facilitating. When you play the recording back, if it sounds like you're a little over the top in your delivery, it's probably exactly where you need to be to provide the right level of energy for your virtual classroom.

Conclusion

Facilitating a class, whether in person or virtually, can be a rewarding experience. You have front row seat to watch your class learn and experience new ideas and relationships, as well as grow as professionals. Take pride in what you do. It's not always easy, and it's not a skill everyone possesses. Realize that as a talent development professional, you have a gift to share.

CHAPTER 3

INSTRUCTIONAL DESIGN

DAWN MAHONEY

Effective training is not about innovative tools or learning content delivery methods. It is first and foremost about the work of instructional design. This chapter is provided to pique your curiosity: to spark ideas, clarify how to best craft a learning strategy, determine the best way to circumvent obstacles before they appear, and discover ways to help learners maximize learning retention. We'll cover the steps in the ADDIE model (analysis, design, development, implementation, and evaluation) and offer best practices to succeed at each stage. But let's begin with your learners and determining who they are.

Who Are the Learners?

What comes to mind when thinking through instructional design for healthcare? Here's one thought: "unique and diverse needs."

Crafting learning programs in healthcare encompasses a wide variety of learning audiences, including:

- Physicians and nurses
- Surgery and anesthesiology
- Emergency services and trauma unit
- Laboratory
- Radiology
- Laundry and housekeeping
- Facilities and maintenance
- Food service: dieticians, line cooks, dishwashers
- Security and parking attendants
- Administration, information services, and operations
- Social workers
- Pharmacy
- Volunteers

They may also include:

- Patients of all ages—from infant through advanced age
- Patients and staff who may not have learned English as their first language
- Three to four different generations

Sometimes, they will overlap and use the same content. At other times, each learning audience will need content uniquely suited to them. Additionally, within each group, you may encounter diverse staff education levels. For example, learners may have no diploma or degree, a high school diploma or GED, a one-year specialized degree or certificate, a two-year specialized degree, a baccalaureate degree, or one or more advanced degrees, possibly with a specialty in more than one area.

You'll need to approach the instructional design process for every project by crafting learning goals for each specific audience. You can't rely on what is easy or quick to produce. Instead, establish standards and priorities for each group, including reading level standards. Generally, learning content should be written at a sixth-grade reading level, which ensures the content is more accessible and easier to consume on a mobile device.

Your content should always be aligned to those you are designing it for—regardless of the subject matter. This is why it is imperative to begin the instructional design process with empathy. In fact, empathy is an excellent starting point for all types of learning content. One way to do this is to craft empathy maps (sometimes called learner personas) that you and your team may revisit often. Doing this reminds the learning team who is going to be consuming the learning content—real people with real needs, real jobs, and real lives. Product designers and marketing professionals use empathy maps when seeking to better align with their ideal consumer's needs and wants. According to Connie Malamed (2020), "personas are well-developed fictional profiles that reflect audience member groups for whom we are designing a course." When used in this way, empathy maps help align the content, design, and development strategy to the learners' needs and wants.

Job Aid

Have you and the learning team crafted empathy maps of the various learner groups before? If so, when was the last review and revision cycle? Or are empathy maps a completely new concept? If so, then there is some work to do—and it should be illuminating and fun. Job Aid 3-1 (which you'll find at the end of this chapter) will help you begin or update your empathy maps.

Meet ADDIE

Instructional systems design (ISD), the core structure for how work gets done, was originally developed by the US military for creating training programs. While ISD and ADDIE are not project management methodologies, they do provide a framework to ensure nothing is missed. Other popular frameworks include the iterative methodologies like SAM (which is based on the Agile project management methodology), Lean, and lean learning (Mahoney 2018). The content in this chapter is based on the ADDIE framework (Figure 3-1), with a few less obvious elements called out and explained further.

Clarify the Business Need

The business need is the impetus for embarking upon the instructional design process. It may be related to overall business performance, or it could be related to learner groups who need additional skill and knowledge to be more effective in their work. The business need might relate to new software applications or business systems, updates to existing systems or processes, new skills or processes, or changes to job skills or tasks. In short, the business need relates to changes in behavior necessary to improve performance.

Understanding the business need is essential for executive buy-in and to demonstrate the value of training. "Persuade the C-suite to see that learning is an investment and tie it to business results," says Jacque Burandt (ATD 2019). For training that involves topics like compliance, Burandt recommends that "TD professionals focus their conversations with leaders on the consequences that may result if learners do not receive training, such as noncompliance fines."

Figure 3-1. The ADDIE Framework

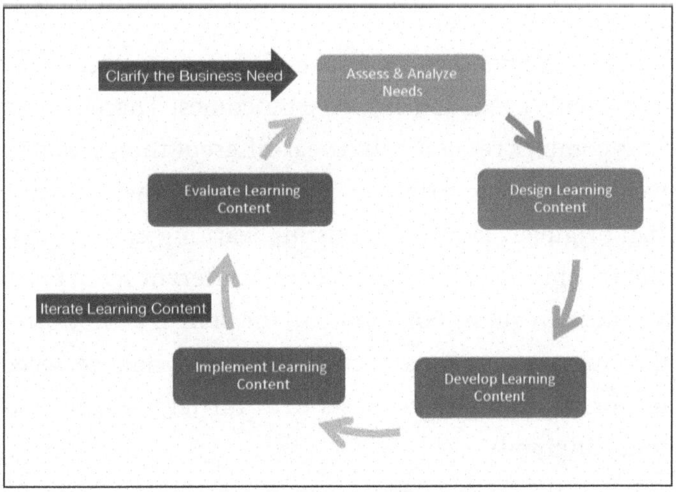

Conducting a needs assessment and compiling a needs analysis are two key instructional design activities TD professionals can use to clarify the business need for developing learning programs.

Conduct a Needs Assessment

Think of conducting a needs assessment as assuming a learning detective persona—begin to look for clues that will solve the mystery. In other words, when a request aligned with a stated business need appears, the learning team's next move should be to assess what is actually needed. The initial request shouldn't drive what happens next. The cause analysis model can help determine whether learners have everything they need to be successful on the job. (Use Job Aid 3-2, Cause Analysis Model, to help identify performance gaps.)

The more complex the business need, the more in-depth the needs assessment must be. But don't fail to assess needs for less complex requests as well. Remember, it is mission critical to do the work, regardless of the request's visibility and exposure. Uncovering the needs of the learners and seeking clarity is important no matter what.

"If all you have is a hammer, everything looks like a nail," warns Beth McGoldrick, instructional designer at RiverSource Insurance and co-author of *Needs Assessment Basics*, 2nd edition (ATD 2018). "When someone brings me a training assignment. . . . I start with a needs assessment on what's going on with the business and why there is a problem. When (or if) training has been identified as one of the possible solutions, then I start doing a training needs assessment."

The requests that accompany less complex learning content have their own unique and specific needs and expected outcomes. Therefore, conducting a needs assessment for a less complex request will reveal different things than a more complex request—and may even reveal some surprises. For example, the learner group may be larger or different than originally stated. Or existing learning content may need further investigation and repurposing. Or you may discover a different set of needs once you dig a little deeper into the initial request. For example, the staff may not have everything they need, which is affecting one or more aspects of their performance. Needs assessments are just as important for less complex requests than for large or more complex projects, even if they're done differently.

Here's what is essential for *every* needs assessment:

- Get very curious.
- Ask lots of good questions.
- Get the full story from as many people as possible.
- Challenge assumptions.
- Get creative.
- Pinpoint the actual problem.
- Confirm the problem with all involved.
- Craft a list of several potential solutions.
- Set goals for the needs assessment.

The next step after gathering information and collecting data is talking to the people who do the work. Here are some best practices for collecting needs assessment data:

- Obtain permission from key stakeholders to complete the needs assessment, being certain to ask for the names of individuals to contact for information.
- If you need access to certain computer apps, systems, or physical locations before starting the needs assessment, be sure to complete any required forms and contact the person or department responsible.
- Contact all individuals assigned to the needs assessment as early as possible. Request their preferred communication method, availability for meetings, and so on.

There are many methods to collect data, including surveys or questionnaires, focus groups, nominal group techniques, interviews, social curation, and secondary sources. See Job Aid 3-3 for a tool to determine which methods fit the learning content, your organization, business need, and expected performance.

Review everything you've collected, looking for trends and anomalies. Quantify how often elements reappear. Review business results. Scrutinize the roles and job descriptions of the affected learners. Clarify and get permission to use testimonials. In other words, pay attention to anything and everything that informs the learning project and expected outcomes. One way to organize your needs assessment efforts is with a data collection plan. See Job Aid 3-4 for a tool to plan what questions to answer and problems to explore, key resources, key data sources, and which methods you'll use.

To communicate the data and information gathered during the needs assessment, you'll use a needs analysis report.

Compile a Needs Analysis Report

Once the business need and expected outcomes are clear, compile the information and craft a plan that makes achieving the expected outcomes a real possibility. This report is called the needs analysis. It brings structure to the various sets of results and is where you'll propose an appropriate learning strategy. Narrate the data and information gathered while assessing needs using infographics, video testimonials, quotations, images, diagrams, pictures—whatever illustrates the story of the data best.

The needs analysis should include:

- The identified learning goals
- The performance gaps
- Definitions of the performance objectives
- Details about the learner groups who will complete the learning content
- The overall design plan for the learning content, the evaluation strategy, and how the content will be reinforced back on the job
- Any resources the learning team needs to complete the learning program, such as additional people, new software applications, or system access for developers
- Explanations of how existing learning content might be reworked for use in this learning program
- The development schedule
- Specifics on the implementation or deployment of the learning content (for example, details about a pilot group that will lead to a revision and iteration plan, or the schedule for deploying each phase of e-learning)
- Explanations of how the learning content will be evaluated, how and how often the results will be provided to key stakeholders, and any plans for acting on the results
- Evidence of when a learning event isn't the best solution to address the business need (for example, if a system enhancement or a change to the environment or process are needed instead)

That final bullet point is provided as both permission and a reminder for the learning team. The request might appear to address a business need through the completion of learning content. However, not all business needs are best addressed through behavior change. Do the work. Take a holistic approach to assessing not only the skills and task of the learners, but also the work environment and organizational capability to address the business need, as well as how the culture and orientation will support behavior change.

As shared in a case study of New York–based St. Charles Hospital about its effort to improve patient care through on-the-job performance support, training might not be the best solution for healthcare professionals' learning needs (ATD Staff 2019). Instead, "look for training alternatives that suit the schedules of busy learners. Performance support tools, which can include job aids, checklists, and templates, provide learners materials they can learn from and reference later. At St. Charles Hospital, where healthcare providers were not always available for on-the-job training, [Andrew] Osso and [Joan] Grothmann provided performance support through step-by-step e-mails."

You can use Job Aid 3-5 to compile your needs analysis findings into a report to share with stakeholders.

Develop Learning Goals

The framework of an effective needs analysis includes a set of learning goals that align with the business need and expected outcomes. Learning goals are more than objectives—they use measurable and clarifying statements to show the impact of the learning program on the business, not the behavior change of the learners or learner groups. Learning goals should also be SMART:

- Specific
- Measurable
- Achievable
- Results oriented
- Time focused

Learning goals can include:

- Statements about how the learning content addresses the business need and initial request
- An outline of the entire learning population (if relevant, include role, department, leadership team, and other groupings)
- Timeframe to begin to realize business impact
- Overall budget and resource expectations
- Other items relevant to the organization

What are the overarching goals for the learning content? Write them out and include them in the needs analysis report.

Craft Performance Objectives

While learning goals reflect the overall expectations for the learning program, performance objectives explain the expected behavior changes after completing the learning content.

Crafting performance objectives is as much art as skill. The art side comes from Benjamin Bloom and his colleagues, who created Bloom's Taxonomy, a set of models that classify educational objectives into three domains: affective, cognitive, and sensory. Each domain is further classified to establish what the learners will be able to do after completing the learning content (Figure 3-2).

Figure 3-2. Bloom's Taxonomy

Affective *(Emotion Based)*	Cognitive *(Knowledge Based)*	Sensory or Psychomotor *(Action Based)*
• Receiving • Responding • Valuing • Organizing • Characterizing	• Knowledge • Comprehension • Application • Analysis • Synthesis • Evaluation	• Perception Set • Guided Response Mechanism • Complex Overt Response • Adaptation • Origination

Source: Bloom (1956); Longman (2001).

When drafting performance objectives, use action-oriented and measurable language to guide completion of the learning content. Ensure each performance objective aligns with the stated business need and defines exactly what you want the learners to be able to do and by when. Design, development, learner support, and evaluation plans that are based on the data gathered when assessing needs are required to achieve the goals and performance objectives.

Here are a few examples of performance objectives:

- Operate a new surgical tool with precision and accuracy after X hours of instruction and Y hours of practice.
- Demonstrate confidence using the newly implemented XYZ accounts payable system within X days of completing the learning content and all simulation practice exercises.
- Reproduce the new admission process including additions after completing the learning content and all simulation assignments.

Behavior change takes time to become fully implemented into the work environment. Therefore, "by when" might be explained using increments of time:

- Learners who complete the learning content will be able to demonstrate skill A in their work environment within the first 10 days.
- Once they've completed the learning content, learners will be evaluated on skill A after 30 days.
- After six months, supervisors will present various work scenarios to evaluate each learner's level of proficiency with skill A.
- Supervisors will use the coaching guidelines to evaluate each learner fairly and provide clear and consistent coaching.

The performance objectives also help shape the evaluation plan by stating what is evaluated, applicable metrics, relevant timeframes, and time intervals.

Crafting performance objectives takes practice. Write many, then refine them. Ask others to review and critique them. Then revise accordingly. It is important that they are clear, measurable, and include a "by when." Include the stakeholder and subject matter experts in the review and critique process to ensure the performance objectives align with the business need and the results of the needs assessment. Use Job Aid 3-6 to help craft action-oriented and measurable performance objectives.

Develop the Evaluation Strategy

Crafting the learning content is only half of the story. An evaluation strategy is a key element of your program's success. It may also include planning for iteration. The evaluation plan is part of the design, development, and implementation stages—it should not be tacked on after everything else is finished.

To best evaluate the success of any learning content, list all relevant dimensions and standards that shape the content. For example:

- **Delivery method.** Ask learners to weigh in on their experience using the learning content's delivery method or methods. Also, ask for suggestions for updates or improvements.
- **Design.** Ask learners to comment on which aspects of the learning content design made it favorable for learning.
- **Relevance.** To what extent was the learning content relevant to completing the job tasks?

- **Technology.** Ask learners to rate how easy or difficult the learning content, registration, and learning support tools were to access and complete.
- **Timeframe and timeliness.** Ask learners to rate their experience with respect to the amount of time allocated to completing the learning content.
- **Value.** Ask learners how valuable they found the learning content and their learning experience. Invite them to share what they plan to put into practice immediately.

Design and Develop the Learning Content

"How we design and deliver training is key to our organization's success," says Elaine Biech (2018). Learning content crafted only to check a proverbial box is a waste of valuable resources and doomed to fail. The design process should focus on proposing immersive learning experiences, not just courses or classes. Immersive learning experiences should challenge the learners to stretch beyond what they already know and know how to do, and think more broadly and apply top-notch critical thinking skills.

Here are a few real-world examples that didn't take environment into account when planning the learning content:

- E-learning courses that require healthcare workers, who are constantly on the move during their shifts, to sit at a computer for an hour or more are not easily accessible, nor do they simulate real-world experience.
- Learning requires focus. Patient care requires 100 percent focus and no distractions. Healthcare workers whose sole responsibility is patient care learn more effectively from e-learning content when not sitting (or standing) at an open workstation computer on the work floor. Having to complete e-learning courses while analyzing patient data, managing med passes, answering phones, greeting visitors, and listening for alarms isn't fair to the staff or the patients.
- Likewise for culinary and custodial staff. Their work requires them to be on the move. Accommodate them by creating learning programs that don't interrupt their workflow and provide the ability to focus only on what they are learning.

Just because it is convenient to develop e-learning does not mean it will provide a quality learning experience with high levels of retention. Some learners are more focused in instructor-led classes and some learning content is better disseminated this way. Others learn most effectively in real work situations with a coach or when completing a project that is then reviewed with feedback. The work is not one size fits all, so learning content shouldn't be either. Remember, it is an art and a science, with a whole lot of common sense thrown in.

Here are a few examples of what might work better:

- Distributed practice with spaced repetition.
- Peer learning where the group attends a classroom training session or completes an e-learning course. Peers are equipped with observation and coaching guidelines and a sign-off sheet for use when their peer masters a new process or procedure.
- Weekly or monthly learning hours that are scheduled in a designated learning environment.

Designing learning content is more than making things "pretty." In fact, "pretty" is only a small part of the design process. Designing is really about crafting a strategy for how learners will interact with the content. User experience (UX) designers refer to it as the user interface (UI), which is how we should think of the learning content design process too. We should consider how the learning content will look, while also considering what the learners' experience with the content will be.

Ask subject matter experts (SMEs) to help you develop real-world scenarios and situations—and get them right. SMEs can explain the tasks and role-specific aspects of the work, as well as clarify what successful outcomes look like and the metrics associated with performance and successful outcomes. Use these scenarios and real-world situations to:

- Challenge learners to step into a new role. Use this mechanism for learning new skills and tasks, fostering empathy for others, and raising awareness of other aspects of a process.
- Complete quests that use actual work settings, processes, and procedures to learn new skills or tasks—or review familiar ones, like safety procedures.
- Take staff on new work journeys. Whether paper or digital, maps make great tools and have a variety of uses in learning.
- Complete critical thinking activities using prompts like "What would you do?" "When would you do x, y, or z?" and "What action would you take?"
- Play serious games that present learners with real-world situations requiring critical thought and strategy to win. They could include increasing levels of complexity so learners can level up to reach the added or new expectations on the job.

Reinforce the Learning: Part of the Design Plan

Part of your design plan should consider how to reinforce the new information after the training program ends. Here are a few best practices:

- **Link to other learning content participants have previously completed.** Getting at least a little bit of someone's time is tough—especially in the healthcare setting. So, help the learners out by linking the program's learning initiatives to previous training they've participated in.
- **Support the learners once they're back on the job.** Develop a coaching plan their leaders can use to assess and coach after participants have finished the training program.
- **Don't assume that building the content, assigning it, and reporting on it is enough.** Do this at the peril of the learning team and its credibility.

Ensure the Content Is Accessible

Learning should always be accessible to all staff, and that's especially true in healthcare. This means that your content needs to stay compliant with Universal Design for Learning (UDL) standards, often referred to as 508 compliance (referencing the US regulations for making content accessible to all learners).

Here are some tips:

- Check the reading level of all text.
- Shorten and rename all links to more descriptive words, which makes them readable to screen readers.
- Update the Alt+Text associated with every image so screen readers can describe them.
- Use color, texture, and contrast intentionally.
- Only use web-safe fonts to ensure that mobile and assistive devices and screen readers will be able to read them.

Check the Reading Level of All Text

Establish a slightly lower reading level for learning content. This not only improves access for assistive devices and education levels, but also helps with retention and mobile learning.

Ensuring readability and reading levels is important because:

- English may not be a staff member's first language.

- Learning disabilities, like dyslexia, are common.
- A slightly lower reading level actually raises the level of reading comprehension for everyone.
- Lowering reading levels removes barriers, making it possible for more people to learn.
- When reading on screens, high-literacy readers scan text, rather than reading word-for-word; when the reading level is lower they'll comprehend better too.

To test readability, copy and paste your text into an online readability tool or use your word processor's built-in program. For example, Microsoft Word's spelling and grammar tool displays the document's Flesch Reading Ease and Flesch-Kincaid Grade Level.

To reduce the reading level of your content:

- Write in the active voice.
- Shorten all sentences.
- Avoid compound sentences.
- Use simpler, shorter words instead of more complex ones.

Reword and Shorten Links

Screen reading equipment only knows to read out all letters and characters that comprise links. Help learners out by updating link names to recognizable words.

Here's how in Microsoft Word:

Right-click on the page to reveal the selection menu and choose the "Link" option.

- Select the "Address" field, right-click, and choose "Paste."
- Move to the "Text to Display" field. Type something that makes sense when spoken out loud. This text will be hyperlinked in your document, so the URL is accessible, but not visible. It is OK to use more than one word, but don't go overboard.

Update the Alt+Text Associated With Every Image

An image that is important enough to be included in the content deserves accurate alt+-text too.

Here's how to add alt+text to an image in Microsoft Word:

- Click on the image and then right-click.
- Select "Edit Alt Text."
- Type an appropriate description for the image in the Alt Text field. (Note, less is more!)

Microsoft Word also has a feature that can generate the description for you. However, if you use this option, make sure to scrutinize the text carefully to make sure it's accurate.

Work Differently With Color, Texture, and Contrast

Use high contrast when crafting learning content—light background with dark text or dark background with light text. Keep the background clear of any interference, like textures, images, or shadows.

Where possible, avoid using red, magenta, orange, neon green, and bright yellow. Use them only sparingly, for example as highlights or spot color. Corporate style guides, palettes, and templates can make this difficult. The learning design team should do their best to finesse the palette available to craft better and more accessible learning content. For example, using difficult colors from the corporate palette as highlights, headers, footers, borders, or frames.

Craft Better Graphs and Charts

Many graphs and charts can be difficult for many people to read. They can even be difficult to work with if they've been provided by subject matter experts. Resist the temptation to just use the generic graphs and charts generated in Microsoft Excel.

Here's how to rework them for maximum impact:

- Only key details or metrics—fewer details mean better focus and better readability.
- Rebuild charts and graphs using shapes, fills, colors, and lines.
- Infographic-style images can tell the data's story quite well.
- Boost font size and weight of key metrics to ensure they are readable.
- Tell a visual story. Don't just plunk in numbers.

Use Fonts That Assistive Devices and Screen Readers Can Read

Fancy, curly fonts are difficult for some people to read, especially on mobile devices and when using screen reading equipment. Stick with simple, usually sans serif, fonts at reasonable sizes.

Here are a few best practices:

- In documents and e-learning content, use 11- or 12-point type for body text.
- If text is going to be projected on a big screen from several feet away, make the fonts larger. Test readability by stepping three to four feet away from your computer. If you can't read the copy at that size, boost it up.

- Use no more than two different fonts in a document.
- Use no more than two different font sizes.
- Use italics sparingly.
- Bold and all caps are for headings (occasionally to emphasize a word or two).

Working With Difficult Corporate Templates

Most organizations have a corporate branding and style guide that designates which logos to use where and what sizes are acceptable. There are also color formulas, suggested image styles, and fonts. The team responsible for the style guide has likely also crafted slide deck and document templates. However, were they crafted to best showcase learning content? Probably not.

Well-crafted learning content isn't a set of business-as-usual materials. For this reason, the learning team should ask to meet with the team responsible for setting the design standards to open a dialogue and explain what works best for different types of learning content. They can work together to craft templates that optimize learning for everyone, as well as e-learning content optimized for mobile.

Possible discussion items:

- Colors or fonts that do and don't work well in mobile and learning content
- Which fonts are not as accessible for the learning population
- The use of soft colors and "fancy" fonts that are difficult to read may become barriers for learners and limit their success
- Screen real estate is valuable in e-learning content and needs to be considered. Discuss whether required use of certain assets (such as larger images or logos) takes up valuable space that could be used to enhance the learning content. Note: The logo doesn't have to appear on every screen

Job Aid 3-7 can help you design your content and make decisions about the learning content to customize it to your organization.

Implement and Iterate the Learning Content

Content development should move almost seamlessly into the implementation stage (and back). Think of this phase as "implement to iterate; iterate to implement." Why? Because you should never consider the work "finished." Instead, move forward into every learning content development project with an iterative mindset. Put the revision plan on meeting agendas and the TD team's calendar from the beginning.

Before going live with the program, test everything. Make sure that:

- All expected learners in the group have access to everything they need
- The learner registration process is working
- All hyperlinks are active
- User access points, including login credentials, are active
- Webcast platform is set and learning content is in place
- Audio and video streams are working properly
- You've viewed the learning content on multiple types of screens and at various sizes
- Any books or print materials have been distributed as required
- You've double checked whatever else is relevant and necessary to the learning content

If you find areas lacking, move on to iteration. In her book *Training and Development for Dummies,* Elaine Biech (2015) explains, "Even after an excellent job of preparing, there is no guarantee that the program will go off without a hitch. That's why some trainers pilot a program with a group of pseudo-learners who provide feedback before the session is ready for prime time."

Don't be in such a hurry to deploy learning content and move on to a new project that you decide testing is not worth the effort. This is especially true if the learning content has high visibility and encompasses a broad group of learners. In addition to just making sense, pilot programs are an excellent way to capture testimonials and user experience information that you can share up the proverbial chain.

Ask the pilot group to provide qualitative and actionable feedback. Learners can rate:

- The level of difficulty to access the learning content
- The ease of navigation in the registration process, the course itself, and any assessments
- The method used to deliver the learning content
- The level to which the learning content was directly applicable to their work
- How the learning content aligned to its purpose and expected outcomes, based on their knowledge of the intent

Review all feedback and, if necessary, devise a plan for revising the learning content accordingly. You may want to convene a second pilot group before declaring everything final.

Before wrapping up, note that we touched on the importance of starting your evaluation plan at the beginning of the instructional design process. For more information on evaluation, see chapter 4 by Timothy R. Brock.

Conclusion

Instructional design should be all about the learners—what they need and what they need to know how to do. It is easy to overthink things and craft more than what they need. Or, to craft learning content using tools instructional designers prefer, rather than what works best for the learners and their environments. Make sure an empathy filter is fixed in place and that it informs every new request for learning content received. And don't forget to implement to iterate and iterate to implement.

Job Aid 3-1. Empathy Mapping the Learners

Craft empathy maps for each unique learner group in the organization. Customize this sample to reflect what is true in the organization. Note: This information is only for TD team use.

- Embark upon this project with eyes and ears wide open.
- Craft learning content that is more effective for the learners.
- Consider all information as relevant.
- No detail is too large or too small to include, at least during the information gathering stage.

1. Learner group:

2. What is known:

3. What this learning group needs, with respect to learning content, to be more successful on the job:

4. Primary needs:

5. Compliance and required learning content:

6. Ongoing learning needs:

7. Accessibility needs:

8. Language and translation needs:

9. Key concerns:

10. Target reading level for learning content for this learner group:

Key Attributes	Primary Roles	Primary Tasks and Responsibilities
• Level of education attained • Age range • Ethnicity • D&I considerations • Avg number of years of service	• Job title • Job codes • Job classifications	• Task 1 • Task 2 • Task 3 • Responsible for 1 • Responsible for 2 • Responsible for 3

Work Environment	Key Influences or Influencers	Technology Considerations
• Work environment is loud • Staff is on the move during their entire shift	• Role is in collective bargaining unit • Role is exempt • Learners fall into protected class	• Able to access a mobile device on the job • Access to a computer • Tech constraints • Apps and tools roles have access to include:

Job Aid 3-2. Cause Analysis Model

Use this tool when conducting a needs assessment to determine whether the learners have everything they need to be successful on the job—and whether the learning content will actually address the performance gap identified by the key stakeholders.

Potential Performance Gap Identified ______________________

External to Staff						Internal to Staff	
Environmental (Intangibles)			Resources (Tangibles)			Internal to Staff	
1. Organizational Systems/Processes	2. Incentives	3. Coaching and Reinforcement	4. Cognitive Support	5. Tools	6. Physical Environment	7. Skills and Knowledge	8. Inherent Ability
· Clear goals · Clear roles · Job design · Clear policies · Authority · Appropriate workload · Access to right people · Effective processes and systems	· Compensation · Positive reinforcement · Interesting, meaningful work · Positive incentives	· Coach · Encourage · Observe · Provide feedback · Acknowledge	· Job aids · Documentation · Performance support	· Computers · Software	· Noise · Lighting · Temperature · Physical space · Work area layout	· Training (self-study, on-the-job, etc.)	· Intellect · Ability · Physical attributes · Education · Level of motivation

Source: Adapted from Wile (1996).

Job Aid 3-3. Data Collection Methods

Use this worksheet to craft a data collection plan. Select the data collection methods that fit the learning content request, the organization, the business need, and expected performance.

Method	Approach	Reason to Use	Type of Data Collected
Survey or Questionnaire Types: • Exit • Engagement • Satisfaction • Informational	• Paper and pencil • Web-based survey tool • Email	• Conducive to using objective questions • Short or long narrative responses possible • Low or no cost to implement • Quick and easy to implement • Able to blend objective items with subjective items	• Personnel and staffing challenges • Working conditions • Organizational culture indicators • Staff level of commitment to the organization and the work • Information on what the staff needs
Focus Group	• In person • Web meeting • Phone • Teleconference	• Ability to observe facial expressions, body language, gestures, vocal tone, group dynamics • Low or no cost to implement • Relatively easy to plan and implement • Ability to uncover information that is or may not be known	• Additional information that may not be widely known
Nominal Group Techniques	• Brainstorming • Mind mapping • Affinity diagram • Cause-and-effect diagram • Statistical process control • Simulation • Problem analysis • SWOT analysis • Force field analysis	• Ability to see what was true, what is true, and what may be true in the future • Able to interpret what staff believe the risks, barriers, and threats to success may be • Possible to "blue sky" solutions with people integrally involved • Ability to uncover information that is or may not be known	• Staff ideas of current state • Ideas for improvement to get to future state • Potential barriers or risks • Conscious or unconscious biases

Interviews Type: • Probative • Exit • Informational	• In person • Web meeting • Phone • Teleconference	• Short timeframe • Quick turnaround • Small group • Data is sensitive and best presented in person	• Additional information that may not be widely known • Individual perspective • Potential barriers or risks • Biases (whether conscious or unconscious)
Observation	• In person	• Need to see the work performed • Test assumptions made from higher-level learning program discussions	• How the staff completes their work tasks • Real-world perspective • Systems, tools, and procedures used to perform the work
Curation, Contribution, Voting, Polling, Social Media Sites	• Internal tool (e.g., Yammer, SharePoint, Intranet) • Social media sites (e.g., Pinterest, Twitter)	• The power of the like button • Garner consensus at a high level • Low or no cost to implement • Quick and relatively easy to implement	• Number of people who "like" the proposed item • Follow the organization • Comment • Contributions by staff
Secondary Sources	• Industry periodicals • External market research • Consumer research and comments • Web sites • Relevant publications	• Comparative analysis • Add dimension from external sources • Information not encumbered by organizational history and lore	• Data points not previously known • Pure metrics and calculations • Relevant industry data

Source: Adapted from Tobey (2007).

Job Aid 3-4. Data Collection Plan

Use this worksheet to craft a data collection plan. Adjust the column and row headings to fit the learning content request, the organization, the business need, and expected performance.

Initial Request: ______________________________

Needs Assessment Item	Questions to Answer and Problems to Explore	Key Resources	Key Data Sources	Data Collection Methods
Business Need				
Performance Gap or Need				
Learning Content Requested				
Learner Needs				

Best Practices

- Obtain permission from key stakeholders to complete the needs assessment, being certain to ask for the names of individuals to contact for information.
- If you need access to certain computer apps, systems, or physical locations, be sure to complete required forms or contact the person or department responsible before starting the needs assessment.
- Contact all individuals assigned to complete the needs assessment, as early as possible. Request their preferred communication methods, availability for meetings, and so on.

Source: Adapted from Tobey (2007).

Job Aid 3-5. Compile the Needs Analysis Report

The needs analysis is a report written to reflect the findings of the needs assessment. Customize this worksheet to suit the needs of the organization and the learning content request.

Getting Started

Executive summary or overview of what to expect	
Stated business need for the learning content.	Outcomes the key stakeholder expects from the learners once they've completed the program.

Body of the Needs Analysis Report

Did the needs assessment validate that the stated business need is a learning, training, or skills issue? (Yes or No)

About the Data Collected	About the Learners
How data was collected	Explanation of exactly who the learners or learner groups are.
Trends and observations	Performance metrics

Performance Objectives	About Existing Learning Content
Relevant job descriptions, job codes, job groups, etc.	Learning methods
Performance metrics	Completion rates
Expected performance after completing the learning content	Evaluative feedback received over time.
What are learners expected to be able to do: • Immediately after the program? • After 30 days? • Within xx days or weeks? How is success defined at each of these intervals? Who is responsible for assessing the learners? Which methods will be used to assess the level of learner adoption?	Relevant industry data and helpful organization-specific information used to support the initiative. For example: • Trending reports • Periodic reports • Personnel reports • Material handling data
Do the staff have what they need to be successful on the job? (See Cause Analysis Model Job Aid)	
Does the organizational culture support implementing learning content?	

Proposed Learning Content Strategy

Timeframes for finishing the learning content and evaluation plan development.

About the Learning Content	
Proposed Design Plan	**Proposed Development Plan**
Key design elements (e.g., design style, color palette, fonts, style of the images and how they might be used, music and narration, accessible and universal design principles to be applied to the learning content, learner interaction, facilitation techniques)	Development tools to be used
Learning methods that work best for the learners (e.g., job aids, performance support tools, e-learning courses, classroom instruction)	Resources (e.g., budget, people, purchases, software applications—whatever is needed to complete the learning content successfully)
Design and development team communication plan	Schedule for completion of development
Strategy for supporting the learners back on the job	Implementation plan
How to beta test learning content or roll it out to a small group of learners before the full roll-out	

Proposed Evaluation and Feedback Strategy	
Plan for gathering learner and leader feedback (e.g., interviews, focus groups, survey, or simulation)	Revision and iteration plan
Specific items to address during the evaluation and feedback process (e.g., learning content design, timeframe for completion, delivery methods, technology, and program content value)	

Any Final Observations, Needs, or Thoughts

Summary

Job Aid 3-6. Craft Performance Objectives

These verbs are part of Bloom's Taxonomy's cognitive domain. Use them to craft action-oriented and measurable performance objectives.

Formula for crafting clear and measurable performance objectives:

Action-oriented and measurable verb + Knowledge, skill, or task to learn + By when

Cognitive Domain Knowledge-Based Verbs

Knowledge		Comprehension		Application	
Learners recognize or remember facts, terms, basic concepts, or responses.		Learners demonstrate an understanding of facts and ideas.		Learners use prior knowledge and acquired knowledge to solve problems.	
Arrange	Order	Describe	Illustrate	Apply	Operate
Define	Outline	Classify	Infer	Change	Practice
Describe	Recognize	Convert	Locate	Choose	Predict
Duplicate	Relate	Defend	Paraphrase	Compute	Prepare
Identify	Recall	Distinguish	Predict	Construct	Produce
Label	Record	Estimate	Recognize	Demonstrate	Relate
List	Repeat	Explain	Rewrite	Discover	Schedule
Match	Reproduce	Express	Review	Dramatize	Show
Memorize	Select	Extend	Summarize	Employ	Sketch
Name	State	Give examples	Translate	Illustrate	Solve
	Tell			Interpret	Use
				Manipulate	Write
				Modify	

Analysis		Synthesis		Evaluation	
Learners examine and break things down into component parts to determine how the parts relate to one another.		Learners assemble information provided to produce something new.		Learners use a set of criteria to formulate opinions to present and defend the validity of their ideas, quality of work, etc.	
Analyze	Modify	Categorize	Plan	Assess	Explain
Apply	Operate	Collect	Prepare	Attach	Judge
Categorize	Practice	Combine	Rearrange	Choose	Justify
Compare	Predict	Comply	Reconstruct	Compare	Interpret
Contrast	Prepare	Compose	Relate	Conclude	Relate
Change	Produce	Construct	Reorganize	Contrast	Predict
Choose	Relate	Create	Revise	Defend	Rate
Compute	Schedule	Design	Rewrite	Describe	Select
Demonstrate	Separate	Develop	Set up	Discriminate	Summarize
Dramatize	Show	Devise	Summarize	Estimate	Support
Employ	Sketch	Explain	Synthesize	Evaluate	Value
Illustrate	Solve	Formulate	Tell		
Interpret	Use	Generate	Write		
Manipulate	Write				

Examples:

- Operate new surgical tool with precision and accuracy after XX hours of instruction and XX hours of practice.
- Demonstrate confidence using the newly implemented accounts payable system within XX days of finishing the training program and all simulation practice exercises.
- Reproduce the new admission process including additions after finishing the training program and all simulation assignments.

Job Aid 3-7. The Design Plan

Use this job aid to craft the design plan and make decisions about the learning content project. Customize this job aid for the learning content and the organization.

Color Palette If the color palette is specified in the corporate style guide and not well suited for the program, work with the marketing and communications department to select colors that work best for learning content.	**Fonts and Text** Fonts and text styles are likely prescribed in the corporate style guide. If they are not well suited for learning content, work with the marketing and communications department to select fonts that work better for learning content.	**Images and Audio Handling** • Style • Music • Scripted narration • Narrator specifics • Localization
Delivery Method Method used to deliver the learning content: • In-person classroom (ILT) • E-learning course • Virtual instructor-led training (vILT) • On-the-job training (OJT) • Job aids or other performance support tools • Video tutorial • Microlearning • Mobile app • Simulation • Spaced practice and repetition	**Development Tools** These are applications used to craft the learning content. There are many potential tools; selection is largely dependent upon the delivery method.	**Accessibility Features** The way the learners will interact with the content informs the design and decisions with respect to accessibility. Reminder: No one is required to self-report a need for reasonable accommodation. Choosing to build more accessible content is better for everyone.

Learner Support Plan The learner support plan determines how the content will be supported back on the job. This plan is very important. It could include: • Coaching guide or other type of plan • How completion of learning content is added to the talent development or talent management system • Refresher or reinforcement training plans, and at what intervals • Job aids or other performance support tools • Electronic performance support system	**Team Roles and Responsibilities** Make sure to outline and explain everyone's roles and responsibilities. Some roles include: • Key stakeholder • L&D leader • Instructional designer • Content developers • Subject matter expert • Graphic designer • Project manager • Training coordinator • Training facilitator • Training manager • Others integrally involved	**Communication Plan** This is your design and development team communication plan. Document: • Every project team member's communication preference (i.e., if someone is unable to read emails during the business day, what's the best way to reach them?) • How will meetings be conducted and how often? • How often will the full project team meet? • How will project updates be shared? • How often will project updates be shared and with whom?
Evaluation Plan Needs assessment informs the evaluation plan. • How to implement the evaluation plan. • Timing to launch the evaluation plan. • How feedback reporting will be disseminated. • Distribution of the feedback reporting. • Reporting effects of learning content on business results. • Whatever else is relevant to the organization and the learning content.	**Iteration Plan** This is the plan and schedule for making any necessary changes to the learning content or in the workstream.	**Schedule for Completion** This is the schedule for completing the various phases of the project.

CHAPTER 4

EVALUATING LEARNING IMPACT

TIMOTHY R. BROCK

A talent development (TD) team supporting a group of hospitals in a metro area learned the hard way the wisdom of that great philosopher, futurist, and Nobel Laurette, Bob Dylan, when he pronounced, "The Times They Are a-Changin'" (1964).

The TD team had worked hard to develop a learning program for several hospitals focused on reducing excessive vascular catheter central line blood infections in ICUs. They involved the right healthcare professionals as subject matter experts while applying assessment, analysis, design, development, implementation, and evaluation (A^2D^2IE) process. Based on their needs assessment and analysis (A^2), the stakeholders agreed the best performance improvement solution was to institute a checklist system for doctors, nurses, and technicians to follow, which would reduce practice variation and resulting infections. This checklist empowered nurses to challenge anyone who deviated from the standardized procedures without fear of negative consequences. The solution would also involve revising some ICU policies and performance support systems, which they would cover in the learning program.

The course was simple to design and develop (D^2). It used deliberate practice simulations to improve the ICU team's competence and confidence as they applied these new procedures and evaluated (E) their learning progress. They also decided to include a final evaluation simulation *challenge*, which involved teams competing for compliance points to ensure everyone could apply the new procedures to safeguard patient safety while delivering quality care. They planned to include their usual end-of-course survey evaluation for participants to rate the course using a five-point Likert scale on what they specifically liked about the learning solution and what could make it better.

Before the TD team finished their design and development work, however, hospital executives added new expectations for the program that made them uncomfortable. Instead of the typical evaluation data, the executives wanted to see successive sets of data that causally linked the program to the outcomes and results they expected to see at the ICUs. They wanted to know how much credit should go to this performance improvement program for decreasing these infection rates rather than other actions taken in the ICUs to reduce this same measure. Even more, they wanted evidence to establish the program's value to all the key stakeholders, including the chief financial officer.

The TD team was now unsure how evaluate this program.

This situation is occurring more frequently in healthcare systems. As a result, healthcare TD professionals must know how to evaluate their learning programs consistently and credibly to the impact level. Evaluating the impact of learning programs changes the evaluation's focus from learning outcomes to an organizational team effort focused on business results to keep the doors open for current and expanding healthcare services.

This chapter describes the best practices of typical and best-in-class organizations around the world that are evaluating their TD programs to the learning impact level using measures that matter to the organization—both business and economic not to mention humanistic. You will learn why measuring the impact of learning or performance improvement programs helps healthcare TD professionals remain relevant and value-added. You will then learn about the five elements required of a comprehensive system to evaluate healthcare TD programs to the organization's impact level. Those five elements are an evaluation framework, process model, guiding principles, applications and practice, and implementation.

Why Evaluation Matters in Healthcare Talent Development

Even though healthcare is already a highly regulated and measured industry, it faces increased scrutiny because of its high costs and societal importance. The Medicare-driven shift in the United States from a pay-for-service to a pay-for-value model is probably the beginning of what is to come. The rules have changed to a triple focus on decreasing costs, increasing value through improved outcomes and services, and expanding healthcare coverage for communities' health (Buzachero et al. 2013). Linking Medicare and Medicaid reimbursement amounts to patient satisfaction scores is a significant quality care value motivator. This increased accountability level requires healthcare systems to emphasize more accountable care and deliver improved outcomes through talent development programs. For example, hospitals must reduce their costs by up to 17 percent to break even with Medicare reimbursements (Buzachero et al. 2013). This reality requires healthcare TD professionals to show their programs' value to justify tight funding, as these programs are often among the first cut or reduced in scope to save money.

Evaluating learning impact is one of the 23 capabilities in ATD's new Talent Development Capability Model. According to the Capability Model, the purpose of an evaluation is to collect, analyze, and report data relevant to business strategies. This data must help executives make data-driven decisions to drive the business. The data must also show the TD programs' value to senior leaders and business stakeholders. Evaluation informs the key stakeholders about what is working, what is not working, and recommended actions for improvement.

Evaluating the impact of healthcare TD programs also enables TD professionals to provide insights about the value of the programs business executives are funding and establishes them as consulting and business partners. The triple aim mandate is making this theory's relevance to all healthcare TD professionals even greater.

Evaluation is more than giving learners a test—it's focused on evaluating the program, not the learners. In this context, Hale wrote that "evaluation is about the efficiency and effectiveness of what you did, how you did it, and the degree to which the solution produced the desired results" (2007).

Therefore, evaluation is about showing value using measures that matter to key stakeholders. The challenge is that value is in the eye of the beholder. Healthcare TD professionals, healthcare system executives, functional managers, and patients and their families each define value differently.

When evaluating healthcare learning programs, it is imperative to show the value of expenditures that resonate with all stakeholders using measures that matter to them. This new value imperative drives healthcare systems to build internal systems that deliver better quality and data that *proves* it (Buzachero et al. 2013). Healthcare TD professionals must provide credible data to prove that their learning programs make a difference to the organization and are worth funding. To do this, you must have a results-focused evaluation methodology that justifies funding.

Learning to Think Differently to Evaluate Differently

Why is this important? To think like a business owner, you must know how a business owner thinks. In 2009, the ROI Institute and ATD conducted a study of CEOs from Fortune 500 and large private organizations to learn how they measured success in their talent development programs (Phillips and Phillips 2009). Their thinking transcends for-profit and not-for-profit industries and professions, including healthcare systems.

Figure 4-1 breaks down the questionnaire data into eight measures, what the CEOs reported that they currently measure, what they should measure, and the importance of each measure. The results indicated a large gap between what talent development professionals were reporting and what CEOs wanted to see.

Figure 4-1. Measures CEOs Want to See

Measures	Currently Measure	Should Measure	Importance
Inputs and indicators	94%	86%	6
Efficiency	78%	82%	7
Reaction	53%	22%	8
Learning	32%	28%	5
Application	11%	61%	4
Impact	8%	96%	1
ROI	4%	74%	2
Awards	40%	44%	3

Phillips and Phillips (2009)

The first five measures (inputs and indicators, efficiency, reaction, learning, and application) communicate program costs that TD professionals typically measure and report. The last three (impact, ROI, and awards) communicate the program benefits that are typically measured and reported that are useful when determining if the costs were worth the investment. Program impact was the top measure the CEOs wanted to see but did not, by a wide margin. Return on investment (ROI) was a second impact measure because they wanted to weigh the program costs against the program benefits to ensure costs did not exceed benefits. ROI was an essential economic accountability impact measure to executives.

Awards are an intangible benefit, which have value without being assigned a monetary amount. Awards help engage, retain, and recruit quality people as well as improve the organization's reputation. The study results showed that executives rank intangibles third on their list because they are impact measures.

Is it any wonder why healthcare TD professionals must fight for funding or defend their budgets from cuts or elimination when the only data they're reporting to executives are considered costs? We must provide evidence establishing healthcare TD programs as investments (which are maintained, enhanced, and protected) rather than costs (which are controlled, reduced, or eliminated). The solution is to change the perception of healthcare TD programs from avoidable costs to necessary investments. Learning impact is about producing organizational results. In summary, healthcare TD professionals cannot afford to ignore the accountability trend to provide executives with evaluation data that show their programs' value to drive the business.

Key Takeaways

- Determine what measures are important to the executives who approve and fund them to achieve triple mandates and why they are important.
- Take proactive steps to anticipate the growing accountability trend and provide evidence of the programs' the value and impact by moving from an activity-based to a results-based focus.
- Use the Talent Development Capability Model as a road map for applying the three domains when evaluating learning impact.

The Five Evaluation System Components

There are many evaluation methods. Some organizations have adopted a default evaluation method simply because it is familiar. How do healthcare TD professionals judge and select the most appropriate and credible method? That is a difficult question to answer.

Figure 4-2 shows the five critical components of a comprehensive evaluation system that must fit together like a puzzle (Phillips 2017). If a piece is missing, the evaluation picture is incomplete. Any best practice method to evaluate the impact of healthcare TD learning programs must include all five elements.

Here is a brief description of each:

Figure 4-2. The Evaluation Puzzle

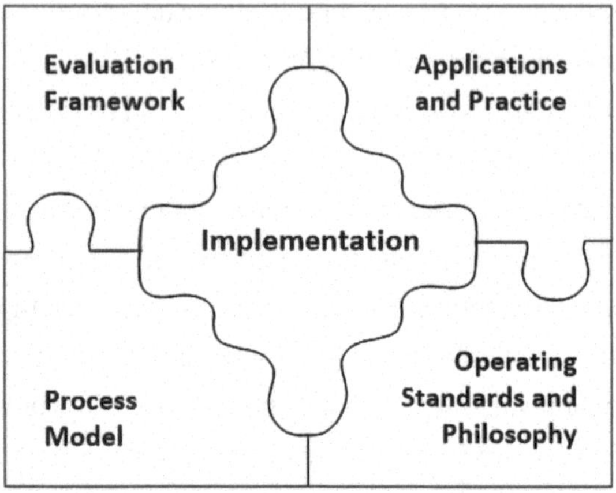

Source: Phillips (2017).

- **Evaluation framework.** The evaluation framework establishes the data categorization schema. What types of data must the healthcare TD team collect, analyze, and report to tell a learning impact evaluation story that includes an evidence-based value chain various stakeholders will believe?
- **Process model.** The process model provides the specific, necessary steps to plan, collect, analyze, and report the evaluation framework data. Quality guru W. Edwards Deming puts it succinctly with the oft-repeated statement, "If you cannot explain what you are doing as a process, you do not know what you are doing."
- **Operating standards and philosophy.** The operating standards and philosophy element define the guardrails that provide a consistent practice using the process model to compare results. These operating standards protect the healthcare TD team's credibility with the stakeholders, especially the executive who controls the fate of the program's funding.
- **Case applications and practice.** The case applications and practices element provides real-world examples of how organizations apply the evaluation methodology in different disciplines, industries, and professions. More importantly, it provides evidence of program success.
- **Implementation.** The implementation piece falls in the middle of the puzzle because it holds everything together. Anyone can learn to collect and analyze data to evaluate programs. The key is to create sustainable change in how learning and development programs add value to the healthcare learning system.

This chapter reviews each evaluation component in more detail as we look at the ROI Methodology. It integrates the operating standards and philosophy (or guiding principles) with the process model to ensure consistent, conservative, and credible decision-making guidelines while applying each step.

The Evaluation Framework

The Phillips' ROI Methodology evaluation framework aims to establish data categories so you know what data to collect and how to categorize it after it is collected. This framework sets a meaningful schema to analyze the data and interpret the results to tell a compelling evaluation story.

Figure 4-3 shows the six types of evaluation data that make up the framework, as well as the focus and typical measures different stakeholders want to see at each level. This evaluation framework is built on the four levels of evaluation created by Raymond Katzell in the 1940s and published in articles written by James Kirkpatrick in the late 1950s and 1960 (Thalheimer 2018). In the early 1970s, Jack Phillips, who was an electrical engineer at the time for an international aerospace company, added the fifth level, ROI, to account for the missing economic measure executives wanted to see when making funding decisions about a cooperative education program. Phillips later added Level 0, Input, to include program costs in the data collection strategy since costs are required for the ROI calculation. However, Level 0 is not an evaluation level—it is a data level that management wants to see for every TD program evaluation effort.

According to Patti and Jack Phillips (2017), an evaluation framework must establish a chain of value (or chain of impact) that links data evidence at each level to show a cause-and-effect relationship. Each level, when arranged sequentially, establishes this cause-and-effect relationship (indicated by the arrows). The levels progress from the costs involved to create the program to the business impact expected in return for the program's investment.

Level 0, Input, represents the input-activity-output elements of a basic logic model (Kellogg Foundation 2004). The input includes the assessment and analysis work that establishes the need for the program. Evaluation Levels 1 through 5 represent the outcomes (Levels 1–3) and results (Levels 4–5) of the program's logic model.

For example, failure at a lower level produces failure at higher levels. If the learners do not perceive the program as relevant, important, or useful (Level 1), they will not commit to learn it (Level 2) or use it (Level 3). If they do not or will not learn it (Level 2), nothing will change in the healthcare workplace (Level 3). If nothing changes in the healthcare workplace, the Level

4 healthcare business impact measures will not improve. The healthcare impact level is why the program was funded (that is, to sustain or improve one or more business measures). If the program does not sustain or improve business measures, a negative ROI (Level 5) will occur.

Figure 4-3. Evaluation Framework

Six Measurement Data Levels	Measurement Focus	Typical Measures
0. Input ⬇	The input into the program, including indicators representing scope, volume, time, costs. and efficiencies	Types of programs, number of programs, number of people involved, hours of involvement, costs
1. Reaction and Planned Action ⬇	Reaction to the program, including participants' perceived value, and planned actions to make them successful	Relevance, importance, usefulness, appropriateness, intent to use, motivation to act, recommend to others
2. Learning ⬇	Knowledge and success gained, learning how to develop concepts and how to use skills and competencies to drive program success	Skills, learning, knowledge, capacity, competencies, confidences, contacts
3. Application and Implementation ⬇	Application and use of knowledge, skills, and competencies, including progress made and implementation success	Behaviors, extent of use, task completion, frequency of use, actions completed, success with use, barriers to use, enablers to use
4. Impact ⬇	The impact of the programs and processes expressed as healthcare business impact measures	Length of stay, infant mortality, medication errors, vaccinations, readmissions, accident costs, nurse retention, patient satisfaction
5. ROI	Comparison of monetary benefits from project-to-project costs	Benefit-cost ratio (BCR), ROI, payback period

Impact measures are classified as either hard or soft. Hard measures fall into four categories (output, quality, costs, and time). Soft measures involve five categories (work climate and satisfaction, employee development and advancement, customer services, initiative and innovation, and image). Figure 4-4 lists examples to help healthcare TD professionals understand the types of business measures that executives want TD programs to help improve or sustain.

Figure 4-4. Level 4 Hard and Soft Data Measure Examples

Hard Data Examples	
Output	Inpatient or outpatient revenue, new patients, clinician productivity, screenings, births
Quality	Error rates, rework, medication event rate, bloodstream infections, incidents
Costs	Operating expenses, treatment costs, accident costs, budget variance, cost per case
Time	Length of stay, overtime, time to proficiency, response rate, patient wait times
Soft Data Examples	
Work climate and satisfaction	Grievances, complaints, satisfaction, engagement, intent to leave
Employee development and advancement	Promotions, readiness, performance appraisal ratings
Customer service	Patient complaints and satisfaction, patient loyalty and retention
Initiative and innovation	Suggestions, new technology and services, innovation, process improvements
Image	Reputation, social responsibility, diversity, community awareness

This framework works well with formative, summative, and confirmative evaluation efforts. According to Van Tiem, Moseley, and Dessinger (2012), summative (Levels 1–3) and confirmative (Levels 4–5) evaluations occur when TD programs are implemented. Formative evaluation occurs during the A^2D^2 phases (Level 0). You must decide if a summative or confirmative evaluation is necessary for your program. This framework enables a scalable methodology.

This scalability is framed by evaluation level targets and criteria for evaluating programs at different levels. Executives or policy decide what level of evaluation is appropriate for a TD program during the process model's planning phase. The decision is based on the evaluation's purpose, program evaluation data needs, the program's profile, and stakeholder needs.

Figure 4-5 illustrates how you can plan and communicate your evaluation strategy. It shows "how often" (by percent) ROI Institute recommends evaluating TD programs at each level (Phillips and Phillips 2017). It also shows the results of a 2020 benchmark study indicating how often organizations evaluated their programs at each level in practice (McLeod 2020).

Finally, it provides reasons to evaluate at each level. Remember, you should not evaluate the impact of every learning program—you must have a business case to justify the added expense of going beyond Level 2 learning objectives.

Figure 4-5. Criteria to Evaluate at Each Level

Evaluation Type	Level	Recommended by ROI Institute	2020 Benchmark	Purpose
Summative	1	90–100%	80%	• Program design • Program delivery • Potential use • Overall satisfaction
	2	60–90%	70%	• Learning progress • Participant and facilitator feedback • A^2D^2 accountability and feedback • Learning system effectiveness
	3	30–40%	49%	• Close workplace performance gap • Address workplace safety issue • Determine training transfer • Assess a pilot program
Confirmative	4	10–20%	37%	• Close organizational performance gap • Cost savings (reduce or avoid) • Improve satisfaction (staff or patient) • Contribute to societal good
	5	5–10%	18%	

This figure corrects a misunderstanding about the ROI Methodology. ROI is in the title because this evaluation methodology provides the necessary road map to evaluate to Level 5 (ROI) when appropriate. However, you can limit the evaluation to any level based on your purpose.

The Process Model

Designing, developing, and implementing a learning program that affects business measures requires knowing which measures the program is expected to improve, how much they must improve, and by when the results are expected. The process model used with this evaluation system is an advanced logic model that includes inputs, activities, and outputs.

Because talent development focuses on improving organizational performance by improving human performance, the process model must have a human-centric foundation.

Figure 4-6 shows the 12-step evaluation process developed by ROI Institute, and integrates 10 human-centric design thinking principles from the world of innovation (Phillips and Phillips 2017; Mootee 2013).

The four process phases—evaluation planning, data collection, data analysis, and optimize results—make it simpler for healthcare TD professionals to apply and explain their evaluation methodology to executives.

Evaluation Planning Phase

Failing to plan for results is the main reason why learning programs that matter to executives have no impact on an organization and why program evaluations fail. This process model accounts for that dangerous oversight.

The first three steps lay the foundation for a successful program evaluation using A^2 results to provide D^2 inputs.

1. Start With Why: Align Programs With the Business

This first step establishes the necessary results-based mindset that links the learning program to specific business needs. When executives decide to fund a TD effort, they must first believe the effort will result in a positive payoff, with the benefits of the program exceeding the cost. The payoff is the economic measure that executives expect in return for their investment. This is Level 5 on the evaluation framework. Next, the executives state the business measures that must improve to achieve the desired business results. This is Level 4 of the evaluation framework. Executives want results, not activities. They want to improve the business measures because they are either unsatisfactory or believe the organization can do better. The business needs are the gap between the "as-is" results and the "should-be" results identified by a needs assessment. These payoff and business measures come from executives.

Winston Churchill summed this step up well when he said, "However beautiful the strategy, you should occasionally look at results." Too often, we focus our efforts on course design and development without considering the business impact expected from our TD programs. You always want to start with knowing why executives decided to fund the program. However, while you do not have to evaluate every program to these business and economic payoff levels, you still must know why the program is considered necessary and what business measures are involved. This ensures you align your solution to address the organization's need and thus justify funding the program to the executives.

Figure 4-6. ROI Methodology Process Model

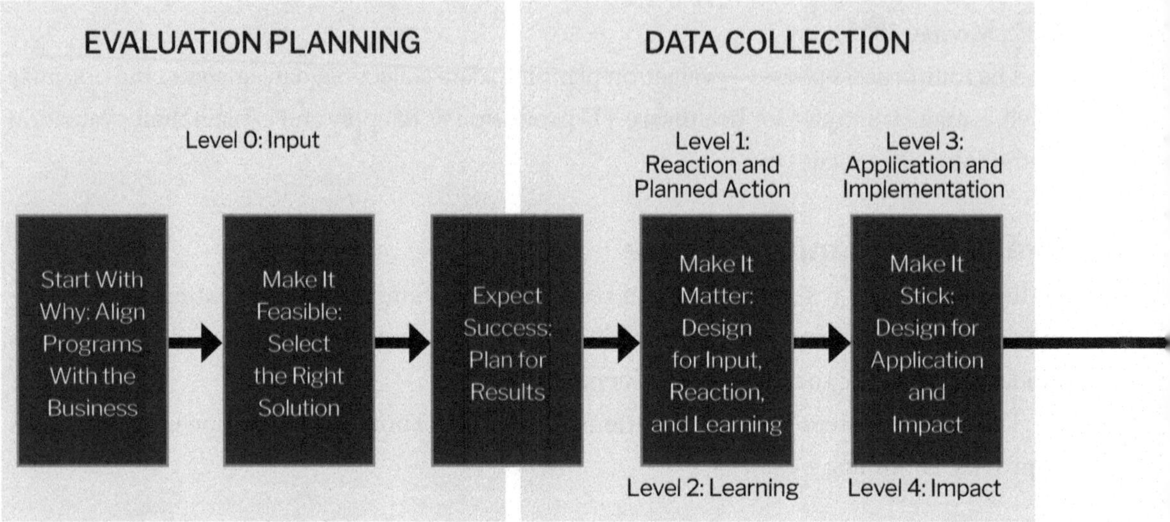

2. Make It Feasible: Select the Right Solution

Once you know the results the executives expect in return for their funding, you can identify the most feasible solution to improve those business measures. You want to learn what is or is not happening in the workplace that is causing the underperforming business measures. This is your needs analysis. Let's go back to the central line infection example from the beginning of the chapter. We want to learn what the ICU staff must start doing, stop doing, or do differently to improve the ICU business measures the executives expect the TD team to improve.

You must also look at organization processes and systems. Do you require new or updated technology to improve workplace performance? Maybe a new or revised policy or procedure is necessary. Is there a contributing communication problem? Are there workplace barriers

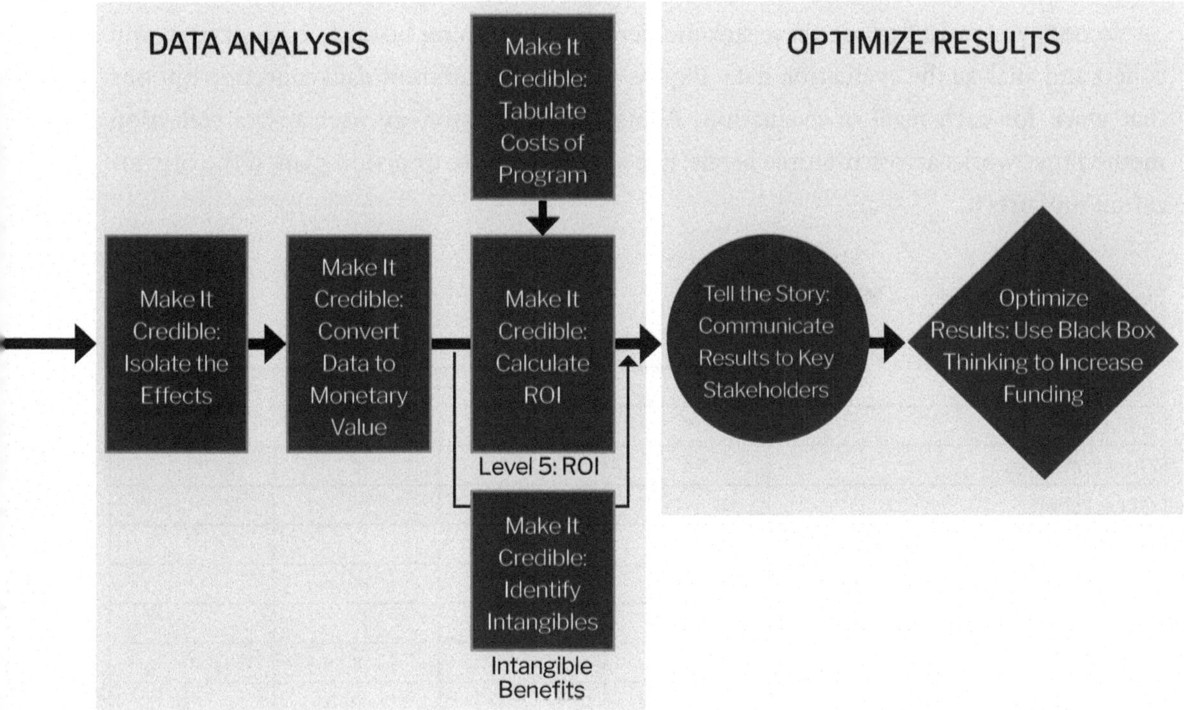

that the organization must remove or missing enablers we must include in the solution? If the planned TD learning solution does not align to improve the workplace behaviors required to improve the defined business measures, the TD learning solution will fail.

3. Expect Success: Plan for Results

When it comes to planning, too many of us have the attitude a friend of mine used to repeat humorously: *"We have no plan and are sticking to it."* This step addresses two planning issues that are critical to gaining the support of your stakeholders.

First, if you evaluate a program to determine if it was successful, you must know how each stakeholder defines success. The best way to learn this is to ask them. Each one monitors, manages, and improves a different area of responsibility—executives focus on payoff and business result measures; managers and supervisors focus on workplace output measures.

Second, you must include these stakeholders when planning how the organization will collect and analyze the evaluation data. Figure 4-7 lists the different data collection options that work for each level of evaluation. A money-saving strategy uses a data collection method that works across multiple levels, like a questionnaire or action plan, if the organization supports it.

Figure 4-7. Data Collection Methods

	Typical Levels			
Method	1	2	3	4
Surveys	✓	✓	✓	
Questionnaires	✓	✓	✓	✓
Observation		✓	✓	
Interviews	✓	✓	✓	
Focus groups	✓	✓	✓	
Tests		✓		
Action planning			✓	✓
Performance contracting			✓	✓
Performance monitoring				✓

Suppose stakeholders cannot agree on a data collection plan. In that case, you will evaluate the program to the level you can by using the data the organization allows you to collect. If you collect impact data, you can work with the stakeholders to plan how you will analyze it to ensure your evaluation findings and recommendations are credible. You will also avoid pitfalls during the evaluation if you cannot get the data that you expected to collect.

Evaluation is geared toward learning how well the program did to achieve the funded objectives, which come from the "as-is" and "should-be" needs. *How well* means how effective (the business impact objective) and how efficient (the ROI objective) the program was to close the needs gap. Figure 4-8 shows the relationship between the program needs assessment and analysis (A^2; as defined by Kaufman and Guerra-Lopez, 2013), objectives, and evaluation.

Figure 4-8. Program Needs, Objectives, and Evaluation Alignment

Needs	Objectives	Evaluation
• **A needs assessment** determines the gap between the "as-is" and "should-be" business results. • **A needs analysis** (or cause analysis) determines the cause that prevents achieving the "should-be" result.	The "should-be" criteria defined by stakeholders that the initiative must meet to consider it a success.	Comparing or judging the effectiveness and efficiency of the initiative to achieve the defined degree of "should-be" results established by the program objectives.

You can use the business alignment model to show executives that you are focused on results that matter to them. Figure 4-9 uses the ICU example from the beginning of this chapter to show how the TD initiative was aligned vertically to address the business needs, and how each objective was aligned horizontally to evaluate the needs-driven "should-be" outcomes (Levels 1–3) and results (Levels 4–5). All stakeholders found this visual immensely helpful when designing the initiative for results.

Suppose you decide to evaluate an existing program. Completing this business alignment model can reveal holes in your needs assessment or analysis, the program or business needs alignment, and program objectives. You must remedy this before you can evaluate the program. If you cannot align the program with business needs, why does it exist? Executives, managers, and TD professionals welcome this business alignment model because it shows how the TD effort is aligned to deliver and evaluate results that matter to all stakeholders.

Even more, with this model, everyone can see what role they play to implement and evaluate the program to improve the business measures and achieve a positive payoff. This benefit includes the TD design and development team who must craft a solution to go beyond learning objectives to achieve the higher-level objectives. If you want to gain the confidence and support of everyone to assist your evaluation effort, convince them that you are collecting the measures that will determine how well the program did in meeting the objectives that matter to them.

Figure 4-9. Business Alignment Model

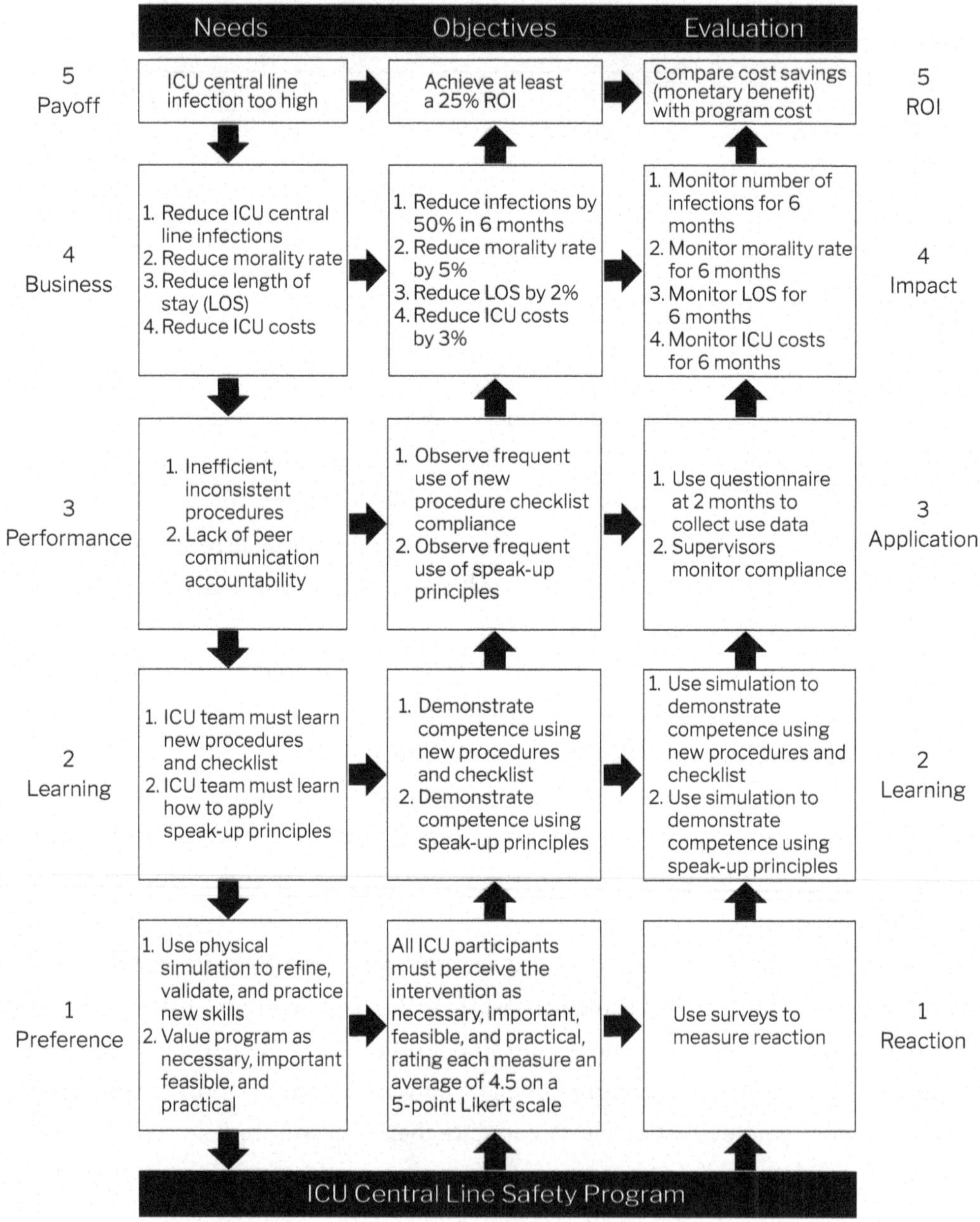

Data Collection Phase

This phase implements the data collection plan. Stakeholders agree to the qualitative and quantitative data collection methods you will use at different times during program implementation. No surprises should occur for anyone.

When you develop your data collection plan, apply three guiding principles to conduct a credible evaluation:

- **When conducting a higher-level evaluation, collect data at lower levels.** Failing to identify the lower-level outcomes and how they affect the following levels will cast doubt on your higher-level evaluation results. Early measurements that indicate the program is not achieving objectives at the lower levels also become red flags to take corrective action and notify management to prevent surprises.
- **When planning a higher-level evaluation, the lower-level evaluations don't need to be comprehensive.** The cost to evaluate a program increases when workers move outside the learning environment and back to their jobs. It is best to conserve evaluation resources at the lower two levels by evaluating the data to a "good enough" state for the stakeholders. This ensures you have the necessary resources to evaluate the higher levels. You should make this "good enough" decision with the stakeholders during the planning phase.
- **When collecting and analyzing data, use the most credible sources.** If people do not consider the evaluation sources credible, they will not believe your data or analysis outcomes or results. TD professionals should define credible sources (as determined by the stakeholders) during the planning phase.

The data collection phase has two process steps: make it matter and make it stick.

4. Make It Matter: Design for Input, Reaction, and Learning

This step is called make it matter for a reason. Failing to make it matter creates a metric called scrap learning, which according to Mattox and Van Buren (2016) is learning that is delivered but does not transfer to the workplace. Scrap learning is the opposite of impactful learning or learning transfer. Benchmark studies using the Metrics That Matter software system show that scrap learning is a significant problem across industries (Mattox and Van Buren 2016; Phillips 2020). The system found that the scrap learning rate was 48 percent in healthcare; the average was 45 percent. You prevent scrap learning by making the program matter to your participants and addressing workplace barriers at the next process step.

5. Make It Stick: Design for Application and Impact

Next, you want to find out if the program design and implementation resulted in participants applying what they learned to meet the Level 3 application objectives. This step requires careful planning because collecting data from people is challenging once they are back in their daily routines.

You also want to discover if the organization did its part to remove any barriers preventing participants from applying what they learned. If not, what are those existing barriers so you can compensate for them to achieve the desired outcomes and results? Some common barriers include:

- Lack of management support
- No time to use
- No opportunity to use
- Systems and processes do not support use
- Work group culture does not support use
- Lack of tools and resources necessary to support use
- Learning material does not apply to my job situation
- Changed jobs and skills no longer apply

Making it stick requires TD professionals to remain mindful of scrap learning during different phases of the process model. Without organizational support at this step, nothing will change in the workplace. Even worse, stakeholders will conclude your learning program failed. Making it stick is another reason why gaining supervisor and management support during the planning phase is critical.

For Level 4 impact, improved impact measures are the consequence of improved workplace measures and vice versa. These are the measures that supervisors and workplace managers report to the executives as key performance measures. Your evaluation will determine how well your learning program did to achieve the business impact objectives to close the "as-is" and "should-be" gap identified during the needs assessment.

If you collect data at all four evaluation levels, you must then analyze the impact data before reporting the program's impact results to the executives.

Data Analysis Phase

The analysis phase is designed to ensure you have the information required (and the data to back it up) when you report a program evaluation's impact results. Executives ask hard questions that require credible answers with supporting evidence. These steps protect your credibility and the credibility of your evaluation data. Two operating standards influence multiple steps of this phase:

- **When analyzing data, select the most conservative alternative for calculations.** Failing to choose the most fiscally conservative alternatives can lead to suspicions about the numbers' credibility. If you're in doubt about whether to include something in your calculations, remember this: If it's a cost, put it in; if it's a benefit, leave it out. The goal is to minimize the isolated impact results and calculated ROI, so it does not appear that you inflated the numbers to make the program look better. You make the data analysis calculation decisions with the appropriate stakeholders during the planning phase.
- **If no improvement data is available for a population or from a specific source, assume that little or no improvement has occurred.** Make no assumptions for nonrespondents. If 50 percent of the program participants do not provide any improvement data, conclude they had no improvement. That is the data you have and can defend.

There are five data analysis process steps that focus on making the program's impact data results credible.

6. Make It Credible: Isolate the Effects of the Program

How can you claim your program improved an impact measure if you do not know how much credit the program deserves for this improvement? Will you claim 100 percent, 50 percent, 10 percent? How did you come up with that number? This step is essential because many other factors influence the same business measures. In fact, this step is so important that it has a dedicated operating standard: *Use at least one method to isolate the effects of a project.*

It is not possible to credibly isolate your learning program's impact (to give credit where credit is due) without a chain of evidence at the lower levels leading up to the impact level (Phillips and Phillips 2019). Proper attribution is the logical step because it increases the credibility of your claim and the accuracy of your learning impact analysis and ROI calculations.

ROI Institute conducted a benchmark study in 2020 to determine how often practitioners used each impact isolation method based on its feasibility and support within their organizational setting (McLeod 2020). These methods are listed below in order of accuracy and credibility, along with their frequency of use, as determined from the study:

- Control group (34 percent)
- Trendline analysis (40 percent)
- Mathematical modeling (28 percent)
- Participant estimates (57 percent)
- Manager estimates (49 percent)
- Senior manager estimates (42 percent)
- Expert input (37 percent)
- Customer input (38 percent)

Together, these methods offer a set of tools to satisfy any stakeholder who asks this important question.

The benchmarking study also showed that practitioners use estimates most often to satisfy executive attribution expectations. Whenever we use an estimate as an isolation method, we must apply another operating standard to ensure it is credible: *Adjust estimates for improvement for potential errors of estimation.* This guiding principle adds credibility to your estimate by taking the additional step of decreasing it based on the estimator's level of confidence in their estimate. Let's look at an actual example from a healthcare setting (Buzachero et al. 2013).

A community hospital with 620 nurses was having a persistent nurse turnover problem, so it decided to take action to reduce the turnover rate. The hospital decided to implement three programs to address the issue:

- It tasked the HR department to develop a career pathways program so nurses could make faster promotion progress in their system.
- It tasked the finance team to create a pay-for-performance program for nurse managers that would link nurse pay to patient satisfaction scores.
- It tasked the talent development team to create a leadership program for first-level managers working with nurses so they could improve their skills engaging and motivating nurses, treating them with respect, and creating a great work environment.

A year after implementing these three programs, nurse turnover fell from 23 percent to 11 percent—with a decrease of 1 percent for each of the previous 12 months (Figure 4-10). Part of the TD team's evaluation process was to isolate the effect of their program. They also anticipated hospital leadership would ask what effect each of these three programs had on turnover reduction. The TD team considered nurse managers the most credible sources to answer this question, so they conducted a focus group with a sample of them. They asked each nurse manager in this sample group to estimate how much credit they gave to each program for the turnover reduction and then asked how confident they were in their estimate. The TD team also asked if there was any other factor that could have contributed to this reduction. From this data, they averaged the estimate and confidence level of the group (Figure 4-10).

Figure 4-10. Estimate Adjustment Example

FACT: 620 Nurses—Turnover Went From 142 (23%) to 68 (11%) = 74 (12%) Avoided Turnovers					
Influence Factors	Avoided Turnovers	Percent Contribution	Estimated Impact	Confidence Level	Adjusted Impact
Career Pathways	74	25%	18.5	70%	13
Pay-for-Performance	74	35%	25.9	90%	23
Leadership Development	74	35%	25.9	80%	21
Other	74	5%	3.7	60%	2
Total		100%	74		

The executives accepted the nurse managers as credible sources of these estimates because they were the ones doing the job and had no vested interest in giving any factor more credit than they believed it deserved. This estimate adjustment increases the reliability of an answer because executives prefer to work with understated estimates.

7. Make It Credible: Convert the Data to a Monetary Value

If management wants to calculate a program's ROI, this step provides a way to put a monetary value on the isolated impact measures. Nobody expects TD professionals to know how to do this. Instead, during the planning phase, ask your finance and HR departments for help. If no one helps you, the evaluation effort cannot go any further. It is better to know this during the planning phase with the organization's stakeholders than to plan it without their support and learn that it was a mistake later when you try to do it during the analysis phase.

This step is not difficult to do if you know how to place a monetary value on the appropriate impact measures. These monetized benefits go in the numerator of the ROI calculation. Figure 4-11 lists various conversion techniques to complete this step (Phillips and Zuniga 2008).

Figure 4-11. Methods to Convert Data to Monetary Value

Standard Values	Other Methods
• Converting output to contribution • Converting the cost of quality • Converting employee's time	• Using historical costs and existing data • Using internal and external experts • Using data from external databases • Linking with other measures • Using participants' estimates • Using supervisors' and managers' estimates • Using staff estimates

This step is essential to determine the monetary value of a program impact measure. It is challenging, especially for soft measures. However, it is currently being done credibly by organizations globally.

8. Make It Credible: Identify the Intangible Measures

It is not always necessary, or wise, to convert every impact measure to a monetary value. Sometimes it is best for the impact measure to remain an intangible benefit. One of the operating standards guides how to handle intangibles: **Intangible measures are defined as measures that are purposely not converted to monetary value.** This means you must decide which impact measures to convert and which ones to leave intangible, based on the four considerations identified in Figure 4-12.

We ask the third question about resources because the cost to convert the measure is a program cost. The fourth question about executive reaction protects our credibility; if the executives do not understand how the conversion was calculated, they will not believe it.

Example intangible benefits for healthcare TD professionals include:

- Improved work–life balance
- Improved health status
- Enhanced image
- Improved networking
- Improved hospital outpatient quality reports
- Improved hospital inpatient quality reports
- Increased engagement
- Improved service
- Improved quality of life
- Fewer complaints

- Increased brand awareness
- Reduced conflict
- Less stress
- Enhanced patient satisfaction

Figure 4-12. Tangible-Intangible Decision Tree

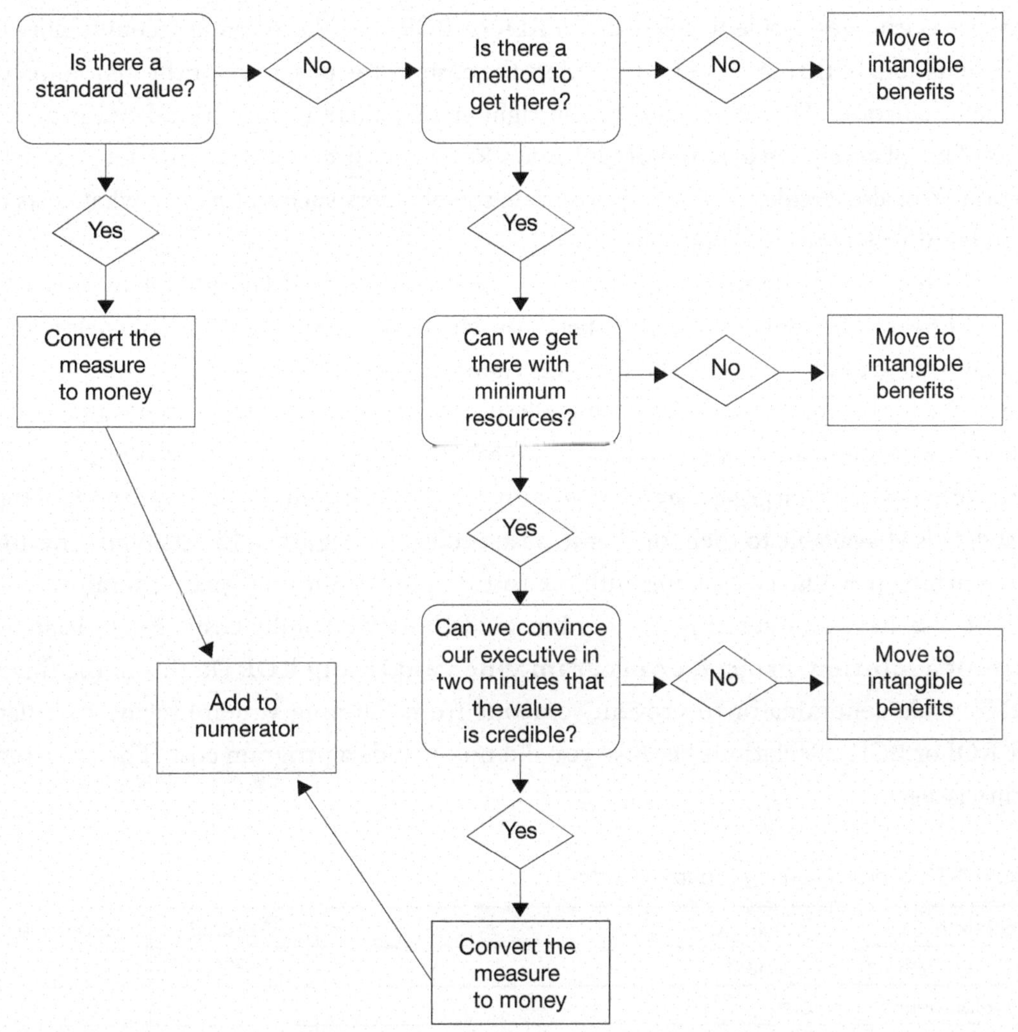

If executives want an ROI calculation, your goal should be to convert every impact measure to a monetary value. Hard business data are typically converted to monetary value. Soft business data conversion is possible but isn't as accurate or credible, which can undermine your credibility. However, it is still appropriate to list these impact benefits as intangibles because they have value to executives. Sometimes, an intangible value can outweigh a tangible value (for example, reputation vs. profit).

9. Make It Credible: Tabulate the Costs of the Program

Suppose executives decide to calculate an ROI or BCR to add economic accountability to the evaluation. In that case, you must collect the costs of the program for the denominator of the calculation. This step requires the right stakeholders to capture related program costs. This planning ensures the organization knows what costs to capture for later tabulation. You also decide, with the appropriate stakeholders such as finance, what costs to prorate for programs used multiple times.

Some healthcare organizations may not allow the healthcare TD team to have this data. That is fine. It is better if your finance team, or whichever department the data belongs to, tabulates these costs for you. If stakeholders cannot agree on this step during the planning phase, the evaluation stops at the business impact level. You can isolate, make a tangible-intangible decision, and convert a business measure to monetary value. Planning to capture costs prevents surprises later—otherwise, the TD team might find out too late that cost data isn't available to them or that it wasn't collected. Figure 4-13 lists typical healthcare learning program costs along with the costs to prorate for multiyear programs.

We also have an operating standard to guide how we handle costs: **Fully load all costs of a solution, project, or program when analyzing ROI.** Do this in the financial formula denominator to prevent someone from claiming you are trying to inflate the ROI or BCR calculations because you did not include a program cost. This is a credibility issue.

Figure 4-13. Typical Learning Program Costs

Cost Item	Prorated	Expensed
Initial analysis and assessment	✓	
Development of solutions	✓	
Acquisition of solutions	✓	

Cost Item	Prorated	Expensed
Implementation and application		
Salaries and benefits for program team time		✓
Salaries and benefits for coordination time		✓
Salaries and benefits for participant time (if appropriate)		✓
Program materials		✓
Hardware and software	✓	
Travel, lodging, and meals		✓
Use of facilities		✓
Capital expenditures	✓	
Maintenance and monitoring		✓
Administrative support and overhead	✓	
Evaluation and reporting		✓

10. Make It Credible: Calculate an ROI

Earlier, this chapter stated that executives use two economic impact calculations: ROI and BCR. ROI is frequently used in healthcare from a business perspective and is now being applied to clinical applications involving quality and safety (Page 2010). TD professionals can collaborate with organizational stakeholders to calculate this economic measurement when evaluating the impact of their clinical and nonclinical learning programs. Two operating standards guide how we calculate the ROI:

- **Avoid use of extreme data items or unsupported claims when calculating ROI.** Good research omits extremes. It is safe to consider anything outside two standard deviations as extreme. Also, if a claim is unsupported or not credible, do not include it. No one will believe it.
- **Use only the first year of annual benefits in an ROI analysis for short-term solutions.** Healthcare TD teams typically support short-term programs because stakeholders do not want to wait two to three years to learn if the TD program was an effective and worthwhile investment, as defined by the Level 4 and 5 objectives. Therefore, the data analysis steps annualize the impact results and ROI, so a year-to-year comparison is possible with other programs. This operating standard helps us calculate the ROI to meet executive expectations.

The BCR is expressed as a ratio and calculated by dividing the program benefits by the program costs.

$$\text{BCR} = \frac{\text{Program Benefits}}{\text{Program Costs}}$$

The ROI is expressed as a percentage and calculated by dividing the net program benefits (program benefits minus the program costs) by the program costs. Since ROI calculates the investment return, you must remove the investment amount (the program costs) from the equation. Multiplying by 100 converts it to a percentage.

$$\text{ROI} = \frac{\text{Net Program Benefits}}{\text{Program Costs}} \times 100$$

The calculations are simple. The challenge is getting the numbers. This evaluation methodology process includes steps to overcome this challenge.

Let's look at an example: If you had a TD program that cost $425,000 to implement and the monetary benefit was $750,000, the equations below show how to calculate the BCR and ROI:

$$\text{BCR} = \frac{\$750{,}000}{\$425{,}000} = 1.76{:}1$$

$$\text{ROI} = \frac{\$750{,}000 - \$425{,}000}{\$425{,}000} \times 100 = 76\%$$

The BCR shows that the organization gets $1.76 back in monetized benefits for every dollar invested. This benefit includes the $1 investment. The ROI removes this investment amount and indicates the program benefits exceeded the program costs by 76 percent. Thus, for every $1 invested, the organization gets that dollar investment back, plus a $0.76 gain (or return).

Optimize Results Phase

The final phase details the evaluation chain of impact, which provides evidence that the learning program delivered the impact the stakeholders agreed upon during the planning phase. They can use this evaluation analysis and your recommendations to take appropriate actions based on the business and economic impact measures. There are two steps in this phase.

11. Tell the Story: Communicate the Results to Key Stakeholders

Design thinking includes a storytelling process to inspire senior executives. You must communicate to all the stakeholders the success of the program as quickly as possible to comply with the last operating standard: *Communicate the results of ROI Methodology to all key stakeholders.*

If the program falls short of meeting the objectives that define success, you now have data to improve the learning program as it is implemented in the workplace. Your story includes numbers and narratives. Facts are just that, facts. Stories, on the other hand, are how we learn. We can remember stories and tell them to others. They give context and meaning to the numbers. People pay attention to stories and get lost in facts.

The data collected using this evaluation methodology includes financial and nonfinancial numbers and stories in the form of interesting antidotes and comments from participants giving evidence about the program's chain of impact. Following this evaluation process generates six types of data that reflect the qualitative and quantitative data collected at different times and levels; this data tells a compelling story about the learning program's impact. You are reporting credible evidence that proves the impact of the learning program. Failing to report the program evaluation results can imply nothing positive is worth reporting to the stakeholders.

12. Optimize Results: Use Black Box Thinking to Increase Funding

This step represents another design thinking principle that is critical for healthcare TD professionals. This principle uses the learning impact evaluation results as part of a new competitive logic of business strategy. You want to ensure the learning programs are adequately supported and funded. You also want to apply black box thinking (which TD professionals have adapted from the airline industry) to analyze your program evaluation results. You want to learn how well the program did to achieve the program objectives and where it fell short, as well as make recommendations to improve the program. Even a learning program that meets all of its objectives can be improved to deliver higher value. Doing this converts your learning impact evaluation program into a process improvement program.

After having reviewed all these process steps, you may be thinking that this sounds too expensive and time-consuming. Remember, best practice research indicates that at least 60 percent of programs will not require evaluating beyond Level 2.

Key Takeaways

- Implement a proven, comprehensive evaluation system that is designed to evaluate both organizational and economic impact measures that are important to the organization.
- Begin every evaluation by knowing which organizational measures executives want to improve, ensuring the solution is aligned to address those measures, and defining the evaluation baseline measures.
- Engage all TD program stakeholders to write measurable program objectives that define the success of the evaluation program and determine how well the program did in meeting those objectives.
- Follow the 12-step process model to gain stakeholder support and generate credible data executives will believe.

Case Applications and Practice

This section addresses the fourth element of a successful evaluation system. Many evaluation methods look great on paper and may include one or two use case examples. But are these methods practical for the TD professional?

A growing number of executives are implementing policies that mandate evaluating the impact of appropriate TD programs. However, doing so does not always get them what they want. According to Drucker, "the test of any policy in management . . . is not whether the answer is right or wrong, but whether it works" (2017).

The ROI Methodology is the most used and implemented evaluation system, and ROI Institute has published more than 400 case studies. Figure 4-14 provides impact measures from healthcare-related program case studies. All are relevant to the healthcare environment.

Figure 4-14. Healthcare-Related Program Case Study Examples

Healthcare-Related Program	Key Impact Measures
Electronic Healthcare Documentation Tool	Productivity, quality, materials costs
Healthcare Leader Development	Time savings, work quality, faster response time
Inpatient Flow	Teamwork, patient and employee satisfaction, fee avoidance, ED stays of more than six hours, percentage discharged by noon
RN Residency Program	Retention, recruitment, employee and patient satisfaction, teamwork
Hospital Staff Sexual Harassment Prevention Program	Internal complaints, external complaints, nurse turnover
Enhanced Recovery After Colorectal Surgery Program	Recovery costs (complications, infections, readmissions) and length of stay
ICU Central Line Blood Infection Reduction Program	Central line bloodstream infections, mortality rates, length of stay, ICU costs

These examples passed the scrutiny of the executives who funded the performance improvement programs and evaluation efforts, and they all had a positive ROI. Refer back to Figure 4-9 to see how the ICU central line infection program's TD learning course was critical to the program's success.

Key Takeaways

- Use published case studies to learn how other organizations have applied this evaluation methodology for similar programs.
- Use internal and external case studies to educate the organization about the benefits of adding this evaluation capability as a TD competency.
- Use case studies and internal impact studies to train TD professionals to evaluate TD programs.
- Create an anthology of internal case studies, which you can use to build the business case for the value of talent development to the organization.

Implementation

The middle puzzle piece of the comprehensive evaluation system is implementation. The purpose of implementation is to create a sustainable evaluation capability within your organization that allows you to collect and analyze impact measures that matter to key stakeholders, especially those who control the budget.

If this results-based focus and evaluation methodology is new to your organization, you will want to educate your leaders and managers about how they will benefit from a results focus and how they can support it with minimal effort. A key to implementation is to routinely conduct impact studies. It is best to start with a simple program to demonstrate the value of a results-based evaluation approach to gain support for other evaluation studies. While this methodology may seem time consuming and expensive, it is not. Many times, you can plan the evaluation with a simple conversation with one or two people.

Key Takeaways

- Set specific goals and targets for implementation.
- Determine specific roles and responsibilities for analytics, measurement, and evaluation.
- Conduct meetings and formal sessions to develop awareness and capability.
- Establish an internal evaluation and analytics network for sharing information (if feasible).
- Conduct impact studies routinely.
- Use tools and templates to make the process easier and more efficient.
- Report progress and adjust tactics.
- Improve management commitment and support for the ROI Methodology.
- Consider determining the ROI of the implementing the ROI Methodology in your organization.

Conclusion

Talent development professionals must learn to think like a business owner. Why? Peter Drucker answered this question well when he wrote that "no organization can do better than the people it has" (1990). Talent development is about improving organizational performance by improving the performance of its people.

By developing the capability to evaluate the impact of learning programs, healthcare TD professionals gain the capability to help their organization see and show the value of their learning programs. This capability will help executives drive healthcare to provide better patient safety and quality care results. In addition, the learning impact evaluation capability earns the healthcare TD profession the respect and funding it deserves by showing how TD programs make a difference by improving measures that matter.

PART 2

ORGANIZATION DEVELOPMENT

CHAPTER 5

BRANDING TALENT DEVELOPMENT

JACQUELINE BURANDT

Eavesdropping on a Conversation in the Cafeteria

Imagine that you are a brand-new employee in the talent development department at a major teaching hospital. In the cafeteria at lunch on your first day, you overhear a group of employees at the next table discussing an upcoming training program advertised on the table tent.

Mario, RN: Look, Carmen, the Center for Learning Excellence has another great program coming up on resiliency. If you're going to sign up, you'd better hurry. Their classes always fill up fast.

Carmen, Respiratory Therapist: That's good to hear since I'm fairly new to the Health System. When I worked at Community, I seldom took classes because they were held at inconvenient times and were overloaded with content. The last one I went to was death by PowerPoint. After I get off work at 7 a.m., I'm too exhausted to sit through an all-day lecture.

Mario: That's certainly not the case here. That facilitator, Daniel, is really good and he always makes training engaging. I'm going to ask the charge nurse about making sure the unit is covered so I can attend.

What you just overheard in this imaginary conversation is a description of talent development's brand. Even if your health system's TD department has a sterling reputation with multiple awards and recognitions, it is always reaffirming to hear it firsthand from the staff.

What about your organization? If you could listen in to what employees say about the talent development function, what do you think you'd hear? Would they sing the praises of your learning offerings and recommend them to their colleagues? Or would it be less flattering?

This chapter explores the relationship between branding principles and techniques and branding learning. It will equip you to move beyond imagination by providing specific ways to determine your organization's learning brand. And it will give you the tools to identify and assess your learning brand; processes to develop and implement your brand; techniques to strengthen, elevate, and expand your brand; and resources for recognition to bolster your brand.

What Is a Brand?

A brand is an identity, reputation, and a promise of delivery—all the ways your customers see you. It is the expectation that a person has of an organization or a product based on actual experience, word-of-mouth, publicity, and advertising:

- **A brand goes beyond the logo or a tagline.** However, the logo itself is the representation of a brand, and consistent use of a logo, tagline, and brand standards help drive recognition.
- **Brands and commodities work in tandem to create a favorable product or service.** Brands lift offerings out of the commodity category. For example, coffee is a commodity, something most of us have to have. Starbucks, however, is a brand that's associated with a particular lifestyle. In the world of talent development, we can think of mandatory compliance training as a commodity; we have to do it. A series of interactive, engaging e-learning programs based on scenarios under a Summer Learning Olympics theme would be part of the learning brand.
- **Branding is what you are; marketing is what you do.** Marketing creates buzz, a lively, positive feeling among a group of people or in a particular place, which in turn promotes your brand. Brand management is the application of marketing techniques to a specific product.

There are two other brand-related terms you should know: brand equity and touch points:

- **Brand equity**, a phrase used in the marketing industry, refers to the perceived worth of a brand in and of itself—the social value of a well-known brand name.
- **Touch points** are interactions with customers that occur during their journey, including emails, website visits, apps, or any other communications. These moments significantly influence customer experience as well as brand perception.

Brands are indelible. William Arruda, branding thought leader, says that if your message is not clear, consistent, and constant (the three Cs of strong brands), you won't be heard.

Branding and Talent Development

Everyone in the talent development field may not realize it, but talent development has a brand. It's made up of every e-learning program you produce, team facilitation you conduct, and presentation you make. And that brand reflects on you and your team.

We all want to be associated with a winning brand. Yet, for TD professionals in healthcare, branding is not always top of mind. There are many reasons for this, including a lack of exposure to branding during their career preparation. Healthcare often has a bias or unwritten rule for not engaging in such salesy behavior in the serious climate of life and death. And of course, there is the tried-and-true excuse that healthcare is famous for: "I'm too busy to take on one more thing."

According to Maria Chilcote and Melissa Smith (2018), talent development professionals are accidental marketers who may not realize they already have two advantages for marketing and branding learning content. First, identifying a target audience for branding uses many of the same skills as a needs analysis. Second, building relationships throughout the organization—a cornerstone of good marketing and branding—is a skill talent development is famous for. It is a matter of fine-tuning your focus.

What Are the Benefits of Branding?

Let's review four benefits of a strong, positive learning brand:

- **Prove value.** This is increasingly important in today's healthcare environment, where profit margins are thin and resources scarce. Using demonstrated results to build a strong relationship throughout the organization, particularly with leadership, increases your chances of preserving staff and budget in tough times.

- **Add credibility.** Many years ago I was involved in a situation in which a new COO was brought in to "clean house." She had her eye on members of the TD function, frequently asking, "What do those people do? Do we really need an assistant director?" It was up to us to call on those who could substantiate the TD brand as a credible contributor to the bottom line.
- **Create buzz.** A sterling brand can lift you out of obscurity and generate excitement among your customers, who have plenty of other worthy causes competing for their attention. With the right branding strategy in place, excitement leads to curiosity, then involvement, then engagement, then loyalty. Voila! You have built brand equity with the staff.
- **Garner support.** As you demonstrate the value your brand adds to employees' careers and personal lives, you will be enlisting champions across the organization—from a member of the C-suite to the environmental services team leader. Whether you are winning a learning award or helping new housekeepers prepare for college, you are building a fan base.

Engage leadership in building your brand by involving them as champions of a particular course. For example, in a business acumen course in the Institute for Leaders at University Health, we worked with the CFO to ensure all examples of patient revenue, budget surpluses and losses, and so on were specific to our organization. These champions of learning will advocate for talent development and market on its behalf throughout the organization because they have experienced the value firsthand (Chilcote and Smith 2018).

Take a cue from social media. Just as influencers promote products on Instagram, talent development can find key individuals on the floors or in units to spread the word about its work. Who of your frequent flyers are well-respected and well-known throughout the organization? Get them to talk up a course you are relaunching through testimonials on your website or intranet ads.

Identify and Define Your Brand

Identifying your talent development brand is both reflective and proactive. You can start by asking yourself some brand-related questions:

- **Think about your own organization and your talent development function.** How would you describe it? Every organization has its own brand. Examples of attributes include *fun, serious, valuable, cutting edge, compliance,* and *unknown to most.* How would others describe the TD function? Do the descriptions match?
- **Think about awareness.** How recognizable is the TD department? What are you known for? Areas such as onboarding, annual compliance, or CPR recertification may label you as a commodity—a place to go for required learning. Are you more than a commodity? Are you coffee or Starbucks? Offering a portfolio of learning that can propel employees' careers will allow you to become a special, integral part of their lives.
- **Think about the emotional connection you have with your learners.** Have you relayed the material with enthusiasm and passion? Do they want to know about the TD function, be a part of it, and wear their connection to it as a badge? At University Health we saw the students in the Leadership Academies attain this emotional connection with The Center for Learning Excellence. The Academies were designed for building competencies and meaningful connections through shared values. Members frequently said with pride, "I'm in the Performance Leadership Academy. That's why I am living the culture."

Key Takeaways

- Your talent development department's brand is your greatest asset, and it is imperative that you know how to build it. Getting clear on your brand and taking deliberate brand-building actions every day will amp up your success and happiness at work.
- Optimize your brand every day through networking. Who do you sit with in the cafeteria or at breaks? Make an intentional effort to engage with those outside your normal sphere. This builds your brand as friendly and approachable.

But defining your brand doesn't stop at what answers you can provide from memory or anecdotal evidence. There is a toolbox of techniques available to help you assess brand identity.

First, establish a thesis, a simple statement or question about what you are trying to learn. For example, what do employees think of talent development's brand? The answer can be found in multiple ways, including:

- **Focus groups.** These are an established research method that brings people together for a guided discussion that provides in-depth, qualitative data. Study up on how to conduct these if you plan to do it yourself, or hire a professional if you have the budget. See if another department at your organization, such as patient satisfaction or corporate communications, conducts focus groups and could help. Or if you have resources in academia, try reaching out to local colleges and universities. If you have neither the time nor the resources to take a comprehensive approach, you can try the fast focus group method. A fast focus group usually involves no more than two focus groups and can be accomplished virtually and in a few weeks.
- **Surveys.** You can customize surveys to a particular group or target audience. Develop your own questions based on what you want to know about your talent development brand. Keep the survey short and simple. Make sure you write the questions at a reading level appropriate for everyone.
- **Employee engagement surveys.** Ask the department responsible for employee engagement surveys (which are typically administered annually organization-wide) if they can extract comments regarding talent development. If they will allow you to see the survey results, search for data in the qualitative comments, which are usually at the end. Ask if it is possible to add a customized question on learning.
- **Needs assessments.** Annual system-wide needs assessments or special requests for group needs assessments provide an opportunity to ask questions concerning talent development's brand. For example, asking if programs are offered at convenient times will elicit answers that indicate whether you are seen as responsive.
- **End of program evaluations.** These can provide a goldmine of feedback to use in identifying and strengthening your learning brand. Evaluations provide insight into how relevant and engaging the learning content is.

Once you have assembled the data for your thesis statement, it is time to conduct a self-assessment of your brand promise. If possible, schedule a mini-retreat or series of meetings, and invite your champions, learning team, and C-suite sponsor.

Here are some questions to spur group discussion:

- How do you want the talent development brand to be described? For example, trusted, cutting edge, useful, reliable, innovative, fun, world class, indispensable, successful, engaging, warm, efficient, or valuable.
- Name five key attributes (descriptive words) that identify the brand now.
- What car, song, or celebrity would the TD brand be?
- Would you swipe right on the brand?
- What makes talent development distinct? What sets us apart from other competing activities? (Is it exciting speakers, CEUs, providing lunch or snacks, first-class video production?)
- What is talent development's reputation? Does it inspire trust and credibility? Do facilitators in instructor-led courses arrive early to ensure the room is in order and greet each attendee? Is the LMS well-maintained so learners don't run into technical difficulties when finishing up last-minute compliance courses?
- What do you know or think about learners' inspiration and motivation to participate in talent development offerings? What makes people sign up, log in, attend, and complete your courses?
- Is what talent development delivers congruent with what it promises?
- Does the TD brand incorporate values that are important to multiple generations?
- What is the one thing for which talent development wants to be known?

Identifying your brand is a process that cannot be skipped. It is essential that you commit the time to a complete analysis before beginning to work on your branding strategy. You'll need this data to build an authentic brand.

Develop Your Brand Strategy

Just as your healthcare organization has a well-developed strategy for communicating its brand to stakeholders, talent development's branding strategy must be in congruence with the larger organization. This alignment includes close coordination with corporate communications and strategic marketing functions, which helps solidify the perception of talent development as a strategic partner.

Without a strategy, your messaging is more likely to come across as scatter shot, failing to connect with important target audiences. This kind of piecemeal communication is often confusing and can do more harm than good to your brand. Healthcare workers, who are under enormous time and work restraints, need to see immediately how the message relates to them. If they don't find value in the brand or the message, they will quickly reject it and move on. If you have the time and interest to pursue branding in more depth, there are many resources out there. *Branding for Dummies,* for example, is an inexpensive handbook for those getting started.

There are three principles that have particular relevance in the healthcare environment: align to the organization's culture; identify key target markets and audiences; and determine all the touch points that reinforce your brand.

Align to the Organization's Culture

Aligning your department's brand to the culture of the organization is a key component for success and consistency. If your hospital serves a diversified patient population, you will want to be sure that it is mirrored in the composition of the talent development department. If you are an academic medical center, talent development staff will be viewed as more credible if they are highly credentialed. It is often said that no one values credentials more than an academic medical center, which is why you see name badges with long lists of initials on them. For example, a University Health performance development consultant's badge reads: Pamela Mann, RN, MSN, NPD-BC.

Consider the influential relationships within your organization. What is the most popular method of communicating—formal or informal? How is information spread? Which marketing and communication media are most appropriate? These are crucial considerations when developing brand strategy.

Identify Key Target Markets and Audiences

Define your target markets, as well as their demographics, preferences, and challenges. This is something you are probably already in doing your needs analysis, goal analysis, or task analysis when you are called in to solve a problem with learning as a possible solution. Like with creating a training program, do not assume you know what your end users need or expect from your brand. Attend their meetings and conduct surveys or focus groups. Listen closely and ask questions about their needs, interests, motivations, barriers, work styles, and work environments. Insert yourself into their world by spending time observing their work on the floor or in the unit (with the supervisors' permission, of course). This will build relationships and bolster your credibility, while building your brand equity. Let's look closer at some examples of key markets and audiences.

Executives

Although executives in healthcare do not usually have the time to take advantage of the learning opportunities talent development provides, they are still a key market. Make every effort to include them in your branding. Their presence and implicit stamp of approval can elevate your brand. Inviting them to participate as course champions or to appear at kick-off sessions, graduations, and onboarding (whether on video or in person) will give credibility to your work.

At University Health, executives played a prominent role in the leadership academies. The proposals for capstone projects in the academies were approved by a trio from the C-suite. Midway through the course, the teams presented their projects in a Shark Tank–format and the C-suite "sharks" coached them on any changes needed.

Managers

This group experiences organizational pain points the most directly; thus, they can be your most staunch advocates and defenders if you offer learning solutions for their problems. How can you earn their trust? Establish the TD brand as a partnership by showcasing what you've achieved with other departments experiencing similar challenges. For example, helping pathology build a pipeline of leaders can get you in the door with radiology management. Proactively attending manager meetings will allow you to stay visible and up to date on their concerns. Go to lunch or take a break or walk with a manager from a different department every week to find out what is going on and how you can help.

Managers are more likely to approve their staff's training requests if you have established a brand as a skill-builder. When new leaders are hired, send them a handwritten note welcoming them and offering your services, and attach your business card. Then follow up with a phone call or email inviting them to coffee or lunch. If new leaders see the value your department offers, they will be more likely to support time away from work for training.

Frontline Workers

Your brand appeal to frontline workers should be inspirational, motivational, and resourceful. Since most are looking to advance, you can connect them to resources, such as educational reimbursement funds, grants, and community college courses. You want them to see you as a career-builder. At University Health we kept a database of any frontline worker who graduated from our School at Work program. We tracked their promotions, salary increases, and education attainment, and then used the data to promote the program and justify the budget.

Nurses

You definitely need to have "street cred" with nurses, and you need to respect their work in direct patient care. You can build credibility by listening to their concerns and spending time on their units observing. I worked in a learning department that required all clinical nursing educators to spend at least one day a week on the floors to stay relevant. When scheduling training content, remember that nurses run on 24/7 schedules, so be as accommodating as possible by offering sessions at their convenience and choice of venue. Typically, nurses prefer to be as close to their units as possible in case they need to return quickly.

Physicians

Physicians are notoriously difficult to target due to their busy schedules. It is imperative that you work with them on their terms like with nurses, and schedule learning programs when they're available, such as in the evening. Or better yet, offer at-the-elbow training, where you literally go to them on the patient floors. This personalized method of learning, which is particularly prevalent for training electronic health record (EHR) systems, builds a brand of flexibility and adaptability. It never hurts to provide meals along with your training content, as physicians do have to step away from their shifts to eat. Offering CMEs also adds credibility.

New Hires

You have the opportunity to make an indelible impression of the talent development brand as new hires begin their career journey. If their first experience with you is engaging, they will want to avail themselves of more learning opportunities that talent development has to offer.

Determine All the Touch Points That Reinforce Your Brand

Do an inventory or assessment of these touch points:

- **Your staff.** These are your brand ambassadors. Do they reflect your brand in the best possible way? If not, it is time for coaching on representing the brand.
- **Website.** Is it inviting? Friendly? Easy to use? Does it have pizzazz?

- **Email signatures.** Do they promote special learning initiatives or awards won?
- **Telephone messages.** Call your department's phone lines and listen for clues about your brand. Is the person who answers the phone friendly, enthusiastic, and helpful? If you get a recording, are there options for you to receive assistance at another number? Having the highest-ranking member of the department on the recording sends a signal that you are valued.
- **Learning management system (LMS).** Sometimes the only contact staff has with your department is through the LMS. This is particularly true of the night shift or float pool. University Health always rebrands any new product it brings in, such as an LMS. For example, when we purchased the Health Stream LMS, we renamed it Learning Central to fit and reflect the University Health Center for Learning Excellence's culture. When the Center for Learning Excellence implemented Slack to foster social connections among its leadership academies, it changed the name to Flow.
- **Materials.** Are your materials aligned with the brand? Are they visually pleasing? Do they follow brand guidelines set up by corporate communications? Are they error free?
- **Facilities.** Look at your shared spaces, such as classrooms, offices, and meeting rooms. Are they comfortable, welcoming, modern, and well-equipped?
- **Systems and processes.** Are your systems and processes designed to please and increase inclusivity, not alienate employees? You must inspire people to check out the TD function, join, and want to stay.

Key Takeaways

Congruence to the organization's culture and branding is the key to success as talent development builds its brand strategy. This, along with a careful analysis of the target audiences and their specific needs and desires, will guide you in developing your branding strategy. You'll be able to fill in the details as you assess the many touch points that can reinforce your brand. Integrating these three tactics—aligning to the organizational culture, identifying key target markets, and determining all touchpoints—will produce a well-thought-out approach to an effective brand.

Now that we've covered the tactics for developing your brand strategy, let's turn to building on your brand to get more butts in seats (in-person or virtual).

Build Your Brand Through Learning Events

You and your team have spent hours developing a new learning program and listed it in the LMS. Yet after a few days, the response has been tepid. What can you do to get staff to participate? The competition for healthcare staff's time and attention is steep. There are patients or customers (internal and external) to take care of, supplies to order, and meetings to attend; there's hardly enough time to take a break or have lunch, much less squeeze in a class. Sometimes your competition for learning is inertia. Let's look at a few ways to increase attendance through your brand.

Create a Compelling Description

Your job is to get people excited enough to sign up for a learning program—and then to show up, either virtually or in person. This requires creating a vivid, intriguing description that is compelling enough to justify the commitment of time and attention in the hectic world of healthcare. It is not the time or place for learning objectives, which are part of the TD professional's internal language. You need to attract participants by putting an outcomes spin on your programs. For example, instead of "Mandatory training on the new performance development tool," say "Learn how to increase your evaluation scores."

Set the radio station to WIIFM (What's in it for Me?). Let potential learners know exactly how they will benefit from the content you are offering. Describe clearly why it is important. When they acquire a new skill, it not only helps the organization achieve its goals, but it also becomes theirs to keep. At the executive level, you must highlight the benefits to the business. Use language that creates and interest and piques curiosity. Choose your words carefully—"mandatory" never evokes a positive reaction. Try "essential" instead.

Overcommunicate

Healthcare is a noisy environment with multiple priorities constantly competing for staff's attention. It is easy to forget about learning when you are giving patient care or are facing what seems to be an endless stream of customers. Use a variety of methods to reach staff and use them often. Analytics can also help you learn which methods produce the best results. For example, do emails sent out on Monday mornings generate the highest engagement? Or is it announcements at daily huddles? Communication cocktails (multiple communication methods) can also ensure success when trying to reach different audiences.

Create a Campaign That Builds Awareness and Excitement

Campaigns involve three distinct yet overlapping phases:

- **Pre-release.** Raise awareness, establish expectations, and increase the perceived value of the learning program through targeted invitations and possible incentives. For example, "The first 20 environmental services workers who sign up and attend an information session on the new GED program will receive a bus voucher."
- **At release.** Include a launch celebration and a call to action. Post photos and quotes from speakers and attendees. For example, "At today's Leadership Academy kick-off, President and CEO George B. Hernandez Jr. will share updates to the Health System's strategic plan."
- **Post-release.** Keep the momentum going and reinforce the learning. Give certificates or badges for participants to post on cubicles or walls or to place in the signature line of emails. Ask the CEO and TD facilitator to sign the certificates.

You should also share the results. For example, send out an email that says, "Congratulations to ninth-floor Cardiac Cath Lab CNAs who received their basic life support (BLS) cards today!" and include a photo of the group. When your organization reaches a goal, thank individuals for their part in the success. For example, "Congratulations to University Health on being named number 1 in the San Antonio market in patient satisfaction." Include a photo of employees attending a recent empathy class offered through talent development.

Key Takeaways

Here are some additional ways to promote learning and build your brand:

- Create a newsletter on the health system's intranet.
- Offer the ability to sign up for updates to certain intranet pages.
- Post or email weekly about new or highlighted courses and resources, such as upcoming deadlines for scholarship applications.
- Make announcements during regularly held leadership meetings.
- Get learning events on the agenda for daily huddles.
- Create an internal certification, such as Customer Service Institute Certificate Program, Medical Interpreters Training Certificate Program, or Cash Handling Certificate Program.
- Collect training success stories to share in promotion.
- Interview super learners. How did they find time to learn? What advice can they give?

- Use themes that coincide with holidays, seasons, or major events going on at the hospital. For example, Share the Love—Attend With a Friend for Valentine's Day; Bring Your Supervisor to Class on Bosses' Day in October; or a Summer Learning Olympics. If you are building a new facility, remodeling, or moving offices, "Get Your Move On!" works well.
- Gather testimonials. Ask participants from the pilot or previous courses to share what they got out of the course. This can be in a linked video on the website or LMS, on a flyer or a poster, or a table tent in the cafeteria.
- Nudge learners to other courses. Use analytics to aggregate learner data to make recommendations, something Kahn Academy does well. For example, "If you enjoyed our class on how to buy a house, check out these other offerings in our financial wellness series."
- Start an email campaign to create interest. Use follow-up emails to extend the enthusiasm and motivation and gently remind them to attend.

Receiving External Recognition to Reinforce and Sustain Your Brand

Today's competitive landscape for talent in healthcare demands that TD departments establish an external brand to recruit talent. Many associations and publications—including ATD, Best Places to Work, *Chief Learning Officer,* and *Training* magazine—offer awards to recognize companies' efforts in being high-quality places of employment. As you and your team embark on a branding effort, look to these associations and their award-winners for insights to help you on your journey.

Submitting for an external award is a highly recommended, yet time-consuming process. Here are the top 10 benefits:

- Establishing TOMA (top of mind awareness)
- Talent recruitment for the organization
- Talent recruitment for the learning department
- Employee retention
- Differentiation from the competition
- Building morale
- Benchmarking against other organizations with winning brands
- Free publicity
- C-suite respect
- Feedback on areas needing improvement

While writing the October 2019 *TD at Work* guide, "Create an Exceptional Learning Culture," I found that organizations with an exceptional learning culture all followed the same five-step process:

- Develop a road map by determining your goal and plotting your course.
- Align with strategic partners, both internal and external.
- Create an anchor program connected to organizational needs.
- Assess results using internal data and external feedback.
- Celebrate and share success by spreading the word within your organization and to your peers in the industry.

Being intentional about your workplace culture and brand creates a strong, self-sustaining cycle that attracts like-minded employees who thrive on excellence.

Conclusion

Branding is an inescapable part of everyday life, and it is integral to talent development as well. While you may not have much had exposure to branding, the activities you engage in regularly as TD professionals, such as conducting needs analysis and developing relationships throughout the heath system, will be valuable as you begin to brand your learning content. The techniques outlined in this chapter provide a framework for growing an authentic, differentiated, and compelling brand for your talent development department. Developing an effective brand will likely also take a change of mindset, some extra time, and fine tuning your focus—turning on your "marketing brain." But it's worth the effort.

The repercussions to good branding are extensive. If you are intentional about building a strong learning brand, you will see ripple effects throughout the organization. Your input metrics will rise as more employees choose to participate in learning events. Your reactions on Level I evaluation data (smile sheets) will also improve if you focus on your audience's WIIFM. This even extends to higher levels of evaluation, including ROI. If you spend time and resources on a project that does not attract participants, you will have little or no ROI and your results won't justify continued expenditures. "If you build it, they will come" may be true for baseball, but not so much in healthcare. There are too many forces competing for an employee's time and attention. You need a message and a campaign that reaches and resonates with them. Good branding will take learning programs from being viewed as a commodity (something mandatory) to being embraced as part of the organization's lifestyle.

At University Health, President and CEO George B. Hernandez Jr. often stated publicly that being a learning organization was an integral part of the University Health brand. When the Health System received international recognition for its talent development work, Hernandez stated, "Learning put us on the map."

Good branding is like good parenting—it requires consistency. In an analogy of the body and an organization, the heart is the mission, the eyes are the vision, and the brand identity is the face. Learning must be intentional in putting its best face, or brand, forward.

CHAPTER 6

CHANGE MANAGEMENT

YON SUGIHARTO AND RYAN KANE

Change management is a term you have probably heard, particularly when a new policy, program, or process is introduced. You've also likely heard it when initiatives have struggled, as in "What are we doing to manage this change?" Too often change management is seen as a "nice to have" during the planning stages of a transition, but then is later called upon to save the day. So, what is change management and why is it so critical to the success of a transition?

Change management seems to be one of those terms that is used frequently, but has different meanings for different people. To some it means formal training. To others it means telling people to perform a new task. Still others take it to mean to just rolling with the punches. While some aspects of these meanings may exist in change management (learning, communication, and resilience), experts agree that change management is a process that involves individuals, how they experience the change, and the application of tools to achieve a desired outcome. Here are a few definitions of change management that may ring true to you:

- "Change management is the process by which individuals and organizations adapt to changes, be they necessary for growth or thrust upon them" (ATD 2019)
- "The process, tools, and techniques to manage the people side of change to achieve a required business outcome" (Prosci nd)
- "Change management is the systematic approach and application of knowledge, tools, and resources to deal with change" (SHRM nd)

The healthcare industry is unique for many reasons including:

- The shift from treatment-focused services to healthcare maintenance and prevention
- The growing emphasis on the patient experience and service-oriented workstreams
- Adapting to the ever-increasing cost of healthcare while reimbursements decrease
- Talent shortages in the physician and nursing populations while patient volumes increase

- Increasing and changing health regulations and policies
- Emergence of telehealth and home-based care

The unique aspects of healthcare create a challenging, somewhat volatile, industry where administrative talent often wears two shoes: patient care and operations. A typical change management project in healthcare must be highly agile, because ongoing staffing shortages may require project members to drop everything and take on a clinical shift. It is also common for healthcare operations leaders to have very little exposure or experience in organization and talent development. This means change management leaders must ensure processes are simple and easy to understand, and allow time to bring any inexperienced clinical leaders up to speed on various aspects of the change. Finally, the volume of potential change management projects is limitless due to the healthcare industry's need to constantly change to meet government regulations, policy developments, and other factors to manage risk. It's vital for the change management leader to focus on the highest-priority items and projects that will have the most impact with the lowest effort.

Change management can occur at the individual level, as it is personal and emotional, and the same change can affect people differently. Imagine if you are told you have been promoted, will receive a raise, and have more responsibility. However, you will also have to relocate. You probably feel like your hard work has been acknowledged, and you may be excited to take on a new challenge. Maybe you have always wanted to relocate. However, what if you were comfortable in your current job? You may not want to be in a position of authority over your colleagues. Or perhaps you would like the promotion, but you can't relocate. There could be any number of reasons why you would not want the promotion or feel conflicted about accepting it. Remember, you cannot assume how a change will affect others—dealing with change is complex and can cause internal conflict.

The role of talent development in a change management process will vary depending on the specific type of change, who's involved, and what was assigned to your unit. In some cases, you are there to facilitate, drive, and lead the change. Other change projects require you to simply offer consultative advice and expertise and perhaps conduct training sessions to prepare the people within the organization for the change.

This chapter describes how critical it is to define roles and responsibilities that are aligned with change objectives. But first, let's look at the types of change.

When managing a change project, large or small, it's critical to apply a systematic approach to ensure all appropriate documents and activities are complete. The five stages to follow before, during, and after a change management project are initiate, plan, execute, control, close (Figure 6-1).

Figure 6-1. Stages to a Change Management Project

Stage	Definition	Activity
Initiate	This stage emphasizes the development of a vision and establishes clear goals. Key individuals form the core change management team.	• Determine what needs to be accomplished. • Define the overall goal. • Set down the general expectations of customers, management, and stakeholders. • Outline the general scope. • Select the initial team members.
Plan	Planning involves defining the resources needed to complete the change initiative, devising a schedule, and developing a budget. It also includes identifying objectives and describing means for achieving them.	• Refine the project scope. • Establish a balance among results, time, and resources. • List tasks and activities that will achieve the project's goals. • Sequence project activities in the most efficient manner. • Develop a schedule and budget (if appropriate) by assigning resources to activities. • Get the plan approved by the stakeholders.
Execute	When executing a project, it's important to coordinate and guide team members to get the work done according to the plan and keep resources and people focused on priorities.	• Lead or facilitate the change team to meet their set goals. • Check in and meet with team members. • Communicate with stakeholders. • Resolve problems as they arise. • Secure the resources to carry out the plan.
Control	This stage requires monitoring the project to measure progress and correct deviations. It's critical to expect and respond to the unexpected and either solve problems independently or address them with the change team to resolve.	• Monitor deviations. • Take corrective actions. • Receive and evaluate project changes from stakeholders and team members. • Adapt resource levels as necessary. • Change (usually reduce) project scope. • Return to the planning stage to adjust goals and gain approval by stakeholders.
Close	The end of a project is time for celebration and reflection. In this stage, it's important to ensure effective closure and acceptance of the final product.	• Acknowledge achievement and results. • Shut down and disband the team. • Learn from the project experience. • Review the change initiative's processes and outcomes with team members and stakeholders. • Write a final report or presentation.

Types of Change

Change can be organized into several high-level categories including strategic, process-oriented, and people-centered:

- **Strategic change** involves changes in leadership, structure, re-engineering, rules, mergers, acquisitions, consolidation, or deep and complex organizational systems.
- **Process-oriented change** includes initiatives involving technology and information systems, performance and quality improvement, service expansion, and streamlining the delivery of care.
- **People-centered change** includes anything affecting the workforce and labor, organizational culture, and patient and provider relationship management.

When conducting an initial needs assessment you may uncover a combination of factors involving different types of change. Therefore, it is necessary to assess the level of impact each category may have on the outcomes of the proposed solutions. With any type of change initiative, it is critical to understand why the change is happening from a local and global perspective. This will help you find best practices and approaches that fit your plan.

Forces of Change

The ever-changing field of healthcare continues to pose a challenging and complex landscape for talent development professionals. The TD department must always assess how new programs and organizational changes will be influenced by internal and external forces of change such as new regulations, a new system-wide electronic medical record upgrade, or a newly acquired hospital. In some cases, these operational changes can reschedule, reformat, or pause talent development programs altogether to ensure leadership and staff at all levels can prioritize and pay attention to the right things.

Let's review a few examples of forces of changes that we should be ready to have a frank discussion about with the appropriate change management team members:

- **The speed of progress.** The healthcare industry is experiencing rapid progress due to the local and global economy, innovations with systems and technologies, and increasing expectations from people—both healthcare workers and patients. Today's leaders and organizations must keep up with this rapid pace of change to succeed. They cannot do this through traditional top-down control mentalities, nor can they do it without formal structure or processes (Senge 2006).

- **Information overload.** Workers at all levels of the healthcare system are overwhelmed with information. For example, as the amount of regulatory training increases, clinicians must stay current on their healthcare knowledge to maintain their credentials. Organizations must find ways to help their workers learn, retain, and sustain this constant, increasing stream of knowledge.
- **Increasing complexity of tasks.** Ongoing updates and an increased use of complex healthcare systems and medical protocols are put in place to support the quality and performance requirements to run hospitals and provide patient care. Healthcare workers must adapt their workflow to integrate newer and, possibly, more time-consuming ways of providing care.
- **Global and local competition.** There is increasing competition within the healthcare industry—between organizations, private practices, and larger systems. Whether it's competing for patients or competing for healthcare workers in a thin talent market, organizations must constantly change how they operate to attract, retain, and grow people and the services they provide.
- **Other forces of change.** A driving force of change could include restructuring organizations, increased turnover, insufficient training, decreased loyalty to employers, increased importance of employee engagement and job satisfaction, preparing and building new leaders, or increased diversity. It's important to embrace these driving forces to provide a targeted change management approach for your organization.

Limiting Factors of Effective Change Management

Most organizations have limiting factors that can impede the success of change management initiatives. These existing, hard-to-move variables should be embraced in the change strategy. It is critical for TD professionals to identify, define, and communicate as early as possible in the change initiative development whether a limiting factor exists and if it will affect the change management plan or process. There are two types of limiting factors:

- **Leadership.** It is essential that all levels of leadership are aligned, support the change initiative, and serve as role a model for whatever behavioral changes are required. Change results never reflect a perfect leadership structure, so the initial assessment process is instrumental for adapting the process to the organization. To ensure leadership alignment and support, organize periodic individual or group discussions with key stakeholders to remind them of the program's objectives and their specific role to in accomplishing them.

- **Culture.** Change agents and facilitators must be aware of any potential cultural limitations and, ideally, use the change initiative to begin to shift the organization's culture as a complementary reinforcing part of the process. TD professionals should assess whether elements of the organization's culture can be improved or adjusted in time to benefit the change initiative (for example, normalizing giving feedback) or if there are too many variables to effectively address the issue (such as problems with employee morale). Once again, this must be assessed against the current and future state of leadership.

As healthcare workers, we face change in almost every aspect of our careers. We also have to assume many different roles when facilitating change, including change agent, leader, facilitator, sponsor, coach, and, ultimately, a champion of the change strategy. By establishing ownership of the initiative, TD professionals will be called upon to plan, assess, implement, support, and evaluate all phases of the change process.

Key Takeaways

- Engage leadership early in the planning stages.
- Be clear about what role leadership should play.
- Identify potential barriers posed by organizational culture and identify solutions.
- Review past change initiatives. What made them successful? What could be improved?

Before the Change

Before an actual change occurs, it is important to lay the foundation for it to be successful. Start by gaining or confirming your understanding of the organization's culture. What unwritten rules and values do employees follow to do their jobs?

Leadership involvement is crucial to a successful change management initiative. Consider the organization's current leadership structure. Is it matrixed, flat, or hierarchical? Are leaders transparent about the change or do they have a hidden agenda? How has the organization handled change before? What made the change successful or unsuccessful? What kind of resources are available? Will the necessary time be allotted to complete the change without cutting corners? Are the appropriate funds budgeted for communication, training, and reinforcement? Do employees have the bandwidth to participate in necessary training while performing their everyday job functions?

Getting the answers to these questions can be a daunting task, so it may be helpful to review an example of how this was accomplished at a large healthcare organization based in the New York, New Jersey, and Connecticut area: First, a group of professionals from the talent development team convened to discuss the organization's history with change, share knowledge about the impetus for the change, and determine what leaders would be playing a role in the change. Next, the team interviewed those leaders to uncover any concerns they might have about the change initiative. That information gave the talent development team insight on how leaders were thinking about resource allocation, scope, and expectations of the change. The team was then able to identify key roles for implementing the change in clinical areas, nonclinical areas, and human resources. Then individuals were nominated by their department heads to fill these roles. The process not only resulted in answering foundational questions about the change initiative, but also helped create the project's change team.

Change Management Roles and Responsibilities

Ideally, a change team consists of cross-functional members with specific roles and responsibilities. Prosci, a global leader in change management, recommends the including a few different roles when planning for a change.

Primary Sponsor

The primary sponsor is the person who charters and authorizes the change. For large changes, this is typically a senior manager or corporation officer. For smaller changes, this could be a supervisor or department manager.

The primary sponsor has two qualities:

- Authority to authorize the change
- Resources to enable and support the change

Sponsors

Anyone who supports the change is a sponsor. They promote the change with their actions, behaviors, and conversations, and can be from anywhere in the organization. Middle managers and supervisors can be the most powerful sponsors of change.

The term *stakeholder* can be confused with a *sponsor*. However, the terms are not interchangeable. A stakeholder is any management-level person who may be affected by the change; but, they may or may not support the change. Stakeholders can also be sponsors if they exhibit sponsor behavior, namely they:

- Actively and visibly participate in the change
- Promote the change with their direct reports
- Help manage resistance to change

Stakeholders

Stakeholders include managers who are affected by the change but may not have direct oversight or influence over the project. When properly coached, stakeholders can become sponsors. However, they can also be wildcards and prove to be a source of resistance.

Project teams and managers may not understand what you mean by the term *stakeholders*. In these cases, we recommend the generic description "key managers and business leaders who are required for successful implementation of the change." These managers may have people reporting to them who are affected by the change, or they may control systems or processes that are influenced by the change.

Other examples of stakeholders include employees who are end users of a technology, department heads, and certain patient populations.

Project Team

The project team is the group that designs and implements the change, whether it is process, technology, organizational, strategy, and so on. Members of the change management team are often part of the project team as well. Project teams could include:

- A group of Six Sigma black belts (process improvement experts)
- A cross-functional team improving business processes
- A quality improvement team
- Process engineers
- A merger and acquisition team

Change management can be applied to make a variety of business changes successful. Thus, the relationship between the project team and change management team will depend on the size and type of project.

Other examples of people or roles who could be on the project team include talent development professionals from organization development and learning, operations managers, IT analysts, and project managers.

Change Management Team

The change management team is the group that develops and implements the change management plan. The change management team is often made up of members of the project team (or the entire team itself). Best practice research indicates teams should allocate dedicated resources (that is, full-time employees) to change management.

While this team develops the change management plans, they are not the primary actors. Primary sponsors, senior managers, mid-level managers, and supervisors are all important advocates who play the primary role in change management. The change management team's responsibilities include coaching these groups to ensure change is successful.

Managers and Supervisors

When it's time to send messages informing employees how they're going to be personally affected by the change, managers and supervisors are best suited for the task. They are essential to convey the WIIFM or "what's in it for me" message to their employees. Supervisors are also in the most effective position to manage resistance to change at an individual level and to correct any misinformation about the change.

Managers are instrumental in your overall success. However, a common mistake made by change management teams is forgetting to train managers and supervisors in the basic principles and tools for managing change. TD professionals can address this by creating training programs for managers and supervisors that not only include content specific for what is changing, but also information on how to manage the change with their employees.

Change Agent

A critical role in organizational change is the change agent—the person or group of individuals within or outside talent development who drive the change initiative by developing and implementing a change strategy. If change is needed within a healthcare organization, the primary change agent could be a leader within operations, facilities management, or even IT, rather than the talent development professional. Change agents assume the role of advisors, facilitators, communicators, coaches, and, at times, referees.

In many ways, change agents need to become catalysts for change and possess the courage to ask tough questions. By being a resilient change champion, they can hold leadership and stakeholders accountable throughout the change process. Figure 6-2 illustrates the role of the leader or sponsor and that of the change agent.

Figure 6-2. Different Responsibilities of Change Sponsors and Change Agents

Leader or Sponsor	Change Agent
• Develop the vision. • Provide input to the business case. • Establish a sense of urgency. • Show credible and unwavering commitment. • Display endorsement in actions and words. • Remove barriers in the system. • Direct the change implementation team. • Hold others accountable to implementation. • Support practices to institutionalize change. • Stay the course.	• Collect and analyze data. • Measure organizational readiness. • Build a plan and business case. • Coach the leadership. • Recommend team members. • Ensure milestones are met. • Design a communication plan. • Recommend measures of success. • Identify rewards and consequences.

Source: Biech (2007).

The reality is that you may not be able to fill every role, and sometimes roles may be blurred. When this happens, you may need to have a conversation with the primary sponsor. Make sure that you not only keep them abreast of potential risks to success, but also to see if they can use their influence to fill any vacant roles.

Key Takeaways

- Ensure the change project has a clear sponsor.
- Work with sponsors to secure the necessary resources for change management.
- Identify key stakeholders.
- Establish which critical competencies the project team needs and staff accordingly.
- Recruit project team members from different disciplines throughout varying levels of the organization.

Change Management Models

To ensure all critical actions are taken, many professionals refer to a change management model. Some examples include the Prosci ADKAR Model, the Bridges Transition Model, and the Kotter 8-Step Process for Leading Change (Figures 6-3 to 6-5).

Figure 6-3. The Prosci ADKAR Model

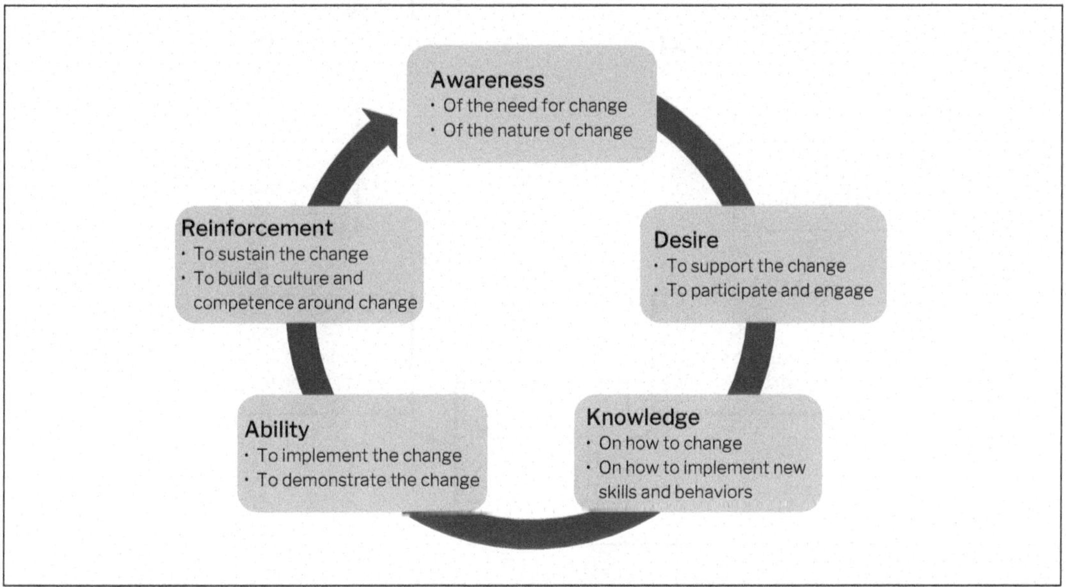

Figure 6-4. The Bridges Transitions Model

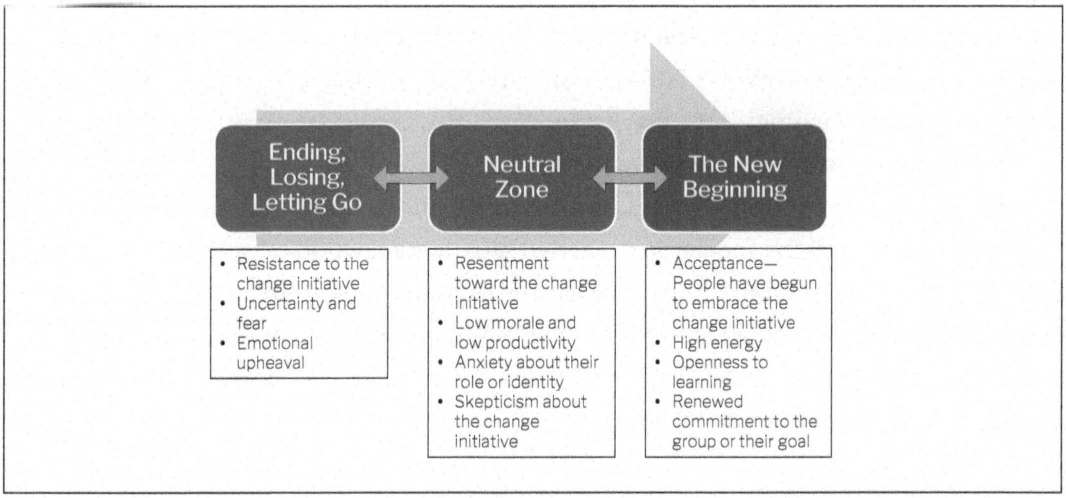

Figure 6-5. The Kotter 8-Step Process for Leading Change

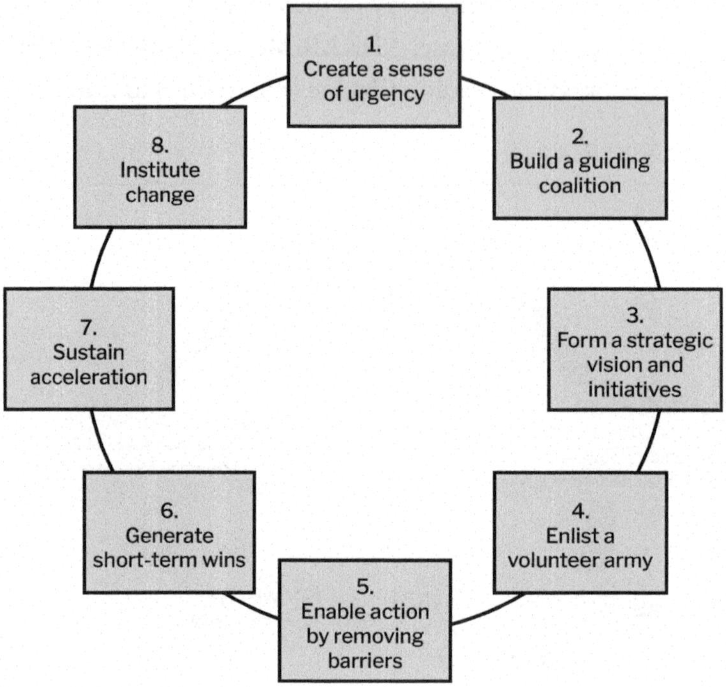

Defining the Change

As a change facilitator, it is critical to clearly define what needs to be changed and for all leadership and sponsors involved to agree on why. Ask stakeholders and leadership, "What is the risk of not changing?" One way to approach this conversation is through a form of action research known as appreciative inquiry.

David Cooperider, Suresh Srivastya, and their colleagues at Case Western Reserve University developed appreciative inquiry in the early 1980s. It is a methodical, affirmative approach to personal and organizational change; a concrete, data-driven, and efficient process that produces clear results. The approach assumes that positive questions and conversations about visions, values, successes, and strengths have the power to enliven possibilities and engage people in creating exciting new realities.

The appreciative inquiry model consists of a four-dimensional cycle that guides participants through the approach in five phases: topic, discovery, dream, design, and destiny (Figure 6-6).

Figure 6-6. The Appreciative Inquiry Model

Phase	Detail	Example Topics
Topic	Identifying the topic and defining the item the team wishes to discuss and reinvent. Good topics focus the conversation in a positive and powerful way and communicate what's important.	• Provide the best patient experience. • Allow more time for patient interactions. • Achieve zero patient readmissions.
Discovery	Typically, the change facilitator conducts formal and informal interviews with individuals or as a group to identify what worked well with the current state and what should be improved to make it work better for the organization. Ideally, the goal is for the change team to share stories illustrating their successes.	• Describe an outstanding patient experience and what made it so. • What types of patient interactions should we do more of? • What are some trends and patterns with patients who have zero admissions?
Dream	Participants discuss what's possible and share their visions, hopes, ideas, and dreams for the future. The goal is to create a clear and measurable vision of the topic's ideal future.	• Describe your vision of the best possible patient experience. • What is the best practice for time spent with patients? • What is the current process to prevent patient readmissions?
Design	The output is a view of the desired state expressed in powerful statements called provocative propositions. According to Cooperider, Whitney, and Stavros (2003), provocative propositions are statements that bridge the gap of "what is" and "what might be," based on current processes, constraints, and operational capacity.	
Destiny	Positive momentum allows highly motivated people to sustain the future they created and continue to invest in it. After the change has been accomplished and celebrated, create a subcommittee with individuals whose sole focus is to ensure continued compliance with the change, updated training, and that measures of success are made visible to appropriate leadership.	

Adapted from Haneberg (2005).

Consider this example of appreciative inquiry in action: A large academic health system asked the TD team to develop a more streamlined approach to onboarding their new faculty physicians. The current faculty onboarding was fragmented; physicians had to use multiple registration systems provided by different organizations to sign up. Details about required tasks were communicated by different departments and included conflicting information.

The change facilitation role was assigned to a medical practice manager, whose goal was to lead an onboarding committee to develop and execute a "one stop shop" approach for all physicians. Talent development was asked to develop a multichannel communication strategy to describe the actions associated with the changes, led by clinical department faculty leadership, their managers, and the physicians. The team was also asked to develop a more centralized training curriculum to bring the onboarding experience under a single entity instead of being taught inconsistently by local department resources.

Using a series of existing meetings early in the process, the manager asked committee members questions to clearly define their vision for the onboarding program. Through the dream process, the manager got commitment from the various institutions and departments to centralize function coordination into one office using a core set of resources. This approval allowed talent development to execute on their communication and training deliverables. By focusing on a positive approach and allowing the stakeholders to envision what could be possible based on current successes, the manager received buy-in to have design conversations and pioneer a joint-institutional approach to a more streamlined onboarding program. Appreciative inquiry allowed individuals to focus on what could happen, rather than be held down by fears and prior negative experiences.

Identifying Stakeholders

After establishing the organization's vision, the next step is stakeholder identification. While you may think you know who your stakeholders are, it is important to make sure you've created an exhaustive list. Collaborating with your colleagues could help identify stakeholders you may have overlooked. You may want to create a document or spreadsheet to help you monitor how stakeholders are responding to the change during the project.

For example, when a group of leaders in a radiology department came together to prepare for a change in staff responsibilities, they each created a list of who they thought their stakeholders were. They then read their lists aloud, writing each unique stakeholder group on a whiteboard. By the end of the exercise, none of the leaders had identified every stakeholder on the group's collective list.

After identifying your stakeholders, think about the impact of the change, the magnitude of the change, the level of resistance to the change from stakeholders, and reasons why they are resisting the change. Use your answers to generate an outline for how to manage your stakeholders and allocate your time and resources accordingly. Figure 6-7 shows a stakeholder management document you can use to track your thoughts.

Figure 6-7. Stakeholder Management Template

Stakeholder	Impact of Change	Magnitude of the Change	Level of Resistance	Reason for Resistance
Stakeholder 1				
Stakeholder 2				
Stakeholder 3				
Stakeholder...				

Here's a tip: Stakeholder management is an ongoing process. Keep the stakeholder management template updated and track your changes. This may provide insights on why certain stakeholders are adapting faster than others and how to help them along. But note that this tool is for you—not one to share with your stakeholders.

Creating a Change Strategy

Once your vision and stakeholders are identified, create a change strategy that will be accepted in your organization. There are several ways to implement change. In healthcare organizations, it's best to apply a combination of approaches, stitching together elements that best fit the scope of your change project and organizational culture. There are four strategies you can use to influence the organization and motivate them to adopt your change management approach (Figure 6-8):

- **Facilitative.** Create shared responsibility and involve everyone in the organization.
- **Informative.** Deliver education or knowledge to everyone in the organization.
- **Attitudinal.** Recognize the need to change mindsets and as a result change behavior.
- **Political.** Navigate the complexities around giving, withholding, competing, or bargaining for scarce resources to accomplish the objectives.

Figure 6-8. Uses of the Four Change Strategies

Type of Strategy	Rate of Implementation	Impact	Consequences	Acceptance Tactic
Facilitative	Faster	Surface	Short term	Helping
Informational	Slower	In depth	Long term	Helping
Attitudinal	Slower	In depth	Long term	Persuading
Political	Faster	Surface	Short term	Persuading

Source: Biech (2007)

This framework can help change agents discuss roles and responsibilities with the organization's change leaders, provide guidance as to the "what" and "why" of change, and gather strategic input.

Communicating the Change

Regardless of what model you or your organization chooses to follow, the importance of communication remains constant. Prosci suggests delivering the key messages of the communication plan five to seven times to be effective. It may sound obvious, but before people can get onboard with a change, they have to know what that change is. It is also helpful to share the risks of not changing (such as losing clients, becoming passe, and falling behind competitors).

There are a variety of methods for effectively communicating the change process. Change agents and facilitators must be persuasive and communicate why it's within an organization's best interest to change behaviors. Whether formal internal communications resources are used or the responsibilities are assigned to the change team, it's vital to examine how information is shared and received in an organization. Some items to consider when developing a plan include:

- What messages are being received
- Credibility of the communications
- How leadership is perceived
- How information moves through the organization
- The quality and quantity of the information
- Preferred sources of information compared with actual sources
- Preferred forms of media for sharing different types of messages

Formal and informal communication channels can be used to provide information about the change (Figure 6-9). It's important to develop a communication approach using a combination of channels because it will allow you to appeal to a broad population with a variety of interests.

Figure 6-9. Formal and Informal Channels for Communication

Formal Channels	Informal Channels
• Department and team meetings • Town halls • Emails and bulletins • Leadership memorandums • Newsletters • Institutional kick offs • Grand rounds	• Advisors and thought leaders • Confidants and trust networks • Operations leaders • Organizational influencers, people of power, and culture leaders • Patient experience initiatives and programs

Once you've thought through the appropriate channels of communication for managing the change, you can put together a communication plan. A clear communication plan can help address various nuances and logistics, such as level of detail to be communicated, whom to include, the appropriate time to deliver information, and the best medium to communicate through (Figure 6-10).

Figure 6-10. Communication Plan Template

	Audience	Key Messages	How	To Whom	When
Before Change					
During Change					
After Change					

One important tip to keep in mind: No news *is* news. If you are a leader during a change, and the process is in a holding pattern or is moving along as planned without a lot of fanfare, let your team know. A lack of communication creates a fertile environment for speculation, and people will inevitably start making up their own stories. Stop this before it starts!

Remember that for a change to be managed successfully, a great deal of communication is necessary. However, change management also requires more than thorough communication.

Now that the foundation has been laid, let's look at the activities that need to happen when the change is active.

Key Takeaways

- Review the models of change and change management. Select one that fits your organization.
- Create a robust communication plan that outlines the roles of those involved in driving the change.
- Compose messaging that becomes more specific as it cascades down.
- Remember that stakeholders may need to be managed throughout the change process.

During the Change

When you're managing change during the change, you need to be aware of a few key concepts: overcoming resistance and complacency, building trust, and knowing when to hit pause.

Overcoming Resistance and Complacency

It's common for people to have a difficult time with change, and their reactions can vary from passively ignoring any new processes or behaviors to more actively voicing their resistance and negativity to the change effort. Both resistance and complacency are behaviors that need to be addressed because they undermine the efficacy of your change management initiatives.

In 2013, Prosci found five primary reasons employees resist change:

- Lack of awareness of why the change was being made
- Impact on current job role
- Organization's past performance with change
- Lack of visible support and commitment from managers
- Fear of job loss

They further proposed these tips for managing resistance to change:

- Do change management right the first time
- Expect resistance to change
- Address resistance formally
- Identify the root causes of resistance
- Engage the "right" resistance managers

Force field analysis, created by Kurt Lewin, recognizes two types of forces: driving and restraining (Figure 6-11). Driving forces are those that help implement a change, whereas restraining forces are defined based on their positive or negative effect regarding the change. Once driving and restraining forces have been identified, you can develop plans to take advantage of drivers or reduce the effect of restrainers.

Figure 6-11. Driving and Resistance Forces to Change

Driving Forces	Restraining Forces
• People • Economic benefits • Environmental factors • Employee needs and desires • Availability of technology	• People • Traditions • Organizational politics • Employee attitudes • Costs

Regardless of their organizational position or involvement in the change team, everyone can and should model the behaviors the change initiative is targeting. This creates a social contract and discourages undesirable behaviors that could emerge, such as creating workarounds in an effort to resist the change.

The most common reason line employees give when asked why they haven't embraced a change is, "If my boss isn't doing it, then why should I?" For example, when an organization began implementing a new HR software platform, their process was rife with potential obstacles: an unwillingness to learn the new software, a preference and comfort with the previous software, the absence of a thorough learning needs assessment, lack of time to ramp up usage while the benefits are emerging, and so on. However, the organization's senior leaders were all trained on the new software and they then encouraged their teams to use the new software as well. This top-down approach of role modeling led to a drastic reduction of resistance to the new HR platform from employees and increased organizational usage.

Building Trust

Whether you are the leader of a change management initiative or are facilitating a change team through their plans, it's important to build trust with the change leaders and stakeholders. One way to build trust is to recognize the change team's interaction and leadership styles—some leaders are extroverted and very comfortable being in the spotlight. Other leaders can be more introverted and prefer to work behind the scenes, relying on analysis and data to illustrate their presence. Most leaders fit somewhere in the middle. Adapt your approach and styles of influence to the types of leaders you're working with and clearly define what's in it for them and which part of the change will most benefit them and their teams.

The way anyone deals with change is personal and varied. Identifying a person's WIIFM (what's in it for me) and uncovering their motivation to get onboard is crucial to the success and sustainment of the change initiative. This also helps build trust. President and CEO of Central Maine Healthcare Jeffrey Brickman (2016) shared four techniques to accomplish this with healthcare workers:

- **Rounding and listening.** Be inclusive and involve clinical, administrative, and operational staff.
- **Unlock the power of purpose through teams.** Connect individual purpose with the organization's overall purpose. This will also boost employee engagement.
- **Pick up speed and measure progress.** Track and measure change efforts; reinforce and recognize desired behaviors. Building on successes creates an environment in which people can generate incisive solutions as hurdles emerge.
- **Lead in a new way.** Listen, learn, collaborate, and eliminate silos.

Knowing When to Hit Pause

Throughout the change management process, it's important to maintain an objective perspective. Stakeholder analysis is evergreen and should be conducted as needed. Constantly reassess how communication is received and observe how employees are applying the new behaviors or processes. Also monitor how the change management team is responding and adjusting its course as any issues arise. How are team and organizational leaders fulfilling their roles to champion the change message and acting as role models to persuade people to follow through on commitments? You or the change team may need to provide informal leadership coaching and periodic updates to ensure clear optics and prevent mixed messaging.

No change process ever occurs without hitting a speed bump that could risk the plan's success or outcomes. Think about all the change projects that were under way in healthcare organizations when the COVID-19 pandemic hit. Other examples could include a major change in leadership, mergers, bankruptcy, economic shifts, or a natural disaster. These will likely influence the change management team, timeline, organization, and outcome of the change management plan. In cases like this, it is imperative to have candid and transparent discussions with the change management team and stakeholders about whether to continue the original plan or hit pause until the unexpected variables have subsided. The organization is looking to the change facilitator to advise of potential landmines and risks to the organization, its people, and its leaders. Much time, effort, resources, and money are invested in the initiative, and it's critically important to ensure they are protected and used appropriately. Continuing the status quo instead of hitting pause on the initiative could jeopardize the success of the change management project as well as your reputation as a change facilitator and change agent.

Let's look at another real-world example. In February 2020, an academic medical group was well on their way to launching a program that would enhance patient provider relationships by implementing several empathetic behaviors. The change management team had been established and the scope of the project was identified. The team was about to transition into the execution phase by implementing its communication and training strategy. However, when COVID-19 struck the United States in March, administrative staff were asked to work from home and all clinicians were redirected from administrative projects to care for the incoming surge of patients. The change team, many of whom were directed to patient care, decided to pause the initiative. They realized that all members of the team were vital and organizational culture and processes would be likely be affected and reshaped by the pandemic. Thankfully, the change team had created comprehensive documentation and project plans during the previous change management stages, so they would be prepared to begin where they left off. This story also highlights how fluid and nimble the change management process needs to in the face of unexpected forces of change.

Key Takeaways

- Resistance is to be expected. Make sure you have a plan to overcome it.
- Be transparent in communicating progress.
- Create a feedback mechanism employees can use to share their experiences with the project team.
- Adjust your change plan if necessary due to unforeseen internal or external factors.

After the Change

Just because a change has taken place doesn't mean that change management is over. Reinforcing the desired behaviors is necessary for sustaining the initiative; however, a third of organizations surveyed by Prosci in 2014 indicated they did not have a plan for change reinforcement and sustainment. Unfortunately, without a sustainment plan, all the effort used to implement the change will be for naught.

Managers need to know not only *what* specific behaviors to reinforce, but also *how* their employees want to be recognized. A systematic recognition program run by the talent development function would be ideal, but the desired effect could also be attained by leaders taking fairly simple approaches toward employee recognition, such as:

- Having conversations with employees about how they want to be recognized during a team meeting, inclusive or exclusive of the change initiative.
- Creating a short questionnaire and asking employees to indicate their preferred method of recognition. Options could include a handwritten note, an email, a shout out in a team meeting, a formal award at an all-hands meeting, or even just giving an employee their favorite candy bar.

Keep in mind that the most powerful type of recognition is timely, specific, and done in a manner that is comfortable for the receiver. It is also important to mention that recognition does not solely fall on the manager's shoulders, as each employee plays a role and should be valued.

Once the change management project is complete, the change facilitator should close the project and provide a summary of its outcomes, successes, missed opportunities, and possible next steps. Providing closure allows for an explicit expert reflection on the change management project to prompt discussion and generate a shared mental model for performance by key stakeholders and team members. As mentioned earlier, items to discuss in a report or presentation are a celebration of successes, initial post-implementation performance metrics, a set of recommendations for next steps, and suggested enhancements. This process is also a good opportunity for all members of the change management team, stakeholders, and key leaders to have a formal discussion about what worked well and should be continued in the next project, as well as what items should be modified to improve future change management initiatives.

Conclusion

Change management can be a simple and straightforward process, but often is quite complex. With the constant influx of new processes and implementations in healthcare, most leaders know to quickly give attention to and invest in change management initiatives.

The challenge for change management facilitators is to be diligent and intentional about selecting the approaches and activities that have the most influence in the most efficient way. Based on your organization's culture, a successful change management initiative may rely primarily on a combination of communications and surveys or it could prefer metrics, training, champions, and so on. When planning the right mix of change management activities, you'll need to balance the organization's workforce, resource availability, budget, and historical leadership behaviors. Whether the change management approach is lean or has a full array of items, communication is key throughout the process—before, during, and after the change has happened.

As a final word of advice: Although its enticing to advocate for additional time to plan and review various lenses, data analysis, and benchmarks to ensure the change strategy is perfect, it may be wise, and as just as effective, to simply weigh the facts, make a decision, and roll out a plan that is simple and actionable for all healthcare workers.

CHAPTER 7

DIVERSITY, EQUITY, AND INCLUSION TRAINING

IMELDA WICKS

> Diversity is not a liberal ideological movement, to be supported or resisted. Rather, it is a reality in today's business environment. Managed well, diversity provides benefits that increase success. However, when ignored or mismanaged, it brings challenges and obstacles that can hinder the organization's ability to succeed. The right question then is not, do we have to deal with diversity, but rather, how do we manage it to reap its potential benefits.
>
> —Lee Gardenswartz and Anita Rowe

In my early 20s, while working on my undergraduate degree, I took a course called Intercultural Communication. But to be honest I didn't understand how it would help me in my future career. What is intercultural communication anyway, I wondered? Don't we all communicate the same? And where does one culture stop and another start? How are cultures created, maintained, and dissolved? Fortunately, the class was able to answer all these questions and many more.

For a girl who lived in a predominately Latino neighborhood growing up and attended school with a predominately Latino population, these questions sounded so foreign. Every single member of my family—on both my father's and mother's side—was married to another Latino/a. So, you can imagine that I didn't have many intercultural experiences at home. I can honestly say this course was the first time I consciously thought about culture, diversity, equity, or inclusion. However, it was the first of many classes that eventually helped me understand what Stephen R. Covey means when he says, "We see the world, not as it is, but as we are—or, as we are conditioned to see it."

Unfortunately, not every student is required to take a course on cultural competency. Consequently, many people, including healthcare employees, join the workforce with no cultural intelligence, knowledge, or skills. Organizations then have to spend millions of dollars teaching employees about the impact of diversity, equity, and inclusion in the workforce, workplace, and marketplace. Being culturally competent is a soft skill we need to succeed and help organizations be more innovative and adapt more easily in a fast-changing, diverse environment. Successful organizations know this, and they are constantly looking for ways to enable members, at all levels, to acquire this soft skill.

In this chapter we will explore the most important topics you need to know about diversity, equity, and inclusion (DEI) in the healthcare setting. We'll address its importance in a healthcare organization and the impact of DEI and cultural competency education and training in healthcare. I'll identify some best practices in DEI training. Last, we'll go over other ways to educate healthcare workers on issues related to diversity and inclusion.

Why the Lack of Attention on Diversity, Equity, and Inclusion?

Let's start by musing on something that seems like common sense: Why doesn't every organization offer DEI training? Why isn't everyone aware of the impact and benefits of diversity, equity, and inclusion?

The main reason is that for many years organizations have not done a good job of tying DEI to their mission, vision, or strategic plan. Instead, they operated DEI as an office or program rather than through the day-to-day operations needed for a diverse workforce, workplace, and marketplace.

DEI is not meant to be practiced in isolation—it is the work of every single member of any organization. Everyone has an active and important role in creating a culture of equity and inclusion. Therefore, it is imperative that diversity, equity, and inclusion be integrated into the organization's mission, vision, and strategy, and as a core value. This will create a road map for the organization's DEI education and training efforts. In many instances it is also the first step and foundation of meaningful and impactful DEI training endeavors.

DEI training can help any organization move in the direction that was established in the vision and strategic plan. It can also help align the work being done across the institution. However, education and training as a standalone DEI initiative will never be enough. Any initiative, including DEI training, that is not grounded in the organization's vision, mission, strategy, and core values will likely lose focus and have a minimal impact or value across the organization.

Another possible reason for the lack of attention to DEI initiatives is that few people really know how to embed DEI in the overall work of a healthcare organization. In this chapter, we'll be working from these definitions:

- **Diversity.** The characteristics that make us who we are as people.
- **Equity.** The absence of avoidable or remediable differences among groups of people, whether those groups are defined socially, economically, demographically, or geographically.
- **Inclusion.** A sense of belonging, feeling respected and valued for who you are, or feeling a level of supportive energy and commitment from others so that you can do your best.

The Impact of DEI Training in Healthcare

For years many have questioned the impact of diversity, equity, and inclusion (DEI) training in healthcare. This is often rooted in mere opinion. However, we've made remarkable advances in demonstrating the impact of diversity, equity, and inclusion training at the institutional, local, and national level.

In my more than 15 years as a diversity professional, I have seen well-intended organizations offer training to address or measure institutional needs, but failing to root that training in a strategic goal. Although offering some training is better than not offering any, not being able to demonstrate the impact of cultural competency training can make employees doubt the value of their efforts. Therefore, it is critical that healthcare organizations assess their institutions and identify strategic goals that can be aligned and supported by DEI training.

While it's not realistic to discuss the full range of diversity, equity, and inclusion resources in this chapter, I do want to highlight two. The Human Rights Campaign and Think Cultural Health offer insights into how you can partner your healthcare organization with outside groups to enhance your DEI offerings.

Healthcare Equality Index Survey

The Human Rights Campaign (HRC) offers a considerable number of educational tools related to equality and healthcare, and they're available to healthcare institutions at no cost. Its Healthcare Equality Index Survey is a national benchmarking tool that evaluates a healthcare facility's policies and practices related to the equity and inclusion of their lesbian, gay, bisexual, transgender, and queer and questioning (LGBTQ) patients, visitors, and employees. At the University of Texas Medical Branch, we used HRC's survey and educational tools to develop a strategy to educate members of our institution on issues important to the LGBTQ patient population.

We offered training opportunities at all levels of the organization. For example, at the executive level, we used the executive training program developed by the Human Rights Campaign. We asked five C-suite leaders, based on their role in the organization, to take the LGBTQ patient-centered care training program. The program introduced LGBTQ identities to C-suite leaders, addressed diversity as a health issue, and highlighted discrimination (specifically in healthcare), social issues, and strategies for delivering accessible and affirming healthcare. In addition, policy and accreditation changes related to serving LGBTQ patients were discussed, and participants identified ways to assist healthcare facilities in creating inclusive environments for LGBTQ patients. We were able to get senior leader buy-in for the program by demonstrating how their participation would help the organization establish a commitment to the LGBTQ patient population and workforce.

At the University of Texas Medical Branch's student level, a diversity council member developed a one-hour LGBTQ cultural competence training for medical students. It was offered on the weekends by medical students to medical students as an opportunity to further their knowledge on how to best serve the LGBTQ community. A faculty member served as a mentor to the project, and the training program was supported by the university's LGBTQ student organization and the office of diversity and inclusion. Hundreds of medical students have benefited from this training.

Material offered by HRC and the National LGBTQIA+ Health Education Center was embedded into our training as well. Our existing DEI training incorporated material specific to healthcare settings, included content directed toward improving interactions with LGBTQ communities by increasing providers' knowledge and skills, and was grounded in evidence using citations of relevant research and best-practice guidelines.

We also created a website for LGBTQ patient services, including a list of LGBTQ healthcare providers at the University of Texas Medical Branch, patient navigation assistance, and transgender hormone therapy information, among many other resources.

For three consecutive years our healthcare institution at the University of Texas Medical Branch was recognized by the HRC as a Leader in LGBTQ Equality Healthcare. The Healthcare

Equality Index survey measured and assessed our institution in the following four LGBTQ patient care and workplace criteria: LGBTQ nondiscrimination and staff training, patient services and support, employee benefits and policies, and patient and community engagement.

Demonstrating how DEI training directly influences patient care is a great opportunity for healthcare facilities to quantitatively and qualitatively show a commitment to equality, equity, and inclusion.

The HRC is just one of the many national organizations that provide educational tools and opportunities for healthcare facilities to measure where they stand in their efforts to advance a culture of inclusion through education and training. Other organizations include:

- National Healthcare Diversity Council
- American Nurses Credentials Center
- The American Hospital Association's Institution for Diversity & Health Equity (IFDHE)
- Forbes
- Disability Equality Index
- Employer Support of the Guard and Reserve
- Talent Dimensions and Prism Inc

Health Disparities

There are also organizations that help healthcare institutions advance in other aspects of diversity, equity, and inclusion, such as reducing health disparities.

As the US population continues to become more and more diverse, those involved in healthcare delivery will continue to have more and more interactions with patients from many different cultural and linguistic backgrounds. It is important that healthcare organizations understand and prepare their staff to meet the needs and preferences of these culturally and linguistically diverse patients. According to the World Health Organization (WHO 2012), "individuals across the United States from various cultural backgrounds are unable to attain their highest level of health for several reasons, including the social determinants of health, or those conditions in which individuals are born, grow, live, work and age, such as socioeconomic status, education level, and the availability of health services." This means that health disparities will not improve without a well-trained, diverse workforce.

A good starting point would be to familiarize yourself with an organization like Think Cultural Health, which is sponsored by the federal Office of Minority Health and dedicated to improving the health of racial and ethnic minority populations through the development of health programs that help eliminate disparities. This organization offers training opportunities and resources for healthcare professionals to learn about culturally and linguistically appropriate services (CLAS). Healthcare institutions can take advantage of these free, pre-made training programs addressing health disparities. In addition, most of their content is eligible for Continuing Medical Education (CME) credit.

Another option is to include the national standards for CLAS in health and healthcare in your training opportunities. In 2013, Think Cultural Health produced "A Blueprint for Advancing and Sustaining CLAS Policy and Practice" to help healthcare organizations advance and sustain culturally and linguistically appropriate services. The report also offered practical information on how to use the national standards for CLAS. In certain states, licensed physicians who practice general medicine, pediatrics, obstetrics, or gynecology are required to complete CME in cultural competency and unconscious bias to renew their registration permit to practice medicine.

While many medical schools include a health disparities course in their curriculum, many medical students have never been exposed to the topic of disparities in healthcare. Many of the students taking my health disparities course for healthcare professionals have told me that my class was the first time they had heard about health disparities. It is imperative that healthcare institutions offer continuing education to those involved in healthcare delivery and continue to prepare them to address the needs of their diverse patient population.

When developing or selecting diversity training courses for your healthcare organization, take into consideration the national standards required for your healthcare providers and offer training opportunities that address their needs by either including those standards in your diversity training or offering diversity training that already includes the information. This will also be beneficial for healthcare institutions that are part of or want to be part of a magnet recognition program.

Awareness, Skills, and Integration-Based Training

When creating diversity training for your healthcare facility, one of the things trainers need to identify is what the training is supposed to accomplish. For example, one of the healthcare facilities I worked for offered several diversity training opportunities. However, when reviewing the content, it was clear that all of the existing diversity training programs were geared to help employees "have a better understanding of XYZ." In other words, the diversity training courses were all awareness based.

Awareness-based training is typically used to enhance an employee's understanding of and sensitivity to cultural and other differences. This training style is critical to the bigger picture, but one should understand that it is not the only answer; in some cases it may even cause more problems than it resolves if done in isolation.

Now, there is nothing wrong with creating diversity training with the sole purpose of helping employees have a better understanding of a topic. However, research shows that a combined approach to training is most effective. This means that organizations also need to offer skill-based diversity training opportunities. *Skill-based training* is a more proactive diversity training approach that provides tools to help employees develop the necessary skills to address challenges in the workplace.

Helping employees move from awareness to skill development and integration is crucial to the success of strategic diversity goals that include training. For example, University of Texas MD Anderson Cancer Center has created skill-based training that focuses on awareness and integration of diversity and inclusion topics, such as unconscious bias. The program operates on three levels:

- The first level is awareness, which introduces the topic of unconscious bias in healthcare. The focus is on terminology, theory, and awareness of unconscious bias in self and others.
- The second level is the skill-based training. Employees are given tools to mitigate their biases in a healthcare setting and then they practice how to address everyday biases in the workplace.
- The third level is the integration-based training, which is a simulation of unconscious bias interactions. Employees are shown a simulation of what biases look like in the workplace. After a group of actors simulate different scenarios related to biases in health care, employees are invited to reflect on what they have witnessed. Then they create a strategy for how to address biases in their work areas.

The unconscious bias training is tied to our institutional diversity, equity, and inclusion practices, procedures, and goals for attracting, hiring, developing, and retaining a diverse workforce.

It is important to offer a variety of diversity training options—remember, one size does *not* fit all.

DEI Training Methods

In the same way that diversity training needs to focus on different areas and at different levels of the professional development, it also needs to be offered through different platforms, such as instructor-led, online, hybrid, and virtual simulations.

Instructor-Led, Live Training

The most common DEI training method comes in the form of courses held in a physical or virtual classroom and led by a diversity and inclusion trainer. An advantage of instructor-led training is that employees have the opportunity to ask questions and learn from one another. When employees are in a classroom setting, their attention is also more likely to be engaged with the material. Another great advantage of instructor-led training is that the trainers have more flexibility to adapt the content to their audience, instantly address challenges, and expand on the content based on participant needs.

Instructor-led, live DEI training doesn't always have to occur in-person. For example, when the COVID-19 pandemic hit in March 2020, institutions had to adapt to new physical and social distancing regulations that prevented in-person training. However, thanks to technology, it was possible to offer instructor-led training in a virtual classroom. At University of Texas MD Anderson Cancer Center, we adapted all our in-person instructor-led training to instructor-led virtual training. This allowed us to continue with business as usual, while also adapting to the change.

Virtual instructor-led training is perfect for healthcare institutions with multiple locations because employees from remote areas can access it more easily. However, the institution still needs DEI trainers to lead the live conversations.

Asynchronous Online Training

Effective DEI training does not require employees be physically present in an on-site or virtual classroom. Asynchronous online training allows employees to read the material at their own speed and go back and review the information whenever they need to. All the material in an online course is formatted and recorded. An obvious downside is that if employees have questions or need more information, they will need to contact the person responsible for the training and then wait for a response.

An advantage of online DEI training is that it's available 24/7, which is especially beneficial for remote employees. At MD Anderson Cancer Center most of the diversity and inclusion programming happens during business hours, and unfortunately that tends to exclude night-shift employees from accessing these opportunities. So, we developed a fully online cultural competency training curriculum that night-shift employees could access anytime, anywhere. Healthcare institutions must provide DEI professional development opportunities for all their employees, especially those who work the night shift and weekends. Online diversity and inclusion training provides this opportunity.

Online training is perfect for healthcare institutions that might not have DEI trainers who can lead live conversations, but do have staff who can monitor the participants' progress.

Hybrid Training

Healthcare organizations can also consider a hybrid approach to DEI training, with courses divided into two parts: a short prerequisite online course followed by a virtual or physical instructor-led training program. This style of learning contains the best of both worlds—virtual and physical instructor-led training. The online portion of hybrid diversity training is typically awareness-based while the virtual or physical instructor-led content is skill- and integration-based.

Hybrid training is perfect for healthcare institutions that have DEI trainers who can develop online content and also conduct live virtual or in-person training.

Virtual Cultural Simulations

The cultural simulation is a new form of virtual training that takes employees out of their normal listening and discussion role and asks them to participate in activities relevant to the DEI courses.

Current research supports this style of delivering cultural training. Organizations such as Kognito, a health simulation company, are harnessing the power of conversations with virtual humans to provide an interactive learning and assessment experience that improves social, emotional, and physical health by offering simulations to support military veterans, LGBTQ, and other dimensions of diversity. These evidence-based simulations prepare individuals to create a more inclusive environment where employees and clients feel safe, valued, and respected. They also allow people to practice having conversations with an individual who has identified as LGBTQ, a military veteran, or another dimension of diversity to understand how to address biased language in the workplace. These simulations prepare nurses, doctors, social workers, and other clinical professionals to use motivational interviewing to encourage behavior change and support patients in need of treatment.

Kognito's "Veterans on Campus" training, for example, helps participants build real-life skills in a virtual environment. In the simulation, the participant assumes the role of a peer and talks with three virtual veterans or service members who are struggling to readjust to civilian life. Participants are able to try different approaches to see what works best in each scenario.

Regardless of the training platform or vendor you select for DEI training, make sure it is supported by your institution and meets the needs of your workforce.

Key Takeaways

- Align your DEI training efforts to the institution's mission, vision, strategy, and core values.
- Make use of educational and measuring tools offered by national organizations to track DEI progress.
- Remember that one size does not fit all. Develop DEI training opportunities that touch on awareness, skill development, and integration.
- Offer different platforms that fit your employees' learning and working styles.
- DEI training must be accompanied by institution-wide initiatives to successfully demonstrate change and help advance a culture of inclusion.

Best Practices in Diversity and Inclusion Training

DEI training is more effective when it's rooted in a clear knowledge of what specific need or needs the healthcare organization wants to address, what skill the institution wants its employees to develop, and what method of delivery fits its workforce. The next step when creating and delivering diversity, equity, and inclusion training in healthcare is knowing your audience.

Healthcare professionals, just like in any other profession, are required to meet certain standards. It is vital that diversity professionals of healthcare institutions be familiar with any required national, local, and state standards. Incorporating these standards into professional development opportunities will also help alleviate employee burnout.

Creating and offering diversity and inclusion training opportunities that align with institutional goals and national standards is a good starting point. Therefore, it is imperative to adapt DEI content to meet the needs of the different healthcare professionals within the organization.

Clinical Staff

Many healthcare organizations are still determining the most effective way to educate nurses and other clinical staff in cultural competence and diversity issues. However, several cultural competency models have emerged to meet the challenges of providing healthcare to our growing diverse population. For example, in 1998 Joesepha Campinha-Bacote developed the Process of Cultural Competence in the Delivery of Healthcare Services.

The Process of Cultural Competence in the Delivery of Healthcare Services "is a model that views cultural competence as the ongoing process in which the health care provider continuously strives to achieve the ability to effectively work within the cultural context of the client (individual, family, community). This model requires health care providers to see themselves as becoming culturally competent rather than already being culturally competent. This process involves the integration of cultural awareness, cultural knowledge, cultural skill, cultural encounters, and cultural desire."

A perfect way a healthcare institution can incorporate Campinha-Bacote's model in DEI training is to incorporate the five cultural constructs in the institution's cultural competence certification program. For example, at the University of Texas MD Anderson Cancer Center we offer a four-part certification program using education (online and instructor-led), engagement, practice, and application. All aspects of our cultural competence certification program address a construct of cultural competence from this model.

The certification program's courses were specifically developed and designed to help healthcare professionals learn more about these five cultural constructs. The online portion consists of eight modules:

- Module 1: Intro to Diversity, Equity, and Inclusion
- Module 2: Cultural Competence: Awareness of Self and Others
- Module 3: Cultural Competence: Knowledge
- Module 4: Cultural Competence: Skills
- Module 5: Health Disparities
- Module 6: Diversity Servant Leadership
- Module 7: DEI, EEO & AAP
- Module 8: Your Diversity Story

Healthcare professionals who have taken our cultural competence certification program are active and essential members of our institution's DEI strategy, goals, and initiatives. The most popular cohort of our cultural competence certification program is the clinical night-shift staff.

Trainers must familiarize themselves with cultural competence models developed specifically for clinical staff and incorporate them into diversity training. It is also crucial to incorporate content and information that has been approved or accredited by organizations such as the American Nurses Credentialing Center (ANCC), the Accreditation Council for Continuing Medical Education (ACCME), the Accreditation Council for Pharmacy Education (ACPE), and the Joint Commission.

For example, the Joint Commission published the report *Advancing Effective Communication, Cultural Competence, and Patient-and Family-Centered Care: A Roadmap for Hospitals* in 2010, along with many other tools that could be incorporated in diversity training for clinical staff. The class I teach on health disparities devotes an entire chapter to this report, and my students are given an assignment that is geared to help them see the applicable aspect of the document to healthcare. As new healthcare professionals prepare to join the workforce, it is extremely important that they join healthcare organizations with a clear understanding of cultural competence in relationship to the standards of the Joint Commission.

Another entity that provides accredited resources geared toward addressing DEI issues in medicine is the Association of American Medical Colleges (AAMC). This association is well-known to healthcare professionals, and represents a spectrum of healthcare institutions, health systems, medical schools and faculty, resident physicians, medical students, and clinical staff. In May 2020, the death of George Floyd and subsequent protests precipitated a national American reckoning on topics of racial injustice. In response, the AAMC created a platform of resources geared to address racism in health. When creating DEI training opportunities, consider using resources from entities such as AAMC and the Joint Commission that provide reliable content, research, and case studies in health and healthcare.

When it comes to deciding what topics your diversity training should focus on, do not follow trends—instead, look at the strategy of the organization and how DEI training can advance its mission, vision, and strategy. Make sure you know your organization's challenges and needs before you create the DEI road map. Identify how diversity, equity, and inclusion training will equip employees with the skills and tools they need and use the road map to designate a beginning and end to their journey.

New Employees

Nothing says proactive better than starting to address DEI from day 1. Incorporating DEI training during new employee orientation sets the tone from the beginning, and it's an opportunity to immediately connect new employees to the organization's mission, vision, and strategy.

One healthcare institution I worked for included a 60-minute presentation on diversity, equity, and inclusion in the new employee orientation. The presentation's objective was to:

- Establish from day 1 the importance of diversity, equity, and inclusion at our institution.
- Share day-to-day examples of how DEI is and will be part of their work in healthcare and the impact it has in the marketplace, workforce, and workplace.
- Exemplify how to be an inclusive ambassador.
- Familiarize new employees with available opportunities to advance their cultural intelligence and skills.
- Demonstrate how DEI allows the institution to provide the best care to our patients and makes us an employer and hospital of choice.

Meeting employees on their first day on the job and sharing how crucial they will be in helping the organization advance a culture of inclusion is extremely important. It makes DEI not the responsibility of a single person, office, or division, but rather the work of all. Therefore, it is vital that all employees know how DEI fits in the organization from the start, and what their role is in advancing a culture of inclusion at all levels of the institution.

Senior Leaders

Topics related to diversity, equity, and inclusion carry sensitivity and often seem daunting for leaders; however, it is important for leaders to be culturally intelligent and have the skills and knowledge they need to actively address DEI topics. Avoiding topics related to DEI out of fear of saying or doing the wrong thing has never been a proactive approach for leadership.

Minorities make up 37 percent of the current US population, and that's expected to climb to 57 percent by 2060. The US Department of Commerce projects nonwhite ethnic groups will represent 85 percent of US population growth in the next three decades. As these changes transform healthcare, being comfortable talking about topics related to diversity will be increasingly important. To meet these challenges, many organizations, including academic health centers, are identifying DEI as a component of their strategic direction. Diversity, therefore, has become more than a value, and is seen as a strategic lever for moving organizations forward.

Several years ago I had the opportunity to collaborate in a very robust project at a healthcare institution that was establishing its first DEI division. We were spearheading its first comprehensive strategic diversity initiative and establishing the infrastructure and key metrics to advance an environment of inclusion for the center's academic, health system, business, and finance entities. Since one of the initiative's main strategies of was bringing leadership on board, we assembled a three-part strategy for senior leaders.

The first part of the strategy was to arrange interviews with every senior leader at the healthcare institution. The interviews served as an assessment component—we got a better understanding of their thoughts and feelings about DEI, helped measure commitment for change, and assessed each senior leader's need for support.

The second part of the strategy was launching a diversity climate survey across the institution. The survey was developed in conjunction with AAMC and the University of Massachusetts Medical School; it was administered by DataStar, an independent survey management firm. (This survey has also been used by many other academic medical centers to measure and assess DEI in academic medicine.)

The third part of the strategy consisted of a DEI executive briefing for senior leaders, which shared innovative and proven DEI strategies and tactics to meet workplace and marketplace goals. It also provided leaders the opportunity to understand how DEI concepts and initiatives contribute to the institution's overall mission, vision, and business objectives, and to learn the importance of the executive's role in the DEI process, including annual goals.

We also gave senior leaders recommendations for next steps to advance diversity, equity, and inclusion across the institution. Our suggestions were based on the results and analysis of our executive interviews, diversity climate survey, and the executive briefing.

Diversity training for leaders helps ensure that they understand diversity as a strategy to accomplish business objectives and that they are equipped to lead the effort. Also, the training encourages senior leadership to tie diversity and inclusion to the overall vision, values, mission, and identified business drivers. It is imperative that your DEI training and education include all leaders, but especially senior leaders across the institution.

Creating Partnerships

A best practice in diversity and inclusion training is to never make this the work of an office or department. Advancing a culture of inclusion, equity, and equality is the job of every single member of a healthcare organization. Therefore, forming alliances in the organization can elevate DEI training.

Departments and offices benefit from alliances with each other and together can create diversity, equity, and inclusion training that addresses institutional needs. When I was working at the University of Texas Medical Branch in Galveston, Texas, the office of diversity and inclusion partnered with the office of health disparities to deliver cultural competency training to physicians. We were able to develop a three-hour cultural competency course. I was representing the office of diversity and inclusion and was responsible for the first part of the training, which included establishing the importance of diversity at the institution, tackling unconscious bias for physicians, analyzing demographics of our patient population, and addressing dimensions of diversity. The second part of the training was led by one of the physicians responsible for all the research that was coming out of the office of health disparities. We were able to demonstrate current projects we were working on to address disparities at the institution and share what physicians could do to help us address these disparities. It was a match of both theory and practice. This was one of the most gratifying DEI trainings I've helped put together.

I have used this same formula in many of the other diversity trainings I've created. Inviting key organizational stakeholders to assist with DEI training helps illustrate the applicable aspect of diversity. For example, we asked nurses to assist our cultural competency training for nurses, and managers assist the cultural competency training for managers. A representative of the office of diversity and inclusion would deliver the theory and importance of DEI at the institutional level, and then we had experts deliver the applicable piece.

Remember, partnering up with your organization's stakeholders is a good starting point for all your cultural competency training opportunities or your DEI training.

Key Takeaways

- It is imperative that training content incorporates recommendations by institutions that regulate healthcare, such as the Joint Commission, in topics related to diversity, equity, and inclusion.
- Senior leaders of healthcare organizations need to be the first to demonstrate cultural knowledge and practice cultural intelligence.
- Day 1 is crucial for the developing inclusive practices in the organization. Incorporating diversity training in new employee orientation can set the tone for your workforce.
- Creating partnerships with stakeholders can elevate your diversity training.

Other Venues to Offer DEI Education and Training

As we continue to identify opportunities to advance diversity, equity, and inclusion in healthcare institutions through education and training, it is important to take into consideration other venues that are unconventional and yet effective. In this section we'll explore how employee resource groups and other tools can serve as places to educate the workforce on diversity, equity, and inclusion.

Employee Resource Groups

Employee resource groups (ERGs), also known as employee networks or employee business groups, are a critical piece of an organization's strategy. ERGs are voluntary, employee-led groups that foster a diverse, inclusive workplace aligned with an organization's mission, values, goals, business practices, and objectives. They enable change at all levels of the organization and can help advance inclusion.

Historically, ERGs have typically been focused on influencing employee engagement and satisfaction. Another important contribution is supporting the organization's efforts to provide professional development opportunities to all employees through training, mentoring, career advancement, workshops, and events.

Employee resource groups are great allies to advance DEI education and training across the institution, and organizations can leverage their work. For example, ERGs were leading the cultural competency efforts at an organization I worked for. They provided training and volunteer opportunities for employees to become diversity champions in the organization. This was a great way to get employees up to speed on the importance of DEI across the institution. Diversity champions even led some of the DEI efforts. Employees who prefer learning in a peer-to-peer setting might be more receptive to receiving cultural knowledge and skills at a workshop, panel discussion, or webinar offered by an ERG. Throughout my career I have met many employees who were introduced to DEI after joining an ERG at their organization. Some of the most passionate and impactful employees at the organization started as ERG members.

ERGs can help you expand on topics that otherwise would make a DEI training program too long or formal. You can invite external experts to serve as panelists and help facilitate the rich discussions that are necessary to advance a DEI strategy. For example, the curriculum at one organization's DEI training only briefly discusses the dimensions of diversity; however, in partnering with our ERGs, we were able to create a whole yearlong series of workshops, panel discussions, and activities focused on the dimensions of diversity of self and patients. On a different occasion an ERG created a series of workshops to discuss fasting in different religions and cultures and the impact of those practices on patients.

You can reach out to an ERG based on the dimension of diversity you want to address. For example, employees in an ERG who self-identify as military veterans can be instrumental in helping the institution advance, recruit, and retain military veterans. They know first-hand what is missing and can make recommendations to address those needs. I recall attending a workshop offered to faculty and adjuncts on how to support military veterans and active-duty service members in a healthcare institution. This initiative was put together by the institution's military employee network.

Stay aware of and support the efforts of the ERGs in your organization and work in partnership with them to advance professional development in diversity, equity, and inclusion. ERGs can help you support your DEI training opportunities, expand the curriculum, and serve as content experts or consultants for your DEI education and training.

Things that can help you start aligning DEI training to ERGs:

- Make sure you know the members of the leadership teams of all organizational ERGs.
- Effectively articulate the mission, vision, and goals of your employee networks.
- Clearly communicate the objectives of the organization's DEI training.
- Identify how your organization's current DEI training can support the work of your ERGs.

- Identify areas where ERGs can assist in expanding on DEI education and training.
- Invite ERG leaders to help make recommendations on current DEI training at your organization (for example, ask members of the LGBTQ ERG to review your training content on LGBTQ cultural competence and help you adapt it to meet the organization's current needs).
- Invest in ERG leaders and provide the tools and resources they need to support the institution's DEI education and training efforts.

Cultural Celebrations

Another great opportunity to support DEI education and training across the institution is through cultural celebrations. For example, when I worked at Lamar University, senior leaders really believed in the importance of celebrating the organization's diverse population, in particular the Hispanic population. Therefore, we created several initiatives, including the Hispanic Excellence Award and Ceremony. This event came about at a crucial time when the university was working hard to be recognized as a Hispanic-serving institution, and we wanted to highlight this population internally and in the community. The university had realized that while the Hispanic population of the neighborhoods surrounding it was growing tremendously, many of the Hispanic students at the institution were not from the surrounding neighborhoods.

So the question arose: How do we attract those prospective students near our campus? Our team created the Hispanic excellence initiative—an award ceremony geared to recognize the positive contributions of the Hispanic population to the institution. The university also hoped to use this award as an inspiration to others in the Hispanic community. It worked. In two years the Hispanic population at Lamar University grew from 17 percent to 23 percent, nearly reaching their goal of 25 percent, which is the percentage needed to receive accreditation as a Hispanic-serving institution.

The Hispanic Excellence Award and Ceremony was the first of its kind at Lamar University. Successful Hispanic alumni were invited to serve as panelists at the ceremony and share concrete actions they took to succeed. The event also provided an opportunity for Hispanics and non-Hispanics support and learn from one another. I remember hearing common participant feedback similar to, "Wow, I wish that back in the day when I was attending Lamar University someone had reached out to me." Or "I never knew so many Hispanic students were in our midst."

This is just an example of how cultural celebrations can affect an institution's DEI efforts, help the institution reach its goals, and tie cultural celebrations to the organization's vision and strategic plan.

Online Videos and Social Media

The internet offers great tools for crowdsourcing DEI education and training opportunities—with a simple search, you can find entire series of DEI training materials. Venues like YouTube host many high-quality videos, most at no cost, that provide extremely important information that can either be standalone or enhance your DEI education and training.

Stanford University created a series of videos called RaceWorks, which expand how people "do race" and ways to "undo racism." This series, hosted on YouTube, is accompanied by a digital toolkit with complementary discussion questions and activities. TEDx has also created an entire series of talks addressing DEI topics. You can use these videos to complement any internal recorded DEI panel discussions, town hall meetings, or keynote speakers you make available to the whole institution.

Social media campaigns offer an excellent opportunity to promote DEI in your organization and they can also feed into your training offerings. For example, a communication plan that includes social media tweets, posts, videos, images, or facts about national heritage months, holidays, or recognizing marginalized groups of people. It's possible to develop an entire campaign on social media to highlight diversity, even offering live events through virtual venues like Facebook.

I have included filmmaking or video recording as part of our DEI work at every institution I have had the privilege of working for. A video can help illustrate and provide narratives that add value to the message you are trying to convey. For example, we were conducting the first diversity engagement survey at one healthcare institution I worked for to help assess the DEI climate, identify opportunities for DEI, and create institutional goals around DEI. Since this was the first of its kind for the organization, it was a much bigger challenge, as people had no reference point and we wanted to get them excited about the initiative. So, we put together a communication plan that included a website dedicated to the initiative, printed messages, tweets, posts, signs, and video. Part of the video creation was developing the script and identifying key stakeholders whose voices we wanted to highlight. We worked with the institution's videographer and were able to create an amazing product. The diversity climate survey was very successful, reaching more than 90 percent of the institution's workforce participation.

Make time to meet with your communication team and find out what resources your institution already has to maximize your DEI educational efforts.

Key Takeaways

- Think outside the box when it comes to DEI education and training.
- Employee resource groups (ERGs) are great resources for advancing an organization's workforce professional development.
- Cultural events can be leveraged into DEI strategic goals and serve as educational opportunities.
- Take advantage of the innovative ways social media and other technological tools can enhance your institution's DEI training opportunities.

Conclusion

In the 21st century, DEI training in healthcare organizations is more needed and important than ever before. Our workforce, workplace, and marketplace presents a much more accurate reflection of today's diverse population. While diversity used to be confined to a box employees checked and DEI training was typically part of compliance, DEI is now directly tied to the organization's mission, vision, and strategy. It is even embedded in the day-to-day business activities of an organization and its culture.

Diversity and cultural competency training in healthcare can positively affect patient care and employee satisfaction and advance a culture of inclusion at all levels of the organization. The days are gone when DEI was merely a program or initiative. DEI is now a skill every employee needs to succeed and something every organization needs to compete in the global market.

The question is no longer if we need DEI training—it's how we can incorporate DEI education into our workplace and workforce. Research shows that there are no signs of this changing or slowing down anytime soon. Being culturally competent has become a critical differentiator in an increasingly competitive economy. DEI education and training is a must-have at any healthcare institution and should be available to every healthcare worker.

CHAPTER 8

TEAMBUILDING

PAMELA MANN

After being on call for 24 hours, the last thing Dr. Martinez wanted to do was admit another patient to the ICU before leaving that morning. Fresh out of medical school and having just started her residency, she wasn't used to these long shifts. Tired and hungry, she set about writing admission orders for her patient. Mr. Singh was diabetic and since his blood sugar was so high, he needed insulin now. Dr. Martinez asked the night nurse, Robert, if he would stay past his 12-hour shift to finish the nursing admission and administer Mr. Singh's first dose of insulin, since the other nurses were still getting started with their shifts. "Sure," Robert replied, "I'm off tonight, I've already done my four 12s. I'll get some coffee and that will give you time to get those orders in."

Coffee in hand, Robert logged into Mr. Singh's electronic medical record, found the insulin order, and went to the medication room. The pharmacy technician had already brought up the insulin and stored it in the unit's medication refrigerator. Standing in front of the med cart, Robert scratched his head. "This order doesn't look right," he thought. "Seems like the dose is too high. I'd better check with the pharmacy before giving this."

One of the new pharmacy residents, Dr. Kim, answered the phone. Robert asked Dr. Kim to review the insulin order and together they determined that, if administered, the dose of insulin Dr. Martinez had written would have resulted in Mr. Singh's death. If not for teamwork, this situation could have been the perfect storm leading to a disastrous patient outcome.

Everyone attended the team conference two days later, including pharmacy, medicine, nursing, social work, dietary, case management, physical and occupational therapy, and leadership. As the unit's patient safety representative, Robert presented the case and thanked the pharmacy team for confirming his suspicion that the dose could have been fatal as written. A nurse with more than 25 years of ICU experience, Robert knew his role was to be supportive of his team. To him, this meant presenting objective facts, giving well-deserved praise, and using this experience as a teachable moment for the new resident. In the world of healthcare, where life and death are in the hands of caregivers, there is no place for shaming or blame.

Yet, just a few months ago, this situation's outcome would have been starkly different. Until recently, when talent development had been called in to help, Robert's unit had been struggling. Unit metrics were poor and patient satisfaction surveys reflected substandard care inconsistent with the organization's mission, vision, and values. The TD team's consult with unit leadership identified a few barriers: New residents weren't included in any unit-based or team orientation in this ICU when they started their residencies. Resident physicians were trained in their traditions and professional culture, particularly medicine's history of hierarchy, but not interprofessional collaboration. Pharmacy residents stuck to their work on the unit and in the pharmacy. There was role and leadership ambiguity and the team was not working together to ensure patient safety.

The impact of high-performing teams in healthcare is evident from the moment patients and families step through the door and well beyond discharge. There is a complicated coordination among these teams that is not seen in other industries—doctors, nurses, patient care technicians, dietary, environmental services, and other supportive personnel are in and out of patient rooms all day and night, giving the appearance of a well-rehearsed orchestra. When healthcare teams collaborate and "get it right" by overcoming the environmental challenges unique to patient care, most will tell you there is no other feeling like it.

This chapter builds upon what you already know about teams and teambuilding, focusing on specific healthcare applications. It also includes actionable strategies to create and sustain high-performing healthcare teams in your organization.

Why Teambuilding Is Important

Teams are a group of people bound together by a common purpose who perform interdependent tasks (Adair 2009). Healthcare teams are multidisciplinary, meaning that the complementary skills and expertise individuals from various departments bring to the team contribute to the overall effort. As Charlotte Hughes (2018), senior manager of talent development at ChenMed, says, "a successful multidisciplinary health team strives to make the most comprehensive assessment of a patient's situation and to follow it up with a full-range plan of treatment." Quality patient care demands team cohesiveness and collaboration. Patient outcomes rely on the ability of many teams working as one.

Few industries match the scale of healthcare and the degree to which people interact with both the industry broadly and healthcare teams specifically. In the United States, an estimated 85 percent of the population has at least one healthcare encounter annually and at least a quarter of them experience four to nine encounters annually (Rosen et al. 2018). A single visit requires collaboration among a multidisciplinary group of clinicians, administrative staff, patients, and patient loved ones. And there is an increasing reliance on teams from a variety of specialties (nursing, physician specialties, physical therapy, and social work) to deliver that care.

A recent study by the *British Medical Journal* found that failures in inter-professional teamwork and communication led directly to compromised patient care, staff distress, tension, and inefficiency, making a substantial contribution to medical error and contributing to 61 percent of sentinel events—patient safety events that result in death, permanent injury, or severe temporary harm (Weller, Boyd, and Cumin 2014).

It is well-known that healthcare occupations experience higher levels of stress than workers in other industries. According to National Institute for Occupational Safety and Health (2008), common stressors in healthcare settings include:

- Low staff levels and excessive workloads
- Long work hours and sleep deprivation
- Role ambiguity
- Exposure to infectious diseases and hazardous substances
- Dealing with difficult or seriously ill patients, as well as death and dying
- Interpersonal conflicts with other staff
- Lack of social support at work

All of this stress inevitably leads to errors. According to My Medical Score's medical error statistics, roughly 12 million Americans are misdiagnosed each year, leading to serious harm—surgical errors, billing errors, and death (My Medical Score 2020). Medical error is estimated to be the third-most common cause of death in the US, and teamwork failures account for up to 70 to 80 percent of serious medical errors (Mayo and Woolley 2016).

Yet we have not made effective use of a simple solution: teamwork. Only by health professionals working together will the cost and injury associated with medical errors be mitigated.

Characteristics of Healthcare Teams

Healthcare teams have several universal characteristics that are important to consider before designing any teambuilding solutions.

Diversity

Effective healthcare teams value diversity. They see the values, beliefs, and opinions of others as opportunities. Having a culturally relativistic belief about the world enables caregivers to relate more easily to and interact more effectively with individuals and groups.

George Washington University's healthcare MBA program stated in 2020 that "teams whose members are of different races, ethnicities, and genders are shown to perform more effectively." Diverse teams leverage skill sets that have a direct influence on positive patient outcomes and the highest employee engagement and patient satisfaction scores. Talent development can lead or contribute to cultural inclusion efforts.

Clear Roles

High-functioning healthcare teams must adapt in real time to rapidly changing environmental conditions, such as when the patient's condition changes rapidly outside the intensive care unit (ICU). For teams to respond quickly, they must have well-understood, clear roles and responsibilities to develop shared accountability for patient care. Amy Edmonson (2015), a professor of leadership and management at Harvard University, calls it "teamwork on the fly, a fluid, collaborative interdependent work, shifting the focus from the structure to the activities of teamwork."

Trust

Teams must have mutual trust, which leads to reduction of duplication and enhanced efficiency and involves knowledge of how teammates respond individually and collectively to changing conditions. Talent development professionals can develop trust through routine practice of simulated, team-based patient scenarios. Case studies with a focus on team roles are also useful table-top exercises during team conference meetings.

Continuous Learning

Healthcare professionals and teams also demonstrate a commitment to continuous learning and development. Hospital physicians conduct grand rounds using case studies as an instructional tool. Nurses conduct nursing grand rounds on patient care topics relevant to the patient population they care for.

Healthcare licensing bodies mandate continuing education hours for all licensed healthcare practitioners. Nurses, physicians, social workers, and occupational therapists, to name a few, all have mandatory continuing education requirements for relicensure.

Nonclinical employee teams, such as those in environmental services, financial accounting, and food service, support direct patient care teams and must have access to learning materials and continuing education opportunities. Organizational support and employee commitment to lifelong learning, growth, and development is embedded in the most successful teams.

This is great news for training and development departments. By linking educational plans to strategic initiatives and meeting employee continuing education requirements, they remain relevant and solidify their place at the table, while reinforcing effective team development.

Key Takeaways

- Effective healthcare teams value diversity. Diverse teams leverage skill sets with a direct influence on positive patient outcomes and the highest employee engagement and patient satisfaction scores.
- High-functioning healthcare teams must adapt in real time to rapidly changing environmental conditions—"teamwork on the fly."
- TD departments that successfully link their education plans to strategic initiatives remain relevant to business operations and organizational success.

The Stages of Team Development

Teams fulfill the needs caregivers have to socialize with others while working toward a common goal. Understanding the theory behind healthcare team formation provides the necessary foundation to fully appreciate the complexity of care delivery.

The World Health Organization wrote about Bruce Tuckman's team model in its publication, "Team Building" (Salas 2007). First proposed in 1965, Tuckman's model includes four necessary, inevitable phases for teams to grow, face challenges, tackle problems, find solutions, plan work, and deliver results. The four phases and identifiable behaviors are:

- **Forming.** Teammates are polite, but untrusting. At this stage, little progress is made.
- **Storming.** People experience blame and frustration, challenge leadership, react or defend, don't listen, and express a full range of emotions.
- **Norming.** Teams exhibit a shared leadership, employ methodical ways of working, are receptive to change and mutual problem solving, and have an open exchange of ideas. Team spirit develops and the team starts to perform better.
- **Performing.** Teams exhibit openness and trust, shared leadership, strong relationships, a high flexibility of contribution, and acceptance of differing views. The team performs as a unit and members work to their strengths. This is the most productive stage of team development.

Let's review a professional example of these four phases in action. A history of low evaluation scores in nursing orientation at University Health necessitated a redesign in 2017. As the project leader, I assembled a multidisciplinary team of key stakeholders across the organization. It seemed easy enough—just bring together the subject matter experts and any end users invested in the outcome. It was anything but. Here's what we looked like using Tuckman's model:

- **Forming.** Management and non-management staff didn't know each other well, had not worked together, and didn't trust opposing opinions. Trust wasn't established and there were varying agendas.
- **Storming.** As the group became more comfortable expressing their views, strong opinions emerged. Many didn't want to let go of the content. In one case, divisiveness ensued over whether the course should continue to use a controversial video.

Our team was supposed to deliver a new course in 12 months. We had to get out of the forming and storming stages fast! Two strategies helped. First, as the meeting leader, I used my influence to include everyone in discussions. Because some people retreated into themselves during the meetings, I continually scanned the room to observe body language and ask quieter individuals their opinions. Second, I would informally check in with those on the team who seemed to leave the meeting with something on their minds. This was very effective for teasing out unresolved individual issues and getting people back on track. These actions increased my credibility, and team members seemed to have more confidence in my leadership and the final outcome.

Now back to Tuckman's model:

- **Norming.** Fortunately, the group moved quickly toward mutually sharing opinions in more constructive ways, leading to a much more open exchange of ideas. All were quick to volunteer to work on action items for the next meeting.
- **Performing.** This is when the project really accelerated. We incorporated action items, as those responsible worked to their strengths. There was a palpable excitement in the room before, during, and after each meeting. People arrived early and began connecting informally, which often led to work beginning before the work sessions even started!

A lesson we can take from this experience is that leaders (whether newly hired or experienced) should engage talent development to perform an analysis of their team's strengths and assess barriers to progress. Knowledge of the variables that cause teams to slip back into the forming and storming stages, like the addition of new staff, is a required leadership competency. For example, nursing leaders must closely monitor changes in team functioning and the multidisciplinary teams on their units and intervene quickly to avoid untoward patient care consequences.

Talent development at University Health works to foster teambuilding from the first day of employment. When we redesigned the new employee orientation, talent development led a multidisciplinary team that included key stakeholders from throughout all levels of the organization. The resulting orientation brings together newly hired staff on teams and makes it memorable by incorporating gamification. Participants meet new colleagues of varying job titles and positions and their orientation teams compete for points by participating in activities. The team that earns the greatest number of points throughout the day is crowned the winner. University Health–branded incentives are rewarded to them as prizes.

Teambuilding in healthcare is time-sensitive and there isn't a minute to waste when it comes to patient care! Use Figure 8-1 to help you identify what stage your team is moving in or out of. Your diligence will pay big dividends as teams come together more quickly and their projects stay on track.

Figure 8-1. Tuckman's Model Checklist

Stage	Identifying Behaviors	Notes
Forming	• Polite conversation • Team members are guarded in their responses • You observe signs of distraction • You don't see much progress being made	
Storming	• People look to be on edge • You notice closed body language (arms crossed, stiff posture) • Some have withdrawn from the conversation • Some attack by interrupting or dismissing opinions of others • Some may be starting to miss meetings or avoiding patient care rounds	
Norming	• You observe more shared leadership • Interactions seem more natural, more patient-focused • Team members seem more receptive to change or the opinions of others • You notice the team performing better	
Performing	• Openness and trust is evident in all team interactions • Strong working relationships have been formed • You notice a sense of shared leadership • Team members exhibit flexibility to changing patient care situations • You notice an acceptance of differing views and consensus is built before patient care decisions are acted on	

Key Takeaways

- Bruce Tuckman's four-phase model (storming, forming, norming, and performing) gives insight into team formation. All phases are necessary and inevitable for teams to grow, face challenges, tackle problems, find solutions, plan work, and deliver solutions.
- Newly hired and experienced leaders should both engage talent development to perform an analysis of their team's strengths and assess barriers to progress.
- Team development in healthcare is continuous.

Building Effective Healthcare Teams

Agility is essential in responding to the unique challenges of healthcare teams. Talent development professionals must go to the teams and train them in nonideal spaces, such as staff break rooms and vacant patient rooms. While vacant patient rooms are excellent for team-based clinical training like mock code blue drills or new equipment use (specialty beds, infusion pumps), they're less ideal for other training situations. Conference rooms in staff work areas are not always equipped with the space or technology ideal for training either—you may not be able to configure tables and chairs in a formation that promotes team interaction. However, don't eliminate group activities because of a less than ideal room set-up. Be flexible! Scope out the space before your training program and bring any necessary technology with you.

Schedule your training sessions at times that are convenient to staff who work 24/7. Consult with leadership and ask which times are best for teams to assemble, free from patient care duties. This may require you to schedule the program outside regular business hours or give multiple sessions until everyone can attend. If you offer multiple sessions, schedule them at varying times to ensure PRN staff (as needed) aren't forgotten. If you're in the emergency room, be prepared for interruptions, such as patients arriving by ambulance or helicopter; if you're in the ICU, patient conditions may change quickly.

Microlearning and sharing information at team huddles and staff meetings work well for teams with little time. Ask to be a standing agenda item for these meetings. By rounding on teams within the hospital you'll learn more about what they need. Think about this as a mini needs assessment. Your efforts to gather and share information with busy teams communicates that talent development is invested in their work.

Unit training, teambuilding, or strategic planning of four to eight hours requires a team's full attention, making it preferable to move the program off-site. The talent development professional has the skill and expertise needed to handle the logistics, such as reserving the location, making arrangements for handouts, room and technology setup, and food and beverage. The leadership team can arrange coverage for essential staff. A coordinated effort between talent development and the clinical department ensures maximum benefit and justifies the financial commitment.

So, what do you do when clinical leaders contact talent development to help solve a problem within their team? Their requested solution for team dysfunction always seems to be education. And education may be exactly what the doctor ordered, so to speak. However, before you do anything else, you need to learn more to determine how to best help the team.

Start by conducting performance gap analyses and learning needs assessments. Observing teams in action in their work environments helps you better understand the context they're operating within. Partnering with unit or department leadership is essential for credibility, and solutions (like training plans) require management support and involvement.

Use the checklist in Figure 8-2 as an assessment tool to identify team and individual barriers. This can help you to determine what type of teambuilding activity is most appropriate for the situation.

Figure 8-2. Barrier Identification Checklist

Team Barriers	**Yes**	**No**	**Notes**
Lack of a clearly stated, shared, and measurable purpose			
Lack of training in interprofessional collaboration			
Role and leadership ambiguity			
Team too large or small			
Team not composed of appropriate professionals			
Lack of appropriate mechanism for timely exchange of information			
Need for orientation of new members			
Lack of framework for problem discovery and resolution			
Difference in levels of authority, power, expertise, and income			
Difficulty in engaging the community			
Traditions and professional cultures, particularly medicine's history of hierarchy			
Lack of team members' commitment			
Apathy of team members			
Different goals of individual team members			
Inadequate decision making			
Conflict regarding individual relationships to the patient or client			
Individual Barriers	**Yes**	**No**	**Notes**
Split loyalties between the team and their own discipline			
Multiple responsibilities and job titles			
Competition			
Naïveté			
Gender-, race-, or class-based prejudice			
Persistence of a defensive attitude			
Reluctance to accept suggestions from team members who represent other professions			
Lack of trust in the collaborative process			

Adapted from Hughes (2018)

Key Takeaways

- Go to the team and offer training close to where they work.
- Be prepared to have training interrupted; be flexible resuming or rescheduling.
- Expect to train in less-than-ideal environments.
- Train at hours convenient to your internal customers.

Team Development Activities

Team development strategies can look different across different industries. In my healthcare experience, both as a clinician and as a talent development professional, some TD solutions work better than others. Let's take a look at these best-practice team development activities.

Team Training

Teambuilding can seem daunting, even for experienced training and development professionals. The secret is to leverage coaching and design training to break down identified barriers. A joint study by Rice University, Johns Hopkins University School of Medicine, University of Central Florida, the US Department of Defense, and the Michael E. DeBakey VA Medical Center found that team training pays off. According to the researchers, teams who train together developed teamwork skills that improved problem-solving skills. Communication, cooperation, and leadership skills were also learned and developed. The researchers reviewed the results of more than 120 previous studies, and found that teamwork reduced medical errors by 20 percent and improved clinical performance by 34 percent. In addition, staff ability to learn new skills increased by 31 percent and on-the-job skills application improved by 25 percent (White 2016).

Scenario-Based Training

Mock code blue drills give staff the opportunity to learn and practice new skills, make mistakes, and improve in a safe setting. These low-fidelity simulation exercises bring the healthcare team together to treat a "patient" suffering from cardiac arrest. Debriefing should always follow the mock code exercise to give participants a chance to self-reflect and discuss. If you record the simulation and incorporate the video playback, staff will be able to see themselves in action and gain valuable insights into their performance under pressure. Newly formed teams should know in advance if you're going to participate in a mock code blue. Pre-work helps with role clarification and documents what to expect, which greatly decreases performance anxiety. Experienced teams benefit more when given unannounced mock code blue drills, which demand a higher level of skill due to the element of surprise and obligation to treat the patient with unfamiliar team members. An example of a mock code blue scenario might look like this:

> An adult male, age 65, is currently being seen in the clinic for prostate cancer. He arrives at the clinic with his wife. She drops him off at the front door as staff meet him with a wheelchair. As she pulls away to park the car, the wife glances in her rear view mirror only to see her husband collapse before he reaches the wheelchair. You are an RN. Show me what you will do.

American Heart Association courses like ACLS (advanced cardiac life support), BLS (basic life support), or CPR and PALS (pediatric advanced life support) are beneficial for clinical teams. These courses train cognitive and psychomotor skills that enable staff to respond as a team to a code blue incident. Students learn and practice high-performance teamwork and multidisciplinary communication. AHA courses also incorporate role identification and clarification by bringing together RNs, MDs, technicians, pharmacists, and RTs for scenario-based practice.

Debriefing is an important part of the high-performance teams activity. Structured and supported debriefing is an organized, evidence-based, student-focused process that takes place in a non-threatening environment. It assists students in thinking about what they did, why and how they did it, and how they can improve. Instructors ask questions and encourage students to analyze their own performance, enabling them to apply what they have learned in actual clinical care (AHA 2015).

Key Takeaways

- Planning the development of healthcare teams should always start with a gap analysis and a learning needs assessment.
- Team and individual barriers must be identified and strategies implemented to remove them. Be sure to include these strategies in your education plans and incorporate into teambuilding activities.

- Teambuilding activities must be designed to provide opportunities for staff to practice developing skills that are easily replicated in the real world.
- Virtual teams present unique challenges. Managers and employees share equal responsibility for maintaining engagement.

Scavenger Hunts

Newly hired team members can benefit from self-paced activities like scavenger hunts, which, when well designed, enable staff to learn their way around their new professional homes. Locating places and things critical to their work is reassuring—finding the cafeteria or breakroom, knowing where to park and where to store personal items like backpacks and handbags decreases anxiety. You can make the scavenger hunt simple or include a competitive element featuring a prize for the winners. Figure 8-3 is an example of a scavenger hunt in use.

Figure 8-3. Unit Orientation Scavenger Hunt

Locate the following items and make a note of where you found them:

Items	Where Located
Report room	
Fire extinguishers	
Fire pull stations	
Clean utility room	
Dirty utility room	
Supply room	
Staff restrooms	
Clean linen	
Dirty linen	
Personal protective equipment (PPE)	
Equipment (infusion pumps, etc.)	
MSDS (Material Safety Data Sheets)	
Medication Room (Pyxis Med Station)	
Exits	
Code blue cart with monitor/defibrillator	
Pneumatic tube system	
Glucose meters and supplies	

Figure 8-3 (cont.)

Items	Where Located
Bedpans, IV start supplies, and other patient care supplies	
Policy and procedure manual for patient procedures	
Patient care coordinator (PCC) office	
Other:	
Off Unit (D Elevator, Rio Tower)	
Employee ID and registration (Parking) (sublevel)	
Inpatient pharmacy (SL)	
Cafeteria (3rd Floor) Use elevator D	
Sky Tower Lobby Area	
Sky Bistro and Starbucks	
Chapel	
Patient information desk	

Scavenger hunts should be incorporated into a unit-based orientation for new team members. It's a self-guided activity—no instructor needed.

Community-Based Initiatives

Civic-minded teams who volunteer at the local food bank, participate in a Habitat for Humanity project, or support other community-based initiatives practice and refine team skills transferable to their clinical work including collaboration, cooperation, communication, negotiation, and trust. Pre-assignment of roles in which nonsupervisory staff are in leadership and leaders assume lesser roles is effective for developing leadership skills within the first group and the enriching the experience of the second group.

Soft Skills Training

Identified barriers to teams and individuals can be eliminated through soft skills training. High-performing teams who are trained in courses focused on complementing clinical skills—like Crucial Conversations, emotional intelligence, and TeamSTEPPS—perform better together than teams whose sole pursuit is continuing clinical education. Soft skills training is the prescription needed—the most successful clinical staff are those trained in courses that complement their clinical skill sets and target deficiencies.

Key Takeaways

- Self-paced activities like scavenger hunts give newly hired staff and students opportunities to own the learning experience.
- Teams who volunteer through community-based initiatives practice and refine team skills transferable to their clinical work.
- Talent development provides the missing link to team successes through soft skills training that complements their clinical skills.

Leadership Development

Leadership development, often a priority in talent development, must include teambuilding through experiential activities. University Health's leadership academies included community service and organizational improvement projects.

For example, an interdisciplinary team from pathology and admissions, coached by talent development and lean transformation, applied business acumen and process improvement methodologies they learned in the academy to reduce wait times in an outpatient laboratory. These wait times had ranged from 30 to 60 minutes since 2016. Following the program, full cycle wait-times decreased by an average of 12 minutes (a 25 percent reduction). Patients reported that staff conveyed an orderly wait process, and their satisfaction scores increased from 80 to 85 percent. This model is replicable throughout the organization.

Key Takeaways

- Talent development plays a critical role in developing leaders.
- Leadership academies provide opportunities for leaders to grow into their roles or take their leadership expertise to the next level through didactic and experiential learning.

Virtual Teams

Virtual teams working from home or off-site have the same need for engagment as a team that regularly interacts in the office. A number of University Health departments work off-site and away from the direct patient care teams that depend upon them; for example, information technology, financial services, legal services, and durable medical equipment vendors. Virtual teams must be cognizant of the challenges of meeting virtually and take the appropriate steps to ensure they are successful. The Ariel Group (2020) published tips for virtual teams, which are shown in Figure 8-4.

Figure 8-4. Virtual Team Tips for Managers and Employees

Tips for Managers	Tips for Virtual Employees
Schedule regular temperature checks. When you can't count on bumping into the person in the hall or dropping by their office: • Be deliberate. • Plan regular communication. Healthcare managers should: • Schedule a weekly infohuddle with your team and always be present. Healthcare teams working 12-hour shifts will need to plan an infohuddle that both day and night shifts can attend without taking time away from patient care. Good options are 6:30 a.m. for day shift and 6:30 p.m. for the night shift. • Give time for each staff member to report out on projects they are working on or patient care issues that have surfaced. Ask how the team can help.	**Stay tuned in.** It's up to you to be present in the moment: • Be aware of your feelings. • Are you feeling disconnected or isolated? If so, take time to reach out. Healthcare employees should: • Actively participate in the infohuddle. • Communicate the status of your projects or patient care issues. Take the lead on solution-focused strategies. • Take initiative to connect with leaders and co-workers just for fun. Check in with them—ask how their weekend was or acknowledge aspects of their lives they have shared with you.
Monitor any virtual signals you are sending or receiving. Especially in the absence of visual cues, vocal style and pacing can speak volumes: • Be more aware of how your messages are landing. • Ask yourself, "did the nuances come through?" • Is the message resonating? • Pause for a check-in to make sure. Healthcare managers should: • Be aware of the urgency of the healthcare environment and tailor communication to be concise. Listen for verbal cues from the receiver. • Give background to your communication, addressing the "why" to compensate for the struggle to recognize nuances that are critical to patient care decisions. • Use the SBAR template (situation, background, assessment, and recommendation) when communicating healthcare information to virtual teams. • Use teach back techniques to check understanding and ensure patient care decisions are clearly understood by all.	**Communicate expressively.** You won't always be able to rely on face-to-face interactions: • When you have ideas or concerns you want to get across, your ability to communicate in a clear, compelling way is more important than ever. • Consider using webcams to enable you to see your teammates. Healthcare employees should: • Respond clearly and concisely to communications regarding patient care decisions. • Assertively express your opinion regarding patient care decisions. • Use the SBAR template. • Use the teach back method to confirm understanding of any patient care decisions you are about to act on. • Use tools available to you in the clinical documentation system. For example, University Health uses Epic, which allows direct patient care givers like nurses and physicians to send comments to the pharmacy regarding medications.

Encourage virtual employees to initiate reaching out to you and others. Suggest that they connect with their colleagues for the sake of keeping in touch. This can help employees build their confidence and presence by taking ownership of their engagement: • Call with birthday wishes. • Recruit someone to be a sounding board for a new idea. Healthcare managers should: • Devote time during infohuddles or pre-shift meetings to celebrate everyone, including those off-site. • Include virtual teammates on unit-based committees like infection control, pharmacy and therapeutics, and reward and recognition.	**Take advantage of the tools.** Email is great, but don't let it be your sole method of contact: • Schedule opportunities for verbal communications by phone. • Schedule opportunities for visual communication using WebEx or other web conferencing software. Healthcare employees should: • Actively participate in virtual teammate celebrations like the birth of a new baby, a wedding, or a birthday. • Volunteer to chair or participate on a unit-based committee.
Include virtual teams when planning company events and activities. While they may not be able to attend activities in the office, you can still find equivalent alternatives for your staff. This helps them to: • Feel like they're part of the culture. • Know they are not forgotten. Healthcare managers should: • Get together before or after work for breakfast. Night-shift staff love to have breakfast together after a 12-hour shift. • Set aside one day a month to celebrate team birthdays or awards. Maybe you could all go bowling.	**Don't let your imagination get the best of you.** Without context we tend to fill in the blanks of what's going on. If you notice that happening, it's a warning sign that you need to reach out and have a conversation with someone else on your team. Healthcare employees should: • Avoid telling yourself that you know why a patient is behaving a certain way or why a physician made a patient care decision. • Get the facts from the patient or physician directly before you tell yourself the rest of the story.

Adapted from Strong (nd).

Developing Teams Within Talent Development

Let's not forget about the teams that represent talent development in healthcare. You need teambuilding, too! Professional growth and development within the talent development team is essential for providing learners with exceptional experiences. Professional continuing education opportunities, such as conferences, offer teams the opportunity to divide and conquer by attending different sessions. Teams then grow stronger when they reconvene to share the new knowledge.

With any new or existing project, the first step is to convene a team within the talent development function to tackle the problem or opportunity. This is what we did at University

Health when we redesigned the way new employee orientation was facilitated. Everyone had a role, including the instructional designers, e-learning team, facilitators, administrative professionals, and leadership.

For every course we facilitate, whether it's 15 minutes or 16 hours, we use a model similar to that of professional sports. Each course includes the facilitator, support personnel, and a bench for them to rotate in and out. This requires cross-training to permit those on the bench to step in in a moment's notice to support the team and guarantee that the show goes on and classes aren't cancelled. Staff count on us to deliver the classes they need to do their jobs, and rescheduling often is not an option when schedules are set eight weeks in advance.

Key Takeaways

- Talent development professionals who engage in industry-specific continuing education and share with their colleagues develop strong teams.
- Always have a strong bench. Every project needs an identified support system.

Conclusion: Sustaining Healthcare Teams

Like all important relationships, teams nurture one another and exhibit behaviors that work to sustain them. Problem-solving and assessment of team effectiveness are encouraged and supported. Mistakes are seen as process improvement opportunities. Teams self-correct by continuously evaluating their performance and learning—shifting from learning from the event to the process of learning over time. Talent development professionals can support team sustainment by creating training development plans for department teams and coaching to personal and professional excellence.

Talent development's role in team building is critical to the healthcare organization's success. Leadership depends upon skilled talent development practitioners to diagnose and solve problems and eliminate barriers and silos that exist in struggling teams. Clinical and soft skills continuing education and experiential team building activities strengthen patient care skills. Multidisciplinary healthcare teams that collaborate, communicate, and work well together see fewer medical errors, fewer sentinel events, and lower morbidity and mortality. Staff benefit by reporting higher satisfaction with their jobs, less tension, and less distress.

When staff unite to form patient-centered teams, they are at their best and doing what they were born to do. They have to be good stewards of the well-being of those placed in their care at the most vulnerable times of their lives. They need to show love and compassion for the human race, free from bias—they are just people in need and suffering.

> It has become necessary to develop medicine as a cooperative science; the clinician, the specialist, and the laboratory workers uniting for the good of the patient, each assisting in elucidation of the problem at hand, and each dependent on the other for support.
>
> —William J. Mayo in his 1910 commencement address to Rush Medical College

CHAPTER 9

CULTURE OF SAFETY AND RELIABILITY

DANIEL GANDARILLA AND CANDY BAPTIST

Safety and reliability are two critical areas to a successful healthcare delivery system. Without proper safety, major errors can occur, including surgical site errors, diagnostic errors, patient falls, communication errors, medication errors, and even death. While most are preventable, they remain a common cause of injury or death in the United States (Rodziewics, Houseman, and Hipskind 2020). As a learning professional, you play a vital role in helping establish a culture that is open, collaborative, transparent, and adaptive. You may already call this a learning culture.

While safety is critical, it doesn't always rise to the top of the agenda for learning professionals, especially when their focus may lie more on the team, employee health, quality outcomes, and nursing professional development. Trainers are commonly overrun with tasks, such as updating existing lessons, converting material to e-learning platforms, and preparing to fulfill the latest request from a leader. This chapter focuses on the critical role the learning function can play in creating a culture of safety and reliability—one where the appropriate behaviors, methods, language, and tools manifest in daily work. We'll define safety as the act of intentionally placing attention on things that prevent harm to a teammate or patient, while reliability is the act of ensuring an expected practice or process occurs routinely and systematically for every patient, every time, everywhere.

The first section focuses on how to successfully partner in a cultural transformation focused on safety and reliability. This includes adoption of new behaviors, tools, and techniques across a full enterprise of both clinical and nonclinical employees. The second section focuses on how we fundamentally transformed the learning function, putting a specific emphasis on accredited education and interprofessional collaborative education (IPCE) at a strategic level. This transformation includes shifting L&D work processes to match expectations in a culture of high reliability. Each section offers a description of the significance, describes how we made the case internally, and explains our method and approach for driving the successful change. We conclude with some key takeaways to frame your thinking as a leader in the healthcare environment. At the end of the chapter, you'll find a case study from John Muir Health on their high-reliability journey.

Please note that these initiatives were not independent activities, but instead were inclusive, collaborative efforts conducted under thoughtful leadership. We had support from the most senior levels of the organization, including the board of directors. Updates and metrics were reported routinely to senior leaders, and their high levels of engagement continue today. Our CEO even wrote an article for ATD highlighting the necessity of speaking up for safety and ensuring accountability as a component of achieving our 10-year strategic plan (Berdan 2016). Our COO, a physician executive, served as the sponsor for IPCE, calling it a "no brainer" to deliver the quality of care that was needed. In addition, our chief clinical officer and physician executive and chief nursing officer both backed these efforts. This executive support was immensely helpful throughout the life of the project. We also had support from our colleagues in HR, finance, quality, nursing, and physician leadership who helped push forward initiatives, provide support, and celebrate successes.

While the overall journey to creating a safe, reliable organization may be a lengthy one, it is imperative for healthcare delivery systems to focus on these fundamental components. We need to get them right so that a broader strategic transformation can occur.

Creating a Reliability and Safety Culture

It is no secret to healthcare workers that preventable harm, or harm that is caused by human error and can be avoided, is prevalent in healthcare; we also know that patients die from errors that are preventable. In fact, four out of 10 patients experience some version of preventable harm in primary and outpatient care (World Health Organization 2019). For perspective, your risk of dying in an airplane crash is only one in 3 million; your risk of dying while receiving healthcare is one in 300.

If patient safety wasn't enough, healthcare employees also face significant risk in their day-to-day work environment. They typically have extended shifts; are exposed to sharp objects, various chemicals, and stress; and sometimes face aggression from those they care for. It should come as no surprise that "cases of nonfatal occupational injury and illness with healthcare workers are among the highest of any industry sector" (National Institute for Occupational Safety and Health 2017).

This environment is dangerous. Placing the emphasis on safety by reducing harm to teammates seems like it would be easy to do, but it takes strong leaders who are willing to look hard at clinical outcomes and adjust as needed. Gaining support by showing the impact beyond the clinical setting can lead to tremendous buy-in from all involved.

Making the Case

To make the case, consider the three lenses that you can use to help reframe the conversation around what is most important to your organization: reliability and outcomes, finances, and experience:

- **Outcomes and reliability.** This is the strongest case to be made and is a springboard for other parts of the business case. Understanding the baseline rate of preventable errors and impact presents the most powerful case for improvement. Our journey started with dissatisfaction in our quality metrics. Our leadership team and board of directors strongly believed that the organization needed to go in a different direction to improve safety. Cases of preventable harm to a patient were occurring nearly every three days. While the financial impact in terms of legal fees is an important point for the business case, this information also allowed us to compare these outcomes with the organization's mission and values. That got their attention.
- **Finances.** Once the outcomes are established, it is easy to make the case financially. We know patient safety events affect our reputation, lead to lawsuits, and can require additional resources to care for the injured individual, thereby causing repercussions to the financial outcomes of the healthcare system. It is worth noting that "preventable harm results in about $9.3 billion in extra healthcare costs in the United States" (Health Day News 2019). Your chief legal officer and risk department will have plenty of information on lawsuits and their implications on costs paid by the organization. Your finance team may even be able to share the amount they hold aside for litigation. This data can help you make a hard business case for avoiding litigation.
- **Experience.** Patient, consumer, and teammate experiences are very important to consider from a business case. Most organizations have a list of what consumers

want from their healthcare provider. Inevitably, something on that list will center around clinical excellence or reliability for consumers. For teammates, mission-focus tends to be at the top of the list. Focusing on creating a culture that prevents harm allows the organization to address two things: respecting that people deliver care and acknowledging that potential harm is a part of it. Putting tools into place that can respect and enhance the current processes will improve the experiences of all parties.

In addition to these three areas, you also need trusted colleagues and supporters within your organization. You will be a part of convening groups of different teams or departments to learn collectively (rather than in the silos of specialties)—L&D cannot be the sole lead on the effort. It must come from senior management and be led jointly by quality, operational leaders, and learning. Some of your closest allies in advancing the effort will include clinicians (chief nurse, chief medical), human resources (employee health and safety), and finance. Working with them to build the case at the outset can have tremendous impact on the overall success of the program.

Key Takeaways

- How are you currently framing your organizational issue? Is it framed through the most critical lenses?
- What are the current mindsets, attitudes, and behaviors related to safety and reliability? How does your data compare to benchmarks? Peers?
- Do you have a model for change? Does it ensure accountability at all levels of the organization?

Our Method and Approach

The talent or learning function should serve as a co-lead in this cultural transformation initiative, whether you are designated that way or not. This will ensure that the learning and education efforts do not get ahead of the process and implementation of tools and expected organizational practices. While it is easiest to lead with education, you risk becoming a flavor of the month if there are no tactical plans to bring the theory and expectations to life. The learning leaders' role will be to understand current state, future state, and measures of success. Answers to these will drive home how to design the most effective learning program and create strategic change.

Current State: TeamSTEPPs

On paper, our organization ran a perfect training program. Safety was thoughtfully included in new employee orientation, managers were trained on proper submission of incidence reports and how to conduct investigations, and there was an established performance improvement model in place (including a plan-do-study-act model). Our hospitals created councils to focus on our improvement goals, and physicians had routine training on safety. In addition, we hosted an annual quality conference to inspire our leaders to hit quality outcomes. We had keynotes from experts in leadership, change management, and even practitioners who were on their way to "zero harm." Our training model included facilitators who worked through performance improvement issues and assisted clinical staff. Yet, our data suggested we were doing harm to patients at an unsatisfactory rate.

According to our assessment, the training was seen as a "one and done" event with supportive elements of reinforcement to ensure it was a part of the work. What we lacked was a common language, cohesiveness, and enthusiasm around expectations for the entire organization, not just clinical staff. To make safety a high priority for all employees, every part of our organization needed a uniform mental model, language, and resources. This would allow for common ground between corporate functions and operations, clinical staff, and administration. It would foster a sense of commonality and purpose, breaking down the "us versus them" mentality, which can be common between clinicians and nonclinical staff in the healthcare environment.

We had introduced the existing model, TeamSTEPPS, to key influencers across the organization. TeamSTEPPS—developed by the Agency for Healthcare Research and Quality (AHRQ)—used an evidence-based teamwork approach to safety and provided a curriculum that emphasized improved communication and understanding one's role within a team structure. Following an initial needs assessment, the TeamSTEPPS model could be used to methodically plan, train, and implement new safety measures. The model also presented tools for improving processes and outcomes to ensure sustainment.

Early application of TeamSTEPPS, including development of practice labs, was conducted by staff from our quality department. The labs were used to train staff with scenario-based simulation. By simulating common safety situations, the labs were able to provide staff with feedback, encouragement, and remediation when necessary. They proved to be effective for training, depending on the level of communication and how much support was provided by managers.

However, while we had a model in place, application, evaluation, and prioritization was not occurring system wide. Although the training process involved education, our learning teams were not spearheading application of the curriculum or evaluating the impact. At some locations, everyone was expected to attend training; at other locations, training was not viewed as mandatory and thus had minimal manager support. In addition, the training outcomes were not uniformly measured or communicated. Lack of extensive leadership support and no clear ties between the training program's ability to improve financial and clinical impact further minimized program outcomes. Leaders eventually realized that a successful safety program could only be effective if it was supported by all levels of leadership and was uniformly conducted and prioritized across the organization. Success relies on building effective teams, and it was time to explore a new approach.

Future State: High-Reliability Organization

Our quality department did extensive benchmarking on different types of safety programs, and we made a decision to move away from TeamSTEPPS toward a more customized effort. We decided to adapt an approach more commonly used by other industries, such as railroads, aviation, and nuclear energy, and shift our focus to becoming a high-reliability organization (HRO). This decision was difficult because the TeamStepps model was familiar. However, the knowledge that our safety record was much poorer than other high-stakes industries, coupled with an unsuccessful attempt at TeamSTEPPs, required us to make a change.

Understanding the impact of this change, executive leaders and the organization's governing board agreed to focus on adopting the HRO model for the entire enterprise. The plan involved a phased approach to meet the five principles of a high reliability organization (Weick and Sutcliffe 2015). Following these principles was crucial for success:

- **Preoccupation with failure.** Everyone accepts and prepares ahead for failure.
- **Reluctance to simplify interpretations.** Everyone resists the urge to accept simple solutions for complex problems.
- **Sensitivity to operations.** Everyone is aware of processes and systems and how actions are interrelated.
- **Commitment to resilience.** Solutions must be nimble, and everyone accepts that failure does not mean giving up.
- **Deference to expertise.** Leaders listen to everyone, regardless of rank.

The gaps we had to overcome included:

- **Building a language.** Organizations gain status as a high-reliability organization when all levels of staff adopt and integrate the HRO principles in their daily work processes. The principles must be hard-wired and used by the entire organization. We launched the initiative at a quality conference for the organization and were clear that we were expecting this to be a part of the lexicon. Elements from the core principles were woven into our behavioral standards.
- **Selecting a common set of tools.** The principles were accompanied by the adoption of error prevention tools, or simple acronyms and tactics that people could put in place to prevent an error. Through a process of vetting and evaluation, employees across all areas of the organization were brought together to identify a set of communication tools that would help enhance quality, safety, and reliability in both clinical and nonclinical areas. Employees are reminded of these tools every month, as part of the routine staff newsletter. The tools we identified for use in the organization were:
    - **STAR:** stop, think, act, review
    - **CUS:** I am concerned, I am uncomfortable, this is a safety issue
    - **Phonetic and numeric clarification:** specifically using alternate characters when speaking (for example, "I need 15 mg, that is one-five mg")
    - **Three-way read (or repeat) back:** the sender of the message makes a statement, receiver repeats back, sender states "That's correct" or clarifies
    - **Question and resolve:** when in doubt escalate to the expert
    - **Clarifying questions:** ask individuals to present clarifying questions
    - **Cross check:** have someone review your work
    - **5:1 feedback:** provide five positive comments to every one constructive; feedback was not intended to be given all at once, but with more routine positive reinforcement than negative reinforcement
- **Establishing methods to hardwire processes and leadership methods.** In addition to error prevention tools, we identified leadership methods that could be hardwired into employees' daily schedules. Methods demonstrated the importance of high reliability and safety and were not complicated. Some of the activities included:
    - **Start every meeting with a safety story:** This includes finding a safety story, preferably from the real work environment. It needs only be two minutes and highlight the effort of prevention tools

  - **Rounding to influence:** Managers and above in the organization spend time with employees and work on gaining commitment to quality and safety
  - **Safety and reliability huddle:** Every morning at 8 a.m. operational leaders hold a daily meeting to ensure that they pay attention to the day-to-day work and understand any potential errors or issues that occurred and focus on solving them

Key Takeaways

- Meet with your quality and safety teams to identify what models and expected practices are in place and what should occur. Then go observe high and underperforming areas. Note what is happening and why.
- Spend time with recent hires and more experienced hires to talk about what they expect to see and what they really see.
- Clearly define data that supports the plan and explain how measures will change outcomes.

Identifying the Measures

We knew that this process would eventually bring about decreases in serious safety events and more near misses, or events where we almost had an error, but were saved by using error-prevention tools. In the end, it would take about three years to realize our goal as the training rolled out and transformation took hold.

In the meantime, we started by tracking the leading indicators that would help us know whether we were on the right path to a safety culture. We established the following metrics to guide the way:

- **Annual knowledge check.** Because we were using training completion as a key driver, we used a knowledge check as an indicator of information transfer and absorption. All management, employees, and physicians were trained over a three-year period. At the end of each training year, individuals were required to pass a knowledge check on the HRO principles, knowledge, and tools. The results were linked to incentive pay, giving additional motivation to complete.
- **Spot checks.** We also put into place spot check efforts to measure identified leadership methods. The patient safety team focused on attending daily safety briefings to give feedback, and people came to expect a safety story at the start of each meeting.

These measures forced people to shine a light on key issues. We knew that if these stories were in place and done well, they would receive focused attention.

- **Tool adoption.** We established an eye toward observing which error prevention tools were being adopted quickly by the full organization. This would indicate that the organization had started to use the language and approach. Within the first six months we noted that the SBAR method (situation, background, assessment, recommendation) was quickly becoming the standard for sharing safety alerts among staff across the full organization (clinical and nonclinical). Working in tandem with the communications team, we found employees who were sharing stories of how they applied HRO concepts and error-prevention tools in their work. In one of the most powerful moments, a surgeon shared her experience with the error-prevention tools, recording it for use in our new leader orientation.
- **Increase in reporting.** Lastly, we looked for a specific increase in reporting. This data point is counterintuitive but important. By focusing on specific tools and methods to open up conversation, we believed that reporting should increase. This is not bad—instead, it would show that the environment was changing and reporting safety events was seen as a learning experience rather than a punitive matter.

Designing the Program

To get to these outcomes, we created a three-year training program focused on leadership in year 1, staff and physicians in year 2, and physicians and affiliated physicians in year 3. We linked training with a KPI and added monthly segments to the organization's newsletter.

Our organization used a vendor to introduce the HRO program, provide the curriculum, and support planning. We chose an outside vendor because our internal capability around the approach was limited and the scope was broad. Topics about patient and employee safety often require an independent party to present findings in a neutral way. This strategy played out well.

The learning and talent team partnered with the vendor every step of the way to modify the base-level program and incorporate it into our work. Communication promoting a thorough understanding of HRO concepts and error prevention tools was crucial. When designing the training program we took additional caution to ensure we weren't using generic scenarios, but instead asked clinical educators, physicians, and nonclinical staff to provide scenarios they encounter every day. We used those examples in the program.

Because training involves tens of thousands of employees, we formed a committee to work through all aspects of the program from development to evaluation. The committee affirmed with the vendor that using a phased approach over a span of three years would increase the likelihood of successful adoption. The first two years would be used to develop a curriculum specific to healthcare, train all employees, and measure whether training had been completed. Subsequent phases are currently underway and focus on measuring impact and sustainment.

Becoming a high-reliability organization meant undergoing a cultural change. To prepare, leaders were chosen to co-facilitate training for staff alongside a learning and development educator. The leaders were expected to present the curriculum at each class, while the educator, HR professional, or trainer provided logistical support and took notes. A vendor was also given co-facilitator duties in case an educator was unable to be present. Physician leaders volunteered to provide classes for employed and affiliated physicians. As an incentive, they were eligible to apply for continuing education credits by attending training.

To prepare the leaders, trainers, and educators to teach the content, we implemented a train-the-trainer model. We reviewed the content with each facilitator and then provided the materials to deliver once they told us they were ready. Volunteers were made lead trainers and were given feedback by the vendor, who sat through their initial presentations.

By having an array of individuals equipped to facilitate training (leaders, educators, and vendors), we were able to hold multiple classes simultaneously at multiple locations. Classes were scheduled around the clock and on weekends, with sessions lasting approximately an hour. To receive credit, participants were required to attend two sessions. For non-providers, sessions incorporated an opening safety story, followed by a review of a video on specific error prevention tools, and then went immediately into scenario practice and discussion of barriers. Physicians and APPs were encouraged to attend non-provider sessions to make them more interprofessional. However, due to limited time, physicians, with the support of physician leaders, could also choose to attend one longer training session that incorporated leadership methods. We wanted these sessions to maximize face-to-face communication and provide extra time to discuss other non-HRO topics as well. They were encouraged to attend by receiving CME ethics credit.

To ensure accurate record-keeping and ease of accessibility for different circumstances, our learning management system kept track of training schedules and employee status and completions. Facilitators scanned and sent in rosters to a central learning administration team who then recorded them. This data was used to create a compliance reporting schedule, which allowed the team to report out training compliance rates on a quarterly basis (then moving to weekly in the final month before the due dates). In addition, alternative catch-up sessions were organized for employees who missed a training session (due to time off, extenuating circumstances, and so forth). We also worked with the vendor to provide a facilitator who was trained to conduct lessons for ESL employees.

Using a top-down approach, our CEO first communicated the shift to HRO to the entire organization. Employees then learned about crucial details and logistics, including what constituted an HRO and how it would contribute to positive outcomes for the system's safety goals, the plan of action for implementation (phase 1), and the mandatory training requirements. We made it a point to highlight the importance of each employee's involvement in the process, as everyone had a role to play in facilitating a positive culture change. To further enforce participation, attendance was incentivized. Communication modalities included leader scripted announcement, use of the employee intranet, and staff meetings.

Upon completion of the first phase, employees across the organization created a fun, educational video to illustrate how each error prevention tool was being used in a variety of settings. The video is now shown at every new-hire employee orientation to showcase our culture of prioritizing safety measures. As the organization expands to include a medical teaching facility in the future, the HRO program will need to be implemented through an interprofessional approach, which will require new planning, collaboration, and phases of development.

Key Takeaways

- Healthcare is complex and the challenges of diverse learning needs and education differences, preferences, and availability will always be present. Incorporating multiple perspectives upfront is critical.
- Most organizations focus exclusively on the roll out, but we focused on both roll out and how to sustain the initiative within our culture. A successful roll out always incorporates disrupting future expectations in orientation and onboarding, which can lead to difficult decisions.

Reliability and Safety Through Interprofessional Continuing Education

The second component of our cultural transformation around safety included a transformation of the learning function itself. In addition to training healthcare staff, the learning function has the added responsibility of modeling the way and walking the talk. This includes being the first to change practices to promote the culture expected within the rest of the organization. Substantive changes to expectations—such as deferring to expertise and reluctance to simplify—required us to reposition how we did our work in the learning function. We decided to leverage pursuit of joint accreditation through the lens of interprofessional continuing education (IPCE) to enact this culture change. Joint accreditation accredits organizations, giving them the ability to offer IPCE in fulfillment of continuing education hours.

We defined IPCE as accredited education that involves two or more disciplines learning together. We believed tackling it through this lens would provide the necessary weight and incentive for participation. Three main components make IPCE an attractive mechanism to transform L&D and achieve a culture focused on reliability and safety:

- It forces departments to work collaboratively to achieve the accreditation. A fundamental requirement is that at minimum 25 percent of IPCE offerings be designed and delivered for multiple professions collaboratively. This requirement forces departments that typically work separately within an organization (such as medical education and nursing education) to collaborate on a unifying goal. The very fact that they are working together will break silos and improve reliability in content and approach.
- IPCE must be designed by, and for, the participants. As such, this disruptive process requires an integrated planning cycle with individuals who reflect the audience. For example, an interprofessional program created by physicians that nurses attend would not be considered IPCE; whereas an event in which a nursing SME and physician SME contribute to content development is considered IPCE. Again, this forces collaboration in design and delivery.
- IPCE has a set of competencies that need to be included in every program (Joint Accreditation: Interprofessional Continuing Education 2020):
    - Values and ethics

- Roles and responsibilities
- Interprofessional communication
- Teamwork

Due to the cultural ambassador role our learning team had to play, IPCE was a perfect fit. We were able to disrupt typical patterns of thinking and doing that had been focused on individual silos (nursing, physicians, leadership). The learning function also took on new responsibilities in supporting reliability by convening, facilitating, and ensuring a laser-like focus on the root cause problem, rather than producing a quick learning solution to check the box.

Thus, we began working as stewards of our focus on safety and reliability to break through traditional cultural norms.

Making the Case

The primary goal of our L&D transformation was driven by the ability to foster a culture focused on creating safe and reliable outcomes. To make a successful case, consider the degree to which your organization believes that L&D should drive a culture of safety, the investment in current continuing education events, and the overall maturity of the organization related to teamwork and collaboration. We also framed our direction through the lens of reliability and outcomes, finance, and experience:

- **Reliability and safety.** We started using the phrase "how you practice is how you play." If our hope was for people to be collaborative around safety and reliability, we had to provide all relevant parties a broader understanding of the process, roles, and responsibilities, while also focusing on how everyone contributes to the team. Data suggests that when done right, CE can contribute to the thoughtful reflection and improvement of practices (Ahmed, Wang, Ashrafian, Darzi, & Athanasiou 2013).
- **Finance.** This is the hardest information to find. The L&D team was working to reduce the amount of CE departments within the organization—initially there were three nursing CE departments, a corporate nursing CE department, and a continuing medical education department. The staffing, resources, and expenditures all contribute to the business case. For us, while consolidating continuous nursing education providerships and streamlining FTEs would create some synergy, there was also a slight cost net increase of $20,000 for our application period to achieve Joint Accreditation, followed by a slight increase in fees over typical accreditation offerings of between $5,000 and $10,000. We believed and successfully argued that year 1 payback

was imminent by avoiding harm in a single patient or preventing a lawsuit, and we pushed for a centralized financial structure.

- **Program leader experience.** Moving to a standard design process provided an opportunity to streamline application forms for continuing education. One piece of feedback we heard from many program directors was about the volume of paperwork required to get other disciplines credit for the same event. Imagine filling out a similar form three times for three separate organizations just to give people the same experience. Instead of using up to three forms to accredit a single event for different attendees (nursing, allied health, and medical education), the new accreditation used a single form for administrative work. We learned that filling out another set of documents requiring learning objectives, outcomes, and a summary of the program was a simple hurdle that, if achieved, would open the doors to new collaboration. Also, due to the content design requirements, interprofessional SMEs were forced to collaborate rather than work independently. This helped iron out key differences in process, expectations, and care. It also provided the opportunity to eliminate separate programs targeted at different audiences and allow for a clear focus on the problem and audience needed to solve it. It connected them to the bigger picture and clarified roles and responsibilities, as well as identified potential issues.

Our Method and Approach

With our focus on error prevention, reliability, and safety, we understood that how we designed and delivered the content would need to change. And that transformation occurred soon after we began the high-reliability organization journey. We started by recognizing the many different hubs in the current environment. We then gained sponsorship to adopt a new direction, pulled a team together, and built the internal capability to have tough conversations. We collectively spent nearly three years working through the process that led to our accreditation with IPEC in 2020 and more importantly, a cohesive approach.

Current State: The ADDIE Model in Various Pockets

When we began the approach, we first identified every pocket of education and the leader who would contribute heavily to ensuring that area's success. Our nursing education team had a cadre of individuals who worked exclusively with nursing to design, deliver, and accredit hundreds of CE events annually. Getting them to look beyond nursing would require sponsorship from the chief nursing executive and chief operating officer. Our continuing medical education team also designed and accredited hundreds of learning events per year. Getting them to jump onto the interprofessional approach would require sponsorship from our COO, SVP of medical staff affairs, and chief clinical officer. We spoke to them first about next steps, their hesitations, and what to watch out for.

Moving toward an interprofessional approach would require new ways to design content and deal with friction between SMEs who didn't always work well together. Our sponsors understood that pockets of learning professionals worked through analysis, design, development, implementation, and evaluation with lone SMEs, which created silos of information.

As you can imagine, this type of siloed learning environment starts far before the work environment. Consider the academic experience of any healthcare professional—their coursework and clinical rotations are focused on a singular specialty, rather than viewing their work as part of a larger, interconnected system of roles. Schools of healthcare professions (medical schools, nursing schools, and training for allied health professionals) continue to produce students who understand their role, but not the related roles of the team. Our sponsors all fundamentally believed that this lack of exposure to differentiating factors, outside their own area of study, prevented them from seeing the bigger connected picture and thus attributed to preventable harm. Our team was tasked with correcting that by changing how we approached training and development.

Our sponsors' only concern was when to address structure. The move to a single approach could result in a new operational structure, reduction of roles, and potential concerns of teammates. We were determined to address this head on and make the connection between the work and the strategic plan.

Future State: A Single, Championed ADDIE Model

We decided to bring all relevant leadership teammates together to discuss an agreed upon approach for pursuing an IPCE designation. These learning leaders also saw the value of making a broader contribution and thought that if we were truly going to be stewards of the safety and reliability culture, we needed to model the way.

We also learned that to achieve IPCE designation we needed to be accredited through a large national organization and would need to apply when we were up for review of our accreditation. Fortunately, we had a three-year window before our continuing medical education accreditation was due for renewal via the Accreditation Council for Continuing Medical Education (ACCME).

We agreed to work on a three-year plan, carved out clear roles and responsibilities for teammates, put into a place a routine cadence of meetings, and divided up tasks that would get us to 25 percent IPCE events. Collaboratively, we established a standard agenda for each meeting. We would discuss:

- Our progress toward the 25% goal
- Events that could be modified to be IPEC
- Team needs for support and skill building in negotiation
- Leadership involvement

Between all the sponsors, we established a cadence to discuss progress. To keep spirits up, we let everyone know that their jobs were safe and that we were working toward an outcome, not a structure. We specifically kept in mind that teams were working through legacy structures, processes, and activities, and the best way to affect change would be to ensure a common vision, set of activities, and routine support.

Key Takeaways

Healthcare is complex. With so many specialties and subspecialties you will likely find numerous pockets of learning or talent development across different functions. Unless these areas are working collaboratively from the same mental model, language, and practices, the organization will not be able to achieve the best outcomes. As a leader, your job is to create movement in this direction using a delicate balance of authority and persuasion.

Enabling the Team to Change the SME–Learning Dynamic

Working with SMEs can be challenging for a host of different reasons. In our case, we had the unique situation of asking SMEs to bring in additional SMEs from other professions during the assessment and design process. To do this, we created a governance process to review content across nursing and medical education and leveraged relationships between the learning team and SMEs to create the best outcomes possible.

One of the first changes we needed to implement was a governance review of content and new requests. Each request had to be reviewed internally by different team members to ensure multiple perspectives on a potential topic or issue. An example is when our food and nutrition services team decided to pursue new nomenclature and categorization for the types of foods post-stroke patients would receive. Rather than act in isolation when going through the design process, the governance process caught the content change so we could review the proposed content and audience. Using our error-prevention tools, we connected with nursing and physicians and realized that the effort to change the food nomenclature hadn't considered the full impact of the change. We slowed down the request to launch and helped them understand the need to work interprofessionally.

When it came to content selection and creation, our skilled learning professionals asked thoughtful questions and identified potential barriers. They told leadership that having stock content, activities, or processes to help cover the IPCE competencies would go a long way toward getting buy-in. We created a set of activities around the four core areas of IPCE to help the SMEs efficiently build out an IPCE program.

Furthermore, we prepared our learning and talent team to navigate relationships with SMEs, helping them formulate questions that were important for breaking through silos. Instead of jumping quickly into considering the SME's opinion and even watching work be done, we encouraged our teammates to focus on the following questions: "Could any other care team members learn better if you focused on the same topic?" and "What outcomes are important and where are there handoffs with teammates?" This helped the team navigate through the process. Our SMEs also jumped on board quickly. When issues were escalated, it only took a quick conversation with a learning leader to get them back on course.

Measure of Success

Due to our leadership support, diligent processes, and strong learning professionals, we were able to achieve a nearly 35 percent rate of interprofessional activity by the end of 2018 and as we entered the accreditation process in 2019. Our accreditation interviews went well, with limited documentation needed because we had been so thorough. Our conference attendance began to soar, and we saw a surge in program requests with IPCE. In June 2019, we received our accreditation for interprofessional accredited education. However, that was just the beginning of the journey.

While the team continued to work independently, they believed we needed to form an office of accredited education focused on ensuring a cost effective, strategic effort centered on the design and delivery of CE events. Rather than continuing to support a separate department for nursing, social work, and physicians, we agreed to move in a singular direction and saved nearly two full-time equivalent positions via attrition. Team members were also highly engaged in the process, getting a better understanding by connecting with their teammates and working toward an outcome that would affect how the care team worked collectively. The new office sat at the system level, reporting to the chief learning officer; it helped launch and accredit key strategic learning programs including change management, supportive and palliative care, and well-being forums.

Our pain point has always been in the assessment and design, and we continue to work through who needs to be engaged in the process to ensure an effective outcome. If done with diplomacy and a keen sense of authenticity, collaboration, and teamwork, creating IPCE content can serve as a great reflection of the organization's culture and values in action.

Key Takeaways

- Create a frictionless experience for SMEs. Working with SMEs is difficult enough, and getting them to agree to include others and add more voices can be challenging. However, offering easy case studies and doing groundwork helps. Think of scenarios that mirror their workplace, including roles for clinical, support, and administrative staff.
- Have open dialogue with leaders. The phrase "due to our leadership support" is under emphasized. We had strong leadership support to discuss difficult issues of prioritization, what becomes IPCE, and who would lead programming design. This cannot be emphasized enough—any move this direction requires strong senior leadership support and advocacy.
- Create a safe environment for reporting program use. Communicating examples and scenarios that use the reported information will improve understanding.

The High-Reliability Journey at John Muir Health

A Case Study by Lea Toppino, Natasha Maghoney, and Jeff Portwood

When the director of quality and patient safety at John Muir Health overheard the words, "Don't report that, it'll make us look bad," her heart was broken.

Fast-forward two years: A nurse barges into a staff meeting and exclaims, "Oh my! Let me tell you about the error I just made so you don't make the same mistake."

What was the change that led from a culture of fear of reporting to one of learning and sharing?

John Muir Health (JMH) has always been known as a high-quality community health system. But 2014, leadership recognized that despite their high accolades, there was plenty of room to improve, and to grow. Enter high reliability.

Two senior executives had recently joined the organization and brought first-hand knowledge of the impact that high reliability could have at John Muir. Their real-life experiences and insights provided the fodder that influenced key stakeholders to adopt a strategy to become a highly reliable organization.

It would not be an easy lift; however, gaining buy-in and commitment across the system would be key to success. And we knew we couldn't just launch into training. We had to focus on culture change first. This meant becoming a learning organization consistent with high reliability practices.

As the movement began, we spent a significant amount of time educating and raising awareness about the importance of reporting errors. We had to ensure we had accurate information about serious safety events (SSE) and process outcomes, so we could focus on improving systems and implementing error prevention techniques to reduce harm.

Rather than simply directing everyone to reduce SSE—since this may have resulted in reinforcing negative behaviors, such as not reporting to reduce events—we did the opposite. We over-emphasized the importance of reporting every event, even those that were caught before reaching the patient. And we encouraged doing so.

This was an important step because we needed to have an accurate baseline of information from which to work. The number of events that began to flood this system were a testament to the acceptance of reporting to prevent harm, as well as the culture shift from one of blame to one of learning.

Additional traction and buy-in to the HRO initiative came when senior executives jumped on board to co-facilitate training sessions. This made it clear that the organization was committed to high reliability.

To complement training, we implemented several tactical plans:

- We launched a new role—culture of excellence (COE) ambassador—to promote and reinforce error prevention in all work areas.
- We embedded error prevention techniques in all work systems, including job descriptions, competency models, and performance management processes.

- We looked for any and every opportunity to promote and reinforce high reliability and error prevention through all available channels.

At John Muir today, we include high reliability in everything we do, from meetings to celebrations. Examples include:

- Safety stories and error prevention boosters at daily safety huddles
- HRO activities for all employee events
- Rotating screen savers, e-cards, and multi-recognition efforts (for example, HeRO awards encourage reporting)

We also included contractors and volunteers to ensure uniform expectations and alignment in training sessions—and to further demonstrate our commitment to the brand promise "We Listen, We Explain, and We Work Together as a Team."

These activities combined to create a cultural shift and common language, and they continue to reinforce buy in. The health system trained nearly 100 percent of staff (approximately 6,000 employees) in three years.

High reliability has become the JMH culture. In addition to increasing reporting and reducing errors, we have become better stewards of resources and HRO has led to many improved processes around the organization. This new commitment to safety and the disciplines that were put in place has allowed our organization to quickly pivot and adapt, not only to the COVID-19 pandemic, but also to other crises, such as natural disasters (the California wildfires) and racial tensions.

John Muir's journey toward becoming a highly reliable organization continues to produce positive results year over year. We continue to reduce our serious safety events for the 300 thousand lives we touch each year.

Conclusion

For cultural change to be successful, not only does the organization have to change, but also, and often first, the learning function must do so. As a learning leader within healthcare, you play an immense role in ensuring safety and reliability across the organization. Here are three parting thoughts.

First, the learning function is a steward of collaboration, so work appropriately. As you have seen in this chapter, learning was never at a table alone and it was never acting out of self-interest (to alleviate work burden, difficulty with a task, or delays). These efforts rested upon established teams, strong support, and collaborative teamwork processes and goals. Additionally, working in teams for extended periods of time can lead to conflict, so having strong sponsorship and a clear goal and purpose are critical. Ours was to fundamentally change and create a safe, reliable care experience and ensure our learning function delivered on its part of the promise.

Second, the learning leader is always a copilot on an initiative, so own that space. Learning leaders should focus on the future impact the program will have on the individuals doing the current work. Training and education will not work unless hard mechanisms are in place to reinforce the change. In this case, our training and education programs were inherently pragmatic. We focused on the theory of high reliability to move minds, and provided the tools to show them how. Learning leaders must ensure that clear expectations are in place before anything rolls out or it will simply be considered a flavor of the month.

Third, the learning function must act as a cultural ambassador for the organization. This could potentially be the biggest game changing perspective for any learning function—the way the learning function operates should model the way for the organization. If this initiative had been around patient experience, we would have had to fundamentally change how we operated around experience to show and teach while working. We needed to amplify the team skill set with a convening a group and push them to focus on outcomes. Knowing that we didn't have a practical solution to develop quickly, we resorted to tips, key questions, and job aids. We found this worked effectively as long as they bought in to the approach.

John Muir Health is a nationally recognized, not-for-profit healthcare organization east of San Francisco serving patients in Contra Costa, eastern Alameda, and southern Solano counties. It includes a network of more than 1,000 primary care and specialty physicians, 6,000 employees, medical centers in Concord and Walnut Creek (including Contra Costa County's only trauma center), and a behavioral health center. John Muir Health also has partnerships with UCSF Health, Tenet Healthcare/San Ramon Regional Medical Center, Stanford Children's Health, and Optum. The health system offers a full-range of medical services, including primary care, outpatient, and imaging services. It is widely recognized as a leader in many specialties, including neurosciences, orthopedic, cancer, cardiovascular, trauma, emergency, pediatrics, and high-risk obstetrics care.

CHAPTER 10

ORGANIZATIONAL CULTURE

MICHAEL LEE STALLARD AND KATHARINE P. STALLARD

The culture in a healthcare setting has a profound impact on every individual who works in the organization, be it positive or negative. And the way individuals work together influences the patient and caregiver experience. A healthy culture in which individuals are thriving, and therefore the organization is as well, has ripple effects. An unhealthy or relationally toxic culture also has ripple effects that extend beyond employees, such as medical errors, mediocre care, or low patient satisfaction scores. These are all bad for morale and the bottom line, not to mention the emotional and physical health of patients. We know the impact culture can have firsthand.

January 7, 2004, was one of the most sobering days of my (Michael's) life. After hours in the hospital's waiting room, wondering how my wife was doing, I received the news from the surgeon that none of us wanted to hear: "It is cancer, and it has spread. I'm sorry." A year earlier, Katharine ("Katie") had been diagnosed with stage 1 breast cancer and the treatment had been successful. Now we were up against another battle—the pathology report would reveal advanced ovarian cancer. Our daughters were 10 and 12 years old at the time, and the thought of not spending the rest of my life with Katie, our daughters losing their mother, and Katie not seeing the girls grow up was overwhelming. As her caregiver, I was anxious about the future.

Before the cancer diagnosis, I had taken a break from working on Wall Street and was in the midst of a personal journey to better understand organizational culture and leadership. This change was motivated by a desire to know what I should be doing as a leader to foster a highly engaging, collaborative, and innovative environment. Employee engagement levels in the US had been stuck, on average, at around 30 percent for years, and I believed leaders needed to take a fresh look at the workplace to see how they can unleash all the wasted potential (Clifton and Harter 2019). I was following the clues where they led, through the fields of organizational behavior, history, psychology, psychiatry, neuroscience, and social science, among others. What I didn't expect was how my experience as a caregiver would shape my thinking about the X factor that brings out the best in a team and organization.

I vividly remember our first consultation at Memorial Sloan Kettering Cancer Center as we considered next steps in Katie's treatment. I admit, I was anticipating an environment shrouded with a sense of death and dying. However, as we got within sight of the 53rd Street entrance in midtown Manhattan, a friendly, larger-than-life doorman named Nick Medley locked eyes with Katie and smiled at her. This was the first of many happy surprises—few make eye contact with a passerby in New York City, let alone smile! I realized that Nick was probably a seasoned wig-spotter and, recognizing that Katie was a cancer patient, was intentionally reaching out to connect with her. In the lobby, the receptionist called everyone "honey" (again, very unlike Manhattan). Each person we encountered was friendly. Katie's oncologist, Dr. Martee Hensley, spent an hour educating us about treatment options and answering our long list of questions. Her warmth and optimistic attitude gave us hope.

By the end of the visit, I had two reactions. First, I had done the research and knew this was one of the best teams in the world to treat ovarian cancer. My rational reaction was that they were up to the task. I also believed that they cared about us as individuals (my emotional reaction). Even though I knew Katie's chance of survival was less than 10 percent, I was hopeful that these amazing people would get her through the difficult season ahead.

One day while Katie was undergoing treatment, I stumbled upon a meeting in a lounge where employees were discussing the results of an employee survey. Nick was there, and I overheard him say that he loved working at the center because he loved his colleagues, the patients, and their families—and most of all he loved the cause, which is to provide "the best cancer care, anywhere." (This got my attention. *Love* was not a word I was used to hearing in the workplace.) It was apparent that Nick's co-workers also felt a connection with one another, their patients, and their patients' families. During the time we spent at Memorial Sloan Kettering, it struck me how much more joy and esprit de corps I felt in a cancer treatment center than I experienced while working on Wall Street. I wasn't at all surprised when I saw a segment about Nick on ABC's *World News Tonight* and learned that he was a cancer survivor and he gave hundreds of hugs a day to patients and their families.

According to the American Cancer Society, one of the worst things for cancer patients is to feel alone. With the support of our team at Memorial Sloan Kettering, along with our family and friends, Katie and I rarely felt alone. Although many factors are involved in combatting illness, research has shown that the human connection that provides emotional support is associated with positive patient outcomes (Bloom et al. 2001; Devine et al. 2003; Lekander et al. 1996; Levy et al. 1990). I'm convinced that the connections we had with our healthcare workers helped Katie go into remission and protected our family's spirits.

Having had such a good experience at Memorial Sloan Kettering, we enthusiastically recommended it to a friend of ours who was diagnosed with a different type of cancer later that year. The physicians in her specialty were located in a different building, and, surprisingly, her experience was completely at odds with ours. After the initial consultation, she felt alone and eventually decided to seek treatment elsewhere. This was another piece of the puzzle in understanding organizational culture.

Reflecting on these experiences made me realize three things:

- Human connection is a powerful force that creates a positive emotional bond between people.
- Connection contributes to bringing out the best in people and energizes them, making them more trusting and more resilient to face life's inevitable difficulties.
- Connection can vary dramatically across teams, units, and even locations of organizations, depending upon local culture and leadership.

As an aside, when Katie was diagnosed with another type of breast cancer in 2014 we returned to Memorial Sloan Kettering Cancer Center. We quickly established a rapport with a new team of specialists there and we found that the connection was just as strong as ever.

Organizational culture matters. It's one thing for an organization to proclaim that it has a great culture on its website or in marketing materials. But if the actual culture being experienced each day is not bringing out the best in individuals, if things are not working well between members of the team or across the organization, the consequences can be far-reaching. And despite superficial smiles all around, patients and their caregivers can tell when stress and disconnection are prevalent, which only adds to the stress they may already be feeling. Because of the nature of healthcare and all those involved, organizational culture needs to be a priority.

In this chapter, we'll look at three types of relational cultures then provide a vocabulary, framework, practices, and a five-step process to cultivate a sustainable, high-performing work culture in healthcare.

Human Connection: The X Factor That Brings Out the Best Performance

Ask a roomful of people what "culture" means, and you'll likely hear responses such as "norms," "values," "behaviors," and "how we do things around here." In the context of organizations, Merriam-Webster defines culture as the set of shared attitudes, values, goals, and practices that characterize an institution or organization.

Is there a best culture? Applying a one-size-fits-all approach isn't realistic in today's increasingly diverse and global working world, especially in the healthcare industry. That said, organizations that have sustainable high performance often have common elements to their culture that enable them to be their best. Tasks will differ, depending on the industry or the function within an organization, yet when it comes to the relational aspects, the best culture is one that has a high degree of human connection.

Leaders are paid to be intentional about getting tasks done and producing favorable results. The most effective leaders, however, do more. They are intentional about developing both task excellence *and* relationship excellence. It's this combination that makes favorable results *sustainable*. Relationship excellence is where connection comes in.

Research has found that social connection is a primal human need that appears to improve the performance of the body's cardiovascular, endocrine, and immune systems (Uchino et al. 1996). Connection makes us more resilient to cope with stress. One prominent neuroscientist describes connection as a superpower because it makes us smarter, happier, and more productive (Lieberman 2013, 2019). In contrast, disconnection is a super-stressor that's associated with a host of negative outcomes, including poorer cognitive performance, impaired executive control and self-regulation, decreased sleep quality, lower levels of self-rated physical health, more intense reactions to negatives and less uplift from positives, greater feelings of helplessness and threat, substance abuse, depressive symptoms, and suicidal ideation (reviewed in Cacioppo and Patrick 2008).

Loneliness is a hidden systemic risk in most healthcare organizations. Research found that physicians, by self-report, are among the loneliest professionals, a factor contributing to high rates of burnout and suicide (Achor et al 2018). In fact, studies have shown that more than 40 percent of physicians are experiencing burnout (Shanafelt et al. 2019, Kane 2020), and suicide rates among physicians exceed those of the general population (AFSP 2020). Other healthcare professionals such as nurses experience similar struggles (Brusie 2019).

Researchers have also found that greater employee loneliness leads to poorer task performance, poorer team role performance, and poorer relational performance (Ozcelik and Barsade 2018). Employees who lack sufficient connection in the workplace and feel regularly left out, lonely, or out of the loop can't do their best work—and may not wish to.

Assessing Culture Through the Lens of Connection

Does your culture connect people or does it cause people to feel disconnected? Organizational culture can be decoded by examining a group's predominant attitudes, uses of language, and behaviors (Stallard 2020). Attitudes represent ways of feeling and thinking that affect behavior, language comprises the words people use, and behavior is the way people act. It's instructive to look at the attitudes, language, and behavior in terms of whether they connect people, disconnect people, or are neutral in their effect on human connection. Cultures that are disconnecting tend to be excessively controlling or indifferent to human needs.

There are three types of relational cultures: cultures of control, cultures of indifference, and cultures of connection (Stallard 2015, Rugg 2018).

Cultures of Control

In cultures of control, people with power, influence, and status rule over others. A culture of control breeds an environment in which people fear making mistakes and taking risks. It is stifling—killing innovation because people are afraid to speak up. Employees may feel left out, micromanaged, unsafe, hyper-criticized, or helpless.

Cultures of control tend to exhibit many common attributes. They are often hierarchical and formal in nature. An inner circle often develops, comprising favored individuals who have the most power, influence, and status, and receive the most recognition, responsibility, and compensation (Kleiner 2003). This favored group makes the most important decisions while rarely sharing information with and seeking or considering the opinions of others outside it. Individuals in the inner circle may expect those outside it to obey their commands without understanding or questioning their decisions. Questioning is viewed as disloyal and, if continued, may be punished by coercion, degradation, intimidation, and isolation through gradual marginalization (such as not being invited to attend meetings, being ignored in meetings, getting passed up for promotions, or being moved into less important roles with lower power, control, influence, and status).

Individuals outside the inner circle who appease those within the inner circle are more likely to be rewarded over time with greater recognition, more responsibility, promotions, and higher compensation. Like those in the inner circle, they may develop an attitude of superiority, hubris, and a false sense of infallibility. Some individuals may even be invited to join the inner circle.

While most individuals on the outside go along with the inner circle's decisions, they are not enthusiastic, energized, or engaged. They may be able to give their best efforts for a short period of time, but because they are not inspired or energized they won't perform at their best for a sustained period of time. Eventually, most marginalized individuals leave on their own or are forced out.

People who fall outside the inner circle often suffer from a lack of autonomy and input that may lead them to develop what University of Pennsylvania psychology professor Martin Seligman has described as "learned helplessness" (and, we would add, hopelessness). They come to believe that they don't have the power or authority to make a difference, so they adopt a passive survivor mentality and simply do what is necessary to keep their job (and paycheck). Some will even secretly sabotage organizational efforts as a means to exact revenge on a system they view as unfair.

Sometimes cultures of control are led by overly critical perfectionists who have trouble giving others autonomy or seeing their perspectives. This type of leader may be so hypercritical that people feel beaten down, and negativism pervades the workplace. In other instances, the leader of a culture of control may simply have a strong desire for power, control, status, or money that drives them to extreme measures to achieve those ends.

Cultures of Indifference

Cultures of indifference are predominant today. In this type of culture, people are so busy with tasks that they fail to invest the time necessary to develop healthy, supportive relationships. Some leaders don't see value in the relational nature of work. Whether they voice it or not, their attitude is "You are being paid to do a job. I don't care how you feel or if you have friends here. All I care about is your work." People in cultures of indifference often come to feel like they are thought of and treated as mere means to an end, rather than as individuals who are valuable in and of themselves. They may feel like a cog in a machine, unimportant, underappreciated, uncertain, or invisible. Many people across the organization struggle with a lack of connection.

Leaders in cultures of indifference may have good intentions but suffer from blind spots. For instance, they may be insecure, and their anxiety compels them to perform a large number of tasks to prove themselves. This leads to a lack of organizational focus and unreasonable workloads for those under them; people may begin to feel overwhelmed. Instead of having the confidence to focus on a reasonable number of priorities and implement them with excellence, or add people to address the heavy workload, leaders of cultures of indifference expect people to do too much and, as a result, actions are executed in a mediocre way that produces lackluster results.

Disconnection cultures also can reflect a hybrid of cultures of control and indifference. A distinguishing feature of an unhealthy culture is a lack of connection and failure to achieve relationship excellence. Leaders may openly dismiss the need for strong relationships. Others may give it lip service and occasional attention, or see its value without knowing how to bring it about. In disconnecting people rather than drawing them together, these cultures sabotage individual and organizational performance. Feeling consistently unsupported, left out, or lonely takes a toll. Without the psychological resources to cope with the normal stress of modern organizational life, employees may develop unhealthy attitudes and behaviors, many of which are addictive and destructive.

Connection Cultures

To achieve sustainable, superior performance, every member of an organization needs to intentionally develop both task excellence and relationship excellence. In contrast with a culture of control or indifference, a connection culture produces task and relationship excellence.

In a connection culture, people care about others and care about their work because it benefits other human beings. They invest the time to develop healthy relationships and reach out to help others in need, rather than being indifferent to them. They embrace the idea that every individual has something to bring to the table based on their experiences and background, and that a diverse marketplace of ideas and perspectives is a strength. Decision makers have the humility to know that they don't have a monopoly on good ideas, and they seek out and consider the opinions and ideas of others to make the best decisions. This bond helps overcome the differences that historically divided people, creating a sense of community and unity that is inclusive and energized, spurring productivity and innovation.

Put simply, in a connection culture, leaders communicate a vision that inspires and unites people, they value people as individuals and don't treat them as means to an end, and they give people a voice to express their ideas and opinions. Vision + Value + Voice = Connection (Stallard 2020).

The connection culture element of vision exists in a culture when everyone is motivated by the mission, united by the values, and proud of the reputation. A sense of shared identity develops among group members as their attitudes, language, and behaviors communicate that they are doing important work together in a way that's consistent with the organization's values and that produces positive results they are proud of.

The element of value exists in a culture when everyone understands the needs of people, appreciates their positive unique contributions, and helps them achieve their potential. In a group that embraces a connection culture mindset, people recognize that there are universal human needs that must be met to thrive in the work context: respect, recognition, belonging, autonomy, personal growth, meaning, and progress (Stallard 2020). They appreciate that each person has unique contributions to offer, given their experience and perspectives, and the diversity that brings to the table is a good thing. A sense of shared empathy develops among group members as their attitudes, language, and behaviors communicate that they are valued as individuals and not merely for their work.

Finally, the element of voice exists when everyone seeks the ideas and opinions of others, shares opinions honestly, and safeguards relational connections. People believe that they are kept informed about important matters and they have a voice—their opinions and ideas are sought and considered. They appreciate the openness in the culture and the open-mindedness of leaders. A sense of shared understanding develops among group members as their attitudes, language, and behaviors increase communication and bring greater clarity to issues that are important to them.

Let's consider how vision, value, and voice create connection at three renowned health-care institutions.

The power of a connection culture is on full display at Mayo Clinic, America's top-ranked hospital and arguably the best hospital in the world. From the time of its founding in 1889, Mayo Clinic has been intentional about cultivating a culture with a high degree of human connection. Dr. Charlie Mayo, one of the earliest leaders, communicated an attitude that placed a high value on relationships and warned about the dangers of isolation: "Our failures as a profession are the failures of individualism, the result of competitive medicine. It must be done by collective effort" (Burns et al. 2018). More than 100 years later, that conviction still guides the organization, and it is an aspect that is highlighted for those who are considering joining their ranks: "You are never an island at Mayo. You are automatically a member of a team and function as a team member on a daily basis. Teammates are eager to share knowledge and are interested in helping you succeed. It's not about competition, it's about collegiality" (Mayo Clinic 2007).

Dr. Herbert Pardes served as president and CEO of New York–Presbyterian Hospital and New York–Presbyterian Healthcare System from 1999 to 2011, leading it to become one of America's top hospitals. Pardes described his mindset about healthcare this way: "I anthropomorphize disease. I convert it to an evil enemy. I want to slay it before it hurts friends and family. But if anyone is ill—cancer, heart disease, depression, schizophrenia—what we want to do is bring everything we have, the very best, to fix the problem" (Pardes 2014). He advocated for connection among patients, caregivers, and the people who worked at New York–Presbyterian. Pardes modeled connection by devoting time to making bedside visits to patients and connecting with those who worked across the New York–Presbyterian system (Stodghill 2007). Some senior leaders might dismiss that as an inefficient use of their time but, as a well-respected psychiatrist and former director of the National Institute of Mental Health, Pardes understood that human connections help people cope with stress, reduce burnout, and improve patient outcomes.

A best practice at Yale New Haven Health hospitals is the daily morning safety huddle that brings together colleagues across departments within that location. Dr. Stephen Jones, medical director of safety for Yale New Haven Health, observed that "the daily morning safety huddles facilitate connections among colleagues who interact before and after the huddle meetings. The connections made during these times humanize our culture and help develop a sense of community that brings out the best of each of us. Since implementing the daily morning safety huddles in 2012, we've seen an 80 percent reduction in serious safety events across Yale New Haven Health" (Jones 2018).

Articulating that collaboration should be the norm and what it looks like, taking the time to be away from their desks and modeling connection in front of colleagues and patients, and purposely bringing people together in forums to contribute their viewpoints and give them opportunities to foster cross-departmental relationships are a few ways leaders can cultivate connection in their organizations.

Key Takeaways

To assess if a culture connects people or disconnects them through control or indifference, consider these questions:

- Are senior leaders distant or are they approachable and present? Do they consciously or unconsciously project an air of superiority?
- Do leaders at all levels show they genuinely care about employees or do their words and behaviors communicate that they view them as mere means to an end?
- Do leaders show they genuinely care about patients and caregivers or are they merely focused on the bottom line?
- Are leaders encouraging, indifferent, or demeaning to those who have lower status in the organization?
- Do those individuals who have greater power, control, influence, or status bully, belittle, or micromanage others?
- Do leaders have realistic or unrealistic expectations of workloads?
- When giving directions, do leaders ask or order people to do things?
- Do leaders routinely seek the opinions and ideas of others and consider that input, or do they operate as if they have a monopoly on good ideas?
- Are leaders transparent? Are they good at keeping people informed on issues that matter to them or do people feel they are being kept in the dark?
- Do employee surveys indicate a high degree of employee disengagement and burnout? Are there groups of employees who seem to be just going through the motions and doing the bare minimum? Are there groups of employees who seem to be energized and enthusiastic about the work they are doing?
- Is there a high degree of employee turnover or employee retention? Do you see patterns emerging in exit interviews for why employees are choosing to leave the organization?

The Role of Talent Development Professionals

No organization of any size has a uniform culture—most will have a mix of subcultures. Some subcultures are effective, with high employee engagement. Others are not—mired by apathy or high turnover. And many fall somewhere on a continuum between those extremes. The opportunity for talent development professionals is to help leaders improve the subculture they are responsible for cultivating.

As role models, leaders at all levels have the most influence when it comes to developing culture. Because they have the power to make decisions concerning hiring, firing, paying, and promoting, it's also true that people are motivated to please leaders because it's in their self-interest to do so. They look for verbal and nonverbal signals about what the leader likes and dislikes, and attempt to conform to those preferences in hopes of gaining approval and favor. Culture change will not take root and be sustained unless leaders are on board.

Ideally a connection culture will be championed and led with consistency by a healthcare organization's senior leadership team. However, if the drive for culture change is not coming from the top, there is still hope. We have seen significant culture change occur in subcultures led by leaders who care about people and results. Be aware that senior leaders with authoritarian tendencies may feel threatened by those who are gaining positive attention and influence by leading through inclusion and connection. In such cases, the senior leader may try to sabotage culture change efforts and the careers of leaders associated with them.

Leaders are busy and suffer from time poverty. Most are under unrelenting pressure to produce superior results. They will likely have little interest in taking action in regard to culture unless it's clear what specific actions they can take and how those actions will improve results.

Cultivating a connection culture can be organized as a process. In our book, *Connection Culture: The Competitive Advantage of Shared Identity, Empathy, and Understanding at Work*, we lay out a five-step process to operationalize a connection culture. Briefly, the five steps are:

- Develop a connection mindset among the members of your group.
- Cultivate the elements of vision, value, and voice by developing habits of attitude, language, and behavior that connect.
- Measure connection in each subculture to identify connected leaders, connected members, and individuals who need help connecting.
- Mentor and coach individuals to become connected members and connected leaders.
- Celebrate and disseminate acts of connection (stories and practices).

Talent development professionals can play an important and supportive role when working to develop training materials, communications, and processes that support culture improvement. In group training and as they work with leaders individually, TD professionals must be clear about what culture is and isn't, what the best culture is, how the best culture has a positive effect on results, and what the leader can do to cultivate the best culture in the context of their team and the broader organization.

One of our clients, the ambulatory care department at Memorial Sloan Kettering Cancer Center, takes a multipronged approach to spreading the message of connection among its employees across 25 locations. Training professionals are at the forefront of that work. New frontline employees are grounded in connection from the start as they go through three straight weeks of training in cohorts of up to 30 individuals. The training program is led primarily by managers from within ambulatory care, which helps new employees connect with managers in their department early on. Connection is further boosted by the department's mentoring program in which every new employee is assigned a mentor.

The department also hosts cohort-based training for new supervisors and leaders titled "Conversations in Supervision" and "Conversations in Leadership." Supervisors go through an interactive workshop on creating a connection culture. Not only do they emerge with a connection mindset and skills to use with their teams, but they practice and experience building connection as they go through the material. These workshops purposely bring together colleagues from a variety of functions within the department as well as different locations. Through a mix of teaching, small group discussions, self-reflection time, and group exercises, participants learn a vocabulary around connection; scientific research on the positive effects of connection and negative effects of loneliness and social isolation; how to decode cultures; the Vision + Value + Voice framework; examples and practices of leaders who have created a connection culture; and connection tips they can start using right away. As a follow-up, participants receive a monthly email newsletter from Connection Culture Group that shares practices, case studies, and new research on connection.

These deliberate actions were born out of a desire on the part of Memorial Sloan Kettering Cancer Center's vice president in charge of ambulatory care to ensure that patients and their families would have a connected and engaging experience with members of the ambulatory care department, no matter which location they went to.

So, what can you do to make connection more top of mind in your workplace? You may want to start with leaders who already have a connection mindset. Consider where connection is happening in subcultures throughout your organization and which leaders and influencers are currently cultivating it. Offer to provide support in the form of training, coaching, and assessment that will help them boost connection even more. As performance improves, it will gain attention and help build momentum for expanding culture improvement efforts.

We recommend that you also look at any employee engagement information you have, whether from formal surveys or anecdotally, and follow the clues to identify attitudes, language, and behaviors that are hurting connection and engagement.

A Few Best Practices to Boost Connection

The most comprehensive approach to strengthening culture is to implement a top-down, multi-step process similar to what we have already described. We find that most leaders, however, prefer a more bottom-up approach that consists of increasingly implementing specific practices.

A broad range of practices increase connection, from commonsense actions that convey respect, recognition, and belonging to approaches that give people a voice. Following are a handful of actions we have identified through our work with healthcare clients and our research that TD professionals can encourage leaders to take. For more practices and tips, read *Connection Culture: The Competitive Advantage of Shared Identity, Empathy, and Understanding at Work.*

Develop and Use Vision Phrases

Getting immersed in day-to-day tasks makes it easy to lose sight of an organization's vision. To keep vision in mind, we encourage leaders to regularly use brief, memorable, and inspiring "vision phrases" to remind people that their work is meaningful, the shared values in the organization are important, and their organization has a reputation to be proud of.

Organizations may already use a phrase in their internal and external communications that is embraced by employees. We know from our work with Memorial Sloan Kettering Cancer Center that people there are inspired and united by the vision phrase "The Best Cancer Care, Anywhere." Employees at MD Anderson Cancer Center are inspired by its vision phrase "Making Cancer History." And New York–Presbyterian's vision phrase "Amazing Things Are Happening Here" is supported with powerful videos of patients telling their stories about how the healthcare professionals there saved their lives.

Vision phrases can also be reinforced by sharing external evidence that supports them. If you set up a Google alert with the name of your organization, you will receive periodic emails with links to the places your organization appeared online. Use these to identify positive stories and media reports to share with your colleagues or use in training as real-life examples. If you encounter negative stories or comments, consider whether you need to discuss the issues with your team, especially if the message contains inaccuracies or is misleading. You may also want to consider any legitimate issues that were raised and should be addressed.

Hire for Competence and Connection Skills

Most leaders hire for competence but are not as intentional about probing to identify whether the applicant has a connection mindset and skill set. Take time to explore these areas as you do the interview. If the applicant is not a good fit relationally, despite their task skills and knowledge, they will disrupt the connection that is in place.

Get to Know the People You Are Responsible for Leading and Let Them Get to Know You

Psychologist James Pennebaker (1997) found that when you get people to talk, they feel more connected to you, like you more, and believe they learn more from you. And according to organizational behavior professor Ashley E. Hardin (2018), greater personal knowledge leads to a more human perception of a colleague, which results in increased responsiveness and decreased social undermining. Talent development professionals can make leaders aware of these important ideas while leading new supervisor training programs.

Take time to connect with people on a personal level and resist the inclination to skip time spent in conversation getting to know the people you are responsible for leading. This is an important step that begins in the onboarding stage and should continue as trust and connection grow with time spent together and increased openness in the relationship. Find out about their past work experiences, their career aspirations, and how you can help them perform at their best. The deepest connections are formed when you are appropriately open to communicate who you really are, what you really believe, and your relevant struggles in life. For example, consider sharing lessons you've learned from past mistakes if it will help another person. This openness communicates humility and promotes connection and trust.

If you work at the same location, meet with employees over a meal or coffee. When team members who work in a different location or telecommute are on-site, be sure to set aside time with them to connect. For those who work entirely remotely, let them decide whether to use a telephone or video call—introverts can be overstimulated and uncomfortable when using video (Grant 2020).

Encourage Connection Across the Organization

As noted earlier, loneliness, burnout, and suicide are serious issues affecting medical professionals. Given these crises, healthcare organizations need to raise awareness as to the dangers of social disconnection and the benefits of connection and take steps to make it easy for people to connect. Having strong social connections improves collaboration and helps address stress and loneliness. Be intentional about finding ways to increase social connection, otherwise busyness will crowd it out.

Mayo Clinic has demonstrated its commitment to promoting connection through a program it established and studied called COMPASS (colleagues meeting to promote and sustain satisfaction). Under this initiative, self-formed groups of six to 10 physicians get together for about an hour every other week, usually over breakfast or lunch; a stipend is provided toward the cost of the meal. They begin by spending at least 15 minutes using assigned prompts to discuss issues related to the physician experience; for example, "brainstorm ways to promote collegiality in your hallway or work unit" or "choose one stressor that you can control, come up with two concrete ways you can reduce it, and commit to trying one approach within the next week" (Berg 2018). Mayo Clinic's research has found that COMPASS participants experience statistically significant improvements in their well-being and satisfaction, which can help reduce the risk of physician burnout and medical errors.

In addition, to facilitate informal and organic opportunities for connection among colleagues, Mayo Clinic provides dedicated spaces for physicians to gather, complete with free beverages and fruit, lunch tables, limited food for purchase, and computer stations.

Don't Ignore Grief and the Emotional Toll of Caring for Others

Dr. Holly R. Dahlman (2015), an award-winning primary care physician, advises colleagues to grieve well: "Unspoken griefs lie buried beneath ever-increasing piles of tasks. It is no wonder that the incidence of depression and anxiety is higher among health professionals than the general population. Healthcare providers can feel like Atlas, carrying the weight of the world on our shoulders. We hear a lot of hard stories, so it is important to share our burdens. Take time to reflect during periods of rest. Consider processing grief through journaling or talking things over with a friend or a counselor."

Dahlman and her staff sometimes observe a moment of silence during an office meeting to commemorate a patient who has passed away. And everyone on the team signs a card for the bereaved. She has found that this was the best way to ensure that even part-time staff members are informed of a patient's death. It also allows them to acknowledge grief and share in the sorrow of the loss. By sending a card, they are able to show compassion as a team.

During the COVID-19 pandemic, Dr. Robert McLean (2020), past president of the American College of Physicians and a physician at Yale New Haven Health, encouraged physicians to "[make contact] via phone, video, or in person every day with at least one colleague to sincerely inquire about their personal well-being and personal life outside of a clinical context."

Boost Connection With, and Among, Individuals Who Are Not in the Majority

Discrimination—whether it is based on gender, ethnicity, sexual orientation, age, political opinions, or other differences—is a cause of disconnection and a source of stress. Women, people of color, and the LGBTQ community are often at higher risk for disconnection. There is increasing evidence that individuals in these groups experience greater stress than individuals in majority groups, and that stress has a negative effect on their health (Khazan 2018). Everyone in healthcare organizations needs to take appropriate steps to develop a culture of connection and inclusion so that members of these at-risk populations feel safe, stress is minimized, and teamwork is fostered. (For more see chapter 7.)

More women than men report that stress is on the rise and that they rely on social connection as a means to manage it (APA 2010). Research has also found that Black individuals often rely on social connection and that it has a "significant stress-suppressing effect on race-related stress" (Utsey et al. 2008). These studies suggest that efforts employing social connection to support individuals who are at risk for stress caused by discrimination, including employee resource groups and mentoring, are having a positive effect and should be encouraged.

Invest in Training to Strengthen the Connection Mindset and Skill Set

Mayo Clinic's onboarding process for physicians and scientists includes extensive training in professionalism and communication, and assessments to help them develop emotional intelligence, which is instrumental to connecting with others. Physician leaders are selected, developed, and assessed based on their ability to connect, which includes listening to, engaging, developing, and leading other physicians. (For more see chapter 11.)

Key Takeaways

- Identify key vision phrases for your organization and coach leaders in using them in their daily interactions with their teams.
- Offer resources to those who are making hiring decisions to help them assess a candidate's connection mindset and skill set.
- Provide training to new supervisors to help them develop a connection mindset and skill set in their role as a leader.
- Encourage physicians or other healthcare staff to form groups and get together periodically to discuss issues relevant to their experiences.
- Make hospital chaplains or counselors available to employees to address grief, stress, and the emotional toll of witnessing suffering and death.
- Support individuals who are at risk for stress as a result of discrimination with employee resource groups and mentoring opportunities.
- Consider sending out a monthly email newsletter that provides practices, case studies, and new research on the importance of connection.

Conclusion

Positive cultures are consistently linked to better patient outcomes (Braithwaite et al. 2017). Culture is also important because it affects whether healthcare professionals perform tasks at a level that reflects excellence. As Dr. Atul Gawande (2020), the noted surgeon and author, observed in an article in May 2020 that Mass General Brigham was able to keep COVID-19 cases at a minimum among its 75,000 employees despite being in Boston, which was a hot spot for the disease at that time. In addition to his hospital's four-pillar combination strategy—hygiene, distancing, screening, and masks—it was a fifth element, culture, that moved people who knew what to do, to actually do it.

We are optimistic that healthcare cultures in the future will become more relationally connected. Medical educators have been developing curricula for empathy and compassion training for physicians and physicians-in-training that is proving to be effective (Patel et al. 2019). One medical school, the new TCU and UNTHSC School of Medicine—a partnership between Texas Christian University and the University of North Texas Health Science Center—is intentionally developing empathetic scholars using an "interdisciplinary curriculum designed to build skills in awareness, listening, inquiry, and engagement to foster exceptional connections between physicians and their patients, their teams, and their communities." Incorporated in the curriculum is a physician development coaching program, which assigns a coach to student team members. This relationship will "assist in the development of resiliency, collaboration, communication, and continuous improvement for personal and professional development" (TCU and UNTHSC School of Medicine 2019).

As Dr. Holly R. Dahlman (2015) noted:

> In a harried profession, detachment often serves as a defense mechanism, hiding beneath the guise of professionalism. As busy days carry on, disruptions distract and burnout multiplies. Yet, there is hope for the health profession and for our patients. We can work to build connected teams to support coordinated care for our patients and a human touch for those in crisis. We can create the space for innovation, where every team member is thriving and is able to offer his or her greatest gifts to the mission. Where each team member is free to provide input and shape processes, leaders are able to entrust more and more to the team. Leaders are then freed to strategize rather than supervise, to build better systems, and manage bumps in the road.

With the help of talent development professionals, leaders can become a force for boosting connection in the culture of healthcare organizations so that healthcare professionals, patients, and caregivers benefit.

PART 3

EMPLOYEE DEVELOPMENT

CHAPTER 11

ONBOARDING

JACQUELINE BURANDT

It was Tuesday afternoon and Denise was heading back to the office to celebrate another successful session of University Health's onboarding program, The Journey Begins Now. Her team in the Center for Learning Excellence had worked hard for several years to completely revamp the onboarding experience for all new hires, continuing to monitor evaluative data from new employees to ensure a quality experience.

This session's evaluations had continued the positive trend, overwhelmingly validating that new hires left the experience with a commitment to the organization's culture and mission and a connection to the people, places, and resources required for success. This was also often confirmed in conversations with new staff as they left onboarding pumped up about their decision to join University Health.

Before Denise could pat herself on the back or applaud her team, however, she ran into Juan, whom she remembered from a recent onboarding. She was surprised to learn that Juan was leaving the organization. Although he'd had a very positive experience in The Journey Begins Now, he didn't get the support he needed from his department director to be successful in his new job. Disappointed to learn that the health system was losing a valuable new hire, along with a considerable investment in his onboarding, Denise brought the issue to her team.

The talent development team decided to gather data on how pervasive the problem was. They surveyed 300 new hires and a sizable sample of departmental supervisors, finding evidence of significant inconsistencies in information covered, delays in speed-to-competence, and disparities in the conveying of first impressions. The team also discovered that, upon reaching their units, some new employees reported feeling devalued, abandoned, and overwhelmed with administrative data. These "culture killers" were negating the positive experience that the new hires had received in The Journey Begins Now.

This true story from University Health underscores talent development's pivotal role in creating positive experiences for healthcare new hires through a comprehensive, quality onboarding program. This chapter will describe best practices and delineate proven approaches that talent development can follow to ensure onboarding is aligned to the organizational culture and is contributing to the organization's strategic goals. It will discuss the various aspects of onboarding, including definitions, phases, needs assessments, manager and leadership involvement, and evaluating onboarding's effectiveness.

What Is Onboarding?

When it comes to onboarding, it's important to define what organizational processes and programs we're talking about, particularly differentiating between orientation and onboarding. Although both terms are often used interchangeably, there is a generally agreed upon distinction that onboarding is a process, while the orientation program is an event that's a major part of the onboarding process.

Ed Bancroft and George Bradt (2016) explain that "onboarding is the process of acquiring, accommodating, assimilating, and accelerating new team members, whether they come from outside or inside the organization."

This chapter details different elements of an onboarding process, including pre-boarding, system-level orientation, nursing orientation, internships, departmental orientation, re-boarding, and offboarding.

Why Onboarding Matters in Healthcare

While first impressions are always important, they are particularly important in healthcare because new employees have many options for employment and need to know they have made the right choice. How organizations present themselves to new hires can make a critical difference in ensuring they become engaged, productive, and loyal. Extensive research validates that this is critically important to both the individual's and the organization's success. For example, nearly 70 percent of employees are more likely to stay with a company for more than three years if their onboarding experience was great (Hirsch 2017). With onboarding crucial to long-term job success and retention, investments in high-quality onboarding can pay big dividends in achieving healthcare's triple aim of patient satisfaction, quality, and efficiency.

The healthcare industry is undergoing radical transformation thanks to massive changes in regulation, competition, delivery, consumerism, technology, operations, and so on (DDI 2017). This accelerated pace of change does not allow for onboarding mistakes, as it can endanger the business and patients. Controlling expenses continues to be a strategic imperative in healthcare, and onboarding can protect investments in new talent. A survey by the Medical Group Management Association in 2017 found that 28 percent of respondents saw an annual staff turnover rate between 5 and 10 percent, 17 percent reported a staff turnover rate of 16–20 percent, and 6 percent had more than 25 percent turnover. A 2017 study by Bamboo HR found that losing a newly hired employee costs nearly twice that employee's annual salary in wasted hiring and re-hiring activity.

Ongoing shortages in specialty areas, such as doctors, nurses, and radiologists, allow talent to be selective in where they seek employment, causing healthcare systems and related organizations to be forward thinking and reconsider onboarding as a key factor in engagement and retention (Gaul 2017). The evidence is clear. Gallup, in a study of 200 hospitals, found that engaged nurses are the number 1 correlative factor to decreased patient mortality. *HR Solutions* reports that 85 percent of engaged employees displayed a caring attitude toward patients, compared with 38 percent of disengaged employees.

The Role of Talent Development in Healthcare Onboarding

The significance of onboarding in healthcare is great, due to the importance of healthcare's mission, complexity, and highly compliance-driven environment. Patient safety, regulatory compliance, and accrediting bodies require new employees to become equipped quickly in many areas, such as infection control, HIPAA, fire and electrical safety, and emergency codes, before beginning work. This is a challenge for those designing onboarding who need to prioritize *must know now areas* for initial system-level onboarding and then work with departments to ensure a smooth transition to learning the remaining *need to know areas* on the unit.

Best-in-class onboarding, many examples of which are covered in this chapter, addresses the sheer volume and complexity of the information through blended learning. A good mix includes instructor-led, e-learning, virtual, video, simulation, virtual reality, and gamification. The organization's mission, values, and culture should be addressed in the interactivity that live training provides, while compliance topics are often best delivered via e-learning. However, this is only effective in transferring the essential information if the e-learning content is contextual and interactive. Talent development must work with subject matter experts to ensure e-learning programs don't become a data dump. Effective e-learning uses visuals to bridge language and literacy barriers.

Onboarding occurs over time, with some organizations devoting a day to covering the basics, while others invest a week or more to ensure new employees receive in-depth information. In organizations that use internships, onboarding can last up to 90 days. In addition, competency check-offs and initial performance reviews frequently occur at 90 days, making it essential that onboarding and any remediation are completed by that point. This timeframe ensures that managers are accountable for onboarding completion and that employees are accountable for their own development.

Because budgets are often tight in healthcare, some organizations make the mistake of thinking that a one-time "sheep dunk" will work. This penny-wise and pound-foolish approach fails to consider the negative effects on the organization—such as turnover, disengagement, and lack of productivity—from failing to onboard staff effectively.

A truly comprehensive, quality onboarding process must occur at many levels, including pre-boarding, system-level orientation, nursing orientation, internships, departmental orientation, re-boarding, and offboarding. While these are distinct phases, their effectiveness lies in the cohesiveness of their design and delivery. Talent development, working with a multidisciplinary team of stakeholders, should oversee all phases.

Phases of Onboarding

As healthcare organizations promote holistic patent care across a lifetime and discourage episodic care (repeated emergency room visits, for example), talent development has followed suit in promoting holistic onboarding that occurs in phases. Best-in-class organizations have abandoned the "one and done" onboarding approach of sitting someone in a classroom or at a computer for eight hours of boring presentations. Instead, they target the different needs of employees as they progress through the organization.

Pre-Boarding

The pre-boarding phase, often considered an extension of the hiring practice, protects the significant investment in recruiting and acquiring talent by paving a smooth transition to the workplace. After a candidate receives a written offer, pre-boarding bridges the time between acceptance and their first day at work. The focus is on building a relationship with the new hire and providing assistance with paperwork and administrative tasks, such as securing access codes and filling out required forms. It also includes first day logistics, such as parking, badging in, and uniform and dress codes. This phase must be a collaborative process involving human resources, talent development, and the hiring manager, ensuring that scheduling of the new hire's start date, attendance at the orientation event, access, and more are in sync.

Good communication during this phase is essential in reinforcing that the new hire has made the right choice and helping prevent buyer's remorse. According to ICIMS, 40 percent of employees say they have experienced a lack of communication between the time they accepted the job and their first day of work (Oliver 2020).

Texas Health Resources (THR)'s Onboarding Navigator Program is a high-touch approach ensuring every new hire is warmly welcomed, set up for success, and has an easy transition into the company. Navigators, similar to patient navigators, humanize the environment by helping hires adjust to their new jobs and assimilate into the organization. These designated full-time HR professionals take new employees under their wing, meet their needs, and shepherd them from job acceptance to integration. Navigators have the responsibility of being ambassadors of the THR's culture, modeling behaviors and standards and ensuring new hires have a smooth start.

Onboarding navigators start the *Wow!* experience by reaching out to the new hire within 24 hours of receiving confirmation that the candidate accepted the job offer. They send a personalized welcome email explaining the onboarding process, outlining next steps, and linking to a portal on *MyTexasHealth,* where the new hire is greeted with a personalized welcome letter from the CEO. Onboarding navigators also call the new hires to see how they're doing, answer their questions, and schedule their preemployment site visit.

During the site visit, onboarding navigators meet with the new hire to review the job description. Every job description addresses THR values and desired behaviors before outlining the job-specific information to underscore that those are the baseline for performance. The onboarding navigators also review the new hire's benefits, discuss other important information, take their ID picture, answer questions, and provide a "trail guide" that outlines the steps required of the new hire on their journey to integration.

Key Takeaways

Best practices in pre-boarding employees include:

- If a recruiter is used, reach out to the new hire within one to two days of receiving confirmation that the candidate has accepted the job offer.
- Send a personalized welcome email explaining the onboarding process and outlining next steps.
- Assign an HR or talent development professional as an ambassador to take the new employee under their wing, meet their needs, and shepherd them from job acceptance to integration.

Orientation

Historically, orientation has been much maligned, as it frequently focused heavily on policies and procedures presented in lecture and PowerPoint format by a host of subject matter experts, many of whom were not skilled facilitators. The stiff competition for talent in healthcare requires employee engagement from the beginning to ensure retention, which means orientation must move beyond its historic parameters and transition to a showpiece of an organization's culture. A best-in-class orientation shifts the focus toward connection and culture, ensuring that orientation is engaging, relevant, and learner-centric, giving new hires an appreciation for the organization and the important role they will play (Gaul 2017).

As shared in the *TD* article "Onboarding Is Critical," University Health successfully dismantled its previous orientation program, in which a host of subject matter experts came and went, dispensing knowledge on discrete areas, none of which tied together. Based on feedback from former attendees and the collaborative work of an interdisciplinary team, the program's focus moved from compliance to culture and from presenter-led to learner-centric through a unified focus on engagement via techniques such as gamification. Now, two seasoned members of the Center from Learning Excellence facilitate a highly successful program called The Journey Begins Now.

Some organizations have begun virtualizing as much orientation as possible—moving away from live classroom training to accommodate geographically dispersed staff and control travel costs. Furthermore, the COVID-19 pandemic compelled most organizations to move entirely to virtual onboarding, if only temporarily. One example of this is the onboarding program at UCHealth. The training team had been revolutionizing the way they trained for more than a year by converting face-to-face classes to virtual instructor-led training and recording e-learning options (Williamson 2020). With the original goal of reducing the number of trainers needed per class, the IT training leadership team had planned to move all new hire training to an on-demand option that could be assigned through the existing learning management system. The advent of COVID-19 accelerated the need to progress with the virtualization. Recordings of each application began with the credentialed trainers responsible for these classes. In fewer than five days, more than 75 modules within 15 different applications were recorded, and UCHealth began virtual new hire training on March 16, 2020.

Knowing that these deliverables were not enough, UCHealth focused on blended learning by developing 50-minute virtual lab sessions. This would support newly hired staff with walk-throughs, questions, and any needed re-training; it also allowed trainers (now called *coaches*) to stay connected with those receiving training, the organization, and others on the training team. UCHealth plans to continually add new exercises, updated information, and technology upgrades to these modules.

While there are many advantages to UCHealth's agile response—on demand learning, reduced trainer and travel costs, and ability to upgrade and update quickly—there are disadvantages that come with any virtual orientation. These include technology issues, lack of learner engagement, and the diminished personal connection among a new hire cohort. While a skilled instructional designer and facilitator can introduce some interaction virtually through breakout rooms, nothing beats a live orientation for promoting culture and a sense of community. Many of us can still remember the people who sat at our table during our orientation and how excited we were to begin work. Figure 11-1 presents a checklist of what to consider when building live orientations for your onboarding program.

Key Takeaways

Some best practices in orientation include:

- In live orientations design maximum opportunities for interaction and engagement by using techniques such as gamification.
- In virtual orientations, support recorded sessions with blended learning modalities, including virtual lab sessions and exercises.
- Monitor all orientations, live and virtual, to ensure content is up to date and presenter quality is top-notch

Figure 11-1. What to Consider for Your Live Onboarding Program Orientations

Content

- What are your learning objectives for the first day? For the entire program?
- Do your learning objectives align with organizational and departmental goals?
- How will you measure if the course learning objectives were met?
- Is you content focused on answering the question, "Why are we here?"
- Is your content useful and relevant to a new hire?
- Did you involve subject matter experts to ensure your content is accurate?
- Are you meeting all your compliance requirements?
- Is there any duplication of your content?
- How does the first day content fit within your entire onboarding program?

Materials

- Did you create professional, useful materials (such as job aids and participant guides) to help the new hires learn and retain the information?
- Is the reading level of your material appropriate for all employees?
- What prizes or giveaways do you have to help reinforce learning?

First Impression

- Did you provide adequate directions and maps?
- Is adequate parking available?
- Do they need special badge access or parking vouchers before arriving?
- Did you place signage to help them easily locate the room?
- Did you prepare other departments (such as security or reception)?
- Did you schedule your start and stop times to allow for traffic?
- Do you have staff assigned to greet the new hires and provide a warm welcome?

Food

- Do you have a budget for refreshments?
- Will you provide breakfast, lunch, snacks, or drinks?
- Is there adequate refrigeration for those who bring a lunch or their medications?

Environment

- Does the classroom setup encourage interactivity?
- Does the room make the best first impression of you company for the new hire?
- Is the room the right size for your group?
- Do you have all necessary equipment and technology in the room?
- Are you able to adjust the temperature during the day according to participant feedback?
- Are there adequate restrooms available, and close by for the group?
- Did you allot time in your schedule for frequent, short breaks?

Adapted from University Health's The Journey Continues flyer.

Nursing Orientation

Nurses are the largest employee category in most healthcare organizations, particularly hospitals. Always in high demand, nurses typically make up 60 percent of the workforce and account for one of the largest pieces of the labor budget. The highly specialized nature of their work, ranging from neonatal intensive care nurses to emergency room nurses, requires extensive onboarding to their new environment.

In today's competitive market, nurses can work at any organization in any city they choose, which increases the challenge of recruiting, hiring, and retaining them. Research indicates it costs approximately $50,000 to replace a bedside nurse, with health systems incurring an estimated loss of $4–7 million a year.

A 2017 report brief by the Advisory Board found that overall bedside RN turnover rose steadily from 2009 to 2015, landing at just under 12 percent in 2016. Of particular concern: A quarter of nurses who left their facility in 2016 had less than a year of tenure. And, many of those departing nurses were younger than 35, an age group that comprises nearly a third of the nursing workforce (Schulze 2017).

This study—coupled with research indicating a strong correlation between positive experiences in classroom nursing onboarding programs and increased retention—supports implementing a quality nursing orientation. Best-in-class healthcare organizations devote significant time and resources to a comprehensive nursing orientation that occurs after the system-level orientation. To ensure a quality product, it's essential that talent development partners with nursing staff development in the design, delivery, monitoring, and evaluation of the effectiveness of nursing orientation. This requires intentional collaboration among these two groups, which are frequently are siloed or competitive.

Simulations, an essential component of nursing onboarding, allow new nurses to practice high-risk procedures in a physically and emotionally safe environment; receive immediate feedback on their performance; and incorporate a variety of modalities and technologies to create a physically and psychologically safe learning environment, including using manikins with programmable software to customize real-life scenarios and playback capability. Advanced simulations use standardized participants (actors who portray a part in the scenario). One consideration with simulations: Organizations must carve out a dedicated space, called a Sim Lab, to house manikins and other equipment necessary to orient new nurses. When not in use for orientation, Sim Labs can be used for annual or as-needed competency checkoffs, maximizing the organization's investment. (For more see the chapter on simulation laboratories by Gretchen Kolb.)

Memorial Health System in Illinois (ATD's 2020 Innovation in Talent Development winner) used virtual reality, specifically first-person point of view (POV), to further engage emergency nurse orientees in the simulations and build critical thinking skills. Each nurse wears a 360-degree GoPro Max during the simulation scenario, replicating the live environment. Depending on the simulated patient's treatment, the scenario has many deviations from the desired plan, which also includes alternate outcomes. The debrief focuses on how the patient's outcome changed based on decisions made from each point of view.

Using these POV simulations aided in an improved turnover rate in the emergency department from 18.4 percent in July 2018 to 9.1 percent in July 2019. Learning consultants with onboarding responsibility for other departments are now working to incorporate POV simulations into their orientations and education classes for further impact throughout the organization.

Key Takeaways

Some best practices in nursing orientation include:

- Don't skimp on the resources required to produce a best-in-class nursing orientation that promotes retention of this key group.
- Use simulations and new learning modalities, such as virtual reality, to build critical thinking skills, mitigate risk through a safe environment, and appeal to millennial nurses.

Internships and Preceptorships

Clinical areas, such as nursing, use internships to onboard new staff effectively in cohorts. These internships, usually categorized by specialty (trauma nursing internship or medical-surgical internship), can last from several weeks to several months. Ideally, they begin after a new employee has attended new hire orientation and department-specific orientation.

University Health's Trauma Nursing Fellowship (TNF) is one best practice example for internships. It was created by the Center for Learning Excellence in collaboration with the nursing department, which invests in, recruits, fosters, and advances nurses in the complex, inclusive world of trauma nursing. The TNF is a six-month clinical program with rotations in five areas: pre-hospital (ground and air transport), trauma resuscitation, trauma ICU, pediatric ICU, and trauma program administration. The program includes didactic training, integrated with simulation skills lab time and clinical performance rotations.

During their fellowship, the participants actively engage in performance improvement, trauma education, injury prevention, and involvement in regional and state trauma systems, including the Southwest Texas Regional Advisory Council (STRAC). Trauma fellows cross all intradepartmental and interdisciplinary boundaries, as do trauma patients. After graduation, they continue their involvement in the fellowship program, serving as mentors and advocates for new fellows and through the Level I Adult and Pediatric Trauma Programs.

Participants receive a stipend of up to $1,250 during the program and an additional $1,250 upon successful completion of the six-month training and certification in exchange for a two-year commitment to remain with the organization as a full-time nurse in a trauma-related area. These stipends are budgeted for by the Center for Learning Excellence. Successful completion includes mentoring nurses in the TNF, internal and external trauma education, trauma conference posters or presentations, certification as a trauma critical care nurse (TCRN), and serving as instructors for Stop the Bleed, a nationwide campaign to teach everyone how to stop bleeding and save lives.

The Trauma Nurse Fellowship, holding its ninth class, has produced 20 graduates as of 2018 with a 100 percent retention rate and 100 percent serving as mentors; increases in knowledge and compliance to nursing education requirements for trauma accreditation have also been reported.

In preceptorships preceptees are matched with a preceptor (clinical mentor) on the unit who works directly with them at the bedside to orient them to clinical processes and standards of care. This is an extremely important step, as it is the last onboarding phase for a new nurse before performing autonomously. It is an up close and personal view, applying all they've learned in previous onboarding phases. With a 12-hour nursing shift now the standard, preceptees spend this shift shadowing the preceptor, practicing time management, getting a first-hand look at the patient experience, prioritizing tasks, and documenting health information in the patient record. The preceptors, who receive special training in providing constructive feedback, receive differential pay for the extra responsibility.

Some internships provide stipends to new hires upon completion, further incentivizing retention. Internships and preceptorships are an effective recruitment tool, providing a pipeline of competent nurses who can practice safely, efficiently, and independently at the bedside.

Many organizations also use a mentorship approach in non-clinical areas. A new directors' mentoring program at University Health matches new directors with seasoned directors for one-on-one support learning and implementing the policies and procedures at University Health, such as payroll and performance development. New directors complete e-learning modules on the competencies before meeting with their mentors for competency check-offs. This is an ideal solution for getting new directors off to a fast start on an as-needed basis, without waiting for enough new directors to fill a formal class.

Key Takeaways

Some best practices for internships and preceptorships include:

- Use a sign-on and completion stipend to foster recruitment and retention.
- Include a post-internship mentoring commitment as part of the completion requirements.
- Look beyond nursing for areas in your healthcare organization to use internships and preceptorships.

Department Onboarding

Great onboarding can jump-start high levels of employee engagement, promote retention, and significantly contribute to an organization's goals, such as productivity. Yet, great onboarding must go beyond the initial, system-level experience that's frequently sponsored by talent development and HR. After investing considerable time and money in the initial experience, organizations often negate this positive experience by not considering what happens once a new employee arrives at the department or unit level.

Typically, when new hires have finished the orientation event, they report to their departments to begin work. Here at the unit level is where employees can feel a disconnect with the organization because their supervisor does not have the time or training to properly orient them. Too often a new employee winds up alone in a barren cubicle with a binder full of information to learn. A "this is the way we've always done it" mentality and narrow bandwidth between meeting patient needs and staff shortages can lead to a hit-and-miss onboarding experience. Making sure that everything is set up and ready for new hires on their first day sets the right tone about their value to the organization and places the focus on productivity, efficiency, and expectations.

Involving the team in preparation for the new hire is a great way to build camaraderie. Get feedback on what they think would be helpful to a new employee. Many recommend asking the most recently hired employees what they would have liked to have had awaiting them on their first day in the unit. Give each team member responsibility for part of the welcome. For example, one can make a personalized welcome sign; one can procure organization-branded swag, including notepads and pens; and one can obtain the necessary equipment. This investment in the new hire will foster team buy-in and promote a win-win.

Too often, having been "pumped up" about their organization's culture, new employees feel abandoned ("Oh, I didn't know you were coming today"), devalued ("Let me try to find a spot for you"), or overwhelmed with administrative tasks (getting computer access) upon arriving at their units. In essence, department onboarding can be a culture-killing experience. This was the situation encountered a few years ago at University Heath in San Antonio, Texas.

While University Health had made great strides in revising system-level onboarding, departmental onboarding still needed attention. Primary and secondary research indicated a need for a seamless, standardized, yet customizable departmental onboarding. This was the missing link to ensuring long-term success for new hires and protecting the organization's talent investment.

Modeling the steps for success of other initiatives at the organization, such as system-level onboarding in The Journey Begins Now, and nursing onboarding in The Journey Continues, the talent development function convened a multi-disciplinary team. The team, which included representatives from inpatient and ambulatory, firstline supervisors, HR, and talent development, met regularly for almost a year.

After interviewing 300 new employees and a sizable sample of departmental supervisors, the team found evidence of significant inconsistencies in information covered, conveying first impressions and delays in speed-to-competence. The team also researched external best practices, which validated the pivotal role that supervisors play in translating the mission vision, value, and culture into daily work.

The culmination of the team's work was *Team Me UP!*, a guide that serves as a blueprint for supervisors to create a standardized, complete, effective, and positive departmental onboarding experience. Divided into timeframe sections that correlate with organizational deadlines, *Team Me UP!* focuses on four crucial areas:

- Positivity—connecting with the organization
- Information—sharing information about their new role
- People—connecting the new hire with others on the team
- Access—providing entry to physical space and online tools

The timelines include what to do before the employee starts, day 1, week 1, week 2, within 30 days, and after 30 days. The content includes first impressions, assigning the right mentor and buddy, arranging job training and access, being welcomed by the department director, job-specific competencies, service excellence, learning opportunities and career advancement, performance evaluations and continuous improvement, and other areas important to new hires on the unit.

After *Team Me Up!* launched, supervisors received specialized training that is now part of the curriculum of the Institute for Leaders, a professional development program for leaders at all levels. Adjustments are made to the guide quarterly, based on data from participant and supervisor feedback and organizational changes. As revisions are made, new training content updates staff while reemphasizing the program.

Post implementation surveys with the supervisors found that *Team Me UP!* made the onboarding process more efficient (57 percent), enhanced a great first impression (54 percent), and improved consistency (61 percent). A major finding that some supervisors were unfamiliar with *Team Me UP!* resulted in a targeted communication campaign to introduce the guide. A message to new employees' supervisors on the day of system-level onboarding also reminds them of this resource.

Extending the positivity and consistency of system-level onboarding to the unit level can pay big dividends in new hire engagement, productivity, success, and retention. The key is to provide a structured, yet customizable format and to train supervisors on implementing it. A guide, determined by unit-specific needs, can serve to connect the new hire and supply the supervisor with documentation of areas covered, dates, and so forth. Assigning a buddy to work with the new hire can be a great way to facilitate this department orientation. Some recommend choosing the last person hired as the buddy since they can empathize the most with the new hire, while others recommend using a seasoned person in the department.

Key Takeaways

To replicate this success in your organization, employ a multi-disciplinary team, obtain feedback from recent new hires and their managers, use an uplifting theme, communicate the initiative, train leaders on the process, ensure consistency with other onboarding phases, and monitor continuously for any needed upgrades or modifications.

Re-Boarding

Ongoing global volatility and disruption in healthcare has spurred the implementation of a new, best-in-practice onboarding phase called re-boarding, which is designed for employees who are returning to work after an extended absence. Many employees who have been furloughed or were required to work remotely will struggle when returning to the workplace.

To ensure successful reentry, healthcare organizations must prepare these employees to adapt to any changes in cultural norms, policies, health and safety protocols, roles, logistics, workplace etiquette, and other issues. In healthcare, perhaps more than any other field, this will require much focus, as workers in direct patient care have cause for concern. The approach requires a balance of speed and safety. For example, new policies and procedures on temperature checks and social distancing in light of the COVID-19 pandemic had to be implemented immediately, with the focus on the importance of protecting everyone—patients and employees.

Key Takeaways

Strategies for re-boarding include:

- Update and consistently use checklists and competency check-offs, already familiar in healthcare.
- Reassess onboarding employees to determine what resources they will need to get up to speed.
- Check in with returning employees early and often and provide a variety of on-demand resources to learn or relearn what is required of them.
- Seize this opportunity to make a second first impression by re-establishing the human connection, which is particularly fragile during change.
- Reenergize their connection to the work through welcome back events and celebrations over small victories.

Offboarding

The importance of offboarding—the process leading to the formal separation between an employee and an organization through resignation, termination, or retirement—is often minimized in the hurry to get new employees on board. Yet, this key phase can help you keep the employee as an advocate for the organization after leaving employment. This bolsters the organization's brand, can result in referrals for new hires, and opens the door for boomerang employees—those who return to the organization.

Ideally the offboarding process involves a phased transfer of knowledge from the departing employee to a new or existing employee; an exit interview to reveal data for improvement; return of any of the organization's property; and various processes from the company's human resources, information technology, or legal functions.

Having in place an effective offboarding process can reduce the chance of misunderstandings after the employee leaves. Taking the time to understand the employee's experience can provide additional opportunities for networking, development, and growth.

Key Takeaways

To facilitate the offboarding conversation, choose:

- The right time—in healthcare, this usually means getting someone else to cover the job while the employee participates in the exit conversation.
- The right environment—finding a quiet, safe place outside the usual hectic spaces in healthcare requires planning.
- The right participants—include HR or another objective party. Two listeners can capture more meaningful data than one.
- The right tone—you are probing for what could be improved, including needed supplies or collegial relationship issues. This is no time to be defensive.
- The right questions—use open-ended questions, such as, "Did you have what you needed to succeed in your position?" "What suggestions do you have for improvement?" "Would you recommend our organization? Why or why not?"

The Role of the Manager

Managers work closely with HR to recruit and hire staff. Once on board, a new hire's success depends greatly on managerial involvement. High-performing organizations are more likely to involve hiring managers in the onboarding process (Friedman 2016). Talent development supports managerial success in onboarding new staff through development of a manager's toolkit, e-learning modules, videos, coaching, and more formal leadership programs.

Since new hires can be overwhelmed by the tremendous amount of new information they receive in onboarding, managers often play a vital role in ensuring new hires receive clear, comprehensive, and complete information.

I've broken down some best practices you can share with managers for sustainable success in this role into three buckets: on the first day on the unit, in the first week on the unit, and ongoing.

On the first day on the unit, managers should:

- Provide a personalized, warm welcome.
- Celebrate the new employee with the team.
- Present them with a customized welcome kit containing themed gifts, such as pens and notepads.

In the first week on the unit, managers should:

- Explain the new employee's role within the organization and specifically how they can contribute.
- Outline guidelines, policies, and responsibilities.
- Help the new employee set concrete goals or milestones so they can focus on the future from day 1.
- Create a sense of commitment and belonging by connecting the employee's and team's role in the success of the organization's vision, mission, values, and strategic focus.
- Develop a career or learning path and review it often with the employee.

Ongoing, managers should:

- Ensure that others on the team are welcoming, helpful, and display a positive organizational culture.
- Determine that learning content is current and accommodates a variety of learning styles.
- Empower new hires to ask questions, setting aside specific time for this.
- Solicit feedback on how the onboarding process is going.
- Encourage them to work collaboratively by giving them team projects, especially in the beginning.
- Provide frequent positive feedback and appropriate guidance.

The Role of Leadership

Leadership's support for onboarding, which is also vital to it success, can manifest in many ways. Visibility is key. Many CEOs appear at orientation events, whether in person, by video, or in a printed message. In some live, instructor-led orientations, members of the C-suite (CEO, CFO, CMO, CNO, and so on) take turns addressing the new hires. This makes a powerful first impression that new employees are welcomed and valued by the organization.

A comprehensive onboarding program requires executive-level support through budget allocations for facilities, supplies, travel costs (when applicable), and employee hours spent in training. This also sends a tangible signal that investment in new hires is an organizational priority. By communicating onboarding's effectiveness and demonstrating its business impact, talent development helps establish and maintain the budget allocated to onboarding.

Onboarding completion measures can have large repercussions in the organization. Many accrediting bodies, such as the Joint Commission, use onboarding completion as a measure of success for accreditation. During site visits, employee records of onboarding completion (usually obtained from the LMS and other human resources files) must be produced for review. With many competing priorities in healthcare, delinquencies in onboarding completion can occur. Talent development's responsibility is having ongoing communication with leadership on the importance of dedicating time and resources to onboarding completion.

Key Takeaways

Some best practices in working with leadership include:

- Provide regular reports using dashboards that indicate delinquencies in onboarding completion by manager and vice president.
- Encourage friendly competition among VPs based on clearing up these delinquencies.
- Arrange celebrations and organization-wide communication when completion benchmarks are met.
- Enlist a C-suite champion to lead the charge to "clean up" the delinquency list.
- Involve talent development in process improvement or LEAN teams focused on delinquencies who report to senior leadership.

Needs Assessment

When designing a comprehensive onboarding process in the highly compliance-driven world of healthcare, it is easy to become overwhelmed by the vast amount of information needed by new employees. Since new hires need to become competent to perform and ready to contribute to productivity once they're on the job, there are limits to what can be accomplished during training, whether live, virtual, or through e-learning. This frequently results in employees' receiving only what is absolutely critical information for their first few days of employment.

Providing the right content and training at the right time is crucial. Deciding what to include in each phase of onboarding is best decided by a multi-disciplinary team that represents and advocates for different constituencies (nursing, front office, and others). This process of prioritizing, which requires ongoing meetings to reach consensus, should be led or facilitated by the talent development function. Representation from the C-suite will further ensure buy-in and strategic alignment.

The process can be as simple as listing all suggested areas on a flipchart and having the group vote on which areas to include in each phase, while eliminating others. Or the team can use any methodology embedded in its culture. For example, access to systems and facilities should be addressed in preboarding, culture in orientation (live or virtual), HIPAA in e-learning, and so on.

Once the team lists areas of competence for new hires, they can be categorized into buckets, as suggested here:

- Culture:
  - Organizational mission, vision, values, culture, and strategic plan
  - Behavioral expectations
  - Patient experience model and survey or CMS hospitalcompare.gov criteria
  - Product and service knowledge
- Connection:
  - Organizational leadership
  - Computer and equipment skills
  - Employee engagement and recognition, employee value proposition (EVP), performance development, growth, and employee development opportunities
  - Exit interviews during offboarding
  - Evaluations and focus group feedback from new hires completing onboarding
  - Access to systems, facilities, and so on
- Compliance:
  - Organizational policies
  - Employee handbook

- Joint Commission criteria
- State and local health department requirements
- Legal requirements and compliance practices
- Nursing Magnet Criteria from ANCC
- OSHA (when applicable), safety, emergency response plans
- Quality care
- Patient rights, such as HIPAA
- HR-related legislation, including ADA, sexual discrimination, and the Civil Rights Act of 1964

Key Takeaways

Before launching a new or revised onboarding phase, conduct a pilot, evaluate results, revise as needed, and relaunch. University Health's revamp of its orientation, The Journey Begins Now, began with a "soft opening," and early post-program evaluations indicated a need for changes. A major source of frustration for new employees was the 8 a.m. start time, which meant braving rush hour traffic to the inner-city site. In response, University Health changed the start time to 8:30 a.m. and saved money by no longer providing breakfast.

A best practice used by University Health was to have the multi-disciplinary team members attend the sessions to get real-time feedback on what was and wasn't working. Before finalizing the program's details, offer a few sessions, pay close attention to end of session evaluations, and use focus groups to get more qualitative feedback. Ongoing monitoring by the multi-disciplinary team is essential to responding to needed changes in speakers, content, and schedule.

Evaluating Onboarding's Effectiveness

Evaluating learning's impact is a rich, complex field of study. (For more see the evaluating learning impact chapter by Timothy R. Brock.)

Organizations with higher levels of maturity consistently measure the effectiveness of their onboarding programs and continuously look to improve practices. Listed here are some specific ways to measure the effectiveness of onboarding in healthcare.

- **Speed to competence.** The number of new hires who come up to speed quickly is an indication of receiving quality, relevant training in a timely manner. Texas Instruments found that employees who went through an improved onboarding program were fully productive two months faster than employees in a traditional program. In nursing, it can mean that a new nurse has demonstrated competence and can practice without a preceptor. It can be measured in days.
- **New hire retention rate.** More than half of employees who leave their job do so within the first six months. These are called quick quits (Brandon Hall Group 2017). An effective onboarding process will produce engaged, connected employees who remain with the organization. This is measured by comparing the number of new hires who leave the organization in a specific period of time, typically annually. Nursing programs are frequently measured on retention.
- **New hire error rate.** Monitoring the frequency and repetition of new hires' errors provides data on where talent development can remediate. Measuring errors made by claims processors, for example, provides information on the effectiveness of their onboarding practices.
- **New hire referrals.** With talent shortages in clinical areas, referrals from happy employees are valuable to recruitment. This can be captured in the application process and tracked.
- **Manager satisfaction.** Manager satisfaction increases by 20 percent when direct reports have formal onboarding training, according to a study at Texas Instruments. The employee engagement survey can provide measures on managers' satisfaction with onboarding.

Conclusion

Talent development professionals in the rapidly changing world of healthcare must constantly search for different modalities to onboard new staff, be alert to short-term challenges, and be proactive in changing the design and delivery of talent development solutions. Benchmarking onboarding in other industries, such as hospitality or finance, can provide ideas for innovation. In 2016 Mastercard launched a streamlined, interactive onboarding program that quickly immersed new employees in the mission and created a sense of belonging. The company saw a dramatic increase in employee engagement and alignment to the overall mission after just four months (*CLO* 2018).

Traditional, one-size-fits-all onboarding programs lead to decreased engagement, inefficient use of resources, and high variation in knowledge and skills. Successful onboarding is a guided journey—a collection of experiences, tasks, and content delivered in a structured way over time (Friedman 2016). All these elements must come together to ensure a successful, productive, healthy work experience for employees, which will, in turn, produce a successful, productive, healthy organization. That is the win-win that an exceptional onboarding process can deliver.

The transition to learner-centric onboarding will require a design that:

- Shifts from prescriptive to descriptive
- Matches learner expectations with organizational objectives
- Engages participants as part of the learning experience
- Keeps generations in mind, using techniques to engage them
- Focuses on culture
- Has a central theme
- Incorporates experiential, hands-on, interactive learning
- Accommodates different roles and learning styles
- Provides an enjoyable experience

Healthcare talent development professionals serve as influencers who can merge content and engagement to create onboarding experiences that bring new hires up to speed faster, keep them engaged, and make them want to stay at the organization.

CHAPTER 12

RESKILLING AND UPSKILLING

JACQUELINE BURANDT

When speaking with doctors, nurses, and other clinicians, we frequently hear them say that their work is "a calling." They are proud of their choice to dedicate their skills and talents to serving others through healing the sick and saving lives.

Throughout my career in healthcare, I have found the same passion and commitment from talent development professionals who, as change agents, have a calling to elevate employees' skills, careers, and economic well-being. We are fortunate to have within our power and skill set the ability to inspire learning and provide the tools and resources to prepare employees with essential skills for the future, keeping them engaged and employable.

Opportunity Abounds

The opportunity and necessity to positively impact our healthcare workforce through reskilling and upskilling has never been greater. Healthcare is constantly evolving, with complex changes in policy and regulations; a shifting marketplace; an emphasis on innovation, rapid digitization, and automation; and unprecedented disruption. The current climate drives us to develop employees who are agile, critical thinkers with the ability to adapt to future organizational needs.

As this current disruptive culture is predicted to be continuous, it's even more crucial for healthcare organizations to commit to a reskilling and upskilling strategy that prepares their people with skills that will align to the business strategy and helps the organization stay competitive. This strategy of growing a talent pipeline (also known as internal recruiting) through reskilling and upskilling is a win-win. It is an opportunity to develop workers who might not have previously been considered for promotions, while providing opportunities for higher salaried and high demand jobs to entry-level employees.

What Are Reskilling and Upskilling?

While there are many definitions of reskilling and upskilling in the literature, the most commonly agreed upon and most frequently used definitions come from the 2018 ATD research report, *Upskilling and Reskilling: Turning Disruption and Change into New Capabilities*:

- **Reskilling** describes training designed to help individuals gain new knowledge or skills, which then enables them to perform new jobs or enter new professions. For example, if medical assistants' positions are eliminated, they can receive reskilling as medical coders, who are in high demand.
- **Upskilling** describes training designed to augment existing skills with new or significantly enhanced knowledge or skills, enabling individuals to continue to succeed in the same profession or field of work. Upskilling does not refer to normal, ongoing development offered to upgrade knowledge or skills in the course of business. For example, respiratory therapists needed to upskill on advanced ventilator management techniques during the COVID-19 pandemic, when a surge of critically ill patients filled intensive care units.

Reskilling or upskilling might also focus on *adjacent skills* (also known as adjacencies), which refer to skills that are similar to ones you already have but apply to another role. Connecting the skills and abilities already present in the organization's current workforce with those needed now and in the future can accelerate learning. These skills allow workers to transition from their current roles to emerging positions within their organization. A surgical tech and an endoscopy tech may have adjacent skills, making it possible to move from one position to another with minimal reskilling.

A *skills gap* is a significant gap between an organization's current capabilities and the skills it needs to achieve its goals. It is the point at which an organization can no longer grow or remain competitive, because it cannot fill critical roles with current employees who don't have the right knowledge, skills, and abilities (ATD Public Policy Advisory Group 2018).

One instructional approach to address reskilling and upskilling is competency-based learning, which focuses on individual skills or outcomes, known as competencies. (The competencies are usually defined in a competency dictionary or model created from an occupational analysis of the skills required for successful performance.) The approach is focused on individual learners who work on one competency at a time, with the ability to skip a learning module if they can demonstrate mastery of the skills contained within it or if their current or future roles may not require it. The competency-based approach is applied most often to skills-based learning.

Case Study: Reskilling in Action

Medical coders are essential to the financial success of any healthcare organization, as they are responsible for entering the correct ICD-9 codes to ensure reimbursement. As the demand for medical coders is expected to grow 16 percent through 2026, academic medical centers face challenges recruiting and retaining skilled coders. To address this, one healthcare organization launched a partnership, the Certified Professional Coder Program (CPC), with a $52,000 grant from a community nonprofit.

The training involved lectures; a scenario-based, hands-on externship; online learning; home and group study; and one-on-one instructor and career advising to prepare for the CPC Exam. Program participants received new career skills, the opportunity for increased wages and organizational advancement, a new network with the same career goals, the opportunity to telecommute, free training, and the ability to work while training.

By growing its own pool of medical coders through a community partnership, this organization was able to meet a business need while simultaneously significantly elevating its employees' skills and salaries.

Implementing Reskilling and Upskilling With Your Workforce

Preparing employees for advancement can ensure a positive return on talent investment for the organization. Kelly Palmer, chief learning officer at Degreed and co-author of *The Expertise Economy*, writes in "Seven Steps for Upskilling Your Workforce" that organizations that "invest in advanced upskilling strategies create a more vibrant culture, see higher employee engagement, and do a better job attracting and retaining talent. More importantly, they can accelerate digital transformation, innovate faster, and quickly react to market opportunities."

Yet, developing a reskilling and upskilling strategy can appear daunting due to its many layers of complexity. Assessing every role and its requisite skills, while also predicting what future skills will be required, is a lengthy and dense task. Given the fast-paced nature of healthcare, it can feel a bit like changing the tires of a moving car. In response, healthcare organizations frequently begin this process by narrowing the focus to the top three to five skills that will be increasing or declining in the next one to three years based on business priorities, strategies, and objectives.

To get started, you need to assemble a cross-functional team, which can be led by talent development, including internal representation from HR, IT, corporate strategy, the executive team, and, ideally, external partners such as the local workforce board and community colleges. You can follow a five-step agile, iterative process to ensure you implement reskilling and upskilling programs successfully: identify future skills needed by your organization, conduct a current skills inventory, leverage resources, maximize manager involvement, and measure results.

1. Identify Future Skills Needed by Your Organization

To identify which skills your organization will need, start by grouping them in three focus areas: organizational level, departmental level, and individual level.

- **Organizational level.** What skills will the organization as a whole require to achieve its business priorities? For example, implementing a new electronic health record (EHR) requires everyone in the organization to be upskilled in this technology.
- **Departmental level.** What specific new skills are required to perform competently at the department level? These often involve new equipment, which has become increasingly digital, such as environmental service workers using Xenex sanitizing machines to kill germs while cleaning patient rooms. Or it could involve upskilling around people skills, such as improving customer service on a floor that has low patient satisfaction scores (frequently referred to as "patient satisfaction hot spots").
- **Individual employee level.** What new skills do employees need to fulfill their roles and support organizational objectives? This personalized learning content will vary greatly across the organization. An increased emphasis on empathy will require upskilling every employee by learning and practicing empathetic listening techniques. A line worker in the cafeteria may aspire to become a supervisor, which could require reskilling through leadership training.

Case Study: Upskilling More Than 10,000 Employees

The greatest change initiative in University Health's 100-year history, the multiyear transition to the new electronic health record EPIC, required building digital skills at all levels of the organization. University Health upskilled 10,914 individuals on EPIC and virtual learning technology. Of 241,555 training completions, 226,181 were virtual.

Some employees, such as environmental services workers, needed basic digital literacy skills. University Health upskilled this group by providing one-on-one hands-on coaching on using computers and using courses from the free online library Bibliotech; this process was referred to as "at-the-elbow support." The EPIC roll-out, which began in early spring 2020, was the culmination of years of planning. The results of this monumental learning initiative continue to have positive impacts on the organization's strategy to develop a future-focused workforce.

If you have limited bandwidth to conduct a thorough identification of the future skills your organization will need to stay competitive, you can start small, perhaps by concentrating on one key department. With communication about your work, other departments will seek you out to work with their reskilling and upskilling needs.

2. Conduct a Current Skills Inventory

Once you have data on future skills, you will need a snapshot or overview of current skills within your organization. Many healthcare organizations have a robust learning management system (LMS), human capital management (HCM) system, or learning experience platform (LXP) that links individual and organizational competencies to career and learning pathways. If you are fortunate enough to have this kind of automated system, you can run queries to obtain the existing skills inventory. This will give you quantitative information. To get a deeper, more qualitative understanding, you can follow up with interviews and focus groups. If you lack the resources to obtain a current skills inventory through technology applications, you can get the information manually and set up spreadsheets for review and reporting.

Fortunately, perhaps more than any other industry, healthcare is based on a solid foundation of competency and skill assessment. At a minimum, employees are typically assessed upon hire, after initial and departmental onboarding, after 90 days, and annually. This ongoing assessment is an integral part of the culture and everyday operation of healthcare organizations, which are accustomed to producing employee competency reports for all levels of employees, due to the Joint Commission and other accrediting bodies' requirements.

Examining the difference between the skills you have identified as crucial for future organizational success and the current organizational skills inventory (the skills gap) will allow you to begin planning your upskilling and reskilling initiatives.

3. Leverage Internal and External Resources

With tight budgets in healthcare, it will be crucial to draw upon existing resources to launch and support your reskilling and upskilling initiative. These resources are likely to be found across your organization in areas such as HR, IT, and clinical services, as well as in talent development. Your previous collaboration record with these groups can pay big dividends when you ask for support in this new endeavor. It is important to address the business case for upskilling and reskilling and how it will benefit these contributing groups.

Likewise, your previous collaborations with strategic partners in the community and public sector will be invaluable as you seek support for upskilling and reskilling.

Internal

Start by taking an inventory of your content library and LMS modules to discover what skill-building content you already have that you can curate for the different roles. Be alert to adjacencies that can apply to more than one role. Reexamine your existing tuition, continuing education, and certification reimbursement programs to ensure they are aligned to the reskilling and upskilling initiative.

Here are some best practices to make the most out of your existing internal resources:

- **Education reimbursement.** Compensating employees for their time and tuition or registration fees will be crucial in supporting their use of external resources.
- **One-stop shop.** To ensure a comprehensive approach in aligning and communicating the link between learning and career growth, establish a one-stop shop for resources in tuition, continuing education, and certification reimbursements and scholarships, discounts, and grant opportunities. Keep everything updated on talent development's website and promote opportunities extensively in regular channels, such as daily huddles and emails. If budget allows, allocate a dedicated position to coordinate this or assign the responsibility to an existing position.

- **Learning and career paths.** Establish learning and career pathways for all levels of employees as part of the performance management process, preparing them for promotion consideration and increased pay. At University Health, employees who go beyond the system-wide annual education requirements are incentivized with bonus points on their performance review score. Continuously review learning and career paths for relevance based on ongoing changes in the healthcare environment.
- **Employee ownership in career development.** It is important to include employee ownership and accountability in reskilling and upskilling initiatives. Ongoing career conversations that help an employee's aspirations align with the organization's goals create buy-in and ownership. Some organizations require employees involved in reskilling and upskilling initiatives to sign contracts promising to work for the organization for a period of time after completing the training. Other organizations believe that contracts are not necessary, preferring instead to focus on getting employees excited about learning new skills and growing their careers inside the company.
- **Job shadowing.** There is no substitute for witnessing firsthand what it is like to perform a specific job function. Allowing employees to preview potential career opportunities can affirm their goals and generate excitement toward achieving them. For example, at a large academic medical center, the job shadowing process is coordinated by the alumni group of the Management Development Academy (MDA). These alumnae, who wanted to give back to the organization based on their positive learning experience, set up a website where hospital employees could sign up to shadow someone in the roles they aspired to.
- **A culture of sharing.** Mentoring and coaching from seasoned, skilled employees can accelerate reskilling and upskilling. Create a culture and systems that reward experienced staff who share their knowledge. This can be built into the performance management system as a behavioral expectation, such as "develops others." Apply this at all levels. Even the most senior (in age) employees can benefit from reverse mentoring in acquiring digital skills from younger, more tech savvy-staff.

External

Support of upskilling and reskilling has been around for decades in the form of apprenticeships, internships, and workforce initiatives at the federal, state, and local level.

ATD's Public Policy Advisory Group has done extensive work in this arena and has published multiple guides to accessing resources, including funding from government and private sources.

If you are new to working with external partners, the following steps will help:

- Regularly assess your talent pool and workforce projections to determine potential gaps.
- Be alert to opportunities for funding partnerships by actively participating in community networks, workforce events, and so on.
- Express your interest in participating in partnerships that that could be mutually beneficial to your workforce and the sponsoring entity.
- Dedicate a staff member to coordinate any partnerships.
- Build strong relationships within the community, including with community colleges, your local workforce board, and faith-based organizations.
- Work closely with human resources to ensure that partnership opportunities and your organization's career paths are aligned.
- Keep leadership informed of progress or any challenges that occur during the partnership.
- Develop a communication plan in conjunction with your communications department to get the word out about the opportunities available through the partnership.
- Keep metrics on the effectiveness of the partnership and track individuals' progress.
- Celebrate successes with graduations, publicity, testimonials, and more.

Case Study: Forming Strategic Partnerships

University Health has a long and proud history of partnering with organizations, locally and across the United States, to secure grants that provide additional resources for employee development.

Faced with a tight budget for talent development and stiff competition for talent, University Health works creatively and strategically to ensure it has a steady supply of skilled professionals by establishing relationships with colleges and universities; the local workforce board, Workforce Solutions Alamo; and intermediary providers, such as ProjectQUEST. These powerful collaborations have become the organization's greatest antidote to scarce resources by extending learning opportunities while promoting recruitment and retention and developing a pipeline from within.

A partner in building this pipeline in 2017, ProjectQUEST is a local nonprofit workforce intermediary provider that addresses the skills gap by collaborating with employers, training providers, workforce development organizations, and other community-based partners to address the employment and career advancement needs of residents of Greater San Antonio. ProjectQUEST also incorporates intensive support services to help participants overcome financial and personal barriers to skills acquisition.

University Health's partnership with ProjectQUEST provided staff access to debt-free (in most cases) funding for higher education, career advancement, and a higher living family wage. ProjectQUEST's statistics indicate that the average annual income is $13,822 at enrollment in ProjectQUEST; at job placement, it rises to $43,425.

Through an $800,000 Kellogg Foundation grant, qualifying frontline staff (low wage, low income, with at least one child 8 years or younger, of minority status), could apply for a two-year healthcare-related degree. Qualifying employees received up to $6,000 for tuition, books, uniforms, and licensing and licensing preparation, and could receive additional funds for mortgage or rent, utilities, childcare, and transportation.

Working with human resources, University Health's Center for Learning Excellence identified 246 eligible employees making less than $14.50 an hour. To reach these individuals, the center implemented an intensive promotion campaign. Information sessions, conducted in collaboration with ProjectQUEST, were advertised on the intranet and in staff meetings in targeted departments. Ninety-five employees attended one of 10 information sessions and 21 employees received funding. Of these, three have completed degrees and one received a Registered Nurse license. Eighteen others enrolled in community college programs including registered nurse, LVN, sonography, respiratory tech, and radiography tech.

In addition to preparing incumbent employees at University Health, ProjectQUEST provided a pipeline of talent from the community. In 2017, University Health hired 12 nurses, three radiology technologists, two ultrasound technologists, and two LVNs from the community, all earning a living family wage of $16 to $25.50 per hour.

This win-win partnership, at no cost to University Health, gave staff a pathway to the middle class, built a pipeline for hard-to-fill jobs, and reduced turnover and the resulting costs to the organization. By developing this internal pipeline, University Health reduced the need for external recruiting, resulting in savings of $249,963. And by drawing upon this outside funding stream, employees did not need to access tuition reimbursement funds, saving the organization $75,600 over two years.

Staff turnover in 2017 at University Health was 14.9%, compared with 19.1% statewide for healthcare organizations. By developing its own, University Health is investing in staff who are already committed to the organization's culture.

4. Maximize Manager Involvement

To foster success, it is crucial that managers are at the heart of all reskilling and upskilling work. They know the work, the people, their existing skills, the skills needed, and the department metrics that those skills can drive better than anyone else. Involve them early on by inviting some to be on the cross functional planning team and provide information on what's in it for them to develop their staff, even if it means seeing staff leave to take new positions.

Leading from the middle will be a key driver to your organization's ability to respond with agility to changing workforce needs. Managers will need training and access to on-demand coaching tools as they guide employees through the process of learning and applying their skills. This can be incorporated into existing leadership programs or built as a standalone module for micro and e-learning. For the greatest impact, involve managers in creating the content for this learning program. For example, when designing a microlearning video on how to conduct a career planning conversation, cast your real-life managers as the actors in the video.

Tie managers' accountability for upskilling and reskilling to reward and recognition. Examine your performance management system to ensure it rewards managers who are accountable for their staff's development. Create a special recognition for managers who have gone above and beyond in upskilling and reskilling their direct reports.

5. Measure Results

A workforce reskilling and upskilling initiative is no different than any other learning initiative in that it will require pre- and post-measures to determine results. Returning to the first step in our iterative process, "identify future skills needed by your organization," you can track skills at the organization, unit, or individual employee level.

The case studies in this chapter are replete with examples of measuring results from reskilling and upskilling work, whether in reducing staff turnover, saving costs, or staff promotion rates. Study them for applicability to your work. Also study the chapter on evaluating learning's impact for specifics on how to conduct evaluations.

While the type of evaluation conducted will vary considerably depending on the organization, HCI's 2020 report, *The Revolution Is Now: New-Skill Your Workforce to Catalyze Change*, lists these areas as possibilities to track:

- Percent learning goals completed
- High-performer retention

- Leadership bench strength
- Role vacancy rates
- Changes in performance ratings on select tasks
- Credits and certifications earned
- Revenue per employee metrics
- Time to proficiency for new roles or new role requirements
- Assessment scores indicating increased knowledge on a specific topic
- Survey ratings from participants in L&D programs or activities
- Return on investment in the learning function

The metrics you choose will be the most powerful when they demonstrate the impact on the business and reflect the organization's highest priorities. Once you have chosen which metrics to track, create a dashboard for easy reference and use it often in reporting your progress.

University Health partnered with Catalyst Learning to support employees with School at Work (SAW) and ECHO, an on-the-job learning and career development system that jumpstarts mid-level employees on allied health, clinical, or management pathways. Through college readiness skills and professional competencies, this three-hours-a-week program prepares staff seeking degrees. SAW and ECHO provide the tools and educational foundation for staff to transition to more advanced roles in the organization. With a delivery format designed for adult learners, SAW and ECHO incorporate multiple learning modalities, while at the same time providing increased confidence, academic discipline, and formal career planning.

The first cohort's results were impressive. Of the 11 ECHO graduates in 2015, six enrolled in college and formed a study cohort. One received a coding certification and one completed an associates' degree. The 2016 ECHO class graduated 12 staff.

For the SAW/ECHO courses, eight received credentials, including certificates in medical coding and Microsoft; and LVN, associate's, and bachelor's degrees in healthcare. Ten were currently in college programs. Thirty took courses for continuing education credit. There have been 26 promotions with pay increases.

Reskilling and Upskilling During the Pandemic of 2020

While reskilling and upskilling have been around for decades, the COVID-19 pandemic forced or accelerated the implementation of many of these practices. The degree of reskilling and upskilling varied, with most organizations upskilling staff to remote work technologies and virtual learning.

Case Study: Reskilling in Times of Adversity

During the pandemic, when healthcare organizations were laying off and furloughing staff, University Health did not. Instead, its strategy was to redeploy employees to maintain institutional knowledge, protect its employer brand, and decrease costs associated with reductions in force. University Health mobilized its workforce, moving staff from closed units to areas of high demand and equipping them with the skills needed to perform in the new environment.

To fill tremendous needs at University Health during sharp and concerning increases in the number of COVID-19 patients, University Health activated its labor pool, bringing in staff from ambulatory clinics experiencing decreased volume, as patients delayed medical care because of COVID-19 concerns. These employees received reskilling on screening and managing patients presenting at our facilities, obtaining travel histories, wearing personal protective equipment, performing temperature checks, and isolating high-risk cases appropriately. Talent development worked closely with the chief medical officer to create uniform scripts to equip employees for success in these new roles.

During COVID-19, University Health faced challenges in treating advanced ventilator patients. To upskill staff, University Health partnered with Chamberlain University to offer free continuing education and promoted American Heart Association (AHA) e-learning courses and podcasts on cardiac and respiratory health, sharing AHA algorithms, job aids, tip sheets, and infographics.

Upskilling Within Talent Development

As role models, talent development professionals must be intentional about their own upskilling and reskilling needs. The COVID-19 pandemic brought this to the forefront, as live instructor-led training frequently became impossible. Those in talent development who quickly pivoted to learn and deploy new methods of content delivery led the charge within organizations in demonstrating resilience and innovation to meet business needs.

Upskilling on Video Production

During strategic planning for the upcoming year, a healthcare system's talent development department responded to its organization's need for fewer hours spent in the classroom. It analyzed its employees' learning consumption patterns, discovering that video was the most preferred method of delivery. This insight propelled the team to make upskilling in video production a strategic focus. The director budgeted for equipment to capture high-quality video with personal mobile devices and encouraged the team to watch YouTube videos to identify preferred video production styles. This was accompanied by ample hands-on practice, reinforced by peer feedback and coaching. The most-experienced team members were the first to be upskilled so that they could serve as coaches to the others on the team. In one year, 85 percent of facilitators became upskilled in video production, and video production increased by 60 percent. As a result, learners had a larger catalog of higher quality videos and consumed 20 percent more videos. Older videos were retired and replaced with new, higher quality ones.

Upskilling on WebEx

With COVID-19 requiring less face-to-face learning, a faith-based health system in the Southwest reexamined its existing live onboarding program for new hires. Enacting COVID-19 guidelines required transitioning three new hire groups from instructor-led live onboarding to virtual. The talent development team, which had not conducted virtual onboarding and had minimal experience producing WebEx training, quickly mobilized resources, securing the approved WebEx training platform and training themselves to proficiency. This included the use of breakout rooms, polling, and live chat to create engagement and replicate the live experience, as well as converting video files for the chat box. The team was able to transition to virtual onboarding in only two weeks, and they continue to upskill on virtual training techniques through WebEx.

Conclusion

The increasingly volatile, uncertain, complex, and ambiguous (VUCA) world of healthcare offers organizations a silver lining—the opportunity to invest in in-house talent instead of buying costly new talent. Reskilling and upskilling incumbent employees offer many advantages, as these employees are already committed to the organization's mission, vision, and values. They will need upskilling to maintain their current jobs by amplifying their current skill set or reskilling to learn a new high-demand job.

Reskilling and upskilling the workforce is thus a moral and economic imperative and a golden opportunity for talent development to shine in a meaningful and demonstrable way.

While we cannot see the future, we can certainly examine data and trends in our industry, healthcare, and the talent development profession to fill identified skills gaps.

As talent development professionals, we can drive business results by offering the skills training demanded in this digital age. Whether upskilling employees on technology, cybersecurity, human skills (resiliency, collaboration, creativity, emotional intelligence), new products and services, digitization of their current roles, new ways of doing work, or process flow enhancement, talent development is needed to offer a culture of development experiences to improve skill sets in current jobs. This includes strategic certifications, required skill development, and redesigning and refocusing the talent infrastructure.

The pay-off to investing in reskilling and upskilling is enormous for the organization, talent development as a profession, and as individual practitioners. It is time for us to step up and offer our considerable expertise—while continuing to gain more—to change employees' lives for the better. We have what is needed in our organizations to foster trust, inspire confidence, and empower learners to prosper during the disruptive days ahead. Following the five-step iterative process outlined in this chapter and researching additional resources offered in this book will arm you with the tools needed for success.

CHAPTER 13

FRONTLINE WORKERS

M. LYNN FISCHER

Training programs at the Veterans Hospital Administration (VHA) give people countless opportunities to transform their careers, says Imon Muldrow, chief of environmental management services at the VA Health System in Pittsburgh, Pennsylvania. Muldrow has had an interesting career trajectory. Over 12 years, he advanced from housekeeping to being a supervisor of 250 associates who play a key role in patient satisfaction and safety. How? He enrolled in training and eventually became a division supervisor.

"The American Dream," the belief that anyone can attain their own version of success and upward mobility through sacrifice and hard work, is alive and well in the healthcare industry. According to the Bureau of Labor Statistics (2020a), healthcare accounts for most of the fastest growing occupations in the US. The sector has numerous entry points and possibilities for promotion and job advancement. In addition, there are a variety of paths by which entry-level employees with limited education can move from low-wage roles to middle-skill positions with family sustaining wages. Muldrow is just one example of the value of identifying and tapping into the potential of your organization's frontline employees.

Broadly speaking, frontline workers in healthcare encompass all employees who have direct contact with patients and their families. For purposes of this chapter, we will focus specifically on those in positions that require less than a two-year post-secondary degree—nurses, physicians, and higher-level technical positions are not included. Many frontline workers serve in entry-level positions, such as food service, environmental services, nurse aide or tech, personal care aide, transporter, and patient admissions. This group of essential workers are typically employed in lower-wage roles and tends to be very ethnically diverse. They also represent an underdeveloped segment of the healthcare workforce.

This chapter is a guide for expanding your talent development system to include frontline associates, providing suggestions for design through implementation as well as ideas for measuring outcomes. The payback for your organization will be improved employee retention and more comprehensive succession planning. You will witness your frontline colleagues and their families be forever changed by the opportunities you helped to create. Whether you work in an independent operation or a large system, you can put a frontline development initiative in place. On behalf of those of us who have helped drive and seen the success of frontline development programs, we encourage you to advocate for these employees in your organization—and make it happen.

"Who touches and impacts the patient? It's our frontline co-workers," says Sister Claudia Ward, program manager health leads at Mercy. "Who has one of the largest impacts on patient experience? Again, it's the frontline co-workers. When we invest in these co-workers, we enhance the learning and productivity of the organization."

Understand How Much Executive Support You Have and Build From There

Most of those in healthcare want to help people. That's why they get into the field. And at its core, that is what frontline development is all about—reaching out your hand to help associates who want to progress in their careers and need help to accomplish that goal. These individuals love working in your health system, they are loyal, and have a broad idea they want to do more with their jobs and lives. Their family members may not have gone to college—they may only have a high-school diploma and perhaps some college courses. As a result, these employees need help gaining confidence and connecting the dots of the work-college-career path so they can move from low-wage roles to middle-skill, family sustaining wage positions. This is not a quick fix.

In our work to advocate for frontline employee development, the resources are scarce. While everyone enthusiastically acknowledges that "We need to do develop frontline employees!" the reality is that very few health systems actually implement processes to facilitate their long-term development and upward mobility. Something else is always more important. Only organizations that are financially and operationally solid, with people-centered leaders who are able to take the long view, can really make and sustain this commitment.

So, how expansive would you like to be in designing or expanding your frontline worker learning and development program? Whether you're starting from scratch or want to expand your existing offerings, begin by assessing how much you'll have. Before you decide to "start small" or "go big" with your plan, take a look at several things about your organization:

- **Culture.** Is there a stated commitment to growing from within, with organizational values that are lived, recognized, and celebrated? If so, that's a huge plus as you can attach your plan to succession planning that includes all levels.
- **CEO, COO, and CHRO interactions with frontline associates.** If your executives are frequently seen with and are known to have an awareness of and commitment to employees at the other end of the spectrum, you should be able to think more expansively. Brian Gragnolati, CEO of Atlantic Health System, is someone who acknowledges the entry-level worker. "We have a lot of staff members who might be in a job that they want to progress in. They might be a housekeeper or dining service or patient transport, for example. They're in those roles, and they can't progress because perhaps they had a bit of a stumble early on in their lives," he says. "Now it's 10 to 15 years later and feel like they're stuck."
- **Education and human resources.** Take the time to learn what's already in place for frontline worker development, as well as what's worked and what's failed. If you're going to pitch the C-suite on expanding the commitment to frontline development, you need to know the current state. If nothing is in place, you may want to start small, unless you have a C-suite champion and a good-sized budget. If some or all of the elements are already in place, you can think more broadly about what you want to recommend for frontline associate development.

As you begin your learning journey in this area, take advantage of the incredible professional network available through CareerSTAT, a network of hundreds of healthcare and workforce leaders dedicated to promoting investment in upskilling frontline healthcare workers. The CareerSTAT website contains many resources and tools that can help you organize and implement a program for your frontline team members.

The Impact of Labor Cost

The single biggest barrier to providing more education for frontline employees is the impact of labor cost on the hospital's bottom line. Unlike salaried employees, exempt employees typically must be paid for any time spent in training. Time spent in training is often categorized as non-productive time and can carry penalties for direct supervisors if they're measured on labor "productivity."

We offer three suggestions to help you overcome the labor cost impact. Selecting one or all of them may require consultation with HR leadership or negotiation with legal staff.

- Give a bonus upon program completion. Look for alternative compensation options. For example, if employees clock out for class, there is no productivity impact to the manager and no chance that class time will create an overtime pay situation. By rewarding the employee with a bonus of equivalent amount at conclusion, they have a built-in incentive for completion.
- Lobby for a bank of labor dollars in your budget. If you can assure direct supervisors that you have a cost center to charge the labor dollars to when you approach them with a training program idea, you show that you understand one of their key issues and want to partner with them to resolve it.
- Examine your HR policies regarding nonexempt employee training. And, if applicable at your organization, be familiar with union agreements. If policies are a hard and fast—for example that nonexempt workers must always be on paid time—work with the HR and legal staff to change them. Health systems like Mercy (St. Louis) and Tri-Health (Cincinnati) have crafted policies in which required training (paid) and optional self-development (unpaid) are clearly defined for nonexempt workers. This separation allows those who want to advance to do so on their own time. This helps prevent a situation in which someone willing to do self-development on their own time can't access your programs because they'd have to be paid for those hours.

Begin With Your Goal

Once you know more about your organization and its capacity for a frontline worker development program, you need to set out what you hope to achieve with it. The most strategic workforce development programs are driven by a well-defined workforce plan that includes projections for numbers of people needed in various types of positions over a five- to 10-year period. In my experience, a limited number of organizations do this. The Veterans Health Administration, for example, updates its Strategic Workforce and Succession Plan every two years. By identifying high-need jobs at every level, the VHA recognizes opportunities that represent the next rung on the ladder for employees who aspire to be upwardly mobile. Medical centers then recruit and develop employees for those positions. At the other end of the spectrum, there are very impactful single-skill programs that focus on application, such as helping employees improve their English language or computer skills.

As you are conceptualizing your frontline development program, I recommend hosting a meeting of key stakeholders to talk about and gain consensus on target outcomes. To quote Stephen Covey, "Begin with the end in mind." It sounds so obvious, but I've been amazed to see how many healthcare organizations we've worked with proceed with a program because it feels like the right thing to do, but without a solid business-related justification. This approach may bring a short-term positive result, but it likely won't stand the test of time.

Examples of different types of outcomes you might discuss with your stakeholders include identifying and upskilling people for a high-need position, increasing the ethnic diversity of people in middle-skill and supervisory positions, and retraining loyal employees whose jobs are in jeopardy due to automation. Your knowledge of future workforce needs combined with stakeholder input will help you prioritize your options. From there, you'll be able to define the tactical elements, such as types of participants, assessments, career planning support, and education programs (both cohort based and individual) that are needed to meet the organization's goals.

Main Line Health CEO Jack Lynch has been outspoken and intentional about achieving more diversity at the leadership apex of the health system. "If we're going to develop more diverse team leaders, we have to grow our own. Top to bottom, employees must see opportunity," he explains. "We want all employees to know Main Line Health is interested in their growth."

Remember that effective workforce development programs:

- Involve a number of different groups within the health system. The work of championing your frontline development program typically falls under the umbrella of talent acquisition, talent management, or learning and organization development or effectiveness (L&OD or L&OE).
- Have two pillars: career planning and related HR-support issues and education.

Let's look closer at some specific recommendations for these areas.

Career Planning and Advising

By talking to stakeholders about target outcomes and priorities, you can begin to help frontline workers plan for career advancement.

Healthcare is a singularly unique industry in the breadth of positions available for individuals with every possible level of education. I have long been astounded by the huge dollars spent on external recruiting of new employees compared with what's often spent on developing internal staff. If you are in an organization that will allow you to establish or expand an internal career center, go for it. Your return on investment will be demonstrated over a period of years as the percentage of internal hires grows.

"There's a lot of competition in this region for entry-level employees, so we started to look at how to better retain talent at EAMC," says Karen Gresham, RN, director of education services at East Alabama Medical Center in Tuscaloosa. "Our frontline employees wanted opportunities for development and promotions, and we realized we had a gap in what we offered at the entry level."

Career planning is also game changing for the lives of the frontline workers and their families. According to 2020 data from the Bureau of Labor Statistics, entry level positions, such as food preparation and cleaning, average $11.68–14.66 an hour ($24,300–30,490 per year). Helping an employee identify and attain a middle-skilled position that is a good fit can result in a wage jump by 45–50% an hour (for example, a phlebotomist makes $17.92 an hour; medical assistant $17.75 an hour; and EMT $19.41) in 18 months.

"When I talk to School at Work (SAW) participants, I tell them that they are in charge of their future," continues Gresham. "It's too important for them to leave it in anyone else's hands. We give them the tools and knowledge to succeed in what they want to do."

To best assist frontline workers in developing their careers, healthcare organizations need highly integrated talent acquisition, education, and HR support elements. Tight planning and communications are required to achieve scalable success that capitalizes on the career pathways available to advance your low wage employees. The simple diagram in Figure 13-1

Figure 13-1. Healthcare Career Ladder Examples

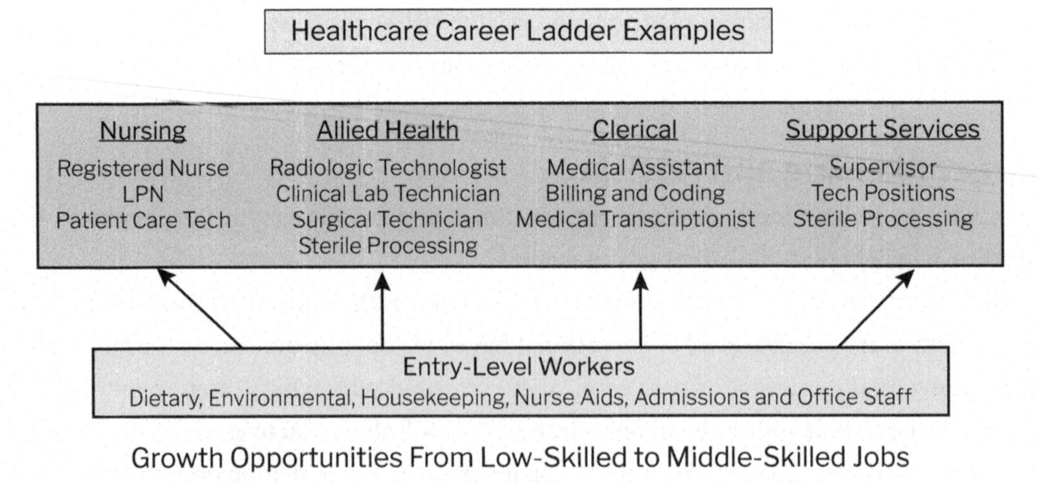

Source: Catalyst Learning Company.

illustrates some of these opportunities. More detailed pathway diagrams can be found on the websites of Baltimore Alliance for Careers in Healthcare and Missouri Health Careers.

Providing a systematic approach to frontline development requires a commitment to having career planning in place. The classic four-step career planning process includes self-exploration, job research, exploration of job options, and taking action (Figure 13-2). For entry-level frontline workers, this way of thinking will likely be new and require structured support. Those who are already employed in certificate-level positions may be more autonomous once you get the right tools in their hands.

Figure 13-2. A Four-Step Career Planning Process

Career Planning Phases	Sample Activity and Tools	Desired Outcome
Self-exploration	• Time for self-reflection • Interest and aptitude assessments	• Define the types of jobs and job titles you like and could be good at.
Job research	• ONET, BLS data, and other research • Job descriptions in your organization • Career coaching or mentoring	• Learn more about the daily work in each job. • Narrow your list to the top four to six positions.
Job exploration	• Informational interviews • Job shadowing	• Prioritize your options. • Narrow the list to your top two.
Taking action	• Career and learning plan • Career coaching or mentoring wrap-up session	• Complete the plan, including next steps with education. • Gain confidence and the motivation to make it happen.

Staff recruiters will be your key allies in placing entry-level employees in higher-level roles. They understand your health system's job needs and, very importantly, they know and work with the hiring managers. Encourage the talent acquisition group leader to dedicate at least one person to career advising. Important skills for the internal developer are nurturing talent and facilitating connections within the organization, which makes the position different from a typical recruiter.

Operationalizing career planning and advising for your frontline employees can take several forms:

- At the small end of the spectrum, you can create a focused area on the organization's website for autonomous employees to learn what tools are available to them and contact points for related activities, such as job shadowing and tuition support.

- Entry-level employees will need more structure and assistance. Think about developing a class called Building Your Career at <Our Health System>. A cohort that is built around the four-step model, includes other frontline employees, has in-person and virtual activities, and a fixed schedule typically results in the best outcomes. This will help them complete a career and learning plan, confidence in their future, and motivation to act on the plan.
- Access to an advisor or mentor will also be essential for entry-level employees to successfully complete their career plan. Career coaches housed within the HR talent acquisition function are a great option. If staffing that type of position isn't feasible, a network of mentors who want to help frontline workers advance can be very effective. Key characteristics of your mentor cadre are less about being "certified" and more about having:
  - the heart to treat entry-level associates with dignity and respect
  - the communications skills and industry and organizational knowledge to ask good questions and encourage thoughtful preparation of the career plan
  - the internal connections to make introductions and put in a good word for the associate with people related to job shadowing experiences, open positions for which the associate is qualified, and so forth.

Remember our story about Imon Muldrow? He benefitted early in his VA career from the support of mentors, EEO/Diversity Program Director Elizabeth Jenkins and Chief of Food and Nutrition Julia Gilmer. "Every good organization needs good people who feel like there's an opportunity to grow," says Jenkins. "Imon had so many skills and abilities that he didn't realize he had, a diamond in the rough. The more we polished, the more he shined."

Setting Up for Success

I'm going to assume that you already know how to address adult learning needs and how to design, develop, and deliver effective training; other chapters in this book address those topics thoroughly. Instead, I'd like to focus on a few points related to education and training that are critical to having a robust set of offerings for frontline workers, particularly those at the entry-level: access to technology, building learner confidence, tuition support, and partnerships with community and technical colleges.

Do Frontline Workers Have Access to Technology?

Ensuring your learners have access to, and comfort with, any technology required for their learning is essential, and their ability to use certain technology is not to be taken for granted. (Think digital divide.) Covering your organization's technology-related bases will improve employee confidence, completion rates, and outcomes.

As I write during the COVID-19 pandemic, the framework for healthcare training delivery is changing. The pandemic has limited our ability to meet in traditional classroom settings, while also accelerating the addition of virtual delivery options.

Without proscribing specific technology recommendations, my guidance is to research your learners' access to and comfort level with technology-delivered education and training. It is likely far different from your own. Be realistic—plan, design, and budget your proposed offering based on what you need to remove technology-related barriers of all types. You may have to be creative and collaborative with internal IT leaders or volunteer groups who are often willing to purchase, loan, or donate laptops for these employees.

How Can You Build Learner Confidence?

As you attend recognition ceremonies for adult learners at this level, the comment you're likely to hear most frequently is something like, "I never would have thought I could have accomplished <education, career or life goal>, but now I believe I can." Makes sense, right? If I had problems in school or other life experiences that made me doubt my potential, that would limit my expectations for my future options.

It requires a lot of motivation for frontline associates to decide to go back to school to achieve a certificate or degree or develop a new skill. At this point in their career, they likely have family and other responsibilities that go well beyond those of a college student who's enrolling as a single person immediately after high school. In addition, since many are currently low-income workers, they may not have the financial freedom to shift their responsibilities, afford after-hours childcare, or take time off work to attend classes. Thus, those who choose to take on the goal of going back to school must be highly confident.

You can build learner confidence by providing a supportive setting that results in program completion (Figure 13-3). An instructor or facilitator who has educational competence and treats individuals with empathy and respect is paramount. Also key is developing a cohort model in which other employees from similar circumstances are able to learn together and provide moral support through class challenges and inevitable life ups-and-downs.

Figure 13-3. Model for Entry-Level Associates Starts With Confidence

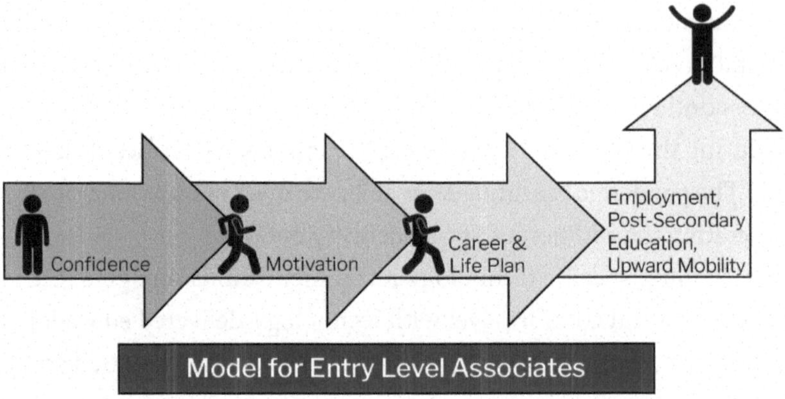

Source: Catalyst Learning Company

Ken Bishop, formerly of AtlantiCare in Atlantic City, New Jersey, sums up the change in confidence by describing students as nervous when one of his adult education classes begins. However, by the end of the program they are standing in front of their classmates, making presentations, and sharing newfound knowledge. "I joke that they've grown three inches," he says. "It's because their posture changes. You can see it in how they carry themselves and interact with each other."

"The program has made me a risk-taker and a goal setter," says JaQuita Newsome, who graduated from the program at Palmetto Health. "I have been able to learn new ideas, make new friends, meet new people, and advance my work skills and job performance. It has made me push further toward job advancement."

Do You Offer Tuition Support?

Upward mobility almost always hinges on advanced education. In fact, health systems spend millions supporting their employees' continuing education. Look at your organization's structural elements to see if there's a level playing field for employees seeking their first credential or degree. Here are two tactics you can take to address any tuition support questions your frontline workers may have:

- **Ask about the organization's tuition reimbursement policy.** Does it support community colleges and technical schools? Does it support attainment of healthcare-specific credentials and roles that are employed within the organization? Both of these are critical for your efforts to advance working adults. Properly credentialed certificate programs can move an employee from a low-wage role to a family-sustaining wage job in 12 to 18 months. For those who wish to keep going, they can also provide a confidence-building steppingstone to an associate's or bachelor's degree.
- **Lobby and partner for tuition advancement.** The cost of higher education can be a barrier for low-income individuals. If they don't have upfront funds to pay for school, post-program reimbursement may not solve the problem. Jenny Skinner of TriHealth in Cincinnati overcame this challenge by partnering with the system's foundation. She and her team identified, prepared, and mentored entry-level employees who wanted to go to college, and then the Foundation advanced the funds for tuition. As the employees completed their courses, the education team then repaid the foundation using the tuition reimbursement budget. This was a creative solution that helped low-wage employees avoid a cash outlay.

Do You Have Active Partnerships With Community and Technical Colleges?

Your organization likely already has a vibrant relationship with the local community college. If not, someone needs to build one. You can foster potential first-generation college students' confidence by inviting college staff to speak and provide a personal point of contact. Think about taking the group for a campus tour to improve their familiarity and comfort level. Get online with them and navigate around the college website. Work with them in advance of taking the placement test, and, if needed, provide preparatory classes in algebra and other subjects. Do whatever you can to make sure newly motivated employees score at a level on their placement test that puts them immediately into credit-bearing courses—remedial math or English classes are total demotivators and often referred to in my work with the community college as the graveyard of student success.

A Word About the Hardest to Serve

In my experience, the most difficult aspect of the work described in this chapter is encountering individuals who want so badly to do better, yet whose reading or math levels are not high enough to qualify for entry into your program. (The minimum suggested reading level for Catalyst Learning programs is eighth to ninth grade.) These situations can be heartbreaking. My best suggestion is to try to connect the individual with someone who can work with them on a one-on-one basis or in a small group of employees with similar challenges. You may be able to recruit retired teachers from the hospital volunteer pool or a local literary organization for this. Ideally, this person can help the employee elevate their basic skills to the point where they can effectively participate in your program.

Win Over Direct Supervisors and Hiring Managers

Whether you've decided to start small or go big with your frontline development program, there are key people in other parts of the organization on whom your success will depend. Increase your odds for success by understanding the needs and drivers of your participants' current supervisors and those of the managers you hope will hire them.

Direct Supervisors

If you don't have the hearts, minds, and actions of the frontline employees' direct supervisors, your program may see some modest success, but won't net transformative outcomes. It's really that simple. You can have the world's greatest learning and career planning programs, but if the employee doesn't make it to class because "it's too busy on the floor" or "we can't work short today," all your effort will be for naught.

The direct supervisors are in many ways the unsung heroes in the whole continuum of frontline employee development. Think about it. You're asking them to let you train their best people, with the full knowledge that this will likely cause them to leave that department. And their department has to "work short" while employees are training. It's a big ask!

So, how do you gain a direct supervisor's support?

- Emphasize the near-term gains to the workgroup: a more knowledgeable, motivated, proactive employee with improved communication skills and initiative.
- Work with HR to ensure the manager won't be penalized by labor costs or productivity measures in a performance review or bonus.

- Recognize effusively the contributions of these supervisors! Some ways to do that are call-outs at graduation ceremonies, in notes to system leadership, and by inviting them to talk with your classes and in leadership forums.

"My employee has become more professional in his actions and attitude," says Richard Miller, project manager at Norton Healthcare. "His work ethic has dramatically improved."

Hiring Managers

We've considered how to win the current supervisor's support. What about the managers of the next-level jobs we're trying to move employees into—the hiring managers? Why do they warrant a mention? This one came as a surprise to me. When the Catalyst Learning team began developing solutions to help entry-level employees advance within healthcare organizations, it was obvious that the individuals enrolled in our programs would need to make a lot of changes to be successful. What was less obvious was other organizational changes necessary to enable their success. One of those top changes is the attitudes of hiring managers.

We sometimes typecast individuals—it's human nature. So, if a hiring manager knows an employee as the friendly and efficient person who takes their payment in the cafeteria or cleans their office, they're probably not thinking of that individual as the next candidate for a billing and coding or medical assistant opening. That's where you, your internal partners in frontline development, and an organizational belief in hiring for attitude and training for skill come in.

These ideas can gain a hiring manager's support:

- Invite them to visit your classes. Observing a support employee participate in a medical terminology module can change the manager's mindset.
- Invite them to attend graduations and other closing ceremonies for your programs. If the hiring manager's mental typecast is based on regular interaction, witnessing that employee as a public speaker can automatically change that impression.
- Work closely with recruiters who are filling open positions. Recruiters screen applicants and are in a position to influence the hiring manager by recommending specific applicants. For example, they could say something like, "She's demonstrated her persistence and motivation by *<insert accomplishment>* and is praised for *<insert competencies>* by her current supervisor."

When you close the circle of relationships surrounding your upwardly mobile frontline employee, their chances for success go up exponentially. The two most important are the current supervisor or department manager and the hiring manager who controls the offer for the new position.

Document the Outcomes

For your frontline development program to be sustainable over the long term, it's critical to have a systematic approach to defining and documenting outcomes. You should expect business cycles to occasionally threaten your program's survival—even in normal times the annual competition for budget dollars can be fierce. It's important communicate in the language of executives when you advocate for your program, which means documented quantitative and qualitative outcomes.

Quantitative Data—The Language of the Mind

Like in all businesses, healthcare leaders expect hard data showing whether organizational initiatives are delivering results. You can choose from several evaluation frameworks—the most notable being the Kirkpatrick's Four Levels of Evaluation and the Phillips's ROI Methodology—to measure the effectiveness of your programs, including frontline worker development.

At Catalyst Learning, we use the Kirkpatrick's Four Levels of Evaluation when communicating with our customers about developing, measuring, and reporting on outcomes. (For more on measurement, see the chapter on evaluating learning impact.)

Only concentrating on Level 1 evaluations (smile sheets) and Level 2 evaluations (post-course knowledge mastery via assessment) is common. However, please don't limit yourself to that with your frontline development programs. A first-rate measurement strategy can be the difference between a program that's perceived as a "need to have" versus a "nice to have" (and thus a candidate for the chopping block when budgets are tight).

"While our staff member has always displayed good customer service, I believe that her desire to go above and beyond for patients has increased since participating in the program," says Juliet DeLeon, patient access manager of admissions at University Health System. "She extends her customer service to assist nursing outside her typical role when they are short staffed without a unit clerk and proactively provides information for patients before they themselves would think to ask."

The outcome that department managers are most interested in is typically the transfer of the learned skill to performance and behavior on the job, which is measured by Level 3 evaluations. But a warning: It takes real commitment to obtain quality Level 3 outcomes! You can get qualitative feedback on behavioral skills, such as communications and teamwork, from the manager. If your project requires you to collect and compile Level 3 data, consult a specialist, your vendor, and refer to in-depth descriptions of the Kirkpatrick model.

Level 4, impact on the operation, is what CFOs and other executives will be most interested in. These impacts include measures such as employee engagement, employee retention, and internal promotions. To place your program in a "need to have" category and make it sustainable for the long term, make your measures as quantifiable as possible.

An important step to take your quantitative reporting to the next level is to work with your organization's HR analytics function to embed measures in your HR information system (HRIS). Too often well-meaning individuals keep track of student successes on a spreadsheet that decision makers can't access. For regular business impact evaluation and sustainability, this data needs to be embedded in your HRIS. Make a friend in the HR data group who can help you design an automated report that shows data on retention and promotions. See if you can get post-secondary program information and dates incorporated into the system too, since education is often the precursor to upward mobility.

Another possibility is developing a gold star designation in the HRIS for individuals who have completed the professional development program for entry-level co-workers. Work with the person in HR who is responsible for nurturing internal talent to create a special flag in the HRIS that records completions of professional development programs that demonstrate commitment and determination. Make recruiters aware of the significance of this gold star designation and use it to define candidates to present to hiring managers.

Adapt the organization's current open position policies so that internal applicants who meet job description requirements and are actively participating in professional development programs are guaranteed an interview. Don't let frontline employees who've been motivated by your program become unengaged because they can't get an interview for jobs for which they meet the qualifications.

Qualitative Data—The Language of the Heart

The most moving testimonials are those spoken by the frontline employees who have benefitted from your programs. When a front-line employee completes a substantial professional development program, it's a big deal! Celebrate their achievement with a memorable recognition or graduation ceremony where they can share their success with peers, family, and health system leadership.

An important part of being an advocate is exposing all stakeholders to what the employee has accomplished, so make the most of your group's recognition ceremony. Schedule it well in advance at a time when key executives can attend. Ask your internal communications team to assist with video recordings and graduate interviews that you can publish in internal newsletters and other formats. You may even be able to get coverage from the local news, as East Alabama Medical Center has done.

There are other opportunities for one-on-one storytelling that humanize the impact of investing in frontline employees. While senior leaders are generally numbers people, you can have an emotional impact by sharing success stories and making them realize their role in enabling that transformation. Think about other platforms where your graduates can share their success, for example at quarterly mid-level and upper management meetings or at a coffee or lunch with C-suite executives.

Conclusion: Be an Advocate

This chapter outlines the lessons the Catalyst Learning team and I have learned over the last 15 years about how to make systemic change to increase entry-level healthcare workforce development. I hope you will find it of value. We need more people in this world who think about how to bridge the economic divide. Even more importantly, we need people who are motivated and will act with persistence and urgency to make things happen.

A key element of this work is communicating the needs of the often voiceless and sometimes invisible hardworking people to those in positions of power. They want to help, but are often busy, so you'll need to be able to quickly explain what you want them to do. Be ready to answer to that question.

This chapter referred to Imon Muldrow as a diamond in the rough. We know that there is hidden gold in every organization's often-overlooked frontline employee population. Find it. Unleash it. Watch them soar!

CHAPTER 14

LEADERSHIP DEVELOPMENT

SCOTT KASHMAN

On Friday, March 6, 2020, I was having dinner with my family. We were eating at a local restaurant. It was busy, the mood was positive, and there was laughter all around. Then I received an urgent text and took a follow-up call—our health system's first COVID-19 positive patient had just passed away and they had scheduled a leadership call within the hour. As I went back to the table and looked around the restaurant and at my family, I was hit with a surge of emotion knowing this was just the beginning. The next day, our health system opened an incident command center. A month later, 90 percent of the US population, and many countries around the world, would be sheltering at home.

Once the pandemic hit, the US and the world would see millions of cases and rising deaths. Yet less than a year before, COVID-19 was not even on our radar for a potential global impact. The pandemic served as a great leadership lesson—it was a catalyst, shedding light on any gaps in our emergency preparedness plans, supply chain, labor management, health system and community relations, and true value-based care.

On top of this, political unrest was starting to further divide the country and world. Unemployment rates spiked to 14.7 percent from less than 5 percent. On May 25, 2020, George Floyd, a Black American man, was arrested after allegedly using a counterfeit $20 bill that was later found to be real. During the arrest, Derek Chauvin, a white police officer, knelt on Floyd's neck for nearly 8 minutes. Floyd later died from this incident. This sparked protests against police violence toward Black people and a rise in the Black Lives Matter movement.

As a nation, debate began over whether communities should wear masks to stop the spread of the virus. Then came conversation on how we could safely open schools. Then debates over the initial Center for Disease Control (CDC) guidelines compared to what they finally recommended.

These issues go much deeper than the immediate lessons from the pandemic. As a world, nation, and community, we need to take a deep look at how public health and social justice plays into our leadership development and actions. These issues have created an incredible opportunity for us to rise up as leaders and showcase how we would move forward. The leadership development lessons from the past are valuable. We need to build on this foundation and understand how to go deeper and get to the root cause of creating change and strengthening current and future leaders. We need leaders who know what they stand for and are willing to make bold moves, take a stance, engage key stakeholders, and bring people together to solve problems. If we cannot solve even small problems together, we will never be able to fix global issues that are already in play. We need interconnected leadership. We need to make big and complex issues smaller, and then navigate toward solutions.

Leadership Development in Healthcare

While the story of 2020 reflects a point in history, it also echoes similar times throughout history where leadership had to bring people together. It mattered before COVID-19 and it will always matter going forward because we are in a constant state of evolution.

Cultivating the power of diversity, equity, inclusivity, and global practices will fuel individual potential and, in turn, solve meaningful organizational problems. Leadership development is critical for synchronizing and reinforcing preparedness. It's about helping individuals thrive so they can help the organization reach its full strategic objectives and long-term sustainability. According to a January 2020 article in the *Harvard Business Review*, one often-overlooked skill to lead effectively is talent management (Chamorro-Premuzic and Kirschner 2020).

So many organizations invest in organization development without clear expected outcomes in leadership development. The article goes on to state that great managers are also talent agents. Organizations have many support positions to help leaders, including finance, legal, and information systems; human resources and organization development are typically support areas as well. It's time for talent development professionals to reimagine their role and how they can unleash talent within their organization while supplementing with external talent as needed.

Talent development professionals can guide the organization by understanding gaps in leadership development, root causes, and tailored tactics, which will help strengthen future leaders. And their ability to develop others starts with the same reflection on their own development needs.

This chapter will cover why traditional leadership development strategies need to transition toward understanding what drives individuals to better lead their organization. We will explore why leadership development fails, the role of TD professionals, and six recommended content areas.

The Challenges of Healthcare Leadership Development

When people do not connect with or understand an organization's "why" or purpose, they're not motivated by the "what and how." This is especially true in healthcare organizations. Healthcare is a unique environment in that those who work within the setting may be employed and paid by different entities. In addition, payment incentives are often not aligned to the most optimal, safest way to care for their patients. Thus, it's critical for everyone to want to work toward common goals. As the "why" becomes clear, people will understand "how and what" they provide to help the organization.

As a leader, you need to embrace diversity so all can show up empathetically and authentically, sharing different ideas and experiences. Healthcare is a highly regulated industry with many talented individuals and differing views; nurses, housekeepers, physicians, social workers, human resource and organization development leaders, administrators, advanced providers, pharmacists, radiology technologists, care coordinators, respiratory therapists, phlebotomists, attorneys, community board members, regulatory experts, supply chain, legislative liaisons—the list goes on. The workforce also includes employees who are full time, part time, on-call, travelers, temporary, and seasonal. Moving this entire workforce together toward a shared vision is a challenging undertaking. At the same time, it is collectively impactful when done well—it takes leadership, coordination, and staff willing to lean in to make it happen every minute of every day.

For example, healthcare systems may have independent and employed physicians practicing in the hospital together. How they align their respective views with system's goals must be reviewed and explored regularly. Being the best surgeon, specialist, or caregiver is a wonderful trait, but it does not necessarily make them a better leader. Longevity may offer incredible experiences and organizational history, but that is just one dimension that needs to be brought together with others.

Leaders need to provide a psychologically safe space where respectful tension can be experienced and used as a growth catalyst. They should strive to create a culture where people can thrive and know their leaders care about their well-being—an environment where they know they matter, can take care of themselves, and, in turn, can take better care of their colleagues, patients, and others. This is why it is also important to understand and integrate well-being strategies to deepen the impact of leadership development.

Traditional and Emerging Leadership Development Tactics

Leadership needs to facilitate a shared vision, provide clear priorities, and cascade that vision and those priorities to their team, ensuring every person knows what part they play. To understand the ways TD professionals can transform their approach to leadership development programs, let's explore some traditional and emerging leadership development focus areas that will strengthen an organization's culture and performance.

There are different ways to train leaders and design leadership development programs. The key is to provide both system and scalable development options, along with smaller group and individual plans. Many traditional leadership development efforts are probably already in place in your organization. Some of these approaches include:

- In-person and online training
- One-on-one coaching
- Annual retreats
- Shadowing leaders
- Feedback through 360-degree tools
- Attending conferences and sharing knowledge gained with colleagues upon return
- Training using social media and other digital platforms
- Orientation for new employees
- Re-orientation and recruitment of current employees
- Policy development with subject matter experts

However, traditional methods might not always be appropriate for what you need to develop in your leaders. Experiential learning opportunities are an effective way to test how people respond in real-world situations, such as through stretch assignments or projects. For example, at a healthcare organization I worked for, we gave a leader the opportunity to lead a major facility expansion project. She learned all aspects of the system strategy and operational priorities of this expansion, and ultimately moved into a new promotional opportunity. The experience allowed her to connect with others across the organization and show how they could solve broader system challenges together. She continued to develop others in the same way. As leaders, we must always train future leaders to ensure the long-term organizational sustainability. In turn, patients, families, and their communities are better served.

Developing a Culture of Evolving Leadership Development

I view leadership through the lens of health and well-being. My personal purpose is to cultivate insights to fuel potential and healthier lives, and I love saying "Training for Life!" To me, this represents a mindset of self-reflection and continuous improvement, as well as the need to build a culture of evolving leadership development.

I have found the 10 principles of personal leadership, introduced by Mark Sasscer, Founder of LeadQuest Consulting, to be helpful as I reinforce and guide my leadership efforts:

- **Be in the moment.** Stay present while connecting with others.
- **Be authentic and humanistic.** I would also add be vulnerable to this principle. Overall, you say what you mean, believe, and think. You are consistent in and out of meetings.
- **Volunteer discretionary effort constantly.** This happens when employees move from compliance to commitment. Once they do, people will put in the time as they become more engaged.
- **Model high performance.** Desired behaviors drive desired results. I would add that this comes from a leader's consistent role modeling.
- **Respect and leverage separate realties.** Each person sees life through a unique lens; in other words, every individual is living a separate reality. This could lead to blind spots based on your own experiences. Establish a common vision and values along with common operating systems—such as planning, goal setting, communications and performance management—that provide organizational focus and alignment.
- **Be curious rather than judgmental.** There is so much judgment and criticism these days without understanding other viewpoints. That's the reason for cultivating actual diversified views and inclusivity to drive change.

- **Look in the mirror first.** Be accountable and look at your own behaviors before pointing the finger and blaming others.
- **Have courageous conversations.** When gossip goes unchecked and conversations take place without the actual person you are concerned about, it leads to significant triangulation, lack of trust, and a toxic culture.
- **Provide timely, clear, and specific performance expectations and feedback.**
- **Teach, coach, and mentor**—spend at least half of your time developing others.

By incorporating these 10 leadership principles, the TD professional can reinforce a culture of leadership development.

To take this one step further, talent development professionals should focus on ways to enhance leadership development in five key development areas. I've shared stories within each section to bring to life ways we can support current and emerging leaders.

- **Take a stance.** Demonstrate leadership and personal responsibility.
- **Listen, lead, and deliver.** Cast an aspirational vision and develop a plan.
- **Learn.** Encourage leaders to shadow their teams.
- **Provide and solicit feedback.** Work through conflict or "respectful tension."
- **Enhance business acumen.** Apply current and emergent business aspects of healthcare.

Take a Stance

Now more than ever we need leaders to show the courage to take a stance and bring people together toward a shared vision. We need to foster flexibility and compromise while staying true to each other and ourselves. There is enough division in companies, across the nation, and around the globe. When was the last time leaders on "different sides of the aisle" role modeled and came together with a shared solution in your organization? Think about how much further we can go in strengthening leadership talent around improving gaps in equity.

Leaders could do this by getting involved with different community groups, especially those with differing views. The emerging and future workforce has been raised with technology and social media, and are much more comfortable embracing changes and accepting of the differences among groups, regardless of race, gender, ethnicity, age, or sexual identity. They want to hear what an organization stands for and how they will be part of that.

In addition, local coalitions and national health care organizations are sharing data and learning from one another. Healthcare organizations are typically strong pillars in their community and are able to serve as a community influencer. The Healthcare Anchor Network, a national organization bringing health systems together as "anchor organizations," is focused on creating equitable health outcomes for America's communities by tackling the underlying economic and racial disparities that drive them—the structural determinants of health. Leaders meet regularly with key stakeholder groups to share an open exchange of ideas, build trust, and collectively make changes as a community.

As leaders make sure you are well-versed in how you express your corporate social responsibility (CSR) to the organization, its stakeholders, and the public. This will help you navigate through ongoing change management and communication toward a stronger culture.

Key Takeaways

Leverage coaching sessions and 360-degree reviews to review actual situations and further develop your leaders.

Listen, Lead, and Deliver

A vision cannot be realized without a plan. This is a major gap in leadership at all levels. To create and disseminate a successful and aspirational vision, start by listening to key stakeholders. This helps others understand the vision so they can weigh in and share the opinions of their team about departmental priorities.

Consistent and succinct communication is key for leaders as they guide and inspire others to lead, manage, and influence their areas of responsibility. Years ago, I used to host an annual retreat with my leadership team. The standard retreat provides a time to reflect on annual performance and where we want to move into the future. It builds strong camaraderie by making sure everyone understands the annual objectives and how they align with the organization's multiyear strategic plan. About 10 years ago, a physician approached me and asked how we were going to engage more of our medical staff. I told him that we would have a retreat to share our vision, goals, and strategies. He said, "Kashman, we've retreated long enough. It's time to advance this organization." So, we renamed the event "the Advance," and have continued the tradition ever since. This also led to continued performance improvement. The first Advance set the foundation with the theme "Inspire Excellence: Inspiring Leaders, Inspired Team."

Once annual objectives are clear, leaders need to create a strategic framework and operating model to show how the mission and strategies cascade to operations at every level, from chief officers, vice presidents, directors, managers, and supervisors to staff. Keep goals and focus areas transparent through department huddle boards that show the system and department goals and focus areas. Develop a consistent standard review cadence. The key is to improve through cycles of learning based on your key goals (such as quality, safety, patient and provider satisfaction, financial performance, or keeping patients at home). Drive priorities using data to understand performance, gaps, and root causes. Staff need to take ownership for sustainable outcomes—a top-down approach or culture of fear will ultimately destroy any chance for the organization to achieve its potential.

Key Takeaways

Talent development professionals need to stay focused on their leaders' ability to cascade a vision and develop clear plans. You should help other leaders facilitate diversified views to provide a well-rounded approach to solving problems. Build this into your leadership selection process, coaching, and even re-recruitment and engagement strategies.

Learn

Leaders should help support and mentor their team in achieving the organization's strategic priorities through daily or weekly huddles and weekly protected time to round on units. This gives them a chance to see the great work their team is doing and identify areas that need more support. Shadowing is another way for leaders to learn, observe, and provide feedback. It's a process I have found extremely valuable for showing staff you care and for aligning strategies to operations at every organizational level.

Before you begin shadowing, ask yourself: "What goals and standard processes does your team set to improve the patient experience and departmental performance?" Then, as you shadow:

- Determine whether the team has clear standard processes to support the system's goals. If not, explore what your leadership team could do to facilitate the necessary development support.

- Evaluate what communication systems are in place for frontline staff and leaders to provide feedback. This should include what's working well and what processes could be improved.
- Solicit the team members' feedback, thank them for sharing, and let them know what action, if any, will be taken based on their feedback. More leaders need to proactively ask for feedback—and accept it graciously.

I once followed a new leader in the transport department. He started the day with a staff huddle, during which I observed how supportive he was of his team and how he well encouraged them. When I asked how he empowered his team to own the organization's strategic priorities, here's what he told me:

> His team's long-term goal has been to establish a culture that promotes a sense of comfort for the employee within their workplace and instills a sense of ownership. That culture is evidenced in staff-led huddles. For example, on a team member's first day, they participate in a huddle that shows the warmth and compassion of the entire transport team. Each member of the team introduces themselves and share a unique thing about themselves; new team members then reciprocate. This breaks the ice and relieves any anxiety about the new job. **Because his team is comfortable, they are more likely to take ownership of patient care by voicing concerns and proposing solutions to any issues that arise during transport and during other departmental huddles.**
>
> The safety of the patients and staff is their top concern. His team is transparent with one another during their daily safety huddles. For example, when they discussed how they could play a part in reducing infections, their thoughts were relayed back to the staff at daily huddles and then recapped as protocols for transporting patients with a higher risk for infections. **The process for the right patient care was already in place; the team just needed to be reminded of the right practice to ensure consistent high-quality patient care.**
>
> Their transport leaders complete rounds multiple times a day to get feedback from other departments and patients. They also monitor daily operations by checking in at frequent transport destinations. But they take rounds one step further by

incorporating "protected time" once a week, in which department heads meet to hold a more in-depth discussion. The leaders work together to evaluate interdepartmental goals and develop a progress report they can bring back to their daily transport huddles. **Because transport has developed a sense of ownership, team members are engaged and work to break down barriers to interdepartmental goals.**

Transport leadership recently rolled out a new model of empowering staff to self-assign runs. That tactic has reduced wait times for patients returning to their rooms from testing sites. In the past, requested transports were entered into a queue and then dispatched by a transport team member at his or her discretion. Self-assigning, on the other hand, allows the transporter to gauge the proximity and urgency of requested transports and immediately take the one with highest priority. This eliminates unneeded phone calls between the dispatcher and the transporter, allowing a transporter to respond more quickly. **This model has improved his team's cycle time and greatly improves its finances. In fact, the self-assign model has caught the interest of other campuses, whose leaders have asked to observe and potentially adopt it.**

I've experienced other shadowing experiences that showcase where leaders could focus their development efforts, for example:

- Shadowing the hospital's administrative house supervisors made me appreciate the challenges they were up against. While placing patients in a timely manner was a main function of their role, it seemed to involve 700 jigsaw pieces to pull it together. In addition, placing patients was just part of their role—they need to maintain a strong grasp of the entire hospital's operations while taking call after call. In one situation, the house supervisor pointed out an ICU supervisor, who was in the ED looking for clinically appropriate patients to bring to the ICU. You could tell the ED team enjoyed having him there, and it made it much easier to coordinate care from one level of the hospital to the next.
- While shadowing a couple of our physician advisers, I saw a multidisciplinary team discuss patients, understand the key clinical issues, and address care coordination with post-acute care facilities. They had great dialogue whenever challenges arose,

which really showed that one person could not make every decision. I saw that it truly takes the input of many to care for patients.

- In another experience, I went undercover. Well, not really—I put on scrubs and worked for one of our emergency techs in the ED. I was about to let him know he could be direct with me and feel comfortable to provide direction. However, that proved unnecessary—before I could open my mouth, he asked me to help him lift a patient and assist him to the bathroom. He paused, looked at me, and said, "and keep up with me!" He was a great teacher and stuck with me even as I fumbled my way through some things.

The best healthcare leadership development programs make job shadowing and learning from those experiences a top priority. Not only does this build interdepartmental awareness in leaders, but it also helps them see how the organization's strategic priorities affect every team and individual.

Key Takeaways

Observe other leaders with their staff—whether they are coaching, in huddles, in staff meetings, or shadowing staff. This will also help show TD leaders any potential gaps in leadership development. For example, the shadowing experience helps leaders look in the mirror and better understand how their role must include support to frontline staff. It also provides a way to solicit staff feedback to make processes better. In turn, our patients and families are the benefactors.

Provide and Solicit Feedback

Many leaders have trouble clarifying the problem your organization is trying to solve, which leads to another gap where feedback is not consistently solicited or provided. Think about how often you solicit, accept, or take action on feedback provided to you. Most leaders will say they love feedback, yet they rarely ask for it. And then if they get defensive when they do receive feedback, people will be less likely to provide more feedback in the future. This leads to a vicious cycle in which leaders and teams fail to provide and accept feedback while unintentionally creating a culture of fear and scarcity. This prevents people from seeing infinite potential and opportunities, which limits the organization's ability to move toward abundance, innovation, and evolution. Organizations thrive when they are open to ideas.

Years ago, I shadowed a clinical area to better understand their workflow. In this department, each therapist was expected to treat about eight patients each day. However, after shadowing them I noticed they were only getting to about 50 percent of the treatment orders. So, I asked the therapists for feedback because they know their workflows best. They noted that since their patient schedule kept shifting them from one end of the hospital to the next, it could often take as long as 10 minutes just to get from one patient to the next. And if a patient was unable to receive treatment when they arrived, the therapist usually did not have time to go back. Their recommendation was assigning a dedicated therapist to one or two units (which is now a more routine practice). It is much more effective to get to know patients when you are on dedicated units. Then, if a patient is unavailable, the therapist can return in a timely manner because they've remained in close proximity. Ultimately, making this change in the department led to 100 percent alignment between orders and treatment.

Here are some tips for providing and soliciting feedback:

- Listen and accept feedback from the people closest to the patient or the problem you are trying to solve.
- Promote data-driven decision making and continuous improvement. Make a commitment to the cycles of learning.
- Leverage the uniqueness of others who may not have had their voice heard otherwise. These people often have untapped insights and experiences.
- Leverage relationships that will lead to greater collaboration and partnerships.
- Acknowledge your appreciation for the feedback you've received and what, if anything, you plan on doing with it. This will foster trust and transparency.

Key Takeaways

Coach leaders in soliciting and accepting feedback. Doing this on a regular basis will bring out the authenticity of their team and build trust, collaboration, and better organizational performance. It is an effective way to move leaders from transactional to relation-based. Imagine how the organization could thrive if everyone provided feedback on improvement ideas.

Enhance Business Acumen

Healthcare has seen a continued rise in hybrid leadership with a collective understanding of clinical, regulatory, and business matters. This starts with having the end in mind and aligning the organization's vision with the strategic objectives and actual performance. Where does your organization want to be in three, five, or 10 years? While that may be too far out to know, it is important to understand key goals you want to accomplish beyond one year and then work backward from there. For example, in 10 years, your organization may want to cover more lives, show a measurable improvement in the chronic care health outcomes, and have a certain amount of money to ensure financial sustainability.

This takes business acumen, also known as business savvy or business sense. It reflects the keenness and quickness to understand and deal with a business situation, including any risks and opportunities. It has emerged as a vehicle for improving financial performance and leadership development. (See the chapter on business acumen for additional details.)

Key Takeaways

Business acumen is a top priority in healthcare that is specific to leadership development. Combining business acumen and healthcare expertise, TD experts should facilitate leadership development opportunities for leaders to navigate the complexities within health systems while also collaborating across functional areas. Knowing how to present "sources of truth" data to help align others is also key. Review the data so that you can understand and know how to take action.

Charge Nurse Leader Development Program

The following case study focuses on a health system's charge nurse leader development program, which was developed in collaboration with nurse leaders and organizational and talent development professionals. The case study includes examples of the criteria and course outline developed by the team; see Figure 14-1 for a sample.

Figure 14-1. Sample Leadership Curriculum

Week 1: Leading Others

- Mindful Leadership
- Emotional Intelligence
- Mood Elevator
- Mindful Breathing
- Leading From the Middle

Week 2: Communication

- Sender Receiver Communication Model
- Nonverbal Behaviors
- Communication Styles (Assertive, Aggressive, Passive, Passive Aggressive)
- Active Listening
- Frame Messages Using SBAR and CUS (or Escalating Concern)

Week 3: Patient Experience

- Patient Experience and 8 Specific Areas to Make a Difference
- Rounding
- Acknowledging With Empathy and the Four Steps of Empathy

Week 4: Collaboration

- Multifunctional Teamwork to Healthcare Collaboration
- Team Development Stages
- Negotiation Steps and Techniques

Week 5: Decision Making

- Decision Making, Problem Solving, and Creativity—a Critical Thinking Model
- Four-Step Decision-Making Process
- Moral Decision-Making Model

Week 6: Conflict Management

- Types of Conflict, Including Conflicts in Nursing
- Conflict Resolution Styles
- Coaching to Resolve Conflict

Week 7: Change Management

- Charge Nurses as Change Agents
- Recap and Wrap Up
- What Now?
- Knowledge, Application, and Reflection
- Opportunities to Grow
- Career Plan

Graduation

The charge nurse leader development program was an intensive seven-week course comprising seven 3.5-hour long modules.

A charge nurse is a nurse who has been given the responsibility of running the nursing unit during their shift. They are required to ensure that everything runs as it's supposed to under their watch. However, that "everything" can represent many different things because their role, duties, and responsibilities will differ depending on the unit they are working in. There are also inconsistencies in selecting, onboarding, training, and deploying charge nurses.

Some typical charge nurse responsibilities include determining staffing needs, facilitating patient assignments, coordinating a patient's plan of care with direct care nurses and other healthcare providers, handling patient complaints, mediating conflicts between patients and unit staff, coaching unit staff, and intervening with physicians.

The Current State

Charge nurses are typically appointed to the role based on availability, volunteering, or interest. The nursing director may notice a nurse's leadership qualities and provide assignment as a learning opportunity to take on additional responsibilities. However, this form of appointment may not accurately assess the individual's desire, ability, characteristics, or attitude to perform effectively in the role. Furthermore, mandating a nurse to take on the responsibility of a charge nurse during a shift can set a negative tone on the unit and have risky implications in patient safety and experience.

Charge nurses are usually trained and developed in an informal setting. Some shadow other charge nurses or supervisors; others are given a "charge nurse binder," which contains unit-specific policies and procedures, and are then trained to use the binder effectively. Most charge nurses are not clear on what their responsibilities are until they have stepped into the role and are learning on the job. Few health units maintain a checklist of duties that charge nurses are expected to complete during their shift.

Once selected and trained, charge nurses take on an informal leadership role. While these responsibilities are significantly different from those of a regular RN, the hour pay differential is only $1 more per hour, which does little to incentivize or recognize their significance. Although they are frequently supported by house supervisors or department supervisors, charge nurses receive little, if any, formal evaluation on their performance.

To build toward the future desired state, we used the PDCA (Plan-Do-Check-Act) model.

Plan (January–June 2018)

The clinical learning department, in collaboration with leadership and the OD department, initiated a thorough needs assessment to understand the current state of the health system's charge nurses. The needs assessment revealed a dire need to empower and support staff assigned the charge nurse role.

With the leadership support from the chief patient care officer and vice president of operations and the chief nurse executive from one of the system hospitals, we formed a steering committee that included representatives from each hospital in the system. The steering committee agreed to meet 10 times in a span of six months, with the goal of:

- Validating the current state of charge nurses
- Creating a charge nurse program that would provide a realistic description of the charge nurse's role and responsibilities
- Providing recommendations on the selection, orientation, and development of charge nurses
- Being a subject matter expert to provide case studies and scenarios for building a charge nurse development program
- Providing feedback and validating new processes that are piloted by the nursing units

The steering committee assembled a comprehensive job profile for the charge nurse leader role. A competency analysis tool was used to understand the essential skills and competencies required to be successful in the role. Selection and orientation criteria were then recommended.

Do (June 2018–March 2019)

The steering committee, with support from nursing leadership at all the acute care facilities, decided to pilot the whole process in one unit at every acute care facility.

The pilot units agreed to follow a standard process of posting an application for the charge nurse leader, practicing behavioral interviewing techniques with all candidates, and selecting enough charge nurses for day and night shifts. All charge nurses were then required to attend a charge nurse leader development program. The pilot units were only allowed to deploy charge nurses who were chosen and developed through this process. And each charge nurse was required to fulfill the roll at least once a week.

Check (March–June 2019)

We evaluated the program on four levels:

- Level 1: participants' initial reactions
- Level 2: a pre- and post-test to measure knowledge transfer

- Level 3: pre- and post-program self-assessments of participant leadership skills; pre- and post-program staff perceptions of charge nurse performance; and post-program interviews with nursing directors regarding charge nurse performance
- Level 4: pre- and post-program Hospital Consumer Assessment of Healthcare Providers and Systems (HCAPHS) patient satisfaction scores for three nurse-sensitive questions.

Participants' initial reaction surveys are overwhelmingly positive, with 96 percent saying they could apply the information to clinical practice. We also saw an improvement in knowledge from the pre-test (57.9 percent) to the end of the program post-test (75.9 percent). Charge nurse self-assessments improved from pre-assessment to post-assessment on all 20 questions. Director interviews were also very affirmative, with reports of positive behavioral changes and improved decision making by charge nurses who had attended the program. Staff post-assessments were gathered in March 2019, and patient experience scores were gathered in June 2019.

Act (June–September 2019)

Phase 2 of the charge nurse leader program was launched in April 2019. Four units at each acute care hospital were chosen by their respective VPs to go through the prescribed process of selection. They nominated 10 nurses per unit in this role. All the selected charge nurses attended the orientation e-learning module and shadowed the required number of hours. Once selected and oriented, these charge nurses were required to attend the charge nurse leader development program.

Phase 2 of the charge nurse leader development program took place from June to September 2019, and about 200 charge nurses participated. Seven different workshop cohort-groups—each with between 25 and 35 participants—went through the seven-week training program. Once they'd completed the program, charge nurses were rewarded a certification of completion and a lab coat with their name and credentials.

By the end of phase 2, we had established a critical mass of charge nurses who had gone through the process. We would launch a few more cohorts the following year to assign charge nurses in the rest of the units at the acute care facilities. Figure 14-2 shows the data behind expanding the program to the acute care facilities, while Figure 14-3 shows how the program can achieve sustainability over five years.

Figure 14-2. Charge Nurse Leader Development Program Phase II (Fiscal Year 2018–2019)

Project Description

- 4 units per acute care hospital, each nominating 10 charge nurses per unit, equals 200 charge nurses
- 200 charge nurses complete the seven-week training program, which totals to approximately 4,900 hours
- Average pay for a charge nurse is $32 per hour

Budget Requisition

Charge nurse pay: 4,900 hours x $32/hour	$156,800
Training program logistics (venue, marketing, enrollment, program management, transportation, printing material, and food)	$15,000
Charge nurse leader graduation lab coats ($37.95 x 200) and certificates ($3 x 200)	$8,190
Total cost for the fiscal year (Oct 2018–Sept 2019)	**$179, 990**

Figure 14-3. Charge Nurse Leader Development Program Sustainability (5 Year Plan: 2019–2024)

Project Description

- Conduct 4 training programs per year accommodating 30 charge nurses per cohort group equals 120 Charge Nurses
- 120 charge nurses complete seven-week training program, which totals to approximately 2,940 hours
- Average pay for a charge nurse is $32 per hour

Budget Requisition

Charge nurse pay: 2,940 hours x $32/hr	$94,080
Training program logistics (venue, marketing, enrollment, program management, transportation, printing material, and food)	$10,000
Charge nurse leader graduation ceremony lab coats ($37.95 x 120) and certificates ($3 x 120)	$4,914
Total cost per fiscal year	**$108,994**

Opportunity for Collaboration

Charge nurse leaders have a unique opportunity to advocate, enable, and mediate health and wellness with the community. They can advocate on behalf of their patients and the community at large by supporting causes the health system promotes. By providing the right set of circumstances, charge nurse leaders can empower patients and the community to take proactive approaches to their health and well-being. Finally, to promote health for all citizens, charge nurse leaders can act as a mediator between healthcare providers, governments, businesses, and the media.

A charge nurse leader is usually the first and last person a patient interacts with. This allows them to assess the patient's experience and receive valuable feedback on the organization's performance. And charge nurses can then use that information to raise awareness on funding options. TD professionals could create a process and communication guide to assist charge nurses in supporting this mission.

The clinical learning department and the leadership and organization development department maintained a separate cost center for the program. In addition, it is critical that human resources be involved. Unfortunately, despite early indications of success, this program was put on hold due to the COVID-19 pandemic and has planned to re-convene as the pandemic subsided.

Conclusion

Healthcare organizations focused on leadership development and staff well-being provide an environment where collaboration, vulnerability, and authenticity are foundational. Bringing along and developing leaders who excel in systematizing and communicating business resolve needs to take priority over tenure and clinical capability. This means putting aside self-serving individual needs and ego for the greater good of the patient and the organization's mission.

As technology evolves, change will occur at a more rapid rate. This can lead to burnout and exhaustion but also resiliency and employee engagement. It's important to note that we need to consistently develop ourselves, other leaders, and staff to help each other thrive. The influence of authentic leadership and the importance of positive psychology will make a deeper difference in leading our organizations into the future. We need the right talent and relationships in place in to make this difference. Talent development leaders have the ability to facilitate and coach leaders on the five key development areas within this chapter.

PART 4

BUSINESS ACUMEN FOR THE HEALTH SYSTEM

CHAPTER 15

BUSINESS ACUMEN AND WELL-BEING

SCOTT KASHMAN

Healthcare organizations remain committed to the Centers for Medicare and Medicaid Services's triple aim framework for value-based programs: better care for individuals, better health for populations, and lower cost. In more recent years, there has been an added focus on a fourth aim, which introduces the clinician's experience and a focus on their well-being. This means reviewing what work conditions and support systems need to be in place to help staff thrive at work. This, in turn, will allow staff to take better care of their patients and one another. Creating high-performing teams and highly reliable and consistent outcomes requires business acumen, a strong workplace structure, and a foundation emphasizing staff well-being. This leads to the cultivation of business opportunities.

Improved Well-Being, Greater Business Results

Consider the effect that making well-being a priority can have on an individual level. A well-respected surgeon I know told me that once he stopped "squeezing every dollar out of a transaction" and remembered his calling into medicine he started loving the work again. This has allowed him to take a more well-rounded, holistic approach to caring for his patients, including spending the necessary time during appointments. He now gets to know his patients and their families on a deeper level and is even broadening his own skills in how he treats them. While he acknowledged he makes about 10 percent less than his counterparts, he is still "energized at the end of the day." As for his colleagues, he said that while they may have a little more money, he still makes a good living. He believes he will want to work longer because of the joy he has in his work. Healthy teams foster healthy businesses!

And yet, too many organizations focus on determining the return on investment for wellness. Instead, they should be asking how we can focus on workplace well-being to create an environment in which our leaders and employees thrive and become high performing teams, delivering on all business and clinical outcomes. It's not an either/or issue. Leaders and teams need to deliver top performance. Forward-thinking organizations should proactively work with their leaders and staff to create a work environment that values long-term, sustainable results instead of quick, unsustainable outcomes.

Now more than ever, after realizing the long-lasting effects of the COVID-19 pandemic, organizations have to redefine how to build back the health of their teams. While new built-in efficiencies have emerged, including constant video meetings, there are downsides. For example, the sense of belonging we felt at the start of the pandemic began to dwindle as fatigue set in. Many employees began to feel a lack of belonging and high levels of loneliness. This, in turn, can lead to mental health struggles and substance abuse. Organizations can use this as an opportunity to reimagine how to reengage and inspire their teams in the post-COVID era. Talent development professionals should work in collaboration with leaders and staff to understand what environmental enhancements would address well-being and achieve the organization's long- and short-term goals.

Having strong business acumen includes understanding the organization's strategic and operational priorities and asking the right questions to trigger insights and potential. These insights bring us to an individual's purpose. Most healthcare professionals went into the field to make a difference and help others. Therefore, healthcare business operations should be deeply rooted in empathy to connect their mission with the hearts and mind of staff. This emphasis on staff well-being should also extend to patients and the community. Unfortunately, healthcare has essentially transformed into a large business, becoming transactional instead of relational. We must ensure our business models serve our patients and their clinical needs, support our providers, and move toward prevention and healthier communities.

I was a mental health counselor at a private psychiatric hospital in Oakland, California, in 1990. On my way into work, I would pass very impoverished neighborhoods and see people who struggled getting access to good food, transportation, and attainable housing. There were also racial tensions and stress, which led to mental and behavioral health issues. One day when

I walked into work I noticed that the receptionist had moved from the hospital entrance and into a storage closet. The closet had been converted to an office and the sign on the door read "managed care office." When I asked why she moved into the storage closet she pointed to the sign and said it was her new office and job. She told me that one of my patients was almost out of insurance and would need to leave the hospital within the week. I said he was still working with his physician to better manage his medications so we could connect on the deeper issues that had led to his hospitalization. He would need to stay at least another two to three weeks. Her response was that we'd need to pursue more aggressive treatments because the patient was out of insurance, unless we got the patient judge to review the case and determine clinically that he needed to stay longer. Ultimately, we got a judgement hearing to extend my patient's stay based on treatment needs. Would kicking my patient out of the hospital prematurely have improved his mental well-being? Surely not. But that's the logic with which healthcare institutions have operated for many years.

Whether it's 1990 or 2021, healthcare organizations and communities face similar medical, physical, mental, and social health issues. Population health and healthcare reform are all versions of "managed care" and there's a movement toward focusing on who and how we would pay for healthcare. Yet, with reimbursements declining for the past 30 years, we cannot change overnight, and we cannot do it alone. We need to prioritize our efforts, collaborate with others, and make a collective change toward broader community health.

Key Takeaways

This is an exciting time when we could rally around new collaborative models and transform health for the next 25 years. Talent development professionals are in a great position to rethink how they do their work and move the industry toward greater health, which ultimately has a positive influence on healthcare costs. A reimagined mindset will help move other leaders toward stronger business acumen while continuing to make a meaningful impact on why they went into healthcare.

Think about new workplace models. How can you develop staff who are working more at home or are more comfortable with video meetings? Cultivate the potential for sharing ideas and development globally. Build learning opportunities using global best practices. Then bring in thought leaders from around the globe to share and discuss best practices. You can do the same thing with clinicians from around globe, allowing them to collaborate and learn from one another.

Why Healthcare Organizations Need Business Acumen

Healthcare providers work tirelessly to improve care every day. And yet our focus on population health, volume to value, and how to reduce costs with better clinical outcomes does not necessarily lead to greater health. In 2020, the top leading causes of death included heart disease, cancer, and complications due to the COVID-19 virus. Health systems still struggle to coordinate care at scale throughout the care continuum. Even more troubling is that 70 to 80 percent of healthcare-related issues are preventable, yet payment models are not providing enough focus on actually keeping people healthy.

We need payment models and community health strategies that are aligned to health creation. This also means a more coordinated approach to address the social determinants of health (SDoH) in communities—not only through health systems but beyond to include public-private partnerships and changes in policies. The issues run deep and have been created over decades, and we need to build skills and competencies to address them. Strong business acumen includes knowing when you have to change the future health model, and that will include a focused and collaborative effort between health systems and key community stakeholders.

So how can your health system get started on this, without feeling like you're trying to boil the ocean? Look internally for support. The business case for coordinating care and focusing on keeping people healthy and outside of the hospital should be clear. Excess days in a hospital stay can cost between $500 and $1,000 per day over the expected stay. We had more than 120,000 excess days in another health system I worked for. This presented a $30 to $60 million opportunity. That is a significant business issue, and we need leaders who have the capabilities to lead with new and more forward-thinking ways. One solution for this particular problem is partnering with community organizations to transition patients safely out of the hospital. When incorporating the extra $500 to $1,000 per day beyond what the system gets paid, there is plenty of opportunity to partner. Health systems do not have to solve this issue alone.

Healthcare organizations would benefit from enhancing the business acumen of their staff and leaders, while also ensuring they're meeting the well-being needs of patients and staff. The rest of this chapter details the top five business acumen topics for healthcare organizations and approaches for talent development professionals:

- Understand your business.
- Provide clarity of vision and get leadership and staff engagement.

- Create scalable business models.
- Cascade strategic priorities through an operating model.
- Develop high-performing, healthy teams.

Understand Your Business

Healthcare is a major business. Talent development professionals should partner with leaders and design workshops that help everyone get a core understanding of the business. Key financial aspects include:

- **Revenue.** How do you make money in your organization? In healthcare, there are so many contracts with varying rates that the revenue has to be shown as gross revenue (what the organization billed) and net revenue (what the organization actually collected).
- **Costs.** What are the expenses to support your business? The most common and highest costs in healthcare are:
    - ***Labor costs.*** It is important to understand the type of employee needed to do the work and to ensure they work at the top of their license (that is they have the highest and best use of their degree and experience). Leaders should also learn to manage to productivity standards based on national benchmarks and understand the actual net revenue per employee or full-time equivalent (FTE). This is a benchmark used by top corporations to ensure they optimize revenue per employee as a reflection of effectiveness and efficiency.
    - ***Supply costs.*** These can be broken out by general office supplies, medical surgical, pharmaceutical, and laboratory supplies.
    - ***Purchased services.*** These can include services you purchase, such as a consulting company or services you outsource. It is important to understand how they are helping your organization advance its strategy without turning over the strategy to others. Organizational leaders should own the strategy so they can continue to provide vision and direction.
    - ***Corporate and overhead costs.*** Make sure you understand the supporting costs that keep your organization running. These expenses are not directly interacting with or supporting the consumer. They may be considered

back-office functions, such as finance, information systems, or legal. It also could be considered human resources or organization development. Talent development professionals should understand and be able to measure the added value they are providing organizations.

   - ***Depreciation.*** This reflects the costs of capital items, including new buildings and equipment, that depreciate. For example, equipment depreciates over the span of three to seven years, while buildings depreciate over 25 to 30 years. This needs to be accounted for in the financial statements.

- **Operating margin.** This reflects the profit the organization makes after subtracting all expenses from net revenue. Healthy systems should reinvest around 4 to 7 percent in their organization and communities, although this may vary depending on the type of healthcare organization and whether they are for-profit or nonprofit. Even a nonprofit still needs to make a margin to support their mission, hence the saying, "no margin, no mission and no mission, no margin."

How can talent development professionals help staff understand how the organization's business runs? In the past, I've worked with the finance department to put on budgeting basics classes for newer leaders. There is no doubt that most organizational leaders would be willing to provide this information in a lunch & learn or provide online video training. In fact, talent development could also benefit from these sessions to better serve the rest of the organization.

When it comes to educating their own department, talent development professionals should explore the Healthcare Management Financial Association website, which serves as a good resource to better understand healthcare financials. As TD professionals want to better serve their organization, it is important that they also continue their education.

Encourage the talent development team to meet with the department leader. This will give you the opportunity to understand how your department manages its financials, as well. Some of the measurable financial data points for your own department include:

- **Productivity.** What's the workload for the department and how is it determined in terms of necessary staffing? How does the department decide how many TD professionals are needed? Is it based on hours of work? Cost as a percentage of the company's net revenue?
- **Expenses.** What are the department's total salary costs? What are the supply costs to run the department? Are there any other costs associated with running the department?

- **Revenue.** Does the department bring in any revenue? If so, how? For example, does it provide continuing education to other organizations? I once worked for an organization with a nationally known continuing education arm that trained hundreds of professionals every year. This alone more than offset the costs of their department.

In addition, talent development professionals need to ask how their work correlates with improved revenue in the departments they are assisting. How is that being measured? One example is to track the performance of another department before and after assisting them. Agree to the expected outcomes and where the talent development professional will provide support. Then, show the results through visual management. I recommend visual management boards or huddle boards, which are used to post key organization and department performance metrics and important messages. Each day or week, the department should gather around the huddle board and review their priorities, performance metrics, and any follow-up. It is a great opportunity to collaborate with their TD colleagues, share best practices, and go back to the departments they supported to help close any lingering performance gaps.

Provide Clarity of Vision and Get Leadership and Staff Engagement

Simply put, are your leaders clear on the direction they are taking the organization? They need to bring others together and let them weigh in so the organization can move toward a shared aspirational vision and rallying point. Everyone in the organization wants to know how they fit into the vision. So, keep it simple.

Start by setting the foundational principles. For example:

- Grounded in empathy
- Know what matters
- Know your business and key metrics

Get buy-in from leaders to determine the strategic priorities, as well as the stakeholders and partners who will help you achieve this vision. I've worked with key leaders to get their buy-in around creating a healthier community, which I discussed in *Mindful Healthcare: Healthy Team, Healthy Business,* a book I co-wrote with Joan Odorizzi in 2017.

The goal was to transform the hospital campus to the center for health, wellness, and well-being, which would serve as a reflection of a healthy community. The campus was to be dedicated to the employees, physicians, and volunteers who tirelessly took care of their patients every day. It was also open to the community. The vision was to create a pathway to discovery, which was a 1.6-mile trail consisting of the pathway around an on-campus pond and a walkway around the campus.

The organization wanted to show its commitment to taking care of the health and well-being of its team so, in turn, they would take better care of themselves, their colleagues, patients, families, and community. This included a firm dedication to their business priorities including:

- Quality, safety, and regulatory compliance
- Coordinated care
- Patient experience
- Staff engagement
- Financial sustainability

So how does this tie into business acumen? The revitalized campus became a rallying point, unifying the leadership team. They then shared the plan with their staff until everyone understood our direction without losing sight of why we were all there: to take care of the health of our patients. Ultimately, the hospital saw improvements, including their strongest financial performance in years, and achieved an "A" grade in Leapfrog Safety Scores (a great improvement from their previous "D" grade). The hospital also saw improvements in staff engagement and patient experience, and went from only having a few donors to receiving hundreds of thousands of dollars in support because the community wanted to be a part of it.

Create Scalable Business Models

Helping healthcare leaders and staff can get overwhelming very fast for TD professionals. There are often so many different areas where you could focus your attention. Map out some major challenges and look to areas where you can make a short- and long-term impact. As I shared earlier in the chapter, many of today's issues are not new; they could be the result of years of neglect and build-up. We need business models to support that we can innovate around.

Take the example of malnutrition among patients. In a hospital I worked with, an employee who was also a registered dietician brought forward an idea for addressing patient malnutrition and moving us toward our vision of being a center for health, wellness, and well-being. She had started to screen her patients for malnutrition and found that one out of every three were malnourished. Preventable chronic diseases make up a significant part of our healthcare costs, and access to healthier food and better nutrition plays a major role in alleviating or avoiding those diseases. The effects of malnutrition also result in higher complexity of care and co-morbidities. Insurance also paid more to cover the additional complexity in costs. She wanted to reflect her findings in the patient's chart, which was not common practice at the time.

Based on her feedback, we started a small program and then used the additional net revenue to scale up and spread the program across another 300-bed hospital in our system that was also seeing same one out of three patients with malnutrition. This time we decided to study patients who were screened and then given nutrition education, along with 30 days home delivery of healthier meals, against those who did not receive the meals. We found that the group who received meal delivery saw a 39 percent readmission reduction compared with second group. The cost savings and net revenue more than covered the 30 days of meal delivery. Next, we scaled the program to all four hospitals in the system and ultimately started integrating it with our insurance plans. This malnutrition work kept people healthier at home and was ultimately provided as part of our Medicare and Medicaid product offerings.

What made this work? We tied the idea into the hospital system's broader vision and strategic priorities. Start small, get some wins, and then scale the idea, keeping the team excited while still making sure it is financially sustainable. Without the passion and vision of that original employee, and the sustainable outcomes, the program would not have been a success. Business acumen must connect to purpose and include the secret ingredients—blending empathy and passion with sustainable business models.

Cascade Strategic Priorities Through an Operating Model

Cascading a vision and strategy into operations at every level means everyone understands their part to play and how they connect their work to the organization's strategies. Every health system will have quality, safety, and patient satisfaction as a goal. Using an operating model simply means that you have a defined way to get work done in your area. Are there agreed upon protocols? How do you ensure they are followed? How do you assess and measure their success? When there are gaps compared to the expected outcome, how does the team develop a plan to improve? Overall, your team develops a continuous improvement model to support the department's and organization's operational and strategic priorities. Everyone can positively contribute under this model.

Talk with leaders and staff to see if they know their part to play, how priorities and goals are visible to the team, and how they know they are successful in their efforts. An effective tool includes tiered team huddles and huddle boards. Tiered huddles cascade information from the top of the organization to every department. They are brief, address high priority issues, and provide an opportunity to escalate issues from the department to senior leadership in a more structured way. Huddle boards serve as a communication vehicle to review organizational and departmental performance so staff can see how their work aligns within the department and the system. Talent development professionals should ensure their own department can showcase the same so they can share what they've learned too.

Rarely are organizations short on ideas. Work with your leaders on how they systematize strategies and cascade those into operations. This is often a major gap with healthcare leaders, so the key is coaching them to take their aspirational visions and strategies and develop cascading plans at every level.

Some core elements of the operating model include:

- Provide an aspirational vision and why this is important: Align to purpose.
- Reinforce your organization's mission, vision, values, principles: What do you really stand for?
- Share the expected performance outcomes and connect to the purpose.
- Determine strategies to positively influence the outcomes.
- Implement operating plans with key roles, responsibilities, timelines, and root cause assessment plans (for example, the five why model).
- Determine what communication plans are in place at every level. They should include outcomes and what matters to staff and the organization.
- Review and incorporate changes. Following a simple PDCA improvement model (plan-do-check-act) is very helpful for creating cycles of learning and change.

Key Takeaways

Retrain healthcare workers and leaders for the future. As healthcare evolves, talent development professionals play an instrumental role. They need to work with the senior leadership teams to understand the new roles. In addition, they should provide feedback in terms of where they're starting to see gaps. Put in place talent development and talent mobility plans so you can proactively move people around the organization.

Develop High Performing, Healthy Teams

According to the American Institute of Stress, *job stress is the top source of stress for American adults* and this has escalated over the past few decades. According to the *Harvard Gazette,* Workplace and Health survey data showed that 36 percent of workers suffer from work-related stress, which then costs US businesses $30 billion a year in lost workdays. In addition, a 2019 survey by the National Academy of Medicine found that nearly half of doctors and nurses in the US suffer from extreme burnout. That leads to emotional exhaustion, cynicism, loss of enthusiasm and joy in their work, and increased detachment from their patients and their patients' ailments. Worse, this burnout rate is linked to higher rates of depression, substance abuse, and suicide. Of course, this then affects the overall business of delivering quality healthcare, keeping people well, and taking care of patients when they are sick. Unsurprisingly, the COVID-19 pandemic has escalated the need to focus on workplace well-being and how to better serve the overall mental and behavioral health needs of our colleagues, patients, and community.

A culture of health and well-being needs to be foundational to everything you do in your organization. It is not a wellness program. In fact, that mentality is why many wellness programs fail—they focus on the program's return on investment rather than the deeper purpose that it drives for staff. If you want to immediately cut healthcare costs, focus on benefit design and high screenings for high-risk populations. If you want to engage your workforce in a meaningful way, show them how they matter. You can do this by focusing on the different dimensions of well-being, such as emotional, intellectual, physical, social, spiritual, and environmental.

For example, I once co-led a pilot well-being program with a self-insured health plan. Approximately 100 participants ultimately went through this voluntary program, which measured health improvement over 12 months in key health outcomes based on a blood test and physician screening (for example, cholesterol, A1C, and blood pressure). The pilot program included coaching, membership to a fitness center, and nutritious meals. We also measured the change in overall participant healthcare costs. In the program's first year, 65 percent of the participants improved their health outcomes. In addition, even including all associated program costs (such as meals, testing, fitness membership), the overall return on investment (ROI) was 2:1. (While only focusing on a financial ROI is not advised, leadership will likely want to know what it is to determine if they're going to continue funding the program.)

The key to a successful well-being program is to support staff in their journey to achieve improved health outcomes—healthier employees will lead to lower healthcare costs and a more engaged workforce. It takes courageous leadership to focus on being a role-model organization. While many leaders say they want a healthier workforce and community, it takes a very intentional effort to create the workspace and environment that can achieve this. These efforts will contribute to a true health transformation leading to healthier communities and measurable population health outcomes (including lower cost of care and better access and equitable outcomes across all populations).

Fostering and coaching leadership to support a healthy workplace will evolve the organization toward a culture of health and well-being. A majority of leaders struggle to role model how they take care of their own well-being. However, doing so is critical and leads to:

- Reduced stress
- Ability to address work problems more effectively
- Strengthened creativity and imagination
- Putting leaders in touch with their subconscious
- Preventing the build-up of negative emotions
- Helping leaders make more integrative decisions
- Improved overall physical, mental, and emotional health

At a different health system, we focused on six wellness areas, created by Christin Collins, who headed the system's health and wellness division. The "wellness wheel" included: purpose or your "why," nutrition, physical activity, sleep, stress management, and mental and behavioral health. Talent development professionals should work with leaders on ways they develop plans around and implement these strategies.

Some practical applications toward promoting intuition and a culture of health and well-being include:

- Start a speaker series to address each of the six areas of health and well-being. Or focus them on the areas most important to your organization and staff.
- Provide cooking contests, healthier meal choices, and discounts so employees can save money and get healthier (including lower A1C levels which affect diabetes), lower cholesterol, and attain a healthier weight. Just as importantly, if not more so, they will feel more engaged and mentally present in the workplace. At a previous health system, after going through one of our nutrition and lifestyle classes, an employee shared with me, "I never really knew how unhealthy I was until I felt the energy I now have today."

- Start a "food is medicine" group with clinicians to discuss how they integrate nutrition into their medical and clinical practice.
- Support or lead community-wide collaborations for greater regional health. For example, one health system I worked at focused on lifestyle management and mental and behavioral health. We offered the LIFT Project, which focused on combining lifestyle medicine and positive psychology to improve mental health and emotional well-being.
- Provide mindfulness and meditation classes, tips, and resources.

The COVID-19 pandemic heightened the need to provide additional support to leaders and providers, specifically in dealing with trauma, grief, self-care, and potential post-traumatic stress disorder (PTSD). Leaders need to further develop their understanding of how they can support a culture of health and well-being, including a well-rounded focus on their own care needs, sleep, mindfulness, and the importance of laughter and humor. The reality is that leaders need to focus on developing their intuition, with a focus on health and well-being, to help their team and organization reach its full potential.

Conclusion

Healthcare costs continue to rise and, most of the time, health system employees' healthcare is no better than that of the general population. We need healthcare systems to become role models for creating health in the community. Talent development professionals should embrace the fact that healthcare systems are typically major employers in their communities and serve as strong drivers of economic growth and development. By helping leaders and staff achieve their full potential, so too will the organization. This, in turn, could provide more jobs within the health system and around the community. Start by supporting the need to understand how business acumen is grounded in well-being.

Do your part to ensure leaders are personally role modeling better health and well-being. As a leader in healthcare, look for ways to develop leadership intuition. Promote and encourage greater health and well-being for your staff and yourself. Start by creating space and having discussions with your team on ways to improve the workplace to facilitate greater well-being. When you and your team take better care of yourself, you will be in a better position to support your colleagues, patients, and the communities you serve.

CHAPTER 16

PERFORMANCE IMPROVEMENT

JENNY HARSHMAN

Linda worked in talent development for a small financial company for five years. In her time there she provided formal training and innovative technology-based development opportunities while learning skills in performance improvement. Linda was proud of how she identified gaps to create inclusive and far-reaching development experiences for the whole company. She understood the importance of creating development initiatives that supported the goals of the organization and strived to frequently evaluate these experiences to ensure sustainability.

With this confidence, Linda accepted a job as a member of a hospital's talent development team. This hospital had a positive reputation for patient-focused care and was highly ranked nationally. While Linda had never worked in healthcare, she felt confident in her skills.

After a few weeks in her new role, Linda started to realize how different performance improvement was in the healthcare industry. She was called to join a group reviewing a case in which serious harm had come to a patient. The organization's clinical and corporate leadership wanted her to create a performance improvement plan to avoid similar events in the future. Linda felt overwhelmed and didn't know where to start. This performance improvement plan would involve implications she had never had to consider before, such as harm to a patient, emotional investment of the patient's family, emotional investment of the clinician who caused the harm, reimbursement of the care required after the harm, and prevention of this harm occurring in the future.

Scenarios like Linda's are all too frequent in the healthcare setting. Human errors, drifting from best practice, and changing processes to align with evidence-based practice all depend on performance improvement, either to fix a problem or to avoid one.

Performance improvement is not a healthcare-specific concept, but there are components unique to the healthcare world. Talent development (TD) professionals in healthcare must consider performance improvement on two levels: the macro-level and the micro-level. The macro-level focuses on industry trends and rankings, organizational goals and objectives, and quality improvement, while the micro-level deals with specific events, individual performance and competence, and processes. For this chapter, we'll focus on the micro-level of performance improvement and how a healthcare TD professional directly affects patient outcomes, individual competence, and interdisciplinary collaboration. Along the way, I'll share practices to identify gaps, respond to needs, and support a successful performance improvement plan to create safe practices.

Overview of Performance Improvement

The Talent Development Capability Model defines performance improvement as a "holistic and systematic approach to meeting organizational goals by identifying and closing human performance gaps" (Vital, Hirt, and Galagan 2020). Performance improvement is a purposeful set of actions to improve outcomes. These actions focus on individual training and performance, systematic policies and processes, or both. According to the ATD research report *Organizational Performance Improvement: Methods and Skills to Drive Business Results* (2018) there are three elements for effective performance improvement: partnering with leaders, stakeholders, and end users; concentrating on business priorities; and focusing on desired results.

Partnering With Leaders, Stakeholders, and End Users

Successful performance improvement must bring leaders, stakeholders, and end users together. Each role offers a different perspective and objective when identifying performance improvement opportunities.

The leader focuses on the business outcomes, the macro-level of performance improvement, bringing considerations on how the change supports the mission and any allocation of resources to support the plan. Some key healthcare leaders include clinical leaders, finance leaders, physician leaders, and information technology leaders.

Stakeholders bring a more focused perspective of the need and downstream effects of a specific process. While stakeholders can be leaders, it is important to have a stakeholder who speaks to past best practices and current processes, and is affected by any change proposed. Some stakeholders in healthcare are clinical managers, electronic documentation developers, and quality and safety department members. Often, they are most invested because the process directly affects their teams or workflow.

Partnering the end user with leaders and stakeholders allows a 360-degree view of the area of improvement and proposed solution. The end user offers the micro-view of performance improvement and can speak for the individual contributor and advocate on their behalf. There are many end users in healthcare, including clinical and nonclinical team members, because the end user is anyone whose work process will change as a result of the performance improvement plan.

When you bring these different voices to the table, you can complete a thorough analysis of the need and create a comprehensive plan.

Concentrating on Business Priorities

Performance improvement must align to business priorities. At first glance, business priorities seem like macro-level performance improvement; however, they are reflected in the day-to-day workings of the end users. For example, if there is a business priority around customer service, a performance improvement plan would focus on organization-wide customer service and what the individual employee could do every day to support a positive customer experience.

Focusing on Desired Results

The final component of successful performance improvement is the most important—framing the conversation around desired results and not jumping directly into solutions. Performance improvement is about the analysis, and gap identification and needs assessment are two important parts of that. It is through the analysis that you identify the real point of improvement and define the desired outcomes. Once you have the confidence of knowing where there is an opportunity and what the desired behaviors and outcomes are, you can create a performance improvement plan outlining different solutions to bridge that gap.

The Role of Talent Development Professionals

When it comes to performance improvement, TD professionals leverage their expertise in development, understanding of adult learning, and use of project and change management techniques. To be successful they must demonstrate understanding of a variety of performance improvement methods, including performance improvement models, change management skills, technology and resource availability, learning and development expertise, and collaborative partnerships with leaders and stakeholders (all of which are discussed in different chapters of this book). Tools for successful performance improvement include an understanding of personal motivation, performance gap assessments, root-cause analysis, implementation, and evaluation. It is the responsibility of the TD professional to create systems and tools to bridge the gap between the identified need and desired outcomes.

Key Takeaways

- Effective performance improvement includes partnering with leaders, concentrating on business priorities, and focusing on desired results.
- Successful performance improvement includes an understanding of personal motivation, performance gap assessments, root-cause analysis, implementation, and evaluation.
- Understanding the macro-view of performance improvement enhances the development of micro-level performance improvement plans.

Author's Reflection

I was asked to create training about the chain of command for post-discharge phone calls. I developed a quick reference guide before collaborating with leaders, stakeholders, and end users. Upon sharing the guide, I discovered that not only was the process different depending on who was making the calls, but in the calls leaders in insurance reimbursement were focused on something different than the clinical leaders. I had to start over. This time I created resources specific to each end user. My lesson? Even if you think you know what training is needed, don't skip the analysis.

Performance Improvement in Healthcare

Performance improvement in healthcare encompasses improving patient health outcomes, increasing process efficiency, avoiding costs associated with errors, proactively identifying processes to avoid errors in the future, and improving internal communication. Typically, when a performance improvement request comes to a TD professional, it has been triggered by a poor patient outcome or a drift from best practice. For example, the goal of my discharge phone call chain of command performance improvement plan was to decrease emergent patient readmissions after discharge.

Before diving into the micro-level of performance improvement, we need to take a brief dip into the macro-level. As mentioned, it is the responsibility of the TD professional to have a pulse on the macro-level as they identify needs and create a performance improvement plan. Thorough performance improvement plans are enhanced when you understand the organizational goals and structure, industry trends or shifts, and cultural or global influences. Here are a few resources to support your macro-view of healthcare performance improvement (some are free and some require membership):

- Your organization's internal and external communications
- *US News and World Report*'s list of the best hospitals
- Becker's Hospital Review
- The Advisory Board Company
- World Health Organization (WHO)
- Center for Disease Control (CDC)
- The Joint Commission
- Agency for Healthcare Research and Quality (AHRQ)

The goals for healthcare performance improvement are multifaceted. So, when identifying the need for performance improvement and moving forward with it, the TD professional must consider the clinician, the patient, and the organization. The impact of the processes and changes proposed and supported by the TD professional will reverberate from the patient to the operational stakeholders; even the nonpatient-facing sides of healthcare like finance and human resources will be affected.

The remainder of this chapter covers three steps for performance improvement in healthcare:

- Identifying performance opportunities
- Responding to performance needs and bridging gaps
- Ensuring performance improvement success

Then, we'll close with some education and training methods TD professionals can use to build performance improvement experiences.

Identifying Performance Opportunities

To successfully identify gaps and areas of opportunities, the healthcare organization can conduct different information gathering sessions. It is imperative that TD professionals participate in these events to build collaborative relationships and identify stakeholders, both of which are important parts of the performance improvement process. Three methods of identifying performance improvement opportunities are bedside reviews, root cause analysis, and audits.

Encouraging a Just Culture for Performance Improvement

A healthcare system that embraces a just culture will be able to identify areas of improvement, drifts in practice, or reckless behavior, and staff will feel safe to openly admit errors and near misses to help to prevent errors in the future. According to the Center for Patient Safety (2020), "Just Culture reshapes our understanding of accountability, the role of the system, and the role of human behavior. It provides a framework to support consistent management of operational systems and behaviors. It encourages open reporting of adverse events and risky situations yet holds people and organizations accountable in a just manner."

I've felt the power of just culture early in my career. The first time I made a medication error as a nurse was less than a year into my practice. I was taking care of multiple patients, I felt rushed and overwhelmed, and I drifted from my practice of a thorough medication check.

In nursing, the "five rights of medication administration" should always be verified before administering a medication: right medication, right dose, right route, right patient, right time.

On this day, I did not check the antibiotic dosage, and I gave my patient double what was ordered by his physician. Two things could have happened next: I could have pretended I didn't realize the error or I could report the error. A double dose of antibiotics is not necessarily a bad thing, the patient did have an infection, and it was what the pharmacy sent for the patient, so it would have been easy to ignore it and move on. Luckily, because I worked in a hospital that supported a just culture, I immediately reported the error up the chain of command. My charge nurse and the physician now knew, I entered it into the electronic reporting tool, and I told the patient and his family. No harm came to the patient, the family was appreciative of my honesty, and the physician was not concerned. And, by coming forward, I was able to build trust between the family and the organization.

Because I felt safe to report my error, we were able to identify and execute performance improvement opportunities, and I worked with my clinical educator (TD professional for nurses) to prevent errors like this in the future.

Bedside Reviews

When identifying opportunities for performance improvement, the first practice TD professionals should participate in are bedside reviews. These reviews encourage the idea of getting back to the bedside to identify where gaps occurred.

When bedside reviews are skipped, event reviews and recommendations may come from a quality or safety team and TD professionals may not be involved. In these cases, the recommendation is often more required training for all clinical areas, regardless of error rates or patient outcomes.

Comparatively, bedside reviews occur in the affected department (allowing for assessment of the environment), with all staff invited (allowing for assessment of the end-user), and through a safe, nonjudgmental conversation (allowing for honest feedback and identification of areas for improvement).

Bedside reviews follow this pattern:

- **Brief synopsis** of the situation and the error that occurred
- **Open dialogue** with the department staff to share their experiences with the situation or something similar
- **Review of best practices** around the situation or error:
    - What training have they received about this situation or error in the past?
    - What are the expectations for each role with this situation or error?
    - Have there been similar situations or errors in the past? If so, how were they addressed?
- **Identify areas of improvement** to avoid this in the future, and identify if it's a problem for all staff or just a few individuals
- Group reflection of **action items** and goals for the future

The TD professional plays an active role in the bedside review. First and foremost, they support a safe environment that encourages open and honest dialogue. They speak to any training or clinical competencies that teach and verify the expectation for safe practices about the given situation or error. The TD professional also shares any just-in-time resources available for staff when faced with a similar situation. Being involved in the bedside reviews allows the TD professional to understand the perspective of the end user, the perspective of leadership, and even the perspective of the organization through the safety and quality team. You walk away understanding the gap and knowing the expectation for improvement.

Root Cause Analyses

A root cause analysis (RCA) is "an approach used to analyze serious problems before trying to solve them, by which the main root cause of a problem is isolated and identified" (SixSigma 2017). It's a problem-solving technique that results in more corrective actions to prevent reoccurrence of an event. The difference between a bedside review and an RCA is the severity of the event, the broad-reaching implications, and the need to maintain confidentiality. The goal is to identify the systems or processes that contribute to the event and create a plan to reduce the risk of error in the future. While an RCA is often used for patient-centered events, they can be used for any process in the healthcare setting.

Like the bedside review, and the support of a just culture, the goal is not to be punitive to an individual.

RCAs follow this pattern:

- **Brief synopsis** of the facts of the event and the outcomes that occurred:
  - How it happened
  - Why it happened
  - How it can be prevented in the future
- **Review of best practices** around the event:
  - What relevant training has been done in the past?
  - What are the expectations for each role with this event?
  - Have there been similar events in the past? If so, how were they addressed?
  - Review of the processes involved in the event and where drift from best practice occurred
  - Review any relevant connection to National Patient Safety Goals (if it was a patient-centered event)

The TD professional has an important opportunity in an RCA because of the broad-reaching performance improvement collaborations. By focusing on processes, systems, and implications, the TD professional can look at all levels of the care team who need performance improvement action items. For a patient-centered error this could include clinical staff, healthcare providers, customer service individuals, and interdisciplinary care providers (such as therapy services, respiratory services, or social services).

Chart Audits and Skill Audits

Auditing is a practice that allows for real-time awareness of the gaps and application of the performance improvement action items. The two main types of audits, chart audits and skill audits, can be used for any employee in a clinical or nonclinical healthcare role.

Chart audits are used when performance is documentation based. Documentation in the chart occurs at all levels of healthcare and serves as an important point of reference around practices. Advancements in data mining and analytics offer the ability to see broad trends in documentation or drill down to a group's specific behaviors. While maintaining confidentiality, the TD professional can enter a patient's chart to see what actions were taken for their direct and indirect care. This provides insight about best practice follow-through, performance improvement application, and ongoing needs for safe and efficient patient care. Chart audits serve an important function for evaluating performance improvement plans and how sustainable action items are.

Skill audits are used when the performance focus is on actions. They can be either demonstrations of technical skills in a work or simulated environment or observations of using skills in daily practice (Wright 2005). Skill audits are only successful when using a checklist or policy of criteria, because the audit uses the detailed criteria of correct practice to identify whether it is being followed. The TD professional can use skill audits to gather information prior to creating a performance improvement plan or to evaluate practice after the performance improvement plan has been implemented.

Let's go back to Linda and identifying opportunities for performance improvement. Since this event resulted in serious harm to the patient, Linda participated in the RCA. Through this, they identified that the event occurred because the process for patient medication reconciliation was not being followed. Linda was able to determine performance improvement action items related to understanding the process and working it into daily workflow, interdisciplinary communication to ensure completion, and understanding regulatory guidelines around medication reconciliation. Now that she understands the needs and gaps, she can start planning the performance improvement.

Key Takeaways

- TD professionals should start a performance improvement plan only after performing an analysis to identify performance opportunities.
- There are three practices for identifying performance opportunities: bedside reviews, RCAs, and audits.

Author's Reflection

To update our education session evaluation, I participated in a workgroup to rewrite our Level 1 survey. We used the outline of an RCA to help identify gaps in the current survey and needs for future usable feedback. The new Level 1 survey focused on the learner experience and the direct application implications to daily practice. Just because the project is small or department specific doesn't mean you can't identify more needs.

Responding to Performance Needs and Bridging the Gaps

After gaps have been identified, you can begin to plan for performance improvement. While there are many different performance improvement methodologies, this chapter focuses on two that work particularly well in healthcare settings: plan, do, study, act (PDSA) and define, measure, analyze, improve, control (DMAIC). PDSA is for rapid-cycle implementation and evaluation with a focus on different methods; DMAIC is data-driven and used when a process or program requires change but the direct cause is not immediately known.

Plan, Do, Study, Act (PDSA)

A TD professional can use the PDSA cycle when they have a performance goal in mind, but are unsure of the best way to carry out performance improvement or when rapidly testing a few options. The PDSA method can help when several roles are affected by the performance improvement plan or when multiple steps of training are required to reach the desired outcome (Jackson 2018). Figure 16-1 shows the four steps in the cycle.

Let's review each in turn:

Figure 16-1. The PDSA Cycle

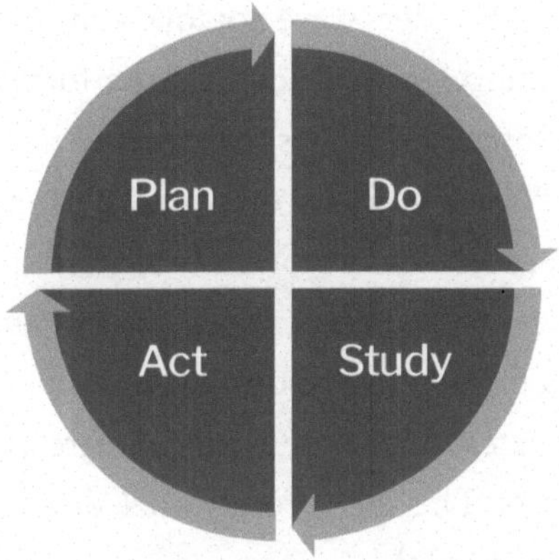

- **Plan.** The TD professional identifies the problem (using a method for identifying opportunities), collects and analyzes data, and outlines the training goal. While there may be several action items for improving performance, the TD professional focuses all efforts on those affected by training and evaluation. This is also the phase in which the TD professional collaborates with stakeholders and leaders to ensure support for the plan. This is like the analysis and design phases of the ADDIE model.
- **Do.** Next, the TD professional develops training initiatives, outlines steps to implement, and then executes the plan. They create an action plan with clear steps and deadlines while identifying other possible implementation team members. Frequent contact with the stakeholders and leaders is important, as their involvement supports success. This phase has parallels to the development and implementation phases of the ADDIE model.
- **Study.** This step involves measuring the effectiveness of the training based on the outcomes produced. When thinking about this step, consider Level 3, behavior, and Level 4, results, of the Kirkpatrick's evaluation model. The TD professional uses this step to monitor understanding and compliance for the training plan, and identify any barriers to implementation. This phase is like the evaluation phase of the ADDIE model.
- **Act.** The final step of this cyclical method is to act based on what the evaluation showed. If the training method improved performance to the desired outcome, it is incorporated into daily practice and spread throughout the system as appropriate. However, if it did not improve performance to desired outcome, changes are made and the PDSA cycle restarts to see if the new version achieves the goal.

Let's review an example of the PDSA method in action: It was discovered that coders were not charging patients correctly for research study interventions in the outpatient setting.

This had negative implications for insurance reimbursement and the organization's ability to continue conducting research. In assessing the root cause, TD professionals identified that research coders were not following the proper process for documenting and charging patients for the research study. The performance improvement opportunity involved training and reinforcement of best practices to mirror policy.

Plan: The TD professional performed a chart and skill audit to see the documentation and observe the daily workflow around charging for research study interventions. They met with leaders of the research department and finance team and the lead researchers to gather feedback for possible resources and solutions. The TD professional identified a goal of increasing accurate documentation by 25 percent by the end of next month.

Do: The TD professional developed a performance improvement plan for this goal (Figure 16-2).

Figure 16-2. Research Coder Performance Improvement Plan

Problem and Goal	Action	Person Responsible	Due Date and Reassessment Date
• Research coders incorrectly document research intervention, resulting in 48% reimbursement lost • Goal to increase accurate documentation by 25%	• Create a quick reference guide outlining the process for documentation • Create a video demonstrating the step-by-step documentation process • Require research coders to watch the video and demonstrate where to find the reference guide (These resources will be provided to all new hires in the research department)	• TD professional	• End of the month • Ongoing reassessment
• No system exists for performing frequent documentation audits. • Goal to create a sustainable method for auditing documentation and providing feedback.	• Create an audit tool that lists criteria for correct documentation • Complete an audit on each research coder quarterly (If there are knowledge gaps, they will complete just-in-time training using the reference guide and video)	• Business owner • Finance team	• End of the month • Ongoing reassessment

Study: At the end of the month, the TD professional gathered the training completion reports and audits. While 90 percent of the research coders completed the training and could correctly demonstrate where to find the resources, the accuracy of documentation only increased by 6 percent. So, the TD professional circled back with the leaders and stakeholders and identified how to modify the improvement plan and reinforce points of accountability the leaders could support.

Act: The TD professional supported more frequent audits and created a competency for new hires to complete. They also created reminders and case studies to share for reinforcing processes during staff meetings. Reassessment would occur at the end of the coming quarter.

Define, Measure, Analyze, Improve, Control (DMAIC)

DMAIC is a data-driven improvement cycle for improving existing process problems with unknown causes (Swan 2019). This method is particularly helpful when the opportunity for improvement lies within a process and not just an individual situation. Often, if DMAIC is being used for performance improvement through process improvement, the TD professional is part of a larger improvement team. Figure 16-3 shows the five steps in the DMAIC cycle.

Let's review each step:

- **Define.** Like the plan stage in PDSA, the TD professional must not only define the problem but also define a goal statement. It is during this phase that they determine the target audience, stakeholders, and leaders directly involved. The audience is identified by taking a thorough look at the process in question and mapping out the team members involved in each step (Business Performance Improvement 2020). The team creates a project charter, and it's the TD professional's responsibility to include training validation, reinforcement, and sustainment.
- **Measure.** This step is all about data measurements, including baseline measures, collection methods, and outcome measure

Figure 16-3. The DMAIC Cycle

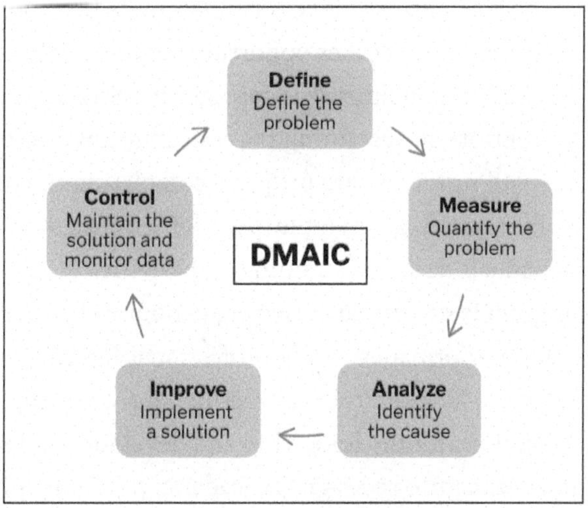

identification (Swan 2019). The required measurements are identified by thoroughly understanding the current process and specific problem. This may require the project team to gather data to understand where to start when creating outcome measures (Business Performance Improvement 2020). The TD professional should use this step to consider the overall measures of the performance improvement goal and those directly related to training. It is important to gather data on any previously offered training and the baseline knowledge of the process. Without this starting point, the TD professional will not have accurate outcome measurements for training application.

- **Analyze.** This step is critical because it brings the information from the first two phases together to identify the causes of the problem. This analysis phase mirrors an RCA—the TD professional's responsibilities are the same as in an RCA and focused on where training has or can affect the process. The goal of this phase is to identify the area of improvement that will yield the highest impact.
- **Improve.** This step is for brainstorming, narrowing down, and prioritizing improvement options (Business Performance Improvement 2020). Once the team identifies improvement options, they can create and implement an improvement plan. This stage takes the most time, collaboration, and planning. While the TD professional partners with the whole team to support the implementation, they also focus on the accompanying training content—not only training to implement the plan but also reinforcing the training to support the plan.
- **Control.** This step focuses on maintaining and sustaining the improvement plan once implemented. The plan must be monitored, outcomes measured, and the cycle restarted if other opportunities are identified. This is also when success is shared and efforts duplicated as appropriate (Swan 2019). The TD professional should focus their effort on sustaining the training plan or creating onboarding competencies to ensure all new hires are properly completing the process.

Let's review an example of the DMAIC method in action. To succeed as a healthcare leader, individuals need both training and experience. In this hospital setting, the leadership training program is structured as two eight-hour lecture days. In responding to a call to improve leadership performance, a TD professional found that the initial healthcare leadership training needed to be more robust, offering long-term support for new leaders. The TD professional partnered with the leadership and development team, instructional designers, and organizational leaders to redesign the leadership training program.

Define: The workgroup identified all new leaders as the target audience. There were currently 750 leadership positions in the organization, with an annual turnover rate of 15 percent. Whenever a new leader was promoted or hired into the organization, they were supposed to attend a new leader orientation (NLO), which was currently offered every other month. It was the hiring manager's responsibility to ensure NLO completion. The NLO program featured a two-day lecture series combined with 10 hours of computer-based training and a 60-day follow-up reflection session. It covered timekeeping, annual reviews, payroll and compensation, just culture leader training, regulatory and accreditation implications, healthcare outcome tracking, internal and external networking, and resource identification. The program was offered through the training department and supported by subject matter experts for each topic. Following their review of the program, the TD professional defined the training problem to be a lack of modern learning techniques, and believed there was opportunity to use adult learning theory and create ongoing reinforcement and resources for new leaders.

Measure: While the workgroup focused on the effectiveness of leaders after attending NLO, the TD professional tracked Levels 1–3 in Kirkpatrick's evaluation model. They considered how the current NLO training was being evaluated and the best method moving forward, as well as the knowledge checks that were scattered throughout the training sessions and afterward. The TD professional also considered application assessments both in the training session and after the leader was practicing in their day-to-day role.

Analyze: The workgroup identified the point of concern for new leader training to be a lack of focus on healthcare-specific needs, sustainability, reinforcement, and long-term evaluation of application.

Improve: The TD professional began to think through different learning modalities that enhance sustainability and encourage application. With the support of the workgroup, they moved the training to an online-based environment and introduced cohorts for leaders to go through the learning together. Instead of sitting through two days of didactic information, participants would engage in discussion boards, reflection activities, synchronous and asynchronous learning sessions, and mentoring over the course of their first nine months in the role. Social learning was encouraged through cohort discussions and the curated leader resources provided support long after the sessions ended. Content was updated to include moral distress in healthcare, data tracking and transparency, pace of change, change management, and patient- and family-centered care.

Control: The first session of the new NLO was a success—89 percent of the cohort stayed engaged through the nine-month program, and new leader turnover fell by 3 percent. Level 1 evaluation results led to changes in some of the discussion prompts and asynchronous learning activities to enhance knowledge acquisition and application opportunities. Lessons-learned discussion posts encouraged leaders to share difficult situations and promoted networking across clinical and nonclinical specialties. Cohorts were launched when at least five new leaders, and not more than 15, could be grouped together. The workgroup planned to continue evaluating, and the TD professional was ready to keep a pulse on minor changes for the content and delivery methods.

Before Linda can choose the best methodology to approach performance improvement for medication reconciliation, she must consider a few key aspects of the situation. First, with the serious harm potential, there is a rapid need to improve the situation. Second, there is already a process in place and it's not being followed consistently. Last, there are multiple ways to reinforce a well-established process. With these considerations in mind, Linda decides to use PDSA.

Key Takeaways

- After needs are identified, the TD professional chooses the performance improvement cycle that best supports the timeline and goal.
- Coupling a performance improvement cycle with ADDIE (or another learning design methodology) creates education and training to support the performance improvement plan, due to their significant overlap.

Author's Reflection

I find that I am frequently in a hurry to create a solution to an identified problem; in my haste, I don't think about a performance improvement model until I have already designed or implemented my original idea. It is only as I am gathering feedback and evaluation, that I remember the cyclical approach of performance improvement and the benefit it provides when trying to implement a solution to realize a goal. I have added a spot for identifying a performance improvement model to my analysis form, as a way to remind myself to consider one from the beginning.

Ensuring Performance Improvement Success

As described throughout this chapter, TD professionals are essential to the performance improvement process; however, in healthcare, they don't have to tackle it on their own. As seen in Linda's situation, when a performance need is identified in healthcare there is rarely just one thing to address. Even when most healthcare-related performance improvement is directly linked to clinical processes, the ripple-effect touches multiple departments. Because of these wide-reaching implications, setting up performance improvement for success cannot be overlooked.

At the beginning of the chapter we shared the three aspects for successful performance improvement: partnering with leaders, stakeholder, and end users; concentrating on business outcomes; and focusing on desired results. TD professionals who want to be successful with performance improvement in the healthcare setting need to account for two additional components: data transparency and early involvement.

Data Transparency

In the healthcare setting data is always being collected around processes, practices, and operations, regardless of a specific problem being addressed. Having this data internally available to all team members—for example through reports, dashboards, meetings, or internal communications—while ensuring patient privacy, supports a culture of data transparency. Creating a culture of data transparency allows for a multitude of performance improvement assessment and analysis. If the data is not completely shared, a piece of the improvement puzzle could be missed, hindering the goals of the performance improvement plan.

Another benefit of sharing data is that it allows TD professionals, leaders, and others to find answers and outcomes. As the TD professional creates performance improvement plans, best practice is to advocate with leadership for data transparency as an important method to encourage buy-in from everyone involved. Data transparency supports the improvement and demonstrates that change is not happening just for the sake of change.

Early Involvement of Talent Development

Even though the importance of education and training has been demonstrated in healthcare, when a serious safety event occurs, bringing the TD professional to the table isn't always the first thought. Since the initial focus is on risk mitigation, patient safety, and moral distress, the team may not think to bring a TD professional into a performance improvement project until after the assessment has been completed, the design created, and the implementation presumed ready. While a TD professional can affect change from whatever point they join the project, the most impactful training performance improvement plan needs a TD professional to be present through the whole process.

The other important role TD professionals play in the process is that of the historian. They can speak to previous education or training efforts around the performance improvement opportunity as well as which competencies already exist. TD professionals can outline a performance improvement plan that builds on what has been done in the past, assessing what did or did not work. After the historical review, the TD professional can partner with the leaders to identify if there is a knowledge or skills gap or if the issue is being caused by an accountability or motivation opportunity. Education gaps are easily addressed by TD professionals, while accountability is an expectation set by the leaders.

Education and Training for Performance Improvement

While performance improvement has its roots in gap identification, brainstorming, implementation, and evaluation, the type of supporting education and training provided is essential to the plan's success. Without going through the full tool kit TD professionals bring to the table, there are a few methods to enhance performance improvement:

- **Design thinking.** While performance improvement methodologies look at the whole picture, design thinking allows TD professionals to design education and training for the target learner. Design thinking is a mindset, as well as a process, that puts the learner at the forefront when creating, refining, and providing education (Boller and Fletcher 2020). This empathetic approach aligns with the empathetic nature of the healthcare setting. Healthcare TD professionals, who often used to be clinical healthcare workers, are equipped with an empathetic mind that carries over into empathy for their learner's needs. A learning experience designed specifically for the learner encourages the adoption and application of new processes.
- **Learning campaigns.** Performance improvement plans typically aren't successful when a single one-and-done education and training approach is used. Learning campaigns outline education delivery, reinforcement, and sustainment over days, weeks, or even months to support the performance improvement. They are especially important in the healthcare setting because of healthcare's 24/7/365 nature. It is not

easy, or often even an option, to give everyone training in the same way; learning campaigns allow TD professionals to plan for different methods of training, reinforcing, and sustaining. Each time reinforcement is provided, it is delivered through a different learning modality. Evaluation is completed at each stage of the campaign.

- **Competencies.** A performance improvement plan occasionally results in significant changes to practice, setting new standards for care and process. When a new standard is created, the TD professional should consider updating the impacted roles' competencies, which are the application of knowledge, skills, and behaviors that are needed to fulfill organizational, departmental, and work setting requirements under the varied circumstances of the real world (Wright 2005). This includes both initial competencies that are completed upon hire and need-based competencies. The new competency should mirror the new standard and serve as the expectation for practice from that point forward. The TD professional, along with the project team, will decide if a need-based competency is required for a performance improvement project. Need-based competencies are best used when the process includes a regulatory standard and the competency of all staff performing the practice must be validated. Documented competencies have become a regulatory standard in healthcare and are useful for demonstrating competency validation across a group of workers.
- **Simulation.** A unique opportunity for TD professionals in healthcare settings, simulations provide a safe environment in which team members can practice. Learners are not only able to apply new knowledge, they can also receive immediate and constructive feedback, encouraging them to practice safely in the real-world setting. TD professionals should create simulations that allow those affected by the changes to demonstrate the correct way to safely perform new practices. Simulations can be used to practice technical skills, critical thinking, or interpersonal skills. Some organizations even leverage simulation experiences in their RCAs to recreate an event.
- **Resources.** Regardless of the method TD professionals use for performance improvement education and training, they can use resources to provide ongoing reinforcement. Examples include quick reference guides (electronic or printed), policy links, QR codes to video resources, and reviewable computer-based training. Resources are especially helpful for supporting the frequent and rapid changes in the healthcare field because they are easy to review, update, and share. By assessing the audience, their work area, and the technology available, TD professionals can create resources that provide the most use for the specific learners.

Linda knows that to be successful with her PDSA performance improvement plan for medication reconciliation, she needs to develop a learning campaign (Figure 16-4) and evaluation goals.

Figure 16-4. Linda's Learning Campaign

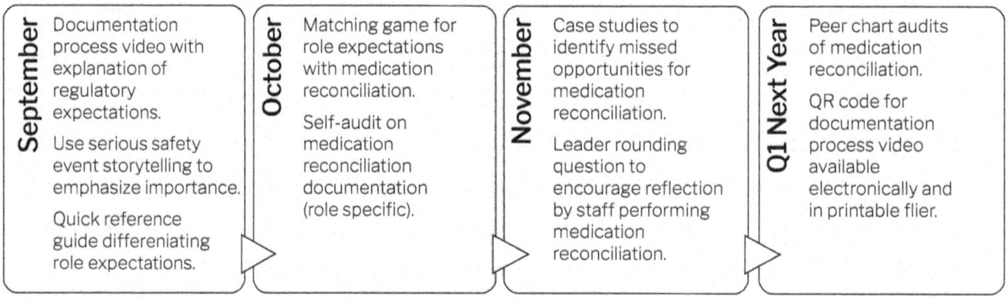

Her performance improvement plan training needed to include:

- Medication reconciliation process reinforcement
- Documentation updates on medication reconciliation completion:
    - Nurse expectations
    - Physician expectations
    - Care coordinator expectations
- Regulation requires medication reconciliation to be completed and documented within the first 24 hours of hospital admission
- Differentiation of role expectations for medication reconciliation

Her evaluation goals during the performance improvement plan were:

- Electronic medical record chart review:
    - 90 percent of patients with completed medication reconciliation within the first 24 hours by end of October.
    - 95 percent of patients with completed medication reconciliation within the first 24 hours by end of year.
    - 1 percent reduction of serious safety events related to incorrect or missed medication reconciliation each month after education.

Key Takeaways

- TD professionals should advocate for two additional components for successful healthcare performance improvement: data transparency and early involvement.
- TD professionals are the historians and training developers for a performance improvement training plan and encourage leaders to tackle accountability opportunities.
- Engaging content, thoughtful reinforcement, and ongoing sustainability of a performance improvement training plan are enhanced using design thinking, learning campaigns, competencies, simulations, and just-in-time resources.

Author's Reflection

When creating training content for charge nurses, we knew a single in-person session would not be enough to support the adoption of correct practices. Instead, we reviewed how charge nurses were trained in the past, gathered information from current charge nurses, and surveyed department leaders to identify gaps in practice. These gaps directly affected the relationships on the unit, the financial stability of staffing, and charge nurse satisfaction. With this information we created a multi-layered approach to training. We focused the in-person session on conflict resolution and communication skills, a website housed just-in-time resources, and an initial competency provided a list of skills each charge nurse should be able to perform. Using continuous evaluation, we added content to support charge nurses with difficult conversations and a second in-person training session to build systems thinking and encourage social learning. Just because you have a great plan in place for performance improvement, don't shy away from adding to it or changing it to meet new needs.

Conclusion

Throughout this chapter, we have shown how performance improvement in healthcare is multifaceted, and its outcomes carry an enormous impact when patients are directly affected. TD professionals have an important role to play in performance improvement in the healthcare setting, and the sooner they are brought into the process the more they can support the organization's goal.

Performance improvement means applying a systematic approach to analyzing and closing human performance gaps. TD professionals can identify those gaps through bedside reviews, RCAs, and chart and skill audits. Once gaps are identified, TD professionals can use cyclic performance improvement implementation and evaluation. This includes creating training that fits into the cycle and supporting sustained performance improvement with design thinking, learning campaigns, competencies, simulations, and just-in-time resources. Throughout the performance improvement process, TD professionals can find further success in a just culture environment supported with data transparency and a performance improvement department.

As you approach your first, or 20th, performance improvement plan as a TD professional, don't forget how Linda did it. While healthcare performance improvement carries a sense of urgency because of patient outcomes, don't let that stop you from gathering more information. Analyzing the whole situation increases the likelihood of success for the performance improvement training plan and reduces the probability of having to revisit the training content in the future.

Take the time to pick a methodology that allows a systematic approach to design, implement, evaluate, and sustain the performance improvement plan. Linda set a great example by using quick cycle improvement with PDSA and supporting that with a learning campaign.

Remember your target audience, learning styles, and environmental factors—the training plan should be varied, sustainable, and frequently evaluated. Linda created a performance improvement plan that helped reduce serious safety events related to medication reconciliation, and through that improvement the hospital continued to receive insurance reimbursements. The decrease in negative patient outcomes also led to improved reviews of the hospital and a positive financial outcome.

As a TD professional focusing on performance improvement, your impact ripples through the organization and allows continued care of the community.

CHAPTER 17

COMPLIANCE TRAINING

CJ WOLF

Why is the healthcare industry so heavily regulated? Because people's lives depend on it! Let's consider the case of Jesse Gelsinger, an 18-year-old who died in September 1999 during a research experiment involving a gene transfer at the University of Pennsylvania School of Medicine. His death raised concerns and debate about the protection of human subjects in medical research, financial conflicts of interest, the appropriate reporting of adverse events, informed consent of participants, and properly following research protocols. Of course, this was an extreme example, but it drives home the point. These areas were all well-known to compliance professionals who provide training in many of these regulatory areas, especially those involved in human research.

Not all compliance regulations are directly tied to life or death situations. Other regulations are aimed at protecting scarce financial resources, such as Medicare and Medicaid funding. The Federal False Claims Act, for example, is the government's primary enforcement tool for ensuring healthcare providers are not committing fraud, wasting, or abusing these essential tax-payer dollars. As a result, many compliance regulations are aimed at the claims hospitals, or physicians submit to government payor programs. Additionally, patient privacy is a key tenant of ethical healthcare. The Health Insurance Portability and Accountability Act of 1996 (HIPAA) is a law that helps protect the privacy and security of patient information. This is a key subject that compliance training often focuses on.

Compliance training is an essential aspect of every healthcare organization. In fact, training is formally recognized as one of the seven key elements of an effective compliance program (DHHS 1998). ATD defines *compliance* as "an action that is mandated by a law, agency, or policy outside the organization's purview. It is generally accompanied by a training program requirement," which is consistent with how it is used in this chapter. Additionally, *training*, as used in this chapter, is a process that "helps individuals improve performance by facilitating learning in a traditional or virtual classroom, one-on-one, or on-the-job in an organization."

This chapter outlines best practices as they relate to compliance training and accreditation in the healthcare industry. Included are the purpose and elements of an effective compliance program, training expectations, the role of the compliance professional, compliance topics for training, applying adult learning theory to training, general versus specific training, frequency of training, and accreditation.

What Is the Purpose of Healthcare Compliance?

Considering the greater history of healthcare in general, compliance programs are young. The first formal compliance programs didn't begin in healthcare organizations until the late 1980s. And even then, it was typically the larger organizations (as well as those that were experiencing significant fines and settlements) that spent the money and made the effort to create formal compliance programs.

Some of the earliest formal compliance programs began as a result of investigations and settlements involving Physicians at Teaching Hospitals (PATH) audits. The basis of the PATH audits involved accusations that teaching physicians were being paid for professional services that were actually performed by medical residents. The government claimed that the teaching institutions were already being paid for services of residents through the direct or indirect GME (graduate medical education) payments that were being made directly to the hospitals. As a result, they claimed that teaching physicians should only be paid an additional professional fee if the teaching physician personally performed and attended to professional medical services. Some of the initial institutions involved in these settlements and the accompanying settlement amounts included the University of Pennsylvania ($30 million in 1995), Thomas Jefferson University ($12 million in 1996), University of Virginia ($8.6 million in 1997), and University of Pittsburgh ($17 million in 1998) (USGAO 1998).

Many of these settlements led to the creation of compliance programs, which went beyond hiring honest and ethical people. Within the highly regulated healthcare industry, formalized compliance programs are designed to prevent, detect, and correct noncompliance with the law and regulations, as well as to create a culture of awareness, prevention, detection, and correction for noncompliance with the law. Because practitioners have busy schedules and receive information through a constant stream from various sources, it can be challenging for them to keep current on the most recent rules; they may also require structure and support to implement laws and rules in an organized, thoughtful, and practical way.

What Are the Elements of an Effective Compliance Program?

A formal compliance program might sound like a good idea, but what are the specific elements that make up an effective compliance program? Most compliance professionals would agree that chapter 8 of the United States Sentencing Commission's Guidelines Manual is one of the foundational documents outlining the elements of an effective compliance program. This chapter outlines the sentencing of organizations and describes mitigating factors that should be accounted for in penalizing and fining them. In the simplest of terms, the sentencing guidelines allow for credit to be given to organizations if they can demonstrate they had an effective compliance program in place. The chapter goes on to describe the elements of an effective compliance program (USSC 2018).

The United States Sentencing Commission

"The Sentencing Reform Act of 1984 created the United States Sentencing Commission as an independent agency in the Judicial Branch, and directed it to develop guidelines and policy statements for sentencing courts to use when sentencing offenders convicted of federal crimes. Moreover, it empowered the Commission with ongoing responsibilities to monitor the guidelines, submit to Congress appropriate modifications of the guidelines and recommended changes in criminal statutes, and establish education and research programs. The mandate rested on congressional awareness that sentencing is a dynamic field that requires continuing review by an expert body to revise sentencing policies, in light of application experience, as new criminal statutes are enacted, and as more is learned about what motivates and controls criminal behavior."

The manual can be viewed in its entirety or downloaded at ussc.gov/guidelines/2018-guidelines-manual-annotated.

The US Department of Health and Human Services Office of the Inspector General (HHS OIG) also developed compliance program guidelines incorporating the Sentencing Commission's Guidelines Manual (HHS OIG nd). The OIG Compliance Guidance documents will be described in further detail later in the chapter.

There are seven key elements of an effective compliance program. Though they may be worded slightly differently by different entities, they include:

- Written policies and procedures
- Designation of a compliance officer and a compliance committee

- Conducting effective training and education
- Developing effective lines of communication
- Enforcing standards through well-publicized disciplinary guidelines
- Auditing and monitoring
- Responding to detected offenses and developing corrective action initiatives

It should be noted that variations on these key elements of an effective compliance program are not uncommon. For example, New York State's Office of the Medicaid Inspector General outlines eight compliance program requirements for certain Medicaid participants in the state of New York (OMIG nd). The first seven elements are basically the same as already outlined. However, the eighth element requires:

> A policy of non-intimidation and non-retaliation for good faith participation in the compliance program, including but not limited to reporting potential issues, investigating issues, self-evaluations, audits and remedial actions, and reporting to appropriate officials as provided in sections 740 and 741 of the Labor Law.

Effective healthcare compliance trainers and talent development professionals will make sure to learn the nuances of compliance programs for the jurisdiction in which they operate.

Compliance Training Expectations of Key Enforcement Agencies

The OIG's compliance guidance documents are based on the seven elements. In addition to providing this proactive guidance, the OIG also leads investigations and enforcement actions throughout the healthcare industry. They've published specific compliance program guidance documents for the following provider types: hospitals; home health agencies; clinical laboratories; third-party medical billing companies; durable medical equipment, prosthetics, and orthotics industry; hospices; medicare+choice organizations; nursing facilities; physician practices; ambulance suppliers; and pharmaceutical manufacturers (HHS OIG nd).

For example, the OIG's Compliance Guidance Document for Hospitals stresses using a variety of teaching methods. These include interactive training, flexibility to train in different languages as needed, and tailoring training to the job role or function such as focused training on risk areas like medical coding, billing, and reimbursement. The OIG has also provided physicians with similar direction and offers additional insights into specific topics on which compliance training could focus, including coding requirements; claim development and submission processes; proper documentation of services rendered and protocol for physician signatures and authorizations; proper billing standards and procedures and submission of accurate bills for services or items rendered to federal healthcare program beneficiaries; and the legal sanctions for submitting deliberately false or reckless billings.

In the OIG's guidance for hospitals and physicians, coding and billing are emphasized as key areas of compliance training. This makes sense because hospitals and physicians are major provider types who submit claims to the government. In contrast, pharmaceutical manufacturers are usually not as involved in the assignment and submission of bills and codes. Thus, the OIG's Guidance Document to Pharmaceutical Manufacturers emphasizes other types of healthcare laws and regulations, such as periodic training for sales and marketing professionals on the Anti-Kickback Statute and its safe harbors.

The Anti-Kickback Statute (AKS)

"The AKS [42 U.S.C. § 1320a-7b(b)] is a criminal law that prohibits the knowing and willful payment of 'remuneration' to induce or reward patient referrals or the generation of business involving any item or service payable by the Federal health care programs (e.g., drugs, supplies, or health care services for Medicare or Medicaid patients). Remuneration includes anything of value and can take many forms besides cash, such as free rent, expensive hotel stays and meals, and excessive compensation for medical directorships or consultancies. **In some industries, it is acceptable to reward those who refer business to you. However, in the Federal health care programs, paying for referrals is a crime.** The statute covers the payers of kickbacks—those who offer or pay remuneration—as well as the recipients of kickbacks—those who solicit or receive remuneration. Each party's intent is a key element of their liability under the AKS.

"Criminal penalties and administrative sanctions for violating the AKS include fines, jail terms, and exclusion from participation in the Federal health care programs.

"Safe harbors [or specific published scenarios] protect certain payment and business practices that could otherwise implicate the AKS from criminal and civil prosecution. To be protected by a safe harbor, an arrangement must fit squarely in the safe harbor and satisfy all of its requirements. Some safe harbors address personal services and rental agreements, investments in ambulatory surgical centers, and payments to bona fide employees." (OIG HHS nd)

In addition to these guidance documents, the OIG also published a tool kit for measuring the effectiveness of compliance programs, including training and education expectations (OIG 2017). Some of these expectations include:

- **Create an established compliance training plan.** The organization should make sure training is executed according to the compliance training plan. The plan should also be updated or refreshed periodically, including any documentation such as sign-in sheets and tracking of completion rates.
- **When appropriate, offer continuing education units for completion of the training.** This can be an incentive to complete training, especially for busy clinicians or key decision makers.
- **Keep training content current.** There should be established processes, policies, and procedures to communicate and provide training on new laws and regulations, in addition to internal policies and procedures.
- **Tie training to policy or compliance failures.** Organizations should monitor incidents of noncompliance and should revise training to address these issues in the organization.
- **Provide new-hire orientation and training.** There is a specific training and education process for orienting new employees to a compliance program and its accompanying policies and expectations.
- **Focus on learners' needs and application of training.** Those receiving the training should perceive it to be useful and applicable to the compliance issues they face in their jobs.
- **Expand your training population.** Training on certain policies and procedures should extend to vendors, business partners, and volunteers, not just employees. Some examples might include technical security and privacy measures required by HIPAA or mandatory timelines for repaying identified overpayments.
- **Measure and evaluate effectiveness.** Measure the effectiveness of training through post-training testing or knowledge assessments. Require training evaluation forms and surveys for those who have recently completed compliance training.

The OIG is not the only enforcement agency with compliance program expectations. The US Department of Justice (DOJ) also has published guidelines on what it considers an effective compliance program (DOJ 2020). Similar to the OIG and Federal Sentencing Guidelines, the DOJ's guidelines include key elements, one of which is effective training and education.

The DOJ document states:

> Some companies, for instance, give employees practical advice or case studies to address real-life scenarios, and/or guidance on how to obtain ethics advice on a case-by-case basis as needs arise. Other companies have invested in shorter, more targeted training sessions to enable employees to timely identify and raise issues to appropriate compliance, internal audit, or other risk management functions. Prosecutors should also assess whether the training adequately covers prior compliance incidents and how the company measures the effectiveness of its training curriculum.

The DOJ's guidance does not set the expectation that all the items mentioned must be implemented—instead they are to meet the needs the of the organization. Other key aspects of the DOJ's expectations include:

Risk-Based Training

- What training has been given to employees in relevant control functions? Examples of these positions include those who authorize the final submission of claims to government payors such as Medicare or Medicaid; IT personnel who control access to confidential patient information protected by HIPAA; and frontline healthcare providers who have access to locked and controlled drugs or substances.
- Has the company provided tailored training for high-risk and control employees, including training that addresses risks in areas where misconduct has occurred? High-risk employees include those who job duties, if improperly performed, could immediately lead to noncompliance. For example, those in charge of physician contracting are often reviewing and approving financial arrangements with physicians; if done improperly this could violate the Stark and Anti-Kickback statutes. Another example might include an employee who approves electronic health record computer access to others. As electronic health records contain protected health information under HIPAA, only certain individuals should be allowed to access them.
- Have supervisory employees received different or supplementary training?
- What analysis has the company undertaken to determine who should be trained and on what subjects?

Form, Content, and Effectiveness of Training

- Has training been offered in a form and language that is appropriate for the audience?
- Is the training provided online or in person (or both)? What is the company's rationale for this choice?
- Has the training addressed lessons learned from prior compliance incidents?
- Whether online or in person, is there a process for employees to ask questions during or after the training sessions?
- How has the company measured the effectiveness of the training?
- Have employees been tested on what they learned?
- How has the company addressed employees who fail all or part of the testing?
- Has the company evaluated the extent to which the training has affected employee behavior or operations?

Key Takeaways

Enforcement agencies have published very clear guidelines on what they expect healthcare compliance programs to institute by way of training and education programs. Compliance trainers and talent development professionals should make themselves aware of any guidelines governing the staff they're responsible for training.

The Role of Compliance Professionals

Compliance professionals come from a variety of backgrounds. Without overgeneralizing, it is safe to say the compliance professionals in your organization likely come from one or many of these backgrounds:

- Legal
- Accounting and finance
- Auditing
- Nursing and other clinical practice areas
- Quality improvement
- Medical records, coding, or billing

Many healthcare compliance professionals choose to join the Healthcare Compliance Association (HCCA) and become certified in healthcare compliance through them. This professional organization has more than 12,000 members across all areas of the healthcare industry and it provides resources, education, and networking opportunities, as well as regional and national conferences.

When it comes to training, compliance professionals could serve as subject matter experts (SMEs) and, depending on whether they have professional education or training credentials or skills, might also serve as the trainer or educator. How involved compliance professionals are with training design often varies depending on the organization's resources. In some cases, compliance professionals are responsible for training from start to finish; in organizations with more robust internal training departments, the compliance professional may serve only as the SME. Regardless of where the compliance professionals fall within the organization, they will likely need to collaborate with other departments, colleagues, and specialists, such as HR, learning and development, legal, internal audit, operations, or clinical leadership.

For example, assume a hospital is interested in participating in a multisite, clinical trial research study. Individuals at the hospital may need compliance training on safeguarding the protected health information of potential clinical trial participants. In this case, compliance personnel will likely act as the SMEs regarding HIPAA and other privacy laws and regulations. Legal may be involved as they negotiate agreements between the hospital and the sponsor of the clinical trial, which might assign information security responsibilities to certain parties. Training developers or educational technologists may be asked to assist with developing a mobile device–friendly training module. The clinical or research administration and leadership teams will want to know which members of the research teams will need to complete the training and how long it will take. This all requires collaboration.

To collaborate effectively on compliance training, consider these tips:

- **Operational lines.** Which department or service is overseeing the activity? For example, is it the department of anesthesia or surgery? Outpatient laboratories? Or the pharmacy.
- **Compliance department.** Who in the compliance department has the needed expertise for the given subject area? For example, will the activity involve patient privacy (HIPAA), medical coding and billing, payment to or financial relationships with physicians, healthcare practitioner licensing, informed consent, or confidential data security?

- **Legal department.** Will the activity need to be performed under attorney–client privilege? For example, is there pending or likely litigation, such as in malpractice claims? Or is there significant repayment of overpayments from Medicare or Medicaid that could implicate the Federal False Claims Act?
- **Human resources.** Does the activity potentially involve employee disciplinary action? For example, did an employee fail to follow a policy or procedure, not complete a required training program, or perform an illegal or noncompliant action for which the employer (the organization) could be held accountable?
- **External parties.** Will non-employed, external parties be involved in the activity? For example, does the activity involve a business partner and if so, are the provisions of the written contract being followed? Is the external party a government agency or health department that has authority under state or federal law? Are the external parties volunteers or community members served by the healthcare organization?

Last, keeping accurate and thorough records of training completion is essential in compliance training. If a more serious incident of noncompliance was investigated or audited by an external enforcement agency, those investigators would likely ask how the compliance program attempted to prevent the noncompliance. Thus, a robust, multi-faceted compliance training program, built on sound talent development principles, is a key to demonstrating any compliance department's good faith efforts at preventing noncompliance. By maintaining accurate and thorough training records a compliance program can prove these efforts were made.

Common Subject Areas for Compliance Training

Although healthcare compliance training topics will vary from organization to organization and provider type to provider type, a few healthcare compliance topics do apply to most organizations.

For the purposes of this chapter, we will focus on HIPAA privacy and security. Additional topics for compliance training not covered in detail include:

- False Claims Act
- Medical coding and reimbursement
- Stark and Anti-Kickback Statute
- Conflicts of interest

The Health Insurance Portability and Accountability Act of 1996 (HIPAA) encompasses much more than just the privacy and security of protected health information (PHI).

However, most people who have interacted with a healthcare provider or organization within the United States equate HIPAA with privacy and protection of health information. And they would be right—those are some of the most well-known and pertinent compliance topics associated with HIPAA. As a body of legislation, along with amendments over the years, HIPPA has led to the publishing of multiple administrative rules by the US Department of Health and Human Services. The two administrative rules most likely needed for compliance training in healthcare are the Privacy Rule and the Security Rule, which can be found on the Health and Human Services website. While training and talent development professionals typically aren't expected to become SMEs in HIPAA, a basic understanding can be helpful.

The US DHHS Office for Civil Rights (OCR) is the federal agency and office charged with enforcing HIPAA compliance. According to OCR,

> The Privacy Rule standards address the use and disclosure of individuals' health information—called "protected health information" by organizations subject to the Privacy Rule—called "covered entities," as well as standards for individuals' privacy rights to understand and control how their health information is used. . . . A major goal of the Privacy Rule is to assure that individuals' health information is properly protected while allowing the flow of health information needed to provide and promote high quality health care and to protect the public's health and well-being. (OCR 2013)

In relation to the HIPAA Security Rule, OCR states that:

> The Security Rule operationalizes the protections contained in the Privacy Rule by addressing the technical and non-technical safeguards that organizations called "covered entities" must put in place to secure individuals' "electronic protected health information" (e-PHI). . . . A major goal of the Security Rule is to protect the privacy of individuals' health information while allowing covered entities to adopt new technologies to improve the quality and efficiency of patient care. Given that the health care marketplace is diverse, the Security Rule is designed to be flexible and scalable so a covered entity can implement policies, procedures, and technologies that are appropriate for the entity's particular size, organizational structure, and risks to consumers' e-PHI.

Figure 17-1 breaks down the differences in scope of the two rules.

Figure 17-1. HIPAA Privacy and Security Rules

Privacy Rule	Security Rule
Protects the privacy of individually identifiable health information, called protected health information (PHI). • Permitted uses and disclosures: To the individual (unless required for access or accounting of disclosures); treatment, payment, and healthcare operations; opportunity to agree or object; incident to an otherwise permitted use and disclosure; public interest and benefit activities; and limited data set for the purposes of research, public health, or healthcare operations. • Limiting uses and disclosures to the minimum necessary • Privacy practices notice • Personal representatives and minors • Business associates • Authorized uses and disclosures	Protects a subset of information covered by the Privacy Rule, which is the individually identifiable health information a covered entity creates, receives, maintains, or transmits in electronic form. The Security Rule calls this information "electronic protected health information" (e-PHI) • Ensure the confidentiality, integrity, and availability of all e-PHI they create, receive, maintain, or transmit • Identify and protect against reasonably anticipated threats to the security or integrity of the information • Risk analysis and management • Administrative safeguards include security management process, security personnel, information access management, workforce training and management, and evaluation • Physical safeguards include facility access and control and workstation and device security • Technical safeguards include access control, audit controls, integrity controls, and transmission security

Key Takeaways

The OCR's website is a valuable resource for those trying to develop training content about HIPAA privacy and security. Here are a few major highlights:

- The Training Materials page is especially helpful as it provides guides, and in some cases, actual training modules from which trainers could adopt material or use the resources as prepared and offered free of charge by OCR (hhs.gov/hipaa/for-professionals/training/index.html)
- HIPAA FAQs for Professionals (hhs.gov/hipaa/for-professionals/faq/index.html)
- Case Examples (hhs.gov/hipaa/for-professionals/compliance-enforcement/examples/index.html)
- HIPAA for Professionals (hhs.gov/hipaa/for-professionals/index.html)
- The HIPAA Privacy Rule (hhs.gov/hipaa/for-professionals/privacy/index.html)
- The Security Rule (hhs.gov/hipaa/for-professionals/security/index.html)

Applying Adult Learning to Compliance

Adult learning theory is especially important for compliance training. In his book *The Adult Learner* (2014), Malcolm Knowles characterized five assumptions of adult learners and four principles of adult learning.

Knowles' five assumptions of adult learners are:

- **Self-concept.** As a person matures, the self-concept changes from dependence like a child to one of self-direction.
- **Adult learner experience.** During maturation, a person gains a set of experiences that become a resource for learning.
- **Readiness to learn.** Readiness to learn becomes more and more tied to the developmental tasks of social roles as a person matures.
- **Orientation to learning.** Adult learners' time perspective changes from one of postponed application of knowledge to immediacy of application. Because of this, the orientation to learning changes from content focused to problem focused.
- **Motivation to learn.** Adult learners' motivation to learn is internal.

Knowles' four principles of adult learning (or andragogy) are:

- Adults need to be involved in the planning and evaluation of their instruction.
- Experience (including mistakes) provides the basis for the learning activities.
- Adults are most interested in learning subjects that have immediate relevance to and impact on their job or personal life.
- Adult learning is problem-centered rather than content-oriented.

When planning, developing, delivering, evaluating, and revising compliance training, Knowles' four principles of adult learning should be kept at the top of mind. Let's walk through the four principles and how they apply in healthcare compliance training.

Involve Learners in the Instruction Design

A common area of healthcare compliance training includes medical record documentation related to Medicare requirements for medical coding and billing. Most often this means meeting with busy physicians.

Unsuccessful training approaches for physicians often begin with materials that outline the regulations and requirements for medical documentation in a very didactic manner.

Unfortunately, this almost always turns physicians off from the very beginning. A more successful approach often results when Knowles' first principle is followed—that of involving the learners in the planning and evaluation of their instruction. For physicians, this can be as informal a sending out a survey asking for their top three questions about Medicare coding documentation and then tailoring the training to those. Alternatively, since compliance personnel are often aware of the results of proactive compliance billing and coding audits, they could identify the top three mistakes on the physicians' most recent audits and ask if they could be the basis of the training. Either approach involves the adult learner in the planning of their training.

Allow for Mistakes to Happen in Training

Another common compliance training topic involves HIPAA or patient privacy protection requirements. Training in this area should lead to better decision making regarding these regulations, especially for frontline healthcare workers who interact directly with patient confidential information. These frontline workers are often faced with scenarios in which they have to decide whether the regulations allow them to share protected health information.

Knowles' second principle of adult learning works well for this type of training, which would include actual patient privacy scenarios an employee is likely to face and allow the learner to make choices about their response. They should be allowed to make a mistake and choose an incorrect response. After selecting a response, the learner should be informed as to whether it was correct or incorrect. In both cases, the trainer can offer explanations as to why the answer was accurate or inaccurate. This approach allows experiences, including mistakes, to be the basis for training on compliance regulations surrounding patient privacy and HIPAA.

Ensure Training Has Immediate Relevance and Impact

Effective compliance programs not only provide training to frontline employees, but they also incorporate a regular cadence of compliance training to a governing board or committee that oversees the compliance program, such as an audit and compliance committee of the board. However, since board members are not typically involved in management decisions, the compliance training should be tailored to address the role of a board member as it relates to compliance program oversight.

Knowles' third principle is applicable in this example; when training board members about compliance, use tools and resources that have immediate relevance to their role, as opposed to what a frontline healthcare worker needs to know about the compliance program. One such tool is the Office of the Inspector General's guidance document, "Practical Guidance for Health Care Governing Boards on Compliance Oversight," which outlines a board member's role in overseeing compliance programs (AHIA et al. 2015). This content is obviously very role-specific and differs significantly from the compliance training a new nurse or clinic manager would receive.

Focus on Problems First, Not Content

As the field of healthcare compliance is heavily directed by laws and regulations, a common mistake many new compliance trainers make is focusing on the content and language of the law or regulation as opposed to actual problems. That is not to say that it's not important to note the precise language of the law or regulation, but it's much more effective to put the law in context rather than simply reading it to learners. For example, a common healthcare compliance training topic is the Federal Anti-Kickback statute. Following Knowles' fourth principle, training should focus on actual problems that a healthcare organization might face in navigating compliance with the Federal Anti-Kickback statute.

Key Takeaways

To ensure your compliance training meets the learning needs of your healthcare staff, ask these questions:

- Are training sessions designed in a way that allows learners to contribute to the direction the training should take?
- Are the examples and content used immediately applicable to the learners' day to day jobs?
- Does the training incorporate examples that highlight problems and solutions, as opposed to simply regurgitating legal text or regulatory requirements? In other words, does the training apply the compliance principles taught to scenarios learners are likely to encounter and allow them to solve the problem?
- Is the training designed in a way that tests learners and allows them to safely make and learn from common mistakes?

General vs. Specific Compliance Training

In addition to incorporating Adult Learning Theory into effective compliance training, talent development professionals can also recognize the unique circumstances surrounding general versus specific training.

When designing compliance training, general training is typically reserved for large audiences with diverse job duties and backgrounds. For example, general compliance training is usually delivered to all new employees upon hire regardless of their job description or role. General training is also used when an organization completes the entire workforce's annual compliance training requirements.

In contrast, specific compliance training is rarely given to everyone in the organization because its content is job or task specific. For example, an employee working in a laboratory billing position should receive specific compliance training on laboratory billing and reimbursement regulations and rules. An employee working in the medical records department would not need the laboratory billing compliance training, but they might need specific compliance training in state laws regarding medical record retention and the appropriate destruction of obsolete medical records.

General training typically includes those compliance topics that apply to the entire organization, including:

- **The importance of, and executive support for, the corporate compliance program.** This kind of messaging can often be delivered in a welcome letter (for new employees) or short video reminders or other delivery methods from a chairman of the board or the CEO to emphasize the "tone from top" that compliance is an important aspect of everyone's job.
- **Code of conduct or code of ethics.** These foundational documents outline, in very broad strokes, the key values or appropriate compliance conduct the organization expects. Employees receive general training on the content of the code and typically sign a statement of acknowledgment that they are aware of and agree to follow the code. This is typically done upon initial hiring, as well as a regular cycle (such as annually).
- **Compliance program awareness.** Healthcare organizations need to ensure employees can find and access more detailed policies and procedures. Additionally, this training tends to focus on an awareness that there is a compliance program or depart-

ment, a chief compliance officer, compliance personnel with various subject matter expertise, a system for reporting concerns of noncompliance, and that the organization takes all concerns seriously and the employee will not be retaliated against for reporting concerns in good faith.

Specific training is typically developed based on distinct risk areas and provided to employees in high-risk positions. A way to ensure this is being done is to monitor the high-risk positions (such as coding, billing, physicians) and establish training requirements for them. The training should focus on the job duties and responsibilities of positions that, if not performed in compliance, could expose the organization to risks.

Some examples of specific training include:

- **Coding, billing, and claims submission.** These activities and the employees who perform them could be considered high-risk—if coding, billing, and claims submissions are performed incorrectly, the organization could face penalties under the Federal False Claims Act. Thus, training for these individuals should focus on proper use of medical codes, billing processes, and appropriate claims submission functions.
- **Medical records.** Individuals responsible for the integrity and security of medical records and patient health information need to be trained in detailed HIPAA privacy and security policies, procedures, and regulations. These personnel are often the gatekeepers to this highly confidential information and so should receive training on what is prohibited as well as authorized disclosures of this information.

The Frequency of Compliance Training

It's often debated how frequently compliance training should be provided. The appropriate frequency will likely depend on the topic, and whether issues of noncompliance have been identified. Most healthcare compliance programs mandate some sort of compliance training for newly hired employees; however, the depth and breadth of such training might vary depending on the individual's role. A newly hired cook in the cafeteria, for example, will likely have different compliance training than a new employee in the medical records or billing department. More mature compliance programs tailor the type and frequency of training to the job role. However, almost all compliance programs require at least some sort of annual training after the initial hire.

Many compliance programs focus their efforts on shorter, more frequent training sessions throughout the year to reinforce the concept that compliance should always be top of mind, rather than as a once-and-done annual event. If noncompliance is identified, training is often one of the required corrective actions. For example, if a medical coding and billing audit identifies an employee's lack of understanding of a regulatory requirement, focused training about that requirement might be mandated as corrective action. A follow up audit can verify whether compliance has improved, and repeat training might be required either until compliance is achieved or disciplinary action is taken.

There is no single right answer about frequency of training. An effective compliance program will provide training as frequently as needed to be most effective. Answering these questions can assist in determining frequency:

- How frequent is employee turnover in a given department or area?
- How frequently are regulations and rules updated or promulgated in a specific compliance content area?
- What is the volume of complaints or reports concerning a given topic, department, or area?
- What are the results of compliance audits and monitoring for certain areas or departments? Do the results warrant increasing or decreasing the frequency of training?

Accreditation

Accreditation in the healthcare industry is the process by which healthcare organizations try to meet certain standards, which are usually associated with patient care and quality. One of the most well-known accrediting organizations in healthcare is the Joint Commission, although there are many other recognized accrediting agencies. For example, Centers for Medicare and Medicaid Services (CMS) has deemed some accrediting agencies as meeting CMS requirements, such as conditions of participation, also known as CoPs. Accreditation is not the same as licensing, which is typically done at the state level.

Organizations that seek accreditation often have departments or teams that focus on patient quality standards. Sometimes accreditation professionals work in the compliance department, but the two functions are typically separated in practice.

Accrediting standards may vary from one agency to the next, as well as by the type of organization seeking accreditation. For example, most standards applicable to hospital accreditation fall into these common categories:

- Patient's rights
- Emergency preparedness
- Quality assessment and performance improvement program
- Medical record services
- Infection control

The principles outlined in this chapter apply to accreditation training as well as compliance training. The obvious differences include the content and the fact that learners tend to be directly involved in patient care, quality, and organizational operations, but there is still great overlap.

Conclusion

Compliance programs are critical to all healthcare organizations. Effective compliance programs provide training and education to staff, volunteers, and key business partners, ensuring they understand the intersection of healthcare laws and regulations and healthcare tasks they perform. Major examples of compliance content include privacy and security (HIPAA); the medical coding, billing, and claims process and the Federal False Claims Act; and financial relationships with physicians and others (Stark law, Anti-Kickback Statute).

In addition to legal and regulatory content, the approach taken in training should focus on sound principles of adult learning theory and practice. Compliance trainers and talent development professionals should be well-versed in these key educational psychology principles and how they influence developing and delivering compliance training to healthcare staff. The most significant of these principles comes from the work of Malcolm Knowles, whose four principles of adult learning (or andragogy) include:

- Adults need to be involved in the planning and evaluation of their instruction.
- Experience (including mistakes) provides the basis for the learning activities.
- Adults are most interested in learning about subjects that have immediate relevance and impact to their job or personal life.
- Adult learning is problem-centered rather than content-oriented.

Following these principles in both design and delivery will make compliance training more effective.

Admittedly, compliance training is not everyone's favorite topic. It can be hard for learners, and those designing and delivering the compliance training often feel like they are force feeding the message. But, following the training principles and concepts discussed here can make compliance training more palatable to both the learner and the designer or trainer. When that end is achieved, employees and organizations truly benefit from better compliance knowledge and can avoid costly and reputation-killing investigations, headlines, and interruptions in patient care. When compliance training is more thoughtfully designed, delivered, and assessed, patients ultimately win because their care givers are focused on providing life-saving care instead of the results of noncompliance.

CHAPTER 18

WORKING WITH SUBJECT MATTER EXPERTS

GREG OWEN-BOGER AND DALE LUDWIG

It was late afternoon and the hospital's newest cohort of nurses was in the home stretch of a long day of nursing orientation. Donna, a seasoned instructional designer, was observing the session. Emmet, an RN and infection control expert, was delivering his portion of the training—a module about exposure to blood.

Emmet had been delivering this module off and on for a few years, but Donna had recently updated it to comply with new regulations that were put in place after a merger. She had sent the new module to Emmet a week ago with a heads up and asked for a few minutes of his time to run through the content. Unfortunately, Emmet's a busy guy and time got away from both of them.

As Emmet began the session, it became clear to Donna that he hadn't put much thought into how he'd deliver the new information. He was struggling to deliver the slides, some of which he hadn't realized had been animated to show each step in a procedure separately. He later admitted to Donna that he hadn't used slideshow mode when he reviewed the new slide deck, so he was surprised when he had to click so many times to bring in each piece of information.

Issues with the newly animated slides wasn't all Donna noticed about Emmet's delivery. The reason she was in the room in the first place was because she'd been hearing some negative feedback on his performance during recent orientation sessions. Sure enough, as she observed Emmet, she started to understand why. Not only was he not prepared, he was treating the training like a lecture. His delivery was dull and lifeless. He sounded like he was delivering the content to a group of first-day nursing students rather than 22 well-educated professionals. He failed to acknowledge what they already knew and that this training was supposed to focus on the procedures *at this hospital at this particular point in time.*

As she walked away from the session, Donna realized that the training was failing on two levels: Emmet was focusing on the wrong learning objectives and his delivery was condescending to the nurses. She thought they deserved better than what they got, and she knew it was up to her to address the situation before the next orientation, which was scheduled for the week after next.

This chapter is for two types of readers:

- First, it's for talent development professionals, like Donna, who work in the healthcare field and design training to be delivered by SMEs. We'll show how talent development professionals support SMEs (for example, they may consult with SMEs during the design phase, create facilitator guides and other support material, and coach SMEs on training delivery). We recognize that the work you do may include all or only some of these steps.
- Second, it is for SMEs, people like Emmett who deliver training in their area of expertise. There is a section at the end of this chapter that focuses specifically on their needs.

The Challenge of Working With Healthcare SMEs

When subject matter experts (SMEs) are brought into the learning and development process, it can feel like two worlds colliding. While their experience, knowledge, and insight are crucial to the success of the learning initiative, finding the best way to tap into it for the benefit of learners is a challenge. No matter what a SME's expertise may be, communicating it to learners in a way that leads to understanding and application on the job is not easy.

The challenge is acutely felt in healthcare because the stakes are high. Not only is the learning content crucial to the well-being of patients, it also affects the organization's ability to remain compliant and, ultimately, earn the trust of the community it serves. In healthcare, learning also takes place in an environment where time is short and scheduling is challenging.

Helping SMEs bring their expertise into the learning process is a matter of easing the tensions found in all live, interactive training programs. Here's what we mean:

- Regardless of industry, there is always a tension between the work that is done in advance of training and the work that is done during its delivery. What is prepared—the plan and its structure—must be delivered in a way that is spontaneous and interactive. This is not the same as a Q&A session after a lecture, where the interaction is very controlled and is in response to what has been said. A learning conversation is a lively dialogue, driven by learner needs and perspective. This is often counterintuitive for SMEs, and it is made more difficult when SMEs are delivering training designed by others.

- There is also a tension between possessing a high level of expertise and the ability to help others understand that expertise. This is strongly felt in healthcare. In an article in the *New York Times* titled "Those Who Can Do, Can't Teach," Adam Grant writes that Albert Einstein was a poor teacher, famously delivering lectures that were uninspiring and disorganized. But Einstein wasn't alone in this struggle. As Grant points out, the more expertise someone has, the more difficult it is for them to help others understand it.

Healthcare SMEs need to find a way to manage these tensions, making the work of talent development professionals supporting them more complicated. We've found it helpful to think of adult learning events not as lectures, but as Orderly Conversations, which we wrote about in *The Orderly Conversation: Business Presentations Redefined.* We define an Orderly Conversation as an outcome-oriented communication that is prepared, well-organized, *and* takes place in a responsive, conversational way. By using this to define training delivery, we can put a finer point on what the interaction between SMEs and learners should be—not lecture or casual conversation, but something that shares characteristics of both. We can also help them understand that their strengths and weaknesses are often connected to a preference for the "orderly" part of the process or a high level of comfort with the "conversation."

Getting Started With SMEs

Let's begin with the assumption that everyone involved in the design and delivery of learning is an expert in their own area. This idea is put forward very persuasively by Chuck Hodell in his book *SMEs From the Ground Up.* Hodell says that while the SMEs you're working with may be experts in their field, you and your L&D peers bring different types of expertise to the process—knowledge of learning design, virtual delivery platforms, adult learning, and coaching, for example. This expertise is crucial to the learning process.

The challenge you face, of course, is finding the best way for people with different types of expertise to work together. This begins by assuring SMEs that your job is to help them be successful in the classroom, and that you will focus on efficiency and ease for them and their learners.

Roles and Responsibilities

Many healthcare SMEs come to the L&D process with assumptions and approaches they learned as students in college or medical school. This is natural, but it can be a problem because the relationship between a university professor and a student is very different than the relationship between a SME and their learners. Unlike students in nursing school, the nurses Emmett was teaching came into orientation with a broad range of experience. His failure to take that into account was one of the problems Donna observed.

As Figure 18-1 shows, the differences between academic and workplace learning can be broken down in terms of power and authority, evaluation of learning, and application of learning. Each one influences the assumptions that SMEs make.

Figure 18-1. Differences Between Academic Teaching and L&D in Healthcare

	Academic System	Healthcare System
Power and authority	Professors have the power and authority to shape learning as they want.	The healthcare system holds the power and authority. SMEs work to meet the needs of the system.
Evaluation of learning	Professors set standards and evaluate learning when they choose.	Learning is evaluated in the moment, during training delivery. It is the SMEs responsibility to help learners learn, not judge their performance.
Application of learning	Real-world application is not the professor's primary responsibility. Each class is part of a student's long-term development.	On-the-job application is crucial for every learner and is the reason training is taking place.

While most SMEs recognize these distinctions, you may find that some academic assumptions still hold sway over their teaching habits. Figure 18-2 highlights what we mean.

Figure 18-2. Overcoming SME Assumptions and Concerns

	SME Concern	Your Response
Power and authority	"I don't think the information you're asking me to deliver has been thought out correctly."	If the plan cannot be changed, remind the SME that their teaching must support the needs of the healthcare organization. They are not the final arbiter of the learning goal. Their expertise serves it.
Evaluation of learning	"I said it. They just didn't understand."	SMEs may show frustration when learners don't immediately understand a particular point. This is an example of evaluating too quickly and blaming learners for not immediately grasping an idea. When this happens, SMEs need to be patient and remember that they are responsible for learning, not merely information delivery.
Application of learning	"They should be able to understand how this applies."	Sometimes the final step in the learning process—application in real-world situations—is easy for a SME to gloss over. Application is, of course, the most important step in workplace learning. Encourage SMEs to remember that every learning point needs to be clearly connected to the learners' jobs and responsibilities.

Two Hats

A good way to help SMEs understand their role is to help them understand that they wear two hats; that is, they have two distinct but equally important responsibilities. The first hat, which we'll call the SME hat, is about their knowledge and experience, as well as their ability to talk about it clearly and persuasively. This is why they are brought into the learning process. The second hat is the trainer hat, which is less comfortable for SMEs because it's about managing the learning process as it takes place.

A good way to explain these dual responsibilities is to point out that learning succeeds through the conversation that takes place between SMEs and their learners. So, while on one level the SME needs to deliver information clearly and persuasively, on another level they need to manage the Orderly Conversation that takes place in the moment of delivery.

When SMEs are comfortable wearing both hats, they will understand that success occurs on two levels. Meeting the first level, the learning objectives, requires managing the second level, the learning conversation (Figure 18-3).

Figure 18-3. How SMEs Can Wear Both Hats Successfully

Meet Learning Objectives	Manage the Learning Conversation
• Follow a learner-centric plan. • Deliver material in a clear, understandable way. • Use their expertise to serve the learning content.	• Engage learners in a fruitful conversation. • Be open and curious about learners' experience and connect it with what they are learning. • Make participating easy. • Manage the give and take. • Summarize conversations to keep them in the context of learning goals. • Connect dots between learning points. • Ask questions and encourage discussion. • Create thinking opportunities. • Reinforce what was previously learned.

Key Takeaways

Your role as a talent development expert is to teach SMEs how to teach. To succeed, SMEs need to understand their responsibilities, including these principles:

- The academic model of teaching does not work in healthcare learning and development. SMEs need to focus instead on initiating and managing a learning conversation.
- SMEs succeed in the training environment when they understand that they wear two hats. The SME hat helps bring their experience and expertise into the learning process. When wearing the trainer hat, SMEs keep an eye on learning goals, training design, and efficiency.

Helping SMEs Initiate and Manage a Learning Conversation

While a successful learning conversation takes place in the moment of delivery, there are things you can do during the design phase to make that easier. In this section, we'll talk about three of them:

- Framing the learning conversation
- Creating facilitator guides and slide notes that function as job aids
- Designing slides for ease of delivery and understanding

Framing

Every learning conversation requires a strong frame. While the primary frame is delivered at the beginning of the training session, it is more than a traditional introduction. A good frame assures learners that the training they are about to receive is important and appropriate to their work. It also communicates a specific goal and easy-to-follow structure.

If you're an instructional designer, build a frame using four components: current situation, goal, agenda, and benefits (Figure 18-4).

Figure 18-4. Four Components of a Strong Frame

	Purpose	Answers These Learner Questions
Current situation	Sets context and helps the SME meet learners where they are	• "Why am I here?" • "Why do I need to learn this?"
Goal	Communicates a sense of purpose and helps the SME set clear expectations	• "What will I be able to do or understand when this is over?"
Agenda	Communicates structure and a sense of direction and efficiency	• "How is this organized?" • "Is it going to be easy to follow along?"
Benefits	Communicates how learners, patients, or the system will benefit from this learning program	• "What's the takeaway from this?" • "How will this benefit me, my patients, or the hospital?"

If your training involves PowerPoint slides, use a few slides to support the frame. You may want one for each step, but you could also use fewer by combining steps on a single slide. Another option is to eliminate the steps from the slides but include them in the facilitator guide.

Let's look at an example: A training session delivered by a nurse to other nursing staff members at a hospital. The nurses are learning about new procedures to reduce the number of hospital-associated infections (HAIs). Figure 18-5 outlines what she might say.

Figure 18-5. Example of a Strong Frame

Current Situation	Good afternoon everyone, as you all know, starting this week we have new procedures in place to reduce HAIs.
Goal	My goal today is for you to leave this training confident in your ability to follow the procedures that are now part of your daily work.
Agenda	We'll be focusing on three things: • New PPE requirements that are more stringent than in the past • Improved cleaning procedures for patient and nonpatient areas • New intake procedures for patients transferring from another healthcare facility
Benefits	When we're finished, you will walk away with: • Confidence in your ability to follow the new rules • Knowledge of where to get support if you need help • Belief in our ability to reduce HAIs by following some pretty easy procedures

This frame brings learners into the training conversation and gives them a sense of relevance and efficiency. It also helps the SME keep their expertise in the context of the learning process, not as something that exists apart from it.

While the frame needs to be strong, it also needs to be adaptable. If training is delivered multiple times to different groups of learners—for example nurses working different shifts—the frame will be slightly different for each delivery because the learners are not the same. They may have different levels of experience or knowledge, which may lead to slightly different goals or benefits. Your SME may make these adaptations naturally, but you still need to communicate that they are being made so the learners know their perspective is being taken into account.

You'll notice that the goal in the frame is related to but different from the learning objectives. In our experience, learners' eyes glaze over when learning objectives are brought into the training room. It's not that learning objectives aren't useful. They are. As talent development professionals, we need learning objectives to get the design right. It's just that the way they are often written isn't useful to learners because they're too formal and usually very specific. Instead, think of the goal as the bucket that the learning objectives fit into, and have the SME focus on that.

Framing doesn't have to be limited to the beginning of a session or module. You can use a new frame when you move from module to module, when coming back from a break, or when setting up an activity. Anytime context shifts, learners will appreciate the focus provided by the frame.

Whenever you ask the SME to develop their own content, we recommend that you help them create the frame because it doesn't always come naturally for them.

Facilitator Guides and Slide Notes

Facilitator guides can take different forms. They can be stand-alone documents or text placed in PowerPoint slide notes. Regardless, they should support SMEs in two ways: to prepare for the training and as a job aid during delivery. Doing so will help the SMEs:

- Understand the overall structure of the training, answering the question, "Why is this laid out this way?" Their comfort will increase once they understand how the design flows and what it is intended to do, and sometimes just as importantly what it is not intended to do.
- Gain focus and flexibility. The SME will be able to focus on the learning that should take place, not just the content being delivered. This will give them the freedom they need to deliver content in their own way.

No matter what type of support you offer, always avoid scripting. Even if your goal is to communicate the meaning of a slide or simply a possible way to deliver its content, scripting it will make things more difficult. When given a script, SMEs may rely on it too much, trying their best to follow it, reading or memorizing it, or even asking questions exactly as they are written in the script. Or, as is far more common, the SME will ignore the script altogether, treating it as a hinderance. In both cases the learning designer is failing to supply what the SME needs during delivery.

If the design allows, give your SMEs options. There may be a range of examples they could use to support a learning point. Let them decide which one to use or give them permission to use their own. Or you could offer optional slides that the SME can use, or not, given their preferences. You may want to include a couple slides intended to make the same point and let the SME choose; for example, one SME may prefer a drawing of a medical device because of its accuracy, while another may prefer a photograph of the device in use. Either is fine because from the learners' perspective, both slides work.

Encourage SMEs to share their experiences and stories, which can make otherwise dull training come to life. It would be a good idea to insert story reminders in the facilitation guide from time to time.

Slide Design

When we're working with SMEs and there are slides involved, the most push back and frustration always concerns slide design. No one—trainer, SME, or anyone else—feels immediately comfortable delivering slides designed by someone else. So, the frustration is understandable.

Sometimes the issue stems from slides that are over-designed. They may include too many colors, too many highlighted or bolded words, overuse of slide animation, redundant graphics, and wordy bulleted lists. While these design decisions were likely intended to make the meaning of the slide clearer, they usually don't.

On the other side of the spectrum, some slides are confusing because they don't include enough information to be helpful. This may be due to vague slide titles, graphics that are poorly labeled, metaphors that don't quite work, or bulleted lists that are jumbled or confusing.

When designing slides, focus on ease of delivery as well as ease of understanding. Once the content has been collected and organized into a slide deck, you can make adjustments such as:

- Create slide titles that are meaningful to learners and helpful to the SME. Too often slide titles simply refer to what is on the slide. Adjust them to communicate why this information is important or how learners will use it back on the job.
- Streamline bullet points so they're concise, readable, and parallel in structure. Parallel bullet points each start with the same part of speech (noun, verb, or adjective).
- Decrease the amount of animation on slides used in live face-to-face settings. For virtual delivery, more animation can help virtual learners stay focused.

It's not realistic to assume that SMEs will be as prepared to deliver the training as an expert facilitator would be. But this isn't because they're lazy. It's because they lack the training and practice talent development professionals have. They also don't have the time or bandwidth to think through every single "what if." Because of this, think of slides and facilitator guides as in-the-moment job aids. The SME should be able to look at a slide title or page in the facilitation guide and be reminded immediately of what they should say. This is very different from developing materials for talent development professionals.

Key Takeaways

Designers should create support materials that help SMEs initiate and manage an effective learning conversation:

- Training should be framed to bring learners into the conversation. The frame promises relevance and efficiency for learners via the current situation, the goal of the training, the agenda, and learner benefits.
- Facilitator guides or slide notes should be designed to act as in-the-moment job aids, not a script.
- If slides are used, they should be designed for easy delivery and understanding, with meaningful slide titles, concise bullets, and easy-to-grasp visuals.

Coaching SMEs on Training Delivery

As shown throughout this chapter, part of working with SMEs as a talent development professional means demonstrating how to deliver training effectively. They'll often require coaching as they progress from lecturing to facilitating effective learning programs. Providing coaching on their training delivery can involve tapping into how they talk to and treat their patients.

Using a Bedside Manner

A few years ago, we were coaching a physician who served as his hospital's chief quality officer. We'll call him Dr. B. In this role, he communicated externally to the community the hospital served, as well as internally to the board and staff members. While working with him, we noticed that Dr. B consistently interrupted people as they were talking, jumping in a bit too quickly to offer his comments.

When we pointed this out to him, he smiled and said, "I get that all the time. You should hear my kids call me out on that. I guess I always interrupt them." He went on to say, "I think I picked up the habit in medical school because when you're a med student you want to be first with the answer. Conversations move fast. So, you never wait for the other person to stop talking before you jump in." We asked if he interrupted his patients. "No," Dr. B said, "that's a completely different thing."

The completely different thing Dr. B was talking about is the difference between interacting with his peers and interacting with patients; that is, his bedside manner. He learned that communicating with patients required listening and self-awareness, focusing on tone and body language, clarity, simplification, and emotional intelligence. Good bedside manner builds trust, communicates compassion, and improves results because patients feel heard and understood.

Everyone working in healthcare recognizes the importance of having an effective bedside manner when working with patients and their families. Whether they are nurses, technicians, or the people sitting behind the desk in the lobby, the effort is made to treat patients and their families with care and concern.

There's a strong parallel between patient interaction and the two levels of success required for effective training delivery. When a healthcare worker's bedside manner isn't good, patients can't listen or focus as well because they are feeling nervous, frightened, or intimidated. No matter how clear and concise a nurse's instructions might be (meeting Level 1 success), the patient's emotional state prevents understanding (managing Level 2 success).

The same lack of understanding can occur in the training room, but for different reasons. During training, SMEs need to be highly aware of how the information is being received. They need to express empathy and check in frequently to make sure the learners are understanding the information. The reason for this is not because learners are frightened or worried about their health—as is the case with nervous patients—instead, learners may be overwhelmed or distracted by work or worried about how they will be judged by the SME or their peers if they don't understand. They don't want to seem confused in public.

It's the SMEs job, therefore, to normalize confusion, to make it OK to be unsure about what's being learned, and to show they're allowed to be frustrated or resistant. It's important to make these feelings and concerns part of the learning conversation. It's one of the primary ways SMEs can demonstrate their concern for learner understanding, not merely demonstrating expertise.

For your SMEs to do that, you need to help them:

- Be open and curious about the learner's experience and concerns.
- Listen well without judgement; probe for more information when necessary.
- Connect the dots; take responsibility for helping learners see the forest and the trees.
- Embrace the learning opportunity of wrong answers by using them to uncover the thinking behind the answer.
- Understand the power of admitting their own frustration or past errors in approach or response—doing so will build trust and empathy.

Engaging Learners in the Conversation

One of the most fundamental and sometimes most challenging things for SMEs to do is to initiate a genuine conversation with learners. When SMEs are engaged with learners, they are in the moment, focused on others, and connecting.

We recommend focusing on engagement from the very beginning of the training session, specifically when the frame is delivered. The frame is, in its broadest sense, a conversation starter that's focused on learners and their needs. It provides the headline for what's to come through its "We're all here, let's get started" nature, almost as if it's an invitation to begin. Thus, this is the perfect time for SMEs to concentrate on the skills that help them connect with learners and get focused. The two required skills, eye contact and pausing, also happen to be the same skills used during patient interactions.

Eye contact, a natural part of face-to-face communication, should be used intentionally at the beginning of a training session. There is no magic length of eye contact that is necessary, and approaching it from that direction is really missing the point. What's important is that individual learners should feel they are each being addressed. If your SME has a habit of avoiding eye contact or merely scanning the room in a scattershot sort of way, encourage them to slow down and hold eye contact a bit longer than feels necessary. This will make their eye contact seem more intentional and effective.

SMEs need to be aware of and use pausing confidently as well, because it provides time to think, stay focused, and respond to what someone else has just said. It's crucial to the learning conversation as we pointed out in the Dr. B example. From the learners' point of view, pausing gives them time to take in information and an opening to ask a question if they need to.

Facilitating Activities

Healthcare L&D often includes activities, which might focus on trying out new equipment, hands-on experience with new software, or practicing patient interactions. Help SMEs facilitate activities to assess understanding and reinforce learning. Do this by encouraging them to:

- Frame each activity for relevance and context.
- Debrief the activity to reinforce learning and uncover any confusion learners may have experienced.
- Trust the activity to achieve its goal, which sometimes takes patience.

Planning for Virtual Delivery

If your SME is delivering training virtually, encourage them to do a dry run beforehand. Remind them that the purpose of a dry run is not to perfect training delivery, but to get comfortable with the virtual platform, iron out technical problems, fit the training into the time available for it, and develop flexibility. We strongly recommend using a virtual host (or producer) to support the SME during delivery. With the host focusing on virtual technology, the SME can focus on learning.

Delivering Feedback to a SME

Depending on the amount of time available and the SME's openness to it, you may have the opportunity to coach your SME before training is delivered or offer feedback afterward. Regardless of when or how you deliver it, giving a SME feedback can be a challenge. Defensiveness, impatience, lack of time, and ego can all affect a SME's willingness to accept feedback, no matter how well-intentioned it may be.

Here are some recommendations to make the process easier and more effective for everyone:

- Coaching and feedback are always about building self-awareness. It's better to point out what you have observed rather than evaluating their performance.
- Be sensitive to the fact that some SMEs tend to follow the plan too strictly while others improvise too much. The first type needs to work on being more flexible; the second needs to trust the learning design to keep training focused. There is nothing wrong with either approach but understanding what each SME prefers is useful.
- Begin every coaching session with a self-assessment. Ask SMEs how they feel about the training program they delivered. They may feel good or bad, effective or not, they may even be unsure. No matter their response, build your feedback from there. This will help you avoid prescriptive, rules-based guidance so you can focus on building self-awareness and reinforcement instead.
- Keep your recommendations simple and actionable. This is important whenever you're coaching someone, but with SMEs in the training room, it's especially necessary. Asking SMEs to pause a bit more or ask more open-ended questions is much better feedback than saying "your speaking pace was fast and some of the learners looked confused."

Key Takeaways

When coaching SMEs to deliver training, keep these ideas in mind:

- Healthcare SMEs should consider the similarities between patient interaction and successful training delivery. Both types of communication require high levels of self-awareness and awareness of others' needs and concerns.
- SMEs should use eye contact and pausing to engage learners in the learning conversation.
- Individual SMEs improve along different paths. Some need to focus on being more flexible and responsive when training. Others need to trust the structure of their content to be easier to follow.
- When coaching SMEs on delivery, be sensitive to their perspective and keep recommendations simple and actionable.

Conclusion

Working with SMEs is a subtle art, especially within the complex, challenging world of healthcare. While SMEs bring a level of insight and experience to the learning process that is impossible to find anywhere else, they still need our support to succeed in the learning environment. As talent development professionals, it's our job to make SMEs comfortable and effective in their training role. We do that when we:

- Help SMEs understand that training delivery requires skills outside their own area of expertise.
- Help SMEs frame the training they deliver, and each module contained in it, to communicate a sense of relevance and efficiency for learners. It's the SME's job to bring learners into the learning conversation.
- Create facilitator guides that act as in-the-moment job aids for SMEs—avoid scripting and instead focus on the intent of each module.
- Design slides that are easily delivered and understood. Use meaningful titles, clear graphics, and concise, parallel bullet points.
- Coach SMEs to deliver training with the same level of concern and focus that medical professionals bring to patient interactions. Be sure to avoid prescriptive, rules-based feedback; base your recommendations on what you've observed, not what you assume; and provide feedback that is specific and actionable.

Following these guidelines will help you help SMEs succeed and make working with SMEs a much more enjoyable experience.

If You Are a SME

As a subject matter expert, you play a crucial role not only in the training program you're delivering, but also in the success of the healthcare system where you work. Delivering training can often feel like a burden. This is understandable because of your existing workload and lack of free time during your regular clinical activities. Keep in mind that there's a reason you've been tasked with training your colleagues. Rather than thinking of training as a burden, what if you treated it as an honor to be asked? Sometimes this subtle shift in mindset can be helpful. As you work with your TD partner to develop the content, be honest with them about your time and bandwidth limitations. It's their job to help you and make you look good, so your honesty about what you can and cannot accomplish will help them set you up for success.

Here are some additional guidelines:

- **Partner with L&D.** It's common for SMEs to lack a full understanding of the L&D role. Think of the individuals you work with as peers with a common goal. Just as you partner with other healthcare providers when working with patients, you should think of L&D practitioners as partners in learning. They are experts in adult learning and are there to help you look good. Let them do that.
- **Make it a learning conversation.** As you think about how you want the training to go, be careful not to think of it as a presentation. While training can look a lot like a presentation, training needs to be focused on learning and on-the-job application. Focus the content on achieving the learning objectives you've received from your partner in talent development.
- **Keep the big picture in mind.** Pay close attention to learning objectives as you prepare to deliver the training. This will help you stay focused on the most important concepts and distinguish "nice to know" from "need to know" information. Learning objectives don't necessarily need to be read or described to learners though. Sticking with the bigger picture is usually a better idea. As you prepare to deliver the training, review the session's structure or learning arc, which will remind you of the big picture and how each module fits together to form the whole.
- **Greet learners as they arrive.** There's always informal conversation prior to a training event. This happens as people file into the room. We recommend that you include yourself in these moments, and greet people as they arrive. This will ease any tension you, or they, may be feeling.
- **Frame the learning conversation.** Use the framing strategy outlined in this chapter to formalize the conversation and get things started on the right foot.
- **Get comfortable with your slides.** There will be times when you look at a slide or other type of visual aid and be mystified as to why it was designed in such a way or why the order is what it is. This is very common. Before you make changes, ask questions of your talent development partner. There may be very good reasons for why things are laid out as they are. If you get satisfactory answers, stick with the plan you've been given. On the other hand, if you're still confused, have a conversation about what could be made better. Remember, your talent development partner is an

expert in adult learning, and they want you to be successful. Those two things are not mutually exclusive.

- **Share your experiences and stories.** There is a reason you've been asked to deliver training. You are the expert and you have stories to share. Please do! Learners generally appreciate real-world stories. Just make sure they're relevant and help advance learning and on-the-job application.
- **Rely on your bedside manner.** As a healthcare professional, you understand the need for a thoughtful bedside manner. Build off this strength and use it to your advantage in the training room. Learners can be vulnerable, distracted, and uneasy about learning. This feeling is not unlike what patients experience. Being empathetic, connecting through eye contact, pausing to think and let learners think, checking in for understanding, listening closely to questions, and reserving judgment are all skills that can work in your favor in the training room.
- **Debrief activities to advance learning.** Debriefing activities and discussions often get short shrift during learning events. Don't let this happen! Debriefs are your opportunity to evaluate whether your content was learned, so don't shy away from discussing wrong answers or mistakes. Understanding how someone reached the wrong conclusion can offer rich learning opportunities for everyone. Debriefs are opportunities for learners to learn from each other. Rather than being the one with all the answers, facilitate the conversation and let learners share their knowledge and experiences.
- **Accept feedback with grace.** When you receive feedback from your L&D partners, try not to take it personally. Teaching adults is hard, and they've made a career out of it. If they suggest you've gone into too much detail, take that advice and try to be more concise. If they ask you to slow down, it's because you're going too fast for learners to digest what you've said. If they recommend fewer personal stories, it's because of time management rather than being a judgment of your storytelling skills. Remember that they have your back, and everyone's best interests at heart.

PART 5

DIGITAL TRANSFORMATION AND LITERACY

CHAPTER 19

FUTURE OF LEARNING TECHNOLOGIES

MARY E. HOLTSCHNEIDER AND CHAN W. PARK

The use of technology in the current workplace learning environment is continuously changing to meet diverse learners' needs. The healthcare arena is no exception. From the education needs analysis, curriculum design, and course implementation to post-training evaluation, new and existing technologies allow TD professionals to tailor learning content to address the different needs of healthcare professionals. Indeed, in today's complex and demanding healthcare learning environments, the efficient use and seamless integration of advanced technologies has become an essential skill for successful TD professionals.

Practicing clinicians with direct patient care responsibilities and nonclinical employees share the same focus of providing optimal patient-centered care. Clinicians must comply with state and federal regulatory requirements for licensure and certification, which are continually evolving to meet growing healthcare challenges. Depending on the individual healthcare facility, clinicians must also meet a variety of credentialing, privileging, and competency-based training requirements. Thus, they must maintain current knowledge of the national standards and guidelines for patient care and demonstrate they can competently perform the clinical skills mandated by their professional role and employer.

High-fidelity learning technologies with enhanced realism play a vital role in meeting many of these growing healthcare mandates. The increasing demand for healthcare professionals to work in interprofessional teams and the importance of effective interprofessional communication are the latest advances in a decades-long trend toward team-based care and greater diversity, equity, and inclusion in the workplace. As the healthcare environment becomes increasingly culturally diverse and technologically complex, the demand on TD professionals to find innovative ways to prepare the modern healthcare staff has grown.

Modern day adult learners often find themselves "distracted, impatient, and overwhelmed," and want their training to be "untethered, on-demand, collaborative, and empowering" (Bersin by Deloitte 2014). On average, only 1 percent of a typical work week is focused on work-related training and development. The educational challenge before healthcare leadership and the TD community, therefore, is to determine how to effectively and efficiently leverage existing healthcare technologies to meet these demands.

In this chapter, we'll start by offering a broad overview of technologies available to TD professionals throughout the healthcare system. From there, we'll look at how these technologies are being used in the healthcare system and the unique challenges they pose to learners and TD professionals. In particular, we will discuss virtual conferencing platforms and simulation technologies (including high-fidelity computerized manikins, immersive environments, wearable training devices, and avatar-based debriefing tools), and how they facilitate improved adult learning environments. We conclude each section with a set of key points and questions to consider when evaluating the use of these technologies.

Technology in the Healthcare Workplace

To capture some of the different possible technology touchpoints in the healthcare setting, let's follow along with Jonathan, a critical care registered nurse (RN) with 10 years of clinical experience. Jonathan was hired into a large academic medical center hospital as the nurse manager for the cardiac intensive care unit (CCU). In past roles, he had attended several days of in-person onboarding before starting his work. As nurse manager, Jonathan needs additional education and training to prepare for his new leadership role, in addition to the overall clinical orientation all newly hired nurses undergo. Although he is generally comfortable with technology, Jonathan has not been exposed to many of the learning technologies he will encounter in this new job.

TD professionals must be prepared to work with new hires with varying degrees of technological ability and propensity to embrace the use of technology in the workplace. We will follow Jonathan through his onboarding and orientation process to see how the integration of advanced healthcare technologies is helping meet each of the four adult learning needs.

The entire onboarding process was conducted remotely using a virtual video conferencing system. Logging on from home, Jonathan joined the other new hires to receive general information regarding employment benefits and professional expectations. Let's see how virtual conferencing technology helped meet Jonathan's learning needs.

Untethered, On Demand, and Empowering

Each employee was assigned courses to complete in the organization's learning management system (LMS). Assignments were sent via email and text, and the LMS recorded Jonathan's attendance and completion times. Every time he finished a course, the LMS automatically checked off the item in his orientation packet and reflected it on his updated competency files. This convenient and reliable automated process meant that Jonathan no longer had to keep a paper record or submit any paperwork to HR. He knew exactly what he'd done, when it was finished, and what he still needed to do. Jonathan felt empowered by the flexibility of the training and appreciated the efficiency of the system.

Jonathan's next step was to update his cardiopulmonary resuscitation (CPR) certificate, which required knowledge and skills demonstrations. He was granted access to a room in the CCU containing a laptop connected to a computerized manikin (a setup devised by the American Heart Association Resuscitation Quality Initiative, RQI). Here he first took an online scenario-based training to satisfy the knowledge portion of the certificate. Once he'd done that successfully, Jonathan was directed to the manikin to perform the skills demonstration, which would be recorded automatically and analyzed by the computerized manikin.

Because this room was accessible 24 hours a day, seven days a week and a CPR instructor didn't need to be present to assess his performance, Jonathan was able to complete his CPR requirements in less than two hours on a weekday evening. Compared to previous methods, which involved signing up for an in-person class during the day at a separate location from the clinical unit, he found this new process both liberating and empowering. Furthermore, he was able to review the cases as many times as needed to successfully complete them and the skills demonstration—he was given specific feedback of what he did correctly and areas where he could improve after each attempt. Jonathan felt psychologically safe training under these conditions. For the first time, he had an internal motivation to learn and improve his skills, not for a grade but personal gratification.

The RQI system's training methods are based on research from the American Heart Association (AHA), which found that refreshing one's knowledge and CPR skills on a quarterly basis resulted in improved performance and retention (Bhanji et al. 2015). Jonathan found this knowledge very empowering. For the first time in a long time, he believed that his employer was invested in his learning and clinical excellence.

Once Jonathan successfully completed this knowledge and skills portion, the LMS immediately updated his file to reflect the achievement. "Why weren't things always this easy and efficient?" he wondered.

Collaborative

After Jonathan completed the LMS and CPR requirements, he was assigned a date and time to for a live session with other individuals using the high-fidelity simulation manikin. The goals for the simulation sessions were to:

- Orient participants to emergency response interprofessional team training.
- Rehearse care scenarios for high-risk CCU patients (such as acute heart attacks, heart failure, or pulmonary embolisms).
- Encourage leadership development for his managerial role, including interprofessional communication, teamwork, and mindfulness.

The training was divided between two locations: the hospital simulation center and the actual clinical space in the CCU (in-situ training). During his CCU in-situ training, Jonathan would interact with other interprofessional team members—including nurses, physicians, respiratory therapists, and pharmacists—and practice clinical skills, team communication, and managing teamwork dynamics. He was pre-briefed with the instructions and expectations via email and text and felt fully prepared and comfortable about what to expect and what he was asked to do.

During the simulation training, Jonathan saw how using life-like or high-fidelity computerized manikins, wearable technology, and procedural task trainers could enhance the immersive learning experience. The collaborative nature of the simulation-based training reinforced several of the key concepts of interprofessional collaborative practice and team-based approaches to patient care that he had learned in nursing school. This was exhilarating and professionally reaffirming. Jonathan was extremely satisfied with the support and training he received during the orientation and was excited to be part of his new team.

Key Takeaways

- TD professionals can employ a variety of learning technologies to meet the needs of modern adult learners (untethered, on-demand, collaborative, and empowering) to enhance new employee engagement with required content. In so doing, this shows how the employer is investing in new staff training and development.
- Because of the potential for enhanced engagement, TD professionals can leverage learning technologies to help advance a new employee's comfort level with technological applications, especially those who have lower technological skills, less formal educational backgrounds, and limited exposure to emerging learning technology, such as high-fidelity simulation.
- TD professionals can implement a wide range of technology in the healthcare environment, depending on their budgets, staff expertise, and physical space. Many applications are affordable and scalable to meet learning needs across a wide spectrum of healthcare facilities.

TD Professionals and Learning Technologies in Healthcare

Let's explore how learning technologies, when used strategically, can enhance the satisfaction and value of the onboarding and orientation experience for new hires. We'll focus on virtual conferencing platforms, simulations, wearables, resuscitation quality initiative equipment, and avatar-based technologies. The viewpoint will be that of Hussein, a TD professional specializing in virtual learning for the hospital.

Virtual Conferencing Platforms

Typically, healthcare facility onboarding processes include a bimonthly live orientation and successfully completing a training checklist, which they would then submit to HR for processing. The consequences of any missing or improperly processed paperwork fell squarely on the new hire and invariably meant a delay in their start date.

The COVID-19 pandemic drastically altered the usual onboarding process, requiring new secure, reliable, and rapidly actionable methods of disseminating key information and education material to all new employees. To comply with social distancing requirements, healthcare facilities turned to virtual conference platforms to deliver onboarding information to new staff. While one could argue that virtual onboarding would have eventually become the norm, even without the pandemic, COVID-19 mandated an accelerated pace of change. This change also brought to light several unforeseen challenges for the healthcare leaders, TD professionals, and administrative staff, including issues of equity, privacy, security, compliance, and overall new employee satisfaction.

When the hospital tasked Hussein to assess which platform would be most useful for onboarding new employees, he investigated the platforms and noted their advantages and challenges (Figure 19-1).

Figure 19-1. Virtual Platform Advantages and Challenges

Advantages	Challenges
• Ability to access and participate in required training from remote locations • Respects social distancing requirements	• Lack of physical space for onboarding training • Complexity of computer and peripherals (camera, microphone, desk, chair) • Potentially unreliable and slow internet connection
• Provides options for breakout rooms mimicking live small group interactions	• Difficult for face-to-face (in-person) learners • Less engagement with the content • Limited social collaboration where participants can leverage their collective knowledge, experience, and skills • Basic or intermediate computer comfort and abilities are required • Unanticipated fatigue from being on virtual platforms rather than live, in-person classes
• Ability to record sessions for future use	• Privacy issues • Unanticipated or unpredictable comments or behavior • Potential over-use and over-reliance on platforms
• General ease of access and intuitive interfaces	• Remote work sites are not always free of distraction • Different devices have different user experiences (laptops, tablets, phones)

Hussein closely monitored the onboarding experience to identify any technical and programmatic issues. During his early observations, he noticed that many users were unable to navigate the virtual platform and appeared confused by all the icons and functional tabs. While a few participants seemed to find the virtual platform intuitive, those who did not voiced their displeasure and appeared visibly frustrated and withdrawn. He also noticed that hardware and connectivity issues disproportionately affected the quality of the training for those with slower internet connections or older computers. In addition, several users had difficulty activating their computer microphones, speakers, and cameras, while others didn't know how to mute or unmute their microphones when listening or answering a question. Still others were unfamiliar with how to engage with the interactive discussion feature. These factors all detracted from the level of engagement, negatively affecting the quality of the learning atmosphere.

Hussein realized he needed improved microlearning aids to help new staff navigate the online environment. In addition, he saw a need to provide quick, real-time answers to commonly asked questions. So, he decided to investigate whether artificial intelligence options or chatbots could help with this situation. As Hussein discovered, the transition to virtual delivery might pose more challenges than anticipated.

Key Takeaways

- Although virtual conferencing platforms are more common now than they used to be, talent development professionals must still ensure that individual learner needs are handled efficiently and appropriately.
- Issues of equitability need to be considered when moving to virtual onboarding. The organization will need to provide a free, accessible internet station that complies with social distancing rules for employees who lack a reliable personal computer or reliable Internet access.
- Clinical staff with patient care responsibilities generally do not adhere to a daytime work schedule, so it is imperative that job aids and other tools are available to them 24/7.
- TD professionals must be prepared to meet the diverse learning needs of new staff with different educational backgrounds, including no college experience, a PhD, a clinical practice doctorate, or other advanced degrees.

Healthcare Simulation Technology

Today, the term "healthcare simulation" is synonymous with advanced technology and innovation. Four examples of widely adopted healthcare simulation modalities are standardized patients, procedural task trainers, high fidelity computerized manikins, and haptics integrated training devices. Let's review a brief description of each modality and their common use for healthcare education.

Standardized Patients

Standardized patients (SPs) are trained healthcare actors who assume the role of patients, clinicians, family members, or other individuals in the clinical environment. SPs offer several advantages to the modern learner:

- They provide dynamic and nuanced human-to-human interaction, which elevates the level of learner engagement.
- They can provide timely and necessary formative feedback to guide the learner during the session.
- They can integrate wearable training devices that allow learners to perform clinical procedures directly on the SP.

With prior formal training, SPs can provide the learner with clinically accurate and relevant responses for real-time experience and feedback that corresponds to what they are likely to encounter when taking care of a live patient.

High-Fidelity Computerized Manikin Simulator

A high-fidelity computerized manikin simulator is an anatomically accurate life-sized human replica capable of providing visual, tactile, and auditory feedback to the learner. Equipped with advanced software, generators, and Wi-Fi internet connectivity, it can be programmed to operate independently or by an instructor working from a remote location. Clinical parameters (such as pulse, respiration, blood pressure, and oxygen saturation), as well as various physiologic properties (such as lung sounds and heart murmurs) or functions (such as pupillary constriction/dilation, tearing, blinking, tongue and throat swelling, and cough reflex) can be controlled to achieve the appropriate learning objective.

The term *high-fidelity* refers to the physical and functional realism of the manikin. An integrated patient monitor shows the real-time dynamic changes in the manikin's vital signs to reflect the appropriateness of the learner's intervention, such as the physiologic response to the administration of intravenous fluid, life-saving medication, or emergent procedure. This creates a realistic and immersive learner-patient interaction that does not pose any harm to an actual person. Many healthcare interprofessional teams use high-fidelity manikins in their leadership, communication, and teamwork training curriculum.

Haptic Devices

Haptic devices provide continuous tactile feedback to the learner to help improve psychomotor development and essential muscle memory. This is useful for procedural training, which requires careful attention to applied force, precision, and technical skill. For example, for surgical training in cricothyroidotomy, a haptic-enabled device can provide valuable feedback to prevent an inadvertent incision of the thyroid gland or carotid arteries or an accidental puncture of the esophagus, which can all be caused by an inappropriately deep incision due to excessive force and incorrect angle of approach. The use of devices with haptic capabilities has been invaluable for training technically challenging and often life-saving surgical procedures.

Procedural Task Trainers

Procedural task trainers are anatomically proportioned to provide a realistic replica of a particular area of the body, such as the head and neck, chest, arms, legs, and abdomen. These are commonly used to teach learners how to perform various invasive skills, such as using endotracheal intubation, cricothyroidotomy, central line placement, thoracentesis, thoracostomy, paracentesis, tourniquet placement, venous cutdown, and damage control packing.

Healthcare simulation modalities can be used alone or in combination, depending on the learning objectives of the simulation scenario. Let's explore the ways some of these modalities can be deployed and how their technological features provide optimal benefits for the learner.

As the new nurse manager of the CCU, Jonathan was required to participate in several simulation-based team training sessions. The goal was to reinforce the four Interprofessional Education Collaborative (IPEC) core competencies:

- Interprofessional teamwork and team-based practice
- Interprofessional communication practice
- Values and ethics for interprofessional practice
- Roles and responsibilities for collaborative practice (IPEC 2016)

These competencies were developed to ensure all newly graduating health professions students are prepared to enter the current complex healthcare environment and work collaboratively with other professions, rather than remain in silos with others from their own professions.

One required program was the code blue, or cardiac arrest, emergency response team training. This simulation training involved a patient who suddenly lost his pulse while getting up out of his hospital bed and a resulting hospital-wide activation of all designated personnel using the actual communication systems.

Jonathan was initially overwhelmed by the realism of the emergency response teamwork simulation. He saw how challenging and stressful it was to navigate the systems to assure optimal patient care.

"Surely, this doesn't happen by chance," he thought. "It has to be rehearsed the same way every time!" Everything from the call for the code blue activation, the assembling of responders, the equipment preparation, the dynamic teamwork and communication, to the actual emergency care rendered seemed like it was part of a well-orchestrated performance.

Jonathan couldn't remember the last time he felt this engaged and empowered. He found himself thinking, "I can do this. No, we can do this. This is a team effort." He could see how important it was to train in all aspects of the healthcare system. Issues he had not previously thought much about came to light during the immersive training, such as disseminating the code activation, assuring correct personnel assembly, availability of essential equipment, communicating with the patient transport service, and the importance of the laboratory and radiology services. He couldn't imagine how this could be learned or taught in the classroom, and appreciated the opportunity to see the code blue response team in action.

Many healthcare systems use high-fidelity manikins for emergency response training. This is especially useful for high-impact situations involving code blue (cardiac arrest), stroke code, and rapid response team training. Once again, Jonathan felt affirmed and validated as an integral member of the diverse hospital staff.

The goal for all healthcare professionals, regardless of educational background or experience, is to provide reliable and high-quality patient care by functioning with a healthcare team structure. Simulation and facilitated debriefing have been shown to increase engagement and provide learners with the opportunity to practice skills with team members, reflect on what went well and what could be done differently in the future, and ultimately transfer that knowledge to the workplace environment.

Key Takeaways

- Clinical realism and role integrity are important for creating high-quality immersive experiences for interprofessional team training.
- Healthcare systems demand that all professionals work effectively and efficiently in an interprofessional team structure.
- An emphasis on teamwork, communication, and behaviors that fosters mutual respect for the interprofessional setting helps promote a culture that is both empowering and collaborative.
- Simulation methods are not necessary if the learning objectives are straightforward and can be accomplished by basic information-sharing, lecture, cognitive aid, or other similar methods.

Wearable Technology

Wearable technology is often associated with fitness, health, and wellness monitoring. For the general consumer, most people have experienced it via smart watches, insulin pumps or glucose monitors, automated internal cardiac defibrillators (AICDs), or nerve stimulators. Different types of wearable technologies exist in the healthcare environment to enhance the fidelity or realism of a patient encounter and improve learner skill development. SPs are often used for this type of training.

Training prehospital, military, and healthcare personnel responsible for managing trauma, battlefield, and mass casualty injury patterns can be a daunting task. Under the Advanced Trauma Life Support (ATLS) guidelines, healthcare professionals must demonstrate competence in various life-saving skills such as hemorrhage control (tourniquet and clamping of bleeding vessels), airway management (placement of a breathing tube via the cricothyroid membrane or the oropharynx), and needle or chest tube placement (for a collapsed lung). Traditionally, these skills were rehearsed using procedural task trainers, live animals, and human cadavers.

Awareness of the strengths and limitations of each modality can guide the TD professional to choose the appropriate technology to meet the learner's need. Such factors include limited realism, availability, anatomical variance, quality of training, learner safety, and cost. Cut-suit technology—a surgical simulator worn by a trained SP that captures injury patterns—offers a cost-effective solution to many of these issues.

In Figure 19-2 a military corpsmen is performing a life-saving needle chest thoracostomy to relieve a tension pneumothorax on an SP wearing a cut-suit. Once the needle is inserted in the correct location, the patient's ability to breathe and vital signs are restored.

The trained SP wearing the cut-suit helps recreate the actual medical emergency by providing the clinical context and stage—the level of realism closely mirrors caring for real-life patients. SPs can offer salient visual, verbal, and psychological cues, which allows the learners to fully experience the challenges, pressures, and heightened emotions associated with caring for a patient with these types of injuries. Expert trainers can also wear the cut-suit and give direct formative and summative feedback from the patient's perspective, which is another critical aspect of healthcare training. This technology currently provides some of the highest levels of realism for learners to safely practice life-saving procedures without risk of injury to the SP.

To add an even greater sense of realism, trainers can immerse the learners in a virtual training environment that includes an audio-visual system producing sensory aspects that recreate conditions that elicit tension, fear, and chaos. The learners can then practice these essential medical interventions, teamwork, and communication skills under duress.

Other forms of wearable technology have sensory features that provide trained SPs with real-time learner performance, which they can use to provide immediate formative feedback or be collected for a more substantive and summative feedback. This type of wearable technology is beneficial for training nurses and respiratory therapists on the proper method and depth for suctioning a patient who has undergone a tracheostomy (Figure 19-3).

To help train healthcare professionals on this skill, the SP wears a specially developed vest with a sensor that sends them a signal if the learner is suctioning too deeply or aggressively.

Figure 19-2. Example of a Cut-Suit

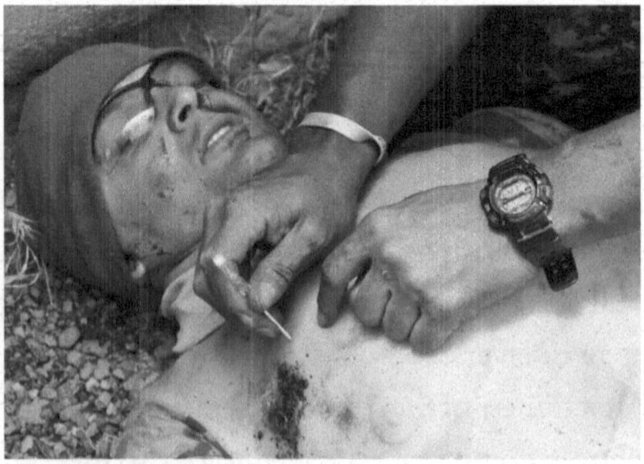

Photo courtesy of Strategic Operations.

The SP is trained to vigorously cough and display extreme discomfort if they receive this signal, which provides learner with a realistic reaction to their incorrect technique.

Prior to the availability of such technology, learners had to rely on skills acquired through practice on a static task trainer. Wearable tracheostomy training now allows the instructor to give precise feedback on the depth, intensity, and duration of the suctioning from a patient's point of view. This combination of wearable technology integrated with SPs continues to push the boundaries of healthcare training.

Figure 19-3. Example of Wearable for Suctioning Skill Training

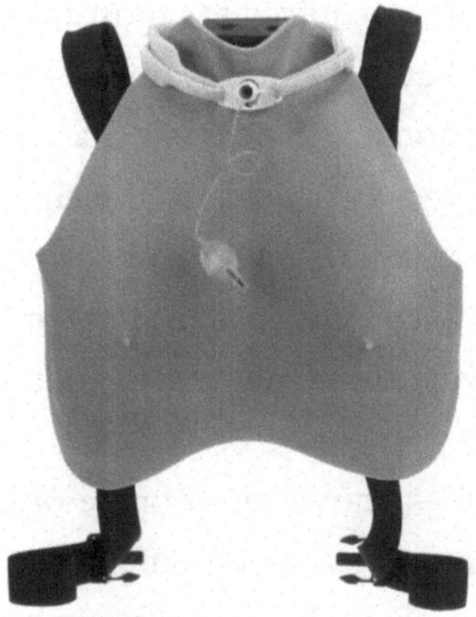

Image courtesy of Avkin.

Key Takeaways

- Wearable technology can be worn by anyone willing to serve as a volunteer; however, we advise that they're only worn by trained SPs who can offer real-time formative and summative feedback.
- When worn by SPs, wearable devices increase the emotional and physical fidelity for practicing essential patient care skills. These devices are affordable, easy to use, and do not require a large amount of storage space.
- Operating and performing life-saving procedures on SPs trained to act the part of the injured patient is an effective way to teach learners how to function under stressful, high-pressure situations.
- Working in interprofessional teams under high-stress and high-pressure situations can forge a stronger team culture by helping learners appreciate one another's clinical and administrative role in patient care.
- Training activities that offer high levels of physical, emotional, and environmental realism can increase learner engagement, which often results in a high level of management support for further training.

Resuscitation Quality Initiative (RQI) Equipment

Since the 1980s, proof of basic life support (BLS) and advanced cardiac life support (ACLS) skills have been required for most healthcare professionals who engage in patient care in the United States. Typically, these courses required practitioners to renew their requisite skills by demonstrating them on a manikin and having them be validated by a certified instructor every two years. RQI technology provides a computerized program and voice-activated manikin (VAM) that does not require verification by an instructor. Instead, the learner independently logs into the automated computer system and performs the requisite skills every three months, including chest compressions and ventilation using the bag valve mask.

Figure 19-4 shows an example of RQI equipment. Here a new employee is completing Basic Life Certification via a voice-activated manikin connected to the hospital learning management system.

Figure 19-4. Example of Resuscitation Quality Initiative (RQI) Equipment

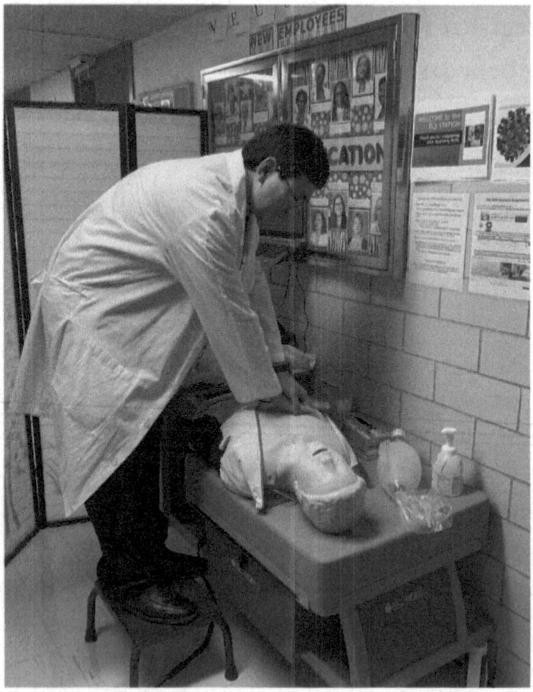

Jonathan, the newly hired CCU nurse manager, had not participated in RQI at his prior employer and was intrigued by both the technology and the science behind it. When he researched this new way of validating CPR skills, he found that the American Heart Association (AHA) strongly favored skills validation using a "low dose, high frequency" CPR training over skills validation every two years. Based on AHA research, the former resulted in better compliance with the guidelines and skills retention.

Jonathan was impressed that this skills validation could be completed so conveniently without requiring an instructor's presence. As a new manager, he readily embraced any technology that would improve employee skills retention and national guidelines compliance. The VAM technology addressed this need.

As Jonathan researched RQI further, he found that many hospital staff members had been resistant to use of the VAM initially, and that technical issues with the computer system had caused some frustration. He also found that many staff thought it would be easier to do the live in-person checkoff every two years. However, once the staff got used to the technology and using the VAM to validate their CPR skills every three months, the resistance faded. Many even appreciated being able to review their content regularly and felt more prepared to perform CPR on a real patient.

Jonathan wondered if the staff's initial resistance to the RQI technology could have been circumvented by employing a better change management strategy. As a new manager, he could see how technology and workforce management were becoming increasingly interdependent. While researching theories of change management he learned some powerful principles, including Kotter's Stages of the Change Process, which include establishing urgency, creating a team to lead the change, developing a vision and strategy, communicating the vision, empowering action, generating short-term wins, consolidating gains, and anchoring new approaches in the culture (Kotter 2012).

In discussion with Hussein, Jonathan learned that because the vision for RQI was not initially clear, it wasn't communicated well to the staff. Hussein had been on the TD team that evaluated RQI and implemented it at the hospital. He said that while there was significant excitement about the new technology, the team hadn't done enough subsequent planning for how to champion the change so the staff would view it positively. Although RQI had now been fully implemented and was generally accepted by staff, Hussein admitted that the whole process could have gone smoother had the team focused more on how to make change work.

As they continued their discussion, Hussein and Jonathan discovered that they both shared a passion for learning technologies and decided to collaborate on ways to further develop them in the hospital. Hussein suggested that they involve other stakeholders, including the simulation educators and the nursing professional development (NPD) practitioners who were responsible for educating staff and being champions for change.

Key Takeaways

- Resistance to change in clinical practice or training curriculum should be expected. TD professionals must effectively educate and gain solid support from various key drivers, who hold influence over their employees within the organization, before rolling out any practice changes or training curriculum.
- During the early adoption phase, live in-person help should be made available to answer any questions employees have. This is essential to working out bugs and systemic issues that arise during this type of independent training.
- In addition to helping increase staff engagement in learning, technology can also help with educational delivery 24 hours a day, seven days a week.

Avatar-Based Technology for Guided Reflection and Facilitated Debriefing

TD professionals and other clinical educators who work in healthcare can employ learning technologies to enhance their own professional development skills. For example, when providing guided reflection and facilitated debriefing after each simulated training session, facilitators must encourage learners to reflect on their strengths, opportunities for improvement, and lessons learned. Furthermore, educators should guide rather than tell, accept rather than judge, and maintain psychological safety rather than create fear.

Traditionally, facilitated debriefing skills were taught via lecture format in a large group setting, however this format has significant limitations, including limited staff and limited time for repetitive practice incorporating self-reflection and the formative and summative feedback received from the expert debriefer. To address some of these limitations, technologies involving avatar-based debriefing programs have been developed, which use avatars that a single expert debriefer operates remotely as they interact with the learner.

To illustrate this further, a new educator wishing to learn debriefing skills can watch a group of avatars (each of which has their own personality, attitude, and behavior) interact in a role-play scenario. After watching the video of the team training session, the new educator can debrief the characters as if they're debriefing real people. Using voice and attitude modulating software, the avatars are all operated by an off-site expert debriefer.

Equipped with the ability to display variations of positive and negative emotions, body language, and speech, the moderator responds in a manner commensurate with how real in-person learners are likely to respond. In this manner, the new educator experiences real-time formative feedback from the avatars as they would from actual learners. Because the expert debriefer can control the avatars' comments, attitudes, behavior, body language, and facial expressions, each session can be customized to address unique educational needs. After the new educator has debriefed the avatars, the expert debriefer can then discuss ways the new educator could improve their debriefing skills.

This learning technology has broad applicability for conducting all types of communication training and assessments for educators and leaders alike (Wong et al. 2020). Prior to the development of this technology, practicing debriefing skills in this manner would have required scheduling a group of SPs to act out this scenario, which would not have been as scalable or cost-effective.

Technological advances have changed the fabric of our healthcare learning environments and opened up doors to educational opportunities that were not imaginable earlier in this century.

Conclusion

TD professionals are in a prime position to evaluate and implement appropriate learning technologies for the healthcare workplace. Before investing in a specific learning technology, consider the following questions and ponder the potential benefits and challenges of the technology before purchasing.

- Who are the targeted learners? Some examples include:
    - New staff requiring onboarding and orientation
    - Current clinical staff who need ongoing training for skills maintenance
    - Nonclinical staff who require education for customer service and other related interpersonal skills professional development
- How will the new technological application enhance the targeted learner's needs for untethered, on-demand, collaborative, and empowering training?
- Where will the device and hardware components be stored? What vendor support exists for education, upgrades, repair, or replacement?

- How often will the technological device be used? Who will use it? What kind of initial and ongoing training will facilitators or operators need?
- What are the initial and ongoing costs to operate the technology?
- What are the current alternatives on the market?
- What overall learning goal will the technological application help meet?
- What is the technological comfort level of the targeted staff? What is the user acceptance level regarding new technology? What change management strategies are in use and supported, and how can they help with user acceptance?
- How scalable is the technology? If more than one device is needed for the targeted learner group, how will they be maintained?
- What is the comfort level of subject matter experts regarding technology and their willingness to educate staff using new technological applications? What is their commitment to learning how to optimize the use of technology?

CHAPTER 20

ELECTRONIC HEALTH RECORDS

CHRISTINE F. REYES

"If you don't know where you're going to sleep tonight," said R. Scott Hawkins, former CIO of the Boston Healthcare for the Homeless Program (BHCHP), "the idea that you need to control your diabetes so you'll be healthier in 10 years doesn't hold as much water as it does in a stable and thriving population" (MeHI 2013). BHCHP provides team-based health services to 12,000 patients annually, using collaborative technology to treat people at 100 locations around Boston, including shelters, clinics, hotels, motels, under bridges, and along back alleys. BHCHP's mobile strategy has roaming physicians and clinicians carrying laptops and Wi-Fi hotspots so they can access the centralized electronic medical records (EMR) housed at Boston Medical Center. BHCHP's primary location, across the street from Boston Medical, has been using an electronic health record (EHR) since 2001 at meaningful use levels, which is well above the federal requirements. This made business sense because the health center didn't know where and when patients would show up—with the EHR, physicians can access a patient's chart in any of the 20 connected sites and see their history, medications, and appointment schedule. The center's clinical measures for meaningful use are focused on women's health, colonoscopies, men's health, smoking, and diabetes.

This example demonstrates the transformative power EHRs can have in a healthcare setting. In this chapter, we'll begin by explaining what EHRs are and why training is needed. Then, we'll examine EHR training from an organizational structure view and a staffing view. Next, we'll review the key components to an EHR training program, including types of training, logistics, and delivery methods. And we'll wrap up by looking at the importance internal governance has for successful EHR implementation, training, and post-live support.

Electronic Medical Record vs. Electronic Health Record

Often the terms *electronic medical record (EMR)* and *electronic health record (EHR)* are used interchangeably. However, there is a difference between them, which the Office of the National Coordinator for Health Information Technology (ONC 2019) defines as:

- "Electronic medical records (EMRs) are digital versions of the paper charts in clinician offices, clinics, and hospitals. EMRs contain notes and information collected by and for the clinicians in that office, clinic, or hospital and are mostly used by providers for diagnosis and treatment. EMRs are more valuable than paper records because they enable providers to track data over time, identify patients for preventive visits and screenings, monitor patients, and improve healthcare quality."
- "Electronic health records (EHRs) are built to go beyond standard clinical data collected in a provider's office and are inclusive of a broader view of a patient's care. EHRs contain information from all the clinicians involved in a patient's care and all authorized clinicians involved in a patient's care can access the information to provide care to that patient. EHRs also share information with other healthcare providers, such as laboratories and specialists. EHRs follow patients to the specialists, the hospital, the nursing home, or even across the country."

Both types bring the benefit of creating an electronic version of a patient's record that enables the clinicians and support staff to have immediate and simultaneous access to their healthcare information. EHRs focus on interoperability and allow shared data between healthcare organizations. This builds a health record over time, across specialties, and beyond geographic borders that enables the healthcare provider, such as a physician, nurse practitioner, or physician's assistant, to get a full picture of the patient's health and enhances the ability for collaboration in treatment plans and preventative care.

The Health Information Technology for Economic and Clinical Health (HITECH) Act was passed as part of the American Recovery and Reinvestment Act (ARRA) of 2009 to promote the adoption and meaningful use of health information technology (HHS 2017). It established incentive payments under Centers for Medicare and Medicaid Services' (CMS) programs for professionals, eligible hospitals, and critical access hospitals that meaningfully use Certified EHR Technology (CEHRT). The "meaningful use" incentive program provided financial incentives for those eligible professionals and organizations that met specific requirements showing they used EHR technology to improve patient care. There were also penalties for those not meeting specific requirements and deadlines. This meaningful use program helped expedite the implementation of EHRs throughout the healthcare industry, so most integrated facilities and providers that are part of integrated facilities are now using EHRs.

Since EHR systems are widely used and highly integrated, we refer to EHRs in this chapter rather than EMRs specifically. However, the training practices and challenges addressed will apply to both EHRs and EMRs.

Why EHR Training Is Important

Through this technological transformation, the implementation of EHRs changed the scope and workflow for the majority of clinicians and many nonclinical healthcare workers over the past several years. In addition to providers, most team members and non-employee workers (including contractors, travelers, volunteers, and students) need EHR access for at least part or all of their daily job responsibilities. At Novant Health, EHR training has become part of the onboarding process for almost everyone and is required to receive EHR system access.

KLAS is a research company that works closely with healthcare providers and payers to evaluate and benchmark healthcare information technology vendor performance. The KLAS Arch Collaborative data illustrates that "training has been shown to impact an end user's satisfaction with their EHR for five years post-go-live" (Jeffery 2018).

Responses to a survey given to collaborative participants show that significant jumps in overall satisfaction with the EHR experience occur for every additional hour of initial EHR education they receive. Organizations that require less than four hours of education for new providers appear to be creating a frustrating experience for their clinicians. These organizations have lower training satisfaction, demonstrate lower self-reported proficiency, and are less likely to report that their EHR enables them to deliver quality care (Longhurst et al. 2019).

Not only does training provide users with increased satisfaction, it improves EHR quality and drives better patient care. "For physicians, feeling safe with tools of medicine is about more than just the user interface. Physicians who report poor training are over 3.5 times more likely to report that their EHR does not enable them to deliver quality care" (Longhurst et al. 2019).

Training is also related to the second highest predictor of EHR adoption success: personalization. During a personalization workshop, a provider receives one-on-one assistance setting up specific items for their specialty, such as templates and order sets. "As provider organizations encourage users to adopt all of the customization features typically available in an EHR, the users' experience with the system improves dramatically" (Jeffery 2018).

The Training Department

With an understanding of what EHRs are and why EHR training is important, let's turn to how healthcare organizations typically structure and staff training to support EHR use.

Organizational Structure

The structure of a healthcare training department generally depends on the type of organization, training phase, and reporting structure. The three common structures for integrated healthcare delivery systems are centralized, decentralized, and blended.

Centralized Model

In a centralized model, the training team generally functions as one work unit, with all members reporting to a training leader. They may be stationed in one or multiple locations depending upon geographical needs. Based on the organization's structure, the EHR training team members may report to a chief learning officer in the HR function, an informatics director in the IT department, or to someone in operations.

Advantages to the centralized model include:

- Enhances team member engagement, ownership, and accountability
- Facilitates cross training of team members
- Promotes career path development and succession planning
- Develops learning competencies
- Establishes standardization of training design
- Supports consistency of training delivery
- Promotes collaboration and shared best practices
- Leverages purchasing dollars and efficient use of resources
- Enables easier outcome measurement

Disadvantages include:

- Less connection with operational departments and specialties
- Geographical expansion of organization may be challenging to support, depending on the structure of the centralized team

Decentralized Model

In a decentralized model, members of the training function are assigned to different teams and often report to different leaders. For example, each instructional designer may be part of the IT team of analysts who are responsible for building the EHR application or module that the instructional designer will support. Often, especially for smaller applications, the IT EHR analyst will not only help build the EHR system but also help develop the training curriculum.

In this model, credentialed trainers (CTs) may report to IT along with the IDs, or they could report to operations and serve as adjunct CTs (see the blended model example). The CT's primary responsibility is ongoing delivery of training via multiple modalities to ensure the end user has the knowledge and skills they need to document appropriately in the EHR system.

Advantages to the decentralized model include:

- Training team members may be more connected to the business
- May be less expensive than employing a full training team

Disadvantages include:

- Lose ability for cross training and career path planning within the training team
- Makes standardization of training development more challenging

When instructional designers are part of the IT analyst team they are more connected with the analyst team and aware of system changes. However, this also prevents them from working as a cross-application team, so they can miss the impact they're having on each other's application and workflow.

Blended Model

In a blended model, the instructional designers are centralized, along with some CTs. They function as one work unit and report to one leader who may have additional responsibilities such as an IT director. An example of this model is when noncentralized CTs report to operational departments. In this case, these designated team members do not report to the training leader and are not part of the training work unit, so they only serve as adjunct, part-time, or as needed (PRN) credentialed trainers.

Advantages to the blended model include:

- Allows the organization to have benefits of the centralized and decentralized models
- Enables the team to handle a large volume of training requests

- Enables trainers to be credentialed in a specialty area that the training team may not be able to handle or may not have the knowledge to handle well
- Allows the training team to develop back-up credentialed training resources
- Provides strong partnerships with other departments

Disadvantages include:

- Difficult to ensure the adjunct trainer stays up to date with EHR system changes
- Scheduling the adjunct CT can be challenging if their primary department has a staffing shortage
- Training defaults back to training team in the event of turnover or other staffing shortages until a replacement is identified, credentialed, and ready to train independently

Novant Health's Training Model

Novant Health has a blended model, with EHR training that's managed by three centralized teams. Each team's members function as one department and report to a training leader. The three teams collaborate and meet monthly to share best practices and learning technology initiatives with all learning professionals in the organization as part of the learning management system (LMS) advisory team. The teams are acute clinical training, ambulatory clinical training, and revenue cycle training:

- **EHR acute clinical training** reports to the vice president of learning and development. This team is also responsible for corporate education and student programs and reports to the chief people officer; it trains roles for all hospitals, outpatient surgery centers, infusion centers, and hospital outpatient departments. Clinical areas that use revenue cycle applications fall within the scope of this training team as well. For example, nurses who schedule chemotherapy infusions do not report to the revenue cycle services leaders and they don't need full revenue cycle training. Instead, they review very specific scheduling training from the EHR acute clinical training.
- **EHR ambulatory clinical training** reports to the senior director of physician services education and training. This team is responsible for all education programs within Novant Health and reports to the vice president of physician network services who reports to senior vice president of the chief operating officer physician network. They also manage the training for all community connect providers, which are affiliate practices that pay Novant Health to use the ambulatory EHR.

- **EHR revenue cycle training** reports to the vice president of acute revenue cycle services. They are responsible for acute revenue cycle services and report to the chief financial officer. This team trains roles for all team members who perform revenue cycle functions for acute (hospital) and ambulatory billing (physician and professional). Team members who join revenue cycle services often have little to no experience in that area, so they are immersed in a 40-hour program that embeds the EHR functionality and workflows throughout.

Staffing

EHR training requires many hands. We'll review the key roles and responsibilities for instructional designers, credentialed trainers, super users, and provider champions.

Instructional Designers

The instructional designer's primary responsibility is to develop and maintain the training curriculum and EHR training environment build. They will likely be required to obtain certification for the application they support through the EHR vendor. In addition, the instructional designer's responsibilities may include:

- Earning EHR certifications for the applications they support
- Mastering EHR applications and the organization's specific workflows
- Meeting regularly with EHR application analyst teams to keep abreast of workflow changes
- Developing and maintaining course curriculum
- Preparing training materials and lesson plans
- Serving as lead for application credentialed trainers (CTs)
- Determining CT resource availability for training and support schedules
- Training and credentialing classroom trainers
- Keeping CTs up to date on EHR system changes
- Monitoring and working in the EHR training IT service system queue
- Building and maintaining the EHR training environment
- Managing, prioritizing, and meeting deadlines for EHR projects related to their applications
- Delivering training as necessary

Previous experience in adult education, instructional design, and healthcare is beneficial but may not be required. For some clinical applications, clinical experience in that area is required because it is imperative to understand the context for those workflows. In all cases, healthcare experience is most important—while adult education and instructional design skills can be taught, the most successful instructional designers are those who have the experience and background for the EHR application they will be supporting.

EHR vendor certification may require multiple classes, exams, and an EHR system build project. Most certifications also require courses in curriculum development and application fundamentals for the EHR application as well as the EHR training environment build.

If the EHR vendor requires a certified instructional designer, the organization may need to hire a certified contract ID if they have a vacancy in their staff. The training manager may want to have contractor available while the full-time instructional designer on staff is obtaining certification, becoming familiar with the organization's workflows, and learning the EHR system and organization's instructional design methodologies.

Credentialed Trainer

In addition to training delivery, the credentialed trainer's responsibilities may include:

- Earning credentialed status
- Keeping current on EHR system changes from the instructional designer
- Preparing for class by reviewing lesson plans and class materials
- Setting up the classroom
- Facilitating training
- Administering end user proficiency assessments
- Completing the course roster and submitting any acknowledgment needed for EHR access (such as crediting course completion in the LMS)
- Following up with outstanding class questions
- Helping IDs update tip sheets or training materials
- Testing lesson plans and the training environment build
- Providing go-live support

Even full-time CTs may have responsibilities in addition to EHR training, based upon their department's structure and needs. For example, they could serve as:

- IT help desk
- A trainer for other IT applications
- An educator for other learning and development programs

Previous experience with adult education, instructional design, and healthcare is beneficial but not required. Clinical experience helps those who train clinical applications understand the context of the workflows; the same holds true for a revenue cycle CT. For initial implementation, it is especially beneficial if the CTs have knowledge of an organization and its workflows. However, Novant Health has had a great experience in hiring trainers with an education background and no healthcare industry experience. There are many ways to provide healthcare knowledge and workflow context for those new to the healthcare industry (job shadowing is one option).

To ensure trainers are ready to train, fully knowledgeable in the EHR application they support, and comfortable with the lesson plans for each role they will be training, they may be required to go through a credentialing or competency training program. Depending on the organization and the number of roles for the EHR application, this four- to seven-week program overseen by an EHR-certified ID or application analyst may include:

- EHR application knowledge
- Train-the-trainer content, including adult learning theory and computer classroom presentation skills
- Job shadowing of end users to better understand their workflows
- Successful completion of EHR proficiency assessments
- Teach backs to practice teaching lessons
- Informal practice in preparation for a final presentation
- A final panel presentation for evaluation of key areas

The panel evaluation rubric evaluates application knowledge, workflow knowledge, ability to answer questions, and presentation skills. A trainer may receive one of three outcomes based on their final panel presentation:

- Credentialed status
- Credentialed with contingencies (for example, additional application training, better use of questions and directional statements, or conduct more job shadowing to better understand workflows); repeating the panel presentation may be required, depending on their panel score
- Not recommended for credentialed status

If the trainer receives a "credentialed with contingencies," then they are credentialed but must work to improve the areas in the contingency. If the trainer receives a "not recommended for credentialed status," they are given a different lesson plan and have 24 hours to prepare for a follow-up panel presentation.

Some of the CT's most important skills are those that connect them with the learner, such as classroom management, verbal and nonverbal communication, passion for teaching, application knowledge, and teaching by asking. "Trainers should have a strong grasp of the application, in part, because when teaching the new system, not all features may be functioning as expected. Often, users are training on a system that is still testing. This shouldn't fluster a quality trainer. The best trainers adapt the lesson plan on the spot and can explain how the application will work once it is live in contrast to any anomalies or bugs that users may experience in the classroom" (Davis 2017). The differences between EHR training environments and production (live) environments exist even after the EHR goes live due to functionality that can't be built or reproduced in a training environment. It is important that a trainer can help the end user bridge the gap to how their workflow will work in the real world. Trainers must fully understand the workflows and use case knowledge. "If the providers don't feel the person guiding them through training and personalization understands them, their workflow, and their patient's needs, every tip, trick, and suggestion will fall on deaf ears" (Jeffery 2018).

EHR Super User

The primary responsibility of the EHR super user is to provide support to their peers during and after EHR implementation. In addition, they:

- Advocate for the EHR system
- Serve as a subject matter expert
- Provide classroom support during implementation training
- Provide elbow-to-elbow go-live support
- Serve as the ongoing point person for workflow questions
- Assist with ongoing post-live training initiatives

Here are some questions to ask when developing a super user program:

- Who manages the program?
- Which areas will have super users?
- When will they be used? Only during implementation?
- What will they be used for? Post-live upgrades only?
- How often will they meet?
- How will they stay current with EHR workflow changes?
- How will they disseminate information to end users and peers?

Provider Champion

The provider champion's primary responsibility is to serve as a point of reference for the provider perspective related to EHR functionality. This person also:

- Reviews curriculum based on area of expertise or specialty
- Verifies training patient scenarios
- Facilitates training and provider practice labs

Training Program

Now that we've reviewed training structure and staffing, let's look at how to put together an EHR training program. Key considerations include the training environment, training phases, types of training, logistics, and delivery methods.

Training and Playground Environments

To provide the end users with a realistic training experience, the training and playground environments should both be copies of the EHR system that are as close to the production (live) environment as possible. They should also contain fictitious patients and patient information, which allows the end user to have a realistic experience without the fear of causing any changes to real information. It is important for end users to have hands-on practice with workflows they will use on the job.

However, the training and playground environments are not the same. The training environment is what trainers use while teaching and learners use while following along and completing practice exercises. In contrast, the playground environment is a practice environment containing fictitious patient data that allows end users to practice accessing the EHR, documenting on a patient's chart, and completing workflows in various patient scenarios. The two environments are separate so that user practice doesn't affect classes that are in progress. Both environments normally reset each night so fictitious patient scenarios can be reused the next day. Playground practice lab exercises may often be used after formal training during implementation or to enhance upgrade training, which may be simple tip sheets or videos.

Training Phase

EHR implementation training is most often provided for groups of individuals whose peers don't know how to use the EHR system, which means that they won't have department support after initial training. This training also includes new workflows and process changes. Therefore, it is important to provide participants with as much information during initial training, hands-on practice prior to go-live, and support during go-live as possible.

Figure 20-1 highlights some of the items Novant Health included in their implementation training and support program.

Figure 20-1. Components of EHR Training

Training Component	Audience	Training Material	Deployment Method
E-learning	All end users	• Virtual, self-paced training with demos, practices, and tests • Prerequisite to instructor-led training • Requires 10–30 minutes per lesson, 3–5 lessons per course	Web-based
Instructor-led training	All end users	• Role-specific, workflow-based training • Includes experiential learning and practice using real-life patient scenarios • Ranges based on role—between 2 and 36 hours	Classroom-based
Playground practice exercises and practice labs	All end users	• Reinforces the "learning by doing" principle through specific role-based exercises • Assists with retention of concepts learned prior to go-live during independent study time or practice labs	Web-based
End user proficiency assessment (EUPA)	All end users	• Role-based assessment administered by super users • Requires end-users to perform key activities to gain access to the system	Super-user administration
Personalization labs	Providers	• Hands-on support • Helps physicians set up patient lists, create favorite order/order sets, and modify onscreen view settings	Classroom-based

Once the EHR has been live in an organization for several months, the current team members should gain confidence and expertise with the system's functionality, workflows, and processes. At this point, the new users will have support from their peers in the department and often won't need as much upfront training. This may be a good time to reevaluate the original implementation training and determine if it can be restructured for new users.

Let's consider an example. During implementation, inpatient nurses were required to take three eight-hour classes, totaling 24 hours of classroom training. After go-live, that transitioned to a five-hour core nursing class and a three-hour inpatient nursing class, totaling eight hours of classroom training. New hires then worked with preceptors on their units following this training.

Here's a more detailed look at the two programs:

- Implementation training: Three classes, 24 hours total
    - **Inpatient Nurse 100.** This eight-hour course is a foundational, 100-level course. Normally this is the end user's first exposure to the EHR in this role or for this specific access.
    - **Inpatient Nurse 200.** This eight-hour, 200-level course expands on the level of knowledge and skill learned during the 100-level course. The 100-level is a pre-requisite to this course.
    - **Inpatient Nurse 300 or Critical Care Nurse 300 or Behavioral Health Nurse 300.** This eight-hour 300-level course expands on the depth and breadth of the participant's knowledge and skills. In this example, the nurse needs to take the 300-level course that focuses on the workflows specific to the nursing specialty where they will be working: inpatient nurse (medical-surgical), critical care nurse, or behavioral health.
- Post live training: Two classes, eight hours total
    - **Inpatient Nurse Core.** This five-hour course includes general nursing information required for all inpatient nurses and is a prerequisite for specialty courses in critical care, medical-surgical, behavioral health, women's services, cardiology, and radiology.
    - **Inpatient Nurse.** This three-hour course includes more specific information about critical care, medical-surgical, and behavioral health.

This transition from pre- to post-implementation training not only shortened the duration of training for the end user, it also consolidated several other courses, which reduced the number of required training hours and classroom space. Another example of post-live transition is that all courses that were offered as five hours or fewer during implementation were reviewed to determine if they could be converted to asynchronous e-learning that could be accessed from any location at any time, which provided scheduling flexibility as well as reducing the required training hours and classroom space.

Type of Training

Many different types of training are required for EHR post-live support, including new hire, new provider, and downtime training.

New Hire

New hire training provides new and transferring team members and nonemployee workers (including contractors, travelers, volunteers, and students) knowledge and skills related to EHR functionality and workflows as they onboard in the organization. Some common structures are instructor-led training, on-the-job training, hybrid training, and blended learning.

Instructor-led training. Traditionally, this is in-person, instructor-led classroom training. However, with the advances in technology and the onset of COVID-19, it is increasingly being offered as virtual instructor-led training, which is accessed remotely online.

Advantages of instructor-led training include:

- Scalable for high volumes
- Improves training content and delivery consistency
- Easy to track training completion
- Provides interaction between the trainer and end users
- Allows end users to ask questions

Disadvantages of instructor-led training include:

- Requires large amount of training team time, including that of a credentialed trainer
- Classrooms are required if the training is in person; if the training is virtual, the end user must have access to the internet, a computer, and audio capability
- Curriculum is designed with the assumption that the end user has only average computer skills (McCain 2018)
- Training is not in real-world context

On-the-job training. On-the-job training takes place in the end user's workplace, often with a designated "preceptor" who is a peer from their department. The preceptor teaches the end user how to complete the workflows in the EHR system, while they're learning how to perform the functions of their role.

Advantages of on-the-job training include:

- Preceptor can adjust training to meet the end user's needs and level of understanding
- Provides training in a real-world context
- Takes little time from training team
- Requires less training resources

Disadvantages of on-the-job training include:

- High volume roles may overwhelm operational preceptors
- Less training content and delivery consistency
- May need additional processes to track training completion

Hybrid training. Hybrid training features portions of training that are instructor-led and portions that are provided on the job. In her 2015 study, "EMR Training Tactics: A Case Study of Clinical Staff Training Experiences, Needs and Perceptions," Victoria Leanne Miller discussed what a focus group and individual participants would consider their perfect EHR training during onboarding. Two types of onboarding training emerged from her data: case-based instruction and shadowing. "For many of the participants, these two types of training went hand-in-hand, with case-based training needed to learn the system and shadowing required to integrate their work environment with their knowledge of the system" (Miller 2015).

Advantages of hybrid training include:

- Can use the instructor-led portion to ensure delivery of standard content
- Frees up some training team time
- Takes up a smaller portion of preceptor time
- Preceptors can focus on items that can't be demonstrated in the EHR training environment
- End users can learn the material during the instructor-led training portion and then experience it on the job in a real-world context

Disadvantages of hybrid training include:

- Requires a dedicated trainer and classroom
- High volume roles may overwhelm operational preceptors
- May need additional processes to track training completion

Blended learning. Blended learning combines electronic or online learning (computer-based learning) and live teaching. This method is used by many organizations and works with any training structure. It provides the training team with flexibility to fit the content and learning structure. Some of the options for training delivery methods are described later in this chapter.

New Provider

New provider training on EHR functionality and workflows is typically part of the onboarding experience. One-on-one personalization workshops are often completed at the end of the new provider training. During these workshops, the trainer works with the provider (physician, nurse practitioner, or physician's assistant) to review the workflows for their specialty and they receive assistance in setting up role-specific items, such as note templates, favorite orders, and order sets.

Other curriculum covered during personalization might include:

- User-specific system settings to enhance usability
- Orders preference lists
- Inpatient order sets
- Note writing macros
- Note smart phrases
- InBasket quick actions
- Report set-ups

Training, clinical informatics, or provider support teams should offer personalization workshops shortly after providers complete their initial training so they can set up their tools and templates prior to their first day using the EHR system in their work environment. Novant Health also offers regularly scheduled walk-in sessions—often set up in physicians' lounges—to assist with any customization features, enhancements, or workflow questions providers may have.

The benefits of personalization sessions include:

- Providing additional education and support
- Improving the provider's efficiency with the EHR system
- Increasing the provider's engagement with and adoption of the EHR system
- Building relationships between the provider and training team
- Providing feedback to training team

Downtime Training

Downtime training instructs the end user how to perform workflows when the EHR system is down, as well as what to do once the EHR system is back online. The protocols are different when the downtime is planned versus unplanned as well as depending on which other systems are available during the downtime.

In the article "A Target Approach to EHR Training Improves Success Rates," Becky Manne, vice president of training and activation at Optimum Healthcare IT states, "most individuals become very savvy on how to use the technology, but they need education on what to do when that technology isn't present. There are employees who have never had to document on paper" (Eramo 2018). She goes on, stating that "Downtime training should be specific to each type of scenario (e.g., downtime due to a power outage, system upgrade, weather-related disaster, or a variety of other reasons)."

Here's an example of Novant Health's downtime training and support process:

- The initial training for new team members is a required scenario-based e-learning program
- Quarterly, in preparation for the EHR system upgrade, all EHR users are sent a PowerPoint document containing instructions and links to all pertinent checklists, tip sheets, and policies
- A facility representative responsible for joining enterprise-wide IT calls is tasked with coordinating the downtime process for each facility for every downtime

Other Training

Let's quickly hit a few other types of EHR training:

- **Upgrade.** Upgrade training typically consists of workflow changes and new functionality related to a new version of the EHR system released by the software vendor. The training environment build will need to be coordinated to ensure any training activities that occur prior to, during, or after the upgrades coincide with EHR system build activities.
- **Refresher.** Refresher training allows users to improve their comfort level with the EHR system and learn functionalities they may not remember from their initial training. It also reviews any upgrades and enhancements that have been implement-

ed since their initial training. This type of training also reinforces core topics and provides tips and tricks for efficiency.

- **Optimization.** Optimization training communicates the optimization build to users and allows them to dig deeper into advanced topics.
- **Efficiency or skills enhancement.** This type of training helps users to learn functionalities that can increase their overall efficiency, including some advanced features.

Training Logistics

Some of the challenges for training logistics encompass scheduling, registration, classroom management, equipment, and training material.

Course Catalog and Training Track

A course catalog or training track document should be developed to communicate to operational leaders and the medical staff office which courses end users and providers are required to take, based on their role. An existing course catalog or training track–type document that could be modified as needed would be used for ongoing new hires or transferring team members and new onboarding providers.

A course catalog is more detailed than a training track document and often looks similar to the college course catalog. It normally includes a table of contents to assist with navigation, as well as a section explaining how to use the catalog, definitions of the training tracks and modules, information about prerequisites, and training policies. It provides information about each course, including the course identification number, name, duration, intended audience or roles required to take the course, a description, objectives, and a list of prerequisites (including e-learning, videos, courses, and pre-work). Figure 20-2 is an example course listing.

Figure 20-2. Course Catalog

EA0123: Research Coordinator	
Audience: Clinical Research Coordinators, Manager	**Course ID:** ADD LMS ID
Course Length: 4 Hours **Description:** In this course, the research coordinator will learn how to modify a research study administrative record from a shell record, associate users with the research study, and mark orders as associated with the study. The research coordinator will also learn how to associate patients with a study, update enrollment status for patients to reflect their study status, and report on study patient populations. **Objectives:** At the end of this course the trainee will be able to: • Demonstrate how to enroll the appropriate patients in a study, update patient demographics, and update patient enrollment status. • Review scheduled visits for research patients and associate these visits with a study from the research patients appointments report to facilitate research charge routing. • Run reports on patient research populations based on the studies and patients you are working with.	**Prerequisites:** **Non-Credentialed Research Coordinator** • EA0069: Specialty Clinicians 100 **Credentialed Research Coordinator** • EA0069: Specialty Clinicians 100 **Oncology Research Coordinator** • EA0001: Inpatient 100 • EA0002: Inpatient 200 • EA0003: Oncology Outpatient Pediatric Nurse & Research Coordinator

A training track document contains less detail and can be created in a spreadsheet. The first tab can act as a table of contents and list each application for end users or specialty for providers—then the applications can be linked to that application or provider specialty's tab (Figures 20-3 and 20-4, respectively). This document may include the training track number, track title, list of roles that should take that training track, and the required training for that track. The training track is typically different for an initial EHR implementation than for ongoing new hire and new provider onboarding training.

Figure 20-3. Training Track

New Hire Training Tracks—End Users All Classes Must Be Taken in the Sequence Listed						
Table of Contents			Computer Based Learning (CBL) Course Name Manager or delegate must enroll team members (Required for access to dimensions)		Instructor Led Training (ILT) Course Name Manager or delegate must enroll team members (Required for access to dimensions)	
Track Number	Track Title	Roles/Positions	Course Number & Title	Time (hours)	"Course Number & Title *All classes must be taken in the sequence listed in this document"*	Time (hours)
DAT400	Tech (CNA): ED	ED Techs, ED CNAI, EDCNAII			EA0670 ED Tech (CNA)	4
			Total CBL Learning		*Total ILT Learning*	4
DAT401	ED Charge Capture	ED Coders, ED Charging Staff, ED Data Specialists	EAE178 ED Charging and EUPA (CBL)	0.5		
			EAE097 Emergency Medicine Reports (to be taken after ILT)	0.5		
			(AT MANAGER'S DISCRETION)			
			Total CBL Learning	1	*Total ILT Learning*	0
DAT402	Unit Recep-tionist: ED	ED Medical Unit Receptionist	EAE154 ED Medical Unit Receptionist and EUPA (CBL)	0.5		
			Total CBL Learning	0.5	*Total ILT Learning*	0
DAT403	ED Reporting	Clinical Shift Managers, Clinical Coordinators, ED Medical Directors, Administrative Specialist	EAE097 Emergency Medicine Reports (to be taken after ILT)	0.5		
			Total CBL Learning	0.5	*Total ILT Learning*	0
DAT404	Manager: ED	ED Managers	EAE097 Emergency Medicine Reports (to be taken after ILT)	0.5	EAN008 ED Nurse 100	8
			EAE022 ED Disaster (to be taken after ILT)	0.5	EAN009 ED Nurse 200	8
			EAE104 ED SANE Documentation (to be taken after ILT)	0.5		
			Total CBL Learning	1.5	*Total ILT Learning*	16
DAT405	Nurse: ED	ED Nurses	EAE022 ED Disaster (to be taken after ILT)	0.5	EAN008 ED Nurse 100	8
			EAE104 ED SANE Documentation (to be taken after ILT)	0.5	EAN009 ED Nurse 200	8
			Total CBL Learning		*Total ILT Learning*	16

Figure 20-4. Provider Course List

Surgical Providers	**All classes must be taken in the sequence listed in this document**					
Table of Contents						
Roles/Positions	**Instructor Led Training (ILT) Course Name**	**Time (hours)**		**Roles/Positions**	**Instructor Led Training (ILT) Course Name**	**Time (hours)**
Provides Inpatient care, WITH admission & discharge Performs procedures within an operating room, endoscopy, or pain procedure room	EA4647 Surgical Provider 100 & 200 (Instructor Led-Acute)	8	**OR**	Provides Inpatient care, WITH admission & discharge Performs procedures within an operating room, endoscopy, or pain procedure room **WITH PREVIOUS EPIC EXPERIENCE**	EA0845 EPIC-Trained Surgeon Provider Course (ILT)	3
	EA0048 Surgical Provider 300 (Instructor Led-Acute)	4			EA0825 EPIC-Trained Inpatient or Surgical Provider (ADT Admit Discharge Transfer) (ILT)	4
	EA0049 Surgical Provider 400 (Instructor Led-Acute)	4				
	Total ILT Course Learning	16			*Total ILT Course Learning*	7
Provides inpatient care, WITHOUT admission or discharge privileges Performs procedures within an operating room, endoscopy, or pain procedure room	EA4647 Surgical Provider 100 & 200 (Instructor Led-Acute)	8	**OR**	Provides inpatient care, WITHOUT admission or discharge privileges Performs procedures within an operating room, endoscopy, or pain procedure room **WITH PREVIOUS EPIC EXPERIENCE**	EA0845 EPIC-Trained Surgeon Provider Course (ILT)	3
	EA0048 Surgical Provider 300 (Instructor Led-Acute)	4				
	Total ILT Course Learning				*Total ILT Course Learning*	3

Novant Health has benefited from creating smaller versions of the training track documents when rolling out new EMR modules or when implementing other clinical integration projects that involve training for multiple roles. This helps the leaders, users, and providers identify which training is appropriate for each role.

Because they've found that course catalogs are large, cumbersome, and rarely used, Novant Health has moved to using only the training track documents for the end user and provider course documents for post-live training. Additional information, such as course description and course objectives, are included in the LMS for each course.

Course Schedule

A course schedule must be developed and communicated to operational leaders early enough to allow for staff scheduling. For implementation training, it's important to consider offering training options on multiple days a week and during multiple shifts.

To assist with class schedule creation, Novant Health uses a spreadsheet to develop a pictorial showing all new hire and new provider EHR classes in each classroom for all markets for the entire year (Figure 20-5). This enables the training coordinator to see any overlaps or gaps and identify available space for other training teams or EHR training projects. Once the training coordinators are satisfied with the pictorial plan, they reserve the rooms for the entire year and schedule the classes in the LMS for the next six months.

Keeping classes scheduled for six months out in the LMS enables the leaders, new hires, and providers to plan their schedules. However, the team doesn't put classes into the LMS that are more than six months out because schedules and course offerings may change.

Course Registration

Course registration is most often done through a system, preferably an LMS. Consideration should be given to whether leaders have to register their team or if team members are allowed to register themselves. If the training will provide new or additional EHR access, it can be important for the leader to enroll the team member. Leaders may also want to schedule their team members so that they can coordinate the staff schedule. However, there are times during implementation initiatives when relying on only one or two leaders to enroll their team members can delay registrations and cause low volume of attendance in classes, which leaves a limited amount of seating in classes held toward the end of the project.

Figure 20-5. Pictorial of Planned EHR Classes

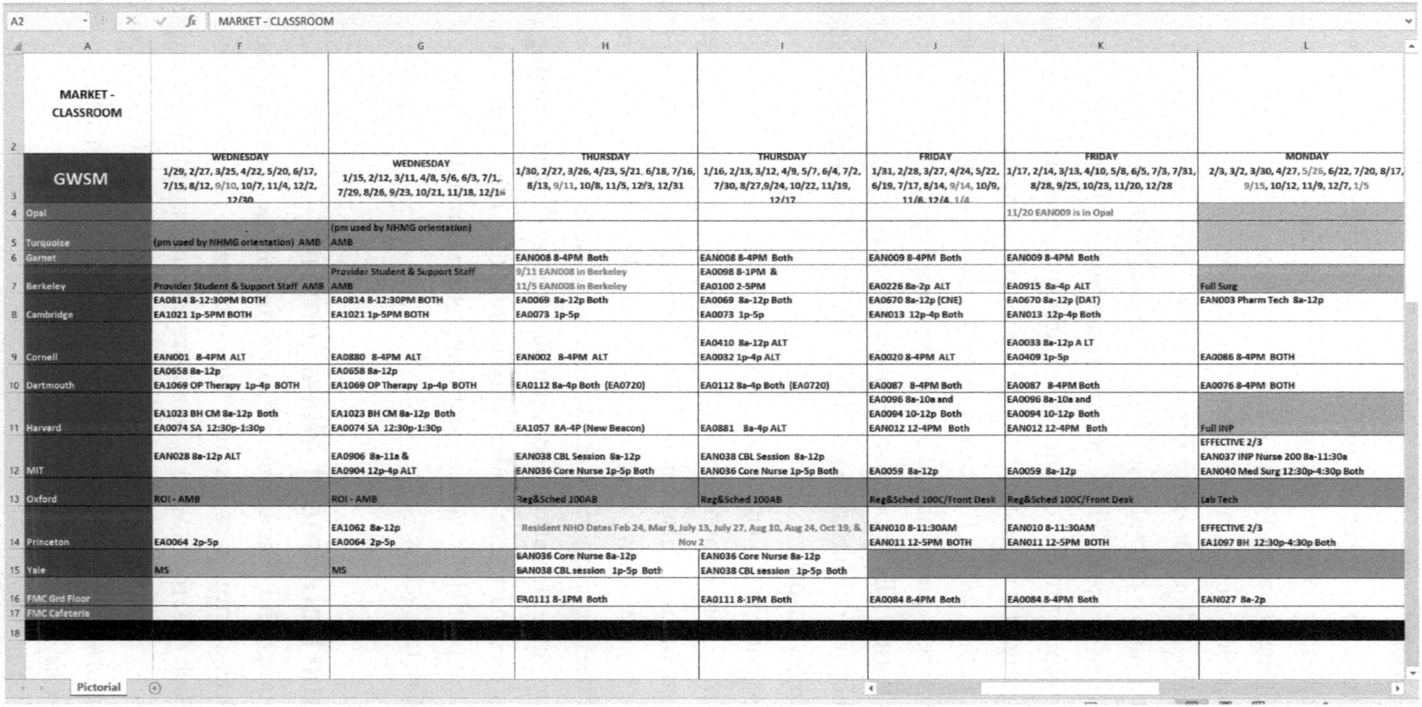

A2 | MARKET - CLASSROOM

MARKET - CLASSROOM							
GWSM	WEDNESDAY 1/29, 2/27, 3/25, 4/22, 5/20, 6/17, 7/15, 8/12, 9/10, 10/7, 11/4, 12/2, 12/30	WEDNESDAY 1/15, 2/12, 3/11, 4/8, 5/6, 6/3, 7/1, 7/29, 8/26, 9/23, 10/21, 11/18, 12/16	THURSDAY 1/30, 2/27, 3/26, 4/23, 5/21 6/18, 7/16, 8/13, 9/11, 10/8, 11/5, 12/3, 12/31	THURSDAY 1/16, 2/13, 3/12, 4/9, 5/7, 6/4, 7/2, 7/30, 8/27, 9/24, 10/22, 11/19, 12/17	FRIDAY 1/31, 2/28, 3/27, 4/24, 5/22, 6/19, 7/17, 8/14, 9/14, 10/9, 11/6, 12/4, 1/4	FRIDAY 1/17, 2/14, 3/13, 4/10, 5/8, 6/5, 7/3, 7/31, 8/28, 9/25, 10/23, 11/20, 12/28	MONDAY 2/3, 3/2, 3/30, 4/27, 5/26, 6/22, 7/20, 8/17, 9/15, 10/12, 11/9, 12/7, 1/5
Opal						11/20 EAN009 is in Opal	
Turquoise	(pm used by NHMG orientation) AMB	(pm used by NHMG orientation) AMB					
Garnet			EAN008 8-4PM Both	EAN008 8-4PM Both	EAN009 8-4PM Both	EAN009 8-4PM Both	
Berkeley	Provider Student & Support Staff AMB	Provider Student & Support Staff AMB	9/11 EAN008 in Berkeley 11/5 EAN008 in Berkeley	EA0098 8-1PM & EA0100 2-5PM	EA0226 8a-2p ALT	EA0915 8a-4p ALT	Full Surg
Cambridge	EA0814 8-12:30PM BOTH EA1021 1p-5PM BOTH	EA0814 8-12:30PM BOTH EA1021 1p-5PM BOTH	EA0069 8a-12p Both EA0073 1p-5p	EA0069 8a-12p Both EA0073 1p-5p	EA0670 8a-12p (CNE) EAN013 12p-4p Both	EA0670 8a-12p (DAT) EAN013 12p-4p Both	EAN003 Pharm Tech 8a-12p
Cornell	EAN001 8-4PM ALT	EA0880 8-4PM ALT	EAN002 8-4PM ALT	EA0410 8a-12p ALT EA0032 1p-4p ALT	EA0020 8-4PM ALT	EA0033 8a-12p A LT EA0409 1p-5p	EA0086 8-4PM BOTH
Dartmouth	EA0658 8a-12p EA1069 OP Therapy 1p-4p BOTH	EA0658 8a-12p EA1069 OP Therapy 1p-4p BOTH	EA0112 8a-4p Both (EA0720)	EA0112 8a-4p Both (EA0720)	EA0087 8-4PM Both	EA0087 8-4PM Both	EA0076 8-4PM BOTH
Harvard	EA1023 BH CM 8a-12p Both EA0074 SA 12:30p-1:30p	EA1023 BH CM 8a-12p Both EA0074 SA 12:30p-1:30p	EA1057 8A-4P (New Beacon)	EA0881 8a-4p ALT	EA0096 8a-10a and EA0094 10-12p Both EAN012 12-4PM Both	EA0096 8a-10a and EA0094 10-12p Both EAN012 12-4PM Both	Full INP
MIT	EAN028 8a-12p ALT	EA0906 8a-11a & EA0904 12p-4p ALT	EAN038 CBL Session 8a-12p EAN036 Core Nurse 1p-5p Both	EAN038 CBL Session 8a-12p EAN036 Core Nurse 1p-5p Both	EA0059 8a-12p	EA0059 8a-12p	EFFECTIVE 2/3 EAN037 INP Nurse 200 8a-11:30a EAN040 Med Surg 12:30p-4:30p Both
Oxford	ROI - AMB	ROI - AMB	Reg&Sched 100AB	Reg&Sched 100AB	Reg&Sched 100C/Front Desk	Reg&Sched 100C/Front Desk	Lab Tech
Princeton	EA0064 2p-5p	EA1062 8a-12p EA0064 2p-5p	Resident NHO Dates Feb 24, Mar 9, July 13, July 27, Aug 10, Aug 24, Oct 19, & Nov 2		EAN010 8-11:30AM EAN011 12-5PM BOTH	EAN010 8-11:30AM EAN011 12-5PM BOTH	EFFECTIVE 2/3 EA1097 BH 12:30p-4:30p Both
Yale	MS	MS	EAN036 Core Nurse 8a-12p EAN038 CBL session 1p-5p Both	EAN036 Core Nurse 8a-12p EAN038 CBL session 1p-5p Both			
FMC Grd Floor			EA0111 8-1PM Both	EA0111 8-1PM Both	EA0084 8-4PM Both	EA0084 8-4PM Both	EAN027 8a-2p
FMC Cafeteria							

Pictorial

Communication

It's important to communicate the training schedule to the operational leaders along with the instructions for how to register team members in the LMS. Keep in mind that there are new leaders all the time, and some leaders who have been with the organization for a long time don't onboard new team members very often.

During new EHR rollout or other project implementations (like a new EHR module), Novant Health has found it helpful to hold webinars for leaders to explain the training enrollment and EHR access process. These webinars can include information about reading the course catalog or training track documents and accessing the LMS registration function, as well as answering any other questions the operational leaders may have. We offered these webinars in partnership with IT access and provisioning so we could share information regarding security access questions and help leaders identify the EHR system access the users would need. This is especially important for users who serve in more than one role. We also held office hours between webinars to provide individual assistance to managers and supervisors, which proved invaluable.

The EHR access and enrollment webinars were not mandatory. Depending on the department, the person enrolling team members into training might have a different role (manager, supervisor, lead, or unit administrative support); this made it difficult to track mandatory attendance. In the beginning, webinar attendance was low, but it increased as word spread about the value of the information shared during the sessions.

In addition, for implementations, communicate the end users' training registration and completion status to department leaders throughout the training process. This is critical because training and proficiency assessment completion is required before the end user can receive their EHR system access.

Classroom and Equipment Management

Classroom and equipment management can be one of the most frustrating points for a trainer when things do not go as planned. Novant Health set up a process and assigned a trainer to check each classroom weekly to ensure all equipment (including computers, bar code scanners, remote control devices for projectors, and cords for large screen monitors) was in the room and set-up properly. There's also a checklist and sign-off process for each room (Figure 20-6).

Figure 20-6. Classroom Signoff Sheet

Training Room Sign Off for EHR Trainers

Classrooms should be inspected and signed off at least once every training cycle.
XYZ Classroom

- ❑ All computers are plugged in and turned on; there should be 18 stations in the room.
- ❑ All computer stations have a mouse, keyboard, and scanner; they are connected and working.
- ❑ Each computer in the room has this software:
  - o ACEs, PLY, PRD, and SoftBank
- ❑ All cords and equipment needed to connect the computer to the projector or front display are up front.
- ❑ The facilitator's computer will connect with the projector or front display.
- ❑ If there is a mess or spill in the room that requires attention, go to the security desk and ask them to contact environmental services.

If something is wrong with a computer or the software:

1. Make sure computer is plugged in and turned on.
2. **If special software is missing from a computer (such as WAM, Softbank, Hospice, or SUP),** ask the instructional designer for the application
3. **Call IT for other computer issues (123.456.7899).** DO NOT use ServiceNow as this will create a work request and lower its priority. In addition:
   - o Have the computer name and number ready. (If this information is not on the desktop, go to Control Panel → System → find Computer Name).
   - o Only put a ticket in as an incident.
   - o Be as specific as possible and list the exact problem (e.g., ACE missing or Citrix missing).
   - o Let IT know that this is time sensitive because you are holding classes.
   - o Note the INC number.
   - o Ask to have Max and Deon added to the ticket so they can follow up.
4. Drop an email to Max and Deon so they know a ticket was placed with the INC number.

After you complete your checks, *even if there were no issues*, sign off on the form in the work room by the printer.

If you placed a ticket, add your INC # to the sign-off form so others will know a ticket has been placed. If you contacted EVS, note the date and time on the sign-off form.

Figure 20-7 is an example of the classroom rounding log for a CT assigned to audit the classrooms in a training center. This log ensures classrooms are audited even if they aren't being used that week. CTs review these items for every classroom:

- Each computer . . .
  - Is plugged in and turned on (this ensures it receives all software updates)
  - Works appropriately
  - Has the updated version of the Citrix environment
  - Has the EHR training environments

    ◦ Has the appropriate software, including any additional software required for that classroom (for example, the hospice module, blood bank software, outpatient pharmacy module, EHR playground region, EHR production or live region, or EHR support region)
- Specific equipment required for that classroom (such as touchscreen monitors or barcode scanners)
- The large wall monitor or projector is working properly and the remote control device is in the front of the room
- Classroom is clean and there are no stains on the carpet or chairs

If any issues are found, the CT should open a ticket with IT or environmental services, as appropriate. They should inform training coordinators and give them the ticket numbers for tracking and follow-up. The classroom logs are posted so the training team can see which tickets are placed and when they are resolved.

Figure 20-7. Classroom Rounding Log

Training Room Sign-Off					*For EHR Training Use*		
Please check the training room and fill in when complete. Note if there are any computer or projector issues and place a ticket before you sign off on the room. Send the INC information to Max and Deon. You can have DPS add them to INC when calling.							
NHO Cycle	April 6–17						
Room	Earth	Jupiter	Mars	Mercury	Neptune	Pluto	Saturn
Extra Software							
Name							
Issues Found?							
Ticket Placed?							
Incident #							
Cleaning Needed? (Email Deon or Max)							
Date and Time Contacted Deon or Max							
Additional Comments							

This process works well even when the majority of our training is being performed virtually. We still have some classroom training, so we need to know the classroom equipment is in working order and the software on the computers is current. In addition, some trainers prefer to facilitate their virtual classes from one of our classrooms rather than their home because the internet connection is more stable at the office. They also prefer the large wall monitor in the classroom or conference room instead of the smaller monitors in their home office.

Trainer Scheduling Reconciliation

Novant Health also put a process in place for CT scheduling reconciliation. They keep the training schedule in the LMS, but they also keep the CT schedule in another system so the manager, instructional designer, and CT can see the entire training team's schedule in one place. A training coordinator reconciles the LMS with the CT scheduling system to ensure that every class has an assigned a CT. If a class is missing a CT, they contact the instructional designer for that application and assign a CT so that all classes are covered. This ensures that the end users are never sitting in a classroom waiting for a CT who doesn't arrive!

Training Delivery

When it comes to EHR training delivery, there are important nuances to consider for synchronous and asynchronous learning.

Synchronous

Synchronous learning occurs live and in real time, with a group of people engaging in learning simultaneously. This enables learners to respond to and ask interactive questions, collaborate with co-learners, and engage in discussion threads.

Let's look closer at the different types of synchronous learning and the benefits and challenges of each:

- **Instructor-led training** is live classroom training that occurs in person.
  - Benefits: interactive, end user has immediate assistance, trainer can determine end users' proficiency
  - Challenges: geographically limited, class size is limited to the classroom size and number of computers available

- **Virtual instructor-led training** is live online training that occurs via remote access on a computer or tablet.
    - Benefits: interactive, end user has immediate assistance, anyone can attend from any location, class size is not limited to classroom size
    - Challenges: inability to see multiple student's computer screens at once and verify student proficiency, can't access EHR system from every device (for example, it might not be compatible on a smartphone)
- **Playground practice lab** is an in-person computer lab where end users can practice exercises in the EHR training environment on their own and a trainer or super-user is available to answer any questions.
    - Benefits: end user has immediate assistance, end users can have hands-on practice
    - Challenges: requires a trainer resource and a classroom, may have limited attendance unless registration is required
- **Trainer rounding** is when a CT does rounds in different departments.
    - Benefits: the end user has immediate assistance, trainers can observe end users as they perform workflows on the job
    - Challenges: requires a trainer, takes a lot of trainer time and travel, trainers can only see a few end users at a time

Asynchronous

Asynchronous learning is self-paced and more learner-centered, but without the constraint of a specific place or time. The content can be recorded and posted online for end users to review at a later time, which means participants don't need to be online at the same time.

Let's look closer at the different types of asynchronous learning and the benefits and challenges of each:

- **E-learning** is computer-based learning and often created in modules.
    - Benefits: can be accessed at any time, consistent content, can be accessed from most devices, including tablets and smartphones
    - Challenges: needs to be updated if the EHR is upgraded or workflows change, takes time to create, needs special software to create

- **Video.**
  - Benefits: quick and easy to create, quick to watch
  - Challenges: needs to be updated if the EHR is upgraded or workflows change, may not have storage capability, may not have way to track whether end users viewed the video
- **EHR dashboards** can provide a place for posting links to tip sheets or videos.
  - Benefits: quick for users to access, can be accessed while performing the workflow
  - Challenges: need to be built by analysts and there may be resistance, the dashboard may not exist, there may not be space on the dashboard to post more information
- **QR codes** are "quick response codes" that are a type of matrix barcode and can be used to create a link to a video.
  - Benefits: quick link that can be scanned by a user's phone, a large amount of information can be stored in the code, can create barcode in a shape or word, can put a QR code in a training document or on a piece of equipment for users to scan and bring up quick how-to videos
  - Challenges: requires a phone with a camera to use, user may need to download an app before they can scan a QR code, not everyone is familiar with QR code technology

EHR Access and Provisioning

From the beginning of the EHR implementation program, the Novant Health governance executive leadership team established that training was required for EHR system access. No exceptions have been made to this directive. The user must also complete and pass an end user proficiency assessment (EUPA) to receive EHR access. This means that before accessing the system, users must take mandatory training and prove their proficiency with the system. The decision has been successful so far, and there are formal IT audits in place to ensure processes are being followed and documented.

As stated by Zack Tisch, consulting services executive at pivot Point Consulting, "EHR training is no different than training on a new device for a surgical procedure. If someone is going to use the system and provide patient care, they need to be trained" (Eramo 2019).

The Joint Commission is an independent not-for-profit organization that accredits and certifies healthcare organizations in the United States. As part of its focus on sentinel event prevention and safe use of health information technology, "the Joint Commission recommends that organizations provide training and have users demonstrate competency before accessing the system" (Smailes et al. 2019).

This is why it's crucial for the training team to accurately track and document training attendance and end user proficiency assessment compliance. It also makes the training team's relationship and processes with the IT access and provisioning team critical.

End User Proficiency or Competency Assessment

It's a best practice to require a proficiency- or competency-based assessment that measures the user's ability to perform specific tasks for their role in the EHR system prior to granting access to the system. The proficiency assessments should be designed and maintained by the instructional designers for each specific role, based on the curriculum and criteria required for that role. The assessment could be designed in various methods, such as:

- An interactive assessment in an e-learning program or computer-based learning module that simulates correct use of a workflow in the EHR system. Grading would be part of the CBL interactivity design and development.
- A paper or online assessment with questions for the user to answer based on tasks they complete in the EHR system. Grading would be done manually or using test grading software.

During implementation, Novant Health administered the end user proficiency assessment (EUPA) just prior to go-live, after users completed their playground practice lab. Post-live, Novant Health administers the EUPA as part of new hire and new provider training, at the end of their last required class. EHR system access is granted only after users complete EHR training and the EUPA and it is recorded the LMS.

Learners With Previous EHR Experience

Now that most healthcare organizations are using EHRs, many organizations are considering the options for training users with previous EHR experience, such as accelerated classes or allowing them to test out of new hire or new provider training. Existing proficiency- or competency-based assessments are sometimes used to determine if the user has adequate previous knowledge to test out of a class or take an accelerated class. An option for those who test out of the full content is to have them take an e-learning module, review tip sheets, or work with a department preceptor to learn organization-specific workflows.

This approach is used at Ohio State University, where the training department converted provider training to an e-learning program and offered an approach that included self-paced, personalized learning and the ability to test out of basic content based on demonstrated competency. This reduced the time providers spent in training and increased time they could spend in clinical roles. It also increased learner satisfaction (Sharp 2017).

Curriculum Management

EHR training curriculum content is based on system information from the EHR vendor and organizational workflow information from IT analysts. Training material, including tip sheets, must go through a review and approval process that may include IT analysts, clinical informatics, and, if they're provider related, the chief medical informatics officer.

It is essential for IT analysts, clinical informatics, and training teams to have a collaborative relationship. Instructional designers may find it helpful to attend the analysts' weekly team meetings so they can better understand any EHR workflow changes that occur. It is also important for IDs to share information with one another as their applications often overlap.

Internal Governance

The purpose of governance is to set direction, make timely decisions, and manage risk associated with EHR implementation, upgrades, enhancements, and other changes. This may include integrated projects and organizational initiatives that affect the EHR system and related workflows.

The governance structure should incorporate input from multiple disciplinary areas in the decision-making process for any changes affecting the EHR system; dividing into subcommittees is often necessary due to the broad scope. It is important to employ a formal decision-making framework to manage and document all responsibilities and decisions going to and from each subcommittee. Formalizing and communicating processes, roles, and accountability before and after live implementation is essential. Training professionals should take part in each subcommittee so they can understand the operational area's needs and priorities as well as the organization's strategic initiatives.

"Establishing governance is an important first step to determine who will make the critical decisions at all levels prior to and throughout the project, as well as set the positive tone for change," said Farrell Sanders, Cerner's senior vice president, consulting and application services, in a Healthcare IT News article. "Doing so aims the project in the right direction, with all parties aligned on how the implementation will be carried out" (Siwicki 2019).

Dana Bensinger, client solutions executive for CTG's health solutions practice added, "The EHR touches every part of a health system's work and mission, so the governance committee should be multidisciplinary. . . . It should include representatives from physicians, nurses, ancillary departments such as lab and pharmacy, and senior leaders who bring knowledge of the health system's long-term strategies" (Siwicki 2019).

Figure 20-8 is an example of an EHR governance structure.

Some of the items that the Novant Health EHR governance structure manages and approves include:

- **Training policies.** The Novant Health EHR leadership committee approves system-wide EHR-related training policies. They also approve overall training plans for upgrades. This provides a standardized approach and a governance process for the EHR training methodology.
- **Clinical integration projects.** The EHR leadership committee approves and prioritizes all IT clinical integration projects that are incorporated into the EHR system. This is vital as many of the same analysts and training resources are assigned to the EHR-related projects.
- **EHR system upgrades.** The EHR leadership committee approves any upgrades, as well as which changes or enhancements will go live.

These, along with other EHR enhancements and organizational initiatives, compete for the same resources and could also cause conflicting EHR workflows. Thus, it is critical for priorities to funnel through a centralized governance board to ensure oversight and consideration for the direction of the organization. All key decisions related to the EHR must be approved through the EHR governance structure lead by the chief medical informatics officer.

Figure 20-8. Sample Governance Structure

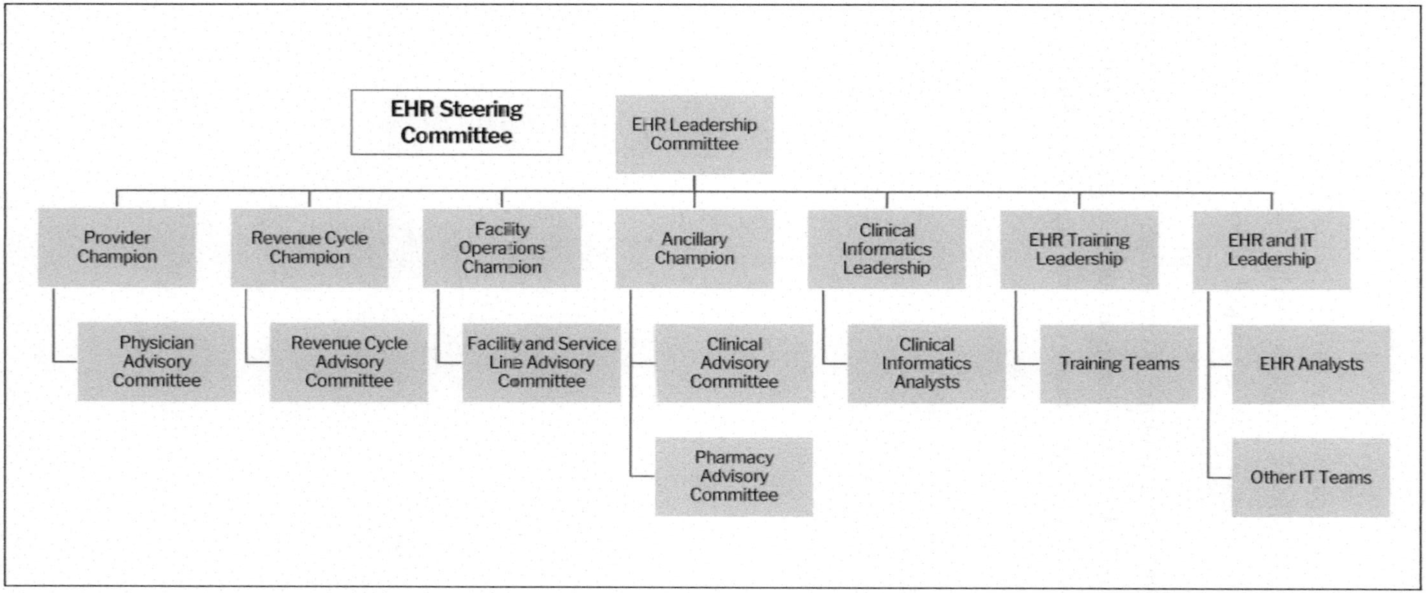

Conclusion

There are many moving parts to an EHR system. However, the most important thing to remember is the EHR affects everyone in the organization and that affects anyone the organization serves. What we do is critical. Communication and change management are key.

Collaborating with other training professionals in the healthcare field is helpful. Sometimes what you think is simple can make someone else's challenge a little easier. We all want what is best for those that are in our care and we can care for them better together!

CHAPTER 21

SIMULATION CENTERS

GRETCHEN MATIKA KOLB

An outbreak of a new, highly infectious disease threatens the lives of millions. Care providers need to be trained to safely don and doff personal protective equipment (PPE) and perform clinical care, including technical skills, with precision and accuracy.

A manager struggles with how best to provide effective performance feedback to a nurse who demonstrates excellent clinical care for his assigned patients but is not perceived as a collaborative team player by his peers.

The intensive care team experiences an adverse event during a patient clinical emergency. A root cause analysis determines that gaps in communication and a lack of role clarity were contributing factors.

A healthcare system announces plans to build a state-of-the-art inpatient facility, which will be its most expensive and ambitious construction project to date. While previous construction projects have engaged end user feedback on the design, costly logistical and safety concerns were always identified the day the facility opened. This time they want to avoid that.

What do these four seemingly different scenarios have in common? They all used simulations to improve healthcare-based outcomes and ensure high reliability.

Simulations are an innovative way to train, assess competency, and improve technical and social skills through immersive experiential learning. It is a technique with varied healthcare applicability that can provide solutions at the individual, team, and system level. Examples of simulation use in healthcare include:

- A high- to low-fidelity task trainer or immersive virtual reality to teach a technical skill, such as intubation or bronchoscopy (fidelity represents the level of realism associated with a particular simulation activity)
- Trained actors, known as standardized patients or participants (SPs), to improve communication skills by realistically portraying patients, their family, or even challenging employees
- High-fidelity patient manikins (controlled remotely via software), which respond physiologically to simulated medications and defibrillators to support interprofessional team training for infrequent, high-acuity events
- One or more of these modalities to test, refine, and improve healthcare processes and even facility design

Based on its broad applicability, simulation is a tool that all healthcare talent development professionals should be familiar with. This chapter focuses on building the larger ecosystem in which simulation activities exist. In some organizations this may be the responsibility of a TD professional, in others it may simply be part of an established simulation center. Regardless of the relationship, it is important to understand the process that goes into the establishment and design of a simulation center, as well as the many ways simulations can be used to advance the organization, teams, and individual employees. From identifying the target audience and their needs to selecting the optimal simulation setting and equipment, this chapter outlines best practices in the exciting, yet challenging process of designing a simulation center equipped to address many different scenarios.

Identify the Target Audience

Whether planning the design and infrastructure of a future simulation event or simulation center, you must start by identifying the target audience. This will dictate who you need to engage with to determine the program's scope of services, medical and simulator equipment, audiovisual (AV), and staffing needs. While the target audience may change over time, understanding who your potential clients are and proactively planning to meet their needs will build a solid foundation for future success.

Ask yourself and the organization whether the center will be expected to provide training and services for anyone employed by the organization, or if it will just be for one department, discipline, or group of student learners. Keep in mind the target audience may extend beyond the institution, such as those in a local healthcare facility or school without similar resources.

Conduct a Needs Assessment

Once you identify the target audience, it is time to assess their needs. Your options through which to conduct a needs assessment with key stakeholders include an online survey, in-person focus groups, individual conversations, or a combination of these. Your stakeholders will include those who partner with the center to establish simulation services suited to their learners, such as the departments of nursing, nursing education, graduate medicine education, surgery, anesthesia, medicine, emergency department, OB/GYN, patient safety, and outpatient services. And, don't forget to include representatives from affiliated health professional schools and any external partners.

When planning a single simulation event or establishing a simulation center, consider focusing your needs assessment on some or all of the categories in Figure 21-1.

Figure 21-1. Simulation Needs Assessment

Category	Considerations
Learner type	• What departments are the learners from? • What are their roles? • Are they new to practice or experienced?
Activity objective	• Is the intent to assess or teach basic or advanced skills, improve teamwork, test new procedures, or identify latent safety issues?
Simulator and equipment needs	• What types of simulators are best suited to meet the stated objectives? For example, do you need a task trainer, patient manikin, virtual reality trainer, or SP? • What medical disposables and equipment (such as ultrasounds, ventilators and bed types) are needed to add fidelity?
Session frequency	• How frequently will the session take place? • Will it be daily, weekly, monthly or quarterly?
Session duration	• Will the session last full days, half days, or an hour?
AV needs	• Does an event need to be recorded, shared, and stored? (This may be the case if it is a formal assessment.)
Instructor needs	• Will the event owner provide their own instructors or are they expecting the center to do so?
Activity location	• Is the stakeholder requesting simulation services at the center or in a clinical area (i.e., in-situ)? (In-situ simulations could have equipment and staff implications.)
Metrics for success	• What can be measured to evaluate the success of the simulation activity or program? • What is the desired change in learner performance or patient outcome? • Can this be measured?

The initial needs assessment is not a documented commitment to use simulation services exactly as projected; it may take some time to build up to this level of anticipated usage. There may also be key clients for whom the needs assessment has not accounted. However, a thorough need assessment will inform next steps in the planning process and help build partnerships with future clients.

Establish a Scope of Services

When building or growing a simulation center, is it essential to establish the scope of services the program will provide early in the process. The scope of services defines where the center will and won't focus its energies. By determining the intended scope of services at launch, you can better determine your initial space, simulator, staffing, and other needs. Some services may not be within scope during the initial planning but will evolve over time, while others may justify the center's establishment.

When defining the center's scope of service, it may be helpful to consider the key areas in which simulation centers can be accredited by the Society for Simulation in Healthcare (SSH): education and training, assessment, research, system integration, and fellowship. Consider a few examples of center scope: A simulation center affiliated with the nursing department within a nonacademic, midsized community hospital, absent of student learners or residents, may focus its efforts on providing simulation-based training for nurses. A simulation center serving a large academic healthcare system, on the other hand, may be tasked with using simulations to train to multidisciplinary healthcare providers, assess student learner competency, improve healthcare systems, and generate research based on their activities.

To maximize the impact of the simulation center, align its scope with the highest priority initiatives of the organization and its learners. How the center ensures its alignment with institutional imperatives will be influenced by its position within the organization, its leadership, and its emerging reputation for high-quality impact outcomes.

Consider the unmet needs of the organization to identify opportunities to return its investment in the simulation center by identifying activities that cannot be as effectively accomplished through other methods—for example, becoming an American Heart Association training center that provides high quality, cost-efficient advanced and basic cardiac life support certification to all on-site providers. Or, if the organization has a large resident population the center could become a site for required certifications, such as the Fundamentals of Laparoscopy Surgery (FLS) or Fundamentals of Endoscopic Surgery (FES), which would improve test access and performance. Finally, if the healthcare organization frequently hires new-to-practice nurses, it may elect to develop a nursing residency program that integrates task and scenario-based training to accelerate the onboarding process.

Key Takeaways

Simulation centers have varying scopes of services based on the key needs of the organization. If you are looking to partner with your organization's simulation center, start by asking:

- What type of skills-based training does the center provide?
- Does the center use simulations to assess technical and behavioral competencies?
- What audience does the center serve?
- Does the center provide team-based training?
- Are simulations used to test policies, processes, systems, and facilities?

Understand Common Team Roles

Depending on the size of the simulation center, there several key roles within the team, such as simulation operation specialist, simulation educator, operation administrator, standardized patient program director, and clinical subject matter expert (SME). It is important to understand each role whether you are developing a simulation center or partnering with an existing one.

Simulation Operation Specialist

Also known as a simulation technologist specialist or simulationist, this individual works with simulation educators and clinical SMEs to support simulation activities by providing technical oversight for AV hardware and software, anticipating the appropriate simulator and medical supplies required for a successful simulation, and programming patient manikin software to model human physiological responses.

The simulation operation specialist may also be responsible for maintaining, troubleshooting, and repairing computerized manikins, task trainers, virtual reality trainers, and related multimedia peripherals and managing center inventory. (A task trainer is a device that specifically trains key elements of a procedure or skill, such as lumbar puncture or chest tube insertion.) Given this wide variety of roles, simulation operation specialists may come from many different backgrounds including IT, healthcare, or even theater.

Simulation Educator

This individual serves as a simulation SME, consulting on the application of simulation-based techniques. The simulation educator partners with the clinical SME (who has in-depth clinical knowledge and expertise) to plan and execute high fidelity, realistic simulation activities.

Simulation educators also work with clinical SMEs to develop clear and measurable objectives and outcomes and leverage the most appropriate simulation-based methodology in response to the initial needs assessment. The simulation educator should also be able to identify if a simulation is not the best learning strategy and advise accordingly. In addition, they may be responsible for hosting post-exercise debriefs, in which learners reflect on their actions and identify areas of strength and opportunities for improvement. They may also mentor others and conduct simulation-based research.

Some centers also include educators who are qualified to train specific skills, such as gowning, scrubbing, phlebotomy, or advanced cardiac life support, in addition to serving as a simulation SME. It is important to understand the boundaries of the simulation educator role at your institution.

Standardized Patients

If the center is affiliated with a medical school, it may include a standardized patient (SP) program for assessing clinical competencies and interpersonal communication. An SP is an individual who is trained to portray a real patient and simulate a set of symptoms or problems used for healthcare education, evaluation, and research. They can help assess the learner's performance. SPs can also be used to portray nonpatient roles, such as a clinical colleague or an employee, to help the learner develop communication skills and other behavioral competencies. This component of the center will necessitate its own director, possibly with additional coordinators, depending upon its size.

Clinical SMEs

These individuals are the clinical subject matter experts responsible for helping to develop simulation-based training and assessment for learner groups within their discipline, which could include physicians or nurses from surgery, obstetrics, and so on. Typically, they're not employed by the center, but they are clients and use its services. Clinical SMEs may be referred to as simulation faculty or instructors, depending on the center, and they collaborate with the simulation educator and operation specialist to design an activity that achieves the stated objectives and desired outcomes.

Operation Administrator

Also referred to as manager or director, the operation administrator is responsible for providing oversight for the center's day-to-day activities. Duties for this individual may include establishing and administering the center's policy and procedures, scheduling events, and managing the center's budget, staff, and equipment.

Executive Director

This individual often provides medical leadership for the center and is ultimately responsible for ensuring that simulation curriculum is aligned with the organization's mission and educational objectives. They should be well connected throughout the organization and have a reporting structure that supports the center's identified scope of services. This individual may have other duties and responsibilities outside what they do for the center.

The executive director is often responsible for developing and implementing the strategic plan and budget. They may also be responsible for pursuing research and grant opportunities and representing the center to internal and external clients. The executive director may also report up to a steering committee that provides strategic guidance and oversight.

When considering your initial staffing needs, keep in mind the extent of your clinical SMEs' simulation experience. If they have significant expertise, the optimal staffing mix may include more operation specialists to partner on course set up, AV, and simulator oversight. However, if they are less experienced with simulations, you may need to hire more simulation educators who can closely oversee the simulation and subsequent debriefing.

Depending on the center's scope of services, staff could also include a research director, additional administrative coordinators, a simulation fellow, and internal or per diem instructors for certification courses such as AHA.

Key Takeaways

Talent selection is key. To ensure your simulation initiatives run smoothly and successfully, you need to have the right people in the right roles. Given how new some of these roles are and the lack of formal training programs, finding experienced candidates can be challenging. For a simulation specialist, learning agility and technical savvy accompanied by a robust onboarding plan might outweigh experience. Ask yourself these questions when selecting and onboarding a high functioning team:

- What are the most crucial technical and behavioral competencies for each role?
- What is the minimum degree and level of simulation experience for each role?
- What interview process or activities would best assess a candidate's simulation capabilities?
- What does the overall onboarding process look like?
- What additional training will be part of the onboarding process?

Design the Space

Finding the space to build a simulation center from the ground up may be challenging, especially if there is a competing organizational need to expand clinical space. It's essential to have strong leadership support to advocate for simulation services above other competing clinical needs. While not always possible, the ideal space is conveniently located either adjacent to or within the healthcare facility. Since the atmosphere will be simulated, it doesn't need to be a former clinical setting; for example, it could be an unused conference room or administrative space. Interview and select design, construction, and AV integration partners early on in the process to ensure the project doesn't expand beyond the allocated budget.

Once you've determined the center's audience and scope of services, it should be fairly easy to identify the spaces required to meet those needs. Similarly, if you're working in an existing simulation center, understanding its space will influence the types of activities you plan. General categories of space found in simulation centers include simulation rooms, a debriefing room, a conference room, a skills lab, an exam suite, a virtual reality room, and a wet lab. Let's review some general descriptions of rooms in the Penn Medicine Simulation Center.

Simulation Rooms

Simulation rooms replicate a specific healthcare setting, complete with human patient manikin and any medical equipment needed to simulate an inpatient, operating, labor and delivery, or emergency room. Keeping these spaces highly flexible to meet the needs of the center's learners and schedule are key to maximizing space usage. In addition, each room should be equipped with AV hardware and software (such as cameras, microphones, and speakers) so facilitators can remotely view and record the interactions.

Figure 21-2 shows two of Penn Medicine's simulation rooms. The picture on the left shows a simulated operating room, complete with table, laparoscopic towers, and booms. On the right is a simulated inpatient room including simulated headwall with gases and bedside monitor.

Figure 21-2. Penn Medicine Simulation Rooms

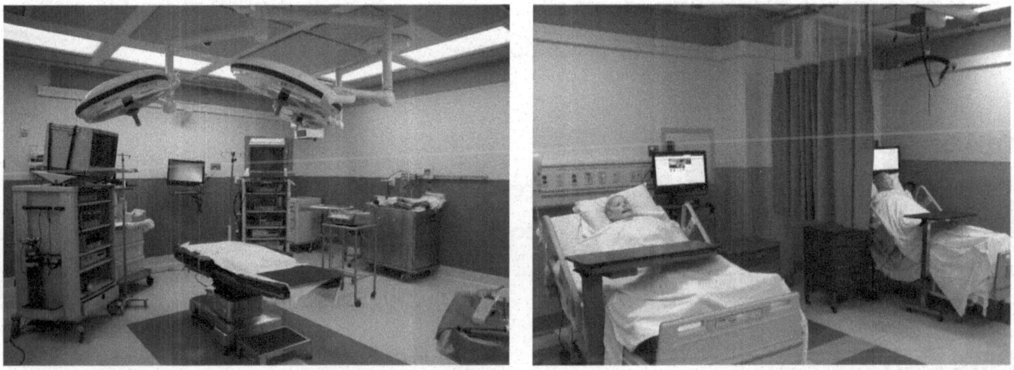

Photos courtesy of Penn Medicine. Used with permission.

Control room

The control room is like the technological brain, which supports each simulation room or the entire center, depending on space configuration. This is the site of AV, data, and voice recording as well as simulator manipulation. The centralized control center at Penn Medicine has multiple monitors that allow facilitators to view and control the manikin, AV, and viewing options (Figure 21-3).

Debriefing Room

Figure 21-3. Penn Medicine Control Room

Photo courtesy of Penn Medicine. Used with permission.

The debriefing room is where the real magic takes place. After they've completed the simulation, learners gather in this room where they're guided by a trained clinical SME or simulation educator to self-identify areas of strength and opportunity. Ideally these rooms are either adjacent to or near the simulation rooms, which allows for a quick transition to the debrief. While debriefing can also be done in the simulation room, that can negatively affect the team's ability to prepare the room for the next session, and thus decrease throughput. Debriefing rooms should be equipped to display video from the recorded scenario if the debriefer chooses to do so.

Conference Room

Although the purpose of simulation is to create highly interactive and realistic scenarios, many courses also include didactic lectures to set the stage. If the center is close to another conference room or lecture space on campus, this dedicated space may not be necessary.

Skills Lab

The skills lab is often used to accommodate multiple task training stations to teach the same or different tasks to multiple learners with support from circulating instructors. Figure 21-4 depicts skills labs at Penn Medicine, which are set up with multiple task training stations to teach skills such as chest tube and foley catheter placement and phlebotomy.

Exam Suite

If the center offers a standardized patient program for competency assessment, it will also require a suite of patient exam rooms. Each room should be equipped with cameras, a microphone, and speakers so facilitators can remotely view and record interaction.

Figure 21-4. Penn Medicine Skills Lab

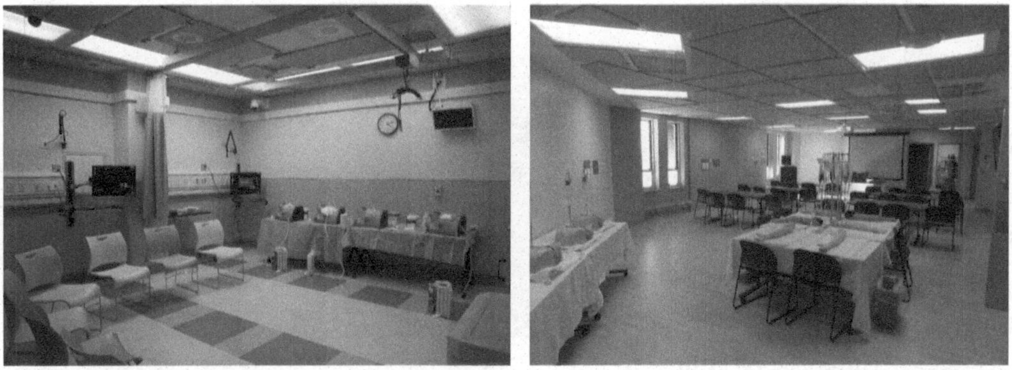

Photos courtesy of Penn Medicine. Used with permission.

Figure 21-5 depicts a typical simulation exam room at Penn Medicine. Computer stations are placed within and outside each room, which allows the learner to simulate exam documentation in the patient medical record and also lets the SP assess the learner's performance.

Figure 21-5. Penn Medicine Exam Suite

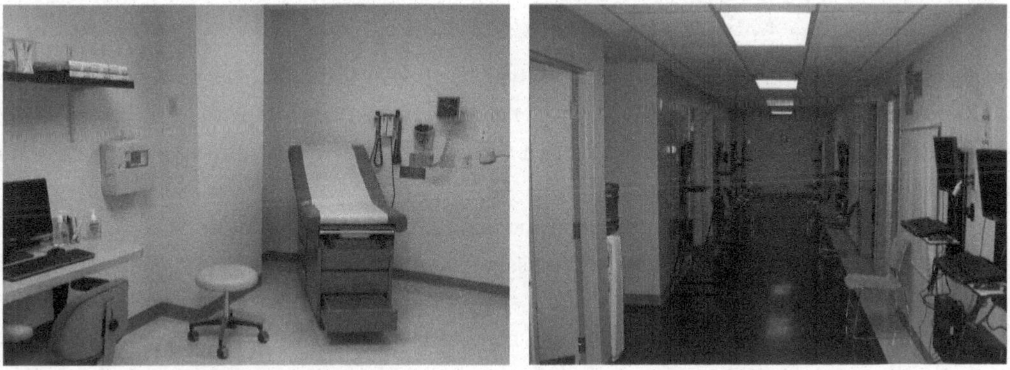

Photos courtesy of Penn Medicine. Used with permission.

Virtual Reality Room

Some simulation centers include a separate room that has the necessary electrical and internet connections to support reality simulators. Figure 21-6 shows virtual reality trainers at Penn Medicine, which use graphics and haptics to teach skills such as colonoscopy, upper endoscopy, and laparoscopy.

Figure 21-6. Penn Medicine Virtual Reality Room

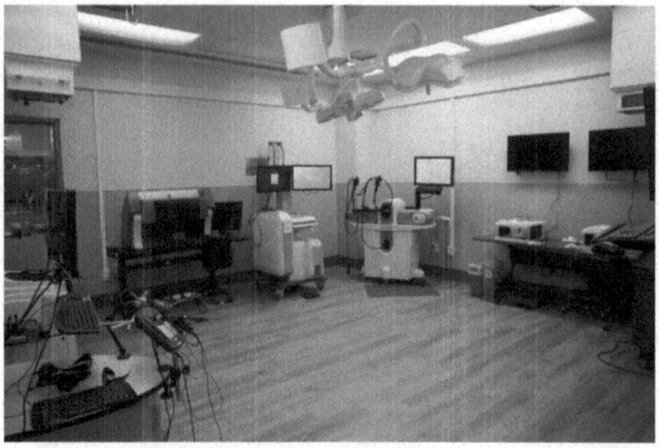

Photo courtesy of Penn Medicine. Used with permission.

Wet Lab

A wet lab is a space where learners can practice a task or procedure using animal parts or other biological matter. If your simulation center's scope of services permits use of animal byproducts, consider confining it to a dedicated space to assist with infection prevention and waste management issues.

Additional spaces in your simulation center might include office space for center staff and storage for medical equipment, supplies, and simulators.

Key Takeaways

Simulation centers can vary greatly in the amount, type, and fidelity of the space. Start by understanding your center's scope of services to guide its space needs and design. Be thoughtful when determining the space configuration and equipment selection. Once made, these decisions are costly to alter and will affect the center's long-term potential.

If you're having trouble finding the space and budget to develop a state-of-the-art simulation center, keep in mind that a lot can be accomplished with simulations even in a minimal amount of space. Scenario-based simulations require a simulation room, an adjacent control room, and a dedicated debriefing space. However, you can convert a 300-square-foot office or unoccupied clinical space into a low-fidelity simulation room using a manikin, appropriate clinical supplies, a doubled sided-glass divider to "hide" the facilitator, and chairs to create a setting for the post-session debrief.

Some simulation centers are even virtual, with the majority of training, assessment, and system integration taking place within clinical areas (referred to as in-situ simulation). These programs are no less impactful for the absence of physical space.

Select Equipment and Audiovisual System

Much like the physical set up of a simulation space, the required medical, simulation, and AV equipment will depend on the scope of services and should be identified in the initial needs assessment.

When determining what simulation equipment is needed, one criteria to consider is the simulator's fidelity. Simulators can be broken into two types—low fidelity and high fidelity—and most centers will have a wide variety of the two:

- **Low fidelity simulators** are not controlled by an external source, so while there may be a degree of anatomical reality, there is minimal interactivity. Examples include a simulated arm for phlebotomy skills or an ultrasound compatible simulated neck for central line placement.
- **High fidelity simulators** are controlled through software and have a high degree of interactivity and realism. Examples include a human patient manikin or a virtual reality endoscopy trainer.

When evaluating simulation equipment, see if the vendor is willing to host an on-site demonstration at the center or healthcare facility. The most efficient way to compare simulators is to arrange side-by-side demonstrations of similar equipment, which instructors and faculty can then try. Develop an evaluation form for each piece of equipment or search online for samples to compare options. (We've included a sample form at the end of the chapter for you to use.) Weigh the cost (including the initial purchase, annual maintenance, warranty, and consumables), ease of use, realism, and projected number of learners and departments that could use the equipment. Another option is to attend industry conferences, such as the International Meeting for Simulation in Healthcare, which often feature large-scale exhibit halls. Consider establishing a selection committee with stakeholders in clinical, information technology, and operations to help inform purchasing decisions.

To create the most realistic and consistent clinical training experience, try to purchase the same medical equipment, furniture, and supplies that the staff use on the job. When requesting vendor quotes, confirm that the equipment is for training and not clinical use, as vendors often offer discounts for educational purchases. Your institution's purchasing department may be able to help secure quotes and obtain the best purchase price. In addition, if the organization is negotiating a large-scale purchase of medication pumps, beds, or other medical equipment, you may be able to acquire additional units for center-based training.

If purchasing new equipment isn't in your budget or is a low priority item, check with clinical departments and the department that services medical equipment. They may have safe, functional items that are simply at end of life for clinical care or expired disposable supplies they are willing to donate for training purposes. Some vendors also sell refurbished medical equipment or rent equipment on a daily or monthly basis. Note: All medical equipment and supplies in the center should be visibly tagged or designated as "not for clinical use." This is even more of a safety concern when conducting in-situ training.

Simulation and exam rooms should be outfitted with AV hardware equipment, such as cameras, microphones, and speakers; many centers also purchase a software system for storage and remote viewing of live or recorded sessions. Consider how the center plans to use the session recordings. Will they be used to enhance the post session debrief, to evaluate the competency of a team or individuals, or as part of a research study? These considerations, as well as budget and data storage issues, can influence vendor selection.

When deciding which and how many simulators to purchase, consider the center's scope of services. Do you need duplicate items to allow for simultaneous use by different groups or to outfit multiple rooms or locations? If the center has an in-situ program, you'll want to ensure the simulators are mobile. While nearly all new high-fidelity manikins are wireless, they can still be heavy and cumbersome to transport. Consider in advance how to make equipment transport feasible.

Build a Budget

Simulation centers typically have two budgets—an operation budget and a capital budget. The annual operation budget covers the center's day-to-day and month-to-month recurring administrative costs. This includes staff salary and benefits, clinical and office supplies, maintenance and warranty agreements, space maintenance, and other miscellaneous costs.

A center may also have a three- to five-year strategic plan and associated capital budget that projects out its growth, including the addition of new employees, simulators, and programs. Capital budgets cover larger purchases, typically those over a certain purchase price. The amount will vary by organization and may even depend on whether the item is equipment, software, or construction or renovation of a space. With high-fidelity manikins and virtual reality simulators costing upwards of $100,000 each (and an additional 10 percent or more of the purchase price to warranty annually), there are significant ongoing costs to keep in mind that are unique from those of a traditional training center.

A significant proportion of a simulation center's financial support typically comes from within the institution. Some centers will charge clients, even internal ones, for their services to generate revenue. If you are a TD specialist looking to partner with an existing simulation center, inquire if there is a charge for the services. This fee may be per event or per learner to offset some or all of the costs associated with the center's space, supplies, and staff time.

Simulation centers can also generate revenue from student tuition, philanthropy, industry support, in-kind donations, grants, or photo or film shoots. While not all centers have a revenue source, it is important to consider since it may offset some expenses.

Key Takeaways

In addition to being resource intense, simulations can be a costly learning solution. A talent and learning development specialist should be able to compare the costs and benefits of a simulation as a learning, assessment, or process refinement technique versus the available alternatives (such as e-learning programs, classroom-based training, or tabletop simulations). Be strategic about when you use a simulation to achieve an objective versus other, potentially more available solutions. Simulations are a limited resource at most institutions, so they should be reserved for challenging situations in which experiential learning is essential. Consider:

- What are the activity's objectives?
- Can these objectives be reached as effectively using another methodology?
- What does the use of simulation contribute to the experience?
- Is simulation a scalable solution based on the number and distribution of learners?

Return the Organization's Investment

Once the organization has committed to providing the leadership and financial support for the simulation center, the TD specialist can help identify which projects fall within the center's scope and provide maximum organizational value.

Recall the four scenarios described at the beginning of this chapter. A simulation might be employed in each to improve healthcare outcomes and ensure high reliability. Let's look at each in more detail:

- Using a simulated environment to train care providers to safely don and doff PPE and provide clinical care to a patient with a highly infectious disease. You could test infectious disease prevention by dusting a high-fidelity patient manikin with a powder containing simulated germs that illuminate under an ultraviolent lamp.
- Improving a new manager's talent development skills. Have the new manager provide performance feedback to an SP playing the role of a nurse who is not perceived as a team player. Then debrief the manager with the SP and an observing talent development professional on the experience and identify areas of opportunity.
- Training and educating staff on team strategies and tools to enhance performance and patient safety (TeamSTEPPS), following an adverse clinical event that occurred due to gaps in communication and a lack of role clarity. Execute recurring simulation-based interprofessional team training across the department and measure the change in team confidence, performance, and patient outcomes before and after implementation.
- Influencing the design of a new healthcare facility. Invite end users to simulate routine and emergency healthcare activities and provide feedback on the experience in a built-to-scale cardboard mock-up. Make sure to focus on safety, efficiency, and the patient experience.

Other high-value uses of simulation include:

- Certifying trauma providers on a new hemorrhage control technique that uses a balloon catheter to temporarily block large vessels. Seek the support of graduate engineering students to modify an available manikin for this training.
- Identifying latent safety issues in a new endoscopy suite. Engage multidisciplinary professionals to simulate routine and emergency procedures in the space prior to opening. Invite departmental leaders and process improvement colleagues to develop a plan to mitigate potential risks before they reach a patient.
- Anticipating changes in clinical workflows upon implementation of new electronic medical records. Have providers document as they normally would during simulated

patient rounds. Disseminate communication and additional training, if needed, regarding workflow changes prior to launch.
- Selecting a low fidelity simulation-based task trainer to orientate new staff to common technical skills. Establish a checklist to assess competency and a plan of action for those who require additional practice.

In addition to working with the center's leadership and steering committee to identify opportunities to use simulation as a lever for change, encourage the inclusion of simulation center representatives on large-scale, high-profile project committees to evaluate any potential applications for simulation. Engage with patient safety, nursing education, and graduate medical education committees to foster a strong partnership.

Best Practices and Tips for Talent Professionals

As we wrap-up this chapter and you work to establish your simulation center or partner with an existing one to support a skilled workforce, engaged teams, strong managers, and effective change, I'll leave you with a few tips to keep in mind.

Focus on the Strategy, Not the Simulator or Space

The impact of a simulation center is not directly tied to how large or state-of-the-art the space or equipment is. Use the principles of identifying and engaging stakeholders and aligning with organizational needs to establish a center to simulate infrequent and high-risk events in a clinical space with an inexpensive CPR manikin. You can also facilitate tabletop simulations with stakeholders around facility design, workflows, and processes to seek their engagement and input without requiring any high-fidelity technology. Do not get lost in the bells and whistles; successful simulation is based on the technique, not the technology.

Prioritize Activities and Monitor Outcomes

Assume that at some point there will be more demand for simulation services than the center is able to deliver. Learn when to say "no" to a request because it is either of low organizational priority or can be accomplished as effectively through an alternative, less resource-intense learning strategy. Your role as a talent and learning development specialist is to provide that guidance to clients.

For any activities in which the simulation center is engaged, identify outcome metrics for measuring success at the project's initiation. Oversight committees appreciate data and may require documentation of the center's impact in return for ongoing support. While assessing learner satisfaction and relevance to practice via a post-session evaluation is important for continuous process improvement, demonstrating the impact of simulation on clinical performance and patient outcomes is the ultimate goal. Since simulation activities are often just one of many institutional mitigation strategies, linking outcomes directly to simulation can be challenging, but it is still important to attempt.

Invest in Talent Development

Maximize the organizational value of simulations by providing ongoing training, monitoring, and debriefing skills for clinical SMEs who aspire to use this technique. Build a cadre of providers knowledgeable about simulation who can support change across the organization and greatly expand the simulation team's capacity.

When procuring new simulation equipment, include vendor-provided training in the purchase and invite end users to attend. Invest in sending key faculty and instructors to external courses on how to design, implement, and debrief a simulation or develop in-house offerings. Consider joining or creating a regional consortium of simulation centers to share best practices, pass on professional development opportunities, and collaborate on research.

Find Where the Value Lies

Unlike clinical departments, the value of a simulation center is not in the direct revenue it generates for the organization but in its ability to promote a highly reliable organization with a positive impact on the patient and employee experience. The center's audience, scope of services, administrative structure, space, equipment selection, staff, and budget are all factors that influence its success and should be weighed carefully throughout its establishment. How each simulation center provides value will vary based on the needs of the institution. It is essential that you anticipate the highest institutional priorities, understand how to appropriately engage the simulation, and secure the organizational support to do so.

Simulation Equipment Evaluation Form

Complete this form as part of the evaluation process. Your input is important and will allow us to evaluate the clinical and educational suitability of this equipment or technology.

Reviewer: ____________________

Medical specialty: ____________________

Product: ____________________

Please rate your level of agreement with each evaluation criteria using a scale of 1 to 5, where 1 means "poor" and 5 means "excellent."

	Assessment Please indicate the appropriate response						
Evaluation Criteria	**Poor**				**Excellent**		**Comments**
Overall clinical realism	1	2	3	4	5	NA	
Ease of use and programming	1	2	3	4	5	NA	
Application to specialty	1	2	3	4	5	NA	
Usefulness in training	1	2	3	4	5	NA	
Comparison to existing equipment or technology	1	2	3	4	5	NA	

Please list any strengths or deficiencies you observed about the equipment or technology. Rate the impact of each using a scale of 1 to 10, with 1 being the lowest level of impact and 10 being the highest.

	Assessment Please indicate the appropriate response									
Observed Strengths	**Low Impact**									**High Impact**
1.	1	2	3	4	5	6	7	8	9	10
2.	1	2	3	4	5	6	7	8	9	10
3.	1	2	3	4	5	6	7	8	9	10
4.	1	2	3	4	5	6	7	8	9	10

	Assessment Please indicate the appropriate response									
Observed Deficiencies	**Low Impact**									**High Impact**
1.	1	2	3	4	5	6	7	8	9	10
2.	1	2	3	4	5	6	7	8	9	10
3.	1	2	3	4	5	6	7	8	9	10
4.	1	2	3	4	5	6	7	8	9	10

Please describe the learner population, type of activity, and frequency with which you would use this equipment or technology.

Do you need an operational or educational function or capacity that this equipment or technology doesn't provide? If so, do you know of any additional vendors we should explore?

CHAPTER 22

ARTIFICIAL INTELLIGENCE

TUSHAR MEHROTRA

Over the past year, clinical quality leaders of Northern Health System, an integrated delivery network, noticed an increase in in-patient admission rates, particularly among those with chronic renal failure. The health system's clinical leaders arranged a meeting with the nephrology group to investigate this issue. The lead nephrologist, Dr. Johnson, had recently attended a training series led by the health system's TD team, in which they discussed the analytics team's ability to leverage artificial intelligence and machine learning techniques to guide clinical decisions and predict patient outcomes. Dr. Johnson suggested that her team work with Northern's clinical and analytics leaders to leverage the health system's machine learning expertise to combat the uptick of in-patient admission rates.

The analytics team reviewed the claims, labs, and vitals data of patients who had interacted with the health system in the past year to stratify them into three risk categories for renal failure: onset tomorrow, onset within six months, and onset in six to 12 months. This predictive data enabled the clinicians to tailor their patient care and outreach, depending on the risk category. This led to a decrease in in-patient admissions, a reduction of costs for the health system, and an enhancement of care for the patients.

This example shows the power artificial intelligence can have in healthcare.

Defining Artificial Intelligence

First coined in 1956, the term artificial intelligence (AI) refers to a machine's ability to perform tasks that normally require human intelligence, such as problem solving and learning, by analyzing data from past events (Marr 2018). Because AI acquires its intelligence from the data it is fed, it is most useful in scenarios that allow for meaningful capture of large data sets. Historically, computers have required human input to draw insights from data.

A common example of how we use AI in our daily lives is the voice assistant features in our smartphones and smart-home devices. These voice assistants understand speech and answer questions; over time, they even learn the user's preferences to give tailored responses and predict future needs more efficiently.

Across several industries, AI can also be used to drive immense value. For example, in the retail industry, stores use robots to scan shelves to identify which items are low in stock and even directly interact with customers by answering their questions in real time. Online retailers use AI to track customers' purchases and give suggestions for other products they might want or need. As more data is collected over time, the recommended products become more specific to the customer's needs (Morgan 2019).

AI has seen considerable adoption outside healthcare, and this trend is only expected to accelerate. Experts project that the AI market will experience a compound annual growth rate (CAGR) of nearly 50 percent, reaching $160 billion in 2025 (Acumen Research and Consulting 2020). Adoption within healthcare has been slower but is expected to intensify. Total investment in AI by healthcare organizations is expected to grow from $1.3 billion in 2018 to $13 billion in 2025 (Global Market Insights 2020). And, according to the 2019 OptumIQ Annual Survey on AI in Health Care, executives across health plans, health systems, and life sciences companies estimate that their own organizations will invest on average almost $40 million in AI by 2025.

AI has numerous potential applications in healthcare, like automating the claim submission process, minimizing clinical variation, and assisting physicians in the diagnosis and prediction of disease progression. This chapter will define the subtypes of AI; examine its application, value, and adoption in healthcare organizations; and discuss solutions to common risks that arise during the AI journey.

AI Within the Analytics Landscape

To fully understand AI, it is useful to consider it in the context of analytics, or the process of capturing and analyzing data to provide actionable insights. Data can be collected and analyzed for almost any event. Collecting healthcare data allows organizations to recognize trends in each population and create a tailored strategy to effectively address them. For example, analyzing historical administrative claims data helps develop a perspective on disease trends and prevalence within a population, or prevent potentially avoidable admissions in a hospital. This enables health plans and providers to more proactively engage community members to seek the right care at the right point in time based on historical health information.

Using advanced mathematics and processing power to predict outcomes from large data sets, AI can produce more sophisticated insights than those produced by other types of analytics. These data sets can be based on information captured in almost any aspect of daily life—including motion sensors, package monitoring systems, and even personal devices—which are then contextualized in relation to historical performance. Incorporating AI into an analytics program can lead to deeper insights for a business or a patient's health.

AI is a type of predictive or prescriptive analytics, as shown in Figure 22-1. Within the realm of predictive and prescriptive analytics, AI can answer questions that typical analytic methods cannot:

- Descriptive analytics provides what happened in the past.
- Diagnostic analytics identifies what happened and why (i.e., what are the drivers behind the data).
- Predictive analytics provides insight into what to expect for future events or outcomes.
- Prescriptive analytics suggests what to do in a predicted future.

Figure 22-1. The AI Opportunity

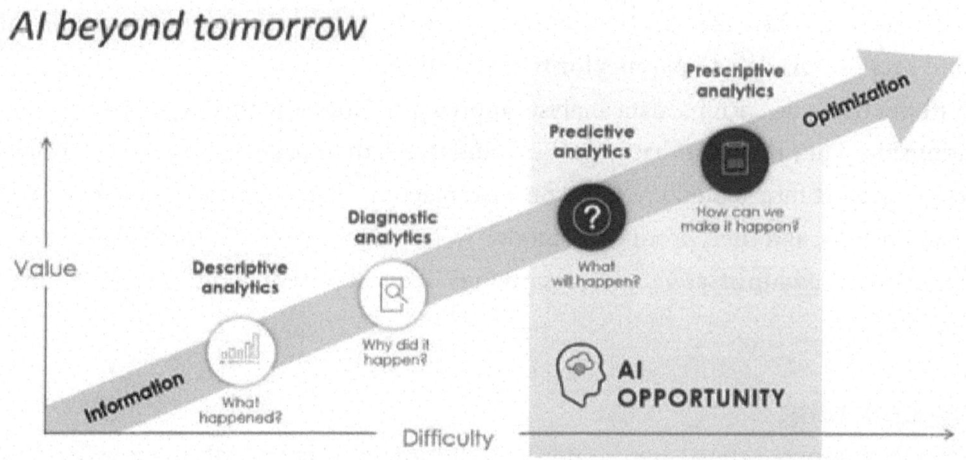

Source: Gartner 2012.

Types of AI

AI is an umbrella term that encompasses three major types: natural language processing (NLP), machine learning (ML), and deep learning (DL). It is important to keep in mind that these three types are not mutually exclusive and are often used in combination with one another.

Natural Language Processing

NLP is a machine's ability to understand speech and text, just as humans give meaning to the words they hear and read. Many customer service platforms use NLP over the phone to analyze information provided verbally by customers to direct them to the correct department to address their concerns. This not only allows customers to quickly access the precise resources they need, but also increases productivity by cutting down the time workers spend routing customers rather than answering questions.

Machine Learning

ML identifies patterns in data to create predictive models. ML algorithms can analyze vast amounts of historical patient data—like symptoms, test results, and demographic information—and create a model to predict disease onset. This can allow clinicians to more effectively implement preventive measures for their patients. Metrics like childhood BMI can be used by ML algorithms to predict whether a patient will develop obesity at a later age. Providers can then use this prediction to take the preventive step of recommending diet and exercise changes to parents for their children.

Without these algorithms, data analysts approach a data set with a hypothesis to explain a relationship. They then test that hypothesis and tweak their pre-existing model until it can accurately predict future outcomes. In contrast, machine learning takes in the data, identifies relationships, and then produces a model. When done correctly, these algorithms can drive significant administrative and cost savings due to the reduction in time required to conduct analyses.

Deep Learning

Commonly compared to the neural networks found in humans, DL is a machine's ability to use data to make decisions. As more data is provided over time, the algorithm driving this decision making adjusts itself to become more accurate and efficient without human input.

In healthcare, deep learning algorithms are used to inform clinical decision making. For example, they can use information from mammography images to better identify patients who are at high risk for developing breast cancer, or they can help doctors make more informed treatment decisions for their patients, ultimately leading to better outcomes (Advisory Board 2019a). This enhanced clinical decision-making capability is one of many valuable applications of AI in healthcare and helps highlight why AI requires a strong foundation to be successful.

Key Takeaways

AI comes in three types: natural language processing, machine learning, and deep learning. But note they are rarely applied on their own—adopting AI for predictive or prescriptive analysis often requires the types to work in tandem. Based on the descriptions provided, ask yourself:

- What problems might natural language processing solve in my healthcare organization?
- What about machine learning?
- What about deep learning?

Use Cases and Benefits of AI

Healthcare organizations are investing in AI more than ever before. The 2020 OptumIQ Annual Survey on AI in Health Care found that 98 percent of respondents were planning to implement or had already implemented an AI strategy at their organizations, marking a 13 percent increase from the year before (Optum 2020).

Health plans showed the highest implementation rate, with 88 percent of survey respondents implementing an AI strategy. However, providers have shown a growing interest and trust in the technology, with a 29 percent increase in implementation from 2018 to 2019. The overwhelming majority of respondents to the Optum survey (97 percent) expressed trust in AI's administrative or clinical capabilities. In addition, most providers expressed trust particularly in AI's administrative capabilities, many of which use NLP. Healthcare organizations have been embedding NLP tools for some time now, allowing health plans to automate their claims processing and providers to transcribe their observations into a patient's electronic health record.

While many providers are still hesitant to fully automate clinical decision making, there is growing interest in leveraging AI as a tool to complement providers' expertise in patient care. The clinical setting offers many opportunities to implement machine learning and deep learning technologies. For example, machine learning models can identify patterns in patient symptoms to give providers insight into potential diagnoses or treatments, and deep learning can be used in tandem with physician expertise to analyze diagnostic images and produce accurate diagnoses (Optum 2020).

How Can AI Be Used?

Generally, use cases fall into two primary categories: task or workflow automation and execution of analysis beyond human capability.

- Workflow automation is when a computer program conducts the steps in a business process without human input.
- Execution of analysis occurs when a computer program processes vast amounts of data (that the human mind cannot process) to draw conclusions and make predictions.

These use cases can be applied in both administrative and clinical functions. Providers have adopted administrative use cases at a far greater rate than clinical, and the first few use cases undertaken are typically within the administrative domain (Optum 2020). This is likely due to the higher risk and greater imperative for accuracy that is required with clinical decision making.

Administrative

The backend operations of health systems are essential for high quality, efficient care. From patient access to coders, these teams provide enabling administrative services, and staff in these roles rely on complicated computer-based workflows and processes. These workflows may be addressed by software like Robotic Process Automation (RPA), which can automate simple repetitive tasks. However, AI provides additional value by making the automation intelligent.

This type of intelligent automation is more common within the coding department, since coders must turn complicated, often unstructured clinical information into standardized codes. Due to the innumerable medical facts that compose coding methodologies, most modern coding platforms are embedded with NLP that can "read" physician notes, understand the medical context, and generate the correct codes based on the evidence (Optum 2021).

Another common administrative deployment of AI is to perform analyses on nonclinical data that increases value. For example, in patient billing the patients' preferences for how to pay for their out-of-pocket expenses varies widely. Some want to pay their bill in full before they leave the facility, while others would prefer to set up a payment plan. Others still might require human outreach to help them understand their obligation. AI has the ability to sift through reimbursement and patient payment data to create a patient profile and customize outreach based on each patient's unique tendencies (StartUp Health 2019). There are a number of factors that make this an incredibly complex issue, including availability of insurance, the patient's socioeconomic status, and overall patient preferences. A human in this position would not have the ability or the time to integrate this information and develop unique interactions based on customer personas.

Clinical

Healthcare providers have started exploring safe and practical ways of applying AI in a clinical setting. Automating workflows in the electronic medical record (EMR), for example, could enable clinicians more time to focus on the patient and provide care in lieu of time spent inputting data into an EMR.

Nurses and doctors with seniority can often anticipate the needs of a patient and the telltale signs of a worsening prognosis as it arises thanks to the experience they've gained from a countless number of past interactions. Similarly, AI can integrate data elements from past encounters allowing it to intelligently predict what may happen or suggest which actions clinical staff could take. For example, a Canadian hospital used AI integrated into its medical equipment, other sensors, building systems, and EMR to alert nurses to patients that were more likely to be at risk for a medical emergency. Through this technology, the hospital was able to reduce the number of ICU admissions and CPR procedures (Rebhan 2018).

Optum has developed a clinical AI methodology to predict a patient's likelihood of developing atrial fibrillation (AFib). By integrating data from a medical group's insurance claims, five years of EMR records, and other clinical indicators, this AI algorithm was able to identify 70 percent of patients diagnosed with AFib. Once they confirmed the algorithm could accurately identify AFib, the next step was to test its efficacy in predicting whether individuals were at risk of developing the disease and identifying those likely to currently have undiagnosed AFib. This innovation enabled clinicians to intervene before the symptoms arose and reduce a patient's risk of stroke and other heart diseases associated with AFib (Optum 2018).

What Are AI's Benefits?

AI plays an important role across many industries, but it is uniquely valuable to healthcare because of its ability to improve human health, reduce total cost of care, and enhance quality of life. Moving forward, we need to continue articulating AI's benefits, as most investments face a rigorous approval process and must be at least budget neutral. Look to these areas for AI to deliver the greatest hard benefits: elevated financial performance (cost reduction and revenue acceleration), increased quality, better patient experience, and clinician and staff satisfaction.

Financial Performance

Because AI can intelligently automate workflows and analysis, it reduces an organization's reliance on staff to perform these tasks. For instance, within the revenue cycle department at a typical hospital or health system, staff make up about 75 percent of expenses, while technology makes up only 2 percent (Advisory Board 2019b). This indicates that if AI were able to intelligently automate some of the repetitive tasks performed by staff, it could have an outsized impact on overall costs, even if technology spend increased.

AI also doesn't have to necessitate staff reduction. Rather, it can enable staff to shift to higher impact activities that lead to higher revenue, such as denial reduction, coding enhancement, and increased collections. Since AI can detect small mistakes in claims submissions that humans might otherwise miss, it can process data on claims submissions over time to recognize patterns and help prevent avoidable denials and coding errors, thus accelerating and increasing reimbursement.

Quality of Care

Leveraging AI can greatly improve the quality of care patients receive by delaying disease progression using better symptom pattern identification and treatment pathways. For example, chronic kidney disease (CKD), which is characterized by diminished kidney function, is often considered a silent disease and is typically asymptomatic in its early stages. However, as CKD progresses into kidney failure, the patient's quality of life also significantly decreases due to a regular need for dialysis or a kidney transplant. Deep learning and machine learning algorithms can enhance providers' ability to detect suspicious kidney scans and use historical data to identify patterns in symptoms and inform care decisions. By delaying onset of end stage renal disease, providers are able to maintain a CKD patient's lifestyle and quality of life.

AI has also shown an ability to reduce hospital readmissions. Algorithms can analyze trends in hospital readmission data to identify root causes that providers and administrators can address. AI can recognize the most minute symptom patterns, indicators of disease progression, and data trends that humans would otherwise miss. This capability is enhanced as more data is collected over time and the algorithms adjust to become more accurate. These analyses allow providers to detect and treat disease symptoms before they become too severe, which in turn helps prevent hospital readmissions.

Patient Experience

From backend office tasks like scheduling and billing to care delivery, AI allows providers to influence the patient experience. As patients are increasingly financially responsible for their care, there has been a market shift toward consumerism—patients have begun "shopping" for care. AI can tailor the patient experience by analyzing past behavior or that of other patients with similar characteristics. For instance, just as AI can be applied to tailor follow-up post-visit billing, it can be used pre-visit to personalize scheduling, initial outreach, and registration upon arrival. Organizations that integrate data from these patient touchpoints and use AI to optimize future pre-visit interactions can improve patient satisfaction and thus reduce cancelations and patient churn.

Clinician and Staff Satisfaction

Employees, both clinical and administrative, are often stretched thin with competing priorities, and recruitment also remains a challenge. In fact, 42 percent of physicians reported in a 2020 survey that they were burned out, and this number is only rising (Medscape 2020). AI could make clinician lives easier by automating mundane workflows or more quickly providing diagnostic insights. This can lead to increased staff retention (avoiding recruiting costs) and increased productivity (Ash, Petro, and Rab 2019).

Key Takeaways

AI has many clinical and administrative applications in healthcare. These include, but are not limited to, coding, reviewing claims, identifying symptoms, improving the patient experience, and helping decrease clinician burnout. Before they implement AI, organizations must identify which use cases will be most impactful in achieving their specific goals.

Risks of AI and Barriers to Adoption

Throughout this chapter, we've mainly focused on the upside AI has to offer within healthcare providers and systems. But it's also important to acknowledge AI's risks and the barriers to adoption. Let's review several potential pitfalls that can lead to an unsuccessful AI adoption that must be monitored and mitigated.

Analytic Maturity

Organizations must achieve an initial level of analytic maturity before introducing AI. For example, they must have clean data that is structured and enriched appropriately before attempting to train algorithms using AI. Moreover, AI should not be regarded as a replacement for the descriptive and diagnostic analytics that are needed for daily reporting—organizations need to have a mature capability in those areas prior to the exploration of AI opportunities.

Technical Expertise and Data Quality

Most health systems have not invested in the in-house technical capability required to build, adopt, and integrate AI into workflows or decision-making processes. It's also possible that these organizations do not have enough clean data to power AI. Organizations should be sure that they have a sufficient historical data that has been collected in a standard way before beginning an AI implementation, because the algorithms are only as good as the data used to build the models. If not enough data has been collected over the years—or if the data has been collected inconsistently or with bias—the insights provided by these algorithms will be reflective of those inconsistencies and biases.

Buy-In

Effective change management plays a critical role in AI implementation. There should be a clear vision, road map, and rollout plan for AI adoption, which the head of the analytics pillar regularly and broadly communicates. Plainly explaining the expectations, outputs, and value of AI to executives and the general workforce will help them develop a clear understanding of how AI will affect their daily operations and the organization's strategic direction. Transition leaders should educate the analytics teams on the differences between the current system's capabilities and AI, the best ways to use large data sets, and how to interpret the results of AI algorithms. Clinicians and administrative staff should learn how AI will increase the efficiency of their workflows. Talent development professionals should tap into their change management expertise to facilitate or lead these conversations.

Effective communication can also help address the general fear that AI will eventually displace employees from their jobs. Administrators may worry that their work will be automated, leaving them without a job, and physicians in diagnostic specialties, like radiology, might harbor similar reservations. Implementation leaders should make sure employees at all levels understand that the new technology is being introduced to complement their efforts, not replace them. For example, instead of spending their time examining images for tumors, radiologists can use AI to examine the images and then shift their efforts to focusing on recommending courses of treatment.

Investment

Investment in new analytical techniques such as AI may not generate an expected ROI or change business outcomes, which can lead to scope reductions or make executives hesitant to approve analytics investment. Starting with simple, concrete use cases can help prove AI's value from the onset while providing important lessons learned for future, more complex endeavors.

Security

Given the high volume of sensitive patient information hospitals collect daily, security is a top concern when implementing any new technologies. HIPAA compliance and privacy parameters are generally built into these algorithms. Incorporating language that is specific to AI into existing data security policies should be part of developing an AI strategy. This presents an opportunity for organizations to partner with an outside group to develop these policies or hire and develop talent in-house (Optum1Q 2019).

Use Case Selection

Starting with the wrong use case can seriously hamper the effectiveness of an organization's AI implementation. Business leaders should first identify an issue they are hoping to solve and then consider whether AI is the best way to solve that issue instead of trying to force the technology to fit into their organization. All stakeholders who will be responsible for setting and executing an organization's technology strategy should be included in the implementation planning process (Mehrotra 2019).

Partner Fit

Just as it is important for all stakeholders within an organization to understand the business need that AI will address, it is imperative that any vendors or outside partners have the same understanding. When evaluating a potential vendor or partner, organizations must make sure that their current goals and plans for future growth are aligned with the vendor or partner organization's expertise.

Healthcare organizations should exercise this same caution when choosing an outside group to partner with on talent development initiatives. All partners should align with an organization's vision for AI adoption, tailor training to specific needs, and deliver tangible results. When partnering with another company, it is important to ensure that their analytics capabilities are firmly established and that they have already successfully adopted AI. Academic institutions should have strong data science research and technical capabilities, along with instructors who have expertise in using data science to drive business value.

To assess overall AI readiness and potential risks, healthcare organizations should conduct a self-assessment using the following questions as a guide:

- Is there enough data available to train the models the right way?
- Was data collection conducted using standardized methods?
- Was the data collected without bias?
- Are there employees at the organization who can build models to analyze the data?
- Are there employees skilled in data visualization techniques?
- Are there employees who can translate the technical jargon across stakeholder groups, including clinicians, administrators, and business leaders?

Key Takeaways

There are several potential barriers to successful AI adoption. Organizations typically face a lack of analytic maturity, technical expertise, organizational buy-in, financial investment, security, focused use case selection, and outside partner fit. Each of these barriers must be systematically addressed during a thorough self-assessment.

Training and Talent Development Implications

The right training and talent development strategy is essential for successful AI adoption at a health system. Optum's 2020 Survey on AI in Health Care found that 92 percent of healthcare executives expected any employee who implemented AI-driven insights to have at least a basic understanding of how the technology worked. Thus, learning and development around AI and its use in healthcare must be a key component of any rollout strategy.

The first tenet of a strong talent development strategy is taking a holistic view of training to develop a shared sense of purpose across all relevant stakeholders. The second is having the right talent and organizational structure. The third is gaining leadership buy-in to ensure the insights gleaned from AI are integrated into daily work and organizational decision making.

Holistic Approach

As organizations set out on their AI journey, it's essential to keep the big picture in mind, namely, what is the larger business problem that AI is serving? For all the challenges involved in implementing new data science projects, a lack of available technology or technical expertise is rarely the reason a solution does not deliver the expected value. Rather, it is more commonly caused by a lack of understanding between data science teams and business teams on how AI and analytics will be most beneficial in increasing business value.

Health systems should therefore provide training for all relevant stakeholders, typically business leaders, operational leaders, product managers, clinicians, statisticians, epidemiologists, healthcare economists, and data scientists. Stakeholders should receive training on fundamentals, such as the organization's guiding principles for developing and deploying AI responsibly, to ensure alignment with the organization's mission and business objectives. In addition, each group should receive targeted training on how AI can transform their business and how they can most effectively contribute in their roles. For example, product managers need to develop a conversational AI and ML literacy so they can collaborate effectively with data scientists on desired AI product enhancements, as well as communicate the value to clients. Operations leaders should learn best practices for accelerating incorporation of AI solutions and process improvement.

Training should focus on material that employees use in the course of their daily work and target concrete skill development. Infrequent formal learning sessions, which are often instructor-led, should be complemented by curated informal content that is made available frequently and on-demand to stakeholders. And the training should evolve as new opportunities—and skills gaps—emerge.

Specialized Talent

Organizations pursuing AI must have specialized talent who are organized in such a way that maximizes impact. With data scientists and translators in short supply and demanding premium pay, many health systems struggle to attract the right talent and organize them at scale. Thus, the most effective operating analytics models with an AI focus feature a separate analytics function with a designated group of data scientists who are responsible for developing and rolling out these models. Another successful approach is to stand up a center of excellence dedicated to AI and innovation. AI should be considered a unique capability that requires its own set of resources and strategies to be most effectively used.

Instead of hiring talent with a data science background, health system leaders may decide to upskill existing employees within the analytics function. These employees should have an established tenure at the organization, as well as the bandwidth and technical ability to take on the additional work. The training can be done through a condensed education series, such as a two-week course, or a long-term partnership, such as a six-month program, developed with an outside group. At a minimum, organizations need a core group of employees with skills in data analysis, science, and translation. In today's job market, these skills are in high demand and there's a known supply shortage. Employers across all industries recognize the power of data and the importance of being able to properly collect and analyze it to drive business value.

Depending on the talent available, as well as existing analytic maturity, provider organizations can decide to either invest in-house or select a partner. Since analytics and software development are not core competencies for many healthcare providers, they might instead consider partnering with other organizations to build out their AI capabilities. Figure 22-2 describes what leaders should consider when making this decision.

Figure 22-2. Benefits and Risks to Investing In-House or Partnering Externally

Build In-House		Partner	
Benefits	**Risks**	**Benefits**	**Risks**
• Provides development opportunities for existing staff • Maximizes institutional knowledge	• Requires specialized talent and staff • Can require significant upfront investment to build models	• Leverages best-in-class talent, regardless of location • Taps into the expertise of a partner with extensive AI experience • Enables the organization to allocate financial resources on core competencies and work with partners where appropriate	• Lack of organizational knowledge and culture • Incompatibility with existing analytics teams • Need for dedicated focus or oversight to ensure value creation

An effective partner will take the time to learn the executive team's organizational objectives and the health system's culture and take accountability for analytics outcomes.

Leadership Understanding and Buy-In

Even with the right talent in the analytics organization, education across the leadership ranks is necessary to ensuring the success of AI adoption across an organization. The first step to generating leadership buy-in is ensuring sufficient understanding of this analytical method.

One particularly effective tactic to help leaders understand AI's potential is peer networking. The widespread use of AI in other industries presents an opportunity for healthcare organizations to connect with other companies to get firsthand knowledge of the adoption process and learn from their successes and failures. Executives should leverage their relationships to connect with other leaders at organizations that have successfully adopted AI. On-site or virtual visits with more analytically mature organizations can help healthcare leaders understand how the AI adoption process is initiated, use cases are chosen, and ROI is demonstrated.

Executive education can also be achieved through partnership with academic institutions or other third-party organizations that provide targeted training in data science. This can be delivered through a learning series, webinars, or one-on-one sessions with senior leaders.

While most opt to take part in existing training programs with these outside groups, organizations with a clearer vision of their AI adoption process might decide to enter a longer-term partnership and co-develop a custom program. This allows executives to combine their vision with the outside group's expertise and create AI models and pilot programs specifically tailored to the organization's needs. Leaders should leave these sessions with the understanding that AI is not a lofty analytics goal for the future, but technology that is currently being leveraged to drive value across various industries.

Key Takeaways

Talent development and acquisition functions play a major role in enabling successful AI implementation. All relevant stakeholders—from executive leaders to clinicians to data scientists—need to understand the organization's overall goals for AI use and how their specific functions align with those goals. Organizations must also decide the best way to go about acquiring specialized talent, whether that's by hiring new employees, upskilling current employees, or partnering with an outside organization.

Key Principles for AI Adoption

Once the core analytics capabilities, people, and organizational structure are in place, analytics leaders can begin to consider use cases that leverage AI. The first step in the AI adoption journey is identifying concrete AI applications. The use cases mentioned in this chapter are good examples, but ultimately all AI use cases should be unique to the organization and its business and clinical objectives.

After a prioritized set of use cases are identified, the organization must rely on its AI team—whether it sits in an analytics group or splits off into a center of excellence—to steer the initiative. This group of business leaders, data scientists, analysts, architects, and translators will act as AI evangelists to spread support throughout the organization. They will be the core change management agents to drive adoption—sharing success stories, helping teams understand how to embed key principles within day-to-day activities, and driving change from legacy approaches to new, innovative AI- and ML-driven models.

After a pilot AI program is successfully launched, most organizations will look to expand and scale to other use cases. Successful organizations often cite organizational structure and talent as two central success factors. As a general guideline, organizations should structure at least 50 percent of their resources toward nontechnical functions like workflow redesign, communication, and training. This may seem like a disproportionate investment, but AI is an emerging discipline that requires adjustment beyond other IT initiatives.

Conclusion

This chapter has sought to demystify AI by putting it in context, showing its value, and outlining its varied use cases. AI application should be considered within the organization's larger technology and analytics strategy and should begin with a focus on specific use cases. A large majority of provider organizations have or plan to dedicate significant resources to build out or mature their AI capability over the coming years.

Organizations that are looking to begin the AI adoption journey can use the following list and questions to guide the development of their strategy:

- Define clear goals for AI and identify specific use cases.
    - What are the organization's overarching goals? How might AI support them?
    - What problems need to be solved that cannot be solved with the current analytic capabilities?
    - How are these problems being solved today? Where are the solutions falling short?
- Consider what skill sets are needed to manage this capability internally, especially when scaling to other areas of the organization.
    - Do these skill sets (such as software development or AI model operation) exist in-house?
    - What training sessions are necessary to upskill current employees?
    - What hiring strategy is in place to attract talent with this highly sought-after skill set?
- Decide how to bridge identified gaps by upskilling, hiring, or partnering.
    - What enhancements are needed for homegrown capabilities to effectively address the use cases?

- How common are the use cases the organization wishes to pursue? (For example, building a model from scratch for common problems like predicting diabetes onset may not be worth the cost when there are many existing models in the market.)
- Who are our trusted enterprise partners? Do they have these capabilities?

With strong organizational buy-in, robust and clean data, properly trained employees, and concrete use cases, progressive organizations can leverage the power of AI to bend the cost curve, free up staff to work at top of license, and improve the health of patients.

PART 6

PATIENT-CENTRIC CARE

CHAPTER 23

FROM PATIENT EXPERIENCE TO HUMAN EXPERIENCE

JASON A. WOLF

In exploring training and development in healthcare, some might ask, "Why address the patient experience?" It is important that we challenge this question and use the opportunity to reinforce the critical role training and development plays. As this chapter will suggest, achieving patient experience success is not simply about ensuring people have the right knowledge or skills, rather it comes from acknowledging the strategic role experience plays for all healthcare organizations in building loyalty and ensuring the best in quality and safe outcomes. Therefore, training and development must champion this strategic view for it to have the greatest impact overall.

In this chapter, we'll discuss how the patient experience is at the strategic heart of healthcare (Wolf 2017). It represents an integrated view of healthcare, supports the drivers of healthcare success, inspires purpose in people, and produces the quality outcomes healthcare aspires to achieve. In fact, each topic addressed in this book influences someone's healthcare experience—whether they're patients and families or those who work in healthcare.

An Emerging Focus and a Challenge

The last decade has seen a rapid expansion of the use of the term *patient experience* in healthcare. In the United States, this has been driven by public policy shifts that use public reporting of the patient experience to determine incentives and reimbursements. It continues to expand globally thanks to a significant transition in healthcare overall, driven by an increasingly involved and engaged patient and family population and the rapid emergence of a consumer mindset for those who engage healthcare. In the wake of this expansion, there has been an increasing acknowledgment that healthcare leaders need to make patient experience a top priority (Wolf 2019). Still, the concept has been applied inconsistently and is often discussed with little explanation of what it actually means.

Many of the ideas framed by patient experience have long been active efforts in healthcare. The evolution toward a patient satisfaction focus has been gradual, beginning with historic roots in patients' rights and advocacy movements; the subtlety of this shift has, in many ways, limited people's views of its potential impact (Press 2014). Experience is about much more than providing a service or addressing how satisfied patients are. By considering experience with a broader lens, we acknowledge that every encounter people have in and with a healthcare system or organization frames their experience, whether there is a formal plan in place or not. Experience is shaped by everything an organization does, in every moment, and in anything patients and families perceive.

The experience an organization provides reflects what it truly is, guides its actions and behaviors, and directs how choices are made and how people are engaged. In that light, those who guide development efforts are essential for elevating the conversations about experience in their organization and across healthcare. It also leads to this key point: What experience is and how it affects all we do in healthcare cannot be left to chance. Experience must be clearly understood by all and comprehensively defined to ensure ownership and aligned action. This may be one of the most critical roles of training and development professionals: to help their organizations develop, understand, and enact the experience they seek to provide both for those they serve and to those who show up to work every day—and then to ensure every member of that organization has the skills and ability to contribute to the consistent execution of that purpose.

Therefore, defining patient experience is essential. It provides an objective target and reinforces purpose. It is a true north for how organizations look to drive their experience efforts and who they choose to be as an organization. It is also important to acknowledge that simply having a definition is not a panacea. Definitions are just inanimate statements if people don't take action to bring them to life. That is why the patient experience must be supported and nurtured in all development work healthcare takes on.

Patient Experience Defined

The Beryl Institute, a global community of practice committed to elevating the human experience in healthcare, formed a workgroup in 2010 of patient experience leaders from a cross-section of healthcare organizations to develop a formal definition of patient experience. This led to a definition of patient experience that has been adopted or adapted by organizations around the world: the sum of all interactions, shaped by an organization's culture, that influence patient perceptions across the continuum of care (Wolf et al. 2014a).

While designed to capture the essence of the idea in simple words, each core concept encompassed in this definition—interactions, culture, perceptions, and a cross-continuum view—has much greater intent and much more significant implications for action. They also provide a foundation talent development professionals can leverage when engaging their organizations in a broader conversation around experience. Let's look closer at these four essential elements (Wolf et al. 2014a):

- Interactions reflect the orchestrated touchpoints for people, processes, policies, communications, actions, and environment. These reach well beyond the clinical realm to reinforce the idea that experience in healthcare happens in many places, primarily those in which we are connecting with one another. Interactions are the basis for any experience someone has in a healthcare organization.
- Culture represents everything an organization thinks and supports in its actions—it reflects the organization's values and is sustained by its people. This plays out in what an organization reinforces as important, the expectations it places on its people regarding behaviors and performance, and the very people it decides to engage when delivering its services. This is done not only for patients, but also to build a highly engaged work environment. Every interaction is rooted in and influenced by what the organization aspires to be—the essence of its culture. (For more on organizational culture, see chapter 10 by Michael and Katherine Stallard.)
- A cross-continuum focus reinforces the idea that experience doesn't just start or end at the traditional boundaries of a clinical encounter. In a consumer-centric world, every interaction an individual has with a healthcare organization directly or indirectly influences how you are seen and what others ultimately share about you. It also acknowledges that the patient experience is not just limited to a hospital, but traverses the overall healthcare landscape.
- Perceptions are influenced by and frame patient experience across touchpoints and through culture-driven interactions—they reflect how those having the experience perceive it. The actions of healthcare organizations can only influence what a patient or family member ultimately determines their experience to be. In experience, perception is truly reality.

This definition has also been reviewed and researched in the context of a broad range of existing literature, and these core concepts link many of the prevailing perspectives that frame the history of this idea and are part of its emerging conversation. "Defining Patient Experience" presented a 14-year synthesis of existing literature on how experience was framed in healthcare (Wolf, et al. 2014b). This article reviewed the overarching concepts and common themes to validate a shared definition of patient experience. As organizations work to develop their own definition for patient experience, they should consider these key elements:

- Ensure the definition encompasses the continuum of care. Whether providing care in one segment of the continuum or within an integrated system, acknowledging the breadth and complexity of the patient experience in today's healthcare environment is fundamental.
- Recognize that experience is about much more than survey results. Experience is not defined by what is asked in surveys or described by policy. Experience is reflected in the eyes and voices of those for whom care is delivered—and in the efforts of all who support and deliver care.
- Focus on expectations. In framing the definition and its purpose, it is important to take the time to understand the expectations of those served and those who deliver care at the systemic level.
- Align with patient-centered care principles. In defining purpose, patient-centered care principles—including respect, dignity, information sharing, participation, and collaboration (IPFCC nd)—help guide how and what to consider in each moment of interaction. While these principles serve as excellent guides for action, it is important to note that experience is about more than "centeredness"—it is acknowledgment of anything that shapes or influences the experience.
- Respect individualized needs. While a definition of patient experience should provide general purpose and direction, it is critical to remember that an individual's experience will always be personal and unique.
- Reach beyond the constraints of satisfaction. Experience is not just about satisfaction—the patient should feel listened to and understand what can or cannot be done. If you're going to provide the best experience, then it will be essential to move beyond thinking of experience as soft encounters to critical interactions across all quality, safety, and service touch points.

These points reflect what healthcare consumers reported when asked how much their healthcare experience matters to them, with almost six in 10 saying it was extremely important (Wolf 2018). In the study, "Consumer Perspectives on Patient Experience 2018," a group of 2,000 people suggested that the experience was a bigger subject than their satisfaction level. Experience is important because people believe it reflects their health, the outcomes they will achieve, and how they are acknowledged and engaged in the healthcare process.

The respondents listed these as the most crucial factors in their experience. They were:

- Listened to
- Communicated to in a way they could understand
- Treated with dignity and respect

Ultimately, this reflects that how people are treated matters—this is not simply a checklist of actions people should take, but a broader call for how an organization behaves overall and what it expects from its people. It is about the kind of organization you want to be in every moment every day, not just the skills or practices you employ. Ultimately, the foundation on which you build an organization will reinforce your ability to provide the best experience for these consumers. It is grounded in a clear set of guiding principles.

Key Takeaways

According to The Beryl Institute, patient experience can be defined as the sum of all interactions, shaped by an organization's culture, that influence patient perceptions across the continuum of care (Wolf et al. 2014a). This idea has been adopted by healthcare systems around the world. How is the patient experience defined in your hospital or healthcare system?

- Does it encompass the continuum of care?
- Does your definition go beyond survey data to incorporate all voices touched by your care?
- What are the "experience" expectations of both your patients and your staff (whether clinical or frontline)?

Setting a Foundation: Guiding Principles for Experience Excellence

A conversation on patient experience must focus on level setting and aligning perspectives to what it means and all it comprises. This starts with a fundamental reality—at its core, healthcare is about human beings caring for human beings. The additional layers of professional titles, technical skills, diagnostic labels, and more are often what causes healthcare to lose touch with this central idea. For healthcare to be effective and meet the needs of those it serves and those who choose caring as a profession, this reality must remain at the heart of every intention and action.

With this in mind, The Beryl Institute established eight guiding principles for experience excellence. Developed from the collective knowledge of the Institute's patient experience community, these actions serve as aspirational and affirmative statements about where individuals, organizations, and the community should focus patient experience efforts. These perspectives are important, as it takes a balance of committed action with clear framing to provide a comprehensive and sustaining experience effort.

It's critical for organizations that are drawn to the quick fix or lured by the latest effort, model, or acronym to acknowledge that despite all the efforts surrounding experience excellence, the solutions are actually quite simple when viewed in terms of human beings caring for human beings. It is about providing good people with the environment to make the right choices while interacting with those they care for and serve, their families, their colleagues, and their community.

The Guiding Principles for Experience Excellence are not boxes to be checked, but rather fundamental commitments that reinforce the central idea that a focus on experience must be relentless, unwavering, and continuous. While there are many tactics that people can and should apply to address experience challenges, they are only as effective as the foundation on which they are built. They are eight foundational actions on which all experience efforts should be grounded. Organizations and systems committed to providing the best in experience will:

- Identify and support accountable leadership with committed time and focused intent to shape, guide, and execute experience strategy. The focused leadership requires a statement of commitment to the importance of experience efforts. There are other strategically defined roles committed to driving outcomes—such as vice presidents of human resources and chief financial officers—but now that organizations are making a clear commitment to experience excellence, it makes sense they would also choose to identify individuals with strategic accountability for experience. In *The State of Patient Experience Study 2019*, 66 percent of responding organizations said they had a specified senior-level leader role with primary responsibility and direct accountability for addressing patient experience (Wolf 2019). Of these organizations, 31 percent said that the individual was focusing on experience 100 percent of the time. This reinforces an important nuance that this principle is not just about having someone called an "experience leader" but having someone with the committed time and the measured accountability to drive strategic outcomes.

- Develop a formal definition of what experience means to the organization. A clear definition is critical to the experience conversation. As noted earlier, without a shared definition that is understood and integrated into the roles of all the people in an organization, there is no basis for action or link to purpose that helps people understand the impact of the role they play. A definition represents an espoused and shared clarity of purpose and direction about "where are we going as an organization and what are we trying to achieve."
- Establish and reinforce a strong, vibrant, and positive organizational culture. Organizations have worked in significant ways to establish and support strong cultures that are built on the right people, framed by clear and shared expectations and values, and focused on alignment to purpose and clarity in how individual roles contribute to organizational success. A commitment to culture is about ensuring the foundation on which every experience is delivered, providing the parameters in which people will operate. Vibrant cultures are rooted in clear and shared purpose, framed by sound core principles and espoused values, and focused on understandable and actionable goals. An organization's culture serves as the lens through which people make good choices. And it is these good choices that are the seed of every positive interaction.
- Implement a defined process for continuous patient and family engagement and community partnership. The value of a focus on patient and family engagement is without question. Yet many still struggle with how to do this effectively. Healthcare, for as much as it is a business, is perhaps the largest community-grounded and consumer-facing industry in existence. Yet, far too often and in many ways for far too long, healthcare has been run from the inside out. This is not to diminish the expertise that comprises healthcare leadership, but rather a challenge to consider the broader scope of all engaged in the healthcare equation. Healthcare leaders must ensure their organizations are listening to those in their care with purpose and the intention to act, as well as capturing feedback and perceptions for use in the immediate situation and more general improvement opportunities. Engagement ultimately means inten-

tionally involving patient and family voices as partners at the systemic level and the individual point of care.

- Engage the voices of staff, clinicians, and healthcare professionals to drive comprehensive and lasting solutions. While the importance of engaging, capturing, and acting on patient and family voice is critical, this cannot and should not be done at the cost of missing what associates or team members have to contribute. Organizations must first get their people in order if they hope to provide the best in experience. This means being intentional in engaging and hearing from those within the institution as well. When engaging all voices, organizations must be committed to looking for, listening to, and acting on what they discover—simply asking with no action is a quick path to undermining intent. The willingness to extend the invitation to all voices reinforces the critical idea that a focus on experience is about more than outcomes; it is about loyalty and consumer choice and the organization's reputation in the communities it serves.
- Ensure an active commitment to health equity and access to care. At a moment in history where the clear inequities in healthcare have been brought to light, it is incumbent on organizations to take a serious look at the issue of racism and discrimination in their midst. In a recent PX Pulse, more than a third of all Black Americans identified as experiencing discrimination in healthcare "sometimes" or "often" (The Beryl Institute and Ipsos 2020). Organizations must reflect institutionally and actively address the issues that affect health disparities and access that challenge their ability to consistently provide the best outcomes. Successful organizations will work to tackle these systemic issues as well as look inward to address the conscious and unconscious bias that affects their ability to provide equitable care. (For more on diversity, equity, and inclusion, see chapter 7 by Imelda Hicks.)
- Expand focus on health outcomes beyond treating illness to promote health, wellness, and well-being. Now that the focus has shifted to the challenges and opportunities of population health, there is a clear acknowledgment that cost will push the system to new interventions and alternative models of care, as well as a shared understanding that keeping people well is much more effective and efficient than healing them once they're sick. This, too, is critical to the experience provided. In recognizing that experience is at the heart of healthcare and in moving from a reactive to an anticipatory model, the experience of those in organizations and more broadly in the system is

recognized first. Acting through the lens of well-being provides more solid footing to think strategically about what ideal experiences look and feel like and affords the opportunity to tackle the experience for all it encompasses. (For more on business acumen and well-being, see chapter 15 by Scott Kashman.)

- Acknowledge that the healthcare experience reaches beyond clinical interactions to all touchpoints across the continuum of care. Experience as framed above is influenced by a wide variety of factors both within the direct experience someone has in a hospital, physician's office, or nursing home and what they experience in the broader system connected to and surrounding that encounter. In moving to a model of integrated systems, someone experiencing those systems will have rapidly increasing expectations of consistency, alignment, and simplicity. Therefore, operational opportunities such as communication, technology, hand-offs, and other points of interaction can and will influence how people perceive an organization.

The eight Guiding Principles for Experience Excellence provide a strategic foundation on which to understand and address all that influences the patient experience. From a development standpoint, the capacity to look at experience from this broad lens reinforces the integrated view it takes to identify and frame actions to ensure the best in experience. But it is critical to look a bit closer at what an organization does that has bearing on a patient's overall experience. The integrated view is seen through the Experience Framework.

An Integrated View: The Experience Framework

Building on the foundation established through the guiding principles, The Beryl Institute introduced the Experience Framework in 2018. The framework offers eight strategic lenses through which any experience effort should be framed (Figure 23-1). We seeing experience as the integration of every area healthcare addresses—from quality, safety, and service to the range of factors that influence the healthcare experience. The Experience Framework provides a means to identify these ideas and a structure to frame them, which expand the strategic view of experience and lead to more comprehensive action overall. It reaches well beyond the clinical experience of patients to the full extent of the human experience in healthcare, representing a macro view of all the elements that must be acknowledged and acted upon to ensure a comprehensive focus on experience.

Figure 23-1. The Experience Framework

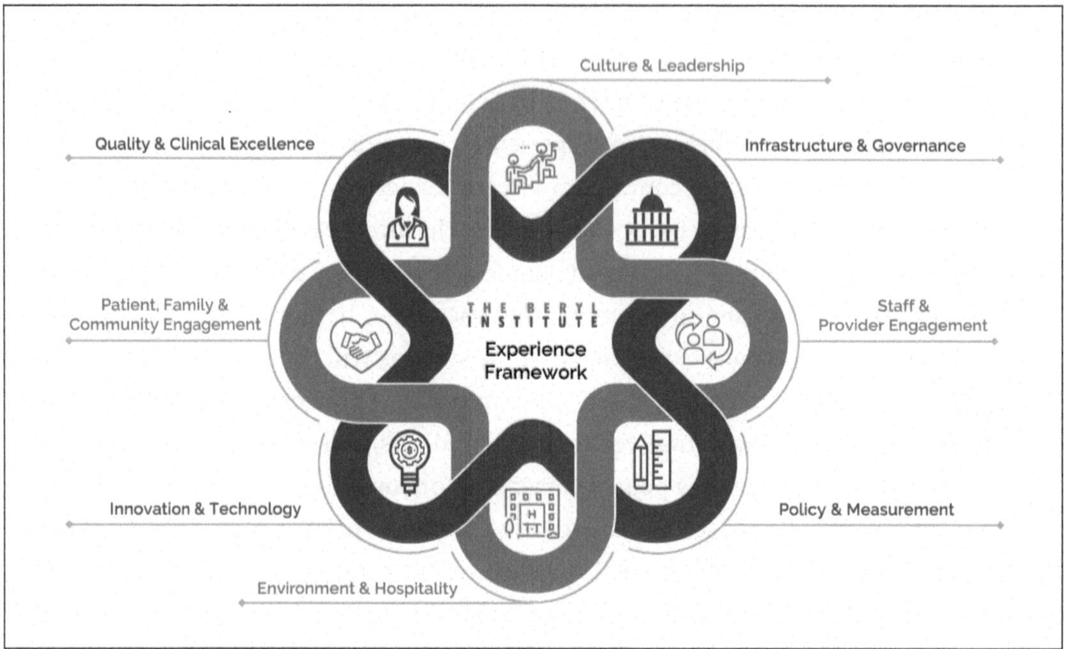

From a systems perspective, experience both influences and is influenced by each of these strategic lenses. It is by taking the integrated view of how they work with, through, and even (at times) against each other that organizations can make the best strategic decisions. This perspective also refocuses leader and associate development to see the role every person and element of their organization plays in shaping the perceptions of those it serves and therefore the experience they have. The Experience Framework also provides a structure for organizations to identify areas where they are excelling or may have opportunities to address and offers a means by which knowledge, resources, and solutions can be identified, aligned, and applied.

The integrated perspective of the Experience Framework reveals how far patient experience has evolved from its roots, which is truly an expansion of the overall perspective of experience for healthcare. If organizations take this broader perspective (and they need to if they want to be successful in today's environment), then this intention leads them to a greater vision for experience today—that of the human experience in healthcare.

Key Takeaways

The eight strategic lenses through which any experience effort should be framed are:

- Culture and leadership: The foundation of any successful experience effort is set on who an organization is, its purpose and values, and how it is led.
- Infrastructure and governance: Effective experience efforts require the right structures and processes by which to operate and communicate, and the formal guidance in place to ensure sustained strategic focus.
- Patient, family, and community engagement: Central to any experience effort are the voices of, contributions from, and partnerships with those receiving care and the community served.
- Staff and provider engagement: Caring for those delivering and supporting the delivery of care and reaffirming a connection to meaning and purpose is fundamental to the successful realization of a positive experience.
- Environment and hospitality: The space in which a healthcare experience is delivered and the practices implemented to ensure a positive, comfortable, and compassionate encounter must be part of every effort.
- Innovation and technology: As a focus on experience expands, it requires new ways of thinking and doing and the technologies and tools to ensure efficiencies, expand capacities, and extend boundaries of care.
- Policy and measurement: Experience is driven and influenced by external factors and systemic and financial realities; it requires accepted and understood metrics to effectively measure outcomes and drive action.
- Quality and clinical excellence: Experience encompasses all an individual encounters and the expectations they have for safe, quality, reliable, and effective care focused on positively affecting health and well-being.

Moving Beyond Patient Experience to Human Experience

Patient experience will forever be central to healthcare. But as the conversation on healthcare experience grows, it fundamentally reaches beyond the patient experience. In reinforcing that healthcare is essentially human beings caring for human beings, we should acknowledge that the work of healthcare is now focused on addressing and affecting the human experience. This focus on human experience calls for an understanding of the breadth of people engaged in the healthcare equation, from patients, family members, and care partners to healthcare practitioners and professionals to the very communities they serve. These components are inextricably linked and are best served when seen for their connected versus disparate nature.

The realities of 2020 and the COVID-19 pandemic have only highlighted the importance of focusing on human experience. While healthcare professionals and organizations responded to the critical needs of patients and their communities, staffing and access to supplies grew challenging, exhaustion overwhelmed the healthcare workforce, and hospitals overflowed with sick patients. The world saw firsthand the power of patient experience—the level of compassion and care that healthcare professionals demonstrated time and time again reinforced the critical nature of the workforce experience. We were also brought face-to-care with the systemic disparities and issues of health equity in our communities. In this moment in our history we are called to forge a new existence that begins with looking beyond the distinct silos of patient experience, employee engagement, or community health to focus on a common thread that binds these areas together—the human experience (Figure 23-2).

Figure 23-2. The Human Experience in Healthcare

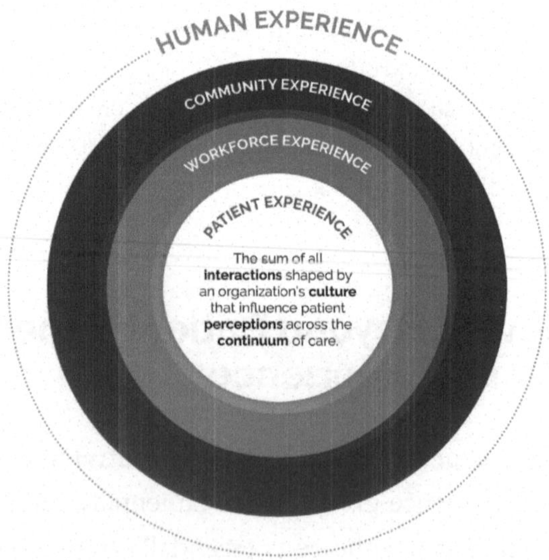

Source: Wolf at al. (2021)

This continued evolution of how we think about experience, of seeing healthcare from this holistic and multi-perspective lens, calls for a shift in some of the very foundations of how healthcare operates. Thus, training and development professionals must play a critical role in helping their organizations move along this path. The paper "Human Experience 2030: A Vision for the Future of Healthcare" outlined three fundamental changes for healthcare, and ultimately the experience it provides (Wolf 2020):

- **A change in perspective from siloed and specialized to integrated and systemic.** Healthcare has worked diligently to establish processes and protocols to manage its intricacies and breadth of scope. This perfect combination of distance between points of work has driven the establishment of specializations, which, while critical for clinical expertise, are damaging to a living system that relies heavily on collaboration, shared information and evidence, and communication to ensure overall success. Healthcare has become a collection of silos, clinically and operationally, that have caused battles for resources and prominence, as well as weakness at the seams of a system that's trying to weave itself together. To truly address the issues that support the best in human experience, we need systemic solutions in which pieces of the systems work with, through, and for one another, not in competition with or against.
- **A change in process from transactional to relational.** To manage the complex and distributed nature of healthcare organizations, transactions have been established and processes and protocols put in place simply to try and bind the parts together. If there is a desire to create a truly integrated and systemic effort in healthcare, then the primary connective tissue must be relational and built on networks and partnerships, collaboration, and seamless processes. Patients and families should not have to travel a transactional path—they should be able to have a relationship with the system that's supported by transactions that expedite and support their journey. The reality is that healthcare is a relational business.
- **A change in focus from aspirational to active.** To the fault of none, and due to the purpose and passion of all, healthcare has always been aspirational. The ability to dream is not the troublesome part; it is the limited action that follows. The opportunity now, but even more so the need, is to move beyond aspirations to the actions it will take to move the experience conversation and other ideas forward. Driving active change for the human experience in healthcare is fundamentally doing the seemingly simple, but practically complex things to create a shared foundation on which to build the future.

A commitment to human experience reinforces why experience is the strategic heart of healthcare. That's why this chapter does not provide techniques or tactics for how to "do" patient experience—by looking at how training and development can play a role, we can begin to see how to achieve success. Every organization will require variations on what practices or processes work for them, but we all must consider the fundamentals around guiding principles, strategic lenses, and fundamental transformations to ensure a sustained focus on human experience.

Key Takeaways

How can you help implement these three fundamental changes for healthcare in your organization?

- A change in perspective from siloed and specialized to integrated and systemic
- A change in process from transactional to relational
- A change in focus from aspirational to active

The Strategic Heart of Healthcare

It is safe to say that patient experience reaches far beyond what happens in the examination room. Experience is something much bigger. It reflects all a patient has lived through and all that is perceived, understood, and remembered from their encounters with health systems. It remains their lasting story. This is no different for those who work in healthcare.

Organizations are now also acknowledging patient experience as a must-do with real strategic significance. When an integrated and strategic perspective is taken, a more sustainable purpose and focus is established for organizations in general—and better outcomes are realized in quality, safety, service, and engagement in experience overall. This has implications on cost and financial performance, clinical outcomes, and even reimbursements.

At the outset of this chapter, you were challenged to look at experience with a broader, more integrated and active lens. In sharing the roots, conceptual evolution, and view for what is next, this ultimately leads to a call to action for those committed to developing both the people in and the organizations that comprise healthcare. If we diminish efforts focused on patient experience as just another thing "to do," the path to what is possible is cut short.

It will be in taking the strategic view, one seeing experience's role at the strategic heart of healthcare, that programs and processes can be built and desired results achieved. There is no easy checklist to experience excellence or a set of proven practices applicable to all. Yes, some efforts may move survey scores, but the intention here and the opportunity called for is to look at this as something bigger.

That is the call to action for development professionals. Be willing to wade into deeper waters and address the big things. That is ultimately what experience is all about, and it is all any individual can ask for from the healthcare organizations they choose. In building organizations that see, engage, and help the totality of each human being they serve, experience will become the heart of healthcare.

Improving the Patient Experience at Stanford Health Care

Stanford Health Care's imaging services and radiology department operates in 12 different locations comprising 300 FTEs and completing about 450,000 patient exams annually. As part of Stanford's system-wide improvement effort "52 and 52" (52 projects in 52 weeks), the imaging team wanted to focus on staff empowerment and staff engagement and provide a platform and an opportunity to effectively solve problems that affect the patient experience.

One example of how individual staff were empowered to bring performance improvement solutions to the forefront came from a radiology nurse who questioned the process for conducting an exam called a cystogram. When patients arrived at radiology with a catheter, there was confusion between the referring physician and the radiology team about who was to discharge the catheter. Urology thought radiology did it, while radiology would tell patients to make an appointment with urology to do it. In the middle was the patient, bouncing back and forth between departments trying to get their catheter removed. This radiology nurse realized what was happening, voiced her concern, and created a project to bring together both services and develop a standard that solved the problem.

What made this specific project and the wider initiative a success at Stanford Health Care? It required rigor, a commitment to process steadiness, and clear and unwavering leadership buy-in, support, and visual presence and engagement.

Adapted from The Beryl Institute (nd)

Experience Excellence: Implications and Actions for Training and Development

In looking at the implications and opportunities outlined in this chapter, it is critical to reinforce a fundamental point: Experience should not and must not be seen as a "thing to do." If working toward experience excellence is seen only as something served by training, it underlines a dangerous course—if experience is simply a "thing to do," it can be prioritized, or not, and may be deemed something people are too busy to address or act on. This does a great disservice to the realities of what true experience excellence represents.

The definitions and frameworks outlined in this chapter call on training and development professionals to push to the highest level of strategic impact with a commitment that the work on experience is about the work on and about your organization. These ideas call on some very clear opportunities for action:

- **Definition.** Work to establish a shared vision or definition of experience for your organization. I have long asserted that without a sense of what you want to accomplish, you will not know that you have. Having a clear and shared understanding of the experience you want to provide must be a critical first step to create a shared north star for any effort. Organizations must first put in place a definition for what they are trying to achieve.
- **Leadership.** Encourage and develop leadership understanding and support of the value and importance of experience. We all acknowledge the importance of leadership when identifying and supporting and sustaining priorities. Leadership not only is needed to focus and then hold the light on experience efforts, but they must be developed at all levels to support on-the-spot efforts to support and sustain the day-to-day efforts of experience excellence. With a definition in place, ensuring clear leadership support becomes the critical next step to align the purpose with a commitment to action.
- **Engagement.** Establish efforts to ensure engaged staff, leadership, patients, families, and communities. This is an effort that requires an integrated and woven effort among the breadth of constituencies in healthcare. Partnership is an essential piece of the experience puzzle that, if missing, breaks the bonds of what is possible. Developing programs and processes for engagement, shared voices, and input must be done with intention. With leadership focus established, an organization can work on the means to engage staff at all levels and include patients and families and the community in their efforts.
- **Culture.** A healthcare organization that's truly committed to experience must have a culture that is grounded in and reinforces expected behaviors. In addressing culture

as a strategic key to experience, there is also the need for clear and measured accountability at all levels. At times, this may not be about creating, but rather removing cultural roadblocks and enabling change. The next component is to build or reinforce the cultural framework required to support an experience effort. This ranges from aligning the organization's vision to the selection and development of the right people to rewards, recognition, and consequences that support positive action. Throughout my research and examination of this topic, culture is consistently found at the center of an effective experience effort.

Training and development professionals focused on ensuring a commitment to patient experience can also acknowledge the need for the basic skills underlying all of these big actions. At the core is the ability to communicate with compassion—not only to those who are receiving care but for all in the healthcare ecosystem. This goes to the heart of healthcare and the broader human experience. If training and development professionals are to be true agents of change in driving experience excellence, we cannot start at this end, but rather know that if we can encourage and support the building of organizations that can nurture and sustain compassion, we ultimately drive the very essence of experience itself.

Conclusion

Experience will forever be the sum of all interactions, human being to human being, shaped by an organization's culture and all we expect it to be. It will always be the perception of those we serve—the experiences created in those small moments of connection, not in new buildings or shiny amenities—that matter most. Building the structures and processes to encourage and nurture those interactions and developing the skill sets to ensure those interactions sing falls squarely in the wheelhouse of training and development. The call to action now is to lead experience efforts forward, knowing your contributions make a difference for all and are needed now more than ever.

So dig in, be relentless, think and act big, and the idea of experience will not just be something your organization measures, it will be what it breathes every moment of every day. That is the opportunity before you and the challenge I hope you will accept.

CHAPTER 24

CLINICAL QUALITY

BEN LOCWIN

Everybody expects to receive "quality" clinical care when the time comes. But what does *clinical quality* really mean? And do we receive quality clinical care when we're patients? It's easy to say the word *quality*, but more difficult to get a standard answer—even from those who work in clinical care—as to what "quality" actually means.

I would argue that clinical quality is "doing the right things when nobody's looking." But too often clinical quality is nonexistent or goes unmeasured, and medical errors contribute to a large proportion of cases of morbidity and mortality in patients under clinical care. Quality goes beyond maintaining proper compliant documentation—it's more about how to *prevent* issues. In this way, quality tools are centered around statistical process control and a structure to repeatably determine and eliminate the root causes of issues so they don't pose a problem in the future. Quality should never be a check-the-box exercise.

So, what's going on here? How can we improve clinical quality? In this chapter, we'll start by answering two key questions: "What does quality mean?" and "What is the cost of quality?" Then we'll review two ethical considerations in clinical quality. Finally, we'll look at clinical quality through the prism of a root cause analysis and describe seven tools you can use to identify problems and improve clinical quality.

What Does *Quality* Mean?

The word *quality* is often used incorrectly across the healthcare, clinical practice, pharmaceutical, and biotech industries. Everyone thinks they understand quality at a deep level, just as 80 percent of drivers think they are "better than average" (McCormick, Walkey, and Green 1986). In fact, no more than 50 percent of the drivers on the road at any given time can be called "better than average." Just as with driving competency, quality expertise is normally distributed at best (meaning half the industry has a lower-than-average expertise at quality); at its worst, the industry has a right-skewed distribution, where only the rightmost tail (representative of maybe 10 percent of the population) has a thorough understanding of the principles, practices, and application of quality concepts (Figures 24-1 and 24-2, respectively).

Figure 24-1. Best-Case Scenario

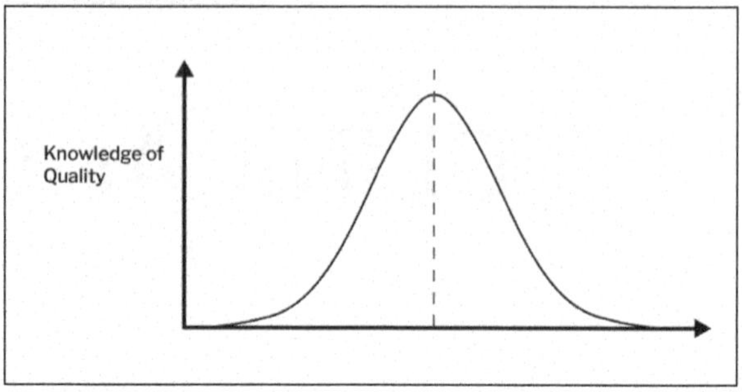

Figure 24-2. Worst-Case Scenario

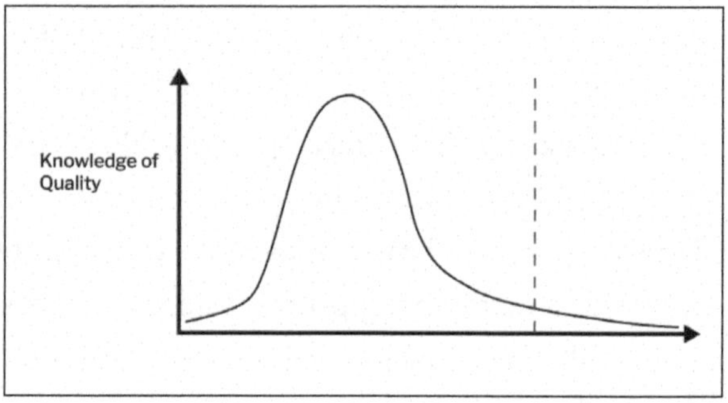

The word *quality* should be very precise—it should call to mind certain requirements. Rework rates, defects, critical-to-quality requirements (CTQs), cost of quality, proportion "good" (such as defects per unit and first pass yield), and other specific terminologies give quality its quantitative robustness and repeatability. Once quality is diluted with discussions about inspections and final product quality assessments, it's no longer proactively ensuring that we can rely upon these processes to produce high-quality outputs without inspections and manual interventions. These are all (inspections, assessments) rework steps and add to the overall cost of quality.

What Is the Cost of Quality?

Let's look at the phrase "What is the cost of quality?" in more detail. The cost of quality comprises a few things:

- Prevention costs
- Appraisal costs
- Internal failure costs
- External failure costs

Each component includes sub-elements that, in totality, add up to an organization's cost of "ensuring" some level of quality. Why have "ensuring" in quotes? Because the only way to systematically ensure that an organization's outputs are of high quality is to design each subordinate process step so that it is repeatable, predictable, and very high quality in and of itself.

Once each process step is chained together in serial order (or parallel, depending upon the activities), it's possible to guarantee quantitatively predictable outcomes to a high degree of certainty. This is the underpinning concept of quality by design (QbD). If each subordinate step's actual performance against expected performance isn't measured or quantified, then as each process step completes and leads to the next, the overall outcome is only structured around the clinically underperforming element of "hope." Let me be clear: *Hope* is never a viable long-term quality strategy, but it is invoked at many organizations where proper process characterization seems like a lot of work.

I intentionally listed the four components in that order to show them in an ordinal list of the most effective ways to apply resources to improve quality:

- **Establishing specifications** for incoming materials and supplies, planning for proactive quality, and looking to improve outcomes are prevention costs.
- **Appraisal costs** include measuring and monitoring, such as quality audits, review of documentation, treatment protocols, and medical stock logs, as well as clinic and hospital survey ratings.
- **Internal failure costs** are those activities that exist to remediate errors and defects within production process steps. Wasted work and excess inventory (as buffers) exist because of poor characterization of processes. Rework, which refers to doing additional work to correct defects, is an internal failure cost, as is analysis of failure (such as deviation investigation processes). Lost material due to expiration and other discards because of significant concerns about material integrity would be included at the tail end of internal failure costs.
- **External failure costs** refer to costs that exist because defective products or services have reached the customers. This can include injuries, adverse events, complaint resolution, and litigation.

Figure 24-3 demonstrates a rolled throughput yield (RTY) across a series of fairly high-quality and well-measured process steps. Step 1 has a success rate of 92 percent (~1 error per 12 iterations), step 2 has a success rate of 97 percent, and so on. However, with the rules of probability, the overall RTY is the multiplicative product of every subordinate step's success rates. This leads to an overall outcome success rate of about 74 percent. So, a quarter of the time, we'll have to explain or justify an unintended effect or outcome in the process or allow it to exist as a failure outcome. More steps in a process, nested sub-processes within a higher-level process, and input factors all work together to dramatically increase the level of complexity and decrease the probabilistic level of success for the final outcome.

Figure 24-3. Process Steps for Rolled Throughput Yield

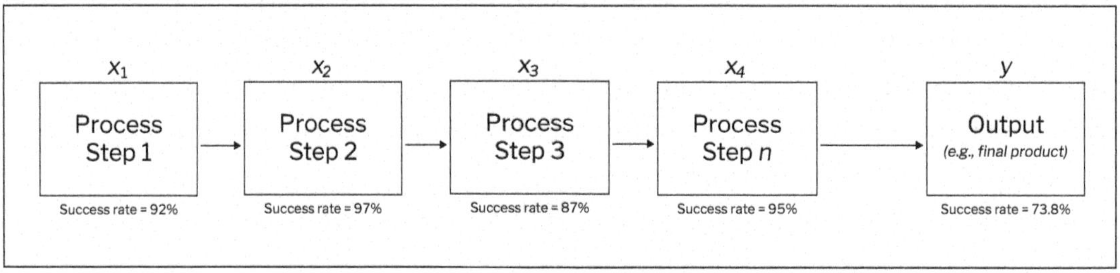

Ethical Considerations in Clinical Quality

While we could tackle many ethical considerations surrounding clinical quality in this chapter, let's focus on two: emergency use authorization and data privacy.

Emergency Use Authorization

The period of authoring this handbook fell squarely amid the COVID-19 global pandemic. Dozens of experimental devices, diagnostics, preventives, and therapies were granted emergency use authorization (EUA) by the US FDA in 2020 and 2021. The EUA is a way to release new healthcare interventions that haven't had time to be rigorously tested for safety and efficacy (which can take several years) for use by the public, under specific conditions where the potential benefit to society can outweigh the risks of unapproved use. The FDA considers an EUA in the following way:

> Under an EUA, FDA may allow the use of unapproved medical products, or unapproved uses of approved medical products in an emergency to diagnose, treat, or prevent serious or life-threatening diseases or conditions when certain statutory criteria have been met, including that there are no adequate, approved, and available alternatives. (FDA 2020)

Of course, dependent on the clinical quality metrics used, an EUA can present a number of untoward risks: Principally, untested medical interventions bring a risk of relative harm; that is, the potential to cause *more* harm than an approach of *no intervention*. This is an important concept: It's not true that simply providing any kind of treatment is better than doing nothing. In fact, the flipside is true: It's much easier to *cause more harm* by trying unproven therapies compared with looking for spontaneous remission or healing.

There's always a fine balance between allowing EUAs for new treatments when we don't have time for rigorous testing. But that won't come with zero risks, by the very virtue of the fact that the interventions have not been tested. We are essentially testing EUA treatments for their safety and efficacy profiles in the wild and experimenting on the public. And that is why Emergency Use Authorization can present bioethical conundrum.

Data Privacy

Data privacy has come to the forefront of medical care over the past couple of decades because of the move to electronic medical records (EMR/EHR). In addition, protected health information (PHI) in clinical trials and the personal data housed within DNA makes for many robust ethical considerations for those involved in clinical practice—both regarding choice of treatment and within the treatments themselves.

While it's sometimes hard to see why these would be quality issues, we need only look to a future where data is handled poorly or improperly, whereafter the quality of the clinical practice could be called into question.

Root Cause Analysis to Identify Problems and Improve Clinical Quality

When things go wrong in clinical care, there needs to be a rigorous investigation to identify the root causes of the errors, and corrective countermeasures must be put into place to prevent their recurrence.

Importantly, good clinical quality isn't about heroics. In fact, acting "heroically" in a clinic usually means there aren't enough gold-standard procedures and protocols in place; if there were, clinical care would be repeatable and look, well, very much non-heroic. In all actuality, *heroism* should be defined as acting during an event with a low probability of survival.

Don't let heroics reflect how you run your clinical quality systems, seeking to survive against all odds. Instead, stack the deck in your favor by implementing the principles and tools listed in here and in this handbook. Before we look at some tools that can help you improve clinical quality within your organization, let's review a real-world example of how to effectively implement clinical quality tools.

Case Study: Reducing Infections Within a Surgical Unit

A surgical acute care unit experienced a significant increase in central line associated bloodstream infections (CLABSI), which is a hospital acquired infection. By September 2018, the unit had reported an unprecedented eight CLABSI cases, compared with none in 2017. To find a solution, a member of the Supervisors' Development Academy took on this problem using a Lean Transformation Project. With talent development's coaching, she conducted a root cause analysis and found that a majority of the affected patients were not given infection-preventing baths with Hibiclens or CHG, an antiseptic soap that creates a skin barrier inhibiting bacteria growth.

When looking at this example, it's striking to note the difference in performance data: moving from a situation of zero infections in the facility's central lines in 2017 to the situation in 2018 where eight instances had been identified. This gives us reason to suspect *special cause variation*—that is, something was different either systemically or with processes and practices in the hospital that allowed for such a marked shift in increased infections.

To conduct a lean transformation, the first step is to define the problem and measure, which allows us to determine the magnitude of the problem and where it's occurring. From there, root cause analysis (RCA) can be conducted to determine which protocols, procedures, practices, and behaviors are associated with the aberrant outcomes. In this example, key actions included re-educating staff on the fingernails policy (ensuring they're clipped short and kept clean) during huddles and required training on how to properly use, order, and document Hibiclens application through a presentation and job aids (flyers, posters, and badge cards). A training video was also created to visually demonstrate the proper use of CHG. Employees were required to review the educational material during staff meetings and discuss barriers to their uptake and use.

After these actions were implemented using lean principles and continuous education, the unit saw zero incidences of CLABSI or catheter associated urinary tract infections for the remainder of 2018.

Incredible, isn't it? I have been personally involved in thousands of such cases to reduce surgical complications, hospital-acquired (nosocomial) infections, medication dispensing errors, and many more critical themes in clinical care. If there's a secret to how it's properly done, it's this: All processes and procedures, even the best ones, have flaws and a nonzero probability of errors.

We need to be clear up front that identifying and solving clinical quality issues is not about blaming people, but about understanding what's actually occurring within the performance metrics that lead to the observed results. Properly identifying and understanding the data of causality and involving the team in its review and solution-set thinking leads to better results. Involving those who get the work done will bring about much more effective collaboration and buy-in for better results. No improvement initiative should ever alienate the people who make the daily operations work.

The Seven Tools of Quality

To identify problems and improve clinical quality, you have seven tools at your disposal: check sheet, flow chart, cause-and-effect or fishbone diagram, histogram, pareto chart, control chart, and scatterplot. They all capture different types of data that might enable you to figure out where the quality breakdown is occurring in your healthcare institution.

1. The Check Sheet

The check sheet is your basic data collection tool—a manual tally of what's going on. It may seem too simple to be true, but in most cases, businesses don't know the actual data underlying their most fundamental problems, where those problems are occurring, and with what frequency. The check sheet allows you to gather data to answer the questions: "What *types* of defects are occurring?" and "What's the relative *frequency* of the defects' occurrence?"

As you can see from Figure 24-4, for example, the check sheet indicates that the painting job wasn't very high-quality painting; although you'll never know for sure until you measure.

Here's my tip: Identify the issues in your organization that are causing errors and defects. Then have employees—who work in the field with the real data—collect the data. If you try to obtain the data second or third hand a lot of important information will get lost along the way.

You can also plot defect data on a concentration diagram, which I also refer to as a visuospatial analog of a check sheet. Using a concentration diagram (like the one in Figure 24-5), you can build up in a spatial layout (or even one that's temporal- or time-based) of *where* (or *when*) defects and failures are occurring.

Allowing anonymity in collecting check sheet defect data may lead to more accurate and true reporting. However, there could be value in capturing the accountability of the data recorder in each iteration of the check sheet. Essentially, you're trying to build up a tally of defects by category or type to help you understand underlying causality in your business and operational processes. Consider these examples: reasons for document review or approval delays, missing materials (including in the pharmacy) at point of use, missed patient treatment targets, treatment failures, and administration delays. If you can think it, you can measure

Figure 24-4. Check Sheet Example

Paint Job Quality Control Checklist
Job: 629555
Inspector:

Problem	Frequency
Chip	卌 卌 |||
Bubble	|||
Run	卌 |
Scrape or scratch	
Inadequate coverage	卌 卌 卌 ||
Other	

Figure 24-5. Concentration Diagram Example

Door Paint Check Sheet

Paint robot number: *832A6* Date: *October 12* Sheet number: *243*
Paint batch number: *A12583*
Paint operator: *Jen Welkens*

Doors painted: 卌 卌

Defect type	Symbol	Count
Bubble	○	卌 卌 卌 ||
Run	△	卌 |||
Scuff	▭	||||

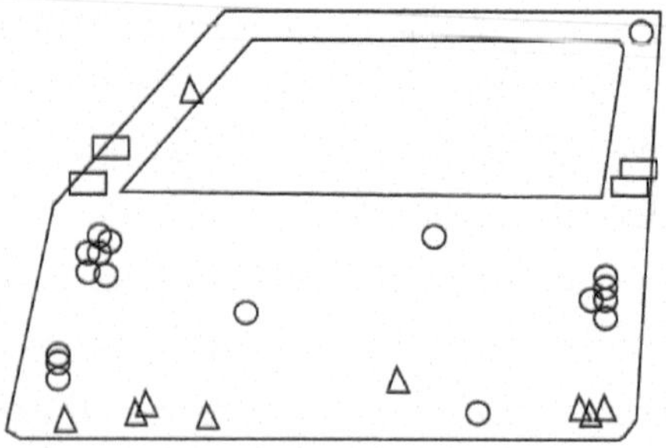

it. (But just remember my other pro tip: Just because you can measure it doesn't mean you should! Rendering everything into numeracy can quickly make you awash in data, but thirsting for information.)

2. The Flow Chart

The flow chart is an engineering favorite, and for good reason: It allows you to document the repeatability by which you expect a process to recur, lest you expect it to fail. The first formal presentation of flow charts was in 1921, and they've been indispensable in process engineering work ever since. Flow charts are algorithmic in nature when done well; that is, they *should* provide unambiguous specifications for how to solve a problem.

To create a flow cart, begin with a terminal shape and plot process steps deterministically in a time-based manner, using arrows to represent the flow of time (typically pointing rightward or downward, depending on the chart's orientation). Each input and output has its own shape to distinguish it from other steps in the process, and decisions (such as do this or this, yes/no) are represented by a diamond shape (called a rhombus). See Figure 24-6 for an example.

Figure 24-6. Flow Chart Example

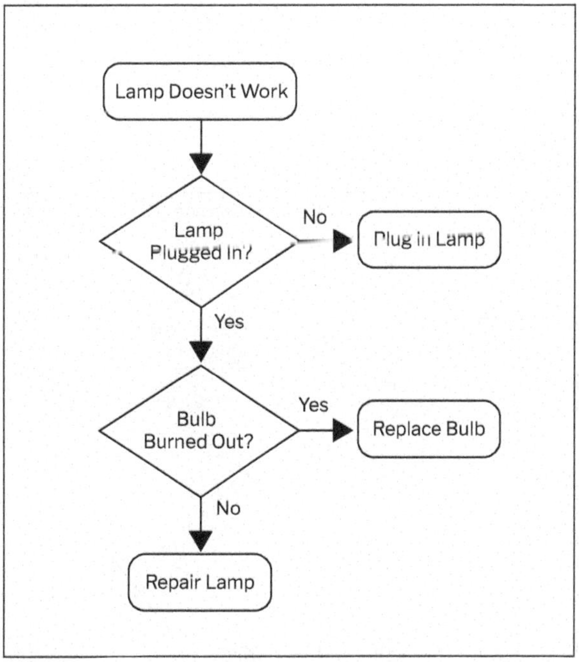

Flow charts are very helpful to include in your standard operating procedures (SOPs) or work instructions (WIs)—because if you can't visualize a "standard," then why are you even calling them *standard* operating procedures?

Neuroscientifically, there are a lot of similarities between flow charts and how humans ritualize behavior. Just think about your morning routine—if you try to disorder or rearrange any part of your normal process, it puts an incredible amount of pressure on your prefrontal cortex and executive brain functions because you can't operationalize your basal functional operations.

3. The Cause-and-Effect (Fishbone) Diagram

The fishbone diagram helps list the main and major causes that lead to some outcome, whether untoward or not. This allows you to arrange and categorize your thinking for further problem solving.

While it's unlikely that simply using a fishbone diagram in isolation will allow you to fully understand and solve your problem to the level of prevention needed, that doesn't stop people from trying to do just that. In fact, this happens all the time. So be better than your peers and competitors—don't just perform a fishbone diagram as part of a deviation investigation, assign corrective and preventive actions based entirely on this one analysis, and then try to close the gap. The fishbone diagram only superficially addresses your issues. Figure 24-7 presents a fishbone diagram to help you start.

The problem statement is placed within the rightmost box, "12-digit production code found incorrectly transcribed on [date]." Then, we probe each causal category to identify

Figure 24-7. Fishbone Diagram Example

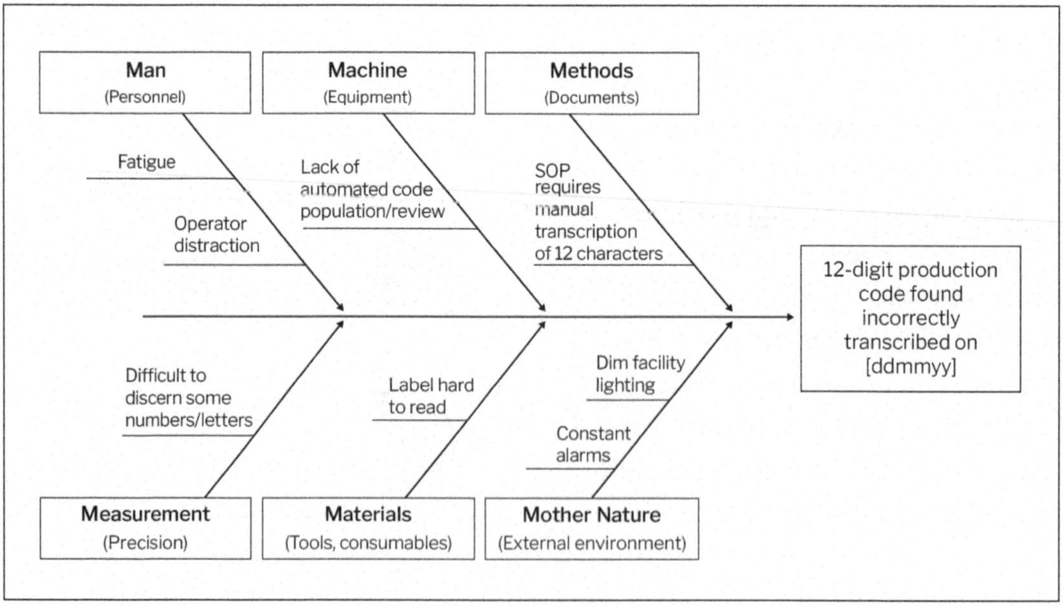

what types of issues could originate from that source. So, for example, under methods, we would list documents that are involved in the contribution to the identified and observed errors—in Figure 24-8, the team noted that the standard operating procedure (SOP) requires a manual transcription of 12 characters. This could indicate that the method itself may be a precursor and contributor to the problem. Moving to the materials category, we might ask the team to determine whether the handwritten labels are hard to read, which could also contribute to transcription errors. We repeat these examinations of each major category until we have exhausted the potential sources of error.

Figure 24-8. Histogram Example #1

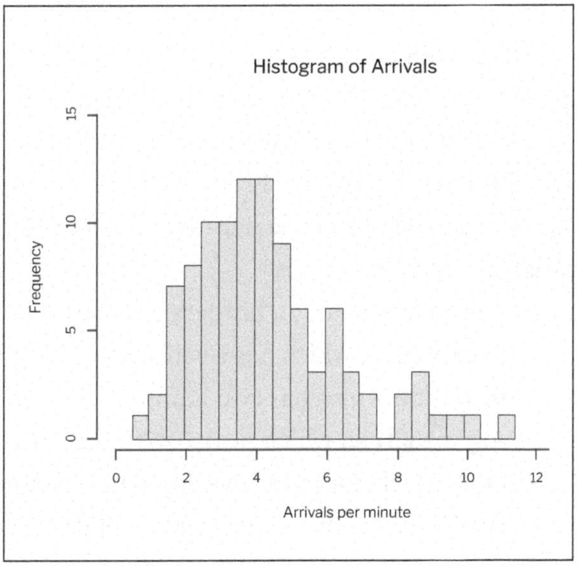

4. The Histogram

A perennial favorite of mine, the histogram allows you to wield your collected data to a greater degree like a quiver loaded with arrows for battle. Named from the Greek *histos* (bar, mast) because the bars resemble the masts of a ship, a histogram is not the same as a bar chart (although it is a chart with bars!). Instead of the x-axis representing another variable, such as time, a histogram's x-axis corresponds to the intervals, or bins, of data being measured. With bins of equal size, the heights of the bars then represent the frequency of data cases in each bin.

Wondering about what the architecture of your data can tell you? Plot it on a histogram and allow it to help guide your investigation.

Maybe you want to know how many radiology documents are arriving per hour so you can more effectively allocate resources. In that case, knowing what your data are telling you is the first step. In Figure 24-8, the data tells us that we receive the bulk of radiographs at a rate of between 2 and 6 per minute, which averages out to about 120 to 360 per hour. If we don't schedule and allocate resources to meet this average demand performance, we will continuously fall behind—or worse—give each document in the queue an insufficient review and potentially compromise the quality of patient care.

The data Figure 24-9—from the 2000 US Census—shows that the vast majority of workers spend about 15 to 40 minutes in their commute to work.

The distribution of the histogram can tell you a lot about the underlying process that manifested the results you see. From its shape you can ask, "Is your data normally distributed?" "Is your data left-skewed (a negative skew) or right-skewed (a positive skew)?" "How much variation is there?"

There are five common histogram shapes:

- **Symmetric**, which has a bell shape, rising or falling in the middle
- **Bimodal**, which has two humps
- **Asymmetric**, which peaks on the left or right side of the graph
- **Flat**, which does not have any significant peak
- **Outliers**, which captures a piece of data that does not connect with the rest

Stratification can also help you uncover interesting features of your underlying data. When everything is combined, you lose the ability to distinguish which effects are due to which factors. Think about separating data out by product line, shift, and so forth to uncover deeper truths about what is really going on.

Figure 24-9. Histogram Example #2

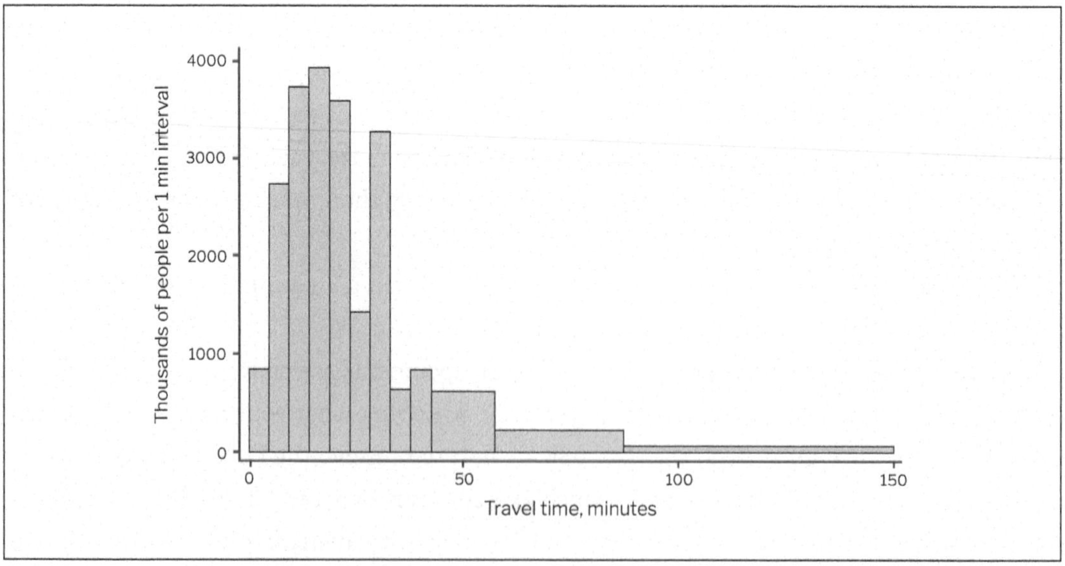

The histogram in Figure 24-10 tells you a lot about the data's underlying nature. The histogram on the left shows that the winning times for the Sydney Marathon clustered around about 136 to 138 minutes in 1960 through 2007. However, the time series plot on the right retains the time-ordering of the data—and indicates that winning time has been decaying upwards for a few years. Plotting the data on a control chart would give you a better indication of whether your gut reaction was accurate.

Figure 24-10. Adding Context to Your Histogram

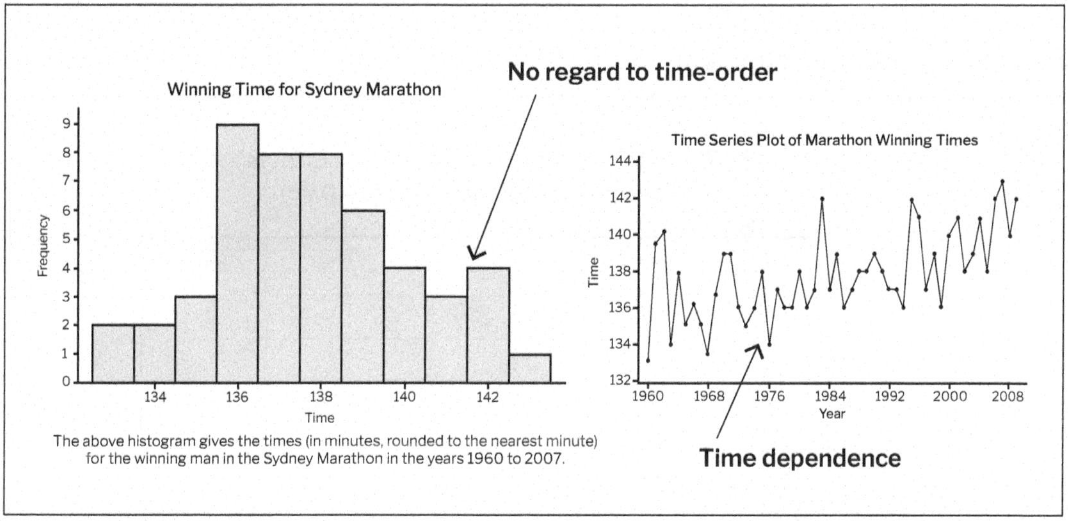

5. The Pareto Chart

Named for the Italian economist Vilfredo Pareto, the Pareto chart provides a very interesting approach to visually show how a small number of "somethings" often contribute disproportionately to something else. Often referred to as the 80/20 rule, the method was used by Pareto himself to plot income distribution and he noted that a small proportion of individuals controlled a large majority of the total wealth (*that is,* an abnormal or rectangular distribution). So many things tend to follow a power law probability distribution that business texts fell in love with the idea of 80/20 in the 1980s. You are guaranteed to have some Pareto relationships within your organization—for example, out of the *millions* (or more!) of things that could go wrong and cause defects in your organization, "critical few" typically have outsized influence and do the majority of the "causing." Find those things and correct them.

A Pareto chart is a combination chart with bars in descending order of frequency, showing the relative proportions, as well as a superposed line plot tallying the cumulative contributions of each category rightward.

For example, in determining critical physiological parameters for a particular process under close examination, not everything has the same standardized effect size. In Figure 24-11, you can see that temperature and pH are absolutely more influential. The takeaway: Some causes have outsized influence when compared with other contemporaneous factors. Don't treat them equally.

Figure 24-11. Pareto Chart Example

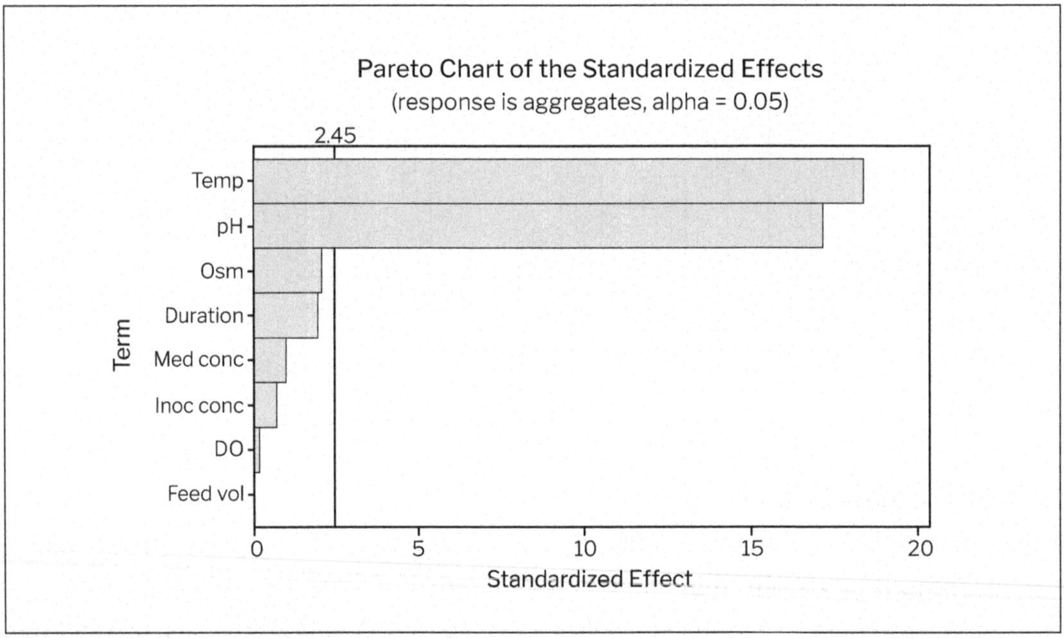

6. The Control Chart

Control charts, sometimes called process behavior charts, are line plots used as part of statistical process control (SPC) to determine if a measured parameter (typically within a manufacturing or business process) is within a state of *control*. In the parlance of control charts, language and nuance matter, and something being in control (or not) is based upon its performance against an accepted rubric of statistical requirements (including the Western Electric, Nelson, Wheeler, or other "run rules" for detecting signals). Control charts have been used since the late 1920s, and even very early in their implementation they taught engineers and scientists about the incredible value of reducing variation from production processes. Using process behavior charts can improve your behavior with respect to how you respond to outputs from your processes.

Here are the basic components of the control chart:

- The data points represent the statistic of interest and are plotted in a time-based way.
- The centerline represents the average (mean) of the data points.
- Upper and lower control limits (UCL and LCL) are calculated, and indicate the upper and lower limits that process data points are statistically unlikely to exceed.

Figure 24-12 shows a control chart examining readmissions to a hospital.

There are a few different methods for establishing control limits and alarm limits (what are called "run rules"), but the basic premise is that the control limits set goalposts of *about* 99.73 percent. The assumption is that, when a process is allowed to run—without tinkering—99.73 percent of the outputs should fall within these control limits and would be called "common cause" variation. Any oddity in output that exceeds the upper or lower control limits is termed a "special cause" variation.

OK now take a deep breath.

Figure 24-12. Control Chart Example

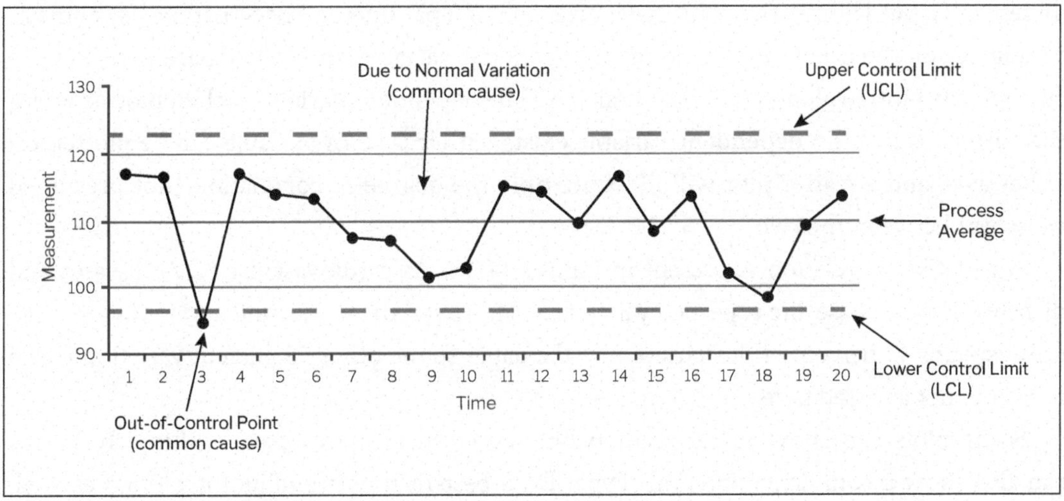

Remember, because we're talking about probabilistic concepts and how they pertain to quality control, these calculations also mean that if you let an "in control" process run 1,000 times, you would expect about three data points to exceed your control limits based solely on chance. That's why interpreting the results of your processes requires you to use your anatomically located false alarm detection tool (that is, your brain).

The bottom line is that *increased variation means lower overall quality* and an increase in costs, so any identified special cause variation should be immediately resolved. There are whole books devoted entirely to control charts, so I can't possibly include all the relevant details here. If you haven't done so already, work with someone in your organization before using this tool to visualize your data. You'll learn much more than you thought you would about your processes and their behavior.

Another thing to consider when you use process behavior charts: Continuously chasing nonconformances by process adjustments (instead of simply improving the overall process) actually *increases* variation and *reduces* overall quality. Don't do that. I see it all the time, and it's basically indicative of process owners not understanding anything at all about quality.

7. The Scatterplot

A scatterplot is a quality tool that allows you to plot data on Cartesian coordinates to better understand the relationship between two variables in two dimensions. (You can also correlate more and more variables, which would give you a scatterplot in three or more dimensions, but I'll just stick with two variables). If a parameter exists that may systematically act upon the other, it is called the independent variable (or control parameter) and is customarily plotted along the horizontal axis. The dependent variable is then plotted along the vertical axis. If no dependent variable exists, either type of variable can be plotted on either axis, and a scatter plot will illustrate only the degree of correlation (not presumed causality) between the two.

A negative correlation is present in Figure 24-13: As cardiovascular (CV) diseases and diabetes rates decrease, life expectancy increases. However, the model underlying these results only explains 42 percent of the variation in the data—so the other 58 percent variation is due to factors not assessed here.

Scatterplots can show visual relationships between two variables, within which you can also show a confidence interval. Typically, a best-fit line (trendline) is plotted as well.

Figure 24-13. Scatterplot Example

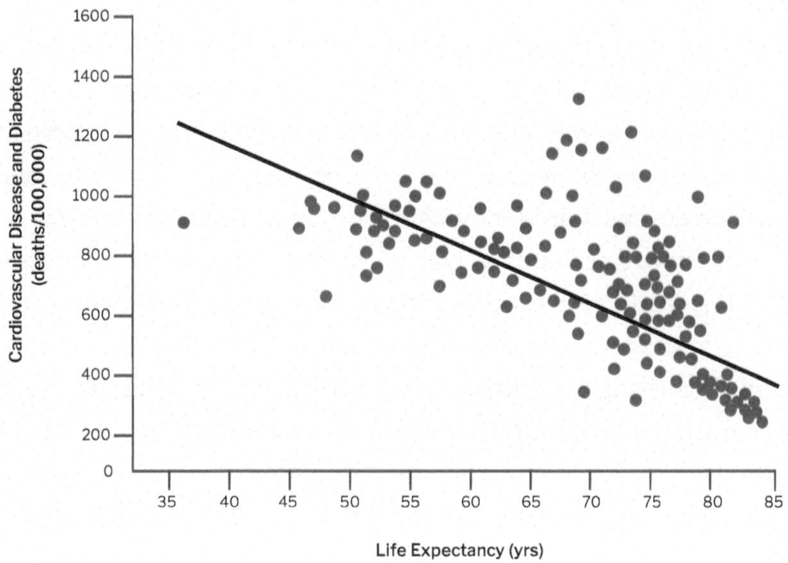

Unfortunately, the focus on trendlines is statistically naïve—their very presence irrevocably biases the viewer to assume the trendline shows the full story, full of assumptions of causality.

Correlation is not causation, so as with all the quality tools, the scatterplot should be used in conjunction with other tools to help you understand your processes. Don't over-rely on output as the answer. Additionally, if someone hands you a scatterplot with a linear fit line but no confidence intervals plotted along with a coefficient of correlation and coefficient of determination, throw it in the trash!

Using the Quality Tools

Kaoru Ishikawa (1985), the progenitor of the Fishbone Diagram, observed that "The seven QC Tools, if used skillfully, will enable 90 percent of workplace problems to be solved." These tools also put you in a position to solve problems several hundred percent better than trying to do so without the appropriate use of the proper tools (this is called gut instinct or the "hope model" of business strategy).

Quality, then, isn't fixing everything. *It's solving what matters.* And you can only find those things through careful and scientific approaches, not guesswork and assumptions. So, read this chapter and think about the things that matter most within your organization—and then distill the trivial many down to the critical few. Every organization is different, and while I could share the 12 quality-related issues that most clinics don't do properly, how you approach and solve these issues within your organization is dependent largely on idiosyncratic organizational structures, business culture, and so on. The only way to make it fit in your situation is to identify the key issues and then work within the nuance of your company to make it stick.

In the case of quality and quality messaging, stickiness is a virtue. You'll often hear me saying in group settings that "perfect is the archenemy of good enough." We can strive for perfection, both personally or professionally, but perfection is an elusive creature. In fact, it's the mathematical corollary of achieving "zero" (in terms of zero defects, zero accidents, or zero errors).

Perfect is a fun aspirational goal for some people and some organizations, but it's impossible on a long enough time horizon. Zero (or perfection) requires achieving a unitary state of improbability and then maintaining it with no variation. Ever. You'll never do this, so don't bother setting such a goal.

Conclusion

Clinical quality isn't synonymous with the approaches to quality in something like potato chip manufacturing. In the food and beverage industry, defects can be individually discriminated at the end of the manufacturing process and removed singularly (through a fairly sophisticated process). But in healthcare, it's not as inexpensive and easy to strike individual errors from the record. At that point, so much effort and risk have been imbued into patient care, as well as fixed and variable costs, that any quality issues that arise are onerous indeed. Not only that, but if final care defect rates (and their associated metrics) are very high, it's a trigger for healthcare regulatory and compliance inspectors to seriously question the quality of the clinical processes that led to such high failure rates.

Instead get better by being proactive in your clinical quality approaches. Implement quality-by-design, which means purposefully designing each step in your critical and important processes—steps that are well-characterized and repeatable so you know what the results will be at the end. Otherwise, you're operating under a model of "hope," and that is not an effective strategy. The future of better patient care need not be that uncertain.

CHAPTER 25

PATIENT SAFETY

BEN LOCWIN

Whether care is delivered in-patient, out-patient, or even managed at a distance via telemedicine or with pharmaceuticals or medical devices, there is no more important healthcare objective than patient safety. As the Hippocratic Oath states, "*Primum Non Nocere*," or "[Of] first [importance], do no harm."

We're never more vulnerable than when we're being taken care of as patient at a healthcare facility. We give up much of what it means to be a healthy and independent member of society when we're under acute medical care: losing our freedom of activity (ability to engage in our normal behaviors), being confined to a situation that's often stressful and fear-promoting, and having to make decisions under duress that are often explained in language we don't fully understand or appreciate.

To patients in these situations, nothing matters more than their *safety*. This chapter's focus is patient safety in all forms, and how the healthcare industry can ensure patient safety to the best of our ability. I also cover how to do this in a patient-centric way.

I have been involved in the regulatory approval of dozens of pharmaceutical treatments and medical devices for a variety of therapeutic indications. The US Food and Drug Administration (FDA) grants approval for new medical treatments based on their demonstrated safety and efficacy. In many of their regulatory documents, the FDA repeatedly states "safety and efficacy" to refer to their expectation of the treatments being developed. It's no accident that they put these requirements in that order—first, safety; then, efficacy. I would phrase this similarly with the Hippocratic Oath to be, "*prima salutis, tum efficacitas.*" If a health treatment isn't safe (interpreted from a broad perspective), it will not be approved by the FDA. If the treatment is demonstrated to be safe enough, *then* the effectiveness data determines how broadly the treatment can be used for its particular indication (therapeutic target).

There is a long history, which others have covered in great detail and insight, of the US FDA and its raison d'être. And that's just one regulatory body in a network of global healthcare oversight. Every major country has a governing regulatory body for drug and device treatments, and they are all similarly tasked with being watchdogs for the public health, ever on surveillance for new treatments that may be more noxious than healing.

Good writing should transcend time periods and be useful for guiding thinking regardless of era. With that said, every piece of writing is informed by the time period in which it was written. This chapter was penned amid the COVID-19 global pandemic, and so my perspective and approach were doubtless shaped by my clinical and public experiences dealing with COVID-19 cases and task force outreach to state and federal government.

A Brief History of Patient Safety in the United States

Patient safety is a topic that, surprisingly, hasn't often been at the forefront of clinical care. Clinical medicine—the practice of literally tending to healthcare "at the bedside" (the word "clinic" comes from the Greek *Klinike,* which means bedside)—has been evolving over the past couple thousand years, but the scientific innovations (that is, the technology, pharmacology, and innovations in approaching diseases and disorders) have been at the forefront, while those topics about the "care" of *healthcare* have taken a lesser role.

Much of the story about patient safety has occured over the past century or so, starting around the mid-19th century, but some of the biggest movement happened between 1937 and 1962 (Figure 25-1). It is a fascinating history, which includes terrible moments of poisonings, untoward noxious health effects, and unintended deaths due to a dearth of regulatory oversight on medicines and consumer products.

As gaps in knowledge were laid bare, the FDA had to rapidly pivot and increase their regulatory fortification to prevent similar issues occurring again. Unfortunately, most of these sweeping changes were in response to public harm and thus didn't precede the harm. But that's how the industry of healthcare has itself evolved over time. FDA remains busy to this day reviewing a continuous cycle of consumer products, drugs, and medical devices for safety and efficacy.

Although the FDA has evolved quite a lot over time, the situation regarding patient safety specifically, surprisingly, has only recently seen much change. A 1999 Institute of Medicine (IOM) report, "To Err Is Human," was the first of three IOM reports addressing medical quality control and patient safety. Their research and content informed and catalyzed congressional action to help safeguard patients, healthcare quality, and safety at the bedside.

Figure 25-1. Evolution of the FDA Response to Public Health Concerns

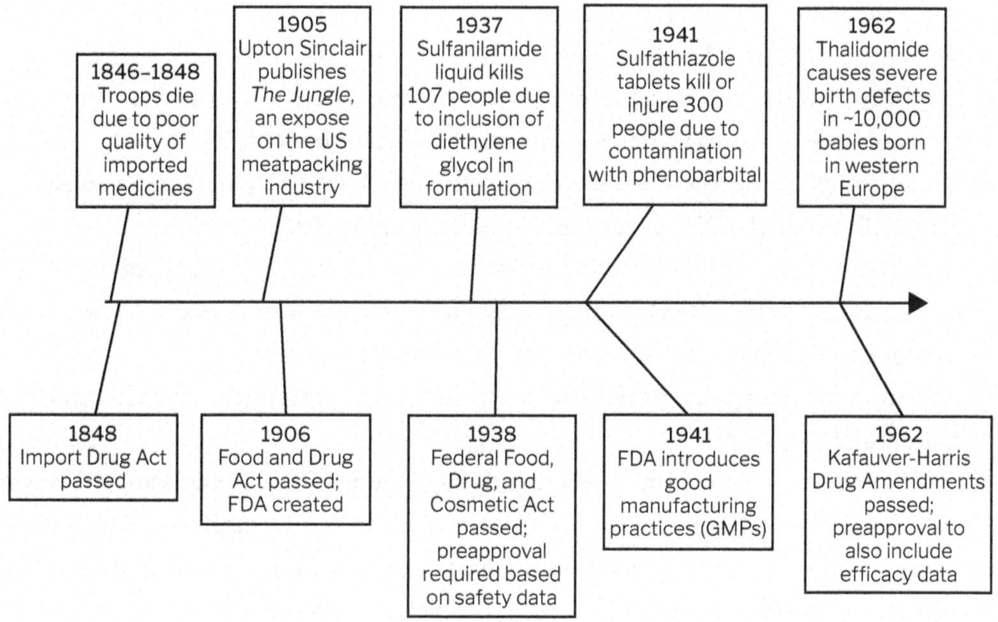

Source: FDA (2018).

Key outputs included:

- Establish a Center for Patient Safety within the Agency for Healthcare Research and Quality (AHRQ).
- Establish a nationwide mandatory reporting system for states to collect data on adverse events that result in death or serious harm.
- Encourage establishment of voluntary, confidential reporting systems for collecting information on errors that result in little or no harm.
- Enact legislation to extend peer review protections to data related to patient safety and quality improvement that is collected and analyzed by healthcare organizations for internal use or shared with others solely for purposes of improving safety and quality.
- Increase focus of performance standards and expectations for healthcare organizations and health professionals on patient safety.
- Require the FDA to develop standards for safe packaging of medications, pretest proposed drug names to avoid look-alike and sound-alike errors, and work with

health professionals and patients to respond to problems arising in post-marketing surveillance.

- Encourage healthcare organizations to commit to improving patient safety and implementing best practices for patient safety.
- Fund through the federal government the National Health Information Infrastructure and include patient safety data standards as a component.
- Fund through Congress a public–private effort led by the Department of Health and Human Services (DHHS) to promulgate patient safety data standards.
- Accelerate via government and industry the development of clinical data interchange standards, with the AHRQ leading an applied research agenda that includes knowledge generation and point-of-care decision support.
- Develop a national patient safety database that contains standard data elements from standardized reports.

While it may seem like the principles and activities behind these 11 points are obvious and should have existed well before the turn of the 21st century, it just wasn't the case. It's interesting to note that the key themes were *patient safety* (four mentions), *reduction of harm* (three mentions), and *increased reporting and surveillance* (seven mentions).

The next chapter of the US patient safety story began on July 29, 2005, when President George W. Bush signed Public Law (PL) 109-41, the Patient Safety and Quality Improvement Act of 2005 (PSQIA). Unfortunately, even though multiple pieces of legislation were introduced during the 106th Congress in response to the recommendations outlined in "To Err Is Human," no further legislation emerged through three successive congressional sessions. A few failed legislative proposals include the Medication Error Prevention Act of 2000 (HR 3672), the Medicare Comprehensive Quality of Care and Safety Act of 2000 (HR 5404), the Medical Error Reduction Act of 2000 (S 2038), the Stop All Frequent Errors in Medicare and Medicaid Act of 2000 (S 2378), the Patient Safety and Errors Reduction Act (S 2738), and the Error Reduction and Improvement in Patient Safety Act (S 2743).

Ultimately, the PSQIA was a fairly impotent approach. It introduced the patient safety work product (PSWP), which deals with information gained during the process of patient safety improvement activities and consists of "any data, reports, records, memoranda, analyses (e.g., root cause analyses), or written or oral statements" that "could result in improved patient safety, health care quality, or health care outcomes," and are assembled for reporting to a patient safety organization, or are compiled *by* a patient safety organization.

What Patient Safety Means to the Patient

The US medical system is home to great innovations that can help preserve or sustain life. However, there are also many associated risks that can actually make a person's health worse.

In 2010 the prestigious *British Medical Journal* published an article by Makary and colleagues analyzing patient outcomes. Their results indicated that about 30 percent of deaths that occurred in the United States could be attributed to medical error. This is obviously the worst outcome possible. Missing a condition or giving a misdiagnosis could, in a more passive sense, lead to mortality or increased disease progression. However, what Makary uncovered was the possibility that the medical system itself had actually contributed to (that is, caused) patient death.

Danielle Ofri, a very accomplished physician in her own right, has also analyzed this situation, and her results suggest that the statistics aren't as dire, and that Makary's work may have misclassified certain conditions and outcomes. However, within an order of magnitude, if it's not a third or even a fifth, a 10 percent medical error-induced mortality rate would still be an incredible number of preventable losses of life and longevity—and something worth improving.

When we put our faith in healthcare providers, we're at our most vulnerable. For the most part, the general public already feels like they're in a compromised position because of their very limited understanding of healthcare and medicine, and this often causes incredible anxiety (the "white coat effect"). The worst we can do is fail to act in their best interest. To this end, communication matters, which means letting patients know what is going on with their care, whether it be inpatient or outpatient. Cleary and colleagues (1991) conducted a moderately sized survey (n = 6,455 eligible patients) and found that 45 percent of patients were not told about the daily routine at the hospital. If you've ever found yourself in a situation with little or no control over your environment, a lack of communication and information is the worst possible state to exist in.

Additionally, upon discharge, more than 20 percent of patients were not informed of important side effects to watch out for with their medications.

As you may imagine, but probably hope isn't the case, surgery is also susceptible to the same sorts of errors at the same frequency. A study published in *JAMA Surgery* analyzed information collected from more than 9,000 surgical procedures and found that surgical complications were highly related in medical error cases (Storesund at al. 2020). Like in any other area, the principles of process improvement and operational excellence can be readily and effectively applied to the surgical realm.

Case Study: Surgical Specimen Discrepancies

A review of surgical performance data in one healthcare system found errors in surgical specimens, which is a critical process. By reviewing data on a weekly and monthly basis, it was found that discrepancies in surgical specimens were occurring 9.44 times per month. In addition to patients potentially not getting correct results, this amounted to a calculated value of $25,687 per specimen (or $242,485 per month).

To reduce the error rate with surgical specimens, the hospital system created a clinical safety effectiveness cohort, involving frontline staff from perioperative services, laboratory, and women's services. After intense data collection and discussion with key stakeholders, the cohort developed the pathology specimen pause (PSP) practice, a step-by-step process of specimen extraction, collection, validation, and processing.

Developing the new process and training the involved staff on the updated procedure was crucial for successfully implementing the new performance improvement approach. The process improvement approach also included:

- On-the-job training for unit clerks on streamlining processes to eliminate patient label batching, which was a primary area of noted discrepancy during the process improvement group sessions
- On-the-job training with laboratory personnel on specimen pick-up and processing best practices
- Training surgeons, nurses, and technicians in the operating room during surgical cases to implement PSP practices.
- Production of a corporate communications video starring operating room staff modeling the correct approach to PSP; this training tool is still viewed by all incoming surgeons and perioperative staff at hiring and onboarding

Importantly, as with any well-run process improvement initiative, measures of performance after the changes were implemented were determined. This allowed the cohort to demonstrate "control" of the process (which is to say, evidence the process was not only changed, but also verified and validated to be successful).

After six months of using the new PSP process, surgical specimen errors dropped to zero (from 9.44 per month) and have remained at zero per month (Figure 25-2). The compliance rate with the PSP process is 90 percent, which is a dramatic improvement that also leaves room for further continuous improvement.

Figure 25-2. A Decreasing Trend in Surgical Specimen Errors

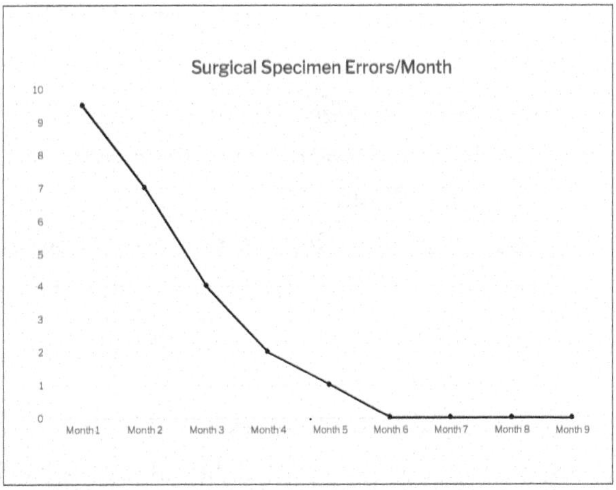

Make Routine Activities a Checklist: Treating Surgery Like Flying a Plane

Anything that can regulate repetitive activities can lead to dramatic improvements in performance outcomes. This is the idea behind preflight checklists in the aviation industry. Author and surgeon Atul Gawande (2009) was a great catalyst for the expansion of checklist use in the healthcare realm (specifically, surgical).

Two well-known surgical checklists are the World Health Organization Surgical Safety Checklist (WHO SCC) and the Surgical Patient Safety System (SURPASS) surgical checklist.

The SURPASS checklist includes:

- **Admission to ward:** Ward doctor checks whether imaging is present and lab work has been done; surgeon checks whether informed consent has been registered and the operation side has been marked; anesthesiologist assesses patient's condition and orders blood products; nurse makes sure premedication is administered.
- **Recovery room or ICU:** Surgeon provides instructions about drains, diet, and medication; anesthesiologist provides instructions about ventilation and medication.
- **Ward boarding:** Surgeon and anesthesiologist specify changes in postoperative instructions.
- **Discharge:** Ward doctor conducts follow-up, checks medications, and writes discharge letter.

The World Health Organization's SCC checklist (Figure 25-3) includes:

- **Before induction of anesthesia:** Patient should confirm their identity, surgical site, and procedure; the surgical site should be marked; the surgical team should know whether the patient has any allergies and whether restrictions to airway exist.
- **Before skin incision:** All team members introduce themselves by name and role; essential imaging should be displayed; confirmation of antibiotic prophylaxis within the prior 60 minutes.
- **Before patient leaves the operating room:** The operating room (OR) nurse should verbally confirm the name of the procedure; the surgeon, anesthesiologist, and OR nurse should identify concerns for the recovery and management of the patient.

As Storesund and colleagues found in their 2020 *JAMA Surgery* article, the use of surgical checklists to reduce the probability of errors has been a very successful undertaking. They found that joint use of the WHO SCC and SURPASS surgical checklist was associated with fewer complications (odds ratio 0.70), reoperations (odds ratio 0.42), and hospital readmissions (odds ratio 0.32). The researchers concluded that: "Findings from this study demonstrate that adding the pre-operative and post-operative SURPASS checklists to the intraoperative WHO SSC may be clinically advantageous. We found that the joint application of the two surgical checklist systems was associated with reduced in-hospital complications, emergency reoperations, and hospital readmissions."

Regardless of where you fall within the spectrum of healthcare providership—whether you're a physician, a PA, a nurse, a medical assistant, a clinical trainer, an educator, or somewhere else in the periphery of healthcare practice and support—the notion of patient safety is one that affects everyone. You're either treating patients, you are a patient, or a family member or friend is a patient—guaranteed. And from this perspective, almost nothing in the nomenclature of clinical healthcare is more important than patient safety.

Practical Tips for Ensuring and Improving Patient Safety

Let's review some best practices from an execution standpoint that you can immediately apply to improve patient outcomes in your professional remit, whether that's in a hospital, clinic, or home-care setting.

Figure 25-3. WHO Surgical Safety Checklist

Surgical Safety Checklist

World Health Organization | Patient Safety
A World Alliance for Safer Health Care

Before induction of anaesthesia

(with at least nurse and anaesthetist)

Has the patient confirmed his/her identity, site, procedure, and consent?
- ☐ Yes

Is the site marked?
- ☐ Yes
- ☐ Not applicable

Is the anaesthesia machine and medication check complete?
- ☐ Yes

Is the pulse oximeter on the patient and functioning?
- ☐ Yes

Does the patient have a:

Known allergy?
- ☐ No
- ☐ Yes

Difficult airway or aspiration risk?
- ☐ No
- ☐ Yes, and equipment/assistance available

Risk of >500ml blood loss (7ml/kg in children)?
- ☐ No
- ☐ Yes, and two IVs/central access and fluids planned

Before skin incision

(with nurse, anaesthetist and surgeon)

- ☐ **Confirm all team members have introduced themselves by name and role.**
- ☐ **Confirm the patient's name, procedure, and where the incision will be made.**

Has antibiotic prophylaxis been given within the last 60 minutes?
- ☐ Yes
- ☐ Not applicable

Anticipated Critical Events

To Surgeon:
- ☐ What are the critical or non-routine steps?
- ☐ How long will the case take?
- ☐ What is the anticipated blood loss?

To Anaesthetist:
- ☐ Are there any patient-specific concerns?

To Nursing Team:
- ☐ Has sterility (including indicator results) been confirmed?
- ☐ Are there equipment issues or any concerns?

Is essential imaging displayed?
- ☐ Yes
- ☐ Not applicable

Before patient leaves operating room

(with nurse, anaesthetist and surgeon)

Nurse Verbally Confirms:
- ☐ The name of the procedure
- ☐ Completion of instrument, sponge and needle counts
- ☐ Specimen labelling (read specimen labels aloud, including patient name)
- ☐ Whether there are any equipment problems to be addressed

To Surgeon, Anaesthetist and Nurse:
- ☐ What are the key concerns for recovery and management of this patient?

This checklist is not intended to be comprehensive. Additions and modifications to fit local practice are encouraged.

Revised 1 / 2009

Source: WHO (2009).

Gather Patient Feedback

This seems so obvious, but gathering patient feedback is the number 1 thing that's either omitted or not properly done during clinical visits. The psychological pitfall known as the fallacy of knowledge states that thinking one has all the answers is associated with a myopic approach to problem solving. In other words, the very fact of having incredibly deep or broad knowledge in a field can in itself be a handicap. Or, as Abraham Maslow opined, "When the only tool you have is a hammer, every problem looks like a nail." Trying to approach each clinical situation with fresh eyes can be incredibly insightful and rewarding (although very tiring). It allows you to break away from thinking about solutions before you've properly incorporated all the available and relevant evidence.

In healthcare, our roles are to improve how a patient feels, functions, and survives. If you're only treating someone based on laboratory blood values, and not asking how they feel, you are doing a tremendous disservice to clinical medicine. There are so many examples I can point to in which discussing how a patient "felt" was just the beginning of unraveling a whole host of under-appreciated or outright missed disease states or disorders. We don't—and can't—know everything. Treating the quantitative patient (that is, only reviewing blood work and other technological diagnostics) seems mathematically rigorous, but it can be more one-dimensional than necessary for a patient's case. Ask them how they feel. Ask what you can do to help.

Ensure You Fully Understand the Patient's Vital Signs

Drawing on the same logic as gathering patient feedback, never be satisfied with the medical status quo. Question everything. This is the only way we truly make progress in science.

I have seen many examples of patients not having their vitals and serology (blood test results) properly assessed. There could be many factors associated with this, including staff fatigue, frequent handoffs or shift changes, overburden at the facility, and documentation errors. These things do happen, but we can surely minimize their existence so they become less impactful on overall patient safety.

Properly measuring and reacting to findings from a review of systems (ROS) can and does prevent many more serious problems when done correctly whether in an inpatient or outpatient setting. This is why they're called vital signs; they are the measurement level that's once-removed from physiological function. However, don't presume that the patient's vital signs are OK, or that they've been properly recorded in the recent past. Check them again if you're new to their case. Do your own primary review of their lab work. It's also incredibly common for serious findings in a patient's bloodwork to be disregarded or not acted upon appropriately. Question everything. *Medical skepticism* is the best way to not fall into the trap of clinical groupthink.

Review the Medication List; Challenge the Regime

I could discuss hundreds of cases where patients were either administered concomitant medications that were contraindicated, or medications were used inappropriately. Obviously, this isn't likely the result of nefarious malpractice, but it's such a common situation that it needs desperate attention.

One example: A patient was awaiting transfer for a multiple cardiac bypass operation, and his intravenous drip included the blood thinner heparin. When I reviewed the patient's chart, I found that he was not only receiving heparin via his IV line, but the prior hospitalist—assuming the patient needed to be in a less-coagulable state—had also added oral heparin (tablets) to his medication list. Fortunately, I detected this error as the first dose was being sent from the pharmacy to the patient's room, so we were able to correct the mistake. But witnessing cases like this truly makes one feel like the probability of similar events occurring is very high.

I've also seen patients who couldn't begin critical dialysis because their blood was too hypocoagulable (too "thinned"). While in the ICU, they had been put on heparin doses that were too high. In some cases, this clinical cascade literally led to patient death.

Ask "What?"

"What can I do to improve how this patient feels, functions, or survives?"

Every patient is a work in progress; many times, they are still under some form of care even after they are discharged and go home. Perhaps it's a medication, an implanted medical device, or behavioral and psychotherapeutic work; it doesn't really matter. The point is: The patient wants to return to normalcy, and there's no better way to make that happen than to challenge the status quo and treat each case as a problem-solving activity. Unfortunately, too many patients don't have someone looking out for their best interest and acting as a healthcare advocate.

Does this sound familiar? Maybe it's your patient. Never assume someone outside the clinical boundary will take up the reins for a patient's care and continued improvement. So, ask yourself, what can you do to make their outcomes the best they can be?

CHAPTER 25

Conclusion

Patient safety and the notion of a continuance of health are inextricably intertwined. When people are at their most vulnerable, they seek or are admitted for healthcare treatment. Whether they like it or not, the trajectory of their healing is in the hands of the caregivers who are working with them. It is not, nor will it ever be, a risk-free endeavor and a seamless partnership. But the magnitude of healing—and even the placebo effect itself—is highly correlated with treating the whole patient as a multidimensional person who matters. Doing so in each case may be the most exhausting and under-appreciated aspect of clinical medicine, but the overall safety and well-being of the patient—and their individual contribution within the aggregate healthcare system—depends on it. You never know when the next complicated case in need of unraveling will be upon you.

CHAPTER 26

VALUE-BASED CARE

CHRISTINA BARSS AND SUZANNE MELL

Sheila was excited about the prospect of automating 12 quality workflows for a value-based care (VBC) program at a large Texas health system. She and her team applied lean methodology when designing the solutions to ensure success and maintain the focus on organizational health, operational efficiency, and the customer's perception of value. As often happens in healthcare, there were many customers: the patient who receives the care, the clinicians who deliver the care, and those in finance who bill for that care. Sheila's team also identified the stakeholders: the clinical support teams, providers, population health team, IT, quality chairman, clinical operations, and the vice president (VP) of population health, who served as the physician sponsor. They also chose pilot departments carefully, and communicated the kickoff date to all stakeholders.

The quality team was made up of seasoned clinical and IT experts who were well-versed in the tenets of VBC and clinical and technical workflows. They possessed the emotional intelligence (EI) to understand their audience and the impact the program would have on patients and the organization. However, the team was missing something crucial to the success of the project: representation from the learning and organization development (L&OD) team.

Instead, they brought the stakeholders and the design team together to identify which 12 VBC workflows to automate. They also developed a plan for the design, implementation, communication, and placement of the tools in the electronic medical record (EMR). The tools were created, tested, and approved by the providers and the clinical teams.

Then they identified the training content and (rather than having L&OD vet the content) developed a PowerPoint presentation to train the clinical teams. The physician champion then requested the population health team to lead training. This team was not familiar with the clinical or digital workflows, which placed them at a disadvantage—especially when the clinical team began asking questions beyond the population health team's scope of knowledge. Unsurprisingly, the training did not go well, which led to frustrations all around.

Driven by the dissatisfaction with and low efficacy of the training, the design team analyzed their process to improve the program based on their lessons learned. They soon realized they had forgotten a vital stakeholder: L&OD. They quickly rectified the situation by bringing on L&OD staff. Now all that remained was re-engaging the clinical teams. The quality manager and director of clinical operations met with the 12 pilot departments in person, took full accountability for the mistake of not including L&OD, and apologized for the oversight.

The L&OD team created an interactive training program that was short and concise, and post-tests showed 98 percent comprehension. Based on feedback and recommendations from the training team, the IT and quality teams scheduled post-training rounding at two weeks, 30 days, and 90 days to answer user questions and obtain feedback.

The project's success was overwhelming. The 12 quality workflows went from 20–30 percent compliance to high 70s and low 80s. Based on these results, L&OD was asked to be a permanent member of the quality team focusing on value-based care. Clinical teams soon requested the automation of 60 quality workflows. In short, L&OD helped this organization realize positive patient safety, outcomes, and bottom-line impact.

Improving patient safety, quality, and service should be the primary goal for every professional in the healthcare industry, no matter the discipline. Adaptable learning organizations are necessary to navigate the transition to value-based care, ensuring patient safety, quality, service, and innovation. L&OD can provide healthcare organizations with a competitive advantage as experts in change management. They bring the necessary skills and understanding of adult learning and human dynamics to drive toward the goal of fiscal fitness. Experts in organizational culture, L&OD professionals are the best to help steward the shift to value-based care. Culture and change management are most successful when augmented by additional areas of L&OD, such as employee engagement, clinician satisfaction, workflow optimization, and talent management.

In this chapter, we start by offering an overview of what value-based care is, three examples of value-based care models, and the risks and benefits of implementing value-based care programs. Then we cover the crucial role L&OD plays when setting up the organization for a transition to value-based care and some organization development opportunities.

What Is Value Based Care?

Michael Porter and Elizabeth Teisberg, Harvard Business School professors and researchers, published *Redefining Health Care* (2006) following the positive reception of their Harvard Business Review article of the same name. Both publications posited that improving the healthcare industry required refocusing the value proposition. Switching focus from being provider-driven to being patient-driven would improve patient safety and quality outcomes. Value would then be defined from the patient perspective—the healthcare outcome divided by the dollars spent.

Healthcare reform is a reality, albeit a slow one. However, Porter and Teisberg's vision of population health and accountable care organizations is becoming more common across the industry. For example, the Cleveland Clinic followed Porter's strategic recommendations under the visionary guidance of then-CEO Toby Cosgrove and restructured the organization. This long-term organizational framework served as a cultural transformation for a patient experience movement where everyone is a caregiver.

Value-based care is a delivery model in which hospitals, physicians, and other licensed providers are paid based on patient outcomes (including quality, patient safety, and patient satisfaction), rather than the volume or quantity of patients treated. (Figure 26-1 provides a breakdown of the differences between volume- and value-based care.) VBC evolved from combining principles of evidence-based practice, patient-centered care, and comparative effectiveness research. Evidence-based practice (EBP) is defined as clinical practice based on research and quantified evidence of improved clinical outcomes. Patient-centered care is defined as care that is centered around the patient and their family. It encompasses the physiologic, emotional, psychologic, spiritual, socioeconomic, and cultural needs of those being cared for. Comparative effectiveness research (CER) is defined as comparing forms of intervention and quantifying the outcomes. The purpose of CER is to ensure the best outcomes for patients and the practice.

The goal of VBC is to improve the quality of patient outcomes while controlling the cost of care delivery. This aligns with the Institute of Healthcare Improvement (IHI) Triple Aim: improving the patient experience of care (including quality and satisfaction), improving the health of populations, and reducing the per capita cost of healthcare (Figure 26-2).

Figure 26-1. Volume-Based Care vs. Value-Based Care

Volume-Based Care	Value-Based Care
Traditional reimbursement model	Known as accountable care, population health management, at-risk contracting
A healthcare provider receives payment for each instance of service. The longer the patient needs treatment, the higher the cost of care. There is no incentive to decrease length of stay or treatment.	Payments are used to incentivize other objectives, such as reducing cost and improving quality. Bundled payments for episodes of care. Provider receives one payment for all services in the episode. Decreases cost of care and length of stay.
Known as fee-for-service care.	Helps healthcare providers.
Incentives are based on volume and cost of care provided.	Manage high patient volume due to increased access to care, which can lead to fewer out-of-network services.
Little or no emphasis on improving quality.	Care for a population that has a higher number of chronic diseases that must be treated.
Success is defined as achieving high profit margins.	Increase their market share now that patients have more options in choosing where to receive care.

Value-based healthcare strives to move the industry from taking a reactionary approach to care to an approach that's proactive toward wellness. Historically, medicine has focused on treating acute illness and physiological symptoms with little analysis of the outcomes or cost associated with the care. This meant the emotional, social, and spiritual needs of patients and their families were not considered. In addition, it also resulted in uncoordinated care between specialists and primary care physicians, which drives up the cost of healthcare per capita.

Figure 26-2. The IHI Triple Aim

One of the major risks of implementing a VBC program is inadequate staffing levels, which can lead to physician burnout. Physician burnout causes decreased patient safety and loss of staff, and it has become a major crisis in our country. In 2017, 50 percent of physicians in primary care reported physician burnout. As of January of 2020, that number decreased to 44 percent, with family health physicians reporting 46 percent burnout and internal medicine physicians reporting 44 percent. Healthcare organizations, the Centers for Medicare and Medicaid (CMS), and the National Institute of Health are taking steps to address physician burnout by improving the provider experience. Experts in the field also recognized the importance of addressing the challenges of the current healthcare environment and the introduction of the EMR. Therefore, Thomas Bodenheimer and Christine Sinsky (2014) called for expanding the IHI Triple Aim to a Quadruple Aim, "adding the goal of improving the work life of healthcare providers, including clinicians and staff" (Figure 26-3). It is important for L&OD professionals to understand this evolution as it affects employee engagement and physician and provider retention.

Figure 26-3. The Quadruple Aim of Healthcare

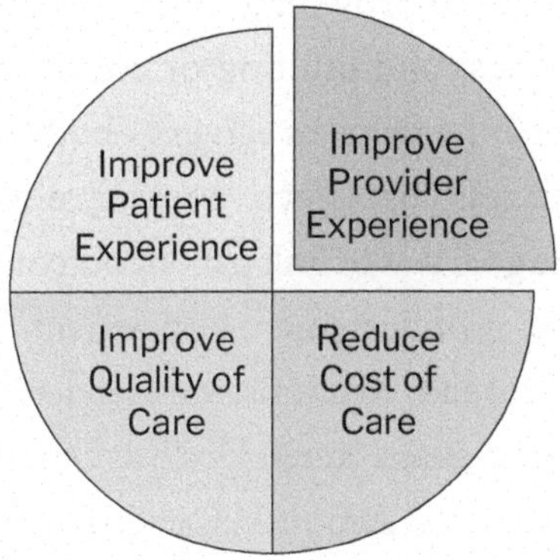

Value-Based Care Delivery Models

VBC, or pay for performance, has many facets and care models. Understanding these different delivery models enables L&OD practitioners to work at both the enterprise and team level. In this section we present a quick overview of the most common models and the financial impact they have on healthcare systems and providers who participate or choose to opt out:

- Pay for Performance model
- Donabedian model
- Accountable Care Organization (ACO) model

At the enterprise level, L&OD can coach executives to mitigate risk and maintain the necessary emotional connection with all stakeholders. At the team level, L&OD can cultivate the "why" to gain buy-in for change, as well as bridge possible gaps regarding communication, tools, and skills required for success.

Model 1: The Pay for Performance Model

The Centers for Medicare and Medicaid (CMS) has shifted from paying for the quantity of healthcare to providing incentives for cost-effective quality healthcare. The focus is now on wellness and limiting or controlling the progression of chronic conditions. Through partnerships with caregivers—both inpatient and outpatient—CMS has several programs that address cost effectiveness, quality, and the patient experience.

The goal was to link patient outcomes and provider performance of quality measures to the provider reimbursement or payment. The five original Pay for Performance programs were:

- Hospital Readmission Reduction Program (HRRP)
- End-Stage Renal Disease Quality Incentive Program (ESRD QIP)
- Hospital Acquired Conditions (HAC) Reduction Program
- Hospital Value-Based Purchasing (VBP) Program
- Value modifier (VM) Program

They later added:

- Skilled Nursing Facility Value-Based Program (SNFVBP)
- Home Health Value-Based Program (HHVBP) (CMS 2020)

In the framework of healthcare delivery, it is shown using a simple formula (Galvin et al. 2019).

$$\frac{\text{the patient outcome achieved}}{\text{the cost of healthcare or value}} = \frac{\text{outcomes}}{\text{cost}}$$

Along with developing quality measures for specific conditions, VBC programs also look at the patient's access to providers, access to preventative care, and access to insurance. This information is also used in developing risk adjustment measures, such as socioeconomic class, absence, and the presence of chronic health conditions (such as diabetes and COPD), multiple chronic conditions, and cultural influences.

Model 2: The Donabedian Model

The Donabedian Model of care is a framework for measuring quality, examining outcomes, and evaluating the outcomes of healthcare delivery. It is structured around three categories: infrastructure, clinical processes, and patient outcomes (Figure 26-4).

Figure 26-4. The Donabedian Model

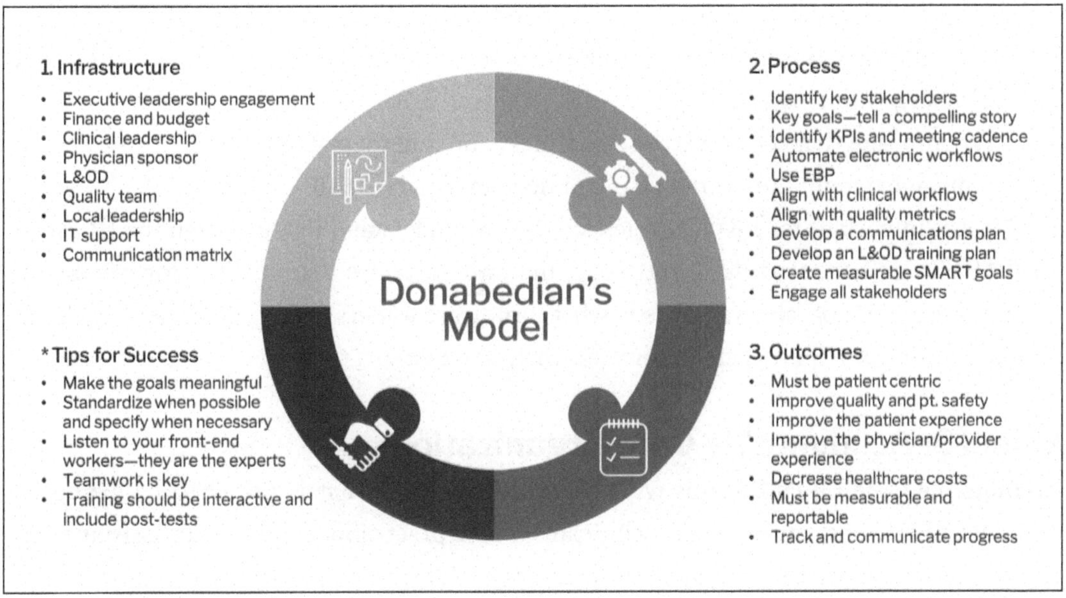

Analyzing infrastructure provides information regarding the provider's or healthcare organization's capacity to offer high-quality or value-based care. Process measures, which are based on the health condition of their patients, identify what the provider does to either improve or maintain a patient's health, whether they are healthy or diagnosed with a condition. Some examples include tracking A1C for diabetics or ensuring that adults and children receive their vaccinations. Outcome measures indicate the impact of healthcare services on the health of their patient population. Outcomes should be reported in a transparent venue so patients can compare the care they've received and its cost (Galvin et al. 2019).

Several websites report the outcomes of care based on the measures in VBC, with the most well-known being HCAHPS (Hospital Consumer Assessment of Healthcare Providers and Systems). HCAHPS scores allow patients to review different providers and make an informed choice, based on quality outcomes and measures, of where and by whom they would like to receive their healthcare. Patients can use these scores to make decisions based on objective comparisons; they also incentivize healthcare organizations and providers to compete for patients based on their engagement and satisfaction.

HCAHPS has seven composites and one global item:

- Six HCAHPS composites: communication with nurses, communication with doctors, staff responsiveness, pain management, communication about medicines and discharge information
- A composite that combines the cleanliness and quietness items
- One global item: the overall rating of hospital (CMS 2020)

What is important for L&OD professionals is to understand that although the HCAHPS (or CAHPS) are answered via Likert scale, the only response that qualifies for reimbursement is a top score of "always." This is what healthcare leaders mean when they say, "all or nothing"—there is no partial credit for a less than "top box" or "top score."

Model 3: Accountable Care Organizations

Accountable Care Organizations (ACOs) coordinate care that is provided by groups of hospitals, physicians, advanced care clinicians, nurse practitioners, physician assistants, dieticians, and pharmacists. The goal of these organizations is to work as a team to ensure appropriate patient access to care by providing the right care at the right time without duplicating services or causing medical errors. If ACOs are successful in delivering cost efficient, quality patient outcomes, they will share in the savings they facilitate for their Medicare patients (NCOA 2021).

Most state Medicaid programs use a combination of value-based programs and more than 70 percent have plans to implement more. Most use HEDIS (healthcare effectiveness data and information set) measures and managed care or managed care organizations that provide incentives based on the provider's healthcare system performance. The majority provide rewards for achieving an attainment threshold. Medicaid programs often focus on the population health of children, women, and adolescents. However, there is little to no qualitative evidence on the effectiveness of these programs to date.

For a talent development professional, what people say during a VBC meeting may feel like it's an entirely different language, especially once the acronyms are thrown around. Some commonly used VBC acronyms include:

- ACA—Affordable Care Act
- EBC—Evidence-Based Care
- PQRS—Physician Quality Reporting System
- PQRI—Physician Quality Reporting Initiative

- MIPS—Merit-based Incentive Payment System
- MACRA—Medicare Access CHIP Reauthorization Act
- HEDIS—Healthcare Effectiveness Data and Information Set
- EMR—Electronic Medical Report

Each of these programs and policies connect, so you'll need to know what their acronyms represent so you can ask informed questions for clarity. For example, Medicare uses the physician quality reporting system (PQRS). This program began as an incentive-based program also based on HEDIS measures, but soon transitioned to a pay for reporting program called the physician quality reporting initiative (PQRI). In turn, this program laid the foundation for the Affordable Care Act's (ACA) Value Modifier program, which began doling out penalties in 2015 for not reporting.

PQRS laid the foundation for the merit-based incentive payment system (MIPS) and the Medicare Access and CHIP Reauthorization Act (MACRA). MIPS is a fee for service program based on quality composite scores, resource utilization, use of an electronic medical record (EMR), and improvement of clinical outcomes. MACRA was signed into law in 2015. MIPS and MACRA then set the stage for reimbursement policies.

Remember how we said everything is connected? MIPS is based on VBC, which is based on HEDIS. Confusing? Yes! However, knowing what the acronyms represent will help you sound considerate when asking strategic questions to support your clinical and financial clients.

Why Make the Transition to Value-Based Care?

VBC improves both the health of an organization's served populations and the organization's financial resilience. It also has the potential to generate additional revenue and increase efficiency. VBC refocuses the attention to the human aspect of patients and providers, raising awareness and improving emotional connections from the initial contact with call centers to delivery with providers to charge for services rendered with finance.

L&OD may assist with the necessary skills and tools to garner lifelong patient relationships. For example, L&OD could provide patient education in different, patient-centric formats, literacy levels, and portals. Or they may facilitate design thinking sessions for innovative problem solving. Interpersonal skills support personalized outreach to the organization's target audiences through their preferred communication channels, whether that's using email, social media, direct mail, phone, or other methods. Patients first have to connect the dots, and

L&OD leads the way in systems thinking, breaking silos, and creating a frictionless experience for healthcare employees and the patient.

Financial Risks and Benefits

The depth and breadth of L&OD's reach is deep and wide within a healthcare organization including operations, administration, and finance. All three areas are affected when implementing VBC, and each is faced with with its own risks. Incentive payments and penalties are associated with meeting the quality measures when participating in advanced care programs. Performers who exceed the top box scores (that is, how often patients select the most positive response category when asked about their hospital experience) are eligible for an incentive adjustment of up to 10 percent annually.

Organizations and providers that do not show improvement or fail to meet their metrics will lose a specific percentage of their Medicare and Medicaid reimbursements. This is important because the long-term impact of losing reimbursement diminishes the organization's financial vitality and can eventually lead to bankruptcy. For example, if a large healthcare organization bills 65 million annually and Medicare is 60 percent of their payor mix, that's equivalent to $39 million. If the organization loses just 4 percent of its Medicare reimbursement, that translates into a loss of $1.56 million. Most healthcare organizations and provider practices only have a small profit margin, so they cannot afford to be penalized. Conversely, if we look at the same model, an organization with exceptional performance may see increased reimbursements from Medicare by 10 percent (a $3.9 million profit). In 2022, these will be increasing to 9 percent (up from 4 percent in 2019; Chee et al. 2016).

Successful Population Health

Population health is a customizable approach that connects the efforts of health departments, health systems, and health practices to work together to affect policy and practice changes at the local community level. Successful population health programs depend on identifying the relevant population, creating an infrastructure to support the program, and identifying and engaging with all relevant stakeholders. With the current shortage in primary care providers, medical assistants, and nurses, one of the major risks facing organizations and providers today is ensuring they have a staff that is stable enough to care for their identified or relevant population. If they cannot deliver quality care, then they run the risk of losing their reimbursement or incurring penalties.

Implementing VBC has increased patient safety, improved tracking of population health, decreased hospital acquired conditions (HACs), and changed the focus of healthcare in the United States from acute interventions to wellness and to maintenance and improvement of chronic conditions. It has also improved the individual's care experience and that of health populations (Whittington et al. 2015). For example, to meet the value-based metrics for diabetics, providers must monitor a patient's A1C and maintain it in a healthy range; if it's not in a healthy range they must prescribe therapeutic interventions. Providers must also complete annual eye and foot exams on their diabetic patients. Another example of value-based care would be controlling hypertension through medication, diet, and exercise.

Improved Primary Care

The cornerstone of the coordination of care is achieved by the primary care provider. Implementation of VBC and the shift in focus to preventative medicine in the United States has strengthened the presence of primary care in this country. The Institute of Medicine identified primary care as crucial in ensuring population health. It has four chief focuses:

- Coordination of care
- Primary first contact access for patients
- Longitudinal patient-focused care
- Comprehensive care inclusive of all systems in the body (cardiac, endocrine, and so on)

Health outcomes are improved when care is referred from the primary care physician, and many organizations require patients to have an assigned primary care provider. An example of this is ensuring schedulers ask all patients who their primary care provider is and document it in their EMR. If the patient does not have a primary care provider, the standard operating procedure is to offer to help the patient make an appointment with one to establish care.

Of utmost importance is ensuring that leadership support, governance structures, and provider engagement are present. Lack of any of these three things will put the program at risk for failure. L&OD professionals may ensure or improve leadership support by acting as a trusted advisor regarding emotional intelligence and providing a toolkit to develop the necessary skill set for success. Governance structures would also benefit from L&OD facilitation and charter development. Improved physician and provider engagement is possible through L&OD initiatives that focus on the voice of the physician and provider, remove the barriers to care delivery, and engage the stakeholders in transformative change.

Rise in Healthcare Consumerism

You may have heard dialogue in your organization switch from "patient first" to "consumer first." The reality is that healthcare organizations are facing more competition than ever. For example, patients can often avoid long wait times and receive quick access to care through stand-up clinics in local pharmacies and grocery stores. These services are often provided at a greatly reduced price (for example, $25 preschool health exams, which may be less than most copays). With more and more readily available information, service ratings, and the proliferation of social media, patients are demanding guaranteed quality at a fair price. In addition, the internet often serves as a self-diagnosis tool and a natural and alternative care resource. People are transitioning from patients to self-care advocates and savvy consumers. To remain competitive, healthcare providers and their organizations must evolve. VBC may assist with the evolution by focusing on personalized medicine, which can happen when we understand how and what healthcare services patients will consume.

So, what is healthcare consumerism? In short, it is about empowering the patient to make informed choices by ensuring they have choices. Value-based care is how the industry ensures those choices continue to exist. Since patients can freely access information on the internet, they now have a better understanding of healthcare issues. So, how do healthcare organizations combat "Dr. Google"? By cultivating patient loyalty, a long-term and hopefully lifelong relationship based on outreach, easily understood evidence-based information, helpful decision-making tools, and transparent financial pricing. With a few clicks, VBC can allow patients to access insight on treatment and care approaches, provider quality and hospital performance, and pricing for common procedures.

There are two sides to consumerism. As organizations make the shift to VBC, providers are often asked to increase their touchpoints with existing and potential patients. Some examples include a nurse advice line, nurse triage, follow-up phone calls, and case management.

However, this is a time-consuming endeavor that cuts into the workload of an already heavily burdened clinical staff.

To meet the healthcare consumer needs of your patients, you can:

- Cultivate strong bonds through frequent and meaningful communications between doctors and their patients.
- Help informed patients better understand the "why" behind their treatment recommendations to increase buy-in and compliance.
- Encourage wellness, lifestyle changes, and improved self-care through preventative medicine practices.

Setting Up for VBC

L&OD is often missing from the table when discussions are happening about organizational strategy on the magnitude of shifting to value-based care. The story we told at the beginning of this chapter is common in healthcare organizations. Unfortunately, this oversight may result in well-meaning tools that were developed in a vacuum, with limited effectiveness and adoption that often stalls or delivers inadequate success. If frontline teams don't receive relevant interactive training, they won't be able to use the tools or program successfully. Value-based care requires healthcare practices to align with patient priorities. Through evidence-based decisions, an organization can focus healthcare professionals on improving patient outcomes.

This section provides an overview of the process of setting up a VBC program so talent development professionals can speak to the opportunities for their support (Figure 26-5). L&OD can serve as tacticians and strategists, supporting the organization to achieve business goals holistically. For example, a best practice to train bedside nurses is to improve their patient interactivity skill set using clear rubrics. This training can be delivered in a dyad format—the nurse is observed by their manager, rated against the rubric, and then given in-the-moment coaching feedback.

This process is simple and repeatable. It can be conducted on any shift in most clinical environments. It can also be adapted into computer-based scenarios, to train managers on coaching skills, and to coach nurses in practice sessions prior to engaging with live patients.

Figure 26-5. Steps to Set Up a VBC Program

STEP 1	Have a clear, concise goal, a compelling story, and the ability to rally caregivers and other stakeholders around that goal
STEP 2	Identify your assigned patient population: • Are you treating Medicare, Medicaid, or pediatric? • What is the quantity or patient numbers?
STEP 3	Identify the VBC program: • MACRA • ACO • MIPS • Medicare Advantage Use the following strategies to help your organization identify which measures to participate in: • Metrics should be clearly defined so they are understood by everyone in the organization • Strategically align your metrics to enable daily operations tracking—this will make it easier to identify issues and react to them • Clearly define how the metrics will affect the bottom line • Document how metrics are sourced to allow for easily tracing cause and effect relationships
STEP 4	Assess the organization or provider's ability to create an infrastructure for the program. This extends to: • Leadership • Governance • Organizational capacity • EMR clinical and reporting capabilities • Culture (collaborative versus siloed) • Staffing levels • Change readiness • Integration of primary and specialty care

Building the VBC Organization of Tomorrow: Organization Development Opportunities

One of the most ambitious enterprise transitions on which to embark is the evolution from fee-for-service healthcare model to one that's value-based. Embracing VBC requires more than simply shifting to a new accounting model. It impacts provider, leadership, and essential support; influences culture, team, and interprofessional behaviors; and affects processes, policies, and infrastructure.

Patient-centered or disease-based care requires care coordination, which is best delivered through teamwork. Breaking functional and cultural silos through interprofessional and cross-disciplinary teamwork will enable the organization to proactively nurture the thoughts and feelings of the organizational collective, positively honoring and supporting its culture. If this is not done proactively, the confusion and power struggle that may ensue from VBC risks haphazardly confirming bias, silos, and work arounds.

TD professionals are in the unique position to have been exposed to each care level and model in the organization. This means that they can act as a conduit connecting caregivers by citing best practices and connecting care teams to improve a patient's continuum of care and overall experience.

Identify Stakeholders

To be successful, the VBC shift demands a deep understanding of stakeholders, including providers, educators, the organization, and policymakers. The risk is that stakeholders won't share a common definition of value and the components thereof, which might be why little progress has occurred in the movement toward VBC adoption industry wide (Pendleton 2018).

To ensure the shift to VBC runs smoothly, L&OD professionals can help identify key stakeholders, including:

- Patients (consumers)
- Organizational leadership
- Clinical
- C-suite
- Operational
- Finance
- Legal
- Nursing
- IT
- Clinical support (front desk, scheduling, medical assistants)
- Training and development

Each of these stakeholders will perceive value, cost, and benefits differently. For example, consumers have personal goals for their health and are invested in achieving them. Providers are expected to expand their focus from personal patient health to include population health and understand the economics associated with each. To uncover the different perceptions, ask each stakeholder about the following regarding VBC:

- Cost
- Accessibility
- Quality
- Safety
- Patient, family, and provider satisfaction
- Outcomes

Match Value-Based Care to Organizational Values

Even with common definitions, value-based care can be a confusing concept. Sometimes it is mixed up with the term values-based care. Both value-based care and values-based care share the same "why"—to deliver the best quality care possible for patients, families, and communities. However, value-based care refers to what and when care is delivered, while values-based care refers to how it is delivered.

An organization's values serve as the foundation for their purpose and passion, guiding the decisions of their leaders, employees, patients, and communities. Values-based care is required for successfully navigating the value-based care transition. During times of change, a recommended tactic is for leaders at all levels to communicate via the organization's values to drive performance. These values are the emotional connection to building trust and loyalty between all stakeholders.

Reinforcing organizational values helps build resilience and the recovery factor for your organization as it experiences change. From moments of recognition and reward to coaching for success, values-based leadership requires fully present leaders who are in constant communication with staff.

To sustain the gains made in organizational culture for VBC, apply a values-based recruiting strategy; for example, speak to the importance of the organizational culture of patient safety and delivering on the Quadruple Aim. This will perpetuate a culture based on VBC within the organization's mission, vision, and values parameters. Hiring for desired culture evolution will also reduce turnover and the learning curve to new role assimilation. This also makes fiscal sense because the estimated cost to replace a role is two times that role's salary.

L&OD professionals have a crucial role to play in an organization's ongoing cultural development through improved hiring practices. Some examples of this are behavior-based interviewing techniques that engage managers in proactive identification and electronic screening tools. HealthcareSource, for example, offers a pre-hire assessment that's aligned to your organization's mission, vision, and values.

Foster a High-EQ Culture

L&OD is key to helping leaders foster meaningful emotional connections with peers, team members, and direct reports. Emotional intelligence (EQ) and interpersonal communication skills refer to a person's ability to recognize their own emotional state as well as the emotional state of others. The key theorists of emotional intelligence are John Mayer, Peter Salovey, Daniel Goleman, and Richard Boyatzis. While healthcare is rich in IQ, it often requires the cultivation of EQ.

EQ is traditionally illustrated through four core dimensions:

- Self-awareness
- Self-management
- Social awareness
- Relationship management

Strengthening emotional intelligence and interpersonal skill sets has many benefits in healthcare, including:

- Improving provider connections with patients, families, and communities
- Decreasing bias in clinical spaces to ensure all patients and families receive the best care possible
- Increasing safety while delivering care by having meaningful and trusted communication at the point of care

We offer two recommendations to improve or coach the EQ skill set in healthcare. The first focuses on individual or team training using an objective measurement device to provide insight into each dimension. There is a wide range of reliable and valid measures of emotional intelligence that L&OD can leverage in talent management and development. The second recommendation focuses on an enterprise approach to create a campaign or program for wide distribution that closes a large-scale gap identified through multiple-source data collection.

When conducting individual or team-based EQ improvements, competency measures are typically delivered through a self-assessment using a multi-rater or 360-degree format. In 360-degree assessments, a predetermined set of others—including the learner's supervisor (manager), peers, and direct reports—provides feedback in addition to the learner's self-assessment.

While conducting in-depth assessments is the best way to collect data, we also recommend collecting data from existing measurement devices and databases, which will help you understand which EQ skill sets are needed at an enterprise level, and then conducting an analysis to identify trends and gaps. Some places to look for existing data include:

- Surveys
  - Employee engagement
  - Customer service, HCAPPS, or CAPPS
  - Exit or stay interviews
  - Culture of safety survey
- Databases
  - Annual performance reviews
  - Succession planning talent pipeline analysis
  - Safety and quality metrics

This approach of citing multiple data points from your organization's existing and trusted tools helps with executive buy-in and championing to implement necessary training campaigns. Emotional intelligence and interpersonal skill sets help fortify a values-based leadership and care tactical approach for strategically shifting to VBC. Personalized patient care and connecting with specific patient populations requires self-awareness, social-awareness, and relationship-building skills.

Analyze the Patient Data

Building and maintaining an electronic reporting structure is key to successful, timely reporting to CMS. If deadlines are not met before the reporting window closes, than the organization runs the risk of incurring penalties or losing its reimbursement. The electronic reporting structure provides ease and speed of data collection. Moving to an EMR positively affects patient safety and quality, improves cross-functional teamwork, and ensures consistent care through the patient continuum.

Reports generated from an EMR help motivate data-driven decisions to create and deliver personalized outreach. Before walking into a meeting, L&OD professionals may want to know where the data sources for VBC come from and how they are used or may be used within their own system. Completing this homework prior to meeting with a stakeholder or executive champion will provide the L&OD professional with a keen insight to the level of change required at the systems and frontline level. It is important to note, however, that

L&OD professionals don't need to provide direction on analysis or IT decisions. Instead, this insight gives the L&OD professional value so they can fully participate in the conversation.

It is important to understand what data is available and the systems used to collect it. One option is the EMR or electronic health record, like Epic or Cerner. A healthcare customer relationship management system (HRCM), which informs personalization and improved patient experiences, is another option. The HRCM is used to collect, store, and analyze patient data.

Another way such data may be used is in applying clinical propensity models, which are robust analyses that identify and help match a healthcare system to specific populations to treat. For example, an organization could use a clinical propensity model to validate if an orthopedic surgery campaign would be successful by tracking consumer behaviors, geographic location, and demographic traits. Healthcare systems can cultivate lifelong patients using clinical propensity models.

Take the Lead on Organizational Transformation

Value-based care is a systems approach featuring new delivery models that require a team-oriented approach vertically and horizontally throughout the healthcare industry. Effective consumer connections require healthcare organizations to break patient data silos between internal functions and between external providers. Only then can they ensure care is coordinated and true outcomes are accurately captured. The value-based payment model requires socially responsible patient education, coordinated clinical care planning, and lifelong treatment implementation. Alignment to the organization's mission, vision, and values needs to be clear to all parties, from RNs to pharmacists to behavioral health providers to social workers and so on.

Securing executive champions is important for every step of the way. Restructuring the organization to better deliver VBC requires significant investment, and it is not a short-term commitment. Transitioning to VBC is a long-term game plan best viewed as an investment, not a financial loss, so having a phased approach is smart. In addition, executive buy-in is critical because some of these changes will be expensive and business balance sheets and budgets will feel the pain. Financial loss and even attrition should be viewed as a short-term issue; coaching leaders at all levels through this transition will help the organization reach its desired goal. For example, a high skill mix staffing model may seem less cost-effective at first, as teams add specialized skill sets such as registered nurses, social workers, pharmacy support staff, or other licensed professionals. However, once the appropriate outcomes are achieved the revenue will be realized through VBC. Such efficient staffing models do pay off through incentive payments or realizing eligibility for other value-based reimbursements.

Support Change Management

Once an organization's values are clearly defined, they become the guiding light for how enterprise, departments, centers of excellence, teams, and individuals are evaluated. This is especially true when organizations are facing change. Values-based leadership and values-based performance evaluation systems need to be put in place. HR performance review systems and talent management mechanisms (such as leadership development, succession planning, or workforce planning) are powerful supporting devices for VBC transitions. It is important to note that when teams experience major VBC changes in structure, care coordination, and performance expectations, yet continue to be measured against old metrics, the cognitive dissonance will erode trust in leadership and the organization. The VBC transition will not be easy, so when L&OD is aware of possible challenges they may feel better prepared to support and guide this change. What do we know about VBC's impact on organizations?

Transitions are never easy and making the switch from volume-based care to value-based care may present a few challenges. Healthcare providers should be ready to make tweaks whenever an unexpected issue arises. Figure 26-6 highlights some ideas for solving challenges related to the VBC transition.

Develop Team-Based Training

As the healthcare industry evolves, requirements in the organizational structure and industry will shift. Conducting workforce leadership analysis will be crucial to continued success. It will also be important to understand the evolution of organizational leadership requirements, such as more clinical leaders assuming operational roles, succession planning, and a global team-based approach. Plan to increase your number of entry-level positions to take the burden off clinical providers and ensure a robust pipeline of leaders and clinical staff. Provide concise, just-in-time training that's geared toward the right role at the right time with the right information. Onboarding should also be considered part of the continued recruiting process. Evolving technology promises to increase the need for technical skill sets with AR, VR, and automation. And leaders will need to master emotional intelligence and an interprofessional skill set to fulfill the VBC imperative.

Figure 26-6. Possible Challenges and Probable Solutions to VBC

Possible Challenge	Probable L&OD Solution
Although it's 14 years in the making, the VBC payment system is still relatively new and evolving.	Help leadership craft a compelling story explaining how the culture change will evolve over many years and will affect patient safety and health as well as population health.
Possible misidentification of quality indicators will negatively affect the bottom line. The organization risks penalties and reimbursements.	Engage front-end users to create meaningful content and training delivery; make sure the content is purposeful and interactive with clear measurable results.
There are limited data, unreliable data resources and analysis, non-actionable data, or analysis paralysis.	Partner with quality and IT to determine if data can be collected from the EMR.
Training and development are designed without a pilot or phased approach, or without the clinical provider in mind	Establish an organizational structure that implements effective processes training and incentives.
Clinicians are burning out due to being overburdened with additional, well-intended responsibilities they don't have time to do.	• Focus on workflows that are time efficient and require fewer clicks • Guide leadership in continuous improvement projects that reduce waste and improve quality to drive value and capacity • Restructure clinical teams to ensure all members can work at top of licensure
There is a lack of understanding of what the patient population needs	• Involve clinical teams when identifying your assigned patient population • Start small and build on your successes • Create a clear and concise picture of what is required of your clinical providers to take care of this population
Providers are confused about how to identify quality indicators that align with payers' expectations (such as insurance and CMS). High error rates on quality indicators are negatively impacting reimbursement.	• Provide clear and concise measures • Align the VBC process with clinical workflows • Automate workflows as much as possible in the EMR to reduce workload on front-end teams • Engage L&OD to ensure concise, meaningful training

VBC programs require that L&OD ensures silos are broken within healthcare training. As we move to team-based care, we must also provide team-based training. By bringing together physicians, advance care providers, nurses, allied health, medical assistants, and front desk personal, everyone learns as a team, knows as a team, acts as a team, and succeeds as a team.

VBC seeks to improve individual patient and overall population health and well-being. It is important to consider the patient or consumer experience. When analyzing the patient journey map, look for the areas lacking continuity of care—that is where you'll find opportunities for continuous improvement. If you don't do this, consumers will be more likely to turn elsewhere for care and organizations likely won't meet their VBC measures. Since VBC models reward organizations that have higher patient or consumer satisfaction numbers, it is imperative to foster excellent patient experiences throughout the care continuum.

VBC is required for the long-term viability of a healthcare organization, so it can remain competitive in the marketplace compared to new entrants like standalone ERs, urgent care and dialysis centers, or primary care subscription services. To survive, cut costs, develop new products, and become more efficient or improve quality, the culture will likely have to transform as well. Leaders at all levels model the behavior of a VBC culture—a new way of thinking to support the new way of doing. Transition is a team sport, and even L&OD benefits from breaking silos and strategically partnering with organizational effectiveness, quality, safety, and continuous improvement personnel.

Team-based care assists in achieving that goal. The World Health Organization (WHO 2010) stated that team-based care in interprofessional practice occurs "when multiple health workers from different professional backgrounds provide comprehensive health services by working with patients, families, care providers, and communities to deliver the highest quality of care." Healthcare professional teams will require learning and development support to foster building these characteristics of responsibility, accountability, coordination, communication, cooperation, assertiveness, mutual trust, and respect.

Key Takeaways

To build the VBC organization of tomorrow, talent development professionals should be able to:

- Support the transition to value-based care through change management and L&OD solutions, such as identifying the key stakeholders who need to be involved in the initiative and securing executive champions.
- Apply organizational values to hiring and staffing decisions to perpetuate a culture of value-based care.
- Foster a culture of high emotional intelligence, which is essential for making meaningful connections with peers, team members, and direct reports, a key to value-based care.
- Develop team-based training that evolves with the breakdown of healthcare silos and the shift to team-based care.

Conclusion

Value-based care is an exciting proposition for healthcare organizations, and L&OD can provide a strategic competitive advantage when implementing and sustaining it. Messaging is important, especially when explaining data-driven approaches to population health. As trusted confidants to executive leadership, coaches to providers, and facilitators of change, L&OD serves by reminding all values-based stakeholders to:

- Be cognizant that no one thinks they are being reduced to a number or classification.
- Be aware that no one feels defined by a demographic or stereotype.
- Be kind, empathetic, and compassionate in a values-based leadership.

In other words, have a high level of emotional intelligence. Each condition, patient, family, culture, and community is different. The healthcare industry is dynamically and rapidly changing. L&OD has the necessary skills and abilities to keep an organization focused on the most important facet of healthcare: the people.

ACKNOWLEDGMENTS

Jacque Burandt

My accidental 30+ year career in healthcare began in the mid-1980s when, after being laid off from a Fortune 500 technology corporation, University Health offered me a position. "This is just until something I really like comes along," I explained to everyone. Then their mission, vision, and values got their hooks in me and I realized there wasn't anything I could possibly like better than being the executive director of the Center for Learning Excellence at University Health.

This book is dedicated to the thousands of employees, volunteers, and patients who engaged with me at University Health during my career. They gave me the experience, expertise, and enthusiasm to edit this handbook and to author three chapters. Their work as everyday extraordinary heroes continues to inspire all of us.

I owe thanks to so many—my parents for teaching me grit, kindness, and humanity. My dad, Jack, who taught me to be fearless, and my mom, Johnnie, who handed down her sterling work ethic. Both my children, Kirsten and Morgan, continue to amaze me with their work ethic, and, thankfully, understand that I am not a traditional mom or grandmother.

My gratitude will always go out to ATD and everyone on staff who has mentored me, involved me, and given me endless opportunities to add to my skill set, resume, and brand. Most recently I had the honor and pleasure to work on this book with Ryan Changcoco, Niranjani Chidamber Papavaritis, and Greg Rider (a.k.a. the Titans). Thanks to Ryan for asking me to co-edit, to Greg for agreeing to be co-editor, and to Niranjani for guiding us through unknown waters.

And thanks to anyone who's reading this tome. I hope you reap the benefits of all the great work inside.

Niranjani Chidamber Papavaritis

I'd first like to express gratitude to my guru for instilling the lifelong value of "love all serve all" and guiding me to this journey in healthcare training. An endless thank you to my parents, who illustrate a life dedicated to helping others, and empower me to pave a path for those with diverse backgrounds. Thank you to my husband, Jon, who champions my career and life goals, and for making (and reheating) endless cups of tea and coffee while I worked on this book.

Thank you to those who have taken me under their wing, providing care and brilliance. To Dr. Arthur Johnson, who ignited the spark for public service, and taught me how to clearly define a problem to find constructive solutions in life. Thank you for always believing in me, and finding humor in my unconventional methods. To Curtis Munlin, who bolstered my first few years in the field and consistently advocated on my behalf for equity. The confidence you instilled in me has carried me to this point. To Len Carter, who motivates me though his leadership and has invested hours in teaching me the ins and outs of HR within health systems. To Briana Whitfield, Fiorella Miranda, and former colleagues in the field, who continue to inspire me as you contribute to the industry's evolution.

A huge thank you to Ryan Changcoco for having my back at every stage of this book's development, and for spending countless hours reviewing drafts and providing advice. Your encouragement and endless jokes have made every working day fun as we navigated the training world of healthcare here at ATD. Thank you to Jack Harlow for playing a key role as developmental editor and patiently working with me to make sure every draft, revision, and chapter fit together perfectly like puzzle pieces. And to the rest of the content team—Lisa, Ann, Eliza, Justin, Kim, Bryan, and Alexandria—thank you for cheering me on and providing resources and excitement through this process.

To my co-editors, Jacque and Greg, thank you for our weekly Friday afternoon calls filled with laughter, vision, and dedication. To each contributor who wrote for this book, thank you for your ongoing work and commitment to the healthcare industry. I am honored to have crossed paths with each one of you and to have been given the chance to showcase your wisdom and experiences. This book wouldn't exist without the collaboration and camaraderie we've all formed.

Greg Rider

I am grateful to Jacque, Ryan, and Niranjani for including me as a co-editor in this outstanding opportunity. I remain grateful for early ATD mentors and colleagues who steered and encouraged me along the way—Dave Jennings, Sardek Love, Dawn Mahoney, and Jacque Burandt. To the colleagues and talent development leaders who guided me onto the CPTD path and then into the world of CPTD volunteer projects—Russell Babcock, Pat Byrd, and Jennifer Naughton—thank you for your attitude of inclusiveness, your sense of humor, and your spirit of giving back.

To Debra Lightner and other leaders who always found time to listen to my ideas, questions, and concerns—thank you. You helped me grow, take more responsibility, and pause to reflect at key moments.

To Andrea Nierenberg, consultant and entrepreneur extraordinaire, thank you for your friendship and guidance and for providing collaborative projects at the most opportune times.

To my parents, John and Barbara Rider, I'm grateful for your love and encouragement and for providing a safe environment for me to read, explore, grow, and try new things.

And to my life partner, Ed Haley, thank you for sharing life, laughter, and love with me, and for championing the professional and personal projects that come across our path.

REFERENCES AND RESOURCES

Chapter 2

Abrahamson, C.E. 2011. "Methodologies for Motivating Student Learning Through Personal Connections." Forum on Public Policy Online (3).

Culatta, R. 2018. "Experiential Learning (Carl Rogers)." InstructionalDesign.org, November 30. instructionaldesign.org/theories/experiential-learning.

Doyle, C., L. Lennox, and D. Bell. 2013. "A Systematic Review of Evidence on the Links Between Patient Experience and Clinical Safety and Effectiveness." *BMJ Open* 3(1): e001570. doi.org/10.1136/bmjopen-2012-001570.

Kenrick, D.T., V. Griskevicius, S.L. Neuberg, and M. Schaller. 2010. "Renovating the Pyramid of Needs: Contemporary Extensions Built Upon Ancient Foundations." *Perspectives on Psychological Science* 5(3): 292–314. doi.org/10.1177/1745691610369469.

Prera, A. 2020. "Self-Actualization." Simply Psychology, September 4. simplypsychology.org/self-actualization.html.

Research History. 2012. "Maslow's Hierarchy of Needs." Research History, June 16. researchhistory.org/2012/06/16/maslows-hierarchy-of-needs.

Sutton, J. 2020. "Socratic Questioning in Psychology: Examples and Techniques." Positive Psychology, September 4. positivepsychology.com/socratic-questioning.

Chapter 3

Anderson, L.W., and D.R. Krathwohl, eds. 2001. *A Taxonomy for Learning, Teaching, and Assessing.* Boston: Longman.

ATD (Association for Talent Development). 2018. *Needs Assessments: Design and Execution for Success.* Alexandria, VA: ATD Press.

ATD (Association for Talent Development). 2019. *2019 State of Healthcare Training.* Alexandria, VA: ATD Press.

ATD Staff. 2019. "St. Charles Hospital: On-the-Job Performance Support to Improve Patient Care." ATD 10-Minute Case Study. casebycase.td.org/st-charles-hospital-on-the-job-performance-support-to-improve-patient-care.

Biech, E. 2015. *Training and Development for Dummies.* Hoboken, NJ: John Wiley & Sons.

Biech, E. 2018. *ATD's Action Guide to Talent Development.* Alexandria, VA: ATD Press.

Bloom, B. 1956. *Taxonomy of Educational Objectives, Handbook 1: Cognitive Domain.* Boston: Addison-Wesley Longman.

Mahoney, D.J. 2018. "Lean Learning Using the ADDIE Model." *TD at Work.* Alexandria, VA: ATD Press.

Malamed, C. 2020. "Learner Personas for Instructional Design." The eLearning Coach, August 29. theelearningcoach.com/elearning_design/audience/learner-personas-for-elearning.

Tobey, D.D. 2007. "Data Collection for Needs Assessment." *Infoline.* Alexandria, VA: ATD Press.

Wile, D.E. 1996. *Why Doers Do: Managing Human Performance to Optimize the Return on Your People Investment.* Self-Published.

Chapter 4

Buzachero, V.V., J.J. Phillips, P.P. Phillips, and Z.L. Phillips. 2013. *Measuring ROI in Healthcare: Tools and Techniques to Measure the Impact and ROI in Healthcare Improvement Projects and Programs.* New York: McGraw-Hill Education.

Drucker, P.F. 1990. *Managing the Nonprofit Organization: Principles and Practices.* New York: HarperCollins.

Drucker, P.F. 2017. *Concept of the Corporation.* New York: Rutledge.

Dylan, B. 1964. *The Times They Are A-Changin'.* Album. Columbia Records, January 13.

Hale, J. 2007. *The Performance Consultant's Fieldbook: Tools and Techniques for Improving Organizations and People,* 2nd ed. New York: Pfeiffer.

Kaufman, R., and I. Guerra-Lopez. 2013. *Needs Assessment for Organizational Success.* Alexandria, VA: ATD Press.

Kellogg Foundation. 2004. *W.K. Kellogg Foundation Logic Model Development Guide.* W.K. Kellogg Foundation. wkkf.org/resource-directory/resource/2006/02/wk-kellogg-foundation-logic-model-development-guide.

Mattox, J.R., II, and M. Van Buren. 2016. *Learning Analytics: Measurement Innovations to Support Employee Development.* New York: Kogan Page.

McLeod, K. 2020. *ROI Institute Benchmarking Report 2019.* ROI Institute. roiinstitute .net/2019-roi-institute-benchmarking-report.

Mootee, I. 2013. *Design Thinking for Strategic Innovation.* New York: Wiley.

Phillips, J.J., and L. Zuniga. 2008. *Costs and ROI: Evaluating at the Ultimate Level,* vol. 5. San Francisco: Pfeiffer.

Phillips, J.J., and P.P. Phillips. 2009. *Measuring for Success: What CEOS Really Think About Learning Interventions.* Alexandria, VA: ASTD Press.

Phillips, K. 2020. "The Cost of Scrap Learning: Use Predictive Analysis to Increase Learning Transfer." *Training Industry* 13(6): 4.

Phillips, P.P. 2017. *The Bottomline on ROI,* 3rd ed. West Chester, Pennsylvania: HRDQ.

Phillips, P.P., and J.J. Phillips. 2017. *The Business Case for Learning: Using Design Thinking to Deliver Business Results and Increase the Investment in Talent Development.* West Chester, PA: HRDQ; Alexandria, VA: ATD Press.

Phillips, P.P., and J.J. Phillips. 2019. *ROI Basics,* 2nd ed. Alexandria, VA: ATD Press.

Thalheimer, W. 2018. "Donald Kirkpatrick Was Not the Originator of the Four-Level Model of Learning Evaluation." Work Learning, January 30. worklearning.com /2018/01/30/donald-kirkpatrick-was-not-the-originator-of-the-four-level -model-of-learning-evaluation.

Van Tiem, D.M., J.L. Moseley, and J.C. Dessinger. 2012. *Fundamentals of Performance Improvement: Optimizing Results Through People, Process, and Organizations,* 3rd ed. San Francisco: Pfeiffer.

Chapter 5

Arruda, W. 2019. *Digital You: Real Personal Branding in the Virtual Age.* Alexandria, VA: ATD Press.

Burandt, J. 2014. "Be the Talk of the Office." *TD* 2(68): 24–26. td.org/magazines/td -magazine/be-the-talk-of-the-office.

Burandt, J. 2019. "Create an Exceptional Learning Culture." *TD at Work.* Alexandria, VA: ATD Press.

Chilcote, M., and M. Smith. 2018. "The Training Clinic." *Training,* March 27.

Phillips, J.J., and P.P. Phillips. 2009. *Measuring for Success: What CEOS Really Think About Learning Interventions.* Alexandria, VA: ASTD Press.

Wallace, D. 2021. "Market Your Internal Learning Solutions Like a Pro." *TD*, March. td.org/magazines/td-magazine/market-your-internal-learning-solutions-like-a-pro.

Chapter 6

ATD (Association for Talent Development). 2019. "What Is Change Management?" Talent Development Glossary Terms, June 21. td.org/talent-development-glossary-terms /what-is-change-management.

Beich, E. 2007. *Thriving Through Change: A Leader's Practical Guide to Change Mastery.* Alexandria, VA: ASTD Press.

Beich, E., ed. 2010. *The ASTD Leadership Handbook.* Alexandria, VA: ASTD Press.

Boogaard, K. 2020. "The 4 Types of Company Culture, Explained." Atlassian, March 23. atlassian.com/blog/teamwork/types-of-corporate-culture.

Cooperrider, D., D. Whitney, and J. Stavros. 2003. *Appreciative Inquiry Handbook: The First in a Series of AI Workbooks for Leaders of Change.* Brunswick, OH: Lakeshore Communications.

Darraugh, B. 1991. "How to Motivate Employees." *Infoline.* Alexandria, VA: ASTD Press.

Jennings, J., and L. Malcak. 2004. *Communication Basics.* Alexandria, VA: ASTD Press.

Haneberg, L. 2005. *Organization Development Basics.* Alexandria, VA: ASTD Press.

Hughes, C. 2018. "Leading and Communicating Change in Organizations." Health Inclusion, July 5. healthinclusion.com/back-up-leading-and-communicating-change.

Koehle, D. 1997. "The Role of the Performance Change Manager." *Infoline.* Alexandria, VA: ASTD Press.

Kotter, J.P. 1996. *Leading Change.* Boston: Harvard Business School Press.

Kotter, J. 2017. "The 8-Step Process for Leading Change." Kotter. kotterinc.com/8-step -process-for-leading-change.

Prosci. n.d. "Definition of Change Management." Prosci, Thought Leadership Articles. prosci.com/resources/articles/definition-of-change-management.

SHRM (Society for Human Resource Management). n.d. "Managing Organizational Change." SHRM,Toolkit. shrm.org/resourcesandtools/tools-and-samples/toolkits /pages/managingorganizationalchange.aspx.

SHRM (Society for Human Resource Management). n.d. "Organizational Culture." SHRM Member Resources, shrm.org/resourcesandtools/pages/organizational-culture.aspx.

Trice, H., and J. Beyer. 1993. *The Cultures of Work Organizations.* Englewood Cliffs, NJ: Prentice Hall.

Chapter 7

"AAMC: Tomorrow's Doctors, Tomorrow's Cures." AAMC website. aamc.org.

"Awards." Healthcare Diversity Council. Accessed January 1, 2021. healthcarediversitycouncil.org/2019-national-healthcare-diversity-conference/awards.

Campinha-Bacote, J. 1999. "A Model and Instrument for Addressing Cultural Competence in Health Care." *Journal of Nursing Education* 38(5): 204–207.

Colby, S.L., and J.M. Ortman. 2014. "Projections of the Size and Composition of the U.S. Population: 2014 to 2060, Current Population Reports, P25-1143." US Census Bureau, Washington, DC.

Covey, S.R. 2004. *The 7 Habits of Highly Effective People: Restoring the Character Ethic,* rev ed. New York: Free Press.

"Diversity Impact Awards for ERGs Diversity Councils & Departments." 2021 ERG & Council Conference. Accessed March 1, 2021. ergcouncilconference.com/erg-diversity-council-awards.html.

Human Rights Campaign. 2019. "Healthcare Equality Index 2019." Human Rights Campaign Foundation, August 16. hrc.org/resources/healthcare-equality-index.

Katz, J.H., and F.A. Miller. 2002. *The Inclusion Breakthrough: Unleashing the Real Power of Diversity.* San Francisco: Berrett-Koehler

Kognito. "Evidence-Based Health Simulations and Training." kognito.com.

Lehner, A. 2021. "Disability Equality Index." Disability:IN, February 18. disabilityin.org/what-we-do/disability-equality-index.

"RaceWorks News." Stanford Center for Comparative Studies in Race and Ethnicity. ccsre.stanford.edu/initiatives/raceworks.

Rowe, A., and L. Gardenswartz, L. 2009. "The Effective Management of Cultural Diversity." Ch. 4 in *Contemporary Leadership and Intercultural Competence,* edited by Michael A. Moodian. Thousand Oaks, CA: Sage.

"Think Cultural Health." Health and Human Services website, thinkculturalhealth.hhs.gov.

The Joint Commission. 2010. *Advancing Effective Communication, Cultural Competence, and Patient- and Family-Centered Care: A Roadmap for Hospitals.* Oakbrook Terrace, IL: The Joint Commission.

Umoh, R. 2020. "Meet America's Best Employers for Diversity 2020." *Forbes,* January 21. forbes.com/sites/ruthumoh/2020/01/21/meet-americas-best-employers-for-diversity-2020/?sh=3a6050c57394.

World Health Organization (WHO). 2011. "WHO | Equity." WHO, June 8. who.int/health systems/topics/equity/en.

Chapter 8

Adair, J. 2009. *Effective Teambuilding: How to Make a Winning Team.* London: Pan books.

AHA (American Heart Association). 2015. *Basic Life Support (BLS).* Dallas: AHA.

DHHS (NOISH). 2008. "Exposure to Stress: Occupational Hazards in Hospitals." National Institute for Occupational Safety and Health (NOISH), July. cdc.gov/niosh/docs/2008-136/pdfs/2008-136.pdf

Edmonson, A. 2015. "The Kinds of Teams Health Care Needs." *Harvard Business Review,* December. hbr.org/2015/12/the-kinds-of-teams-health-care-needs.

GWU School of Business. 2020. "5 Teambuilding Practices that Lead to Organizational Success." GWU Healthcare MBA blog, November 4. healthcaremba.gwu.edu/blog/5-teambuilding-practices-that-lead-to-organizational-success.

Hughes, C. 2021. "Multidisciplinary Teamwork Ensures Better Healthcare Outcomes." ATD blog, April 21. td.org/insights/multidisciplinary-teamwork-ensures-better-healthcare-outcomes.

Mayo, A.T., and A.W. Woolley. 2016. "Teamwork in Health Care: Maximizing Collective Intelligence Via Inclusive Collaboration and Open Communication." *American Medical Association Journal of Ethics,* September.

My Medical Score. n.d. "Medical Error Statistics." Accessed May 17, 2021. mymedicalscore.com/medical-error-statistics.

Rosen, M.A., D. DiazGranados, A.S. Dietz, L.E. Benishek, D. Thompson, P.J. Pronovost, and S.J. Weaver. 2018. "Teamwork in Healthcare: Key Discoveries Enabling Safer, High-Quality Care." *The American Psychologist* 73(4): 433–450. pubmed.ncbi.nlm.nih.gov/29792459.

Salas, I. 2007. "Team Building." World Health Organization. who.int/cancer/modules/Team%20building.pdf.

Salas, I., N. Kumar, C. Sepulveda, and M. Villanueva. 2007. "Team Building." World Health Organization. who.int/cancer/modules/Team%20building.pdf.

Strong, E.P. n.d. "How to Keep Virtual Teams Engaged." Ariel. arielgroup.com/how-to-keep-virtual-teams-engaged.

Weller, J., M. Boyd, and D. Cumin. 2014. "Teams, Tribes, and Patient Safety: Overcoming Barriers to Effective Teamwork in Healthcare." *Postgraduate Medical Journal* 90:149–154. pmj.bmj.com/content/90/1061/149.

White, J. 2016. "Use Teamwork to Cut Back on Medical Errors." Healthcare Business and Technology, July 18. healthcarebusinesstechnology.com/index-103.htm.

Chapter 9

Ahmed, K., T.T. Wang, H. Ashrafian, A. Darzi, and T. Athanasiou. 2013. "The Effectiveness of Continuing Medical Education for Specialist Recertification." *Canadian Urological Association Journal* 7(7–8): 266–272.

Berdan, B. 2016. "Climbing the Healthcare Summit: A Long-Term Strategic Plan Comes to Fruition to the Benefit of Employees, Patients, and the Community." *TD* 70(2): 50–54.

HealthDay News. 2019. "Study: 1 in 20 Patients Victim of Preventable Medical Error." Health News, United Press International, July 19. upi.com/Health_News/2019/07/19/Study-1-in-20-patients-victim-of-preventable-medical-error/5081563540276.

Joint Accreditation. 2020. "Joint Accreditation Framework." Joint Accreditation for Interprofessional Continuing Education, August. jointaccreditation.org/sites/default/files/816_20200806_JA_Framework.pdf.

National Institute for Occupational Safety and Health (NOISH). 2017. "Healthcare Workers." NOISH, January 13. cdc.gov/niosh/topics/healthcare/default.html.

Rodziewics, T.L., B. Houseman, and J.E. Hipskind. 2020. *Medical Error Prevention.* Treasure Island, FL: StatPearls Publishing.

Weick, K.E., and K.M. Sutcliffe. 2015. *Managing the Unexpected*, 3rd ed. San Francisco: John Wiley.

World Health Organization (WHO). 2019a. "Patient Safety." WHO Fact Sheet, September 13. who.int/news-room/fact-sheets/detail/patient-safety.

World Health Organization (WHO). 2019b. "Patient Safety." WHO Facts in Pictures, March 9. who.int/news-room/facts-in-pictures/detail/patient-safety.

Chapter 10

Achor, S., G.R. Kellerman, A. Reece, and A. Robichaux. 2018. "America's Loneliest Workers, According to Research." *Harvard Business Review*, March 19. hbr.org/2018/03/americas-loneliest-workers-according-to-research.

AFSP (American Foundation for Suicide Prevention). 2020. "Facts About Mental Health and Suicide Among Physicians." datocms-assets.com/12810/1578319045-physician-mental-health-suicide-one-pager.pdf.

AFSP (American Foundation for Suicide Prevention). n.d. "Healthcare Professional Burnout, Depression and Suicide Prevention." AFSP. afsp.org/healthcare-professional-burnout-depression-and-suicide-prevention.

APA (American Psychological Association). 2010. "Stress in America: Stress and Gender." Press release, November 9. apa.org/news/press/releases/stress /2010/gender-stress.pdf.

Berg, S. 2018. "4 Lessons Mayo Clinic Learned from Group Meetings to Cut Burnout." AMA, April 4. ama-assn.org/practice-management/physician-health/4-lessons-mayo-clinic-learned-group-meetings-cut-burnout.

Bloom J.R., S.L. Stewart, M. Johnson, P. Banks, and P. Fobair. 2001. "Sources of Support and the Physical and Mental Well-Being of Young Women With Breast Cancer." *Social Science and Medicine* 53(11): 1513–1524. sciencedirect .com/science/article/abs/pii/S0277953600004408.

Braithwaite, J., J. Herkes, K. Ludlow, L. Testa, and G. Lamprell. 2017. "Association Between Organisational and Workplace Cultures, and Patient Outcomes: Systematic Review." *BMJ* 7(11). bmjopen.bmj.com/content/7/11/e017708.

Brusie, C. 2019. "Study Reveals Alarming Statistics on Nurse Burnout." Nurse.org, April 7. nurse.org/articles/nurse-burnout-statistics.

Burns, K., E. Ewers, and C.I. Ewers, dirs. 2018. *The Mayo Clinic: Faith, Hope and Science. Documentary*, PBS. pbs.org/kenburns/the-mayo-clinic.

Cacioppo, J.T., and W. Patrick. 2008. *Loneliness: Human Nature and the Need for Social Connection.* New York: W.W. Norton & Company.

Clifton, J., and J. Harter. 2019. *It's the Manager: Gallup Find the Quality of Managers and Team Leaders Is the Single Biggest Factor in Your Organization's Long-Term Success.* New York: Gallup Press.

Dahlman, H.R. 2015. Correspondence with authors.

Devine, D., P.A. Parker, R.T. Fouladi, and L. Cohen. 2003. "The Association Between Social Support, Intrusive Thoughts, Avoidance, and Adjustment Following an Experimental Cancer Treatment." *Psycho-oncology* 12(5): 453–462. ncbi.nlm.nih.gov/pubmed/12833558.

Gawande, A. 2020. "Amid the Coronavirus Crisis, a Regimen for Reentry." *New Yorker,* May 13. newyorker.com/science/medical-dispatch/amid-the-coronavirus-crisis-a-regimen-for-reentry.

Grant, A. 2020. "Yes, Even Introverts Can Be Lonely Right Now." *New York Times,* April 16. nytimes.com/2020/04/16/smarter-living/coronavirus-introverts-lonely.html.

Hardin, A.E. 2018. "Getting Acquainted: How Knowing About Colleague's Personal Lives Impacts Workplace Interactions." *Academy of Management Journal,* July 9. journals.aom.org/doi/abs/10.5465/AMBPP.2018.14989abstract.

Jones, S. 2018. Conversations with M.L. Stallard during October and November.

Kane, L. 2020. "Medscape National Physician Burnout & Suicide Report 2020: The Generational Divide." Medscape, January 15. medscape.com/slideshow/2020-lifestyle-burnout-6012460.

Khazan, O. 2018. "Being Black in American Can Be Hazardous to Your Health." *The Atlantic,* July/August. theatlantic.com/magazine/archive/2018/07/being-black-in-america-can-be-hazardous-to-your-health/561740.

Kleiner, A. 2003. *Who Really Matters: The Core Group Theory of Power, Privilege, and Success.* New York: Doubleday.

Lekander M., C.J. Fürst, S. Rotstein, H. Blomgren, and M. Fredrikson. 1996. "Social Support and Immune Status During and After Chemotherapy for Breast Cancer." *Acta Oncologica* 35(1): 31–37. 10.3109/02841869609098476.

Levy, S.M., R.B. Herberman, T. Whiteside, K. Sanzo, J. Lee, and J. Kirkwood. 1990. "Perceived Social Support and Tumor Estrogen/Progesterone Receptor Status as Predictors of Natural Killer Cell Activity in Breast Cancer Patients." *Psychosomatic Medicine* 52(1): 73–85. psycnet.apa.org/record/1990-20194-001.

Lieberman, M. 2013. "The Social Brain and Its Superpowers: Matthew Lieberman, PhD at TEDxStLouis." TEDx Talks, video, October 7, 2013. youtube.com/watch?v =NNhk3owF7RQ.

Lieberman, M. 2019. "Matthew Lieberman: The Social Brain and the Workplace." Talks at Google, video. February 22, 2019. youtube.com/watch?v=h7UR9JwQEYk.

Mayo Clinic. 2007. "Rochester, Minnesota, Mayo Clinic." Information packet. mayoclinic .org/documents/mc6028-pdf/doc-20079214.

Mayo Clinic. 2019. "Mayo Clinic Mission and Values." mayoclinic.org/about-mayo-clinic /mission-values.

McLean, R. 2020. "Dr. McLean's Presidential Address." American College of Physicians. acponline.org/membership/physician-membership/acp-fellowship/dr-mcleans -presidential-address.

Ozcelik, H., and S. Barsade. 2017. "Work Loneliness and Employee Performance." *Academy of Management Proceedings,* October 5. journals.aom.org/doi/pdf /10.5465/ambpp .2011.65869714.

Pardes, H. 2014. "Herbert Pardes, M.D.—2014 Inaugural Pardes Humanitarian Prizewinner." Brain and Behavior Research Foundation, October 27, 2014. youtube.com/watch?v =OPHNjlCNKgw.

Patel, S., A. Pelletier-Bui, S. Smith, M.B. Roberts, H. Kilgannon, S. Trzeciak, and B.W. Roberts. 2019. "Curricula for Empathy and Compassion Training in Medical Education: A Systematic Review." *PLoS ONE* 14(8): e0221412. ncbi.nlm.nih.gov /pmc/articles/PMC6705835/pdf/pone.0221412.pdf.

Pennebaker, J. 1997. *Opening Up: The Healing Power of Expressing Emotions.* New York: Guilford Press.

Rugg, J.E. 2018. "The Connection Value Chain: Impact of Connection Culture and Employee Motivation on Perceived Team Performance." PhD dissertation, Biola University.

Shanafelt, T.D., C.P. West, C. Sinsky, M. Trockel, M. Tutty, D.V. Satele, L.E. Carlasare, and L.N. Dyrbye. 2019. "Changes in Burnout and Satisfaction with Work-Life Integration in Physicians and the General U.S. Working Population Between 2011 and 2017." Mayo Clinic, February 22. mayoclinicproceedings.org/article/S0025 -6196(18)30938-8/fulltext.

Stallard, M.L., J. Pankau, and K.P. Stallard. 2015. *Connection Culture: The Competitive Advantage of Shared Identity, Empathy, and Understanding at Work*, 1st ed. Alexandria, VA: ATD Press.

Stallard, M.L., T.W. Hall, K.P. Stallard, and J. Pankau. 2020. *Connection Culture: The Competitive Advantage of Shared Identity, Empathy, and Understanding at Work*, 2nd ed. Alexandria, VA: ATD Press.

Stodghill, R. 2007. "The Doctor Is In." *New York Times*, January 7. nytimes.com /2007/01 /07/business/yourmoney/07hospital.html?.

TCU and UNTHSC School of Medicine. 2019. "Empathetic Scholar: Communication." mdschool.tcu.edu/empathetic-scholar/communication.

Uchino, B.N., J.T. Cacioppo, and J.K. Kiecolt-Glaser. 1996. "The Relationship Between Social Support and Physiological Processes: A Review With Emphasis on Underlying Mechanisms and Implications for Health." *Psychological Bulletin* 119(3): 488–531.

Utsey, S., N. Giesbrecht, J. Hook, and P. Stanard. 2008. "Cultural, Sociofamilial, and Psychological Resources that Inhibit Psychological Distress in African Americans Exposed to Stressful Life Events and Race-Related Stress." *Journal of Counseling Psychology* 55(1): 49–62.

Chapter 11

Bancroft, E., and G. Bradt. 2016. "The Total Onboarding Program." ATD blog, December 7. td.org/insights/the-total-onboarding-program.

CLO (*Chief Learning Officer*). 2018. "Mastercard Motivates New Hires With Sleek Digital Learning Model." Learning in Practice Award Spotlight. *CLO* magazine, May.

Friedman, D. 2016. "Have Organizations Really Changed Their Onboarding Practices?" Brandon Hall Group, August 9. brandonhall.com/blogs/have -organizations-really-changed-their-onboarding-practices.

Gaul, P. 2017. "Onboarding Is Critical." *TD*, August. td.org/magazines/td-magazine /onboarding-is-critical.

Hirsch, A.S. 2017. "Don't Underestimate the Importance of Good Onboarding." SHRM, August 10. shrm.org/resourcesandtools/hr-topics/talent-acquisition/pages/dont -underestimate-the-importance-of-effective-onboarding.aspx.

Oliver, A. 2020. "How Successful Onboarding Kickstarts Employee Engagement and Retention." ICIMS Hiring Blog, July 31. icims.com/company/blog/article-how-successful-onboarding-kickstarts-employee-engagement-retention.

Schulze, R. 2017. "Millennial Nurses are Headed for the Exit. Here's How to Stop Them." Advisory Board Daily Briefing, September 14. Republished June 11, 2019. advisory.com/en/daily-briefing/2017/09/14/millennial-nursing.

Walker, D., and B. Schneider. 2017. *Better Hires, Better Outcomes. Organizational Impact Summary.* Pittsburgh, PA: DDI.

Williamson, K. 2020. "Online Training, Stat." *TD,* August. td.org/magazines/td-magazine/online-training-stat.

Chapter 12

ATD (Association for Talent Development). 2018. *Upskilling and Reskilling: Turning Disruption and Change into New Capabilities.* Alexandria, VA: ATD Press.

ATD Public Policy Advisory Group. 2018. *Bridging the Skills Gap: Workforce Development and the Future of Work.* Alexandria, VA: ATD Press.

Daniel, M. 2020. "Embark on a Reskilling Initiative." *Training,* September-October.

HCI and Cornerstone People Research Lab. 2020. *The Revolution Is Now: New-Skill Your Workforce to Catalyze Change.* Cincinnati, OH: Human Capital Institute.

Palmer, K. 2020. "7 Steps for Upskilling Your Workforce." Degreed. get.degreed.com/en/7-steps-for-upskilling-your-workforce.

Schwartz, N.D. 2019. "Training Can Change Lives. See How San Antonio Does It." *New York Times,* August 19. nytimes.com/2019/08/19/business/economy/worker-training-project.html.

Weinstein, M. 2020. "The Right Stuff." *Training,* September-October.

Chapter 13

US Bureau of Labor Statistics (BLS). 2020a. "5 out of 20 Fastest-Growing Industries From 2019 to 2029 are in Healthcare and Social Assistance." The Economics Daily, September 4. bls.gov/opub/ted/2020/5-out-of-20-fastest-growing-industries-from-2019-to-2029-are-in-healthcare-and-social-assistance.htm.

US Bureau of Labor Statistics (BLS). 2020b. "May 2020 National Occupational Employment and Wage Estimates United States." Occupational Employment and Wage Statistics, May. bls.gov/oes/current/oes_nat.htm#35-0000.

Chapter 16

Boller, S., and L. Fletcher. 2020. *Design Thinking for Training and Development.* Alexandria, VA: ATD Press.

Business Performance Improvement. 2020. "What Is DMAIC?" PBI. biz-pi.com/what-is-dmaic.

Center for Patient Safety. 2020. "Just/Accountable Culture." CPS. centerforpatientsafety.org/just-culture.

Jackson, B. 2018. "Performance Improvement (PI) in Healthcare." Presentation Transcript. slideplayer.com/slide/12356846.

Robinson, S. 2018. "Why Performance Improvement Is Essential." ATD blog, May 16. td.org/insights/why-performance-improvement-is-essential.

SixSigma. 2017. "Root Cause Analysis (RCA) for Beginners: Root Cause Analysis Tools." Six Sigma, March 8. 6sigma.us/etc/root-cause-analysis-for-beginners.

Swan, E. 2019. "DMAIC." Go Lean Six Sigma, October 25. goleansixsigma.com/dmaic.

Vital, C., M. Hirt, and P. Galagan. 2020. *Capabilities for Talent Development: Shaping the Future of the Profession.* Alexandria, VA: ATD Press.

Wright, D. 2005. *The Ultimate Guide to Competency Assessment in Health Care.* Minneapolis, MN: Creative Health Care Management.

Chapter 17

Association of Healthcare Internal Auditors (AHIA), the American Health Lawyers Association (AHLA), the Health Care Compliance Association (HCCA), and the Office of Inspector General (OIG) of the U.S. Department of Health and Human Services (HHS). 2015. "Practical Guidance for Health Care Governing Boards on Compliance Oversight." AHIA, AHLA, HCCA, and OIG HHS, April 20. oig.hhs.gov/compliance/compliance-guidance/docs/Practical-Guidance-for-Health-Care-Boards-on-Compliance-Oversight.pdf.

Centers for Medicare and Medicaid Services (CMS). 2020. "CMS-Approved Accrediting Organizations Contacts for Prospective Clients." CMS, August 25. cms.gov /Medicare/Provider-Enrollment-and-Certification/SurveyCertificationGenInfo /Downloads/Accrediting-Organization-Contacts-for-Prospective-Clients-.pdf.

DOJ. n.d. "Justice News." justice.gov/news?f%5B0%5D=field_pr_topic%3A3936.

Knowles, M.S., E.F. Holton III, and R.A. Swanson. 2014. *The Adult Learner: The Definitive Classic in Adult Education and Human Resource Development.* New York: Routledge.

New York Office of the Medicaid Inspector General (OMIG). n.d. "Compliance." Accessed June 29, 2020. omig.ny.gov/compliance/compliance.

Office for Civil Rights (OCR). 2013. "Summary of the HIPAA Privacy Rule." HHS.gov, reviewed July 26. hhs.gov/hipaa/for-professionals/privacy/laws-regulations/index.html.

US Department of Health and Human Services Office of the Inspector General (HHS OIG). n.d. "A Roadmap for New Physicians." Office of Inspector General US Department of Health & Human Services (OIG HHS). oig.hhs.gov/compliance/physician -education/01laws.asp.

US Department of Health and Human Services Office of the Inspector General (HHS OIG). n.d. "Compliance Guidance." U.S. Department of Health and Human Services, accessed June 29, 2000. oig.hhs.gov/compliance/compliance-guidance/index.asp.

US Department of Health and Human Services Office of the Inspector General (HHS OIG). n.d. "Enforcement Actions." oig.hhs.gov/fraud/enforcement/index.asp.

US Department of Health and Human Services Office of the Inspector General (HHS OIG). 1998. "Publication of the OIG Compliance Program Guidance for Hospitals." *Federal Register* 63(35): February 23.

US Department of Health and Human Services Office of the Inspector General (HHS OIG). 2017. "Measuring Compliance Program Effectiveness: A Resource Guide." March 27. oig.hhs.gov/compliance/compliance-resource-portal/files/HCCA-OIG-Resource -Guide.pdf.

US Department of Justice (DOJ). 2020. "Criminal Division Evaluation of Corporate Compliance Programs." Updated June. justice.gov/criminal-fraud/page/file/937501 /download.

US General Accounting Office (US GAO). 1998. "MEDICARE: Concerns with Physicians at Teaching Hospitals (PATH) Audits." Report to the Chairman, Subcommittee on

Health, Committee on Ways and Means, House of Representatives, July 23. GAO /HEHS-98-174. gao.gov/assets/hehs-98-174.pdf.

US Sentencing Commission (USSC). 2018. "Guidelines Manual, §3E1.1, §8B2.1." November.

Chapter 19

Allen, R. 2019. "Innovative 'Cut-Suit' Brings Life to Trauma Simulations." UC Health, August 28. uchealth.org/today/cut-suit-trauma-training.

Bersin by Deloitte. 2014. "Meet the Modern Learner." Infographic. deloitte.com/content /dam/Deloitte/global/Documents/HumanCapital/gx-cons-hc-learning-solutions -placemat.pdf.

Bhanji, F., A.J. Donoghue, M.S. Wolff, G.E. Flores, L.P. Halamek, J.M. Berman, E.H. Sinz, and A. Cheng. 2015. "2015 American Heart Association Guidelines Update for Cardiopulmonary Resuscitation and Emergency Cardiovascular Care." *Circulation* 132(suppl 2): S561-S573.

Cowperthwait, A.L., et al. 2015. "Tracheostomy Overlay System: An Effective Learning Device Using Standardized Patients." *Clinical Simulation in Nursing* 11:253–358.

Fox, D. 2020. "Learning Engagement in a Time of Zoom Fatigue." ATD blog, May 11. td.org/insights/learning-engagement-in-a-time-of-zoom-fatigue.

Goolsby, C. 2014. "New Wide Area Virtual Environment (WAVE) Medical Education." *Military Medicine* 179:38–41.

Harper, M.G., and P. Maloney, eds. 2016. "Nursing Professional Development: Scope and Standards of Practice." Association for Nursing Professional Development (ANPD).

Holtschneider, M.E. 2017. "Expanding the Fidelity of Standardized Patients in Simulation by Incorporating Wearable Technology." *Journal for Nurses in Professional Development* 33(6): 320–321.

International Nursing Association for Clinical Simulation and Learning (INACSL). 2021. "Healthcare Simulation Standards of Best Practice." inacsl.org/inacsl-standards -of-best-practice-simulation.

Interprofessional Education Collaborative. 2016. "Core Competencies for Interprofessional Collaborative Practice: 2016." IPEC. aamc-meded.global.ssl.fastly.net/production /media/filer_public/70/9f/709fedd7-3c53-492c-b9f0-b13715d11cb6/core _competencies_for_collaborative_practice.pdf.

Kotter, J.P. 2012. *Leading Change.* Boston: Harvard Business School Publishing.

Meaney, P., et al. 2013. "Cardiopulmonary Resuscitation Quality: Improving Cardiac Resuscitation Outcomes Both Inside and Outside the Hospital—A Consensus Statement From the American Heart Association." *Circulation* 128:417–435.

Torgerson, C., and S. Iannone. 2019. *Designing Microlearning.* Alexandria, VA: ATD Press.

Wong, N., C. Peng, C.W. Park, J. Pérez, A. Vashi, J. Robinson, and Y. Okuda. 2020. "Debrief Live: A Pilot Study of a Virtual Faculty Development Tool for Debriefing." *Simulation in Healthcare* 15(5): 363–369.

Chapter 20

Davis, V. 2017. "5 Critical Skills to Look for in EHR Trainers," Healthcare IT Leaders (blog), January 9. healthcareitleaders.com/blog/5-critical-skills-to-look-for-in-ehr-trainers.

Ermo, L.A. 2019. "A Targeted Approach to EHR Training Improves Success Rates." *For The Record* 30(9): 22. fortherecordmag.com/archives/1018p22.shtml.

Gray, C. n.d. "Blended Learning: Why Everything Old is New Again—But Better." ATD Links, td.org/newsletters/atd-links/blended-learning-why-everything-old-is-new-again-but-better.

HHS (U.S. Department of Health & Human Services). 2017. "HITECH Act Enforcement Interim Final Rule." HHS, June 16. hhs.gov/hipaa/for-professionals/special-topics/hitech-act-enforcement-interim-final-rule/index.html.

Jeffery, J. 2018. "Training Matters! Don't Sell your EHR Experience Short." KLAS blog, July 17. klasresearch.com/resources/blogs/2018/07/17/training-matters-dont-sell-your-ehr-experience-short.

Longhurst, C.A., T. Davis, A. Maneker, H.C. Eschenroeder Jr, R. Dunscombe, G. Reynolds, B. Clay, T. Moran, D.B. Graham, S.M. Dean, and J. Adler-Milstein. 2019. "Local Investment in Training Drives Electronic Health Record User Satisfaction." *Applied Clinical Informatics* 10(2): 331–335. doi: 10.1055/s-0039-1688753.

McCain, C. L. 2008. "The Right Mix to Support Electronic Medical Record Training: Classroom Computer-Based Training and Blended Learning." *Journal for Nurses in Staff Development* 24(4): 151–154. doi: 10.1097/01.NND.0000320673.65824.db.

MeHI (Massachusetts eHealth Institute). n.d. "Boston Health Care for the Homeless Program (BHCHP) Puts Meaningful Use in Perspective." Accessed October 24, 2020. mehi.masstech.org/education/spotlights-stories/massachusetts-ehr-success-stories/boston-healthcare-homeless-puts.

Miller, V.L. 2015. "EMR Training Tactics: A Case Study of Clinical Staff Training Experiences, Needs and Perceptions." PhD thesis, University of Arkansas. scholarworks.uark.edu/etd/1086.

ONC (Office of the National Coordinator for Health Information Technology). 2019. "What Are the Differences Between Electronic Medical Records, Electronic Health Records, and Personal Health Records?" ONC, May 2. healthit.gov/faq/what-are-differences-between-electronic-medical-records-electronic-health-records-and-personal.

ONC (Office of the National Coordinator for Health Information Technology). 2019. "Improved Diagnostics & Patient Outcomes" ONC, June 4. healthit.gov/topic/health-it-and-health-information-exchange-basics/improved-diagnostics-patient-outcomes.

Sharp, K., M. Williams, A. Aldrich, A. Bogacz, S. Denier, A.S. McAlearney. 2017. "Conversion of Provider EMR Training From Instructor-Led Training to eLearning at an Academic Medical Center." *Applied Clinical Informatics* 8(3): 754–762. doi: 10.4338/ACI-2017-03-CR-0040.

Siwicki, B. 2019. "Implementation Best Practices: The Keys to Launching an HER." HealthcareITNews, April 18. healthcareitnews.com/news/implementation-best-practices-keys-launching-ehr.

Smailes, P.S., J. Zurmehly, C. Schubert, J.M. Loversidge, L.T. Sinnott. 2019. "An Electronic Medical Record Training Conversion for Onboarding Inpatient Nurses." *CIN: Computers, Informatics, Nursing* 37(8):405–412. doi: 10.1097/CIN.0000000000000514.

Chapter 21

Levine, A.I., S. DeMaria, A.D. Schwartz, and A.J. Sim. 2013. *The Comprehensive Textbook of Healthcare Simulation.* New York: Springer.

Lioce, L., ed. 2020. *Healthcare Simulation Dictionary,* 2nd ed. Rockville, MD: Agency for Healthcare Research and Quality. ssih.org/Dictionary.

Palaganas, J.C. 2015. *Defining Excellence in Simulation Programs.* Philadelphia: Springer.

Society for Simulation in Healthcare. n.d. "SSH Accreditation of Healthcare Simulation Programs." ssih.org/Credentialing/Accreditation.

Chapter 22

Acumen Research and Consulting. 2020. "Artificial Intelligence (AI) Market Exceed US$ 160 Bn 2026." Acumen Research and Consulting, January 23. acumenresearchandconsulting.com/artificial-intelligence-ai-market.

Advisory Board. 2019a. "How Deep Learning Dramatically Improved Breast Cancer Prediction Modeling—Especially for African American Patients." The Advisory Board, May 21. advisory.com/blog/2019/05/deep-learning.

Advisory Board. 2019b. "Your First Look at our 2019 Revenue Cycle Benchmarks." Advisory Board webinar, October 16. advisory.com/topics/classic/2019/10/your-first-look-at-our-2019-revenue-cycle-benchmarks.

Ash, M., J. Petro, and S. Rab. 2019. "How AI in the Exam Room Could Reduce Physician Burnout." *Harvard Business Review*, November 12. hbr.org/2019/11/how-ai-in-the-exam-room-could-reduce-physician-burnout.

Gartner. 2012. "Best Practices in Analytics: Integrating Analytical Capabilities and Process Flows." Gartner, March 27.

Global Market Insights. 2020. *Healthcare Artificial Intelligence Market Size by Application (Medical Imaging & Diagnosis, Drug Discovery, Therapy Planning, Hospital Workflow, Wearables, Virtual Assistants) Industry Analysis Report, Regional Outlook, Application Potential, Competitive Market Share & Forecast, 2019–2025.* Global Market Insights, February. gminsights.com/industry-analysis/healthcare-artificial-intelligence-market.

Marr, B. 2018. "The Key Definitions of Artificial Intelligence (AI) That Explain Its Importance." *Forbes*, February 14. forbes.com/sites/bernardmarr/2018/02/14/the-key-definitions-of-artificial-intelligence-ai-that-explain-its-importance.

Medscape. 2020. *National Physician Burnout & Suicide Report 2020.* Medscape, January 15.

Mehrotra, T. 2019. "Lessons Learned: Experience With AI in Healthcare." Becker's Healthcare, January 2. beckershospitalreview.com/healthcare-information-technology/lessons-learned-experience-with-ai-in-healthcare.html.

Morgan, B. 2019. "The 20 Best Examples of Using Artificial Intelligence for Retail Experiences." *Forbes*, March 4. forbes.com/sites/blakemorgan/2019/03/04/the-20-best-examples-of-using-artificial-intelligence-for-retail-experiences/?sh=7b36c2aa4466.

Optum. 2012. "Optum Enterprise Computer-Assisted Coding." Optum, September.

Optum. 2018. "AI for Health Care: Supporting Providers in Delivering Better Care." Optum, November 19. healthcare-conversation.com/2018/11/19/ai-for-health-care-supporting-providers-in-delivering-better-care.

OptumIQ. 2019. "Annual Survey on AI in Health Care." OptumIQ, October 8.

OptumIQ. 2020. "Annual Optum Survey on AI in Health Care." Optum IQ, October 27.

Rebhan, A. 2018. "The Artificial Intelligence Ecosystem." The Advisory Board, April 6. advisory.com/en/topics/artificial-intelligence/2018/04/the-artificial-intelligence-ecosystem.

StartUp Health. 2019. "Could AI-Driven Medical Billing Be the Key to Keeping Struggling Hospitals in the Black." StartUp + Health, March 26. healthtransformer.co/could-ai-driven-medical-billing-be-the-key-to-keeping-struggling-hospitals-in-the-black-222c6a25f10b.

Chapter 23

Institute for Patient- and Family-Centered Care (IPFCC). n.d. "Core Concepts of Patient- and Family-Centered Care." ipfcc.org/about/pfcc.html.

Johnson, B.H., and M.R. Abraham. 2012. *Partnering with Patients, Residents, and Families: A Resource for Leaders of Hospitals, Ambulatory Care Settings, and Long-Term Care Communities.* Bethesda, MD: Institute for Patient- and Family-Centered Care.

Press, I. 2014. "Concern for the Patient's Experience Comes of Age." *Patient Experience Journal* 1(1): 4–6. pxjournal.org/journal/vol1/iss1/3.

The Beryl Institute. n.d. "Patient Experience Case Study: Stanford Health Care." The Beryl Institute. theberylinstitute.org/page/CASE1118.

The Beryl Institute. 2018. "Experience Framework: Guiding Your Experience Efforts." The Beryl Institute. theberylinstitute.org/page/ExperienceFramework.

The Beryl Institute and Ipsos. 2020. "Consumer Perspectives on Patient Experience in the U.S." *PX Pulse,* July. theberylinstitute.org/page/PXPULSEJuly2020.

Wolf, J.A. 2017. "Patient Experience: The New Heart of Healthcare Leadership." *Frontiers of Health Services Management* 33(3): 3–16.

Wolf, J.A. 2018. "Consumer Perspectives on Patient Experience 2018." Nashville, TN: The Beryl Institute.

Wolf, J.A. 2019. "The State of Patient Experience 2019." Nashville, TN: The Beryl Institute.

Wolf, J.A. 2020. "Human Experience 2030: A Vision for the Future of Healthcare." Nashville, TN: The Beryl Institute.

Wolf, J.A., V. Niederhauser, D. Marshburn, and S. LaVela. 2014a. *Defining Patient Experience: A Critical Decision for Healthcare Organizations.* Nashville, TN: The Beryl Institute.

Wolf, J.A., V. Niederhauser, D. Marshburn, and S. LaVela. 2014b. "Defining Patient Experience." *Patient Experience Journal* 1(1): 7–19. pxjournal.org/journal/vol1/iss1/3.

Wolf, J.A., V. Niederhauser, D. Marshburn, and S. LaVela. 2021. "Reexamining '*Defining Patient Experience*': The Human Experience in Healthcare." *Patient Experience Journal* 8(1).

Chapter 24

Ishikawa, K. 1985. *What Is Total Quality Control? The Japanese Way.* Translated by D.J. Lu. Englewood Cliffs, NJ: Prentice-Hall.

McCormick, I.A., F.H. Walkey, and D.E. Green. 1986. "Comparative Perceptions of Drive Availability—A Confirmation and Expansion." *Accident Analysis & Prevention* 18 (3): 205–208. sciencedirect.com/science/article/abs/pii/0001457586900047.

US Food and Drug Administration (FDA). 2020. "Emergency Use Authorization for Vaccines Explained." US FDA, November 20. fda.gov/vaccines-blood-biologics/vaccines/emergency-use-authorization-vaccines-explained.

Chapter 25

Aspden, P., J.M. Corrigan, J. Wolcott, et al., eds. 2003. *Patient Safety: Achieving a New Standard for Care. Institute of Medicine Committee on Data Standards for Patient Safety.* Washington, DC: National Academies Press.

Cleary, P.D., S. Edgman-Levitan, M. Roberts, T.W. Moloney, et al. 1991. "Patients Evaluate Their Hospital Care: A National Survey." *Health Affairs* 10(4).

Committee on Quality Health Care in America. 2001. *Crossing the Quality Chasm: A New Health System for the 21st Century.* Institute of Medicine Committee on Quality of Health Care in America. Washington, DC: National Academies Press.

Franklin, S.S., L. Thijs, T.W. Hansen, E. O'Brien, and J.A. Staessen. 2013. "White-Coat Hypertension: New Insights From Recent Studies." *Hypertension* 62(6): 982–987.

Gawande, A. 2009. *The Checklist Manifesto: How to Get Things Right.* New York: Metropolitan Books.

James, J.T. 2013. "A New, Evidence-Based Estimate of Patient Harms Associated with Hospital Care." *Journal of Patient Safety* 9(3): 122–128. journals.lww.com/journalpatientsafety/Fulltext/2013/09000/A_New,_Evidence_based_Estimate_of_Patient_Harms.2.aspx.

Kohn, L.T., J.M. Corrigan, and M.S. Donaldson, eds. 2000. *To Err Is Human: Building a Safer Health System. Institute of Medicine Committee on Quality of Health Care in America.* Washington, DC: National Academies Press.

Makary, M., and M. Daniel. 2016. "Medical Error—The Third Leading Cause of Death in the US." *The British Medical Journal.* bmj.com/content/353/bmj.i2139.

Ofri, D. 2020. *When We Do Harm: A Doctor Confronts Medical Error.* New York: Penguin Random House.

Storesund, A. et al. 2020. "Clinical Efficacy of Combined Surgical Patient Safety System and the World Health Organization's Checklists in Surgery: A Nonrandomized Clinical Trial." *JAMA Surgery* 155(7): 562–570.

US Food and Drug Administration (FDA). 2018. "Milestones in US Food and Drug Law." FDA History, January 31. fda.gov/media/73549/download.

World Health Organization (WHO). 2009. "Surgical Safety Checklist." who.int/teams/integrated-health-services/patient-safety/research/safe-surgery/tool-and-resources.

Chapter 26

Chee, T.T., A.M. Ryan, J.H. Wasfy, and W.B. Borden. 2016. "Current State of Value-Based Purchasing Programs." *Circulation* 133(22): 2197–2205. doi.org/10.1161/CIRCULATIONAHA.115.010268.

CMS (Centers for Medicare and Medicaid Services). 2020a. "The HCAHPS Survey: Frequently Asked Questions." cms.gov/Medicare/Quality-Initiatives-Patient-Assessment-Instruments/HospitalQualityInits/Downloads/HCAHPSFAQ092713.pdf.

CMS (Centers for Medicare and Medicaid Services). 2020b. "HCAHPS: Patients' Perspectives of Care Survey." cms.gov/Medicare/Quality-Initiatives-Patient-Assessment-Instruments/HospitalQualityInits/HospitalHCAHPS.

Galvin, J.W., J.C. Thompson, A.M. Thompson, S.A. Parada, J.K. Eichinger, J.F. Dickens, and B.L. Gillingham. 2019. "A Guide to Understanding Reimbursement and

Value-Based Care in the Military Health System." *Military Medicine* 184 (3-4): e205–e210. doi.org/10.1093/milmed/usy206.

IHI (Institute for Healthcare Improvement). n.d. "The IHI Triple Aim: Initiatives." ihi.org/Engage/Initiatives/TripleAim/Pages/default.aspx.

NCOA (National Council on Aging). 2021. "Accountable Care Organizations and the Benefits of Partnering for CDSME." NCOA, May 13. ncoa.org/article/accountable-care-organizations-and-the-benefits-of-partnering-for-cdsme.

Pendleton, R.C. 2018. "We Won't Get Value-Based Health Care Until We Agree on What 'Value' Means." *Harvard Business Review,* February 27. hbr.org/2018/02/we-wont-get-value-based-health-care-until-we-agree-on-what-value-means.

Porter, M.E., and E. Teisberg. 2004. "Redifining Competition in Health Care." *Harvard Business Review,* June. hbr.org/2004/06/redefining-competition-in-health-care.

Porter, M.E., and E.O. Teisberg. 2006. *Redefining Health Care: Creating Value-Based Competition on Results.* Boston: Harvard Business School Press.

Whittington, J.W., K. Nolan, N. Lewis, and T. Torres. 2015. "Pursuing the Triple Aim: The First 7 Years." *Milbank Q* 93(2): 263–300. pubmed.ncbi.nlm.nih.gov/26044630.

WHO (World Health Organization). 2010. *Framework for Action on Interprofessional Education and Collaborative Practice.* Geneva, Switzerland: WHO Press.

ABOUT THE CONTRIBUTORS

Candy Baptist

Candy Baptist is the director of the career transformation center for Texas Health Resources, where she is responsible for strategic academic partnerships, career pathing, and workforce grants. Most recently she has been creating a program that offers career planning for role-specific competencies, career paths, and learning resources. In prior roles she has led system clinical education, strategic learning initiatives, and workforce pipeline programs. Candy also serves as an associate professor at the University of Texas at Arlington, College of Business MHA program. As a registered nurse, she has incorporated her healthcare knowledge and experience in roles ranging from staff to C-suite to preparing graduate students to take on administrative roles within the complex landscape of healthcare. Candy has a BS in nursing from the University of Texas at Arlington and a master's degree in health management services from the University of Mary Hardin Baylor.

Christina Barss

Christina Barss holds a PhD in management and sustainable systems design from Case Western Reserve University. She leveraged her Lean Six Sigma Black Belt expertise studying successful interprofessional teams during strategic lean transformation at Cleveland Clinic, finding insights into how goals, location, communication, and relationships influence team efficacy. Her post-graduate studies include completing a certificate in applied positive psychology. Christina has extensive experience in talent optimization, specifically in executive education and succession planning. She has taught in higher education for more than 14 years, with a focus on continuous improvement, organizational leadership, and change management.

Timothy R. Brock

Tim Brock is a senior consultant at ROI Institute, where he helps organizations implement the ROI Methodology. He facilitates ATD's Evaluating Learning Impact and Measuring Return on Investment certificate courses, and is a faculty member at Capella University, where he teaches master's and doctoral degree courses in the principles and practices of performance improvement and program measurement, assessment, and evaluation. Tim also serves as a mentor, program reviewer, and school reviewer for doctoral applied research capstone projects. While at his previous position at Lockheed Martin, Tim was responsible for leading a team of 26 people to invent innovative, systemic human performance improvement solutions to solve evolving customer workplace outcome and organization result challenges that included multiple healthcare environments. Tim has a PhD with a specialization in training and performance improvement from Capella University and is a Certified Performance Technologist, Certified ROI Professional, Certified Performance Improvement Facilitator, and Certified Designer of Training with a specialization in simulation and labs. He retired from the US Air Force after serving in both the enlisted and officer ranks. Tim has written chapters about performance improvement and evaluation for two healthcare books, and has published multiple articles on performance improvement and evaluation topics. He has also spoken about these subjects at conferences around the world. Tim lives in Orlando, Florida, with his wife, three grown children, and three grandchildren.

M. Lynn Fischer

M. Lynn Fischer is founder and CEO of Catalyst Learning Company (CLC), which provides high-quality skill and career development programs to healthcare organizations across the US. These programs target the frontline associates of the organization—from entry-level individuals to first-level supervisory nurses. Lynn's passion for helping low-skilled, low-wage employees increase their skills and wages led her and her team to create the School at Work model in 1998. Recognizing that the healthcare employers are uniquely motivated to "grow their own" employees, she began in 2005 to shift CLC's focus to the healthcare sector. Lynn serves on the board of Jefferson Community and Technical College (Jefferson) Foundation, where she has an active role in elevating community understanding of the key role that Jefferson plays in workforce development, serving nontraditional students, and raising per-capita income in the Louisville region. She is a past member of the Jefferson Board of Directors, the Kentucky Medical Licensure Board, Bellarmine University, Kentuckiana Works, and the Louisville Free Public Library Foundation. In 2010, Lynn served as field director in her brother Greg Fischer's successful campaign for mayor of Louisville. She holds a BA in mass communications from the University of Denver and is a graduate of the Goldman Sachs 10,000 Small Businesses program.

Daniel Gandarilla

Daniel Gandarilla serves as the senior vice president and chief talent officer for Atrium Health. In this capacity he is responsible for the strategic oversight of core talent processes including learning, leader development, performance management, succession, career mobility, and employee experience for the enterprise. Previously, Daniel served as the vice president and chief learning officer for Texas Health, where he led a team to Gold Level Learning Elite Awards and helped the organization place in the top 10 Learning Elite companies. Daniel balances his passion for learning and driving transformational change with the most important activities in life: volunteering, quality time with his wife and two daughters, long walks listening to NPR podcasts, finding quality coffee, and completing his taxes. He holds bachelor's degrees in psychology and political science and a master's degree in education from Stanford University. He also has an MBA and EdD, with an emphasis in education leadership, from Texas Christian University.

Jenny Harshman

Jenny Harshman, MSN, RN, NPD-BC, CPN, CCRN-K, is a nursing professional development leader at Children's Health in Dallas, Texas. She serves as the manager of clinical education in the Learning and Leadership Institute and has a special interest in how modern learning design affects outcomes. Jenny has presented on social learning and redesigning learning methods at multiple national conferences and enjoys writing blogs for professional organizations like ANPD and ATD. She was named Educator of the Year in 2018 at Children's Medical Center of Dallas. Jenny is a recipient of D Magazine's Nurse Excellence Award in Education and Research and was named one of DFW's Great 100 Nurses of 2020. Jenny lives in Dallas with her supportive husband and two dogs, and enjoys reading and traveling whenever possible. She is appreciative of the continued support from her leaders and team as she worked through ideas and drafts of this chapter.

Denise Hicken

Denise Hicken, MEd, CPTD, has spent more than two decades working in talent development. Her first talent development position was director of professional development at a large bank in Missouri. After moving to Atlanta, Denise held a contract instructional designer position at AT&T before moving to her current position of senior learning consultant for Atrium Health Floyd, formally Floyd Health System. Prior to working in talent development, she enjoyed a career as a television executive news producer. Denise holds a bachelor's degree in journalism and an MEd in educational technology from the University of Missouri and has earned the designation of Certified Professional in Talent Development from ATD. Denise volunteers as a CPTD test item writer, and has also been a volunteer judge for ATD's BEST Awards and Excellence in Practice Awards.

Mary E. Holtschneider

Mary E. Holtschneider, MEd, MPA, RN, CPTD, is simulation education coordinator and nursing professional development specialist at the Durham, North Carolina, Veterans Affairs (VA) Health Care System. She also serves as nursing program manager for Duke University Area Health Education Center (AHEC), part of the North Carolina AHEC system dedicated to educating healthcare professionals throughout the state. Mary is a co-director of the Interprofessional Advanced Fellowship in Clinical Simulation at the Durham VA Health Care System, a yearlong fellowship designed to mentor future leaders in healthcare simulation and education. Mary also serves as a co-editor for the bimonthly "Interprofessional Learning Environments" column for the *Journal for Nurses in Professional Development.* She speaks and writes frequently on simulation, leadership, mindfulness, interprofessional education, and how best practices from the simulation educational arena can be integrated throughout the healthcare continuum. Mary is an active volunteer for ATD as a CPTD item writer, awards reviewer, and past ATD-Research Triangle Area (RTA) chapter president.

Ryan Kane

Ryan Kane, PhD, is an organization development and talent management professional with a passion for helping others learn, develop, and improve their performance. Ryan is certified in change management execution and industry leading assessment tools. In the last 20 years, he has applied his skills in the fields of healthcare, finance, academia, and consumer packaged goods. Ryan is currently the assistant vice president in talent and development at a financial services firm in New York City, where he oversees global onboarding, manager effectiveness, and employee experience surveys.

Scott Kashman

Scott Kashman is market president for Franciscan Missionaries of our Lady Health's ministries in Jackson, Mississippi. He also leads the St. Dominic Health Services and St. Dominic Hospital. He started his career as a psychiatric counselor and has been in healthcare executive roles for more than 25 years. His most recent positions include serving as the chief officer of hospital operations for a $2 billion health system and system vice president of administration and governance, with a focus on board priorities, advocacy, and the community health improvement strategy in an $8 billion organization. He is an executive coach and advisor and fellow with the American College of Healthcare Executives. Scott is the co-author of *Mindful Healthcare: Healthy Team, Healthy Business.*

Naomi Joan Kinney

Naomi Joan Kinney, CPTD, is an experienced training industry leader, certified instructional designer, and facilitator of professional development training in varying subject matter and across several industries (including mortgage banking and finance, healthcare, retail, insurance, and higher education). Over her extensive training career, she has helped hospitals and Fortune 500 organizations maintain federal, state, and local regulatory compliance. She is a published author in the subjects of leadership development, diversity and inclusion, instructional design, and project management. Naomi has won awards for her community service and training, and is the recipient of the ATD's Certification Institute 2016 CPLP Contributor Award. Always working on an education-focused volunteer project, Naomi is currently co-chair (and one of the original curriculum designers) of the McKoin Leadership Training Academy (for women of color in local politics) via Delta Sigma Theta Sorority, her sorority. In college, Naomi received a scholarship to study, live, and travel in Mexico. Professionally, she has always involved language in her training career, and is now more fluent in Spanish. She eventually became a certified healthcare interpreter, and in 2005 created the Interpreter Services Program at Providence Hospital DC, where she was serving as the education director. She has since taken on several leadership positions in training, training not only audiences, but many trainers along the way. Naomi is now an independent training consultant and owns the Spanish-language training business LingoBits Learning Services. Her lifelong mission of educating and training others in language and other professional development subject matter continues. Currently, she lives in Hyattsville, Maryland, with her college-student daughter, Julia, and pet beagle, Kiki.

Gretchen Matika Kolb

Gretchen Kolb has served as the director of learning innovation at Penn Medicine Academy since 2016, providing leadership and strategic direction on the coordinated application of learning strategies including online, mobile, virtual, microlearning, classroom, and simulation. Prior to this expanded role she was the director of simulation at Penn Medicine, responsible for overseeing all simulation activities, both unit-based and those taking place in the Penn Medicine Clinical Simulation Center, where she began her simulation experience as director of operations in 2008. Under her leadership Penn Medicine Simulation was one of the first programs to receive accreditation by the International Society for Simulation in Healthcare. Gretchen started her career at the Hospital of the University of Pennsylvania in 2002 as director of professional medical education for the department of surgery. She has an MS in genetic counseling from the University of Pittsburgh School of Public Health and worked clinically as a certified pediatric and cancer genetic counselor from 1997 to 2008 at Children's Hospital of Pittsburgh, Thomas Jefferson University Health System, and the Hospital of the University of Pennsylvania. She also has a BA in biology from Colgate University in Hamilton, New York.

Ben Locwin

Ben Locwin is a clinical expert and healthcare futurist. His work has included developing and commercializing pharmaceutical therapies and medical technologies for oncology, cardiology, immunology, neurology, psychiatry, and other indications. This has included work in molecular development, clinical trial design and conduct, and many successful product launches. Ben has ushered in many innovations to clinical care practice and emergent care settings, which have systematically reduced medication errors, surgical complication rates, and improved patient-centric care. During the COVID-19 pandemic, Ben was appointed to various committees and task forces for epidemiology and public health oversight, as well as to improve vaccination rates nationwide. He has worked closely with the FDA, CDC, and WHO. Ben has been widely featured in top-tier media, including *Wall Street Journal, Forbes, USA Today,* and CNN.

Dale Ludwig

Dale Ludwig, PhD, is the founder and president of Turpin Communication, a communication training firm based in Chicago. Along with his colleagues, he provides training and coaching to business presenters, meeting facilitators, and trainers. He founded Turpin Communication in 1992 with the mission of providing the best presentation and facilitation skills training available. Since then, he has worked to do just that. In addition to being one of Turpin's lead instructors, Dale is the chief learning architect when tailoring learning engagements for clients. He holds the Bates ExPI coaching certification. Dale is a frequent blogger and the co-author of three books—*The Orderly Conversation, The Virtual Orderly Conversation,* and *Effective SMEs*—with Turpin's VP, Greg Owen-Boger. Prior to Turpin, Dale taught at the University of Illinois at Urbana-Champaign.

Dawn J. Mahoney

Dawn Mahoney, CPTD, is a talent development professional who is passionate about developing people through better learning content, better learning strategy, and better dialogue. In 2015, Dawn founded Learning in the White Space, a boutique consultancy devoted to planning learning strategies and bringing them to life. Dawn speaks and writes on most things learning and development. She has contributed to several books over the years and authored the *TD at Work* issue, "Lean Learning Using the ADDIE Model."

Pamela Mann

Pamela Mann is a clinical learning consultant at University Health in San Antonio, Texas, where she has worked for 28 years. She designs and facilitates instructor-led and virtual clinical and nonclinical courses to meet the continuing education needs of the University Health staff. She also holds an academic adjunct faculty appointment to San Antonio College School of Nursing and facilitates a critical care nursing clinical rotation at University Hospital for fourth-semester nursing students. Highlights of her career include speaking at the ATD 2019 International Conference & EXPO and earning the APTD credential in September 2019. She has been certified in nursing professional development by the

American Nurses Credentialing Center since 1993. In addition, she has been a registered nurse for 37 years and holds a master of science in nursing from the Medical College of Virginia/Virginia Commonwealth University in Richmond, Virginia.

Tushar Mehrotra

Tushar Mehrotra is SVP of analytics at Optum, where he leads the analytics services and solutions business across payer and provider segments. He is responsible for leading a team of 100+ analytics professionals including data scientists, health economists, and actuaries to serve healthcare clients (payer, provider, and life sciences) on their most pressing data and analytics needs, including data platforms, engineering, actuarial modeling, data science, and AI/ML. Prior to joining Optum, Tushar spent seven years at McKinsey & Company in Washington, DC, as an associate partner, where he was one of the core leaders in the North America Digital and Analytics practice for healthcare. He has published articles on healthcare digital and analytics topics and has served on panels and roundtables with leaders in the industry. Tushar has a BS in electrical engineering from the University of Illinois at Urbana-Champaign and an MBA in strategic management and finance from the Wharton School at the University of Pennsylvania.

Suzanne Mell

Suzanne Mell, MSN, RN, is a dynamic leader with more than 35 years of clinical and operational leadership. Her expertise in clinical workflows, risk analysis, regulatory compliance, technological algorithms, and clinical documentation fills her success portfolio with wins in clinical leadership, operational leadership, access, call center operations, growth strategies, and healthcare reform. She is adept at change management, implementing population health initiatives, value-based care and advanced care models at Cleveland Clinic and Houston Methodist. She is a founding member of the Council for Ohio Health Care Advocacy. Suzanne has a BSN from Elmhurst College, an MSN from Kent State University, and a graduate certificate in health care management from Rice University.

Greg Owen-Boger

Greg Owen-Boger is the vice president of Turpin Communication, a communication training firm based in Chicago. Greg believes in the Turpin vision—a future in which meetings, presentations, and training sessions are the least frustrating parts of doing business. Schooled in management and the performing arts, Greg brings a diverse set of skills and experiences to the organization. He is one of Turpin's facilitators and coaches, and he holds the Bates ExPI coaching certification. When he's not with clients, he manages the day-to-day operations of the company. Greg is an active member of the Association for Talent Development and was president of the ATD Chicagoland Chapter in 2015. He is a popular speaker and blogger, a frequent podcast guest, and the co-author of three books—*The Orderly Conversation*, *The Virtual Orderly Conversation*, and *Effective SMEs*—with Turpin's president, Dale Ludwig.

Chan W. Park

Chan W. Park, MD, FAAEM, is the director of simulation education at the Durham, North Carolina Veterans Affairs (VA) Health Care System, where he also serves as co-director of the Interprofessional Advanced Fellowship in Clinical Simulation, a yearlong fellowship designed to mentor future leaders in healthcare simulation and education. In addition, Chan also serves as an adjunct assistant professor of emergency medicine, a faculty member at the Duke University Medical School Leadership Education and Development program, and a senior faculty advisor for the John A. Feagin Leadership Program, all at Duke University Medical Center. Chan serves as a co-editor for the bimonthly "Interprofessional Learning Environments" column for the *Journal for Nurses in Professional Development*, and he speaks and writes frequently on simulation, leadership, mindfulness, interprofessional education, and how best practices from the simulation educational arena can be integrated throughout the healthcare continuum.

Christine F. Reyes

Christine F. Reyes, MBA, FHFMA, CPTD, serves as the director of Dimensions acute training at Novant Health. There she leads a world-class team in development and delivery of education and learning tools for clinicians to provide remarkable care in their use of Dimensions (Epic) electronic health record and integrated applications and devices. During the pandemic, she led the corporate initiative for rapid onboarding and has been instrumental in the development of hiring and onboarding processes as the organization moved to normal operations. Christine has more than 20 years' experience in healthcare, learning and development, applications management, and revenue cycle management. She is an advocate for adult literacy, upskilling, reskilling, and upward mobility. Christine earned a Certified Professional in Talent Development certification from ATD, is a Kirkpatrick Certified Professional Bronze Level and Strategic Evaluation Planning, and is a Fellow of the Healthcare Financial Management Association.

Katharine P. Stallard

Katharine P. Stallard is a partner at Connection Culture Group. In addition to being a workshop leader, Katie is a contributor to *Connection Culture: The Competitive Advantage of Shared Identity, Empathy, and Understanding at Work*, and has co-authored articles that have appeared in *HR Magazine*, *Leader to Leader*, and *TD* magazine.

Michael Lee Stallard

Michael Lee Stallard is a keynote speaker, workshop leader, and globally recognized expert on how to tap into the power of human connection to maximize the performance of individuals and organizations. He is president of Connection Culture Group and the primary author of *Fired Up or Burned Out: How to Reignite Your Team's Passion, Creativity and Productivity* and *Connection Culture: The Competitive Advantage of Shared Identity, Empathy, and Understanding at Work.*

Yon Sugiharto

Yon Sugiharto is constantly searching for innovative ways to make learning and professional development more accessible to healthcare workers and care providers who are juggling multiple organizational priorities while caring for patients. Yon fell in love with the healthcare industry as an EMR trainer more than 20 years ago. Since then, he has worked in various learning and development capacities at organizations such as BMO Financial Group, New York-Presbyterian Hospital, and Nuvance Health. Yon is currently the executive director of education programs and services at Yale University's School of Medicine, where he oversees programs focused on leadership development, technology training, instructional design services, and continuing medical education.

Imelda Wicks

Imelda Wicks serves as program director of diversity, equity, and inclusion for the University of Texas MD Anderson Cancer Center. There, she oversees the DEI efforts and serves as program advisor and adjunct for the Health Care Disparities, Diversity and Advocacy

Program. Imelda previously worked at Lamar University as their founding executive director of diversity, inclusive excellence, and training. She established the university's first diversity and inclusion strategic plan, cultural competence training program, and a variety of initiatives and events geared to highlight the positive contributions of underrepresented and underserved groups. Imelda also worked as the diversity and inclusion consultant for The University of Texas Medical Branch (UTMB), where she was responsible for providing leadership and strategic direction to the Office of Diversity and Inclusion. She is credited with launching UTMB's ERG and Veterans Day luncheon, creating their train-the-trainer diversity training program, leading the UTMB Diversity Council, and managing the institution's Affirmative Action Plan (AAP). Imelda has lectured across the country at conferences on various topics related to cross-culture and diversity and inclusion. She has a bachelor's degree in communications from the University of Texas at Brownsville and a master's degree in cross-cultural studies, as well as certifications in mediation, affirmative action, and pastoral studies.

CJ Wolf

CJ Wolf, MD, MEd, is an experienced compliance officer and healthcare educator with more than 20 years of professional experience. He is currently a faculty member in the health services department of Brigham Young University—Idaho. He previously served as a clinical assistant professor at the University of Illinois at Chicago College of Medicine in the department of medical education. CJ also provides compliance and training consulting services. CJ has worked in various compliance roles for Intermountain Healthcare, MD Anderson Cancer Center, and the University of Texas System, as well as serving as chief compliance officer for an international medical device company. He has a passion for teaching and has developed curricula and taught adults seeking national coding and compliance certifications, trade workshops, seminars, and university courses. In addition to a medical degree from the University of Illinois at Chicago College of Medicine, CJ has a master of education from the University of Texas at Brownsville and a BS from Brigham Young University. He also holds the following certifications: Certified Compliance and Ethics Professional, Certified in Healthcare Privacy Compliance, Certified in Healthcare Research Compliance, Certified in Healthcare Compliance, Certified Professional Coder—Hospital, Certified Professional Coder—Physician, and Certified Internal Auditor.

Jason Wolf

Jason Wolf is a passionate champion and recognized expert on patient experience improvement, organizational culture and change, and sustaining high performance in healthcare. He led The Beryl Institute to become a leading global community of practice and thought leader on improving the patient experience, establishing the framework for the emerging profession of patient experience. Jason is the founding editor of the Patient Experience Journal, the first open-access, peer-reviewed journal committed to research and practice in the patient experience improvement. He also established and currently serves as president of Patient Experience Institute, an independent nonprofit committed to improving patient experience through evidence-based research, continuing education, and professional certification. Jason is a sought-after speaker, provocative commentator, and respected author of numerous publications and academic articles on culture, organizational change, and performance in healthcare. He has written two books on organization development in healthcare and more than 50 whitepapers and articles on patient experience excellence and improvement. Jason received the American College of Healthcare Executives 2018 Dean Conley Award for his article "Patient Experience: The New Heart of Healthcare Leadership." A recovering marathoner—he's run seven—Jason's proudest "accomplishment" remains his family. He currently resides in Nashville, Tennessee, with his wife, Beth, and sons, Samuel and Ian.

INDEX

Page numbers followed by *f* refer to figures.

D

I

M

N

O

P

U

V

W

Y

ABOUT THE EDITORS

Jacque Burandt, MEd, president of Award-winning Results, is passionate about transforming organizations through people development, creating top performers and leaders at all levels, and enhancing organizational and individual visibility, prestige, and pride through achieving awards and recognition for her clients' great work.

She authored the *TD at Work* "Create an Exceptional Learning Culture" in 2019 and has facilitated this topic at many ATD events, including the closing keynote at the ATD Houston Chapter's 2020 Fall Symposium.

A proven expert in creating an award-winning culture, Jacque led the Center for Learning Excellence at University Health to win eight ATD BEST Awards and ATD's first Innovation in Talent Development Award. University Health has won more BEST Awards than any other nonprofit organization in the world.

Jacque has a bachelor's degree in TV and film and an MEd in adult and continuing education from the University of Texas at Austin; she is also certified in emotional intelligence. Jacque frequently speaks at ATD's International Conference & EXPO, has presented at several of ATD's Healthcare Summits, and has also been a speaker at ATD's CORE 4 conference. She is a member of ATD's Awards Strategy committee.

Jacque served on the Texas Advisory Committee on Qualifications for Healthcare Translators and Interpreters, a legislative subcommittee, for six years and continues that work under the auspices of the Texas Association for Health Care Interpreters and Translators. She is a recipient of the Texas STAR Award for language access in 2016. She's based in San Antonio, Texas.

Niranjani Chidamber Papavaritis is the project manager and head of content for the healthcare industry vertical at ATD. In her role, she creates resources for healthcare trainers, practitioners, and executives by bridging areas of learning and development with topics specific to the industry to improve employee and organizational skill sets.

Niranjani has been passionate about healthcare since her youth, having spent summers volunteering at the Sri Sathya Sai Institute for Higher Medical Sciences—a hospital in rural India that offers patients state-of-the-art services at no cost. Before coming to ATD, Niranjani worked under UnitedHealth Group at Optum, specializing in business development. She served as a trusted partner and business advisor to hospital executives, ensuring health systems provided high-quality patient care.

Placing importance in interpersonal relationships, Niranjani believes that adaptive communication and a strong emphasis on soft skills are crucial to growth, success, and fulfillment for businesses. She values and brings a fusion of cultures through ideas, traditions, and pastimes. It is her core belief that through a blend of dedication, compassion, foresight, and intentionality, the healthcare industry can reach new heights.

Based in Alexandria, Virginia, Niranjani lives with her husband and two cats, Indra and Taco. She holds a BA in political science, with a minor in information systems, from the University of Maryland Baltimore County (UMBC).

Greg Rider, CPTD, is director, corporate compliance for EmblemHealth, one of the nation's largest not-for-profit health plans serving more than 3 million people in New York City and the tristate area. He has more than 15 years' experience in employee training and development, with much of that time spent in healthcare-related organizations. In his role at EmblemHealth, Greg directs compliance communication, training, and other compliance governance functions. He is also the founder and leader of Prism, the LGBTQ employee resource group, and sits on the company's Diversity, Equity and Inclusion Council.

Prior to joining EmblemHealth, Greg worked in compliance education for NYU Langone Medical Center, where he designed, developed, and launched online compliance courses for 20,000 users of the Medical Center's LMS; he also facilitated live classroom training in several sites across New York City. He has held positions as director of learning services and training manager for several medical education agencies and served as an instructional design consultant for Quest Diagnostics, Shire Pharmaceuticals, and Forest Pharmaceuticals and Laboratories.

Greg has served in many volunteer roles at the local and national levels for ATD and delivered workshops at ATD's International Conference & Exposition and the Chapter Leaders Conference. He has been a reviewer for the BEST Awards and the Excellence in Practice Awards, and served on numerous projects for ATD's Certification Institute. Greg is both a Certified Professional in Talent Development (CPTD) and Certified in Healthcare Compliance (CHC). He has a master's in English from Georgia State University.